THE MODERN WORLD-SYSTEM I

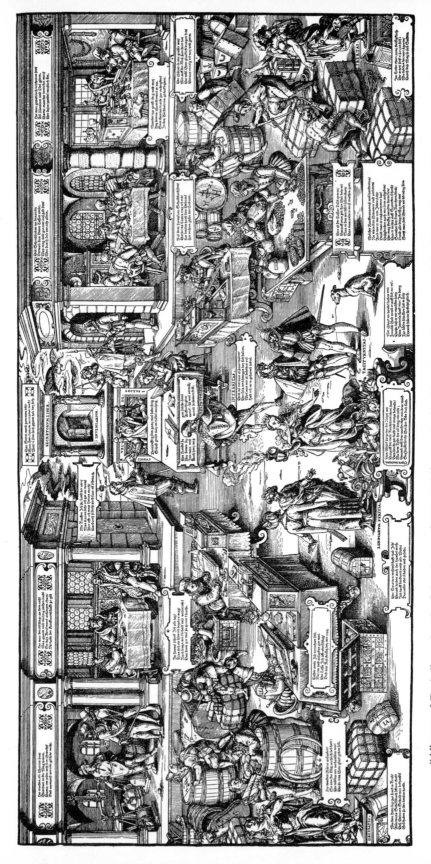

"Allegory of Trade," woodcut by Jobst Amman (1539–1591), who lived in Nuremberg. He was one of the "Little Masters." This bottom detail illustrated the house of a merchant of Nuremberg, still a flourishing center of trans-European trade.

THE MODERN WORLD-SYSTEM I

Capitalist Agriculture and the Origins of the European World-Economy in the Sixteenth Century

Immanuel Wallerstein

ACADEMIC PRESS   New York   San Francisco   London

A Subsidiary of Harcourt Brace Jovanovich, Publishers

This is a volume in the series entitled
STUDIES IN SOCIAL DISCONTINUITY
Under the Consulting Editorship of Charles Tilly, *University of Michigan* and Edward Shorter, *University of Toronto*

ACADEMIC PRESS, INC.
111 Fifth Avenue, New York, New York 10003

United Kingdom Edition published by
ACADEMIC PRESS, INC. (LONDON) LTD.
24/28 Oval Road, London NW1

Library of Congress Cataloging in Publication Data

Wallerstein, Immanuel Maurice, Date
    The modern world-system.

    (Studies in social discontinuity)
    Bibliography: p.
    1.   Europe–Economic conditions.   2.   Economic history
–16th century.   3.   Capitalism.   I.   Title.
II.   Series.
HC45.W35   330.9′4′022   73-5318

PRINTED IN THE UNITED STATES OF AMERICA
81 82   9 8 7 6 5 4 3

To TKH

CONTENTS

LIST OF ILLUSTRATIONS

CHAPTER 7:   *"Richmond Palace," an oil painting by David Vinckenboons (first quarter of the seventeenth century). Cambridge: Fitzwilliam Museum.*

The illustrations were selected and annotated with the assistance of Sally Spector.

ACKNOWLEDGMENTS

It is always difficult to list the immediate sources of ideas and assistance—from authors, colleagues, and students—in the conception and writing of a book, and particularly so in a book that pretends to synthesize other people's empirical work. The great risk is neglect.

In the case of this volume the two authors whose voluminous writings most immediately inspired me on the path I finally decided to go were Fernand Braudel and Marian Malowist.

Once I had written a draft, Fernand Braudel read it carefully and gave me encouragement at a moment when I needed reassurance. Charles Tilly also read it carefully, and by raising pertinent questions forced me to clarify my argument. This was particularly so concerning the role of state-power and "absolutism" in general, and its counterpoint with the phenomenon of banditry in particular. Douglas Dowd put me onto Frederic Lane for which I thank him, since Frederic Lane is very worth being put onto.

As for Terence Hopkins, my debt is to our twenty years of intellectual discussion and collaboration. There is no sentence that can summarize this debt.

This book was written during a year's stay at the Center for Advanced Study in the Behavioral Sciences. Countless authors have sung its praises. Aside from splendid surroundings, unlimited library and secretarial assistance, and a ready supply of varied scholars to consult at a moment's notice, what the center offers is to leave the scholar to his own devices, for good or ill. Would that all men had such wisdom. The final version was consummated with the aid of a grant from the Social Sciences Grants Subcommittee of the Faculty of Graduate Studies and Research of McGill University.

QUOTATION CREDITS

Selections from Violet Barbour, *Capitalism in Amsterdam in the Seventeenth Century*, appearing on pages 211-214, are reprinted by permission of the University of Michigan Press. Copyright 1963 by the University of Michigan Press.

Selections appearing on pages 303, 305-306, 315, 317-318, 320-322 from Jerome Blum, *Lord and Peasant in Russia from the Ninth to the Nineteenth Century* (Copyright © 1961 by Princeton University Press; Princeton paperback 1971), pp. 120-212, partly paraphrased. Reprinted by Permission of Princeton University Press.

Selections appearing on pages 16-340 *passim* from Vols. I and II, *The Mediterranean and the Mediterranean World in the Age of Philip II* by Fernand Braudel (about 2600 words *passim*). Originally published in France under the title *La Méditerranée et le monde Méditerranéen à l'époque de Philippe II*.
© Librairie Armand Colin 1966.
English translation by Immanuel Wallerstein with special permission of Harper & Row, Publishers, Inc.

Selections appearing on pages 26-27, 30-31, 34, 103, 105-106, reprinted from *Rural Economy and Country Life in the Medieval West*, by Georges Duby (Cynthia Postan, translator), by permission of the University of South Carolina Press.

Selections appearing on pages 153, 161, 207, 232-234, 244 reprinted from Christopher Hill, *Reformation to the Industrial Revolution, 1530-1780*, Vol. II of The Pelican History of Britain, pp. 25, 26, 27, 28, 34, 65-66, 96, 101. Copyright © Christopher Hill, 1967, 1969.

Selections appearing on pages 203, 206-209 from H. G. Koenigsberger, "The Organization of Revolutionary Parties in France and the Netherlands During the Sixteenth Century," *The Journal of Modern History*, XXVII, 4, Dec. 1955, 335-351. Copyright © by the University of Chicago Press. Reproduced by permission.

Selections appearing on pages 215, 267-268 reprinted from H. G. Koenigsberger, "Western Europe and the Power of Spain," in *New Cambridge Modern History*, III: R. B. Wernham, ed., *The Counter-Reformation and the Price Revolution, 1559-1610*

C'est par une crise des revenus seigneuriaux que se termine le moyen-âge et s'ouvrent les temps modernes.

—MARC BLOCH

This collapse in real wage-rates [in Europe] formed the counterpart to the revolutionary rise of prices in the sixteenth century. The operation was fully paid for by the increased toil, hardships, impoverishments and dejection of the majority. Contemporaries were often aware that the deterioration was taking place.

—FERNAND BRAUDEL and FRANK SPOONER

The discovery of gold and silver in America, the extirpation, enslavement and entombment in mines of the aboriginal population, the beginning of the conquest and looting of the East Indies, the turning of Africa into a warren for the commercial hunting of black-skins, signalised the rosy dawn of the era of capitalist production. These idyllic proceedings are the chief momenta of primitive accumulation. On their heels treads the commercial war of the European nations, with the globe for a theatre.

—KARL MARX

INTRODUCTION:
ON THE STUDY OF
SOCIAL CHANGE

Figure 1: "The Sack of Rome by Charles V," a woodcut illustrating a book on "Imperial Practices and Prognostication . . ." published in Strassbourg circa 1535. This woodcut celebrates the event that brought the Holy Father to political dependence on the Holy Roman Emperor, and made Charles the uncontested power in Italy.

Change is eternal. Nothing ever changes. Both clichés are "true." Structures are those coral reefs of human relations which have a stable existence over relatively long periods of time. But structures too are born, develop, and die.

Unless we are to use the study of social change as a term synonymous to the totality of social science, its meaning should be restricted to the study of changes in those phenomena which are most durable—the definition of durability itself being of course subject to change over historical time and place.

One of the major assertions of world social science is that there are some great watersheds in the history of man. One such generally recognized watershed, though one however studied by only a minority of social scientists, is the so-called neolithic or agricultural revolution. The other great watershed is the creation of the modern world.

This latter event is at the center of most contemporary social science theory, and indeed, of the nineteenth century as well. To be sure, there is immense debate as to what are the defining characteristics of modern times (and hence what are its temporal boundaries). Furthermore, there is much disagreement about the motors of this process of change. But there seems to be widespread consensus that some great structural changes did occur in the world in the last several hundred years, changes that make the world of today qualitatively different from the world of yesterday. Even those who reject evolutionist assumptions of determinate progress nonetheless admit the difference in structures.

What are the appropriate units to study if one wishes to describe this "difference" and account for it? In a sense, many of the major theoretical debates of our time can be reduced to arguments about this. It is the great quest of contemporary social science. It is therefore appropriate to begin a work that purports to analyze the process of social change in the modern world with an intellectual itinerary of one's conceptual search.

I started with an interest in the social underpinnings of political conflict in my own society. I thought that by comprehending the modalities of such conflict, I might contribute as a rational man to the shaping of that society. This led me into two great debates. One was the degree to which "all history is the history of the class struggle." Phrased another way, are classes the only significant operating units in the social and political arenas? Or, as Weber argued, are they only one of a trinity of units—class, status-group, and party—which exist, the interactions among which explain the political process? Although I had my prejudices on the subject, I found, like others before me, that neither the definition of these terms nor the description of their relations was easy to elucidate. I felt increasingly that

3

this was far more a conceptual than an empirical problem, and that to resolve the debate, at least in my own mind, I would have to place the issues within a larger intellectual context.

The second great debate, which was linked to the first, was about the degree to which there could or did exist a consensus of values within a given society, and to the extent that such a consensus existed, the degree to which its presence or absence was in fact a major determinant of men's actions. This debate is linked to the first because it is only if one rejects the primordial character of social struggle in civil society that the question can even be raised.

Values are of course an elusive thing to observe and I became very uneasy with a great deal of the theorizing about values, which seemed often to combine the absence of a rigorous empirical base with an affront to common sense. Still it was clear that men and groups did justify their actions by reference to ideologies. Furthermore, it seemed clear also that groups became more coherent and hence more politically efficacious to the extent that they were self-conscious, which meant that they developed a common language and a *Weltanschauung*.

I shifted my area of empirical concern from my own society to Africa in the hope either that I would discover various theories confirmed by what I found there or that a look at distant climes would sharpen my perception by directing my attention to issues I would otherwise have missed. I expected the former to happen. But it was the latter that came to pass.

I went to Africa first during the colonial era, and I witnessed the process of "decolonization," and then of the independence of a cascade of sovereign states. White man that I was, I was bombarded by the onslaught of the colonial mentality of Europeans long resident in Africa. And sympathizer of nationalist movements that I was, I was privy to the angry analyses and optimistic passions of young militants of the African movements. It did not take long to realize that not only were these two groups at odds on political issues, but that they approached the situation with entirely different sets of conceptual frameworks.

In general, in a deep conflict, the eyes of the downtrodden are more acute about the reality of the present. For it is in their interest to perceive correctly in order to expose the hypocrisies of the rulers. They have less interest in ideological deflection. So it was in this case. The nationalists saw the reality in which they lived as a "colonial situation," that is, one in which both their social action and that of the Europeans living side by side with them as administrators, missionaries, teachers, and merchants were determined by the constraints of a single legal and social entity. They saw further that the political machinery was based on a caste system in which rank and hence reward was accorded on the basis of race.

African nationalists were determined to change the political structures within which they lived. I have told this story elsewhere and it is not relevant to refer to it here. What is relevant here is that I thereby became aware of the degree to which society as an abstraction was heavily limited to politico-juridical systems as an empirical reality. It was a false perspective to take a unit like a "tribe" and seek to analyze its operations without reference to the fact that, in a colonial situation, the governing institutions of a "tribe," far from being "sovereign," were closely circumscribed by the laws (and customs) of a larger entity of which they were an indissociable part, the colony. Indeed this led me to the larger generalization that the study of social organization was by and large defective because of the widespread lack of consideration of the legal and political framework within which both organizations and their members operated.

I sought to discover the general attributes of a colonial situation and to describe what I thought of as its "natural history." It quickly became clear to me that I had to hold at least some factors of the world-system constant. So I restricted myself to an analysis of how the colonial system operated for those countries which were colonies in the nineteenth and twentieth centuries of European powers and which were "overseas possessions" of these powers. Given this constant, I felt I could make generally applicable statements about the impact on social life of the imposition of colonial authority, the motives and modalities of resistance to this authority, the mechanisms by which colonial powers entrenched and sought to legitimate their power, the contradictory nature of the forces that were able to operate within this framework, the reasons why men were led to form organizations that challenged colonial rule, and the structural elements that made for the expansion and eventual political triumph of anticolonial movements. The unit of analysis in all of this was the colonial territory as legally defined by the administering power.

I was interested equally in what happened to these "new states" after independence. As the study of colonial territories seemed to focus on the causes of the breakdown of existing political order, the study of the postindependence period seemed to focus on the opposite issue: How legitimate authority is established and a sense of membership in the national entity spread among the citizenry.

This latter study ran into problems, however. In the first place, to study the postindependence politics of Afro-Asian states seemed to be a process of running after the headlines. There could perforce be relatively little historical depth. Furthermore, there was the tricky question of Latin America. There were many ways in which the situations there seemed parallel, and more and more people began to think of the three continents as a "Third World." But Latin American countries had been politically independent for 150 years. Their cultures were far more closely linked with the European tradition than anything in Africa or Asia. The whole enterprise seemed to be wavering on very shaky ground.

In search for an appropriate unit of analysis, I turned to "states in the period after formal independence but before they had achieved something that might be termed national integration." This definition could be taken to include most or all of Latin America for all or almost all of the time up to the present. But it obviously included other areas as well. It included for example the United States of America, at least in the period before say the Civil War. It surely included eastern Europe, at least up until the twentieth century and possibly up to the present. And it even included western and southern Europe, at least for earlier periods of time.

I was therefore forced by this logic to turn my attention to early modern Europe. This led me first into the question of what I would take as the starting point of this process, a process I provisionally formulated, for want of a better conceptual tool, as the process of modernization. Furthermore, I had not only to consider the issue of starting points but of terminal points, unless I wished to include twentieth-century Britain or Germany as instances of this same social process. Since that seemed prima facie dubious, terminal points had to be thought about.

At this point, I was clearly involved in a developmental schema and some implicit notion of stages of development. This in turn posed two problems: criteria for determining stages, and comparability of units across historical time.

How many stages had there been? How many could there be? Is industrialization a turning point or the consequence of some political turning point? What in this context would the empirical meaning of a term like "revolution" mean, as in the French Revolution or the Russian Revolution? Were these stages unilinear, or could a unit go "backward"? This seemed to be a vast conceptual morass into which I had stepped.

Furthermore, getting out of the conceptual morass was very difficult because of the absence of reasonable measuring instruments. How could one say that seventeenth-century France was in some sense equivalent to twentieth-century India? Laymen might consider such a statement absurd. Were they so wrong? It was all very well to fall back on textbook formulae of the virtues of scientific abstraction, but the practical difficulties of comparison seemed immense.

One way to handle the "absurd" idea of comparing two such disparate units was to accept the legitimacy of the objection and add another variable—the world context of any given era, or what Wolfram Eberhard has called "world time." This meant that while seventeenth-century France might have shared some structural characteristics with twentieth-century India, they were to be seen as very different on the dimensions of world context. This was conceptually clarifying, but made measurement even more complicated.

Finally, there seemed to be another difficulty. If given societies went through "stages," that is, had a "natural history," what of the world-system itself? Did it not have "stages," or at least a "natural history"? If so, were we not studying evolutions within evolutions? And if that, was not the theory getting to be top-heavy in epicycles? Did it not call for some simplifying thrust?

It seemed to me it did. It was at this point that I abandoned the idea altogether of taking either the sovereign state or that vaguer concept, the national society, as the unit of analysis. I decided that neither one was a social system and that one could only speak of social change in social systems. The only social system in this scheme was the world-system.

This was of course enormously simplifying. I had one type of unit rather than units within units. I could explain changes in the sovereign states as consequent upon the evolution and interaction of the world-system. But it was also enormously complicating. I probably only had one instance of this unit in the modern era. Suppose indeed that I was right, that the correct unit of analysis was the world-system, and that sovereign states were to be seen as one kind of organizational structure among others within this single social system. Could I then do anything more than write its history?

I was not interested in writing its history, nor did I begin to have the empirical knowledge necessary for such a task. (And by its very nature, few individuals ever could.) But can there be laws about the unique? In a rigorous sense, there of course cannot be. A statement of causality or probability is made in terms of a series of like phenomena or like instances. Even if one were to include in such a series those that would probably or even possibly occur in the future, what could be proposed here was not to add a series of future possible instances to a network of present and past ones. It was to add a series of future possible instances to a single past-present one.

There had only been one "modern world." Maybe one day there would be discovered to be comparable phenomena on other planets, or additional modern world-systems on this one. But here and now, the reality was clear—only one. It was here that I was inspired by the analogy with astronomy which purports to explain the laws governing the universe, although (as far as we know) only one universe has ever existed.

What do astronomers do? As I understand it, the logic of their arguments involves two separate operations. They use the laws derived from the study of smaller physical entities, the laws of physics, and argue that (with perhaps certain specified exceptions) these laws hold by analogy for the system as a whole. Second, they argue a posteriori. If the whole system is to have a given state at time y, it most probably had a certain state at time x.

Both methods are tricky, and it is for this reason that in the field of cosmology, which is the study of the functioning of the system as a whole, there are wildly opposing hypotheses held by reputable astronomers. Just as there are in the explanations of the modern world-system, a state of affairs likely to remain so for some time. Actually, students of the operation of the world-system possibly have it easier than students of the operation of the universe in terms of the amount of empirical evidence at their disposal.

In any case, I was inspired by the epigram of T. J. G. Locher: "One should not confuse totality with completeness. The whole is more than the assembled parts, but it is surely also less."[1]

I was looking to describe the world-system at a certain level of abstraction, that of the evolution of structures of the whole system. I was interested in describing particular events only insofar as they threw light upon the system as typical instances of some mechanism, or as they were the crucial turning points in some major institutional change.

This kind of project is manageable to the extent that a good deal of empirical material exists, and that this material is at least partially in the form of contrapuntal controversial work. Fortunately this seems to be the case by now for a large number of the themes of modern history.

One of the major thrusts of modern social science has been the effort to achieve quantification of research findings. Utilizing the heavily narrative accounts of most historical research seems not to lend itself to such quantification. What then is the reliability of such data, and to what extent can one safely draw conclusions from the material about the operation of a system as such? It is a major tragedy of twentieth-century social science that so large a proportion of social scientists, facing this dilemma, have thrown in the sponge. Historical data seemed to them vague and crude, hence unreliable. They felt that there was little to be done about it, and that hence it was best to avoid using it. And the best way not to use it was to formulate problems in such a way that its use was not indicated.

Thus the quantifiability of data determined the choice of research problems which then determined the conceptual apparatuses with which one defined and handled the empirical data. It should be clear on a moment's reflection that this is an inversion of the scientific process. Conceptualization should determine research tools, at least most of the time, not vice versa. The degree of quantification should reflect merely the maximum of precision that is possible for given problems and given methods at given points of time. More rather than less quantification is always desirable, to the extent that it speaks to the questions which derive from the conceptual exercise. At this stage of analysis of the world-system, the degree of quantification achieved and immediately realizable is limited. We do the best we can and go forward from there.

Lastly, there is the question of objectivity and commitment. I do not

[1]*Die Überwindung des europäozentrischen Geschichts-bildes* (1954), 15, cited by G. Barraclough in   H. P. R. Finberg, ed., *Approaches to History: A Symposium* (Univ. of Toronto Press, 1962), 94.

believe there exists any social science that is not committed. That does not mean however that it is not possible to be objective. It is first of all a matter of defining clearly our terms. In the nineteenth century, in rebellion against the fairy-tale overtones of so much prior historical writing, we were given the ideal of telling history *wie es eigentlich gewesen ist*. But social reality is ephemeral. It exists in the present and disappears as it moves into the past. The past can only be told as it truly *is*, not was. For recounting the past is a social act of the present done by men of the present and affecting the social system of the present.

"Truth" changes because society changes. At any given time, nothing is successive; everything is contemporaneous, even that which is past. And in the present we are all irremediably the products of our background, our training, our personality and social role, and the structured pressures within which we operate. That is not to say there are no options. Quite the contrary. A social system and all its constituent institutions, including the sovereign states of the modern world, are the loci of a wide range of social groups—in contact, in collusion, and above all, in conflict with each other. Since we all belong to multiple groups, we often have to make decisions as to the priorities demanded by our loyalties. Scholars and scientists are not somehow exempt from this requirement. Nor is the requirement limited to their nonscholarly, directly political roles in the social system.

To be sure, to be a scholar or a scientist is to perform a particular role in the social system, one quite different from being an apologist for any particular group. I am not denigrating the role of advocate. It is essential and honorable, but not the same as that of scholar or scientist. The latter's role is to discern, within the framework of his commitments, the present reality of the phenomena he studies, to derive from this study general principles, from which ultimately particular applications may be made. In this sense, there is no area of study that is not "relevant." For the proper understanding of the social dynamics of the present requires a theoretical comprehension that can only be based on the study of the widest possible range of phenomena, including through all of historical time and space.

When I say the "present reality" of phenomena, I do not mean that in order to strengthen the political claims of a government, an archaeologist for example should assert that the artifacts he uncovers belong to one group when he in fact believes them to belong to another. I mean that the whole archaeological enterprise from its inception—the social investment in this branch of scientific activity, the research orientation, the conceptual tools, the modes of resuming and communicating the results—are functions of the social present. To think otherwise is self-deceptive at best. Objectivity is honesty within this framework.

Objectivity is a function of the whole social system. Insofar as the system is lopsided, concentrating certain kinds of research activity in the hands of particular groups, the results will be "biased" in favor of these groups.

Objectivity is the vector of a distribution of social investment in such activity such that it is performed by persons rooted in all the major groups of the world-system in a balanced fashion. Given this definition, we do not have an objective social science today. On the other hand, it is not an unfeasible objective within the foreseeable future.

We have already suggested that the study of world-systems is particularly tricky because of the impossibility of finding comparable instances. It is also particularly tricky because the social impact of statements about the world-system are clearly and immediately evident to all major actors in the political arena. Hence the social pressures on scholars and scientists, in the form of relatively tight social control on their activities, is particularly great in this field. This affords one further explanation to that of the methodological dilemmas for the reluctance of scholars to pursue activities in this domain.

But conversely this is the very reason why it is important to do so. Man's ability to participate intelligently in the evolution of his own system is dependent on his ability to perceive the whole. The more difficult we acknowledge the task to be, the more urgent it is that we start sooner rather than later. It is of course not in the interest of all groups that this be done. Here our commitment enters. It depends on our image of the good society. To the extent that we want a more egalitarian world and a more libertarian one, we must comprehend the conditions under which these states of being are realizable. To do that requires first of all a clear exposition of the nature and evolution of the modern world-system heretofore, and the range of possible developments in the present and the future. That kind of knowledge would be power. And within the framework of my commitments, it would be a power that would be most useful to those groups which represent the interests of the larger and more oppressed parts of the world's population.

It is therefore with these considerations in mind that I have embarked on this effort to analyze the determining elements of the modern world-system. It will take several volumes to accomplish this task, even in the preliminary format that this work must necessarily be.

I have divided the work, at least initially, into four principal parts, corresponding with what I think of as four major epochs, thus far, of the modern world-system. This first volume will deal with the origins and early conditions of the world-system, still only a European world-system. The approximate dates of this are 1450–1640. The second volume shall deal with the consolidation of this system, roughly between 1640 and 1815. The third shall deal with the conversion of the world-economy into a global enterprise, made possible by the technological transformation of modern industrialism. This expansion was so sudden and so great that the system in effect had to be recreated. The period here is roughly 1815–1917. The fourth volume will deal with the consolidation of this capitalist world-economy from 1917 to the present, and the particular "revolutionary" tensions this consolidation has provoked.

Much of contemporary social science has become the study of groups and organizations, when it has not been social psychology in disguise. This work, however, involves not the study of groups, but of social systems. When one studies a social system, the classical lines of division within social science are meaningless. Anthropology, economics, political science, sociology—and history—are divisions of the discipline anchored in a certain liberal conception of the state and its relation to functional and geographical sectors of the social order. They make a certain limited sense if the focus of one's study is organizations. They make none at all if the focus is the social system. I am not calling for a multidisciplinary approach to the study of social systems, but for a unidisciplinary approach. The substantive content of this book will, I hope, make it clear what I mean by this phrase, and how seriously I take it.

1

MEDIEVAL PRELUDE

Figure 2: "The Foxhunt," from *Das Mittelälterliche Hausbuch,* ink drawing by an anonymous German artist, active 1475–1490, known as the Master of the Housebook.

In the late fifteenth and early sixteenth century, there came into existence what we may call a European world-economy. It was not an empire yet it was as spacious as a grand empire and shared some features with it. But it was different, and new. It was a kind of social system the world has not really known before and which is the distinctive feature of the modern world-system. It is an economic but not a political entity, unlike empires, city-states and nation-states. In fact, it precisely encompasses within its bounds (it is hard to speak of boundaries) empires, city-states, and the emerging "nation-states." It is a "world" system, not because it encompasses the whole world, but because it is larger than any juridically-defined political unit. And it is a "world-*economy*" because the basic linkage between the parts of the system is economic, although this was reinforced to some extent by cultural links and eventually, as we shall see, by political arrangements and even confederal structures.

An empire, by contrast, is a political unit. For example, Shmuel Eisenstadt has defined it this way:

> The term "empire" has normally been used to designate a political system encompassing wide, relatively high centralized territories, in which the center, as embodied both in the person of the emperor and in the central political institutions, constituted an autonomous entity. Further, although empires have usually been based on traditional legitimation, they have often embraced some wider, potentially universal political and cultural orientation that went beyond that of any of their component parts.[1]

Empires in this sense were a constant feature of the world scene for 5,000 years. There were continuously several such empires in various parts of the world at any given point of time. The political centralization of an empire was at one and the same time its strength and its weakness. Its strength lay in the fact that it guaranteed economic flows from the periphery to the center by force (tribute and taxation) and by monopolistic advantages in trade. Its weakness lay in the fact that the bureaucracy made necessary by the political structure tended to absorb too much of the profit, especially as repression and exploitation bred revolt which increased military expenditures.[2] Political empires are a primitive means of economic domination. It is the social achievement of the modern world, if you will, to have invented the technology that makes it possible to increase the flow of the surplus

[1]S. N. Eisenstadt, "Empires," *International Encyclopedia of the Social Sciences*, (New York: Macmillan and Free Press, 1968), **V**, 41.

[2]A discussion of the internal contradictions of empires which account for their decline is to be found in S. N. Eisenstadt, "The Causes of Disintegration and Fall of Empires: Sociological and Historical Analyses," *Diogenes*, No. 34, Summer 1961, 82–107.

from the lower strata to the upper strata, from the periphery to the center, from the majority to the minority, by eliminating the "waste" of too cumbersome a political superstructure.

I have said that a world-economy is an invention of the modern world. Not quite. There were world-economies before. But they were always transformed into empires: China, Persia, Rome. The modern world-economy might have gone in that same direction—indeed it has sporadically seemed as though it would—except that the techniques of modern capitalism and the technology of modern science, the two being somewhat linked as we know, enabled this world-economy to thrive, produce, and expand without the emergence of a unified political structure.[3]

What capitalism does is offer an alternative and more lucrative source of surplus appropriation (at least more lucrative over a long run). An empire is a mechanism for collecting tribute, which in Frederic Lane's pregnant image, "means payments received for protection, but payments in excess of the cost of producing the protection."[4] In a capitalist world-economy, political energy is used to secure monopoly rights (or as near to it as can be achieved). The state becomes less the central economic enterprise than the means of assuring certain terms of trade in other economic transactions. In this way, the operation of the market (not the *free* operation but nonetheless its operation) creates incentives to increased productivity and all the consequent accompaniment of modern economic development. The world-economy is the arena within which these processes occur.

A world-economy seems to be limited in size. Ferdinand Fried observed that:

> If one takes account of all the factors, one reaches the conclusion that the space of the 'world' economy in Roman antiquity could be covered in about 40 to 60 days, utilizing the best means of transport. . . . Now, in our times [1939], it also takes 40 to 60 days to cover the space of the modern world economy, if one uses the normal channels of transportation for merchandise.[5]

---

[3] And it was a mark of political wisdom to realize this. The first such sign of wisdom was the refusal of Venice in the thirteenth century to take over the political burdens of the Byzantine Empire. Mario Abrate observes:

"The political organism which emerged from the fourth Crusade, the Eastern Latin Empire, placed its entire hope of survival on the continuity of its links with the West.

"Venice, the naval power which had supported the Crusade, and furnished the naval means to conduct it, did not wish to burden itself with the political governance of the Empire (Doge Enrico Dandolo refused in fact the throne that was offered

to him) but assured itself, and that almost automatically, of the monopoly of naval communications and markets for all the territories controlled by the new Latin Dominion." "Creta, colonia veneziana nei secoli XIII-XV," *Economia e storia*, **IV**, 3, lugl.-sett. 1957, 251.

[4] Frederic C. Lane, "The Economic Meaning of War & Protection" in *Venice and History* (Baltimore: Johns Hopkins Press, 1966), 389.

[5] Ferdinand Fried, *Le tournant de l'économie mondiale* (1942), cited in Fernand Braudel, *La Méditerranée et le monde méditerranéen à l'époque de Philippe II*, 2e édition revue et augmentée (Paris: Lib. Armand Colin, 1966), **I**, 339.

still provided a certain cultural and even legal coherence to the area. Christianity served as a set of parameters within which social action took place. Feudal Europe was a "civilization," but not a world-system.

It would not make sense to conceive of the areas in which feudalism existed as having two economies, a market economy of the towns and a subsistence economy of the rural manors. In the twentieth century, with reference to the so-called underdeveloped world, this approach has gone under the label of the "dual economy" theory. Rather, as Daniel Thorner suggests:

> We are sure to deceive ourselves if we think of peasant economies as oriented exclusively towards their own subsistence and term "capitalist" any orientation towards the "market." It is more reasonable to start by assuming that, for many centuries, peasant economies have had both orientations.[10]

For many centuries? How many? B. H. Slicher van Bath, in his major work on European agrarian history, marks the turning point at about 1150 A.D.. Even before then, he does not think Western Europe was engaged in subsistence farming, but rather from 500 A.D. to c. 1150 A.D. in what he calls "direct agricultural consumption," that is, a system of partial self-sufficiency in which, while most people produce their own food, they also supply it to the nonagricultural population as barter. From 1150 A.D. on, he considers Western Europe to have reached that stage of "indirect agricultural consumption," a stage we are still in today.[11]

What we should envisage then, when we speak of western European feudalism, is a series of tiny economic nodules whose population and productivity were slowly increasing, and in which the legal mechanisms ensured that the bulk of the surplus went to the landlords who had noble status and control of the juridical machinery. Since much of this surplus was in kind, it was of little benefit unless it could be sold. Towns grew up, supporting artisans who bought the surplus and exchanged it for their

"European feudalism should therefore be seen as the outcome of the violent dissolution of older societies. It would in fact be unintelligible without the great upheaval of the Germanic invasions which, by forcibly uniting two societies originally at very different stages of development, disrupted both of them. . . ." *Feudal Society* (Chicago, Illinois: Univ. of Chicago Press, 1961), 443.

On the issue of the "money-economy," see also M. M. Postan: "Thus from the point of view of English history, and even from that of medieval and Anglo-Saxon history, the rise of the money economy in the sense of its first appearance has no historical meaning. Money was in use when documented history began, and its rise cannot be adduced as an explanation of any later phenomenon." "The Rise of a Money Economy," *Economic History Review*, **XIV**, 2, 1944, 127.

[10]Daniel Thorner, "L'économie paysan: concept pour l'histoire économique," *Annales E.S.C.*, **XIX**, 3, mai-juin 1964, 422.

[11]B. H. Slicher van Bath, *The Agrarian History of Western Europe, A.D. 500–1850* (New York: St. Martin's, 1963), 24. The author notes that about 1850, a second phase of indirect agricultural production begins, one in which the *majority* of the population is no longer engaged in agricultural production.

And Fernand Braudel adds that this could be said to be the time spa
of the Mediterranean world in the sixteenth century.[6]

The origins and the functioning of such a 60–day European world
economy[7] in the sixteenth century is our concern here. It is vital t
remember, however, that Europe was not the only world-economy at the
time. There were others.[8] But Europe alone embarked on the path of
capitalist development which enabled it to outstrip these others. How and
why did this come about? Let us start by seeing what happened in the
world in the three centuries prior to 1450. In the twelfth century, the
Eastern Hemisphere contained a series of empires and small worlds, many
of which were interlinked at their edges with each other. At that time,
the Mediterranean was one focus of trade where Byzantium, Italian city-
states, and to some extent parts of northern Africa met. The Indian
Ocean–Red Sea complex formed another such focus. The Chinese region
was a third. The Central Asian land mass from Mongolia to Russia was
a fourth. The Baltic area was on the verge of becoming a fifth. Northwest
Europe was however a very marginal area in economic terms. The principal
social mode or organization there was what has come to be called feudalism.

We must be very clear what feudalism was not. It was not a "natural
economy," that is, an economy of self-subsistence. Western Europe feudalism grew out of the disintegration of an empire, a disintegration which
was never total in reality or even *de jure*.[9] The myth of the Roman Empire

[6]See Braudel, *La Méditerranée*, **I**, 339–340. As for Europe in the fifteenth century, Garrett Mattingly argues that it still required smaller-scale units: "At the beginning of the fifteenth century Western society still lacked the resources to organize stable states on the national scale. On the scale of the Italian city state it could do so. Internally the smaller distances to be overcome brought the problems of transport and communication, and consequently the problems of collecting taxes and maintaining central authority, within the range of practical solution." *Renaissance Diplomacy* (London: Jonathan Cape, 1955), 59.

But, says Mattingly, this changes by the following century: "[I]n terms of commercial intercourse, or military logistics, or even of diplomatic communication, European distances were perceptibly greater in the fourteenth than in the sixteenth century. . . ." [*Ibid.*, p. 60].

[7]"When one says 'world', with reference to the 16th century . . . in fact, usually one means Europe by the world. . . . On a world scale, geographically speaking, the Renaissance economy is a regional aspect, no doubt primordial, but nonetheless regional." Michel Mollat, "Y a-t-il une économie de la Renaissance?", in *Actes du Colloque sur la Renaissance* (Paris: Lib. Philosophique J. Vrin, 1958), 40.

[8]"Before the constitution of a truly world economy (still uncompleted in the twentieth century), each nucleus of population is found in the center of a communications network. . . . Each of these worlds corresponds . . . to a nucleus with a high population density. It is bounded by deserts, by seas, by virgin lands. The case of Europe and that of China are particularly clear." Pierre Chaunu, *L'expansion européenee du XIIIe au XVe siècle*, Collection Nouvelle Clio, No. 26 (Paris: Presses Universitaires de France, 1969), 255.

[9]Marc Bloch attacked the basic confusion head on: "Clearly from the fact that a transaction stipulates a price in monetary equivalents or in kind, one cannot legitimately deduce, without more precise evidence, that the payment was really made or not in cash. . . .

Just as the political institutions of feudalism characterized by a profound weakening of the Stat presumed nonetheless the memory and bore th traces of a past when the State had been stron so the economy, even when exchange had becoi minimal, never ended its attachment to a monet; schema, whose principles were inherited from ceding civilizations." "Economie-nature économie-argent: un pseudo-dilemme," *An; d'histoire sociale*, **I**, 1939, 13–14. Bloch further st

products. A merchant class came from two sources: On the one hand, agents of the landlords who sometimes became independent, as well as intermediate size peasants who retained enough surplus after payments to the lord to sell it on the market[12]; on the other hand, resident agents of long-distance merchants (based often in northern Italian city-states and later in the Hanseatic cities) who capitalized on poor communications and hence high disparities of prices from one area to another, especially when certain areas suffered natural calamities.[13] As towns grew, of course, they

[12]Karl Bücher warns us of the confusion that the world "merchant" causes in the medieval context: "Recent literature relating to the origin of the constitution of German towns has overlooked the very wide significance of the word *Kaufmann* and imagined that the innumerable towns existing within the German Empire towards the close of the Middle Ages, from Cologne and Augsburg down to Medebach and Radolfzell, were inhabited by merchants in the modern sense of the term, that is, by a specialized class of professional tradesmen who are as a rule still represented as wholesale merchants. All economic history revolts against such a conception. What did these people deal in, and in what did they make payment for their wares? Besides, the very terms used are opposed to it. The most prominent characteristic of the professional merchant in his relation to the public is not his custom of buying, but of selling. Yet the chapman (Kaufmann) of the Middle Ages is named from the word for buying—*kaufen*. In the State records of Otto III, for Dortmund from 990 to 1000 A.D. the *emptores Trotmanniae*, whose municipal laws, like those of Cologne and Mainz, are said to serve as a model for other cities, are spoken of in the same connection as *mercatores* or *negotiatores* in other records. If the abbot of Reichenau in the year 1075 can with a stroke of the pen transform the peasants of Allensbach and their descendants into merchants *(ut ipsi et eorum posteri sint mercatores)*, no possible ingenuity of interpretation can explain this if we have in mind professional tradesmen. That in point of fact merchant meant any man who sold wares in the market, no matter whether he himself had produced them or bought the greater part of them, is evident, for example, from an unprinted declaration of the Council of Frankfurt in 1420 regarding the toll called *Marktrecht* (in Book No. 3 of the Municipal Archives, Fol. 80). There we find at the beginning that this toll is to be paid by 'every merchant who stands on the street with his merchandise, whatsoever it be.' Then follow, specified in detail, the

individual 'merchants' or the 'merchandise' affected by this toll. From the lengthy list the following instances may be given: dealers in old clothes, pastry-books, food-vendors, rope-makers, hazel-nut-sellers, egg and cheese-sellers with their carts, poultry-vendors who carry about their baskets on their backs, strangers having in their possession more than a matter of cheese, cobblers, money changers, bakers who use the market-stalls, strangers with breadcarts, geese, wagons of vitch (fodder), straw, hay, cabbages, all vendors of linen, flax, hemp, yarn, who sell their wares upon the street. Here we have a confused medley of small tradesmen of the town, artisans and peasants. That buyers as well as sellers on the market were designated as *Kaufleute* (merchants) is evident from numerous records; in fact, passages might be cited in which, when the merchant is spoken of, it is the buyer that seems to be chiefly meant." *Industrial Evolution* (New York: Holt, 1901), 117–118, fn. 23.

[13]There was "long distance" trade and very local trade, but no "intermediate" trade. Carlo Cipolla gives this explanation: "A curious mixture of universalism and particularism dominated the scene. It was economically convenient to get precious silk from China or precious rugs from the Near East, but it was usually not convenient to get poorer commodities from a few miles away. Since mass transportation was impossible for technical reasons, freight costs remained relatively high. Particularly when transportation by water route was impossible, long distance trade had to rely mainly, if not exclusively, on precious objects. For its basic daily needs any community had always to be as self-sufficient and self-sustaining as possible. The interlocal division of labor had to rest mainly on precious objects or other things that by no means could be made locally or were not susceptible of easy substitution. And trade had to rest heavily on aristocratic consumption of luxury goods." *Money, Prices, and Civilization in the Mediterranean World: Fifth to Seventeenth Century* (New York: Gordian Press, 1967), 57.

offered a possible refuge and place of employment for peasants which began to change some of the terms of relationship on the manor.[14]

Feudalism as a system should not be thought of as something antithetical to trade. On the contrary, up to a certain point, feudalism and the expansion of trade go hand in hand. Claude Cahen suggests that if scholars have often observed this phemonemon in areas *other than* western Europe,[15] perhaps they have failed to notice the same phenomenon in Western feudalism because of ideological blinkers. "Having thus noted the possibility of convergence, *up to a certain stage of development only,* of the development of feudalism and of commerce, we ought to reconsider, from this point of view, the history of the West itself."[16]

Yet a feudal system could only support a limited amount of long-distance trade as opposed to local trade. This was because long-distance trade was a trade in luxuries, not in bulk goods. It was a trade which benefited from price disparities and depended on the political indulgence and economic possibilities of the truly wealthy. It is only with the expansion of production within the framework of a modern world-economy that

---

[14]See Paul Sweezy: "[T]he rise of the towns, which was fairly general throughout western Europe, did a great deal more than merely offer a haven of refuge to those serfs who fled the manor; it also altered the position of those who remained behind. . . . Just as wages must rise in a low-wage area, so concessions had to be made to serfs when they had the possibility of moving to towns." "The Transition from Feudalism to Capitalism," *Science and Society,* **XIV,** 2, Spring 1950, 145. It might be noted that in the course of this long debate between Sweezy and Maurice Dobb, in which they disagree about a long list of things, Dobb notes on this point: "Incidentally, I agree entirely with the important consideration which Sweezy stresses that it was not so much the magnitude of the flight to the towns which was significant, but that the threat of it (accompanied perhaps by no more than a small movement) might suffice to force the lords into making concessions, severely weakening to feudalism." "Reply by Maurice Dobb," *Science and Society,* **XIV,** 2, Spr. 1950, 160.

[15]"There is no doubt that forms nearest to feudalism appeared in all their force, both in Byzantium and in the Moslem world, at moments of commercial expansion and not at those of decline. The same thing is undoubtedly true for the Russian and Polish worlds, with the particular feature that the men who materially organized the international trade were by and large foreigners (Hanseatic merchants), while the indigenous landowners took care of producing and assembling the objects of commerce. The profits were divided between the two groups, thus assisting the rise of the seigniorial class by ena-

bling it to acquire the means of dominating the peasants." Claude Cahen, "A propos de la discussion sur la féodalité," *La Pensée,* No. 68, juil.–août 1956, 95–96.

[16]Cahen, *ibid.* p. 96. A. B. Hibbert similarly argues that: "Both fact and theory suggest that in earlier medieval times trade was by no means a solvent of feudal society, but that it was a natural product of that society and that feudal rulers up to a point favored its growth. . . . Feudalism could never dispense with merchants. . . . There were two reasons why. . . . They had to provision large private and public establishments, and they wished to gain profit from trade and industry, either by becoming traders themselves or by tapping the wealth produced by trade and industry through levies and charges upon goods or upon those who produced and distributed them." "The Origins of the Medieval Town Patriciate," *Past & Present,* No. 3, Feb., 1953, 17.

Hibbert further discusses the *two* sources of dominant strata in the towns:

"Two processes are involved in the formation of a patriciate, the internal transformation of an old dominant class and the recruitment of new families from the more successful merchants and artisans, who were often immigrants and descendants of immigrants [p. 23]."

"[This explanation] allows for a source of mercantile capital additional to the windfalls of petty pedlars and porters. Finally it will allow for the idea that the novel techniques or fresh markets might first be exploited by new men who in order to expand relied on association with wealthy men of older standing so that capital was gradually shifted

long-distance trade could convert itself in part into bulk trade which would, in turn, feed the process of expanded production. Until then, as Owen Lattimore notes, it was not really what we mean today by trade:

> As late as the time of Marco Polo (at least) the trade of the merchant who ventured beyond his own district depended delicately on the whims of potentates. . . . The distant venture was concerned less with the disposal of goods in bulk and more with curiosities, rarities and luxuries. . . . The merchant sought out those who could extend favor and protection. . . . If he were unlucky he might be plundered or taxed to ruination; but if he were lucky he received for his goods not so much an economic price as a munificent largesse. . . . The structure of the silk trade and that of much other trade was more a tribute structure than a trade structure.[17]

Thus, the level of commercial activity was limited. The principal economic activity remained food and handicraft production traded within small economic regions. Nonetheless, the scale of this economic activity was slowly expanding. And the various economic nuclei expanded therewith. New frontier lands were cultivated. New towns were founded. Population grew. The Crusades provided some of the advantages of colonial plunder. And then sometime in the fourteenth century, this expansion ceased. The cultivated areas retracted. Population declined. And throughout feudal Europe and beyond it, there seemed to be a "crisis," marked by war, disease, and economic hardship. Whence came this "crisis" and what were its consequences?

First, in what sense was there a crisis? Here there is some disagreement, not so much as to the description of the process as to the emphasis in causal explanation. Edouard Perroy sees the issue primarily as one of an optimal point having been reached in an expansion process, of a saturation of population, "an enormous density, given the still primitive state of agrarian and artisanal technology."[18] And lacking better plows and fertilizer little could be done to ameliorate the situation. This led to food shortages which in turn led to epidemics. With a stable money supply, there was a moderate rise in prices, hurting the rentiers. The slow deterioration of the situation was then rendered acute by the beginnings of the Hundred Years War in 1335–1345, which turned western European state systems toward a war economy, with the particular result that there was an increased need for taxes. The taxes, coming on top of already heavy feudal dues, were too much for the producers, creating a liquidity crisis which in turn

from an older to a new use [p. 26]."

[17]Owen Lattimore, "The Frontier in History", in *Relazioni del X Congresso de Scienze Storiche,* **I:** *Metodologia—Problemi generali—Scienze ausiliare della storia* (Firenze, G. C. Sansoni, 1955), 124–125.

[18]Edouard Perroy, "A l'origine d'une économie contractée: les crises du XIVe siècle," *Annales E.S.C.,* **IV,** 2, avr.-juin 1949, 168. One piece of evidence that Perroy may be right about saturation of popula-

tion is the fact that English archives indicate that in the Middle Ages, a working day in agriculture in fact meant "from sunrise to noon." See Slicher van Bath, *Agrarian History,* p. 183. In fact Ester Boserup derives from this fact the conclusion that a significant aspect of modern agricultural development is "a gradual lengthening of working hours in agriculture." *The Conditions of Economic Growth* (Chicago, Illinois: Aldine, 1965), 53.

led to a return to indirect taxes and taxes in kind. Thus started a downward cycle: The fiscal burden led to a reduction in consumption which led to a reduction in production and money circulation which increased further the liquidity difficulties which led to royal borrowing and eventually the insolvency of the limited royal treasuries, which in turn created a credit crisis, leading to hoarding of bullion, which in turn upset the pattern of international trade. A rapid rise in prices occurred, further reducing the margin of subsistence, and this began to take its toll in population. The landowner lost customers and tenants. The artisan lost customers. There was turn from arable to pasture land because it required less manpower. But there was a problem of customers for the wool. Wages rose, which was a particular burden for small and medium-sized landowners who turned to the State for protection against wage rises. "The disaggregation to manorial production, which becomes ever more severe after 1350, is proof of a continuous slump . . . [of] mediocrity in stagnation."[19]

Stagnation is, on the face of it, a curious consequence. One might have expected the following scenario. Reduced population leads to higher wages which, with rents relatively inelastic, would mean a change in the composition of demand, shifting part of the surplus from lord to peasant, and hence ensuring that less of it would be hoarded. Furthermore, a reduction of population in an economy that was largely agricultural should have led to parallel reductions in demand and supply. But since typically a producer will normally reduce production by eliminating the less fertile plots, there should have been an increased rate of productivity, which should have reduced prices. Both of these developments should have encouraged, not discouraged, trade. Nonetheless trade "stagnated" in fact.

What went wrong in the calculation is the implicit assumption about elasticity of demand. North and Thomas remind us that, given the state of the technology and the range of the volume of international trade, transactions costs were very high, and any reduction in volume (due to a decline in population) would set in train a process of rising costs which would lead to a further reduction in trade. They trace the process like this:

> [Previously] merchants found it profitable to reduce transactions costs by stationing factors in a distant city to acquire information about prices and possible trading opportunities; as the volume of trade shrank, this was no longer expedient. Information flows dried up and trade volume was further reduced. It is thus not surprising that economic historians have found depression (for them meaning a decreased total volume of economic activity) even in the midst of this world where higher *per capita* income would presumably have followed the relatively increased real wage that peasant and worker must have been experiencing.[20]

[19]Perroy, *ibid.*, p. 182.
[20]Douglass C. North & Robert Paul Thomas, "An Economic Theory of the Growth of the Western

World," *Economic History Review*, 2nd ser., **XXIII**, 1, Apr. 1970, 12–13. B. H. Slicher van Bath points to a similar pressure towards "stagnation." He says:

R. H. Hilton accepts Perroy's description of events.[21] But he takes exception to the form of analysis which makes the crisis comparable to one of the recurrent crises of a developed capitalist system, thus exaggerating the degree to which financial and monetary dilemmas affect a feudal system in which the cash-flow element is so much smaller a part of human interaction than in capitalist society.[22] Furthermore, he suggests that Perroy omits any discussion of another phenomenon which resulted from the events Perroy describes, and which to Hilton is central, that of the unusual degree of social conflict, the "climate of endemic discontent," the peasant insurrections which took the form of a "revolt against the social system as such."[23] For Hilton, this was not therefore merely a conjunctural crisis, one point in an up and down of cyclical trends. Rather it was the culmination of 1000 years of development, the decisive crisis of a system. "During the last centuries of the Roman Empire as during the Middle Ages, society was paralyzed by the growing expense of a social and political superstructure, an expense to which corresponded no compensating increase in the productive resources of society."[24] Hilton agrees with Perroy that the immediate cause of the dilemma was to be found in technological limitations, the lack of fertilizer and the inability to expand fertilizer supply by expanding the number of cattle, because the climate limited the quantity of winter forage for cattle. But "what we should underline is that there was no large reinvestment of profits in agriculture such that would *significantly* increase productivity."[25] This was because of the inherent limitations of the reward system of feudal social organization.

What Hilton's emphasis on the *general* crisis of feudalism offers us

"Despite the diminution of the cultivated area and a reduction in the factors of production—which must have indicated a great diminution in the total production of cereals—the price of cereals did not rise in proportion to other merchandise. They even showed a slight tendency to go down. Which indicates that consumption regressed further than production." "Les problèmes fondamentaux de la societé pré-industrielle en Europe occidentale," *Afdeling Agrarische Geschiedenis Bijdragen*, No. 12, 1965, 40.

How great the "stagnation" was is itself an issue. Eugen A. Kominsky doubts that the description is valid other than for England and, to some extent, France. See "Peut-on considérer le XIVe et le XVe siècles comme l'époque de la décadence de l'économie européenne?" *Studi in onore di Armando Sapori* (Milano: Istituto Edit. Cisalpino, 1957), **I**, 562–563.

[21] Michael Postan's description is also close to that of Perroy. See M. M. Postan, "Some Economic Evidence of Declining Population in the Later Middle Ages," *Economic History Review*, 2nd ser., **II**, 3, 1950, 221–246.

[22] Marc Bloch supports Hilton's argument when he warns us against exaggerating the extent of decline in seigniorial income which comes from overestimating the role of cash-flow. It is true that to the extent that rents were fixed, a devaluation of silver would in fact mean an increment to the tenant, provided the tenant paid in silver. But these provisos are bothersome. Bloch reminds us that at this time there was "a terrible famine of metallic money (to such an extent that in England, some peasants, unable to procure the silver needed to pay their rents, themselves asked to pay them in kind)." *Seigneurie française et manoir anglais* (Paris: Lib. Armand Colin, 1960), 110. Hence, says Bloch, there resulted a "lower limit [*palier*] of prices advantageous, obviously, for those who earned fixed rents."

[23] R. H. Hilton, "Y eut-il une crise générale de la féodalité?" *Annales E.S.C.*, **VI**, 1, janv.-mars 1951, 25.

[24] *Ibid.*, p. 27.

[25] *Ibid.*, p. 28.

over Perroy's sense of the conjunctural is that it can account for the social transformation these developments involved. For if the optimal degree of productivity had been passed in a system *and* the economic squeeze was leading to a generalized seignior–peasant class war, as well as ruinous fights within the seigniorial classes, then the only solution that would extract western Europe from decimation and stagnation would be one that would expand the economic pie to be shared, a solution which required, given the technology of the time, an expansion of the land area and population base to exploit. This is what in fact took place in the fifteenth and sixteenth centuries.

That peasant revolts became widespread in western Europe from the thirteenth century to the fifteenth century seems to be in little doubt. Hilton finds the immediate explanation for England in the fact that "in the 13th century most of the great estate-owners, lay and ecclesiastical, expanded their demesne production in order to sell agricultural produce on the market. . . . [As a result], labor services were increased, even doubled."[26] Kosminsky similarly talks of this period as being that of "the most intense exploitation of the English peasantry. . . ."[27] On the continent, there were a series of peasant rebellions: in northern Italy and then in coastal Flanders at the turn of the 14th century; in Denmark in 1340; in Majorca in 1351; the Jacquerie in France in 1358; scattered rebellions in Germany long before the great peasant war of 1525. Peasant republics sprang up in Frisia in the twelfth and thirteenth centuries, and in Switzerland in the thirteenth century. For B. H. Slicher van Bath, "peasant rebellions went with economic recession."[28] Dobb suggests that when such recession occurred, it fell particularly hard not on the lowest stratum of workers who probably never were very well off but on "the

---

[26]R. H. Hilton, "Peasant Movements in England Before 1381," in E. M. Carus-Wilson, ed., *Essays in Economic History* (New York: St. Martin's, 1966), **II**, 79. Hilton points out that rent increases, in the case of poor peasants, might cost him his reserve for the winter. For rich peasants, the result was different: "More irritating to them must have been the hindrances to accumulation, rather than the fear of starvation [p. 86]." Furthermore, legislation designed to hold down costs by freezing wages benefited large landowners more than rich peasants. "Now a large farm is useless without the hands to till it, so the tenant was prepared to pay high prices for the labour he could not get otherwise. In so doing he would also tend to put up the price of labour for the manorial lords. But there was no need for the lords to suffer from the working of economic laws because they had at their disposal the political power which enabled them to circumvent them. They still had reserves of serf labour, and they controlled the distribution of such available wage labour as there was, in their capacity as

Justices of Labourers, or of the Peace [p. 88]."

[27]Eugen A. Kosminsky, "The Evolution of Feudal Rent in England from the XIth to the XVth Centuries," *Past & Present*, No. 7, April 1955, 32. He continues: "The growth of feudal exploitation began to exhaust peasant agriculture and at the same time to whittle down the productive forces of feudal society, destroying the conditions for reproduction of the labor force. . . . This long drawn-out struggle . . . found its clearest expression in the rising of 1381. . . ."

[28]Slicher van Bath, *A.A.G.B.*, No. 12, p. 190. He describes the mechanism in this way: "The peasants felt discontented when they saw the low prices brought by agricultural produce, and contrasted them with the high prices and relatively high wages that obtained in industry. Often some further addition to the taxes, which the government or landowner thought might still be borne, provided the spark that set long-smouldering resentment aflame."

upper stratum of well-to-do peasants, who were in position to extend cultivation onto new land and to improve it, and who accordingly tended to be the spearpoint of revolt."[29]

The sudden decline of prosperity involved more than peasant discontent. The depopulation which accompanied it—caused by wars, famines, and epidemics—led to the *Wüstungen,* the recession of settlements from marginal lands, the disappearance of whole villages sometimes. The desertion of villages should not be seen exclusively as a sign of recession. For there are at least two other major reasons for desertion. One, which was a continuing one, was the search for physical security whenever warfare overtook a region.[30] A second, less "accidental" and more structural, was a change in agrarian social structure, the "enclosure" or "engrossing" of land. It seems clear that this process too was going on in the late Middle Ages.[31] And it is somewhat difficult at this stage of our knowledge to disentangle the three.

Two things seem clear about the cessation of clearings and the recession of settlements. It was, as Karl Helleiner remarks, a "selective process with respect to size of holdings. The percentage of small holdings abandoned in the course of the late Middle Ages appears to have been higher than that of full-sized farms."[32] It was also selective by regions. The *Wüstungen* seemed to have been extensive not only in Germany and Central Europe,[33] but also in England.[34] It was on the other hand far more limited in France.[35] No doubt this is in part explained by the fact

[29]Maurice Dobb, *Papers on Capitalism, Development, and Planning* (New York: International Publ., 1967), 11.

[30]See for example the discussion by Jean-Marie Pesez and Emmanuel Le Roy Ladurie concerning France in the fourteenth and fifteenth centuries. "Le cas français: vue d'ensemble," *Villages désertés et histoire économique, XIe-XVIIIe siècles* (Paris: S.E.V.P.E.N., 1965), 155. They also point out that the search for security may sometimes be forced upon the peasants by nearby towns for strategic considerations (see p. 156). See Carlo Cipolla, *Clocks and Culture, 1300–1700* (New York: Walker & Co., 1967a), 115.

[31]See the discussion by Georges Duby in "Démographie et villages désertés," *Villages désertés, et histoire economique, XIe-XVIIIe siècles* (Paris: S.E.V.P.E.N., 1965), 18–23.

[32]Karl Helleiner, "The Population of Europe from the Black Death to the Eve of the Vital Revolution", in *Cambridge Economic History of Europe.*, **IV**, E. E. Rich and C. H. Wilson, eds., *The Economy of Expanding Europe in the 16th and 17th Centuries* (London and New York: Cambridge Univ. Press, 1967), 15. See Duby, *Villages désertés*, 14, 16; Pesez & Le Roy Ladurie, *Villages désertés*, 181–183.

[33]See Wilhelm Abel, *Die Wüstungen des Ausgehenden Mittelalters*, 2nd ed. (Stuttgart: Verlag, 1955), 5–12.

[34]See Maurice W. Beresford, *The Lost Villages of England* (London: Lutterworth Press, 1954). Beresford dates the high point of depopulation (both total desertion of villages and reduction of population therein) as between 1440 and 1520 (see p. 166). He considers enclosure to be the single greatest explanation of this phenomenon which he sees as a gradual development: "[D]epopulation came to villages where there was already a good deal of grassland alongside a diminishing number of husbandlands of corn; . . . enclosure and depopulation [are] an aim only slowly achieved. . . . [p. 210]."

[35]Pesez and Le Roy Ladurie come up with a figure of 5 to 7% of villages of eastern Languedoc deserted between 1328 and today. As they say: "These figures are not insignificant, but we are far from the 40% rate observed by Abel in Germany, and also from the figures calculated by Mr. Beresford." *Villages désertés*, p.129. The rate differential tends to confirm the agrarian reorganization theme rather than the population decline theme. We know there was considerable difference in agrarian reorganization, and that France, for example, saw the creation of far fewer large domains than either England or Ger-

that France was more densely settled and earlier cleared than other areas of Europe for both historical and pedological reasons.

At this time of contracting demand for agricultural products, urban wages and hence industrial prices were rising, because of the shortage of labor bred by population decline. This in turn raised the cost of agricultural labor while reducing rents (insofar as they were fixed while nominal prices were inflating). This led to what Marc Bloch has called the "momentary impoverishment of the seigniorial class."[36] Not only were profits diminished but the costs of management rose, as they always do in difficult times,[37] leading owners to consider shedding direct management. The economic squeeze led to increased exactions on the peasantry which were then counterproductive, and resulted in peasant flight.[38] One path to the restoration of income for the nobility, one often efficacious for the wealthiest stratum, was to involve themselves in new and remunerative careers with the princes.[39] It was not however sufficient to counteract the effects of recession and therefore to stem the decline of the demesne.[40] And it may incidentally, by removing seigniors from residence, have encouraged disinterest in management.

many. Of course, there may have been differences in the rate of population decline in the fourteenth and fifteenth centuries, but here we are on weaker grounds, as so much of the evidence is inferential, from precisely such phenomena as deserted villages. Hence, we cannot use this evidence, or we would be involved in circular reasoning.

[36]Marc Bloch, *Les caractères originaux de l'histoire rurale français* (Paris: Lib. Armand Colin, 1964), **I**, 122.

[37]Henri Lefebvre, "Une discussion historique: du féodalisme au capitalisme: observations," *La Pensée*, No. 65, janv.-févr. 1956, 22.

[38]"The result of this increased pressure was not only to exhaust the goose that laid golden eggs for the castle, but to provoke, from sheer desperation, movement of illegal emigration from the manors. . . . [So] considerable did the problem of fugitives become and so great the hunger for labor, that, despite treaties and mutual promises, an actual competition developed to entice and steal the serfs of a neighboring domain—a competition which . . . involved the making of certain concessions, and the existence of which imposed its own limits on the further increase of feudal exploitation." Maurice Dobb, *Studies in the Development of Capitalism* (London: Routledge & Kegan Paul, 1946), 46–47.

[39]"In fact the fall in fixed payments, together with the decline in direct management and the necessity to spend money on repairs, significantly affected the financial standing of all lords during [the fourteenth and fifteenth centuries]. Everywhere they

appeared to be short of money and on the look-out for outside profit, and for this reason often launched out into careers or adventures which took them away from their estates. However, the various ways of supplementing their incomes, such as taking employ with the more powerful princes who were in search of allies, or the hazardous path of political intrigue and matrimonial alliance, assured the maintenance of nearly all the great aristocratic fortunes." Georges Duby, *Rural Economy and Country Life in the Medieval West* (Columbia: Univ. of South Carolina Press, 1968), 330.

[40]"[The] ever more pronounced decline in the price of grain compared to rural wages, which were maintained at such a very high level by the competition of town crafts and the spread of textile workers into many country districts of Europe, sealed the fate of all excessively large agricultural enterprises. Indeed it seems as if the eclipse of the demesne and the great decline in direct manorial cultivation occurred in the years after 1380, at any rate in France and England." Duby, *ibid.*, 311.

An earlier statement of Duby was more cautious: "It seems probable consequently . . . that the large estate in the course of the second half of the 14th and during the 15th century, if it was not notably reduced in size and sometimes on the contrary enlarged, at least lost its cohesion." "Le grand domaine de la fin du moyen âge en France," *Première Conférence Internationale d'Histoire Economique*, Stockholm, August 1960: *Contributions* (Paris: Mouton, 1960), 338.

What then happened to the large estates? They were sold or rented for money to the principal group ready and able to engage in such a transaction, the better off peasants, who were in a position to obtain favorable terms.[41]

We must however remember that the social organization of agricultural production was not identical everywhere. The demesnes were the largest in western Europe, in part because denser population had required the relative efficiency of larger units. In central Europe, the effects of economic recession led to the same desertion of marginal lands, but the analysis of these *Wüstungen* is complicated by the fact that they represented in part enclosures as well as abandonment.[42] Further to the east, in Brandenburg and Poland, as we shall discuss later, where population density was even thinner, the lords who collectively previously owned less land than the peasants "saw their estates acquiring all the lands left deserted by the sudden demographic collapse."[43] How profitable this would be for them in the sixteenth century, how profoundly this would alter the social structure of eastern Europe, how important this would be for the development of western Europe—all this was doubtless outside the ken of the participants in the fourteenth and fifteenth centuries. But in the *nonmarginal* arable land areas of *western* Europe, the *excessively large* demesne gives way to smaller landholdings. Thus, simultaneously, there is the rise of a medium-sized peasantry on arable land in western Europe, the beginning of enclosures of less arable lands in western Europe (which would be the basis of expanded animal husbandry), and the concentration of property into large estates in eastern Europe (which would come to serve a new function as grain export areas).

Was this period of economic "collapse" or "stagnation" good or bad for the development of a capitalist world-economy? It depends on the length of one's perspective. Michael Postan sees the fifteenth century as

[41]"The final establishment of money rent took place in circumstances unprofitable for those who received it. It was to a great extent forced on them, since it was the rise of the popular movement which compelled lords to be more accommodating." Kosminsky, *Past & Present*, No. 7, p. 33.

[42]See Duby: "We must constantly be on our guard against considering the abandonment and regrouping in the fourteenth and fifteenth centuries of *all* [italics added—I. W.] the fields into a few coherent village territories subject to strict agrarian constraints as signs of economic malaise, agricultural failure or a too sudden decline of the population. On the contrary, these topographical transfers reflect a critical phase in the growth of the cereal economy, postponed for a century or two, but quite comparable in their development and nature to those of which the Ile de France was the scene in the thirteenth century. Thus, in north-western Germania the lords enclosed their woods whose value was increasing. They surrounded them with hedges, shut out the peasants' swine and henceforth forbade periodic heat burning. The power of the lords enforcing this enclosure, caused the families who in these woodland zones drew much of their subsistence from forest, animal husbandry and related cultivation to change their objectives. They were obliged to alter their way of life and the *Waldbauer* became an *Ackermann*, a genuine cultivator settled on permanent fields." *Rural Economy*, p. 309.

[43]*Ibid.*, p. 315.

a regression from the developments of the fourteenth,[44] a setback which to be sure was later overcome. Eugen Kosminsky sees it as part of the liquidation of feudalism, hence a necessary step in the development of a capitalist economy.[45] The facts are the same. The theoretical perspective is different.

Thus far, in this discussion, we have scarcely mentioned the developments in the political sphere, and in particular the slow rise of the centralized state bureaucracy. In the heyday of western feudalism, when the state was weakest, the landowner, the lord of the manor thrived. However much, in a later era, the state machinery might be utilized by the nobility to further their interests, they were doubtless better served still by the weakness of kings and emperors. Not only were they personally freer of control and taxation but they were also freer to control and tax the peasants. In such societies, where there is no effective link between the central authority with its legal order and the masses, the effect of violence was double, since as Bloch noted, "through the play of custom, an abuse might always by mutation become a precedent, a precedent a right."[46]

Lords of the manor then would never welcome the strengthening of the central machinery if they were not in a weakened condition in which they found it more difficult to resist the claims of central authority and more ready to welcome the benefits of imposed order. Such a situation was that posed by the economic difficulties of the fourteenth and fifteenth centuries, and the decline of seigniorial revenues.

Alongside the economic dilemmas occurred a technological shift in the art of war, from the long bow to the cannon and the handgun, from the cavalry war to the one in which infantry charged and hence in which more training and discipline was required. All this meant that the cost of war increased, the number of men required rose, and the desirability

[44]"The great breeding season of English capitalism was in the early phases of the Hundred Years War, when the exigencies of Royal finance, new experiments in taxation, speculative ventures with wool, the collapse of Italian finance and the breeding of the new cloth industry, all combined to bring into existence a new race of war financiers and commercial speculators, army-purveyors and wool-monopolists. But the race was as short-lived as it was new. The great fortunes were lost as easily as they were made, and the period of reckless finance and gigantic fiscal experiments, passed away with the first stage of war. . . .

The English merchant class responded to the stability and recession of trade in the way of all merchants. They adopted a policy of regulation and restriction, impeding the entry of new recruits into commerce and attempting to share out the available trade. . . . What is sometimes regarded as evidence of a typical medieval regulation is in fact nothing else than instances of fifteenth-century departure from the freer and more speculative conditions of the earlier centuries." M. M. Postan, "The Fifteenth Century," *Economic History Review*, **IX**, 2, May 1939, 165–166.

[45]"We believe that it was not depopulation, but rather the liquidation of the manorial economy, the commutation and the diminution of feudal rent which brought about the improvement of the situation of the peasants and the expansion of simple commercial production which prepared the way for capitalist relations. A moderate reduction of population . . . could only intensify and modify . . . the progress of this development." Eugen A. Kosminsky, *Studi in onore di Armando Sapori*, **I**, p. 567.

[46]Marc Bloch, "The Rise of Dependent Cultivation and Seigniorial Institutions" in M. M. Postan, ed., Cambridge Economic History of Europe, **I**: *The Agrarian Life of the Middle Ages* (London and New York: Cambridge Univ. Press, 1966), 269.

of a standing army over ad hoc formations became ever more clear. Given the new requirements, neither the feudal lords individually nor the city-states could really foot the bill or recruit the manpower, especially in an era of depopulation.[47] Indeed, even the territorial states were having a hard job of maintaining order, as the frequency of peasant revolts shows.[48]

The fifteenth century, however, saw the advent of the great restorers of internal order in western Europe: Louis XI in France, Henry VII in England, and Ferdinand of Aragon and Isabella of Castile in Spain. The major mechanisms at their disposition in this task, as for their less successful predecessors, were financial: by means of the arduous creation of a bureaucracy (civil and armed) strong enough to tax and thus to finance a still stronger bureaucratic structure. This process had started already in the twelfth and thirteenth centuries. With the cessation of the invasions, which had previously preoccupied and exhausted the princes, the growth of population, the revival of trade and hence the more abundant circulation of money, there was a basis for the taxation which could pay for salaried officials and troops.[49] This was true not only in France, England, and Spain but in the principalities of Germany as well.

Taxes are to be sure the key issue. And it is not easy to begin the upward cycle.[50] The obstacles to an effective taxation system in the late Middle

[47]"The rival of the city-state, the territorial state, rich in hopes and in men, showed itself to be more capable of meeting the costs of modern war; it supported mercenary armies, procured the costly material for artillery; it soon would permit itself the great luxury of large-scale maritime warfare. Its rise had been for a long time an irreversible phenomenon." Braudel, *La Méditerranée,* **II**, p. 8.

We must of course be careful not to anticipate. Sir Charles Oman dates the historical break in the art of war as occurring only in 1494. See *A History of the Art of War in the Sixteenth Century* (London: Methuen, 1937), 30. For Oman the two key "tendencies" [Note well, however, this word] were "the progressive importance of firearms, and (partly in consequence of that progress) the utilization of field entrenchments, which would make cavalry charges less and less practicable [p. 33]." Indeed, some authors go further and suggest that the social impact of the new military technology is exaggerated even for the sixteenth century. See for example H. M. Colvin, "Castles and Government in Tudor England," *English Historical Review,* **LXXXIII**, 1968, 226. Nevertheless, if we remember we are describing trends or tendencies, then we can ascertain a cumulative and continuous impact beginning already in the fourteenth century.

[48]"The last two centuries of the Middle Ages, throughout western and central Europe, was an era of rural malaise and of depopulation. . . . The large political constructs of the preceding period . . . appeared provisionally to be unable to fulfill their

mission of police and order which was their very reason for being." Bloch, *Caractères originaux,* **I**, pp. 117–118.

[49]"Thus the State from this time onward began to acquire that essential element of its supremacy—financial resources incomparably greater than those of any private person or community." Bloch, *Feudal Society,* p. 422.

[50]David Lockwood has isolated the theoretical problem involved: "The relationship between bureaucracy and taxation is a highly interdependent one. The efficiency of the bureaucracy depends upon the effectiveness of its taxation system; and the effectiveness of its taxation system depends upon the efficiency of the bureaucratic apparatus. Thus, for whatever reason, any increase in the bureaucratic load or decrease in taxation capacity may generate a vicious circle of decentralization of power. Indeed, it might be argued that the 'taxation' crisis of patrimonial bureaucracy is essentially analogous to the 'production' crisis of capitalism. . . . The points of tension are those which represent an actualization of the potential for 'feudalization': the tendency of officials to 'appropriate' the economic and political resources of the office; the struggle of large land-owners to gain immunity from taxation and/or usurp fiscal and political functions; and the economic and political dependency into which the peasantry are forced in seeking protection against the tax burden of the bureaucratic center. These 'centrifugal' tendencies

Ages seem in retrospect overwhelming. Taxation can only in reality be
on net production, and net production was low, as was the quantity of
money, as well as its circulation. It was extremely difficult to verify taxes
both because of a lack of personnel and because of the low level of quantified
record keeping. It is no wonder that rulers constantly resorted to alternatives to taxation as sources of income: to confiscation, to borrowing, to
selling state offices, to debasing the coinage. But each of these alternatives,
while they may have solved financial dilemmas of the moment, had some
negative long-term effects on the politico-economic strength of the king.[51]
Still it would be false to emphasize the difficulties. It is the magnitude of
the achievement that is impressive. The many compromises might be seen
as essential steps on the road to success. Tax-farming[52] and the venality
of office[53] can be seen precisely as two such useful compromises. Furthermore, the increased flow of funds to the king not only hurt the nobility
by strengthening the state, but also by weakening the nobility's own sources
of revenue, especially in the tighter economy of the fourteenth and fifteenth
centuries, and especially for those not linked to the new bureaucracies.
As Duby puts it: "A large part of the revenues extracted from the soil
by the peasants still found its way into the lord's hands, but the endless

may be seen as both a cause and a consequence of
the possible failure of mechanisms for maintaining
effective taxation capacity and central control."
"Social Integration and System Integration" in
George K. Zollschan and Walter Hirsch, eds.,
Explorations in Social Change (Boston, Massachusetts:
Houghton, 1964), 254.

Gabriel Ardant's formulation of this dilemma
places greater emphasis on the fiscal policy-choices
of the state leading to structural change rather than
the reverse, although it is hard to separate the two.
Ardant says: "Apart from confiscation, which in all
eras tempted governments that were unable to
resolve their fiscal difficulties, but which gave them
only resources that were limited in time and often
wasted, whether we are talking of the profits of
conquest, of expropriation of the church's property,
or of the systematic persecution of certain social
categories, two types of solutions were available to
the authorities:

"The first type, the feudal solution, often preceded by a manorial economy and the venality of
offices, tended to result in a significant number of
cases in actual dismemberment of the state.

"To these formulas we can oppose borrowing
and inflation, financial expedients which we shall
see also depend on the structure of the economy.

"We are to be sure abstracting policies, of quite
different dimensions, by which the State transforms
the social organization of the society." *Théorie
sociologique de l'impôt* (Paris: S.E.V.P.E.N., 1965), **I,**
541 and ff.

[51]For example, Ardant points out that: "To obtain
credits judged necessary within the framework of
an unfavorable financial situation, a state may be
led to make pledges *(gages)* in the broad sense of
this term which signify a restriction of its
sovereignty: a specific source of income may be
turned over to foreign creditors; a degree of supervision of financial administration, extended then to
political administration, may be exercised by the
creditors, or by the State which backs them, etc.
[*Ibid.,* **I,** pp. 549–550]."

[52]Max Weber, in contrasting western Europe to
India, states: "Also in the occidental state at the
beginning of modern times there appeared tax
farming and the commissioning of entrepreneurs
with army recruitment—entrepreneurs to whom
finance had largely to be entrusted. In India, however, under the great kingdoms those central institutions failed to develop which in the West allowed
the princes gradually to take back military and financial administration into their own hands." *The Religion of India* (New York: Free Press, 1958), 69.

[53]"The venality of offices, despite its very severe
inconveniences, had then the political consequence
[of strengthening the state]. It is, for civil administration, the equivalent of the system of paid military
troops, 'mercenaries'—a system denounced with
equal vigor, . . . but one nonetheless tied to the
great and growing fortune of royal power, which
thus no longer depended only on the military force
of feudal nobility." F. Chabod, "Y-a-t-il un état de
la Renaissance?" in *Actes du Colloque sur la Renaissance* (Paris: Lib. Philosophique J. Vrin, 1958), 66.

progress of taxation had greatly enlarged the share taken by the agents of the State."[54]

And as the state grew stronger, monetary manipulation became more profitable. When in the fourteenth and fifteenth centuries, the financial crises of states beset by war were compounded by low profit margins in the countryside that could be taxed, the states had to find other sources of revenue, especially since depopulation meant that princes were offering exemptions from taxation to those who would recolonize devastated areas. Monetary manipulation thus had many advantages. Léopold Génicot points out that there are three possible explanations for the frequent debasements of the period: the reduction of state debts (although debasement also thereby reduces fixed revenues, which constituted the bulk of income from royal domains); scarcity of means of payment, at a time when trade was growing more than the stocks of silver and when public disorder encouraged hoarding of bullion; or a deliberate economic policy of lowering the exchange rate to arrest deflation, combat hoarders, facilitate exports and thus revive commerce. Whichever the explanation of the debasements, they were "very largely inflationary" and "reduced in this way the real value of fixed revenues."[55] The principal recipients of fixed revenues were the seigniorial classes, and hence they were weakened vis-à-vis the state.

The state? What was the state? At this time, it was the prince, the prince whose reputation was lauded, whose majesty was preserved, who little by little was removed from his subjects.[56] And it was the bureaucracy which emerged now as a distinctive social grouping with special characteristics and interests, the principal ally of the prince,[57] and yet one which, as we shall see, was to remain an ambivalent one. And it was the various parliamentary bodies the sovereigns created as mechanisms to assist them in the legislating of taxes, bodies composed largely of nobles, which the kings tried to use against the nobility and the nobility against the king.[58]

This state was a creation which dates not from the sixteenth century

---

[54]Duby, *Rural Economy*, p. 331.

[55]Léopold Génicot, "Crisis: From the Middle Ages to Modern Times," in *Cambridge Economic History of Europe*, **I**: *The Agrarian Life of the Middle Ages*, 2nd ed. (London and New York: Cambridge Univ. Press 1966), 699.

[56]"The importance given to the *reputation* of the prince, both by theoreticians and by men of action (for example, Richelieu), goes with the ever greater attention paid to 'Majesty': all of which little by little created distance between the prince and his subject, placing him on a plane where one could no longer dare to be familiar." Chabod, *Actes*, p. 72.

[57]"If the power of the prince was increasing, another power also grew: that of the bureaucratic 'corps'. Thus was created esprit de corps, linking them one to the other, despite all the personal and private personality disputes, and not only among the *officiers de justice*, the most senior bureaucrats, but among the others as well . . .

"This growing power of the 'fourth estate', the ally—in political terms—of the prince's power, which had been growing simultaneously (administrative centralization and political absolutism going thus hand in hand) is in fact the fundamental element to which we should pay attention [*Ibid.*, pp. 68–69, 72]."

[58]Edward Miller has a brief discussion of how the now far more complex interplay of interests began to take shape in the late medieval period in the various European states. See "Government and Economic Policies and Public Finances, 900–1500," *Fontana Economic History of Europe*, **I**, 8, 1970, 34-40.

but from the thirteenth century in western Europe. Yves Renouard has traced how the boundary lines that determine to this day the frontiers of France, England, and Spain were more or less definitively settled in a series of battles which occurred between 1212 and 1214.[59] It was on the basis of these lines rather than some others (for example, a Mediterranean Occitanian state including Provence and Catalonia; or an Atlantic state including the western France of the Angevins as part of England) that later nationalist sentiments were constructed. First the boundaries, later the passions is as true of early modern Europe as, say, of twentieth-century Africa. It was at this period that not only were the boundary lines decided but, even more important, it was decided that there would be boundary lines. This is what Edouard Perroy calls the "fundamental change" in the political structure of western Europe.[60] In his view, it is between the middle of the twelfth century and the beginning of the fourteenth, in short at the height of commercial and agricultural prosperity of the Middle Ages, that we can date the transformation of Europe.

Why nation-states and not empires? Here we must be prudent about our terminology. Perhaps we should think of France of the thirteenth and fourteenth centuries as a nation-state, of France of the fifteenth and sixteenth centuries as an empire, of the seventeenth century as a nation-state again. This is what Fernand Braudel seems to think.[61] Why this pattern of alternation? Braudel suggests that "there was, with the economic expansion of the 15th and 16th centuries, a conjuncture stubbornly favorable to vast, even very vast States, to these 'thick States'. . . . In fact, history is, in turn, favorable and unfavorable to vast political structures."[62] Fritz Hartung and R. Mousnier suggest the need for a minimum size (but also a maximum?) for the establishment of an absolute monarchy, a form which

[59]See Yves Renouard, "1212–1216: Comment les traits durables de l'Europe occidentale moderne se sont définis au début du XIIIe siècle," *Annales de l'Université de Paris*, **XXVIII**, 1, janv.–mars 1958, 5–21.

[60]"A large unified body, more or less congruent with Latin Christianity, and composed of a multitude of small autonomous cells, the seigniories, gave way to a juxtaposition of vast territorial sovereignties, quite distinctive, the first beginnings of the States of modern Europe." Edouard Perroy et al., *Le Moyen Age*, Vol. III of *Histoire Générale des Civilisations* (Paris: Universitaires de France, 1955), 369–370.

[61]"In fact, the wheel had turned. The [sixteenth] century in its early years favored large States [Spain, Ottoman Empire], which were, as the economists would say, the political enterprise of optimum dimensions. As the century went on, and for reasons that we cannot adequately explain, these large bodies were betrayed bit by bit by circumstances.

Was the crisis transitional or structural? Weakness or decadence? In any case, at the beginning of the 17th century, only middle-sized states seemed vigorous. Thus the France of Henry IV, this sudden splendor; or the little England of Elizabeth, pugnacious and radiant; or Holland organized around Amsterdam; or that Germany invaded by material quiescence from 1555 to the years preceding the Thirty Years' War, in which she would founder, body and soul. In the Mediterranean, such is the case of Morocco, once again rich in gold, and of the Regency of Algiers, the story of a city becoming a territorial state. It is the case as well of Venice radiant, glittering with luxury, with beauty, with intelligence; or of the Tuscany of Grand-Duke Ferdinand. . . .

"In other words, the Empires must have suffered, more than the middle-sized states from the regression of 1595–1621." Braudel, *La Méditerranée*, **II**, p. 47.

[62]*Ibid.*, **II**, p. 10.

did not succeed in little States. "Doubtless, the latter could not constitute military and economic units large enough to sustain an absolute monarchy."[63] These are but hints at answers to a problem worth considerable theoretical attention. V. G. Kiernan helps us perhaps the most with the following conceptual clarification:

> No dynasty set out to build a nation-state; each aimed at unlimited extension . . . and the more it prospered the more the outcome was a multifarious empire *manqué*. It had to be large enough to survive and sharpen its claws on its neighbours, but small enough to be organized from one centre and to feel itself as an entity. On the closepacked western edge of Europe, any excessive ballooning of territory was checked by competition and geographical limits.[64]

Unless, of course, they extended their empires overseas.

What would happen to those empires *manqué* was that they would develop different *raisons d'etat* from empires, different ideologies. A nation-state is a territorial unit whose rulers seek (sometimes seek, often seek, surely not always seek) to make of it a national society—for reasons we shall discuss later. The affair is even more confusing when we remember that from the sixteenth century on, the nation-states of western Europe sought to create relatively homogeneous national societies at the core of empires, using the imperial venture as an aid, perhaps an indispensable one, to the creation of the national society.

We have discussed the crisis of western feudalism in the fourteenth and fifteenth centuries as the background for, prelude to, the expansion of Europe and its economic transformation since the sixteenth century. Thus far the discussion and the explanations have been largely in terms of the social structure (the organization of production, the state machinery, the relationship of various social groups). Yet many would feel that the "crisis" of the fourteenth century and the "expansion" of the sixteenth could be accounted for, let us say in significant part, by factors of the physical environment—climate, epidemiology, soil conditions. These arguments cannot be lightly dismissed and the factors should be assessed and given their due weight in accounting for the social change that did occur.

The case for climate has been put most strongly by Gustaf Utterström. The argument in summary goes like this:

> Thanks to industrialism, thanks not least to technical progress, man in our own day is less exposed to the whims of Nature than he was in previous centuries. But how often is it considered that another factor is that we are living in an age in which the climate, especially in northern Europe, is unusually mild? During

[63]Fr. Hartung & R. Mousnier, "Quelques problèmes concernant la monarchie absolue," in *Relazioni del X Congresso Internazionale di Scienze Storiche*, **IV:** *Storia moderna* (Firenze: G. B. Sansoni, 1955), 47.

[64]V. G. Kiernan, "State and Nations in Western Europe," *Past & Present*, No. 31, July 1965, 35–36.

the last 1000 years, . . . the periods of prosperity in human affairs have on the
whole, though with important exceptions, occurred during the warm intervals
between the great glaciations. It is in these same intervals that both economic life
and the size of the populations have made the greatest advances.[65]

To strengthen his case, Utterström reminds us that climatic change
might have had special bearing on the earlier periods in the transformation of Europe. "The primitive agriculture of the Middle Ages must
have been much more dependent on favorable weather than is modern
agriculture with its high technical standards."[66]

Utterström points for example to the severe winters of the fourteenth
and early fifteenth centuries, the mild winters from 1460 to the mid-
16th century, the severe winters of the second half of the seventeenth,[67]
which corresponds *grosso modo* to economic recession, expansion, and
recession.

> To regard population pressure as the decisive factor does not provide a satisfac-
> tory explanation of these economic developments. The fact that the population
> increased in the way it did raises a question which has not so far been asked:
> why did the population increase? . . . The great increase in population was . . .
> general throughout Europe. In northern and central Europe it got well under
> way during the period when the climate was unusually mild. This can scarcely
> be a chance coincidence: there must be a causal connection.[68]

In addition, Utterström makes epidemiological factors intervening variables. He explains the Black Plague by hot summers which led to the
multiplication of the black rat, the host to the rat flea, one of the two
carriers of the plague.[69]

Georges Duby acknowledges that this hypothesis must be taken seriously. Certainly some of the fourteenth century abandonments of cultivation (cereals in Iceland, the Scandinavian colonies in Greenland, the
lowered forest limit in Sudetenland, the end of viticulture in England
and its regression in Germany) are all plausibly explained by climatic
change. But there are alternative plausible explanations. Most importantly, Duby reminds us that "agrarian recession, like the demographic
collapse, started before the beginning of the fourteenth century,"[70]
hence before the presumed climatic changes. Instead, Duby would see
climatic factors and then epidemiology as being cumulative woes which,

[65]Gustaf Utterström, "Climatic Fluctuations and
Population Problems in Early Modern History,"
Scandinavian Economic History Review, **III,** 1, 1955,
47.
  [66]*Ibid.,* p. 5.
  [67]*Ibid.,* p. 24.
  [68]*Ibid.,* p. 39.
  [69]See *ibid.,* pp. 14–15. However Karl Helleiner,

citing work by Ernst Rodenwaldt, suggests that,
although the human flea is a less important vector
of bubonic plague than the rat flea, it may have
been more significant in the Middle Ages, thus
reducing the import of Utterström's hypothesis. See
Helleiner, *Cambridge Economic History of Europe,* **IV,**
p. 7.
  [70]Duby, *Rural Economy,* p. 307.

in the fourteenth century, "dealt a crushing blow to the already fragile demographic structure."[71] Similar skepticism about the temporal primacy of climatic change in explaining the ups and downs have been expressed by Helleiner,[72] Slicher van Bath,[73] and Emmanuel Le Roy Ladurie.[74]

Obviously, to the extent that there was climatic change, it would affect the operations of a social system. Yet equally obviously, it would affect different systems differently. Though opinions differ, it is probable that such glaciation as did occur was spread over the whole Northern Hemisphere, yet social developments in Asia and North America were clearly divergent from those in Europe. It would be useful therefore to return to the chronic factor of resource strain involved in the feudal system of social organization, or overconsumption by a minority given the overall low level of productivity. Norman Pounds reminds us of "how small the margin for security was for the medieval peasant even under conditions that might be termed normal or average. . . ."[75] Slicher van Bath tends to corroborate this hypotheses of prolonged undernourishment by observing that it was precisely in protein-producing regions that men were most resistant to the plague.[76]

If however there was first economic regression because of the chronic overexploitation and resulting rebellions discussed previously, and then climatic factors added on both food shortages and plagues, it is easy to see how the socio–physical conjuncture could achieve "crisis" proportions. The crisis would in turn be aggravated by the factor that the plague, once it spread, became endemic.[77] Furthermore, although fewer men should have meant more food since the landmass remained the

---

[71]*Ibid.*, p. 308.

[72]Helleiner, *Cambridge Economic History of Europe*, **IV**, p. 76.

[73]"It does not appear likely that the periodic ups and downs observed in the economic life of western Europe after 1200 are the result of climatic changes. . . ." Slicher van Bath, *A.A.G.B.*, No. 12, p. 8.

[74]After pointing out that some of Utterström's evidence is not a priori climatic, he points to methodological flaws in the use of meteorological data. He suggests that Utterström has not given enough long trend data to sustain his generalizations. "Let us imagine a historian or an economist who would claim to demonstrate a long and lasting rise in prices, arguing only from some exceptional 'cyclical' points of the curve he wishes to interpret, while neglecting, not even perhaps knowing, the general shape of the curve in question." Emmanuel Le Roy Ladurie, *Histoire du climat depuis l'an mil* (Paris: Flammarion, 1967), 17.

[75]Norman J. G. Pounds, "Overpopulation in France and the Low Countries in the Later Middle Ages," *Journal of Social History*, **III**, 3, Spring 1970, 245. Pounds talks of a "permanent condition of

undernourishment." Fernand Braudel takes a similar position: "[In a primarily agricultural economy], the rhythm, the quality, the inadequacy of harvests determine the whole of material life. There can result from them brusque harm, like bites, in the sap-wood of trees or in the flesh of men." *Civilisation matérielle et capitalisme* (Paris: Lib. Armand Colin, 1967), 32–33.

[76]"The people of the Dutch coastal areas, who lived for the most part from stock-farming and fishery and consequently ate more animal products and fats than the arable-farming folk, perhaps for that reason, did not succumb to the epidemics of the fourteenth century to anything like the same degree [as other Europeans]." Slicher van Bath, *A.A.G.B.*, No. 12, pp. 89-90.

[77]"For the plague, once it had been introduced [in 1347-1351] did not disappear from Europe until about 350 years after its first outbreak. In endemic or epidemic form it continued to exercise a profound influence both on the long-term average and on short-term fluctuations of the death rate." Helleiner, *Cambridge Economic History of Europe*, **IV**, p. 5.

same, it also meant a shift to pasturage and hence a reduction of caloric output. The demographic decline thus became endemic too.[78] Pierre Chaunu adds that "the collapse of rent, the diminution of profits and the aggravation of seigniorial burdens" may have worsened the situation further by turning capital investment away from the land.[79] And Dobb suggests that the resulting phenomenon of commutation may have further increased the burden of the peasant, rather than mitigating it as usually assumed, thereby adding to the dilemma.[80] Thus, intruding the variables of the physical environment does not undo our previous analysis. It enriches it by adding a further element to help explain a historical conjuncture so consequential in the future history of the world, a further instance in which long-term stabilities and slow secular changes can account for conjunctures which have the power to change social structures which are intermediate from the perspective of temporal duration.

The analysis thus far is as follows. In Europe in the late Middle Ages, there existed a Christian "civilization" but neither a world-empire nor a world-economy. Most of Europe was feudal, that is, consisted of relatively small, relatively self-sufficient economic nodules based on a form of exploitation which involved the relatively direct appropriation of the small agricultural surplus produced within a manorial economy by a small class of nobility. Within Europe, there were at least two smaller

[78]Karl Helleiner puts forth the following hypothesis: "[The] very improvements in the economic position of the lower classes [following the depopulation caused by the Black Death] may have militated against speedy demographic recovery. It is to be assumed on *a priori* grounds, and there is some evidence to support this view, that those improvements led to an upward revision of the living standard, involving a partial shift from a cereal to a meat standard of consumption. This change in consumers' preference is reflected in the movement of relative prices of animal products and grain, which must have intensified [the] *Wüstung* process . . . , one aspect of which was a partial 'decerealization' of Europe in favour of animal husbandry. However, given a certain level of agrarian technology, five or six more times as much land is required for the raising of one calorie of animal food as is needed for the production of one calorie of vegetable food. It follows that whatever relief from pressure of population on land was afforded by the initial demographic slump must have been partially offset by that change in the pattern of consumption and production. This hypothesis helps to explain an otherwise puzzling fact, namely that the later Middle Ages should have suffered scarcely less than previous centuries from death and famine,

even though man's *per capita* supply of fertile land was undoubtedly much bigger in this period [*Ibid.*, pp. 68–69]."

[79]"The regression of population in the 14th and 15th centuries aggravated, rather than resolved, the shortage of space. Therefore it did not diminish the pressure which had been occurring during the 13th century. It may have increased it, by the fall of rent, the diminution of profit, and the worsening of the seigniorial burden. Capital which would have been tempted to turn to the land was attracted to some degree by other horizons." Chaunu, *L'expansion européenne,* p. 349.

[80]"But there were also plenty of instances where commutation involved not a mitigation but an augmentation of feudal burdens. Here it was merely an alternative to direct imposition of additional services. Commutation was most likely to have this character when resort to it was largely at the lord's initiative; the attempt to increase feudal revenue presumably taking this form because of a relative abundance of labour. . . . Probably it was the pressure of population upon the available land of the village, rendering it harder for the villager to obtain his subsistence and hence making hired labour cheap and relatively plentiful . . . that furthered the inducement to this commutation." Dobb, *Studies,* pp. 63–64.

world-economies, a medium-sized one based on the city-states of northern Italy and a smaller one based on the city-states of Flanders and northern Germany. Most of Europe was not directly involved in these networks.

From about 1150 to 1300, there was an expansion in Europe within the framework of the feudal mode of production, an expansion at once geographic, commercial, and demographic. From about 1300 to 1450, what expanded contracted, again at the three levels of geography, commerce, and demography.

This contraction following the expansion caused a "crisis," one which was visible not only in the economic sphere but in the political sphere as well (internecine wars among the nobility and peasant revolts being the two main symptoms). It was also visible at the level of culture. The medieval Christian synthesis was coming under multitudinous attack in all the forms which later would be called the first stirrings of "modern" Western thought.

There are three main explanations of the crisis. One is that it was the product essentially of cyclical economic trends. The optimal point of expansion given the technology having been reached, there followed a contraction. The second is that it was the product essentially of a secular trend. After a thousand years of surplus appropriation under the feudal mode, a point of diminishing returns had been reached. While productivity remained stable (or even possibly declined as a result of soil exhaustion) because of the absence of structured motivation for technological advance, the burden to be borne by the producers of the surplus had been constantly expanding because of the growing size and level of expenditure of the ruling classes. There was no more to be squeezed out. The third explanation is climatological. The shift in European metereological conditions was such that it lowered soil productivity and increased epidemics simultaneously.

The first and the third explanation suffer from the fact that similar cyclical and climatological shifts occurred at other places and times without producing the consequence of creating a capitalist world-economy as a solution to the problems. The secular explanation of crisis may well be correct but it is inherently difficult to create the kind of serious statistical analysis that would demonstrate that it was a sufficient explanation of the social transformation. I believe it is most plausible to operate on the assumption that the "crisis of feudalism" represented a conjuncture of secular trends, an immediate cyclical crisis, and climatological decline.

It was precisely the immense pressures of this conjuncture that made possible the enormity of the social change. For what Europe was to develop and sustain now was a new form of surplus appropriation, a capitalist world-economy. It was to be based not on direct appropriation of agricultural surplus in the form either of tribute (as had been the case for world-empires) or of feudal rents (as had been the system of European feudalism). Instead what would develop now is the appropriation of a surplus which was based on more efficient and expanded productivity (first in agriculture and later in industry) by means of a world market mechanism with the "artificial" (that is, nonmarket) assist of state machineries, none of which controlled the world market in its entirety.

It will be the argument of this book that three things were essential to the establishment of such a capitalist world-economy: an expansion of the geographical size of the world in question, the development of variegated methods of labor control for different products and different zones of the world-economy, and the creation of relatively strong state machineries in what would become the core-states of this capitalist world-economy.

The second and third aspects were dependent in large part on the success of the first. The territorial expansion of Europe hence was theoretically a key prerequisite to a solution for the "crisis of feudalism." Without it, the European situation could well have collapsed into relative constant anarchy and further contraction. How was it then that Europe seized upon the alternative that was to save it? The answer is that it was not Europe that did so but Portugal, or at least it was Portugal that took the lead.

Let us look now at what it was in the social situation of Portugal that can account for the thrust toward overseas exploration which Portugal began right in the midst of the "crisis." To understand this phenomenon, we must start by remembering that Europe's geographical expansion started, as we have already suggested, earlier. Archibald Lewis argues that "from the eleventh to the mid-thirteenth century western Europe followed an almost classical frontier development."[81] He refers to the gradual reconquest of Spain from the Moors, the recuperation by Christian Europe of the Balaeric Islands, Sardinia, and Corsica, the Norman conquest of southern Italy and Sicily. He refers to the Crusades with its addition first of Cyprus, Palestine and Syria, then of Crete and the Aegean Islands. In Northwest Europe, there was English expansion into Wales, Scotland, and Ireland. And in eastern Europe, Germans and Scandinavians penetrated the lands of, conquered, and converted to Christianity Balts and Slavs. "The most important frontier [however] was an internal one of forest, swamp, marsh, moor, and fen. It was this wasteland which Europe's peasants settled and largely put into cultivation between the years 1000 and 1250."[82] Then, as we have seen, this expansion and this prosperity was brought to an end by a "crisis" which was also a contraction. In political terms, this involved the rally of the

[81] Archibald R. Lewis, "The Closing of the European Frontier," *Speculum*, **XXXIII**, 4, Oct. 1958, 475.

[82] *Ibid.*, p. 476

Moors in Granada, the expulsion of the Crusaders from the Levant, the reconquest of Constantinople by the Byzantines in 1261, the Mongol conquest of the Russian plain. Internally, in Europe, there were the *Wüstungen.*

The great explorations, the Atlantic expansion, was thus not the first but the second thrust of Europe, one that succeeded because the momentum was greater, the social and technological base more solid, the motivation more intense. Why however a thrust whose initial center was Portugal? In 1250 or even 1350, few would have thought Portugal a likely candidate for this role. And retrospectively from the twentieth century, it clashes with our sense of probability, our bias against the minor power Portugal has been in modern times and indeed throughout all of history.

We shall try to answer this question in terms of motivation and capabilities. The motivations were European in scope, though some of them may have been felt more acutely in Portugal. What were the explorers looking for? Precious metals and spices, the schoolboy textbooks tell us. And this was true, to be sure, up to a point.

In the Middle Ages, Christian Europe and the Arab world were in a symbiotic relationship in terms of gold and silver. In Andrew Watson's phrase, "in monetary matters, . . . the two regions should be treated as a whole."[83] The former minted silver, the latter gold. As a result of a long-term disequilibrium in prices, whose origins are complex and need not concern us here, the silver flowed eastward leading to an abundance in the Arab world. Silver exports could no longer lead to gold imports. In 1252, Florence and Genoa therefore struck new gold coins. The motive was there. One fact which made it possible was the expansion of the trans-Saharan gold trade in the thirteenth century.[84] Watson thinks it is implausible to talk of a gold shortage, therefore, in western Europe between 1250 and 1500, for it was a time of increasing supply. Still there remained a constant outflow of precious metals from Europe to India and China via Byzantium and the Arab world, although the disequilibrium was lessening. Watson talks, somewhat mysteriously, of the "strong power of India and China to attract precious metals from other parts

---

[83]Andrew M. Watson, "Back to Gold—and Silver," *Economic History Review,* 2nd ser., **XX,** 1, 1967, 1.

[84]"We forget that, in antiquity and during the Middle Ages, what we should now consider as very poor mines were then held to be first rate. The Western Sudan was, from the 8th century until the discovery of America, the chief supplier of gold for the western world; the trade, commercialized first by Ghana, came under that name to the Mediterranean and enhanced the prestige of the kings who owned such

a source of wealth:" R. A. Mauny, "The Question of Ghana," *Africa,* **XXIV,** 3, July 1954, 209.

Marian Malowist argues that it was the North African demand for gold (in order to sell it to Europeans) rather than the need of the Western Sudan for the salt they received in turn which was the primary stimulus for this expansion. See "Quelques observations sur le commerce de l'or dans le Soudan occidental au moyen âge," *Annales E.S.C.,* **XXV,** 6, nov.–déc. 1970, 1630–1636.

of the world."[85] The demand for bullion thus remained high. Between 1350 and 1450, the silver mines in Serbia and Bosnia began to develop[86] and became an important source until the Turkish invasion of the fifteenth century cut them off from western Europe. Similarly, beginning

---

[85]Watson, *Economic History Review*, **XX**, p. 34. See the remarkable collaborative article by R. S. Lopez, H. A. Miskimin and Abraham Udovitch in which they argue very convincingly that the years 1350–1500 see a steady outflow of bullion from north-west Europe to Italy to the Levant to India:
"Both luxury consumption by the non-agricultural population [of England] and extensive investments in the ornamentation of churches . . . exacerbated the already acute shortage of skilled craftsmen which followed the Black Death by causing a relative increase in the demand for their services. As a result, the wages of skilled artisans were considerably augmented and some of the new demand for luxury, not satisfied domestically, was diverted to areas beyond northern Europe by economic necessity as well as in search of the exotic; the inevitable result of this demand was an increase in the export of money. Further, since the use of scarce labour in the production of domestic luxury proscribes its use for the manufacture of export articles, the potential foreign earnings of the northern economies was reduced. . . .
"[W]here had [the money] gone? . . . [T]he papacy was indeed a major drain of the metal supply of northern Europe. In addition to direct transfers of money, however, the more conventional channels of commerce tended, through the medium of luxury consumption, to produce the same result. . . . The continental termini of [the] north-south route [leading from the Hanse cities] were Milan, Genoa, and Venice; . . . it would seem there was an active and probably one-sided trade connecting the northern economy with the southern in such a way as to drain precious metals southward.
"In France, also, we find a widespread increase in the consumption of southern luxuries during the fourteenth and early fifteenth centuries. . . .
"England and France complained bitterly about the drain of precious metals by Italy, but this was largely the counterpart of the drain from Italy into the Levant. . . . [I]n spite of gold imports from north-western Europe, a moderate production of central European mines, and more substantial amounts coming from Senegal, there are abundant indications that the supply of gold was at best barely adequate and often scarce. Granted that man's gold hunger is chronically insatiable, it is certain that trade with the Levant in the fourteenth and fifteenth centuries drained from Italy an ever growing amount of gold. . . . [T]he comparative ascendancy of luxury trade made Italy more dependent

upon the Levant and increased the drain of precious metals in that direction. . . .
"[There is] an absolute contraction of the Egyptian economy by the end of the fourteenth century and . . . an absolute quantitative decline of all its sectors. . . . Egypt's economic crisis was accompanied by a breakdown of its monetary system. Gold and silver currency became increasingly scarce, and copper coins predominated in internal circulation and on all levels of transaction. . . .
"Among the numerous factors contributing to Egypt's shortage of specie in the late fourteenth and fifteenth centuries, the most central was her persistent unfavourable balance of payments in international trade. By the thirteenth century, the Nubian gold mines were exhausted to the point that the gold extracted barely covered expenses. A lively and profitable trade with the western Sudan kept Egypt supplied with gold until the latter part of the fourteenth century, at which time this trade declined and the African gold was siphoned off toward Europe. . . . While the source of Egypt's gold supply was contracting, there are no indications of a correspondingly significant decline in consumption of foreign products and luxury goods, or a parallel reduction of state expenditures for imports. . . .
"Throughout the fifteenth century, Europe was the only area with which Egypt maintained a favourable balance of trade. . . . Egypt, at the beginning of the fifteenth century, was virtually living off the profits of the spice trade with Europe. . . . But only a fraction of this sum remained in the country. The spice trade was a transit trade. In addition, Egypt was also contributing to [the] flow [of gold toward India] by its own internal consumption of spices and other imports from the Farther East. . . .
"Thus, at least a good portion of the gold which began its long trek southward from Northern Europe in search of luxury products, travelling via Italy and Egypt, found its final resting place as additions to the already incredible gold accumulations of India." "England to Egypt, 1350–1500; Long-term Trends and Long-distance Trade," in M. A. Cook, ed., *Studies in the Economic History of the Middle East from the Rise of Islam to the Present Day* (London and New York: Oxford Univ. Press, 1970), 101, 102, 103, 104, 105, 109, 110, 114, 117, 123, 126, 127–128.
[86]See Desanka Kovacevic, "Dans la Serbie et la Bosnie médiévales: les mines d'or et d'argent," *Annales E.S.C.*, **XV**, 2, mars-avr. 1960, 248-258.

in 1460, there was a sudden rise of silver mining in central Europe, made possible by technological improvements which permitted the exploitation of what had been theretofore marginal mines. Perroy estimates that between 1460 and 1530 silver production quintupled in central Europe.[87] Nonetheless, the supply was not keeping pace with the demand, and the search for gold by the maritime route (thus, for Sudanic gold, circumventing North African intermediaries) was unquestionably one consideration for the early Portuguese navigators.[88] When, therefore, the discovery of the Americas was to give Europe a richer source of gold than the Sudan and especially a far richer source of silver than central Europe, the economic consequences would be great.[89]

The bullion was sought to provide a monetary base for circulation within Europe but even more to export it to the Orient. For what? Again, every schoolboy knows: for spices and jewels. For whom? For the wealthy, who used them as the symbols of their conspicuous consumption. The spices were made into aphrodisiacs, as though the aristocracy could not make love otherwise. At this epoch, the relationship of Europe and Asia might be summed up as the exchange of preciosities. The bullion flowed east to decorate the temples, palaces, and clothing of Asian aristocratic classes and the jewels and spices flowed west. The accidents of cultural history (perhaps nothing more than physical scarcity) determined these complementary preferences. Henri Pirenne, and later Paul Sweezy, give this demand for luxuries a place of honor in the expansion of European commerce.[90] I am skeptical, however, that the exchange of

---

[87]"[There was a] sudden rise of mineral production as of 1460, primarily in Central Europe. In this domain, technology became scientific. The invention of better methods of drilling, drainage and ventilation made possible the exploitation of the mines in Saxony, Bohemia, and Hungary as far as 600 feet down; the increased use of hydraulic power increased the strength of the bellows and the drills such that the hearths could come down from the mountainsides, and be located in the valleys. The building of the first blast-furnaces ten feet high tripled the productive capacity of the old hearths. It is not impossible that, between 1460 and 1530, the extraction of mineral quintupled in Central Europe." Perroy, *Le Moyen Age,* **III,** pp. 559–562.

[88]See V. M. Godinho, "Création et dynamisme économique du monde atlantique (1420–1670)," *Annales E.S.C.,* **V,** 1, janv.–mars 1950, 33; Pierre Chaunu, *Séville et l'Atlantique (1504–1650),* **VIII** (1) (Paris: S.E.V.P.E.N., 1959), 57.

[89]America which relieved, in the Mediterranean, the African gold sources was an even more important substitute for German silver mines." Braudel, *La Méditerranée* **I,** p. 433.

[90]"In every direction where commerce spread, it created the desire for the new articles of consumption which it brought with it. As always happens, the aristocracy wished to surround themselves with the luxury or at least the comfort befitting their social rank." Henri Pirenne, *Economic and Social History of Medieval Europe* (London: Routledge & Kegan, 1936), 81.

"When we take account of the fact that warfare took its main toll from the upper orders (since they alone were permitted to bear arms) we may well doubt there was a significant *relative* growth in the size of the parasitic class. . . . On the other hand, there is no reason to doubt the reality of the growing extravagances of the feudal ruling class. . . . But was this growing extravagance a trend which can be explained by the nature of the feudal system, or does it reflect something which was happening outside the feudal system? . . . . The rapid expansion of trade from the 11th century on brought an ever-increasing quantity and variety of goods within its reach." Paul Sweezy, *Science and Society,* **XIV,** pp. 139-140.

Maurice Dobb, however, argues: "The transition from coercive extraction of surplus labour by

preciosities, however large it loomed in the conscious thinking of the European upper classes, could have sustained so colossal an enterprise as the expansion of the Atlantic world, much less accounted for the creation of a European world-economy.

In the long run, staples account for more of men's economic thrusts than luxuries. What western Europe needed in the fourteenth and fifteenth centuries was food (more calories and a better distribution of food values) and fuel. Expansion into Mediterranean and Atlantic islands, then to North and West Africa and across the Atlantic, as well as expansion into eastern Europe, the Russian steppes and eventually Central Asia provided food and fuel. It expanded the territorial base of European consumption by constructing a political economy in which this resource base was unequally consumed, disproportionately by western Europe. This was not the only way. There was also technological innovation which increased the yield of agriculture, innovation which began in Flanders as early as the thirteenth century and spread to England, but only in the sixteenth century.[91] But such technological innovation was most likely to occur precisely where there was dense population and industrial growth, as in medieval Flanders, which were the very places where it became more profitable to turn the land use to commercial crops, cattle-breeding and horticulture, which consequently "required the import of corn [wheat] in large quantities. Only then could the complicated interlocking system of agriculture and industry function to its fullest advantage."[92] Hence, the process of agricultural innovation fed rather than foreclosed the necessity of expansion.

Wheat was a central focus of new production and new commerce in the fifteenth and sixteenth centuries. At first, Europe found in northern forests and Mediterranean plains its "internal Americas," in the perceptive phrase of Fernand Braudel.[93] But internal Americas were not enough. There was expansion at the edges, first of all to the islands. Vitorino Magalhães-Godinho has put forward as a working hypothesis that agriculture was the major motivation of Portuguese colonization of the

estate-owners to the use of free hired labour must have depended upon the existence of cheap labour for hire (i.e. of proletarian or semi-proletarian elements). This I believe to have been a far more fundamental factor than proximity of markets in determining whether the old social relations survived or were dissolved." *Science and Society*, **XIV**, p. 161.

R. H. Hilton sides with Dobb: "The economic progress which was inseparable from the early rent struggle and the political stabilization of feudalism was characterized by an increase in the total social surplus of production over subsistence needs. This, not the so-called revival of international trade in silks and spices, was the basis for the development of commodity production." "The

Transition from Feudalism to Capitalism," *Science & Society*, **XVII**, 4, Fall 1953, 347.

[91]See B. H. Slicher van Bath, "The Rise of Intensive Husbandry in the Low Countries," in J. S. Bromley & E. H. Kossman, eds., *Britain and the Netherlands* (London: Chatto, 1960), 130–153.

[92]*Ibid.*, p. 137.

[93]"These movements of improvement (*bonificacion*) were in response to the requirements of the towns, whose population never stopped growing in the 15th and 16th centuries. Urgent needs of provisioning these towns led them to develop agricultural production in their environs, either by cultivating new terrains, or by practicing irrigation." Braudel, *La Méditerranée*, **I**, p. 62.

Atlantic islands, a hypothesis pursued by Joël Serrão, who noted that the development of these islands was speedy and in terms of "the tetralogy of cereals, sugar, dyes, and wine . . . . [There was] always a tendency towards monoculture, one or the other of the four products always being preferred."[94] The new wheat that was grown began to flow throughout the European continent, from the Baltic area to the Low Countries beginning in the fourteenth century[95] and as far as Portugal by the fifteenth,[96] from the Mediterranean to England and the Low Countries in the fourteenth and fifteenth centuries.[97]

Foods may be placed in a hierarchy in terms of their cost per 1000 calories. M. K. Bennett finds this hierarchy fairly stable over time and space. Milled-grain products and starchy roots and tubers are at the bottom of his eight tiers, that is, they are the cheapest, the most basic of the staples.[98] But on grains alone a good diet is not built. One of the most important complements in the European diet is sugar, useful both as a calorie source and as a substitute for fats. Furthermore, it can also be used for alcoholic drinks (particularly rum). And later on, it would be used for chocolate, a usage which the Spaniards learned from the Aztecs, and which would become a highly appreciated drink, at least in Spain, by the seventeenth century.[99]

Sugar too was a principal motivation for island expansion. And, because of its mode of production, with sugar went slavery. This started in the eastern Mediterranean in the twelfth century and then moved westward.[100]

[94]Joel Serrão, "Le blé des îles atlantiques: Madère et Açores aux XVe et XVIe siècles," *Annales E.S.C.*, **IX**, 3, juil.-sep. 1954, 338.

[95]See J. A. van Houtte, "L'approvisionnement des villes dans les Pays-Bas (Moyen Age et Temps Modernes)," *Third International Conference of Economic History*, Munich 1965 (Paris: Mouton, 1968), 73–77.

[96]"In the 15th century, Portugal became more and more open to Hanseatic traders and to Bretons who supplied the country with wheat and wood, the import of which was already in that epoch indispensable." Marian Malowist, "Les aspects sociaux de la première phase de l'expansion coloniale," *Africana Bulletin*, **1**, 1964, 12.

[97]See Ruggiero Romano, "A propos du commerce de blé dans la Méditerranée des XIVe et XVe siècles," in *Eventail de l'histoire vivante: hommage à Lucien Febvre* (Paris: Lib. Armand Colin, 1953), 149–161.

[98]The eight tiers Bennett lists are (1) milled-grain products and starchy roots and tubers, including plantain; (2) vegetable fats and oils; (3) dried pulses (beans, peas, lentils); (4) sugar; (5) milk and its products; possibly fish; (6) pig meat; (7) beef, mutton, goat, buffalo, and poultry and eggs; (8) vegetables and fruits. See M. K. Bennett, *The World's Food* (New York: Harper, 1954), 127–128. "Why should the general hierarchy exist? It is undoubted-

ly the reflection of relative costs of production and the inherent calorie-bearing qualities of the several foods [p. 128]."

[99]See G. B. Masefield, "Crops and Livestock," *Cambridge Economic History of Europe*, **IV**: E. E. Rich and C. H. Wilson, eds., *The Economy of Expanding Europe in the 16th and 17th Centuries* (London and New York: Cambridge Univ. Press, 1967), 295.

[100]Anthony Luttrell has traced the picture *prior* to 1500: "The Latins were producing sugar with Muslim and other slaves in Syria, Cyprus and other Levantine colonies from the 12th century onward and by 1404, when Giovanni della Padua of Genoa received a royal licence to establish a plantation in Algarve, the Genoese had apparently transferred it from Sicily to southern Portugal. It was largely the Genoese who provided the initiative, the capital, the milling and irrigation techniques for the introduction of sugar to the Azores and Madeiras, and who exported it from the islands as far afield as Flanders and Constantinople. They also helped provide the necessary labor; Antonio da Noli, for example, was carrying Guineans to Cape Verde isles in the 1460's." "Slavery and Slaving in the Portuguese Atlantic (to about 1500)," in Centre of African Studies, University of Edinburgh, *The Transatlantic Slave Trade from West Africa* (mimeo, 1965), 76.

The Atlantic expansion was simply its logical continuation. Indeed, E. E. Rich traces African slavery in Portugal back to 1000 A.D., the slaves being acquired by trade with Mohammedan raiders.[101] Sugar was a very lucrative and demanding product, pushing out wheat[102] but then exhausting the soil, so that it required ever new lands (not to speak of the manpower exhausted by its cultivation).

Fish and meat are higher on Bennett's list of categories. But they were wanted as sources of protein. Godinho cites the expansion of fishing areas as one of the key dynamics of early Portuguese exploration.[103] Meat no doubt was less important than grain, and was considerably and steadily reduced in importance in the period from 1400 to 1750[104]—a proof of a point to which we shall return, that European workers paid part of the costs of European economic development.[105] Nonetheless the desire for meat was one of the motivations of the spice trade, not the Asian spices for the aphrodisiacs of the rich but the West African grains of paradise *(Amomum melegueta)*, used as a pepper substitute as well as for the spiced wine known as hippocras.[106] These spices were "barely capable of making thin gruel acceptable."[107]

If food needs dictated the geographical expansion of Europe, the food benefits turned out to be even greater than could have been anticipated. World ecology was altered and in a way which, because of the social organization of the emergent European world-economy, would primarily benefit Europe.[108] In addition to food, the other great basic need was wood—wood

[101]See E. E. Rich, "Colonial Settlement and its Labour Problems," in *Cambridge Economic History of Europe*, **IV**: E. E. Rich and C. H. Wilson, eds., *The Economy of Expanding Europe in the 16th and 17th Centuries* (London and New York: Cambridge Univ. Press, 1967), 308.

[102]For example, Serrão notes of Madeira: "About 1475, the wheat cycle ended. . . . Sugar had killed wheat." *Annales E.S.C.,* **IX**, p. 340. Serrão points out that when this happened, the Azores became Portugal's wheat-growing area, supplanting primarily Madeira. This cyclical pattern was "true in the 16th century, as in the 17th, and still in the 18th." *Ibid.,* p. 341.

[103]See Godinho, *Annales E.S.C.,* **V**, p. 33.

[104]"What people are generally less well aware of is that the situation sketched in 1750—large rations of bread and a little meat . . . was itself the result of a deterioration and does not apply when we go back in time to the Middle Ages." Fernand Braudel and Frank C. Spooner, "Prices in Europe from 1450 to 1750," in *Cambridge Economic History of Europe*, **IV**: E. E. Rich and C. H. Wilson, eds., *The Economy of Expanding Europe in the 16th and 17th Centuries* (London and New York: Cambridge Univ. Press, 1967), 414.

[105]"From 1400 to 1750 Europe was a great consumer of bread and more than one-half vegetarian.

. . . Only this 'backward' diet allowed Europe to carry the burden of a continually increasing population. . . . The consumption of bread put that of meat more and more in the background until the mid-nineteenth century." *Ibid.* p. 413. See also W. Abel, "Wandlungen des Fleischverbrauchs und der Fleischversorgung in Deutschland," *Bericht über Landwirtschaft*, n.s., **22**, 1938, 411–452, cited in Slicher van Bath, *Agrarian History,* p. 204.

[106]"The early explorations of the Portuguese along the West African coast yielded only one plant of immediate interest, grains of paradise. . . . They could now be obtained more cheaply than by the overland trans-Saharan route, and the trade gave its name to the 'Grain Coast'; but the plants could not be acclimatized in Europe." Masefield, *Cambridge Economic History of Europe*, **IV**, p. 276.

[107]Chaunu, *L'expansion européenne,* p. 354.

[108]G. B. Masefield points out how the link between the Americas and the Eastern Hemisphere changed the agrarian map of the world: "The dispersal of crops and livestock which followed the establishment of these links was the most important in human history, and perhaps had the most far-reaching effects of any result of the Discoveries. Without the American crops, Europe might not have been able to carry such heavy populations as she later did,

for fuel, and wood for shipbuilding (and housebuilding). The economic development of the Middle Ages, and one must assume its crude forestry techniques, had led to a slow but steady deforestation of western Europe, Italy, and Spain, as well as Mediterranean islands. Oak became especially scarce.[109] By the sixteenth century, the Baltic area had begun to export wood in large quantities to Holland, England, and the Iberian peninsula.

One other need of provisioning should be mentioned, the need of clothing. There was of course the luxury trade, the demand for silks, whose ancient history was linked with the demand for jewels and spices. The growing textile industry, the first major industry in Europe's industrial development, was more than a luxury trade, however, and required materials for processing: dye-stuffs for cotton and wool textiles and gum used to stiffen the silks in the finishing process.[110]

Bullion was desired as a preciosity, for consumption in Europe and even more for trade with Asia, but it was also a necessity for the expansion of the European economy. We must ask ourselves why. After all, money as a means of payment can be made of anything, provided men will honor it. And indeed today we almost exclusively use nonbullion items as means of payment. Furthermore, Europe was beginning to do so in the late Middle Ages with the development of "money of account," sometimes deceivingly called "imaginary money."

It would however take centuries before metallic money approached the status of symbolic money.[111] It is not yet totally there even today. As a result Europe was beset by constant mutations of value through debasement, so constant that Marc Bloch calls it "the universal thread of monetary history."[112] Yet no one seriously suggested then dispensing with bullion.

---

and the Old World tropics would not have been so quickly developed. Without the European livestock, and especially horses and mules for transport and cultivation, the American continent could not have been developed at the rate it had been." *Cambridge Economic History of Europe*, **IV**, p. 276.

[109] Braudel speaks of a "wood famine" with reference to various parts of Italy. "The Mediterranean navies became accustomed, little by little, to go looking further and further for what they couldn't find in their own forests. In the sixteenth century, Nordic wood arrived in Seville in boats filled to the brim with planks and beams." *La Méditerranée*, **I**, p. 131.

See Frederic Lane: "When this depletion of the oak woods was first clearly recognized—in the last half of the fifteenth century—the shortage seems to have been peculiar to Venice. At least the Ragusans and the Basques had a sufficiently plentiful supply so that their competition was severely felt. At the end of the sixteenth century the scarcity of oak timber appears to have been general throughout Mediterranean countries." "Venetian Shipping During the Commercial Revolution," in *Venice and His-*

tory (Baltimore, Maryland: Johns Hopkins Press, 1966), 21.

H. C. Darby makes the same point for England: "The growth of England's mercantile marine and the development of the English navy from the Tudor age onward depended upon an adequate supply of oaks for the hulls of ships; fir trees for masts, together with such 'naval stores' as pitch and tar, were imported from Baltic lands." "The Clearing of the Woodland in Europe," in William L. Thomas, Jr., ed., *Man's Role in Changing the Face of the Earth* (Chicago, Illinois: Univ. of Chicago Press, 1956), 200.

[110] See Godinho, *Annales E.S.C.*, **V**, p. 33.

[111] The key element in making metallic money symbolic is to make the coins with a commodity value lower (preferably far lower) than their monetary value. Yet Carlo Cipolla points out this was not adopted for petty coins in England until 1816 and in the United States until 1853. See *Money, Prices*, p. 27.

[112] Marc Bloch, *Esquisse d'une histoire monétaire de l'Europe* (Paris: Lib. Armand Colin, 1954), 50.

There were various reasons why not. Those who advised the governments were self-interested in the system.[113] We must not forget that in the late Middle Ages, it was still the case that mints were commercial propositions serving private interests.[114] But more fundamental than self-interest was the collective psychology of fear, based on the structural reality of a weakly-articulated economic system. The money of account might always collapse. It surely was in no man's hands, however wealthy, to control it either singly or in collusion with others. Indeed, who knew, the whole monetary economy might once again collapse? It had before. Bullion was a hedge. The money of payment might always be used as a commodity, provided only the two uses of money, as measurement of value and means of payment, did not get too far apart.[115] For this, the use of bullion was essential. And hence without it, Europe would have lacked the collective confidence to develop a capitalist system, wherein profit is based on various deferrals of realized value. This is *a fortiori* true given the system of a nonimperial world-economy which, for other reasons, was essential. Given this phenomenon of collective psychology, an integral element of the social structure of the time, bullion must be seen as an essential crop for a prospering world-economy.

The motives for exploration were to be found not only in the products Europe wished to obtain but in the job requirements of various groups in Europe. As H. V. Livermore reminds us, it was the Iberian chroniclers of the time and shortly thereafter who first noted that "the idea of carrying on the *Reconquista* in North Africa was suggested by the need to find useful employment for those who had lived on frontier raids for almost a quarter of a century."[116]

We must recall the key problem of the decline in seigniorial income in the fourteenth and fifteenth centuries. M. M. Postan has called the consequent behavior of the English nobility "gangsterism," the use of illegal

[113]"The majority, if not the totality of experts consulted by the later Capetian [monarchs in France] were merchants, often Italian merchants, at one and the same time long-distance merchants and moneylenders to kings and notables; frequently also mint farmers and sellers of precious metals [Bloch, *ibid.*, p. 52]."

[114]"In most cases the mints were not operated directly by the State, but were farmed out to private persons who coined money out of the metal that other private persons brought to them. The controlling interest of these mint farmers was naturally that of private profit, not that of public utility. In those cases in which a king himself ran a mint he also acted more often as a private entrepreneur than as head of the State." Cipolla, *Money, Prices*, p. 28.

[115]Marc Bloch cites the striking fifteenth century example of the French *Chambre des Comptes* itself which, "when it calculated the transfers from one royal account to another, instead of simply inscribing the sum transferred in *livres, sous* and *deniers*, took care to attach to it a coefficient intended to take account of the modifications which had in the interim occurred to the metallic worth of these units. 'Due from the preceding account 416 *livres* 19 *sous tournois* of weak money . . . which in strong [i.e. current] money is worth 319 *livres* 19 *sous tournois*.' " *Esquisse d'une histoire*, p. 49.

[116]H. V. Livermore, "Portuguese History," in H. V. Livermore, ed., *Portugal and Brazil, an Introduction* (London and New York: Oxford Univ. Press (Clarendon) 1953), 59.

Vitorino Magalhães-Godinho sees a direct link between the cessation of the violent social struggle in Portugal (1383–1385) and the Portuguese expedition to Ceuta in 1415. See *L'économie de l'empire portugais aux XVe et XVIe siècles* (Paris: S.E.V.P.E.N., 1969), 40.

violence to recover a lost standard of income. Similar phenomena occurred in Sweden, Denmark, and Germany. One of the forms of this violence was surely expansion.[117] The general principle that might be invoked is that if feudal nobles obtain less revenue from their land, they will actively seek to have more land from which to draw revenue, thus restoring real income to the level of social expectations. If then we ask why did Portugal expand overseas and not other European countries, one simple answer is that nobles in other countries were luckier. They had easier expansions to undertake, closer at home, using horses rather than ships. Portugal, because of its geography, had no choice.

No doubt overseas expansion has been traditionally linked with the interests of merchants, who stood to profit by the expanded trade, and with the monarchs who sought to ensure both glory and revenue for the throne. But it may well have been that the *initial* motivation for Iberian explorations came primarily from the interests of the nobility, particularly from the notorious "younger sons" who lacked land, and that it was only once the trade network began functioning that the more prudent merchants (often less entrepreneurial than nobles threatened by being déclassé) became enthusiastic.[118]

Was the cause of expansion overpopulation? This is one of those questions which confuse the issue. Braudel tells us that there was of course overpopulation in the western Mediterranean, and as proof he cites the repeated expulsion of Jews and later the Moriscos from various countries.[119] But

[117]"Historians see a connection between the great wars of the 14th and 15th centuries (including the French descent into Italy) and the weakening of the income-level of the nobility. . . . Does not the beginning of the great expansion movements in the 15th century (even in the 14th century with the colonization of the Atlantic islands) belong to the same group of events and was it not provoked by identical causes? We could consider as parallel the expansion in Eastern Europe, and the attempts of the Danish and German nobility to conquer Scandinavia." Marian Malowist, "Un essai d'histoire comparée: les mouvements d'expansion en Europe au XV et XVI siècles," *Annales E.S.C.,* **XVII,** 5, sept.–oct. 1962, 924.

[118]See Malowist: "It seems clear that in the first phase of Portuguese colonial expansion . . . , the element of the nobility plays a dominant role. . . . As the process of development of the Portuguese colonial empire went on, the share of Portuguese merchants in the overseas trade grew. . . . It seems that the process of Spanish colonization of America was analogous." *Africana Bulletin,* No. 1, pp. 32–34. Similarly, Chaunu, citing Godinho as his authority, distinguishes two kinds of Portuguese expansion: "an expansion that was primarily overland, hence by the nobility and political in form, represented

by the taking of Ceuta and the extension of the *Reconquista* into Morocco; and an essentially mercantile expansion, hence primarily by the bourgeoisie, along the coast of Africa." *L'expansion européenne,* p. 363. Chaunu adds, as had Malowist, that he is tempted to extend this explanation to the Spanish conquest of America.

Luis Vitale is ready to go further in assessing the role of the bourgeoisie. He argues: "Portugal, in 1381, witnessed the first bourgeois revolution, four centuries before that of France. The commercial bourgeoisie of Lisbon, connected through trade with Flanders, removed the feudal lords from power. The ultimate failure of the revolution showed that conditions were unripe for the triumph of the bourgeoisie, but their rise was reflected in the trade with the North Atlantic, in the plans of Henry the Navigator, and above all, in the discoveries of the fifteenth century." "Latin America: Feudal or Capitalist?" in James Petras and Maurice Zeitlin, eds., *Latin America: Reform or Revolution?* (Greenwich, Connecticut: Fawcett, 1968), 34.

[119]"[R]eligion was the pretext, as much as the cause, of these persecutions. . . . Still later, as Georges Pariset remarked a long time ago, [the law of numbers also operated] against French Protestants in the age of Louis XIV." Braudel, *La Méditerranée,* **I,** p. 380.

E. E. Rich assures us that, as a motivation for expansion in the fifteenth and sixteenth centuries, "overspill for redundant population was negligible. . . . The probability (for it can be no more) is that the increasing population went to the wars or to the cities."[120] Yes, perhaps, but how were those who went to the cities (or to the wars) fed—and clothed and housed, etc.? There was physical room for the population, even the growing population, in Europe. Indeed that was part of the very problem that led to expansion. The physical room was one element in the strength of the peasantry vis-à-vis the nobility, and hence one factor in the decline of seigniorial revenues, in the crisis of feudalism. European societies could have responded in various ways. One way was to define themselves (at least implicitly) as overpopulated and therefore in need of a larger land base.[121] Actually, what the nobility (and the bourgeoisie) needed, and what they would get, was a more tractable labor force. The size of the population was not the issue; it was the social relations that governed the interaction between upper and lower classes.

Finally, can overseas expansion be explained by the "crusading spirit," the need to evangelize? Again, the question obscures the problem. No doubt Christianity took on a particularly militant form in the Iberian peninsula where the national struggles had for so long been defined in religious terms. No doubt this was an era of Christian *defeat* by Moslem Turks in south-eastern Europe (to the very gates of Vienna). And Atlantic expansion may well have reflected a psychological reaction to these events, "a phenomenon of compensation, a sort of flight forward," as Chaunu suggests.[122] No doubt the passions of Christianity explain many of the particular decisions taken by the Portuguese and Spaniards, perhaps some of the intensity of commitment or overcommitment. But it seems more plausible to see this religious enthusiasm as rationalization, one no doubt internalized by many of the actors, hence reinforcing and sustaining—and economically distorting. But history has seen passion turn to cynicism too regularly for one not to be suspicious of invoking such belief systems as primary factors in explaining the genesis and long-term persistence of large-scale social action.

All that we have said of motivation does not conclusively answer: why the Portuguese? We have talked of *Europe's* material needs, a *general* crisis in seigniorial revenues. To be sure, we here adduced a particular interest of Portugal in solving this problem by Atlantic exploration; but it is not enough to be convincing. We must therefore turn from the issue of motiva-

[120]Rich, *Cambridge Economic History of Europe*, **IV**, pp. 302–303.

[121]This self-definition had of course a long history on the Iberian peninsula. See Charles Julian Bishko: "[T]hose eight centuries of now slow, now rapid southward advance against the Moors were not merely an Iliad of military and political combat, but above everything else a medieval *repoblación*, or recolonization, of the Iberian Peninsula." "The Castilian as Plainsman: The Medieval Ranching Frontier in La Mancha and Extremadura," in Archibald R. Lewis and Thomas F. McGunn, eds., *The New World Looks at Its History* (Austin: Univ. of Texas Press, 1969), 47.

[122]Chaunu, *Séville*, **VIII** (1), p. 60.

tions to that of capabilities. Why was Portugal, of all the polities of Europe, most able to conduct the initial thrust? One obvious answer is found on any map. Portugal is located on the Atlantic, right next to Africa. In terms of the colonization of Atlantic islands and the exploration of the western coast of Africa, it was obviously closest. Furthermore, the oceanic currents are such that it was easiest, especially given the technology of the time, to set forth from Portuguese ports (as well as those of southwest Spain).[123]

In addition, Portugal already had much experience with long-distance trade. Here, if Portugal cannot match the Venetians or the Genoese, recent research has demonstrated that their background was significant and probably the match of the cities of northern Europe.[124]

A third factor was the availability of capital. The Genoese, the great rivals of the Venetians, decided early on to invest in Iberian commercial enterprise and to encourage their efforts at overseas expansion.[125] By the end of the fifteenth century, the Genoese would prefer the Spaniards to the Portuguese, but that is largely because the latter could by then afford to divest themselves of Genoese sponsorship, tutelage, and cut in the profit. Verlinden calls Italy "the only really colonizing nation during the middle ages."[126] In the twelfth century when Genoese and Pisans first appear in Catalonia,[127] in the thirteenth century when they first reach Portugal,[128] this is part of the efforts of the Italians to draw the Iberian

[123]"There does not exist, in all of the North Atlantic, a place more ideally suited for navigation in the direction of the warm waters than the coastal fringe which goes from north of Lisbon to Gibraltar or possibly from Lisbon to the northern tip of Morocco. There alone one will find, alternately, a sure wind to take you from the coast and into the open seas, in the full heart of the ocean, at the low point [*racine*] of the tradewinds, at the moment of the summer solstice, and a wind to bring you back, the counterflow [*contreflux*] of the middle latitudes from autumn to early spring [*petit printemps.*]" Pierre Chaunu, *Seville* **VIII** (I), p. 52. A helpful map is to be found in Charles R. Boxer, *The Portuguese Seaborne Empire, 1415–1825* (New York: Knopf, 1969), 54–55. See Braudel, *Civilisation matérielle et capitalisme*, pp. 310–312.

[124]"It is incontestable that the prodigious colonial and commercial development of the Iberian countries at the dawn of Modern Times was made possible in large part by a gradual growth in their external commerce during the latter centuries of the middle ages." Charles Verlinden, "Deux aspects de l'expansion commerciale du Portugal au moyen âge," *Revista Portuguêsa de História*, **IV**, 1949, 170. See also Charles Verlinden, "The Rise of Spanish Trade in the Middle Ages," *Economic History Review*, **X**, 1, 1940, 44–59. A similar point is made by Michel Mollat in "L'économie européenne aux deux dernières siècles du Moyen-Age," *Relazioni del X Con-*

gresso Internazionale di Scienze Storiche (Firenze: G. B. Sansoni, 1955) **III**, *Storia del medioevo*, 755.

António H. de Oliveira Marques spells out the nature of Portuguese trade with Flanders in the thirteenth and fourteenth centuries in "Notas para a história da feitoria portuguesa na Flandres no século XV," *Studi in onore di Amintore Fanfani*, **II**. *Medioevo* (Milano: Dott. A. Giuffrè-Ed., 1962), 437–476. He notes that already in 1308 there was a Portuguese "nation" in Bruges and that goods were transported on Portuguese ships. (See p. 451). See Godinho, *L'économie portugaise*, p. 37.

[125]K. M. Panikkar points to Genoa's desire to capture the India trade from the thirteenth century on. "Finally, through Spain and Portugal, the Genoese were able to break through Venetian monopoly and Muslim blockade. . . ." *Asia and Western Dominance* (London: Allen & Unwin, 1953), 26–27. While this account of the decline of the Venetian monopoly is oversimple, as we shall see in Chapter 6, Panikkar is correct to point to Genoa's longstanding desire in this regard.

[126]Charles Verlinden, "Italian Influence in Iberian Colonization," *Hispanic American Historical Review*, **XXXIII**, 2, May 1953, 199.

[127]*Ibid.*, p. 200.

[128]See Virginia Rau, "A Family of Italian Merchants in Portugal in the Fifteenth Century: the Lomellini," *Studi in onore di Armando Sapori* (Milano: Istituto Edit. Cisalpino, 1957), 718.

peoples into the international trade of the time. But once there, the Italians would proceed to play an initiating role in Iberian colonization efforts because, by having come so early, "they were able to conquer the key positions of the Iberian peninsula itself."[129] As of 1317, according to Virginia Rau, "the city and the port of Lisbon would be the great centre of Genoese trade. . . ."[130] To be sure, in the late fourteenth and early fifteenth centuries, Portuguese merchants began to complain about the "undue intervention [of the Italians] in the *retail* trade of the realm, which threatened the dominant position of national merchants in that branch of trade."[131] The solution was simple, and to some extent classic. The Italians were absorbed by marriage and became landed aristocrats both in Portugal and on Madeira.

There was one other aspect of the commercial economy that contributed to Portugal's venturesomeness, compared to say France or England. It was ironically that it was least absorbed in the zone that would become the European world-economy, but rather tied in a significant degree to the Islamic Mediterranean zone. As a consequence, her economy was relatively more monetized, her population relatively more urbanized.[132]

It was not geography nor mercantile strength alone, however, that accounted for Portugal's edge. It was also the strength of its state machinery. Portugal was in this regard very different from other west European states, different that is during the fifteenth century. She knew peace when they knew internal warfare.[133] The stability of the state was important not only because it created the climate in which entrepreneurs could flourish and because it encouraged nobility to find outlets for their energies other than internal or inter-European warfare. The stability of the state was crucial

---

[129]Verlinden, *Hispanic American Historical Review,* p. 205. See also Charles Verlinden, "La colonie italienne de Lisbonne et le développement de l'économie métropolitaine et coloniale portugaise," *Studi in onore di Armando Sapori* (Milano: Istituto Edit. Cisalpino, 1957), I, 615–28.

[130]Rau, *Studi in onore di Armando Sapori,* p. 718.

[131]*Ibid.,* p. 719. Italics added.

[132]"The creation of the internal market [in Portugal] reached its high point and felt its first brutal limitations in the 14th century. Probably it was because Portugal belonged to the rich Islamic zone that it had maintained exchange at a rather high level of activity, higher than that of western Europe, one in which there was a *predominance* of monetary payments. . . . Thus it was that the peasantry, uprooted, rebelling against the growing violence of seigniorial exploitation, ruined by the fall in purchasing power of currency, attracted by the large

cities on the coast, contributed to the enrichment of these mercantile cities and to the extension of trade." J.-G. DaSilva, "L'autoconsommation au Portugal (XIVe–XXe siècles)," *Annales E.S.C.,* XXIV, 2, mars–avr. 1969, 252. Italics added.

[133]"An important contributing factor [to Portugal's lead] was that during the whole of the 15th century Portugal was a united kingdom, virtually free of civil strife; whereas France was distracted by the closing stages of the Hundred Years' War—1415 was the date of the battle of Agincourt as well as the capture of Ceuta [by the Portuguese]—and by rivalry with Burgundy; England by the struggle with France and the War of the Roses; and Spain and Italy by dynastic and other internal convulsions." C. R. Boxer, *Four Centuries of Portuguese Expansion, 1415–1825* (Johannesburg: Witswatersrand Univ. Press, 1961), 6.

also because it itself was in many ways the chief entrepreneur.[134] When the state was stable, it could devote its energies to profitable commercial ventures. For Portugal, as we have seen, the logic of its geohistory dictated Atlantic expansion as the most sensible commercial venture for the state.

Why Portugal? Because she alone of the European states maximized will and possibility. Europe needed a larger land base to support the expansion of its economy, one which could compensate for the critical decline in seigniorial revenues and which could cut short the nascent and potentially very violent class war which the crisis of feudalism implied. Europe needed many things: bullion, staples, proteins, means of preserving protein, foods, wood, materials to process textiles. And it needed a more tractable labor force.

But "Europe" must not be reified. There was no central agency which acted in terms of these long-range objectives. The real decisions were taken by groups of men acting in terms of their immediate interests. In the case of Portugal, there seemed to be advantage in the "discovery business" for many groups—for the state, for the nobility, for the commercial bourgeoisie (indigenous and foreign), even for the semiproletariat of the towns.

For the state, a *small* state, the advantage was obvious. Expansion was the most likely route to the expansion of revenue and the accumulation of glory. And the Portuguese state, almost alone among the states of Europe of the time, was not distracted by internal conflict. It had achieved moderate political stability at least a century earlier than Spain, France, and England.

It was precisely this stability which created the impulse for the nobility. Faced with the same financial squeeze as European nobles elsewhere, they were deprived of the soporific and financial potential (if they won) of internecine warfare. Nor could they hope to recoup their financial position by internal colonization. Portugal lacked the land. So they were sympathetic to the concept of oceanic expansion and they offered their "younger sons" to provide the necessary leadership for the expeditions.

The interests of the bourgeoisie for once did not conflict with those of the nobility. Prepared for modern capitalism by a long apprenticeship in long-distance trading and by the experience of living in one of the most highly monetized areas of Europe (because of the economic involvement with the Islamic Mediterranean world), the bourgeoisie too sought

---

[134]"Under feudalism a state was in a certain sense the private property of a prince in the same way that the fief was the private property of a vassal. . . . Princes and their vassals extended the jurisdictions of their courts, the cultivation of their fields, and the conquests of their armies as profit-seeking ventures. Later, much of the spirit and legal forms of feudalism were applied to oceanic expansion." Frederic C. Lane, "Force and Enterprise in the Creation of Oceanic Commerce," in *Venice in History* (Baltimore, Maryland: Johns Hopkins Press, 1966), 401–402.

to escape the confines of the small Portuguese market. To the extent that
they lacked the capital, they found it readily available from the Genoese
who, for reasons of their own having to do with their rivalry with Venice,
were ready to finance the Portuguese. And the potential conflict of the
indigenous and foreign bourgeoisie was muted by the willingness of the
Genoese to assimilate into Portuguese culture over time.

Finally, exploration and the consequent trade currents provided job outlets for the urban semiproletariat many of whom had fled to the towns
because of the increased exploitation consequent upon the seigniorial crisis.
Once again, a potential for internal disorder was minimized by the external
expansion.

And if these conjunctures of will and possibility were not enough, Portugal
was blessed by the best possible geographic location for the enterprise,
best possible both because of its jutting out into the Atlantic and toward
the south but also because of the convergence of favorable oceanic currents.
It does not seem surprising thus, in retrospect, that Portugal made the
plunge.

There is one last issue we must confront before we can proceed with
the main part of the book. Thus far we have been concerned with explaining
what it was that led Europe to the brink of creating a capitalist world-
economy. Since our emphasis will be on how capitalism is only feasible
within the framework of a world-economy and not within that of a world-
empire, we must explore briefly why this should be so. The apt comparison
is of Europe and China, which had approximately the same total population
from the thirteenth to sixteenth centuries.[135] As Pierre Chaunu elegantly
states:

> That Christopher Columbus and Vasco da Gama . . . weren't Chinese, . . . is
> something which is worth . . . some moments of reflection. After all, at the end
> of the 15th century, insofar as the historical literature permits us to understand
> it, the Far-East as an entity comparable to the Mediterranean . . . is in no way
> inferior, superficially at least, to the far-west of the Eurasian continent.[136]

In no way inferior? This requires the traditional comparison of
technologies, and here the scholars are divided. For Lynn White, Jr.,
Europe expanded in the sixteenth century because Europe outstripped
the rest of the world in the technology of agriculture as early as the
ninth century A.D.:

> Between the first half of the 6th century and the end of the 9th century North-
> ern Europe created or received a series of inventions which quickly coalesced into
> an entirely novel system of agriculture. In terms of a peasant's labor, this was
> by far the most productive the world has seen. [White is referring to the heavy

[135]See Fernand Braudel, *Civilisation matérielle et*   [136]Chaunu, *Séville*, **VIII** (1), p. 50.
capitalisme, p. 24.

plough, the three-field rotation system, open fields for cattle, the modern harness and horseshoe].... As the various elements in this new system were perfected and diffused, more food became available, and population rose. . . . And the new productivity of each northern peasant enabled more of them to leave the land for the cities, industry and commerce.[137]

White also argues that northern Europe pulled ahead in military technology in the eighth century and in industrial production in the eleventh. If one asks why this should be so, White attributes this to the profound upheaval of the barbarian invasions, to which the West presumably had a Toynbeean creative reaction.[138]

Other scholars however disagree on the factual assessment. Take military technology. Carlo Cipolla argues:

It is likely that Chinese guns were at least as good as Western guns, if not better, up to the beginning of the 15th century. However, in the course of the 15th century, European technology made noticeable progress. . . . European artillery was incomparably more powerful than any kind of cannon ever made in Asia, and it is not difficult to find, in [16th century] texts echoes of the mixture of terror and surprise that arose at the appearance of European ordnance.[139]

Similarly, Joseph Needham, who is still in the midst of his monumental account of the history of Chinese science and technology, dates the moment of European technological and industrial advantage over China only at 1450 A.D.[140] What accounts for the European surge forward? Not one thing, says Needham, but "an organic whole, a packet of change."

The fact is that in the spontaneous autochthonous development of Chinese society no drastic change parallel to the Renaissance and the "scientific revolution" of the West occurred at all. I often like to sketch the Chinese evolution as represented by a relatively slowly rising curve, noticeably running at a *much higher level than Europe* between, say, the 2nd and 15th centuries A.D. But then after the scientific renaissance had begun in the West with the Galilean revolution, with what one might call the discovery of the basic technique of scientific discovery itself, then the curve of science and technology in Europe begins to rise in a violent, almost exponential manner, overtaking the level of the Asian societies. . . . This violent disturbance is now beginning to right itself.[141]

[137]Lynn White, Jr., "What Accelerated Technological Progress in the Western Middle Ages?" in A. C. Crombie, ed., *Scientific Change*, (New York: Basic Books, 1963), 277.

[138]"The chief factor making for innovation in a community is prior innovation. Applying this hypothesis to the Middle Ages as a whole, it would appear that to some extent the greater originality of the West is related to the fact that Latin Christendom was far more profoundly shaken than the East [Byzantium and Islam] ever was by wave after wave of barbarian invasion, extending, with interruptions, from the 3rd century into the 10th. . . . The West . . . was a molten society, ready to flow into new moulds. It was singularly open to change, and agreeable to it [*Ibid.*, p. 282].

[139]Carlo Cipolla, *Guns and Sails in the Early Phase of European Expansion, 1400–1700.* London: Collins, 1965, 106–107.

[140]See Joseph Needham, "Commentary on Lynn White, Jr., "What Accelerated Technological Change in the Western Middle Ages?" in A. C. Crombie, ed., *Scientific Change* (New York: Basic Books, 1963a), p. 32.

[141]Joseph Needham, "Poverties and Triumphs of Chinese Scientific Tradition," in Crombie, ed., *Scientific Change* (New York: Basic Books, 1963b), 139. Italics added.

Some scholars insist on the crucial role of the development of the rudder in Europe in the fifteenth century.[142] But Needham argues the existence of a rudder in China since ± first century A.D., an invention probably diffused from China to Europe in the twelfth century A.D.[143]

If Needham's account of Chinese technological competence and superiority over the West until the latter's sudden surge forward is correct, then it is even more striking that Chinese and Portuguese overseas exploration began virtually simultaneously, but that after a mere 28 years the Chinese pulled back into a continental shell and ceased all further attempts. Not for lack of success, either. The seven voyages of the eunuch-admiral Cheng Ho between 1405 and 1433 were a great success. He traveled the breadth of the Indian Ocean from Java to Ceylon to East Africa in his seven voyages, bringing back tribute and exotica to the Chinese court, which was highly appreciative. The voyages ceased when Cheng Ho died in 1434. Furthermore, when, in 1479, Wang Chin, also a eunuch, interested in launching a military expedition to Annam, applied to the archives to consult Cheng Ho's papers on Annam, he was refused access. The papers were suppressed, as if to blot out the very memory of Cheng Ho.[144]

The origins of the expeditions and the causes of their cession are equally unclear. It seems to be the case that they were constantly opposed by the official bureaucracy of Confucian mandarins.[145] The question is why. They seem, on the contrary, to have been supported by the Emperor. How else could they have been launched? Further evidence is found by T'ien-Tsê Chang in the fact that, at the beginning of the fifteenth century, the function of the Bureau of Trading Junks, a state institution since the eighth century A.D., was shifted from that of collecting customs (which

[142]See Boies Penrose, *Travel and Discovery in the Renaissance, 1420–1620* (Cambridge, Massachusetts: Harvard Univ. Press, 1952), 269–270.

[143]See Joseph Needham, "The Chinese Contributions to Vessel Control," *Scientia,* **XCVI,** 99, May 1961, 165–167. When Needham gave this paper at the Fifth International Colloquium on Maritime History, he was specifically queried on the possibility of independent invention by W. G. L. Randles. He responded by affirming his doubts, although, as he said, it is inherently difficult to demonstrate a negative. See "Discussion de la communication de M. Needham," in Joseph Needham, "Les contributions chinoises á l'art de gouverner les navires," *Colloque internationale d'histoire maritime,* 5e, Lisbonne, 1960 (Paris, 1966), 129–131.

[144]See William Willetts, "The Maritime Adventures of the Great Eunuch Ho," in Colin Jack-Hinton, ed., *Papers on Early South-East Asian History* (Singapore: Journal of Southeast Asian History, 1964), 38.

[145]"In ±1405, the eunuch admiral Cheng Ho left with a fleet of 63 ocean-going junks who visited many parts of the south seas. . . . During the next 30 years seven such expeditions set forth, returning each time with abundant information concerning geography and sea routes as well as large quantities of the produce of the isles and India. . . . The reasons for these expeditions are not known; they may have been intended to counterbalance the foreign trade which had dried up over the land routes, or to increase the grandeur of the imperial court, or even, as the official annals said, to seek out the emperor's predecessor and nephew (who, in fact, had disappeared underground as a Buddhist monk and was found many years later in a succeeding regime). In any case they stopped as suddenly as they began, again for reasons which are now obscure. Whether or not some feud between the eunuchs and the Confucian bureaucrats was involved, the upshot was that the commerce of the Indian Ocean was left to the Arabs and the Portuguese." Joseph Needham, *Science and Civilization in China,* **I** (London and New York: Cambridge Univ. Press, 1954), 143–144.

now became a provincial function) to that of transmitting tribute, which was to be sure of considerable importance in the era of Cheng Ho. Chang asks of the decentralization of customs collections, which presumably permitted lowered barriers in some regions: "[Did not the Emperor] have an eye to encouraging foreign trade the importance of which to China was only too evident?"[146]

Only too evident, yet soon encouragement ceased. Why? For William Willetts, this has something to do with the *Weltanschauung* of the Chinese. They lacked, it is argued, a sort of colonizing mission precisely because, in their arrogance, they were already the whole of the world.[147] In addition, Willetts sees two more immediate explanations for the cessation of exploration: the "pathological hatred felt by Confucian officialdom toward the eunuchs"[148] and the "drain on Treasury funds occasioned by the fitting-out of overseas missions."[149] The latter seems a strange reason, since the drain would presumably have been compensated by the income colonial enterprises might have generated. At least so it seemed to European treasuries of the same epoch.

There are other explanations which argue in terms of alternative foci of political attention diverting the initial interest in Indian Ocean exploration. For example G. F. Hudson argues that the removal northward of the capital, from Nanking to Peking in 1421, which was the consequence of the growing menace of the Mongol nomad barbarians, may have diverted imperial attention.[150] Boxer sees the distraction as having been the menace from the east in the *Wako* or Japanese piratical marauding bands that preyed on the coast of China.[151] M. A. P. Meilink-Roelofsz suggests that

---

[146]T'ien-Tsê Chang, *Sino-Portuguese Trade From 1514 to 1644* (Leiden, Netherlands: Brill, 1934), 30.

[147]"The question may be asked, what were the practical results of these amazing expeditions, in which hundreds of ocean-going junks and several tens of thousands of men were used? The short answer would be, absolutely none. The Ming Chinese were not empire-builders. Their political pundits had no conception of the horrors of *realpolitik* inseparable from a colonial regime. They had no sense of mission, no idea of *sturm und drang*. Theoretically the Son of Heaven ruled the whole world, *t'ien hsia*, 'all under heaven,' and his envoys considered it enough to show themselves to the non-descript barbarians on the fringes of the civilized world, in order to usher in a millennium activated by the serene presence of the Son of Heaven upon the Throne." Willetts, *Papers on Early South-east Asian History*, pp. 30–31.

[148]*Ibid.*, p. 37.

[149]*Ibid.*, p. 38.

[150]See G. F. Hudson, *Europe and China* (London: Arnold, 1931), 197. May it also have been the result of a population shift northward? "This regional

analysis shows that the loss of population by Southern China [during the Ming dynasty] (12 millions, excluding Nanking) was almost exactly balanced by the gain in Northern China (9 million) and the West and South-West (3 million)." Otto B. van der Sprenkel, "Population Statistics of Ming China," *Bulletin of the SOAS*, **XV**, Part 2, 1953, 306.

[151]"The work of fortifying the coast between the Yangtze and Pearl rivers was compared by contemporary Chinese historians to the building of the Great Wall against the Tartar invaders from the north. This was an obvious exaggeration, but the necessity of maintaining costly coast defenses to cope with these chronic incursions was undoubtedly a severe strain on the Ming exchequer and may . . . have contributed to the abandonment of the great Chinese maritime expeditions to the Indian Ocean [p. 126]." C. R. Boxer, *The Christian Century in Japan* (Berkeley: Univ. of California Press, 1967), 7.

George Sansom, looking at this phenomenon from the Japanese end, sees a suggestive European parallel. "There is no doubt that both China and Korea suffered from the depredations of the Wako. . . . The fault was partly that of the Chinese, for the pull of withdrawal may have been abetted by the push of expulsion by Moslem traders in the Indian Ocean.[152]

Even if all these things are true, it does not seem enough. Why was there not the internal motivation that would have treated these external difficulties as setbacks rather than as definitive obstacles? Was it, as some writers have suggested, that China simply did not want to expand?[153] Pierre Chaunu gives us a clue when he suggests that one of the things that was lacking to China was a lack of "groups with convergent wills" to expand.[154] This is more telling, since we remember that in Portugal what is striking is the parallel interests in overseas exploration and expansion shown by *varied* social groups. Let us review therefore the ways in which the European and Chinese world differed.

There is first a significant difference in agronomy. We discussed the emphasis on meat consumption in Europe, an emphasis which increased with the "crisis" of the fourteenth century. And while meat consumption for the mass of the population would later decline from the sixteenth to the nineteenth century, this did not necessarily mean a decline in the use of land for cattle rather than for grain. The absolute size of the upper classes going up from the sixteenth century on in Europe because of the dramatic rise in population, the same land area might have been used for meat. This would not be inconsistent with a relative decline in meat consumption by the lower classes, who would obtain their grains by import from peripheral areas as well as by more intensive cultivation in western Europe as the result of technological advance.

China by contrast was seeking a stronger agricultural base by developing rice production in the southeastern parts of the country. The emphasis on cattle in Europe led to the extensive use of animal muscular power as an engine of production. Rice is far more fruitful in calories per acre but far more demanding of manpower.

Thus, Chaunu notes, European use of animal power means that "European man possessed in the 15th century a motor, more or less five

they were opposed to foreign commerce, whereas the Japanese authorities would have been glad to promote legitimate trade. But these were also the reasons why the Bakufu [Japanese central authorities] was reluctant to go to extremes in suppressing piracy. It was not entirely convinced of the peaceful intentions of the Chinese, and looked upon the pirate chiefs probably as Queen Elizabeth looked upon Sir Francis Drake—as a freebooter or a naval captain according to circumstances. Moreover, action against the pirates depended upon the Bakufu's control over the Western warlords, and before 1400 Yoshimitsu was not yet firmly established in power." *A History of Japan:* Vol. II. *1334–1615* (Stanford, California: Stanford Univ.

Press, 1961), 177–178.

[152]"[One] is struck by the significant part played by the Chinese in the [Indonesian] archipelago in the 14th century. . . . As the hegemony of trade in this ocean passed into the hands of the Moslems, the Chinese ships began to disappear. There is probably a connection here. . . ." M. A. Meilink-Roelofsz, *Asian Trade and European Influence in the Indonesian Archipelago between 1500 and about 1630* (The Hague: Nijhoff, 1962), 25, 74.

[153]See R. Servoise, "Les relations entre la Chine et l'Afrique au XVe siècle," *Le mois en Afrique,* No. 6, juin 1966, 30-45.

[154]Chaunu, *L'expansion européenne,* p. 335.

times as powerful as that possessed by Chinese man, the next most favored in the world at the time of the discoveries."[155]

But even more important than this technological advance for our problem is the implication of this different relationship of man to the land. As Chaunu puts it:

> The European wastes space. Even at the demographic lowpoint of the beginning of the 15th century, Europe lacked space. . . . But if Europe lacks space, China lacks men. . . .
>
> The Western "take-off" occurs seemingly at the same date (11th–13th centuries) as the Chinese 'take-off' of rice-production, but it is infinitely more revolutionary, to the extent that it condemns the great Mediterranean area to the conquest of the Earth. . . .
>
> In every way, the Chinese failure of the 15th century results less from a relative paucity of means than of motivations. The principal motivation remains the need, often subconscious, for space.[156]

Here at least we have a plausible explanation of why China might not want to expand overseas. China had in fact been expanding, but internally, extending its rice production within its frontiers. Europe's "internal Americas" in the fifteenth century were quickly exhausted, given an agronomy that depended on more space. Neither men nor societies engage in difficult tasks gratuitously. Exploration and colonization are difficult tasks.

One last consideration might be that, for some reason, the fifteenth century marked for China what Van der Sprenkel calls a "counter-colonization," a shift of population out of the rice-producing areas.[157] While this may have relieved the "over-population," a term always relative to social definition, it may have weakened China's industrializing potential without the compensating advantages of a colonial empire. The "take-off" may have thus collapsed.

There is a second great difference between Europe and China. China is a vast empire, as is the Turco-Moslem world at this time. Europe is not. It is a nascent world-economy, composed of small empires, nation-states, and city-states. There are many ways in which this difference was important.

Let us start with the arguments that Weber makes about the implications of the two forms of disintegration of an empire: feudalization, as in western Europe, and prebendalization, as in China.[158] He argues that a newly

[155]*Ibid.*, p. 336.
[156]*Ibid.*, pp. 338–339.
[157]"The Ming period, once the power of the Mongols was broken, seems to have witnessed a strong reaction against these compressive conditions on the part of the over-populated south." *Bulletin of the SOAS,* **XV,** Van der Sprenkel, p. 308. Note that van der Sprenkel, in contrast to Hudson, gives the

declining menace of the Mongols as the explanation for northward shift of emphasis.

[158]In the glossary to Max Weber, *The Religion of China* (New York: Free Press, 1951), Hans Gerth writes: "Prebend: Right of an officeholder to yield from state or church lands or from other public income. Weber terms such office-holders 'prebendaries'. A political social system based upon a staff

centralized state is more likely to emerge from a feudal than from a prebendal system. Weber's case is as follows:

> The occidental seigneurie, like the oriental Indian, developed through the disin-
> tegration of the central authority of the patrimonial state power—the disintegration
> of the Carolingian Empire in the Occident, the disintegration of the Caliphs and
> the Maharadja or Great Moguls in India. In the Carolingian Empire, however,
> the new stratum developed on the basis of a rural subsistence economy. [Hence,
> it was presumably at a *lower* level of economic development than its oriental counter-
> parts.] Through oath-bound vassalage, patterned after the war following, the
> stratum of lords was joined to the king and interposed itself between the freemen
> and the king. Feudal relations were also to be found in India, but they were not
> decisive for the formation either of a nobility or landlordism.
>
> In India, as in the Orient generally, a characteristic seigniory developed rather
> out of tax farming [presumably because the central power was still *strong* enough to
> insist on taxes and the economy *developed* enough and with enough money-circula-
> tion to furnish the basic surplus for taxation; as compared with the presumably
> less developed Occident of the early Middle Ages] and the military and tax
> prebends of a far more bureaucratic state. The oriental seigniory therefore
> remained in essence, a "prebend" and did not become a 'fief'; not feudalization,
> but prebendalization of the patrimonial state occurred. The comparable, though
> undeveloped, occidental parallel is not the medieval fief but the purchase of
> offices and prebends during the papal seicento or during the days of the French
> Noblesse de Robe. . . . [Also] a purely military factor is important for the explana-
> tion of the different development of East and West. In Europe the horseman was
> technically a paramount force of feudalism. In India, in spite of their numbers,
> horsemen were relatively less important and efficient than the foot soldiers who
> held a primary role in the armies from Alexander to the Moguls.[159]

The logic of Weber's argument runs something like this: A technical
factor (the importance of horsemen) leads to the strength of the intermediate warriors vis-à-vis the center during the process of disintegration
of an empire. Hence the new social form that emerges is feudalism rather
than a prebendal state, in which the center is relatively stronger than in
a feudal system. Also, the economy of a feudal system is less developed
than that of a prebendal system. (But is this cause or consequence? Weber
is not clear.) In the short run, feudalization is obviously better from the
standpoint of landlords, since it gives them more power (and more income?).
In the long run, however, a prebendal land-controlling class can better
resist the growth of a truly centralized monarchy than a feudal landowning
class, because the feudal value system can be used by the king, insofar
as he can make himself the apex of a single hierarchical system of feudal
relations (it took the Capetians several centuries to accomplish this), to
build a system of loyalty to himself which, once constructed, can simply

of prebendiaries Weber calls 'prebendalism.' [p.
305]." Eric Wolf discusses the differences of a patrimonial (or "feudal") domain and a prebendal
domain from the perspective of its meaning for the

peasant in *Peasants* (Englewood Cliffs, New Jersey:
Prentice-Hall, 1966), 50–52.
[159]Weber, *Religion of India.* pp. 70–71.

shed the personal element and become loyalty to a nation of which the king is the incarnation. Prebendalism, being a far more truly contractual system than feudalism, cannot be conned by such mystical ties. (In which case, incidentally and in passing, we could see the growing prebendalism of eighteenth century France as regressive, and the French Revolution as an attempt to recoup the regression.)

Joseph Levenson, in a book devoted to the question, why not China?, comes up with an answer not too dissimilar from that of Weber:

> Ideally and logically, feudalism as a sociological "ideal type" is blankly opposed to capitalism. But historically and chronologically it gave it stimulation. The very absence of feudal restraints in China put a greater obstacle in the way of the expansion of capitalism (and capitalistic world expansion) than their presence in Europe. For the non-feudal bureaucratic society of China, a self-charging, persisting society, just insofar as it was ideally more congenial than feudal society to elementary capitalist forms, accommodated and blanketed the embryonic capitalism, and ruined its revolutionary potential. Is it any wonder, then, that even in Portugal, one of the least of the capitalist powers in the end, a social process quite the reverse of China's should release the force of expansion instead of contracting it? It was a process in Portugal and Western Europe generally, of a protocapitalist extrication from feudalism and erosion of feudalism. And this was a process quite different from the persistence in China of a non-feudal, bureaucratic society, a depressant of feudalism—and of capitalism, too.[160]

Here we have an argument we shall encounter frequently: Initial receptivity of a system to new forms does not lead to gradual continuous change but rather to the stifling of the change, whereas initial resistance often leads later on to a breakthrough.

Feudalization brought with it the dismantling of the imperial structure, whereas prebendalization maintained it. Power and income was distributed in the one case to ever more autonomous landlords, rooted in an area, linked to a given peasantry, and in the other to an empire-wide stratum, deliberately not linked to the local area, semi-universalistic in recruitment but hence dependent upon the favor of the center. To strengthen the center of an empire was a colossal job, one only begun in the twentieth century under the Chinese Communist Party. To create centralized units in smaller areas was impossible as long as the center maintained any coherence, which it did under the Ming and then the successor Manchu dynasty; whereas creating centralized units in a feudal system was, as we know, feasible if difficult. Weber outlined the reasons quite clearly:

> A general result of oriental patrimonialism with its pecuniary prebends was that, typically, only military conquest or religious revolutions could shatter the firm structure of prebendary interests, thus creating new power distributions and in turn

---

[160]Joseph R. Levenson, ed., *European Expansion and the Counter-Expansion of Asia, 1300–1600* (Eng- lewood Cliffs, New Jersey: Prentice-Hall, 1967), 131–132.

new economic conditions. Any attempt at internal innovation, however, was wrecked by the aforementioned obstacles. Modern Europe, as noted, is a great historical exception to this because, above all, pacification of a unified empire was lacking. We may recall that, in the Warring States, the very stratum of state prebendiaries who blocked administrative rationalization in the world empire were once its most powerful promoters. Then, the stimulus was gone. *Just as competition for markets compelled the rationalization of private enterprise, so competition for political power compelled the rationalization of state economy and economic policy* both in the Occident and in the China of the Warring States. In the private economy, cartellization weakens rational calculation which is the soul of capitalism; among states, power monopoly prostrates rational management in administration, finance, and economic policy. . . . In addition to the aforementioned difference in the Occident, there were strong and independent forces. With these princely power could ally itself in order to shatter traditional fetters; or, under very special conditions, these forces could use their own military power to throw off the bonds of patrimonial power.[161]

There is another factor to consider in envisaging the relationship of the regional center or the forward point of a system with the periphery in a world-economy versus an empire. An empire is responsible for administering and defending a huge land and population mass. This drains attention, energy, and profits which could be invested in capital development. Take for example the issue of the Japanese *Wako* and their presumed impact on Chinese expansion. In principle, the *Wako* were less of a problem to China than the Turks to Europe. But when the Turks advanced in the east, there was no European emperor to recall the Portuguese expeditions. Portugal was not diverted from its overseas adventures to defend Vienna, because Portugal had no political obligation to do so, and there was no machinery by which it could be induced to do so, nor any Europe-wide social group in whose interests such diversion would be.

Nor would expansion have seemed as immediately beneficial to a European emperor as it did to a Portuguese king. We discussed how the Chinese emperor may have seen, and the Chinese bureaucracy did see, Cheng Ho's expeditions as a drain on the treasury, whereas the need for increasing the finances of the state was one of the very motives of European expansion. An empire cannot be conceived of as an entrepreneur as can a state in a world-economy. For an empire pretends to be the whole. It cannot enrich its economy by draining from other economies, since it is the only economy. (This was surely the Chinese ideology and was probably their belief.) One can of course increase the share of the Emperor in the distribution of the economy. But this means the state seeks not entrepreneurial profits but increased tribute. And the very form of tribute may become economically self-defeating, as soon as political strength of the center wanes, because

---

[161]Weber, *Religion of China,* pp. 61–62. Italics added.

under such circumstances, the payment of "tribute" may be a disguised form of trade disadvantageous to the empire.[162]

There is a link too between military technology and the presence of an imperial framework. Carlo Cipolla raises the question as to why the Chinese did not adopt the military technological advantages they saw the Portuguese had. He suggests the following explanation: "Fearing internal bandits no less than foreign enemies and internal uprisings no less than foreign invasion, the Imperial Court did its best to limit both the spread of the knowledge of gunnery and the proliferation of artisans versed in the art."[163] In Europe with its multiplicity of sovereignties, there was no hope of limiting the spread of arms. In China, apparently, it was still possible, and hence the centralized system backed off a technological advance essential in the long run for the maintenance of its power. Once again, the imperial form may have served as a structural constraint, this time on technological development.

One last puzzle remains. There emerged in China at this time an ideology of individualism, that of the Wang Yang-ming school, which William T. Du Bary sees as comparable to humanist doctrines in the West, and which he calls a "near-revolution in thought," that however failed "to develop fully."[164] Did not individualism as an ideology signal the strength of an emergent bourgeoisie, and sustain it against traditionalist forces?

Quite the contrary, it seems, according to Roland Mousnier. His analysis of the social conflicts of Ming China argues that individualism was the weapon of the Confucian mandarins, the bureaucratic class which was so "modern" in outlook, against the eunuchs, who were "entrepreneurial" and "feudal" at the same time, and who represented the "nationalist" thrust of Ming China.[165] Mousnier argues as follows:

[162]Owen Lattimore shows how just such a tribute relationship of Manchuria to Ming China worked in the sixteenth century: "In the period of Ming decline the 'tribute missions' received at court became a method of taking advantage of the Chinese. The 'tribute-bearers' came with retinues running into hundreds, at the expense of the Chinese authorities, which inflated their political importance. At the same time, they brought 'non-tribute' goods for trade, which cut the profits of the Chinese frontier traders." *Inner Asian Frontiers of China*, 2nd edition (Irvington-on-Hudson, New York: Capitol Publishing Co. and American Geographical Society, 1940), 124. Compare this self-defeating political arrangement to the frank colonialism Portugal and other European countries practiced on the overseas barbarians, what Weber called "booty capitalism." *Ibid.*, p. 135.

[163]Cipolla, *Guns and Sails*, p. 117.

[164]William Theodore de Bary, ed., "Introduction," in *Self and Society in Ming Thought* (New York: Colum-bia Univ. Press, 1970), 24. He develops this theme further in his essay in this volume entitled "Individualism and Humanism in Late Ming Thought": "A type of individualistic thought with strikingly modern features did arise, in conjunction with larger social and cultural forces, out of a liberal and humanitarian movement within the Wang Yang-ming school in the sixteenth century. Thus Confucianism, though the dominant tradition and, to modern eyes, an authoritarian system, proved capable of fulfilling somewhat the same function as . . . medieval Christianity in the rise of Western individualism [p. 233]."

[165]"The insurrection which chased the Mongol dynasty of the Yuan from the throne in 1368 and the coming to power of the Ming were Chinese national reactions against the barbarians." Roland Mousnier, *Les XVIe et XVIIe siècles*, Vol. IV of *Histoire Générale des Civilisations* (Paris: Presses Universitaires de France, 1954), 520.

To advance their career [in Ming China], a large part of the educated classes of middle-class origin voluntarily became castrates. Because of their education, they were able to play a preponderant role and the Empire was in reality ruled by these eunuchs.

Once having obtained high posts, they aided their families, created for themselves a clientele by distributing offices and fiefs, became veritable powers within the Empire itself. The large role played by eunuchs seems to be therefore a function of the rise of the bourgeoisie. The princes of the blood and the men of importance [*les grands*] sought to defend themselves by creating a clientele also made up of educated men of middle-class origin whom they pushed forward in the civil service. . . . [This latter group] were sometimes disciples of Wang Yang-ming and invoked his precepts to oppose the eunuchs who were established in power. The eunuchs were for Chu Hi, defender of tradition and authority [to which the eunuchs had, at this point, primary access]. These struggles were all the more serious since princes of the blood, men of importance, and eunuchs all had a power base as land-controllers [*maîtres du sol*]. The Mings had sought to reinforce their position by creating a sort of feudalism of relatives and supporters. . . . The victim of this state of affairs was the peasant. The expenses of the State grew ceaselessly.[166]

So, of course, did they in Europe, but in Europe, these expenses supported a nascent bourgeoisie and an aristocracy that sought ultimately, as we shall see, to save itself by becoming bourgeois, as the bourgeois were becoming aristocratic. In Ming China, the ideology that served the western bourgeoisie to achieve its ultimate conquest of power was directed against this very bourgeoisie who (having achieved some power too early?) were cast in the role of defenders of tradition and authority. There is much that remains to be elucidated here, but it casts doubt on the too simple correlation of the ideology of individualism and the rise of capitalism. It surely casts doubt on any causal statement that would make the emergence of such an ideology primary.

The argument on China comes down to the following. It is doubtful that there was any significant difference between Europe and China in the fifteenth century on certain base points: population, area, state of technology (both in agriculture and in naval engineering). To the extent that there were differences it would be hard to use them to account for the magnitude of the difference of development in the coming centuries. Furthermore the difference in value systems seems both grossly exaggerated and, to the extent it existed, once again not to account for the different consequences. For, as we tried to illustrate, idea systems are capable of being used in the service of contrary interests, capable of being associated with quite different structural thrusts. The tenants of the primacy of values, in their eagerness to refute materialist arguments, seem guilty themselves of assuming a far more literal correspondence of ideology and social structure (though they invert the causal order) than classical Marxism ever was.

[166]*Ibid.*, pp. 527–528.

The essential difference between China and Europe reflects once again the conjuncture of a secular trend with a more immediate economic cycle. The long-term secular trend goes back to the ancient empires of Rome and China, the ways in which and the degree to which they disintegrated. While the Roman framework remained a thin memory whose medieval reality was mediated largely by a common church, the Chinese managed to retain an imperial political structure, albeit a weakened one. This was the difference between a feudal system and a world-empire based on a prebendal bureaucracy. China could maintain a more advanced economy in many ways than Europe as a result of this. And quite possibly the degree of exploitation of the peasantry over a thousand years was less.

To this given, we must add the more recent agronomic thrusts of each, of Europe toward cattle and wheat, and of China toward rice. The latter requiring less space but more men, the secular pinch hit the two systems in different ways. Europe needed to expand geographically more than did China. And to the extent that some groups in China might have found expansion rewarding, they were restrained by the fact that crucial decisions were centralized in an imperial framework that had to concern itself first and foremost with short-run maintenance of the political equilibrium of its world-system.

So China, if anything seemingly better placed prima facie to move forward to capitalism in terms of already having an extensive state bureaucracy, being further advanced in terms of the monetization of the economy and possibly of technology as well, was nonetheless less well placed after all. It was burdened by an imperial political structure. It was burdened by the "rationality" of its value system which denied the state the leverage for change (had it wished to use it) that European monarchs found in the mysticality of European feudal loyalties.

We are now ready to proceed with our argument. As of 1450, the stage was set in Europe but not elsewhere for the creation of a capitalist world-economy. This system was based on two key institutions, a "world"-wide division of labor and bureaucratic state machineries in certain areas. We shall treat each successively and globally. Then we shall look at the three zones of the world-economy each in turn: what we shall call the semiperiphery, the core, and the periphery. We treat them in this order largely for reasons of historical sequence which will become clear in the exposition of the argument. It will then be possible to review the totality of the argument at a more abstract level. We choose to do this at the end rather than at the beginning not only in the belief that the case will be more convincing once the empirical material has been presented but also in the conviction that the final formulation of theory should result from the encounter with empirical reality, provided that the encounter has been informed by a basic perspective that makes it possible to perceive this reality.

Igritarum ergo opera vſi ſunt Hiſpani initiò in ſcrutandis venis metallicis: verùm poſt-quam illæ fuerunt exhauſtæ, horum miniſterio vti cœperunt ad molas truſatiles quæ ſac-chariferas cannas comminuunt, ad faccharum coquendum & cogendum : in quo mini-ſterio etiamnum hodie magna ex parte occupantur. Nam cùm ea Inſula humida ſit & calida, minimo negotio ſacchariferæ cannæ ſiue arundines ſuccreſcunt ; ex quibus contuſis, deinde in lebetes conieſtis, & decoſtis, poſtremum ritè repurgatis & in faccharum concretis, magnum quæſtum facere ſolent. Vtuntur præterea iſtorum Nigritarum opera in paſcendis armentis , & reliquis rebus adminiſtrandis quæ neceſſariæ ſunt ad ſuos vſus.

2

THE NEW EUROPEAN
DIVISION OF LABOR
C. 1450-1640

It was in the sixteenth century that there came to be a European world-economy based upon the capitalist mode of production. The most curious aspect of this early period is that capitalists did not flaunt their colors before the world. The reigning ideology was not that of free enterprise, or even individualism or science or naturalism or nationalism. These would all take until the eighteenth or nineteenth century to mature as world views. To the extent that an ideology seemed to prevail, it was that of statism, the *raison d'état*. Why should capitalism, a phenomenon that knew no frontiers, have been sustained by the development of strong states? This is a question which has no single answer. But it is *not* a paradox; quite the contrary. The distinctive feature of a capitalist world-economy is that economic decisions are oriented primarily to the arena of the world-economy, while political decisions are oriented primarily to the smaller structures that have legal control, the states (nation-states, city-states, empires) within the world-economy.

This double orientation, this "distinction" if you will, of the economic and political is the source of the confusion and mystification concerning the appropriate identification for groups to make, the reasonable and reasoned manifestations of group interest. Since, however, economic and political decisions cannot be meaningfully dissociated or discussed separately, this poses acute analytical problems. We shall handle them by attempting to treat them consecutively, alluding to the linkages, and pleading with the reader to suspend judgment until he can see the whole of the evidence in synthesis. No doubt we shall, wittingly and otherwise, violate our own rule of consecutiveness many times, but this at least is our organizing principle of presentation. If it seems that we deal with the larger system as an expression of capitalism and the smaller systems as expressions of statism (or, to use the current fashionable terminology, of national development), we never deny the unity of the concrete historical development. The states do not develop and cannot be understood except within the context of the development of the world-system.

The same is true of both social classes and ethnic (national, religious) groupings. They too came into social existence within the framework of states and of the world-system, simultaneously and sometimes in contradictory fashions. They are a function of the social organization of the time. The modern class system began to take its shape in the sixteenth century.

When, however, was the sixteenth century? Not so easy a question, if we remember that historical centuries are not necessarily chronological ones. Here I shall do no more than accept the judgment of Fernand Braudel, both because of the solidity of scholarship on which it is based, and because it seems to fit in so well with the data as I read them. Braudel says:

> I am skeptical . . . of a sixteenth century about which one doesn't specify if it
> is one or several, about which ones gives to understand that it is a unity. I see

"our" century as divided in two, as did Lucien Febvre and my remarkable teacher
Henri Hauser, a first century beginning about 1450 and ending about 1550, a
second one starting up at that point and lasting until 1620 or 1640.[1]

The starting points and ending points vary according to the national perspective from which one views the century. However, for the European
world-economy as a whole, we consider 1450–1640 the meaningful time
unit, during which was created a capitalist world-economy, one to be sure
that was, in Braudel's phrase, "vast but weak."[2]

And where was this European world-economy? That too is difficult to
answer. For the historical continents are not necessarily geographical ones.
The European world-economy included by the end of the sixteenth century
not only northwest Europe and the Christian Mediterranean (including
Iberia) but also Central Europe and the Baltic region. It also included
certain regions of the Americas: New Spain, the Antilles, Terraferma,
Peru, Chile, Brazil—or rather those parts of these regions which were
under effective administrative control of the Spanish or Portuguese. Atlantic islands and perhaps a few enclaves on the African coast might also
be included in it, but not the Indian Ocean areas; not the Far East, except
perhaps, for a time, part of the Philippines; not the Ottoman Empire; and
not Russia, or at most Russia was marginally included briefly. There are no
clear and easy lines to draw, but I think it most fruitful to think of the
sixteenth century European world as being constructed out of the linkage
of two formerly more separate systems, the Christian Mediterranean system[3]
centering on the Northern Italian cities and the Flanders–Hanseatic trade
network of north and northwest Europe, and the attachment to this new
complex on the one hand of East Elbia, Poland, and some other areas
of eastern Europe, and on the other hand of the Atlantic islands and
parts of the New World.

In sheer space, this was quite an expansion. Just taking into account
formal overseas colonies of European powers, Chaunu notes that in the
five years between 1535 and 1540, Spain achieved control over more than
half the population of the Western Hemisphere, and that in the period
between then and 1670–1680, the area under European control went
from about three million square kilometers to about seven (to be stabilized
at that point until the end of the eighteenth century.[4] However, expanding
the space did not mean expanding the population. Chaunu speaks of a
"demographic scissors movement" wherein demographic growth in

[1]Fernand Braudel, "Qu'est-ce que le XVIe
siecle?," *Annales E.S.C.,* **VIII,** 1, janv.-mars 1953,
73. B. H. Slicher van Bath distinguishes the periods
1450–1550 and 1550–1650 in terms of cereal price
levels: "rising slightly" and "rising steeply." *Agrarian
History,* p. 113.
[2]Fernand Braudel, "European Expansion and
Capitalism: 1450–1650" in *Chapters in Western*

Civilization, **I,** 3rd ed. (New York: Columbia Univ.
Press, 1961), 260.
[3]For a discussion of the nature and extent of the
Christian Mediterranean area, see Jaime Vicens
Vives, *An Economic History of Spain* (Princeton, New
Jersey: Princeton Univ. Press, 1961), 260.
[4]Chaunu, *Séville,* **VIII** (1), p. 148.

Europe "is largely nullified at the planetary level by the decline in immense extra-European sectors."[5] Hence, the land/labor ratio of the European world-economy was immensely increased, one fundamental factor in Europe's ability to sustain continued economic growth in this critical early period of the modern era. But expansion involved more than an improved land/labor ratio. It made possible the large-scale accumulation of basic capital which was used to finance the rationalization of agricultural production. One of the most obvious characteristics of this sixteenth century European world-economy was a secular inflation, the so-called price revolution. The connection between this particular inflation and the process of capital accumulation has been a central theme of modern historiography. We propose to try to sift through the complexities of this debate in order that, in the light of the patterns we observe, we shall be able to explain the particular division of labor that the European world-economy arrived at by the end of this epoch.

The cyclical pattern of European prices has a voluminous history behind it, and although scholars differ about dates and even more about causes, the reality of the phenomenon is agreed. If we put together two recent summaries[6] of the prices of grains, we get the following picture:

1160–1260—rapid rise
1260–1310 (1330,1380)—consistently high
1310 (1330,1380)–1480—gradual fall
1480–1620 (1650)—high
1620 (1650)–1734 (1755)—recession
1734 (1755)–1817—rise

If we take the more narrow segment with which we are presently concerned, the sixteenth century, which appears on the above listing as "high," there were of course economic fluctuations within that. Pierre Chaunu has uncovered the following cycle, based on his monumental study of the records of the *Casa de Contratación* in Seville, the key entrepôt of trans-Atlantic trade. By using measures of volume (both overall and for specific merchandises) and of value, Chaunu sees four periods:

1504–1550—steady rise
1550–1562/3—relatively minor recession
1562/3–1610—expansion
1610–1650—recession[7]

---

[5]Pierre Chaunu, "Réflexions sur le tournant des années 1630–1650," *Cahiers d'histoire*, **XII**, 3, 1967, 257.

[6]Eugen A. Kosminsky,*Past & Present*, No. 1, p. 18; B. H. Slicher Van Bath, *Britain and the Netherlands*, p. 150.

[7]See Pierre Chaunu, *Séville et l'Atlantique (1504-1650)*, **VIII**, (2): *La Conjoncture (1504-1592)* (Paris: S.E.V.P.E.N., 1959), 14–25.

Jorge Nadal is skeptical of deriving statements about Spanish prices from the volume of trade passing through Seville, because there is no way of determining how much of the volume is in transit.

Volume and value measures are not to be sure identical. "The index of flow is likened, in an exaggerated fashion, to the fluctuation of prices. The peculiar price curve is flatter than that of trade-flow."[8] Chaunu considers his breaking point of 1610 to fit in with those of Elsas for Germany (1627) and of Posthumus for the Low Countries (1637) for, as we shall see, the decline set in at different times for different parts of Europe.[9]

These time discrepancies remind us that the world-economy was only in the process of emergence. Chaunu points out that in the fifteenth century, the three European trade areas (the Christian Mediterranean, the northwest, and eastern Europe) were at three different price levels, ranging respectively from expensive to inexpensive. The creation of a world-economy can be precisely measured by the "fantastic spread of prices at the beginning [of the century], and in the long run the closing of the gap."[10] Though the long run is longer than the sixteenth century, progress in closing the gap can be seen. If in 1500, the price gap between the Christian Mediterranean and eastern Europe was on the order of 6 to 1, by 1600 it was only 4 to 1,[11] and by 1750 it was only 2 to 1. Henryk Samsonowicz says that from the early sixteenth century on, Prussian wages and prices came "closer and closer" to those in western Europe "despite the diametrically opposed directions of their social and economic development."[12] Despite? Should it not read "because of"?

One major explanation of the price rise of the sixteenth century has been that of Earl J. Hamilton. He first argued it in relation to sixteenth century Andalusian prices, later applying it more generally to western Europe:

> Throughout the period under investigation there was a close connection between the imports of American gold and silver and Andalusian prices. . . . Commencing

"Finally, I believe, that in superposing the tonnage curve on that of prices, Chaunu has been led into the same error as Hamilton in superposing on the latter the shipments of the noble metal. In both cases one compares an authentically Spanish phenomenon—the movement of prices of articles of consumption—with others only tangential to the economy of the country (merchandise largely of foreign provenance, consignments of silver destined for shipment abroad.)" "La revolución de los precios españoles en el siglo XVI: estado actual de la cuestión," *Hispania, revista española de historia,* **XIX,** No. 77, oct.-dic. 1959, 519-520, fn. 55.

[8]Chaunu, *Séville,* **VIII** (2), p. 19.

[9]"Roughly speaking, in 1600 the change in the curve set in for Spain, Italy, and southern France. It occurred only in 1650 in the northern lands, particularly in the Low Countries, where Amsterdam was to assert her dominance on the world scene." Braudel, in *Chapters,* **I,** p. 263.

[10]Chaunu, *L'expansion européenne,* p. 343.

[11]"At the end of the 15th century, the three Europes stood in a relative [price] ratio of 100, 77 and 16; at the end of the 16th, the ratio was 100, 76 and 25. The movement towards closure had begun, but it only affected outer Europe. The distance between Mediterranean and median Europe remained the same throughout the century [*Ibid.,* p. 343]."

The gaps for more peripheral areas might nonetheless remain quite large, as Braudel notes: "The greater the extent of self-enclosure of these archaic economies, the more gold and silver, when they unexpectedly appear on the scene, are overvalued. Life in Sardinia, notes a Venetian in 1558, is four or five times less expensive than in Italy, obviously for someone with a full purse." *La Méditerranée,* **I,** p. 352.

[12]Henryk Samsonowicz, "Salaires et services dans les finances citadines de la Prusse au XVe siecle et dans la première moitié du XVIe siècle," *Third International Conference of Economic History,* Munich, 1965 (Paris: Mouton, 1968), 550.

with the period 1503–1505 there was an upward trend in the arrivals of treasure until 1595, while from 1503 to 1597 there was a continuous rise in Andalusian prices. The greatest rises in prices coincide with the greatest increase in the imports of gold and silver. The correlation between imports of treasure and prices persists after 1600, when both are on the decline.[13]

By 1960, Hamilton's theory had been subject to much attack, both empirical and theoretical. Nonetheless, he reasserted it even more vigorously:

> [The increase of bullion supply since 1500] was probably much greater percentage-wise than the price upheaval. So rather than seek ancillary causes of the Price Revolution, . . . one needs to explain the failure of prices to keep pace with the increase of stock of precious metals. Increased utilization of gold and silver for plate, ornamentation, jewelry and other non-monetary purposes as they became relatively cheaper through rising commodity prices neutralized some of the new bullion. . . . Liquidation of the unfavourable trade balance [with the Orient] absorbed large amounts of specie. . . . Conversion of produce rents into money payments, a shift from wages partially in kind to monetary renumeration and a decline in barter also tended to counteract the augmentation of gold and silver supply.[14]

As many of his critics have observed, Hamilton is working with Fisher's quantity theory of money which states that $PQ = MV$ and implicitly assuming that V and Q are remaining constant (P is equal to prices; Q is equal to the quantity of goods and services; M is equal to the quantity of money; and V is equal to the velocity of circulation). They have doubted the assumption and called for empirical enquiry.

In a major attack on Hamilton, Ingrid Hammarström argued that Hamilton had gotten his sequence wrong, that it was an increase in economic activity which led to an increase in prices which then accounts for the mining activities which produced the increased supply of bullion. To which Hamilton retorts:

> Obviously the "rise in prices" usually resulting from "economic activity which somehow comes about" . . . would curb, not increase, mining of the precious metal through rising costs of production in conjunction with *fixed mint prices* of precious metals. Furthermore, the rise in prices would decrease, not increase, the coinage of existing bullion by relatively cheapening it for nonmonetary use[15]

But why need the mint prices have been fixed? This was a policy decision and it would scarcely have benefited those who would profit by the flow of bullion in expanding times (which included the Spanish crown) to discourage its production when such a large quantity was suddenly available

---

[13]Earl J. Hamilton, "American Treasure and Andalusian Prices, 1503–1660," *Journal of Economic and Business History*, **I**, 1, Nov. 1928, 34–35. For a bibliography that contains all the major items of this literature, see Braudel and Spooner, in *Cambridge Economic History of Europe*, **IV**, pp. 605–615.

[14]Earl J. Hamilton, "The History of Prices Before 1750," in *International Congress of Historical Sciences*, Stockholm, 1960. *Rapports: I. Méthodologie, histoire des universités, histoire des prix avant 1750* (Göteborg: Almqvist & Wiksell, 1960), 156.

[15]*Ibid.*, p. 157. Italics added.

at such low real cost (given the form of labor). As Hammarström points out, the fundamental question is what explains the use to which the bullion was put:

> Why did Western Europe need the American bullion, not to be hoarded as treasure nor to be used as ornaments in the holy places (the use to which it was put in Asia and among the natives of America), but to form an important addition to its body of circulative coin—that is, as a medium of payment?[16]

Y.S. Brenner argues that a look at English data confirms Hammarström. He finds that the changes in the commodity-price level resulted "less from an increase, or lack of increase, in the European stock of metal, than from the manner in which this stock was employed."[17] He notes that the price rise antedates the arrival of American treasure.[18] Brenner argues that one should perceive that *all* the factors in Fisher's equation were variable at this time:

> In conclusion, the rise in prices during the first half of the 16th century was due to a combination of an increased velocity and volume of currency in circulation with a relatively decreased supply of, and intensified tightness of demand for, agricultural products. . . .
> The velocity (V) of the circulation was increased by the development of industry and the expansion of commerce; the sharp rise in the speculation in land and in the legalized market for funds; and by the transition of greater sections of society from rural self-sufficiency into urbanized communities dependent on markets (money-supply) for their food.[19]

Hence, Brenner is arguing, it was the general rise of capitalist activity that accounts for the *use* made of the bullion.

[16]Docent Ingrid Hammarström, "The 'Price Revolution' of the Sixteenth Century: Some Swedish Evidence," *Scandanavian Economic History Review*, **V**, 1, 1957, 131.

[17]Y. S. Brenner, "The Inflation of Prices in Sixteenth-Century England," *Economic History Review*, 2nd, ser., **XIV**, 2, 1961, 231.

H. A. Miskimin, commenting on Brenner, says: "I would go even further, and insist that the population's distribution and its relation to a fixed land supply had a great deal to do with a country's propensity to retain such gold and silver as came across its borders, since the more population pressure there was upon the food-producing land, the greater was the relative share of the country's monetary stock directed toward domestically produced agricultural goods." "Agenda for Early Modern Economic History," *Journal of Economic History*, **XXXI**, 1, March 1971, 179.

[18]Y. S. Brenner, *Economic History Review*, **XIV**, p. 229.

Fernand Braudel makes the same point: "[If] the mines of the New World are a factor, it is because

Europe has the means to take advantage of [their products]." *La Méditerranée*, **II**, p. 27. R. S. Lopez and H. A. Miskimin emphasize however that the economic growth from about 1465 until 'the Reformation' was a process of "slow recovery." Thus the rapid rise after 1520 is compatible with Hamilton's arguments. "The Economic Depression of the Renaissance," *Economic History Review*, 2nd ser., **XIV**, 3, 1962, 417.

[19]Brenner, *Economic History Review*, pp. 238–339. Braudel and Spooner also argue there is an increase in velocity: "This acceleration [of velocity], this rise in the cost of living are the most noteworthy aspect of the Renaissance, or better of the sixteenth century compared to earlier times . . . but that there was a difference in proportions. . . . [There was] in Europe a powerful spurt of 'growth'. . . . But this 'growth' pushed the whole world to the limits of the possible and the impossible, that is to say to the edge of catastrophe." "Les métaux monétaires et l'économie du XVIe siècle," in *Relazioni del X Congresso Internazionale de Scienze Storiche*, **IV**: *Storia moderna* (Firenze: Sansoni, 1955), 245–246.

The bullion theory of economic expansion presumes, if not fixed velocities (V) and quantities of goods (Q), at least upper limits. Is there any evidence in support of this? On quantities of goods and services, it does not seem very plausible. For one thing, it implies, as Jorge Nadal reminds us, the hypothesis of full employment:

> Only then when the volume of goods produced cannot be increased, will any increase in expenditure (equivalent to the product of the quantity of money and velocity [*la masa monetaria en circulación*]) be translated into a proportionate increase in prices.[20]

Let us then not assume that an increase of bullion led to a price increase directly but only via its ability to increase employment. Miskimin argues, for example, that the "early mercantilist obsession with bullion flows" made sense in that:

> Inflows of precious metals would presumably have set men and resources to work, and at the same time, tended to increase the funds available for government finance and thus lower the cost of fighting wars.

In which case, we can analyze which countries *utilized* the bullion most effectively

> in terms of each country's ability, whether institutionally or physically determined, to extend the full employment constraint in order to convert the influx of bullion into real economic growth.[21]

What about limits on velocity? W.C. Robinson in his debate with Michael Postan takes up the question of whether bullion flows are capable of explaining the fourteenth century downturn. He argues that in an economy with primitive credit mechanisms, "the V was something close to the actual physical turnover per coin per time period. . . ." Hence the thirteenth century expansion which was stimulated by dehoarding and increases in velocity was subject to inherent constraints:

> Eventually . . . the money supply reached its upper limit, save for modest annual increases, and velocity could increase no more. At this point trade was constricted and downward pressure on prices was felt. The buoyant optimism and high profits of the earlier period was replaced by pessimism and retrenchment. Hoarding of money began as a hedge against falling prices. In short, the downturn could become self-reinforcing.[22]

Postan, in his reply, argues that Robinson is factually wrong about a limit having been reached since dehoarding was continuing, that credit

---

[20]Nadal, *Hispania*, **XIX**, p. 517.
[21]Miskimin, *Journal of Economic History*, **XXXI**, p. 183.

[22]W. C. Robinson, "Money, Population and Economic Change in Late Medieval Europe," *Economic History Review*, 2nd ser., **XII**, 1, 1959, 67.

mechanisms were more flexible than Robinson suggests, and that the psychological attitudes of businessmen were a minor economic variable at that time.[23] But basically he does not challenge the concept of a limit. Miskimin does, and it seems to me effectively:

> It is also true, in all probability, that, given the level of development of credit institutions, there was a physical upper limit to the velocity of circulation of any given quantity of bullion, once it was struck into a finite number of coins. Debasement, however, by reducing the size of the units in which bullion circulated, would have the effect of raising the physical and institutional upper limits imposed on the velocity of circulation of bullion. Under the combined pressures arising from internal migration, urbanization, and specialization, it would appear possible, indeed likely, that when debasement raised the technical limits on velocity, the new freedom was used, and that the many European debasements of the sixteenth century acted through the velocity term to increase prices *more* than proportionally, relative to the level of debasement itself.[24]

Hence we come back to the fact that it is the overall system with its structured pressures for certain kinds of political decisions (for example, debasement) which is crucial to explain the expansion. It was not bullion alone, but bullion in the context of a capitalist world-economy, that was crucial. For Charles Verlinden, it was specifically the monopolistic forms of capitalism in this early stage that accounted largely for the continued inflation of prices:

> In the explanation of cyclical crises, we must reserve a large place for speculation. "Monopoly" did not regulate price movements. It "deregulated" them in the short run, except for certain luxury products (wine). It is responsible for the catastrophic aspect of these movements. Indirectly it affected doubtless the peculiar movement. After each rise, partially artificial, prices did not come down to the pre-crisis level. Monopoly thus contributed, to a certain degree, to the intensification and acceleration of the long-term rise.[25]

Was the influx of bullion then good or bad? We are not posing a sort of abstract moral question. Rather were the consequences of the bullion inflow salutory for the creation of the new capitalist world-economy? Hamilton certainly seems to say yes. Joseph Schumpeter however thinks quite the opposite:

> Increase in the supply of monetary metals does not, any more than autonomous increase in the quantity of any other kind of money, produce any economically determined effects. It is obvious that these will be entirely contingent upon the use to which the new quantities are applied.... The first thing to be observed [about the sixteenth century] is that, as far as Spain herself is concerned the new

[23]See M. M. Postan, "Note," *Economic History Review*, 2nd. ser., **XII**, 1, 1959, 78–79.

[24]Miskimin, *Journal of Economic History*, **XXXI**, p. 177.

[25]Charles Verlinden *et al.*, "Mouvements des prix et des salaires en Belgique au XVIe siècle," *Annales E.S.C.*, **X**, 2, avr.-juin, 1955, 198.

wealth ... served to finance the Hapsburg policy.... The influx provided ... an alternative to the debasement of currency to which it otherwise would have been necessary to resort much earlier, and thus became the' instrument of war inflation and the vehicle of the familiar process of impoverishment and social organization incident thereto. The spectacular rise of prices which ensued was a no less familiar link in that chain of events. . . .

In all these respects, the evolution of capitalism was indeed influenced, but in the end retarded rather than quickened, by that expansion of the circulating medium. The cases of France and England were different but only because effects were more diluted. . . . All the durable achievements of English industry and commerce can be accounted for without reference to the plethora of precious metals. . . .[26]

This argument is predicated on Schumpeter's firm conviction that "the inflationary influence—which the writer thinks, as a matter of both history and theory has been exaggerated, but which he does not deny—was almost wholly destructive."[27] Without accepting Schumpeter's bias for the rationally controlled as against the possibly impulsive and sometimes unpredictable consequences of inflation, his tirade does force upon us an awareness that the global effects of inflation were far less significant than the *differential* effects.[28]

Let us look first at food supply. Why, given a general economic expansion, was there a *decreased* supply of agricultural products? Well, first, there was not in an absolute sense.[29] It is only if one considers the figures for countries like England or Spain separately rather than the European world-economy as an entity that there is a decreased supply relative to increased population. In those countries where industry expanded, it was necessary to turn over a larger proportion of the land to the needs of horses.[30] But the men were still there; only now they were fed increasingly by Baltic

---

[26]Joseph A. Schumpeter, *Business Cycles* I (New York: McGraw-Hill, 1939), 231–232.

[27]*Ibid.*, **I,** p. 233, fn. 1.

[28]Miskimin, *Journal of Economic History,* **XXXI,** suggests possible lines along which to pursue this question: "In considering the structure of industry and the changes in production processes over the course of the war-torn sixteenth century, we might well ask what role was played by more abundant and perhaps cheaper money. Was private industrial capital accumulation rendered easier when governments could satisfy their needs at relatively lower interest rates without competing with private industry, discouraging reinvestment of profits, and creating a rentier class? Did lower capital costs in turn permit industries such as Dutch shipbuilding to maintain larger inventories of timber and raw materials or the English tanning industry to conserve labor by keeping more hides in the tanning pits, thus raising labor productivity? Perhaps this analysis might provide fruitful insights into the causes of the comparative economic success of Eng-

land and the Low Countries and the relative failure of Spain and France, and in the process convert the term 'profit inflation' from an analytical misconception to a much more useful tool [p. 183]."

[29]Was there even in a relative sense? Robinson argues that newly cleared land is not necessarily marginal in the sense of being less productive or fertile. See *Economic History Review,* p. 68. Postan retorts that, whatever the theory, the fact is that new settlements tended to be on "inferior soils." *Economic History Review,* **XII,** p. 81.

[30]"A secondary factor which may have contributed to the rise of cereal prices [in the sixteenth century] was the increasing number of horses [in western Europe]. The great expansion of commerce and industry, with its attendant transportation, called for more haulage and power, consisting largely of horses. More horses meant a greater demand for fodder. Land used to grow fodder crops is obviously no longer available for crops to feed men." Slicher van Bath, *Agrarian History,* p. 195.

grain.[31] It was, however, more expensive grain because of apparent shortage, transport, and the profits of middlemen.

Was then the increased supply of bullion irrelevant? Not at all. For it performed important functions for the expanding European world-economy. It sustained the thrust of the expansion, protecting this still weak system against the assaults of nature. Michel Morineau points out that in medieval Europe, wheat prices rose and fell in direct response to harvests. What happened in the sixteenth century was not so much that bullion raised prices but that it prevented their fall.[32] Indeed Carlo Cipolla is skeptical there was any *real* price rise at all.[33] Rather he believes that what is truly significant about the financial structure of the sixteenth century was not the rise of prices but the decline of the interest rate. He argues that in the late Middle Ages, the interest rate was about 4–5%, rising to a high point between 1520 and 1570 of 5.5%, and then dropping

---

[31]See Josef Petráň, "A propos de la formation des régions de la productivité specialisée en Europe Centrale," in *Deuxième Conférence Internationale d'Histoire Economique:* Aix-en-Provence, 1962, Vol II, *Middle Ages and Modern Times* (Paris: Mouton, 1965), 219–220.

It is sometimes said that Baltic grain could not have been that important since it represented only a small percentage of total consumption. There are two responses to this. For certain areas of Europe, Baltic grain was a major source of supply. "That one or two percent [of Europe's total consumption] was nevertheless exceptionally important, both because of the prosperity it brought to such seafarers as the Dutch and because it represented the margin of survival for capital cities like Lisbon." Charles Tilly, "Food Supply and Public Order in Modern Europe," (mimeo, 45). See Pierre Jeannin, "Les comptes du Sund comme source pour la construction d'indices généraux de l'activité économique en Europe (XVIe-XVIIIe siècles)," *Revue historique*, **CCXXXI**, janv.–mars 1964, 62, Jeannin cites E. Scholliers as saying that, between 1562-1569, Baltic grain provided 23% of Dutch consumption.

The second answer is that it was marginally crucial to the world-economy as a whole: "Local and international traffic in grain is inextricably interwoven. It would be wrong in the case of a commodity, like grain, to think in terms of a dual economy with two mutually distinct sectors. If this argument is sound, then supplies from the Baltic were marginal in relation to total demand and total supply. From this it follows that relatively slight changes in the total quantities supplied and/or demanded can produce relatively large changes in that marginal sector where Baltic grain was to be found." Glamann, "European Trade, 1500–1700," *Fontana Economic History of Europe*, **II**, 6, 1971, 44.

[32]"In the 16th century, the arrival of precious metals 'sustains' currency, leading to the devaluation of the metal instead of the currency. Precious metals are responsible for the increase in the silver-price (*prix-argent*) but not in the increase of real price." Michel Morineau, "D'Amsterdam à Séville; de quelle réalité l'histoire des prix est-elle le miroir?" *Annales E.S.C.* **XXIII**, 1, janv.-fevr. 1968, 195.

Ruggiero Romano points out that crises appear and disappear according to whether we calculate price increase in terms of gold and silver prices or in terms of the money of account: "[The results of research on sixteenth century prices] are in large part the fruit of an arbitrary transformation into metallic prices originally expressed in money of account: these are therefore not *prices*, but silver-prices and gold-prices and are expressions, to be exact, of aspects not of monetary history but of 'metallic' history. . . . [As for the arguments about whether or not there was a depression in the fifteenth century], the reasons for the opposed interpretations are due in large part precisely to the different constructions of the price curves. Prices in silver? 'crisis' of the 15th-century; prices in money of account? the 'crisis' dissolves." "Tra XVI e XVII secolo. Una crisi economica: 1619–1622," *Rivista storica italiana*, **LXXIV**, 3, sett. 1962, 481–482.

[33]"[American bullion] created a floor below which prices could no longer fall in the course of the long phases of depression. Their role was to intensify or to lessen *general trends*. This was to be sure an important role, but one which can only be explained by and exist through other *trends:* investment trends for example. These are the true mirrors [of change.] One cannot ignore them, nor confine them to a secondary role." Carlo M. Cipolla, "La prétendue 'révolution des prix' ", *Annales E.S.C.*, **X**, 4, oct.–déc. 1955, 515.

suddenly between 1570 and 1620 to an average of 2%. Bullion cheapened money.[34]

What this seems to indicate is that the critical factor was the emergence of a capitalist system which, as Marx said, could be said to date "from the creation in the sixteenth century of a world-embracing commerce and a world-embracing market."[35] The key variable was the emergence of capitalism as the dominant mode of social organization of the economy. Probably we could say the *only* mode in the sense that, once established, other "modes of production" survived in function of how they fitted into a politico–social framework deriving from capitalism. Still it is salutary to remember that, at least at this point, "there was not one capitalism, but several European capitalisms, each with its zone and its circuits."[36] Indeed, it is precisely this existence of several capitalisms which gave importance to the increased stock of bullion, for the velocity of its circulation was precisely less in the beginning in northwest Europe than in Mediterranean Europe. As Braudel and Spooner conclude, "the quantity theory of money has meaning when taken with the velocity of circulation and in the context of the disparities of the European economy."[37]

This brings us to the second half of the Hamilton argument. There was not only a price rise, but a wage lag. Here too the controversy about its existence and its causes is great.[38] Hamilton argued that as prices rose, wages and rents failed to keep abreast of prices because of institutional rigidities—in England and France, but not in Spain.[39] This created a gap, a sort of windfall profit, which was the major source of capital accumulation in the sixteenth century:

> In England and France the vast discrepancy between prices and wages, born of the price revolution, deprived labourers of a large part of the incomes they had hitherto enjoyed, and diverted this wealth to the recipients of other distributive

[34]"Therefore if one takes the period 1570–1620 in its entirety, a period judged to be on the whole an inflationary one—so much so that historians have called it a 'price revolution'—one has the optical illusion of a paradoxical decrease in the interest rate during an inflationary phase." Carlo M. Cipolla, "Note sulla storica del saggio d'interesse—Corso, dividendi, e sconto dei dividendi del Banco di S. Giorgio del secolo XVI," *Economia internazionale*, **V**, 2, magg. 1952, 266.

[35]Karl Marx, *Capital* (New York: International Publishers, 1967) **I**, Ch. IV, 146.

[36]Braudel in *Chapters*, **I**, p. 286.

[37]Braudel and Spooner, *Cambridge Economic History of Europe*, **IV**, p. 449.

[38]Pierluigi Ciocca does say, as he ends his very long pair of articles on the wage-lag hypothesis, that the wage-lag issue is less difficult to resolve than the issue of accounting for the causes of inflation in the sixteenth century. See "L'ipotesi del 'ritardo'

dei salari rispetto ai prezzi in periodi di inflazione: alcune considerazioni generali," *Bancaria*, **XXV**, 5, maio 1969, 583.

[39]Jorge Nadal denies the empirical truth of this assertion of Hamilton, arguing that Hamilton's figures have a faulty methodological basis, in that he used weighted figures for England and France, and unweighted ones for Spain. He points out that when Phelps-Brown and Hopkins took the only published figures available for a comparison of the wages of masons, all weighted in the same way, the analysis was altered fundamentally. "The lesson of these figures is as clear as it is unsuspected: over the 16th century, the purchasing power of the nominal wages received by the mason in Valencia (the only computable Spanish wage) suffered a progressive and very drastic decline, along the same lines as that of the English and French mason." *Hispania*, **XIX**, pp. 523–524.

shares. . . . Rents, as well as wages, lagged behind prices; so landlords gained
nothing from labour's loss. . . .

The windfalls thus received, along with gains from the East India trade, furnished
the means to build up capital equipment, and the stupendous profits obtainable
supplied an incentive for the feverish pursuit of capitalistic enterprise.[40]

The assertion that rents lagged behind prices has been subject to particularly heavy attack, notably by Eric Kerridge for sixteenth century England,[41] as well as by others for other places and times.[42] By 1960, Hamilton had retreated on rents but asserted this did not affect the thrust of the
argument:

[O]ne may assume that at the beginning of the Price Revolution wage payments
represented three-fifths of production costs. . . . I guess that in 1500 the rent
of land may have been one-fifth of national income in England and France and
that, with the tendency for rising agricultural prices to raise rents and the infrequent
removals of rent contracts to lower them offsetting each other, rents rose as fast
as prices during the Price Revolution. The remaining fifth of national income
went to profits, including interest. With three-fifths of the costs lagging far behind
soaring prices, . . . profits must have reached high levels in England and France
in the sixteenth century, continued on a high plateau for four or five decades,
and remained high, into the great, though declining, gap between prices and wages,
until the close of the seventeenth century.[43]

---

[40]Earl J. Hamilton, "American Treasure and the
Rise of Capitalism," *Economica*, **IX**, 27, Nov. 1929,
355–356.

Walter Prescott Webb adds the useful conceptual
distinction of distinguishing between *primary* and
secondary windfalls, both of which occurred as the
result of European conquest of the Americas.
"Leaving aside the land—the greatest of all the
windfalls—let us consider gold and silver, forest
products, furs, and ambergris in a first category. . . .
The primary windfalls were those quickly come at,
things that could be had with a minimum of investment and little preliminary work. The secondary
windfalls involved a long time element of waiting,
and often great expense, too great for the endurance
of a distant and impatient investor. It was the primary windfalls that gave the impetus to capitalism
in the sixteenth and seventeenth centuries and the
secondary ones which kept capitalism going through
the eighteenth and nineteenth centuries." *The Great
Frontier* (Boston, Massachusetts: Houghton, 1952).
181–182.

Fritz Redlich reminds us that the booty resulting
from European warfare, an ancient form of windfall, also remained an important source of capital
creation in the sixteenth century, "De Praeda Militari: Looting and Booty, 1500-1815," *Viertjahrschrift
für Sozial-und Wirtschaftsgeschichte*, Suppl. No. 39,

1956, 54–57. The difference is that booty represent
a redistribution of Europe's existing wealth, not an
addition of new resources.

[41]See Eric Kerridge, "The Movement in Rent,
1540–1640," in E. M. Carus-Wilson, ed., *Essays in
Economic History*, **II**, 208-226. See also Ian
Blanchard: "The evidence so far available in print
for the study of changes in rents during the period
1485–1547 is not unambiguous, and nowhere is this
more clearly illustrated than in [Joan Thirsk, ed.,
Agrarian History of England and Wales, Vol. IV]
where on [p. 204]it is declared that from the 1470's
onward there was a marked increase in the rents
for arable land, whilst on [p. 690] it is stated that
there was no sharp upward movement until well
into the sixteenth century. To resolve this seeming
contradiction one must consult studies of particular
estates, but few of these exist." "Population Change,
Enclosures, and the Early Tudor Economy,"
Economic History Review, 2nd Ser., **XXIII**, 3, Dec.
1970, 443.

[42]Pierre Vilar, "Problems on the Formation of
Capitalism," *Past & Present*, No. 10, Nov. 1956, 25.
In addition, Nadal says of Spain: "[W]e are forced
to conclude, in opposition to Hamilton, that the
inflationary phase was not unfavorable to the large
Spanish landowners." *Hispania*, **XIX**, p. 526.

[43]Hamilton, *Int. Cong.*, **I**, 1960, p. 160.

There have been other criticisms of Hamilton's wage lag hypothesis.[44] One important line of argument was contributed by John Nef, who suggested that recorded money wages were not equivalent to total wages, since there existed wages in kind which might have expanded to fill the gap, and also rises in wheat prices might not have been matched by rises in all basic commodity prices:

> In the first place, the index numbers hitherto compiled exaggerate the increase in the cost of subsistence during the price revolution. Secondly, the increase in the cost of the workingman's diet was borne to some extent not by them but by their employers. Thirdly, many workmen held small plots of land from which they obtained some of their necessary supplies. It follows that they were probably able to spend a more than negligible portion of the money wages on commodities other than food.[45]

Phelps-Brown and Hopkins agree that the deterioration in wages might have been less bad than it seemed, since grain prices did rise faster than manufactured products. Hence processed food products, increasingly important, rose less in price than basic grains, and improvements in manufacture further reduced the cost of such processed items.[46] Nonetheless more recent (1968) evidence, based on better data than Hamilton originally used, including evidence offered by Phelps-Brown and Hopkins, tends to confirm the general hypothesis that there was a decline in real wages in sixteenth century western Europe.[47]

The fall of real wages is strikingly exemplified in Table 1 compiled from Slicher van Bath.[48] It is the real wages of an English carpenter, paid by the day, expressed in kilograms of wheat.

[44]Ciocca summarizes them in *Bancaria*, **XXV**, 4, apr. 1969, 425–426 (footnote 13).

[45]John U. Nef, "Prices and Industrial Capitalism in France and England," *The Conquest of the Material World* (Chicago, Illinois: Univ. of Chicago Press, 1964), 254. Hamilton denies Nef's point in "Prices and Progress," *Journal of Economic History*, **XII**, 4, Fall 1952, 333–334. But Ciocca comments: "The [above] observation of Hamilton that the importance of the two factors in question is less in the historical phase of growing commercialization and the birth of the proletariat, seems to us valid and reassuring. Still the greatest prudence [is] called for." *Bancaria*, **XXV**, p. 428.

[46]See E. H. Phelps-Brown and Sheila V. Hopkins, "Wage-Rates and Prices: Evidence for Population Pressure in the Sixteenth Century," *Economica*, **XXIV**, No. 96, Nov. 1957; 293. See Jean Delumeau on prices in Rome: "Stated more generally, the decennial wheat index was always higher than all others products [various foodstuffs, wine, firewood, wax] throughout the 40 years from 1590 to 1629, with only one possible exception: that of

raisins between 1610 and 1619. And even there it is an exception that proves the rule, for the price of raisins was abnormally high at the end of the 16th century and the beginning of the 17th." *Vie économique et sociale de Rome dans le seconde moitié du XVIe siècle* (Paris: Boccard), **II**, 741–742.

[47]Phelps-Brown and Hopkins present evidence for real wage-shrinkage in the sixteenth century for southern England, France, Alsace, Munster, Augsburg, Valencia, and Vienna in Table II, "Builders Wage-rates, Prices and Population: Some Further Evidence," *Economica*, **XXVI**, No. 101, Feb. 1959, 21. Jean Fourastié and René Grandamy are not sure how real the drop in living standards was from the fifteenth to the sixteenth century, but they point out that between the fifteenth century and the seventeenth and eighteenth centuries, the real price of wheat quadrupled. "Remarques sur les prix salariaux des céréales et la productivité du travailleur agricole en Europe du XVe and XVIe siècles," *Third International Conference of Economic History*, Munich 1965 (Paris: Mouton, 1968), 650.

[48]Slicher van Bath, *Agrarian History*, Table I, p. 327.

TABLE 1 *Real Wages of English Carpenter*[a]

1251–1300	81.0
1300–1350	94.6
1351–1400	121.8
1401–1450	155.1
1451–1450	143.5
1501–1500	122.4
1551–1600	83.0
1601–1650	48.3
1651–1700	74.1
1701–1750	94.6
1751–1800	79.6
1801–1850	94.6

[a]1721–45 = 100.

Three facts are to be derived from this table. The real wages of an English carpenter are not strikingly different in 1850 from 1251. The high point of wages (155.1) was immediately preceding the "long" sixteenth century, and the low point (48.3) was at its end. The drop during the sixteenth century was immense. This drop is all the more telling if we realize that English wages in the period 1601–1650 were by no means at the low end of the European urban wage scale.

This dramatic drop in wages was itself the consequence of three structural factors which were the remains of features of a precapitalist economy not yet eliminated in the sixteenth century. Pierluigi Ciocca spells out in careful detail how these structures operated to reduce real wages in an era of sharp inflation and why each of these structural factors was largely eliminated in later centuries. The three factors are: money illusions, as well as the discontinuity of wage demands; wage fixing by custom, contract, or statute; and delay in payment. By money illusions Ciocca means the inability to perceive accurately gradual inflationary rises except at discontinuous points in time. Even, however, if they were perceived, wages could only be negotiated at intervals. Furthermore in the sixteenth century, the state often intervened, where custom or contract broke down, to forbid wage raises. Finally, at that time, many workers were only paid once a year, which in an inflationary era meant depreciated money. By the twentieth century, money illusions would be counteracted by the organization of trade unions, the spread of education, the existence of price indexes, and the accumulation of experience with inflation. Furthermore, the political organization of workers makes it more difficult for the state to restrain wages. And of course frequency of wage payment is a long-acquired right. But in this early capitalist era, workers did not have the same ability to maneuver.[49]

[49]Ciocca, *Bancaria*, **XXV**, pp. 578–579.

What strengthens the plausibility of this analysis, that there was a wage lag because of structural factors in the sixteenth century European world-economy based on early forms of world capitalism, is not only the empirical data which confirms it but the two known empirical exceptions: the cities of central and northern Italy, and of Flanders. Carlo Cipolla notes that in the late sixteenth and early seventeenth centuries, "labour costs seem to have been too high in Italy in relation to the wage levels in competing countries." The reason, according to Cipolla, was that "the workers' organizations succeeded in imposing wage levels which were disproportionate to the productivity of labour itself."[50] Similarly, Charles Verlinden finds that in the Belgian cities, wages followed the price of wheat products closely in the sixteenth century.[51] Why these two exceptions? Precisely because they were the "old" centers of trade,[52] and thus the workers were *relatively* strong as a politico–economic force. For this reason, these workers could better resist the galloping profiteering. In addition, the "advance" of capitalist mores had broken the old structures partially. It was, however, precisely as a result of the "strength" of the workers and the progress of capitalist mores that both northern Italian and Flemish cities would decline as industrial centers in the sixteenth century to make way for the newcomers who would win out: those of Holland, England and, to a lesser extent, France.

The thought that some workers (precisely those in the most "advanced" sectors) could resist the deterioration of wages better than others leads us to consider what were the *differentials in losses*[53] occasioned by the long-

---

[50]Carlo Cipolla, "The Economic Decline of Italy," in Brian Pullan, ed., *Crisis and Change in the Venetian Economy in the Sixteenth and Seventeenth Centuries* (London: Metheun, 1968), 139, 140. See Brian Pullan, "Wage-earners and the Venetian Economy, 1550–1630," *Economic History Review*, 2nd ser., **XVI,** 3, 1964, 407-426; Domenico Sella, "Les mouvements longs de l'industrie lainière à Venise aux XVIe et XVIIIe siècles," *Annales E.S.C.,* **XII,** 1, janv.–mars 1957, esp. 40–45. Sella calls Venice a "rich city" where the high cost of living was due to "burdensome rents and high wages."

[51]See Verlinden *et al., Annales E.S.C.,* **X,** p. 198. See Herman van der Wee: "Hence Brabant did not experience a catastrophic collapse of real revenues of the masses of wage-earners, as was the case in other European countries during the sixteenth century." *The Growth of the Antwerp Market and the European Economy* (The Hague: Nijhoff, 1963), **II,** 386.

[52]This leads us back to the question of why the "old" centers of trade were the centers. This is another story entirely. Sylvia Thrupp offers this brief explanation: "Flanders and north Italy are by far the most interesting areas because the fertility of their soil and the ease with which they could import extra food from nearby 'breadbasket' regions had favoured high density of population. This gave them not only a large reservoir of part-time peasant labour free for country industrial work but enabled them also to urbanize a greater proportion of their population." "Medieval Industry, 1000–1500," *Fontana Economic History of Europe,* **I,** 6, 1971, 47.

[53]We are referring to differentials according to country. There also were differentials of course according to social groups within countries, which are reflected in our discussion of the relation of rents, profits, and wage-rates. Between categories of wage-earners, however, there do not seem to have been such differentials. Or at least this was the case for the relative pay of craftsmen and laborers in the building industry in England, where "the building labourer's rate [changed] in the same proportion as the craftsman's with great consistency from the Black Death to the First World War." E. H. Phelps-Brown and Sheila V. Hopkins, "Seven Centuries of the Prices of Consumables, Compared with Builder's Wage-rates," in E. M. Carus-Wilson, ed., *Essays in Economic History* (New York: St. Martin's, 1966), **II,** 189.

term inflation. Pierre Vilar suggests a simple core-periphery alternation.[54] This is however too simple a dichotomy. For it is not only the workers of the periphery, those who engage as we shall see in labor in Hispanic America and eastern Europe in the sixteenth century, who lost. Simultaneously the wage workers in most of western Europe lost as well, if not perhaps as much—do we know?—as the workers in eastern Europe (the "loss" being immeasureable for the workers of Hispanic America, since they had not previously been in the same economic system at all). And J.H. Elliott argues that the position of the Spanish worker in this decline more nearly approximates that of the east European worker rather than that of England.[55]

Thus if on some sort of continuum the Polish worker earned least and the Spanish next and let us say the Venetian most, where exactly was the English worker, representing the semiperipheral areas that were in the process of becoming core areas. Phelps-Brown and Hopkins suggest that one way to think of what was happening in these countries is to see that "the contraction of the [English] wage earner's basketful was mostly due to the changed terms of trade between workshop and farm."[56] On the one hand, the changed terms of trade falls most heavily on the wage earner (either landless or whose income from land is subsidiary). Phelps-Brown and Hopkins estimate the number of such wage earners as already one-third of the occupied population in England in the first half of the sixteenth century. As they say, "the other side of the medal [of the impoverishment of the wage earner] is the enrichment of those who sold farm produce *or leased farms at rents they could raise.*"[57] This throws some

[54]"But might we not see [the 'long waves' of prices and economic activities] in terms of a historic alternation between an increase in the exploitation of colonial and European labor, recalling Marx' profoundly suggestive phrase: 'The veiled slavery of the wage-workers in Europe needed for its pedestal slavery pure and simple in the New World.'" Vilar, *Past & Present*, No. 10, p. 34.

[55]"[Hamilton's] hypothesis that Spanish wages kept abreast of prices would seem so far to be quite unfounded. Indeed, further investigation may well show a marked deterioration in the living standards of the mass of the Castilian population during the first half of the century. Such a deterioration, combined with the high level of Castilian prices *in relation to those of other European states,* would go a long way towards explaining the peculiar structure of Castile's economy by the end of the century: an economy closer in many ways to that of an east European state like Poland, exporting basic raw materials and importing luxury products, than to the economies of West European states. Insofar as industries survived in Castile they tended to be luxury industries catering for the needs of the wealthy few and subject

to growing foreign competition." J. H. Elliott, "The Decline of Spain," *Past & Present*, No. 20, Nov 1961, 62. Italics added. The developments in Catalonia were analogous. See the "Comments" of Jaime Vicens Vives made on the "Rapport de M. Malowist" in *IXe Congrès Internationale des Sciences Historiques*, **II.** *Actes* (Paris: Lib. Armand Colin, 1951) in which Vicens makes the comparison between the "second feudalism" in Catalonia and Poland.

[56]Phelps-Brown and Hopkins, *Economica*, **XXIV**, p. 298.

[57]*Ibid.,* p. 299. Italics added.

This analysis is very close to that of Dobb: "It may be asked: how, in these circumstances if the real consumption of the masses declined, could the price-level have risen and enabled the large profits of this period (depending essentially on the margin between prices and money-wages, multiplied by the commodity turnover) to be successfully realized. In other words, whence the expanding demand? The answer apparently lies in the fact that it was the expenditure of the rich and the middling-well-to-do (i.e., the new bourgeoisie and the Crown, and also the rising class of provincial capitalists and larger

doubt on Hamilton's argument that the wage lag was a direct source of capital accumulation, or at least alerts us to the fact that the landowner in western Europe was a key intermediary in the accumulation of capital.

Still, Hamilton's fundamental point, endorsed by John Maynard Keynes, is well-taken. The inflation created a redistribution of incomes—a complicated one, because of the multiple layers of the European world-economy. It was nonetheless a method of taxing the politically weakest sectors to provide a capital accumulation fund which could then be invested by someone.[58] The landlords in particular kept finding new ways to extract payments from the peasants.[59] The argument, remember, is not only that there was a profit windfall, but that inflation encouraged investment.[60]

This brings us to one further objection to the wage-lag hypothesis, that of John Nef. He claims the argument falls because of the case of France, where, although it had the same wage lag as England, it did not make significant progress in industry at this time.[61] Furthermore, Nef points out that he is not dealing merely with a France–England comparison, for in terms of the industrial development, France's situation was, he asserts, comparable to that of southern Germany and the Spanish Netherlands, whereas England was comparable to Holland, Scotland, Sweden, and Liège. That is, the former all slowed down by comparison with the "age of the Renaissance" and the latter all speeded up. Yet wood and

yeomen farmers) that supplied the expanding market; the increased expenditure of this section in a sense creating the conditions for profit-realization. Many of the expanding industries of the period catered for the luxury-consumption of the more well-to-do. There was also an expanded investment in shipping, in building (and to a very small extent) in machinery and craft-implements, also in ordnance and military equipment. To this must be added the important effect of foreign trade—foreign trade conducted on highly favorable terms and balanced by an appreciable input of bullion into the realm." *Studies*, p. 120.

Braudel adds an analysis of why the landowners were not necessarily hurt by the price-inflation in the way initially implied by Hamilton: "The price revolution . . . was not, as by a miracle, obstinately democratic. It lightened those burdens and rents of the peasantry which were payable in money and fixed well before the discovery of America. In fact, feudal claims on peasant holdings were often slight, sometimes less than nothing. But not always. And especially given the fact that the seignior often received payments in kind as well, and those followed the course of the market. . . . Furthermore, in both the Mediterranean area and Europe, the division of land was never made on a once-and-for-all basis." *La Méditerranée*, **II**, p. 51.

[58]"Capitalism required *capital*, and it would not

be easy to imagine a more powerful instrument for providing it than forced savings through a highly favorable price-wage ratio." Earl J. Hamilton, *Journal of Economic History*, **XII**, p. 338. See J. M. Keynes: "Thus a profit inflation is almost certain to bring about a more unequal distribution of wealth —unless its effects are balanced by the direct taxation of the kind which characterizes modern England [1930] but no other place or period." *A Treatise on Money* (London: McMillan, 1950), **II**, 162.

[59]"If this landowning class dominates Europe in the beginning of the 17th century, it is because it has lost hold less than is ordinarily asserted. So it was not madness for so many merchants and urban rich to buy lands or estates." Braudel, *La Méditerranée*, **I**, p. 479.

[60]"Rising prices penalized delay in investment and by lowering the effective rate of interest encouraged borrowing for investment in anticipation of earnings. In short, rising prices and lagging wages provided capital and gave strong incentive to use it capitalistically." Hamilton, *Journal of Economic History*, **XII**, p. 339.

[61]"What we have to explain in the case of France is not, as in that of England, why industrial capitalism made so much progress in the age of the price revolution but why it made so little." Nef, *The Conquest of the Material World*, p. 242.

labor were *cheaper,* not dearer, in France than in England. Possibly the problem is that they were *too* cheap.[62]

But this comparison of Nef only undoes the Hamilton thesis if England and France are compared *in vacuo.* If, however, they are taken within the context of the European world-economy, this comparison merely places the French real wage level somewhere between that of Spain and England. What we could then argue is that within the world-economy as a whole there was an acute reduction of the distribution of produced income to the workers. The rates varied according to the country. The optimal situation for a local investing class would be to have access to profits from low wages in the periphery and further profits from medium (as opposed to high) wages in their own area. A medium wage level was optimum since whereas on the one hand a too high wage level (Venice) cut too far into the profit margin, on the other a too *low* wage level (France, a fortiori Spain) cut into the size of the local market for new industries. England and Holland came closest to this optimum situation in the Europe-wide system. The fact that it was a world-economy, however, was the sine qua non for the likelihood that inflationary profits could be profitably invested in new industries.

Inflation thus was important both because it was a mechanism of forced savings and hence of capital accumulation and because it served to distribute these profits unevenly through the system, disproportionately into what we have been calling the emerging core of the world-economy away from its periphery and its semiperiphery of "old" developed areas.

The other side of this picture, as the reader may already have gleaned from the discussion on the impact of inflation, is that there emerged within the world-economy a division of labor not only between agricultural and industrial tasks but among agricultural tasks as well. And along with this specialization went differing forms of labor control and differing patterns of stratification which in turn had different political consequences for the "states," that is, the arenas of *political* action.

Thus far we have tried to explain why it was that Europe expanded (rather than, say, China), why within Europe Portugal took the lead, and why this expansion should have been accompanied by inflation. We have not really faced up to the question of why this expansion should be so significant. That is to say, why was the creation of this world-economy

[62]"French history suggests that a prolonged decline in the real wages of labor, while undoubtedly an incentive to enterprise, is not by itself a sufficiently powerful influence to cause a great speeding-up in the rate of industrial growth. It is possible that during the last quarter of the sixteenth century the fall in the workman's standard of living was so great as to prevent increases in the demand for some industrial products and that the misery of the poor hindered more than it helped the progress of manufacturers during the religious wars [Nef, *ibid.,* p. 267]."

Nef is also supported by David Felix, "Profit Inflation and Industrial Growth: The Historic Record and Contemporary Analogies," *Quarterly Journal of Economics,* **LXX,** 3, Aug. 1956. Especially see pp. 443–451.

the harbinger of modern industrial development, whereas previous imperial creations in the history of the world, apparently based on a relatively
productive agricultural sector and a relatively strong bureaucratic political
machinery, failed to go in this direction? To say it was technology is only
to push us to ask what kind of system was it that encouraged so much
technological advance. (Remember Needham's metaphor of the sudden
spurt of Western technology.) E. L. Jones and S. J. Woolf see the distinctive
features of the sixteenth century precisely as the fact that, for the first
time in history, an expansion of agricultural productivity opened the way
to the expansion of real income:

> One of the less palatable lessons of history is that technically advanced and physic-
> ally productive agricultures do not inevitably bring about a sustained growth of *per
> capita* real income, much less promote industrialization. The civilizations of Antiquity,
> with their elaborate agricultures, provide a starting-point. None of them, in the
> Middle East, Rome, China, Meso-America . . . led on to an industrial economy.
> Technically their farming organization was superb. . . . Equally, the physical volume
> of grain they produced was impressive. Yet their social histories are appalling tales
> of production cycles without a lasting rise in real incomes for the mass of people
> in either the upswings or the downswings. . . .
>
> The common fact, notably of the empires with irrigated agricultures, was the
> immense power of a state apparatus based on a bureaucracy concerned with defense
> against external threat and the internal maintenance of its own position. Taking
> a grand view of history, it would be fair to conclude that *these bureaucracies aimed
> at, and succeeded in maintaining, vast peasant societies through long ages and at all popu-
> lation densities in a state of virtual homeostasis.*[63]

The authors argue that in such a system, increase in gross production
results simply in "static expansion,"[64] that is, an increase in the supportable
population with a maintenance of the same absolute distribution of goods
in the same relative proportions to different classes of society.

What was it about the social structure of the sixteenth century world-
economy that accounts for social transformation of a different kind, one
that could scarcely be called homeostasis? No doubt the bureaucracies
of the sixteenth century did not have motivations very different from those
Jones and Woolf ascribe to earlier ones. If the result was different, it
must be that the world-economy was organized differently from earlier
empires, and in such a way that there existed social pressures of a different
kind. Specifically, we might look at the kinds of tensions such a system
generated among the ruling classes and consequently the kinds of opportunities it provided for the mass of the population.

We have already outlined what we consider to be the pressures on
Europe to expand. Expansion involves its own imperatives. The ability to

[63]E. L. Jones and S. J. Woolf, "The Historic Role
of Agrarian Change in Economic Development" in
Jones and Woolf, eds., *Agrarian Change and Economic
Development* (London: Methuen, 1969), 1. Italics
added.
   [64]*Ibid.*, p. 2.

expand successfully is a function both of the ability to maintain relative social solidarity at home (in turn a function of the mechanisms of the distribution of reward) and the arrangements that can be made to use *cheap* labor *far away* (it being all the more important that it be cheap the further it is away, because of transport costs).

Expansion also involves unequal development and therefore differential rewards, and unequal development in a multilayered format of layers within layers, each one polarized in terms of a bimodal distribution of rewards. Thus, concretely, in the sixteenth century, there was the differential of the core of the European world-economy versus its peripheral areas, within the European core between states, within states between regions and strata, within regions between city and country, and ultimately within more local units.[65]

The solidarity of the system was based ultimately on this phenomenon of unequal development, since the multilayered complexity provided the possibility of multilayered identification and the constant realignment of political forces, which provided at one and the same time the underlying turbulence that permitted technological development and political transformations, and also the ideological confusion that contained the rebellions, whether they were rebellions of slowdown, of force, or of flight. Such a system of multiple layers of social status and social reward is roughly correlated with a complex system of distribution of productive tasks: crudely, those who breed manpower sustain those who grow food who sustain those who grow other raw materials who sustain those involved in industrial production (and of course, as industrialism progresses, this hierarchy of productive services gets more complex as this last category is ever further refined).

The world-economy at this time had various kinds of workers: There were slaves who worked on sugar plantations and in easy kinds of mining operations which involved skimming off the surface. There were "serfs" who worked on large domains where grain was cultivated and wood harvested. There were "tenant" farmers on various kinds of cash-crop operations (including grain), and wage laborers in some agricultural production. This accounted for 90–95% of the population in the European world-economy. There was a new class of "yeoman" farmers. In addition, there was a small layer of intermediate personnel—supervisors of laborers, independent artisans, a few skilled workmen—and a thin layer of ruling classes, occupied in overseeing large land operations, operating major institutions of the social order, and to some extent pursuing their own leisure. This last group included both the existing nobility and the patrician bourgeoisie (as well as, of course, the Christian clergy and the state bureaucracy).

[65]See discussion in François Mauro, *Le XVIe siècle européen: aspects économiques* (Paris: Presses Univer-sitaires de France, 1966—Collection Nouvelle Clio, 32), 285–286.

A moment's thought will reveal that these occupational categories were not randomly distributed either geographically or ethnically within the burgeoning world-economy. After some false starts, the picture rapidly evolved of a slave class of African origins located in the Western Hemisphere, a "serf" class divided into two segments: a major one in eastern Europe and a smaller one of American Indians in the Western Hemisphere. The peasants of western and southern Europe were for the most part "tenants." The wage-workers were almost all west Europeans. The yeoman farmers were drawn largely even more narrowly, principally from northwest Europe. The intermediate classes were pan-European in origin (plus mestizos and mulattoes) and distributed geographically throughout the arena. The ruling classes were also pan-European, but I believe one can demonstrate disproportionately from western Europe.

Why different modes of organizing labor—slavery, "feudalism," wage labor, self-employment—at the same point in time within the world-economy? Because each mode of labor control is best suited for particular types of production. And why were these modes concentrated in different zones of the world-economy—slavery and "feudalism" in the periphery, wage labor and self-employment in the core, and as we shall see sharecropping in the semiperiphery? Because the modes of labor control greatly affect the political system (in particular the strength of the state apparatus) and the possibilities for an indigenous bourgeoisie to thrive. The world-economy was based precisely on the assumption that there were in fact these three zones and that they did in fact have different modes of labor control. Were this not so, it would not have been possible to assure the kind of flow of the surplus which enabled the capitalist system to come into existence.

Let us review the modes of labor control and see their relation to product and productivity. We can then see how this affects the rise of the capitalist elements. We begin with slavery. Slavery was not unknown in Europe in the Middle Ages[66] but it was unimportant by comparison with its role in the European world-economy from the sixteenth to the eighteenth century. One reason was Europe's previous military weakness. As Marc Bloch has put it:

> Experience has proved it: of all forms of breeding, that of human cattle is one of the hardest. If slavery is to pay when applied to large-scale enterprises, there must be plenty of cheap human flesh on the market. You can only get it by war or slave-raiding. So a society can hardly base much of its economy on domesticated human beings unless it has at hand feebler societies to defeat or to raid.[67]

Such an inferior mode of production is only profitable if the market is

[66]See Charles Verlinden, *L'esclavage dans l'Europe médiévale*, 2 vol. (Brugge: De Tempel, 1955).
[67]Bloch, *Cambridge Economic History of Europe*, **I**,

p. 247. See also Marc Bloch, "Mediaeval 'Inventions,'" in *Land and Work in Medieval Europe* (Berkeley: Univ. of California Press, 1967), 180.

large so that the small *per capita* profit is compensated by the large quantity of production. This is why slavery could flourish in the Roman Empire and why it is preeminently a capitalist institution, geared to the early preindustrial stages of a capitalist world-economy.[68]

Slaves, however, are not useful in large-scale enterprises whenever skill is required. Slaves cannot be expected to do more than what they are forced to do. Once skill is involved, it is more economic to find alternative methods of labor control, since the low cost is otherwise matched by very low productivity. Products that can be truly called labor-intensive are those which, because they require little skill to "harvest," require little investment in supervision. It was principally sugar, and later cotton, that lent themselves to the assembling of unskilled laborers under brutal overseers.[69]

Sugar cultivation began on the Mediterranean islands, later moved to the Atlantic islands, then crossed the Atlantic to Brazil and the West Indies. Slavery followed the sugar.[70] As it moved, the ethnic composition of the

[68]The classic statement of this point of view is Eric Williams, *Capitalism and Slavery* (London: Deutsch, 1964). For a more recent supporting statement, cf. Sergio Bagú "La economía de la sociedad colonial," *Pensamiento crítico*, No. 27, abr. 1969, 53–61.

[69]Eric Wolf notes that *small-scale* mining and *small-scale* cane-farming both proved uneconomic for technological reasons in Middle America and quickly gave way to large-scale capitalist enterprises. In the case of mining, the technological advance was the introduction of the patio process in 1557 in which silver is extracted from ore with the aid of mercury and which needs expensive machinery especially since with the new process it became profitable to engage in deep mining. In sugar production, it was the large-scale grinding mill or *ingenio* which required such a large-scale capital outlay. Similar technological requirements had similar social consequences for indigo production. See *Sons of the Shaking Earth* (Chicago, Illinois: Univ. of Chicago Press, 1959), 177–180.

[70]"The first result of the extention of sugar cane production to Madeira and the Canaries in the fifteenth century was severe competition with existing European producers. This was accentuated as the American colonies came into production. By 1580, . . . the industry in Sicily was moribund. . . . In Spain the industry languished. . . . The small medieval sugar industries of southern Italy, Malta, the Morea, Rhodes, Crete and Cyprus all underwent a similar decline and eventually disappeared.

"In both Madeira and the Canaries sugar production involved the use of African slave labor. . . . This use of slaves may have helped the islanders to undersell other European sugar producers, but Madeira and the Canaries in their turn succumbed respectively to Brazilian and West Indian competition. . . .

"In the American tropics the history of sugar and slavery is even more intimately linked. Of all the tropical export crops of this period, sugar cane demanded the most manual labor, especially for harvesting. The necessity for a mill in close proximity to the fields, to which the transport of cane must be organized within a few hours of cutting, required for the first time the establishment of the plantation system.. . . Without doubt sugar cane was primarily responsible for agrarian slavery in the tropics." Masefield, *Cambridge Economic History of Europe*, **IV**, pp. 289-290.

Islands as stepping-stones for trans-Atlantic settlement are not an exclusively Iberian phenomenon. A. L. Rowse makes the case for the same thing being so in north Europe in three steps: from the Continent to Britain, from Britain to Ireland, and then from Britain to North America.

"We may regard the peopling of North America as an extension across the Atlantic of the process a thousand years before, in the time of the *Volkerwanderungen*, by which Britain was colonized by the original Anglo-Saxon stocks. . . .

"The unification of the islands [Britain and Ireland] gave the basis for the great lunge forward across the Atlantic, the exodus of stocks to North America, the open door for which the Elizabethans had fought. . . . [O]bserve, what has been little observed by historians, that it was the very people who were most deeply concerned with the plantation and colonization of Southern Ireland—Humphrey Gilbert, Walter Raleigh, Richard Grenville—who took the leading part in planting the first colonies in Virginia. It is as if Ireland were the blueprint for America." Rowse, "Tudor Expansion: The Transition from Medieval to Modern History," *William and Mary Quarterly*, 3rd ser., **XIV**, 3, July 1957, 310, 315.

slave class was transformed.[71] But why Africans as the new slaves? Because of exhaustion of the supply of laborers indigenous to the region of the plantations, because Europe needed a source of labor from a reasonably well-populated region that was accessible and relatively near the region of usage. But it had to be from a region that was outside its world-economy so that Europe could feel unconcerned about the economic consequences for the breeding region of wide-scale removal of manpower as slaves. Western Africa filled the bill best.[72]

The exhaustion of alternative supplies of labor is clear. The monocultures imposed on the Mediterranean and Atlantic islands ravaged them, pedologically and in terms of human population. Their soils were despoiled, their populations died out (for example, the Guanches of the Canary Islands), or emigrated, to escape the pressure.[73] Indian populations on Caribbean islands disappeared entirely. New Spain (Mexico) had a dramatic fall in population from approximately 11 million in 1519 to about 1.5 million in circa 1650.[74] Brazil and Peru seem to have had an equally dramatic decline.[75] The two immediate explanations of this demographic decline seem to be disease and damage to Indian cultivation caused by the

[71]"Slavery and the slave trade had flourished in the Mediterranean for many centuries before the Europeans began to expand into Africa, and the Atlantic trade which developed during the fifteenth century was in no sense a mere accidental by-product of African discovery . . . . The most important change, that from trafficking chiefly for domestic consumption to slaving predominantly for plantation or colonial markets was well under way before the discovery of America. In general, the color of the slave changed during the fifteenth century from white to black, and there was a growing tendency to treat slaves in the mass as impersonal items of commerce rather than as individuals who worked for a family or a farm as a domestic servant or agrarian labourer." Anthony Luttrell, *The Transatlantic Slave Trade*, pp. 78–79.

[72]Confirming evidence for the fact that slaves are drawn from outside one's own world-economy can be found in Charles Verlinden's study of Crete in the fourteenth and fifteenth centuries. Crete was then a Venetian colony, serving both as a center of cash-crop agriculture and as an entrepot. In this latter capacity it was a pivot in the slave trade. The slaves were drawn from various parts of southeastern Europe, Russia, and southwest Asia, (all areas outside of the then Mediterranean world-economy) for use in Crete and in other Venetian colonies and for resale to Egypt, southern France, and eastern Spain. See "La Crète, débouché et plaque tournante de la traite des esclaves aux XIVe et XVe siècles," *Studi in onore di Amintore Fanfani*, **III**: *Medioevo* (Milano: Dott. A. Giuffrè-Ed., 1962), 591–

619.

[73]See Braudel, *La Méditerranée*, **I**, pp. 144–145.

[74]Sherburne F. Cook and Leslie Boyd Simpson document a fall from 11 million in 1519 in Mexico to about 6.5 million in 1540 to about 4.5 million in 1565 to about 2.5 million in 1600. See *The Population of Central Mexico in the Sixteenth Century*, Ibero-Americana: **31** (Berkeley: Univ. of California Press, 1948), 10–16, 38, 43, 46. Woodrow Borah adds the figure of 1.5 million for 1650. See *New Spain's Century of Depression*, Ibero-Americana: **35** (Berkeley: Univ. of California Press, 1951), 3.

[75]"The wholesale destruction of Brazil's aboriginal population was equally drastic [to that of Mexico]. The Jesuit, José de Anchieta, observed that 'the number of people used up in this place (Bahía) from twenty years ago until now (1583) seems a thing not to be believed,' and proceeds to give figures that reveal a destruction of population on a scale similar to that carried out in Mexico." Celso Furtado, *Economic Development of Latin America* (London and New York: Cambridge Univ. Press, 1970), 5, fn. 2.

For Peru, see Alvaro Jara: "The devouring mining enterprise would have crumbled had there not existed the reserves of a mass of high density population, capable of supporting for some time the declining demographic curve." "Estructuras de colonización y modalidades de tráfico en el Pacífico Sur Hispano-Americano," in *Les grades voies maritimes dans le monde, XVe-XIXe siècles*. VIIe Colloque, Commission International d'Histoire Maritime (Paris: S.E.V.P.E.N. 1965), 251.

domestic animals that the Europeans bred.[76] But sheer exhaustion of manpower, especially in the mines, must also have been significant. Consequently, at a relatively early point, the Spaniards and Portugese ceased trying to recruit Indians as slave labor in the Western Hemisphere and began to rely exclusively on imported Africans for plantation slaves. Presumably, the cost of transport still did not bring the cost to a higher point than the potential cost of preventing runaways by the remaining indigenous population. Besides the latter were rapidly dying off.

And yet slavery was not used everywhere. Not in eastern Europe which saw a "second serfdom." Not in western Europe which saw new forms of "rent" and the rise of wage labor. Not even in many sectors of the economy of Hispanic America where, instead of slave plantations, the Spaniards used a system known as *encomienda*. Why not slavery in all production in Hispanic America? Probably because the supply of African slaves, however large, was not unlimited. And because the economies of supervising an *indigenous* slave population (the amount of world-available nonindigenous slave labor making this the only reasonable other possibility), given the high likelihood of revolts, made it not worthwhile. This was especially the case since grain production, cattle-raising, and mining required a higher level of skill among the basic production workers than did sugar production. These workers therefore had to be compensated for by a slightly less onerous form of labor control.[77]

Since both the "second serfdom" in eastern Europe and the *encomienda* system in Hispanic America—synchronous be it noted—have been termed by many persons as "feudalism," much useless controversy has been generated as to whether and in what way these systems are or are not comparable to the "classic" feudalism of medieval Europe. The debate essentially revolves around whether the defining characteristic of feudalism is the hierarchical relationship of ownership (the awarding of a fief to a vassal, an exchange of protection for rents and services), the political jurisdiction of a seignior over his peasantry, or the existence of large domains of land upon which a peasant is somehow "constrained" to work at least part of his year in return for some kind of minimal payment (whether in the form of cash, kind, or the right to use the land for his own production for use or sale). Obviously, all sorts of combinations are possible.[78] Further-

[76]See J. H. Parry, *The Age of Reconnaissance* (New York: Mentor Books, 1963), 245–246.

[77]See Gabriel Ardant on the link between skill requirements and forms of labor control, in his discussion of the gradual elimination of legal restrictions: "The logic of a system which asked the serf to produce more while organizing his own work-schedule led both to a system of fixed payments and to greater liberation. . . . That the substitution of payments [*redevances*] for requisitions might increase productivity was realized by the seigniors themselves." *Théorie sociologique de l'impôt*, **I**, pp. 46–47. See also *Ibid.*, **I**, p. 194.

[78]See the discussions in Rushton Coulbourn, ed., *Feudalism in History* (Princeton, New Jersey: Princeton Univ. Press, 1956). See Claude Cahen, 'Au seuil de la troisième année: Réflexions sur l'usage du mot 'féodalité,' " *Journal of the Economic and Social History of the Orient*, **III**, Pt. 1, April, 1960, 2–20; Dobb, *Studies*, pp. 33–37; Lefebvre, *La Pensée*, No. 65; Henryk Lowmianski, "The Russian Peasantry," *Past & resent*, No. 26, Nov. 1963, 102-109; Joshua Prawer and S. N. Eisenstadt, "Feudalism," in *International Encyclopedia of the Social Sciences*, (New York: Macmillan and Free Press, 1968), **V**, 393–403; George Vernadsky, "Feudalism in Russia," *Speculum*,

more, not only the form of the subordinate's obligation to the superordinate may vary, but the degree of subordination may vary also, and as Dobb notes, "a change in the former is by no means always yoked with a change in the latter. . . ."[79]

From the point of view we are developing here, there is a fundamental difference between the feudalism of medieval Europe and the "feudalisms" of sixteenth century eastern Europe and Hispanic America. In the former, the landowner (seignior) was producing primarily for a local economy and derived his power from the weakness of the central authority. The economic limits of his exploitative pressure was determined by his need to furnish his household with the limited degree of luxury determined as socially optimal and by the costs of warfare (which varied over time). In the latter, the landowner (seignior) was producing for a capitalist world-economy. The economic limits of his exploitative pressure were determined by the demand–supply curve of a market. He was maintained in power by the strength rather than the weakness of the central authority, at least its strength vis-à-vis the farm laborer. To avoid any confusion, we shall call this form of "serfdom" by the name "coerced cash-crop labor," although the term is imperfect and awkward.

"Coerced cash-crop labor" is a system of agricultural labor control wherein the peasants are required by some legal process enforced by the state to labor at least part of the time on a large domain producing some product for sale on the world market. Normally, the domain was the "possession" of an individual, usually by designation of the state, but not necessarily a heritable property. The state could be itself the direct owner of such a domain, but in this case there was a tendency to transform the mechanism of labor control.[80] Using such a definition, this form of labor control became the dominant one in agricultural production in the peripheral areas of the sixteenth century European world-economy.

Henri H. Stahl makes very clear the way in which East Elbia's (and more generally eastern Europe's) "second serfdom" is "capitalist" in origin.[81]

XIV, 3, July 1939, 300–323; Max Weber, *Economy and Society* (Totowa: Bedminster Press, 1968), I, 255–256.

[79]Dobb, *Studies*, p. 66.

[80]See the discussion by Charles Gibson in which he indicates how those *encomiendas* directly under Crown jurisdiction, and which were managed by men called *corregidores*, evolved from what we are calling coerced cash-crop labor into a mechanism for taxation of the peasantry in which the *corregidores* became in eff.... tax-farmers. *The Aztecs Under Spanish Rule* (Stanford, California: Stanford Univ. Press, 1964), 82–97.

[81]"This renewal of serfdom, which thus occurred in Germany, was not a return to the former state of things, nor the simple repetition, east of the Elbe, of outdated medieval forms. The influences of the capitalist world market which had loosed 'the second serfdom' imposed new laws on local social develop-

ment.

In the first place, it was necessary to ensure an increased quantity of cereal products. To do that, the technique of 'Dreifeldwirtschaft' dating from the High Middle Ages had to be given up in favor of a more modern technique borrowed by the Junkers from the Dutch, that of 'Koppelwirtschaft' which they adapted to their needs (the 'Preussische Schlagwirtschaft').

In the second place, the goal of agricultural production ceased being consumer's goods for a subsistence economy and became merchandise with a price on the world market.

As a result the feudal exactions on the peasantry took on the character of the 'primitive accumulation of capital'. . . ." Henri H. Stahl, *Les anciennes communautés villageoises roumaines—asservissement et pénétration capitaliste* (Bucarest: Ed. de l'Académie de la République Socialiste de Roumanie, 1969), 15.

A number of other authors recognize that we are calling "coerced cash-crop labor" is a form of labor control in a capitalist and not a feudal economy. Sergio Bagú, speaking of Hispanic America, calls it "colonial capitalism."[82] Luigi Bulferetti, speaking of seventeenth century Lombardy, calls it "feudal capitalism."[83] Luis Vitale, speaking of the Spanish *latifundias,* insists they are "very capitalist enterprises."[84] Eric Wolf sees no inconsistency between a lord maintaining "patrimonial controls within the boundaries of his domain" and running his domain "as a capitalist enterprise."[85]

The pattern already began with the Venetians in Crete and elsewhere in the fourteenth century[86] and became widespread by the sixteenth century throughout the periphery and semiperiphery of the European world-economy. The crucial aspects from our perspective are twofold. One is to see that "coerced cash-crop labor" is *not,* as Pietro Vaccari puts it, "of a form that may be defined as a true reconstitution of the former feudal servitude;"[87] it is a *new* form of social organization. And second, it is *not* the case that two forms of social organization, capitalist and feudal, existed side by side, or could ever so exist. The world-economy has one form or the other. Once it is capitalist, relationships that bear certain formal resemblances to feudal relationships are necessarily redefined in terms of the governing principles of a capitalist system.[88] This was true both of the *encomienda* in Hispanic America and the so-called "second feudalism" in eastern Europe.

The *encomienda* in Hispanic America was a direct creation of the Crown. Its ideological justification was Christianization. Its chief function was to supply a labor force for the mines and cattle ranches, as well as to raise silk and to supply agricultural products for the *encomenderos* and the workers in towns and mines.[89] The *encomienda* was originally a feudal privilege, the right to obtain labor services from the Indians.[90]

When the exaggeration of early *encomenderos* threatened the supply of

[82]See Bagú, *Pensamiento crítico,* No. 27, pp. 34–35, 42–53, 61.

[83]See Luigi Bulferetti, "L'oro, la terra e la società: une interpretazione del nostro Seicento," *Archivio storico lombardo,* 8th ser., **IV,** 1953, *passim.*

[84]Luis Vitale, "España antes y después de la conquista de America, *Pensamiento crítico,* No. 27, abril 1969, 12.

[85]Wolf, *Peasants,* p. 54.

[86]"The fief was awarded [to Venetians] with full liberty of use; it could therefore be exchanged or alienated except to Greeks and to Jews." Abrate, *Economia e storia,* **IV,** p. 262.

[87]Pietro Vaccari, "I lavatori della terra nell'occidente e nell'oriente dell'Europa nella età moderna," *Studi in onore di Armando Sapori* (Milano: Istituto Edit. Cisalpino, 1957), **II,** 969.

[88]Henri Stahl, *Les anciennes communautés:* "Every 'historical epoch' is characterized by the coexistence in a single cultural arena [*aire*] of many countries

having un-equal levels of development. There are always some countries at the forward-point of progress and backward countries. An 'historical era' necessarily takes on the character imposed upon it by the most advanced countries. Those countries that are behind must submit to the law of the 'epoch' [p. 17.]"

[89]"The *encomendero* invested the tribute in enterprises of all kinds: mining, agricultural, husbandry, industrial, commercial. But the investments were most concentrated, as was to be expected, in mining, and later in husbandry," José Miranda, *El tributo indígena en la Nueva España durante el siglo XVI* (Mexico: El Colegio de Mexico, 1957), 186. On the relation of tribute to silk production, see pages 197–204. On the relation of tribute to basic provisioning of the needs of the nonagricultural population, see pages 204–223.

[90]"In legal principle, encomienda was a benign agency for Indian Hispanization. Its essential fea-

labor—for example, the Indians on the West Indian islands died off—a royal cedula of 1549 changed the obligations of *encomienda* from labor to tribute, thus shifting from a system akin to slavery to one we may call coerced cash-crop labor. As Silvio Zavala points out, the new version of *encomienda* was "free," but the threat of coercion lay in the background.[91] When "freedom" resulted in a significant drop in the labor supply, a further legal shift occurred, the institution of forced wage labor, called the *cuatequil* in New Spain and the *mita* in Peru.[92]

Consequently, although it is true that the *encomienda* in Hispanic America (as well as the *donatária* in Brazil) might have originated as feudal grants, they were soon transformed into capitalist enterprises by legal reforms.[93] This seems to be confirmed by the fact that it was precisely to avoid the centrifugal character of a feudal system that the *cuatequil* and *mita* were installed.[94]

Not only did the landowner have the Spanish Crown behind him in creating his capital, in coercing the peasant labor. He normally had an

ture was the official consignment of groups of Indians to privileged Spanish colonists. The grantees, called *encomenderos*, were entitled to receive tribute and labor from the Indians delegated to them. The Indians, though liable to the demands for tribute and labor during the effective period of the grant, were regarded as free for the reason that they were not owned as property by the encomenderos. Their freedom established a legal distinction between encomienda and slavery. . . . A grant of encomienda conferred no landed property, judicial jurisdiction, dominium, or señorío." Gibson, *The Aztecs*, p. 58. See the description of the jurisdiction, economic and social condition of the Indians on ecomiendas in J. M. Ots Capdequí, *El estado español en las Indias* (Mexico: Fondo de Cultura Económica, 1941), 24–33.

[91]"The aim . . . was to establish a system of voluntary wage labor with moderate tasks; but in anticipation that the Indians might not offer their services voluntarily, the order further directed the royal authorities in the colony to deliver laborers to colonists who needed them. From one point of view this order was designed to prevent abuses arising from a direct relationship between the Spanish master and the Indian encomenderos to compel the Indians to work. From another point of view, however, its significance lies in the fact that if the effort to establish a voluntary system should fail through the Indian's refusal to accept work, the state was ready to act as a mediator and to protect public interest by compelling the laborer to work." Silvio Zavala, *New Viewpoints on the Spanish Colonization of America* (Philadelphia: Univ. of Pennsylvania Press, 1943), 94. See also his classic work *Le encomienda indiana* (Madrid: Centro de Estudios Historicos, 1935). See the collection of viewpoints in John F. Bannon, ed.,

Indian Labor in the Spanish Indies: Was There Another Solution? (Indianapolis, Indiana: Heath, 1966).

See also Alvaro Jara on the encomienda in Chile: "The native was constrained to participate in a system of production in which he was required to furnish to Spain a surplus which exceeded considerably his own needs, which were reduced." *Guerre et société au Chili: Essai de sociologie coloniale* (Paris: Institut des Hautes Etudes de l'Amérique Latine, 1961), 46.

[92]Zavala, *New Viewpoints*, p. 95.

[93]This seems to be the view of Bagú. See *Pensamiento crítico*, No. 27, pp. 32-33. The equivalent in Brazil to the abolition of personal servitude in the *encomienda* by the Spanish Crown in 1549 was the process by which the Portuguese crown took back the *capitanias hereditárias*, making them into *capitanias da coroa*. The first such action was done in the very same year of 1549. See J. Capistrano de Abreu, *Capítulos de historia colonial (1500-1800)* (Rio de Janeiro: Ed. da Soc. Capistrano de Abreu, Typ. Leuzinger, 1928), 63–76.

[94]Luis Vitale argues: "During the first years of the conquest the encomenderos attempted to assert their independence. The Spanish Crown, anxious to avoid the emergence in America of a group of lords who might eventually repudiate its authority, set up a strong administration with the aim of counteracting any feudal outbreak. . . . The encomendero was not the master of the Indians, nor could he impose justice, because 'the Indian was not the encomendero's serf but was the king's subject. . . .' Thus the encomienda of services was replaced by the encomienda of money tribute. . . . The salaried worker signified an embryonic capitalist relationship between the classes, and formed a new class of workers." *Latin America*, pp. 37–38.

See José Miranda: "The *encomendero* is, first of

arrangement with the traditional chief of the Indian community in which
the latter added his authority to that of the colonial rulers to the process
of coercion.[95] The strength of chieftaincy was of course a function of pre-
colonial patterns to a large extent.[96] The interest of the chief or *cacique*
becomes quite clear when we realize how laborers were in fact paid. Alvaro
Jara describes the system established in 1559 as it worked in Chile. There
the Indians working on gold washing received a sixth of its value. This
payment, called the *sesmo*, was however made not to individual Indians
but to the collectivity of which they were members.[97] One can guess at
the kinds of unequal division that were consequent upon this kind of global
payment system.

The creation of coerced cash-crop labor in eastern Europe was more
gradual than in Hispanic America, where it had been instituted as a result
of conquest. In the twelfth and thirteenth centuries, much of eastern Europe
(that is, East Elbia, Poland, Bohemia, Silesia, Hungary, Lithuania) went
through the same process of growing concessions to the peasantry and
growing transformation of feudal labor obligations into money obligations
as did western Europe, and also Russia.[98] The process was gone through

---

all, a man of his time, moved by a desire for profit
and making wealth his objective. For his contemporaries, the *encomendero* is the man of action in
whom the ideas and desires of a new world are
most strongly reflected. He is very different from
medieval man. . . . He does not limit his aspirations,
as did the feudal seignior, to the mere enjoyment
of tribute and service, but converts them into the
foundation of multiple gain. . . . Thus, the
encomendero gives primacy to the element of capitalist
labor-conscription [*repartimiento*] of the *encomienda*,
which is the only element which can lead him to
the objective he pursues with such ardor—wealth."
"La función económico del encomendero ₍en los
orígenes del regimén colonial, Nueva España
(1525-1531)," *Anales del Instituto Nacional de
Anthropología e Historia*, II, 1941-1946, 423-424. A
capitalist in outlook and mode of operation, but
not one, as Miranda indicates (see pp. 431–444) who
brings financial capital to the enterprise. His initial
capital is what the state gave him, and he derived
his further capital from his profits.

[95]Fernando Guillén Martínez goes so far as to say:
"The fact is that 'encomienda' and 'mita' could only
survive as institutions in those areas where, by dint
of numbers or force of inertia, Indian tribal institutions were preserved. Insofar as there was the magic
kinship of chieftaincy *(cacique)* and collective slavery
in the soul of the people, the Indian went solemnly
and in a resigned fashion to his work and his
slaughter. But when Christian evangelization and

miscegenation *(mestizaje)* disintegrated the tribe,
making way for individualism, the Indian would
no longer permit himself to be subordinated to an
organized servility. . . ." *Raíz y futuro de la revolución*
(Bogotá: Ed. Tercer Mundo, 1963), 80. On the
definition and origin of the 'mita', see Ots Capdequí
El estado español, pp. 31–32.

[96]Furtado, *Economic Development of Latin America*,
argues in fact that where the traditional local ruling
class was weak, "the *encomienda* proved ineffective
as a form of social organization and the *encomendero*
resorted to more direct forms of slavery, forcing
the men to perform intensive labour in conditions
very different from those to which they had been
accustomed. This system resulted in a rapid depletion of the population [pp. 10–11]."

[97]"Starting from the decree of the *Tasa de Santillan*
in 1559, which assigned a sixth of the gold placers,
the *sesmo*, for the Indian of each encomienda paid
out annually for their labors, it has been possible
to establish that such participation acquired the very
definite characteristic of a social or communal salary,
which came in a lump sum into the treasury of each
Indian community or village." Alvaro Jara, "Una
investigación sobre los problemas del trabajo en
Chile durante el periódo colonial," *Hispanic American Historical Review*, **XXXIX,** 2, May 1959, 240.

[98]Some areas did not have a feudal system at all,
properly speaking, during the Middle Ages. They
knew only the 'second', never the first feudalism.
Stahl argues this for Moldavia and Wallachia. See
Les anciennes communautés, pp. 241-244.

everywhere for the same reasons: the impact of prosperity and economic expansion on the bargaining relationship of serf and lord.[99] The recession of the fourteenth and fifteenth centuries however led to opposite consequences in western and eastern Europe. In the west, as we have seen, it led to a crisis of the feudal system. In the east, it led to a "manorial reaction"[100] which culminated in the sixteenth century with the "second serfdom" and a *new* landlord *class*.[101]

The reason why these opposite reactions to the same phenomenon (economic recession) occurred was because, for the reasons we previously explicated, the two areas became complementary parts of a more complex single system, the European world-economy, in which eastern Europe played the role of raw-materials producer for the industrializing west, thus coming to have, in Malowist's phrase, "an economy which, at bottom, [was]

[99]"The natural wealth of eastern Europe . . . demanded much effort in order to profit by it. A certain balance of power between the states which had been formed in the 12th and 13th centuries meant that reciprocal invasions could bring significant gains to no one. And German pressure on Bohemia and Poland constituted a very serious threat. In these circumstances the princes, the lay and ecclesiastical aristocracy, were forced to take more interest in developing their own resources. This was possible, however, only with the cooperation of the peasants. All the while peasant obligations were uncertain and peasants were afraid of being deprived of their surplus production, they had no interest in improving their working methods. Lords, on the other hand, were in no position to increase their demands on their serfs, for the latter could easily run away. Princes and lords who wished to develop their property economically were thus compelled to encourage their subjects to work more intensively and to introduce new methods, particularly in connection with agriculture. They achieved these aims by introducing the German or rather Western custom whereby peasant dues were not only regulated but also reduced. Commutation of services and renders in kind into money rents, began in Bohemia in the early 13th century and carried into effect a little later in Poland, already reflected the development of agriculture and progress in the social division of labor." M. Malowist, "The Social and Economic Stability of the Western Sudan in the Middle Ages," *Past & Present*, No. 33, April 1966, 14–15. See Jerome Blum, "Rise of Serfdom in Eastern Europe," *American Historical Review*, **LXII**, 4, July 1957, 807–836.

[100]The *Grundsherr*, a rent receiver, became a *Gutsherr*, a direct producer. See discussion in Hans Rosenberg, *Bureaucracy, Aristocracy and Autocracy:*

The Prussian Experience, 1660–1815 (Cambridge, Massachusetts; Harvard Univ. Press, 1966), Ch. I. See the discussion concerning how in Slovenia the nobles overcame their financial difficulties by extending their domain, raising rents due them, and taking over commerce, in Ferdo Gestrin, "Economie et société en Slovénie au XVIe siècle," *Annales E.S.C.*, **XVII**, 4, juil.–août 1962, 665.

[101]"Colonial East Elbia had [prior to the fifteenth century] its individual Junkers but no Junker class, except for the Teutonic Knights. The formation of a closely-knit noble landlord class with great political and social ambitions, displaying solidity and class consciousness, a collective will manufactured in con-; crete defense and aggression, and a caste-like self-assurance and *esprit de corps*, was the work of the 15th and 16th centuries. . . . Chronologically it coincides with the ascent of the gentry in England and Hungary, of the landed nobility in Bohemia and Moravia, and of the *szlachta* in Poland, as well as with the economic and political decline of the leisured *noblesse* of seigniorial rentiers and absentee landlords in France and western Germany." Hans Rosenberg, "The Rise of the Junkers in Brandenburg-Prussia, 1410–1653," *American Historical Review*, **XLIX**, 1, Oct. 1943, 4. Note that Rosenberg includes England in with the eastern European countries. As we shall see later on, this is understandable but confusing. One of the bases of making this link of the English gentry with east European landlords is given by Zs. P. Pach who says that both were "bourgeois-like." See "Die Abbiegun der Ungarischen Agrarentwicklung von der Westeuropaischen," in *International Congress of Historical Sciences*, Stockholm, 1960. *Résumés des communications* (Göteborg: Almqvist & Wiksell, 1960), 155.

close to the classic colonial pattern."[102] A look at the nature of Baltic trade is sufficient to verify this. From the fifteenth century on, the products flowing from east to west were primarily bulk goods (cereals, timber, and later on, wool), although the older exports of fur and wax continued. And from west to east flowed textiles (both of luxury and of middling quality), salt, wines, silks. By the end of the fifteenth century, Holland was dependent on Baltic grain, Dutch and English shipping unthinkable without east European timber, hemp, pitch, and grease. Conversely, wheat had become the east's most important export, reaching even the Iberian peninsula and Italy.[103]

To be sure, this kind of colonial pattern of trade existed previously in terms of trade relations in Europe. There was the relationship of Venice and her colonies plus her sphere of influence.[104] There was Catalonia as a trade center in the late Middle Ages.[105] In the thirteenth and fourteenth centuries Portugal was a primary producer for Flanders,[106] as England was for the Hanse.[107] The production of primary products to exchange for the manufactured products of more advanced areas was always, as Braudel says of grain, a "marginal phenomenon subject to frequent [geographical] revisions." And, as he says, "each time, the bait [was] cash."[108] What was different in the sixteenth century was the existence of a market for primary products that encompassed a large world-economy. Slicher von Bath dates the creation of the international cereals market, centering in the Low Countries, only in 1544.[109]

[102]M. Malowist, "Poland, Russia and Western Trade in the 15th and 16th Centuries," *Past & Present*, No. 13, April 1958, 32. See also M. Malowist, "The Problem of the Inequality of Economic Development in Europe in the Latter Middle Ages," *Economic History Review*, 2nd ser., **XIX**, 1, April 1966, 15–28. Stanislaw Hoszowski quotes an English diplomat of the first half of the seventeenth century, Sir George Carew, who said: "Poland had become the granary of Europe and the storehouse of materials for shipbuilding." "The Polish Baltic Trade in the 15th-18th Centuries" in *Poland at the XIth International Congress of Historical Sciences in Stockholm* (Warsaw: The Polish Academy of Sciences, The Institute of History, 1960), 118.

[103]See Malowist, *Past & Present*, No. 13, pp. 26–27.

[104]The exchange of primary products of the colonies against manufactured goods of the metropole is described in Freddy Thiriet, *La Romanie vénitienne au Moyen Age* (Paris: Boccard, 1959), 304–305. Crete is described as the "breadbasket of the empire [p. 414]." As for similar relations with countries outside the empire, "the wheats of the empire not sufficing," see pp. 327–328.

[105]See Jaime Vicens Vives, *An Economic History of Spain*, ch. 17, esp. 211–215.

[106]See Oliveira Marques, *Studi in onore di Armando Sapori* **II**, p. 449.

[107]See Phillipe Dollinger, *La Hanse (XIIe–XVIIe siècles)* (Paris: Montaigne, 1964), 76–80.

[108]Braudel, *Civilisation matérielle*, p. 94.

[109]B. H. Slicher van Bath, *A.A.G.B.* No. 12, p. 28. See Karl Helleiner: "[B]y the sixteenth century inter-regional sea-borne trade in victuals already had a long history behind it. . . . What may be claimed, however, is that now owing to a more elaborate marketing mechanism, and above all to a greatly increased volume of disposable surpluses in East Elbia, Poland, and Estonia, areas of permanent or temporary grain deficits could be provisioned from abroad more amply and with greater regularity than in previous times. By the middle of the sixteenth century the amount of grain exported annually through the port of Danzig was from six to ten times more than the average in the years 1490–92. . . . Two or three important new sources of animal food opened up to European man in this periods: the rich fishing banks from Cape Cod to Labrador were yielding increasing quantities of rich protein, while the Hungarian and Wallachian plains as well as the Danish lowlands had for some times past become breeding-grounds of vast numbers of oxen for export to Austria, Germany, and Holland." *Camb. Eco. Hist. Eur.*, **IV**, pp. 77–78.

If we take seriously Braudel's notion of "frequent revisions," then we must ask how an area gets defined as periphery rather than as core. In the Middle Ages, even the late Middle Ages, it was not at all clear that eastern Europe was destined to be the periphery of a European world-economy. A number of writers have emphasized the comparability of developments, east and west. Reginald R. Betts, for example, says of the fourteenth century: "Curiously [sic!], payments in specie were preferred not only by French and English large landowners . . . but by Czech, Polish and Hungarian landowners as well. . . ."[110] Similarly, Zs. S. Pach argues that as late as the fifteenth century, "the trend of rural development [in Hungary] was fundamentally concordant with that of the west European countries. . . ."[111]

Why then the divergence? One can answer in terms of the factors—geographical and social—which accounted for the spurt of western Europe. To some extent, we have already done this. One can also answer in part in terms of specific characteristics of eastern Europe. For one thing, the weakness of the towns was an important factor.[112] This was a small difference in the thirteenth century which became a big one in the sixteenth, since, as a result of the complementary divergence, western towns grew stronger and eastern ones relatively weaker. Or one can emphasize the fact that there already was a relatively more extensive cultivation of land in western Europe by the end of the thirteenth century, whereas there remained much more vacant space in eastern Europe.[113] A process of coerced cash-crop labor was relatively easier to institute on "new" lands.

But then we have to ask why even the slight differences between west and east? There is perhaps a single geopolitical explanation: the Turkish and Mongol–Tartar invasions of the late Middle Ages, which destroyed much, caused emigrations and various declines, and above all weakened the relative authority of the kings and great princes.[114]

[110]Reginald R. Betts, "La société dans l'Europe centrale et dans l'Europe occidentale," *Revue d'histoire comparée*, n.s., **VII**, 1948, 173.

[111]Zs. P. Pach, "The Development of Feudal Rent in Hungary in the Fifteenth Century," *Economic History Review*, 2nd ser., **XIX**, 1, April 1966, 13.

[112]"The economic rise of western Europe became one of the most powerful causes of the decline of towns in eastern Europe." Hartung and Mousnier, *Relazioni del X Congresso Internazionale di Scienze Storiche*, **IV**, p. 46. "From the middle of the 15th century to the middle of the 18th century, the characteristic feature of the Polish economy was the diffusion of demesne economy based on serf labor. This in turn hampered the development of the towns and had a negative effect on economic and social conditions in the country generally." Hoszowski, *Poland at the XIth International Congress of Historical Sciences in Stockholm*, p. 117.

[113]See Doreen Warriner, "Some Controversial Issues in the History of Agrarian Europe," *Slavonic and East European Review*, **XXXI**, No. 78, Dec. 1953, 174–175.

[114]Betts argues the parallel of these invasions and the "second feudalism" to the earlier invasions and the creation of the "first" feudalism in Europe. See Betts, *Revue d'histoire comparée*, p. 175. He spells out the impact of the later invasions on the rulers of eastern Europe in pp. 175–180. Doreen Warriner, *Slavonic and East European Review*, **XXXI**, speculates that "if the [European] trade channels had not shifted [relatively speaking] westward [from eastern Europe] in search of bullion overseas, eastern Europe might have continued to follow the same development as Western Europe, with trade and town expansion acting as solvents of the feudal society and economy. Or, alternatively, the fifteenth-century depression in Western Europe might have shifted to the East [p. 176]."

What is at operation here is the general principle that in the course of social interaction small initial differences are reinforced, stabilized, and defined as "traditional." The "traditional" was then, and always is, an aspect of and creation of the present, never of the past. Speaking of the modern world, André Gunder Frank argues: "Economic development and under-development are the opposite face of the same coin. Both are the necessary result and contemporary manifestations of internal contradictions in the world capitalist system."[115] But the process is far more general than Frank indicates. As Owen Lattimore puts it, "Civilization gave birth to barbar-ism."[116] Speaking of the relationship between the sedentary and the nomadic at the frontiers of the world, Lattimore argues that the way to conceive of their origin and their relationship is to observe

> the formation of two diverging types out of what had originally been a unified society. These we may call, for convenience, "progressive" (agriculture becoming primary, hunting and gathering becoming secondary) and "backward" (hunting and gathering remaining primary, agriculture becoming secondary, in some cases not advancing beyond a desultory stage.[117]

Thus if, at a given moment in time, because of a series of factors at a previous time, one region has a *slight* edge over another in terms of one key factor, *and* there is a *conjuncture* of events which make this *slight* edge of central importance in terms of determining social action, then the slight edge is converted into a large disparity and the advantage holds even after the conjuncture has passed.[118] This was the case in the fif-teenth and sixteenth centuries in Europe. Given the great expansion of the geographic and demographic scope of the world of commerce and industry, some areas of Europe could amass the profits of this expansion all the more if they could specialize in the activities essential to reaping this profit. They thus had to spend less of their time, manpower, land,

[115]André Gunder Frank, *Capitalism and Under-development in Latin America* (New York: Monthly Review Press, 1967), 9. Frank continues: "Economic development and underdevelopment are not just relative and quantitative, in that one represents more economic development than the other; economic development and underdevelopment are relational and qualitative, in that each is structurally different from, yet caused by, its relation with the other. Yet development and underdevelopment are the same in that they are the product of a single, but dialectically contradictory, economic structure and process of capitalism."

[116]Owen Lattimore, "La civilisation, mère de Barbarie?" *Annales E.S.C.*, **XVII**, 1, janv.–fevr. 1962, 99.

[117]Owen Lattimore, *Relazioni del X Congreso de Scienze Storichi,* **I,** p. 110. A very similar point is made by Morton Fried: "[M]ost tribes seem to be secondary phenomena in a very specific sense: they may well be the product of processes stimulated by the appearance of relatively highly organized societies amidst other societies which are organized much more simply. If this can be demonstrated, tribalism can be viewed as a reaction to the creation of complex political structure rather than as a neces-sary preliminary stage in its evolution." "On the Con-cept of 'Tribe' and 'Tribal Society'" in June Helm, ed., *Essays on the Problem of Tribe,* Proceedings of 1967 Annual Spring Meeting of the American Ethnological Society, 15.

[118]In fact, awareness of this cumulative effect of small differentials provides a bridge to overcoming the somewhat sterile argument about quantity and quality. I agree with P. C. Gordon-Walker: "The distinction between changes in quality and changes in quantity is an unreal one. If historians looked for changes in quantity, in degree, they would find that 'changes in quality' only in fact result from changes in quantity. This holds good both for changes in ideas and social outlook, as well as for changes in economic organization. . . .

[C]hanges of quality are nothing else but a certain stage of intensity reached by preceding changes in quantity." "Capitalism and Reformation," *Economic History Review,* **VIII,** 1, Nov. 1939. 4–5.

and other natural resources on sustaining themselves in basic necessities. Either eastern Europe would become the "breadbasket" of western Europe or vice versa. Either solution would have served the "needs of the situation" in the conjuncture. The *slight* edge determined which of the two alternatives would prevail. At which point, the *slight* edge of the fifteenth century became the great disparity of the seventeenth and the monumental difference of the nineteenth.[119]

The crucial considerations in the form of labor control adopted in eastern Europe were the opportunity of large profit if production were increased (because of the existence of a world market) plus the combination of a relative shortage of labor and a large amount of unused land.[120] In the sixteenth century eastern Europe and in parts of the economy of Hispanic America, coerced cash-crop labor was thus desirable (profitable), necessary (in terms of the landowner's self-interest), and possible (in terms of the kind of work required). Slavery was impracticable because of the relative shortage of labor. *Indigenous* labor is *always* in short supply as slaves, as it is too difficult to control, and long-distance importation of slaves was not profitable for products that required as much supervision as wheat. After all, the cost of slaves was not negligible.

While presumably the peasant prefers a system of coerced cash-crop labor to slavery because of the minimal dignity and privileges involved in formal freedom, it is not necessarily the case that the material conditions of the coerced cash-crop laborer were better than those of the slave. Indeed Fernando Guillén Martinez argues that in Hispanic America, the Indian on the *encomienda* was more poorly treated than the slave, largely because of the insecure social situation of the *encomendero*.[121] Alvaro Jara argues

[119]Traian Stoianovich argues the same growing disparity of western Europe with southeastern Europe: "If in the fourteenth century, one discovers little quantitative difference between the iron orientation of Balkan societies and [western] Europe's iron orientation, that distinction was significant in 1700, much greater in 1800, and incredibly greater in 1850." "Material Foundations of Preindustrial Civilization in the Balkans," *Journal of Social History,* **IV**, 3, Spr. 1971, 223.

[120]Evsey D. Domar hypothesizes: "[O]f the three elements of an agricultural structure relevant [to the phenomena of slavery and serfdom]—free land, free peasants, and non-working landowners—any two elements but *never all three can exist simultaneously.* The combination to be found in reality will depend on the behavior of political factors—governmental measures. . . ." "The Causes of Slavery or Serfdom: A Hypothesis," *Journal of Economic History,* **XXX**, I, March 1970, 21.

[121]"The creation and constitution of castes, groups permanently subjugated to others, did not succeed in receiving legal sanction [in Hispanic America] except embryonically and provisionally. Official legislation on the personal labor of the Indians never quite accepted intrinsic judicial

inequality between whites, Indians and mestizos. . . .

"Precisely because of its precautions and extra-legal charades, the exploiting class (of land owners and allied bureaucrats) came to have characteristics of moral irresponsibility, rapine, and inhuman violence, unknown where there coalesced an aristocratic strata firmly supported by the State in its privileged economic situation, as in Germany, France or Italy.

"Evidence of this is to be found in the fact that, when the importation of Black slaves to New Granada was authorized, to work in the mines of Antioquía and to be agricultural laborers in the region of Río Cauca or on the Atlantic Coast, the paternal treatment they received from their masters was much less cruel, immoral or barbaric than that which the Indian tribes assigned to the encomenderos had previously received. The proprietor of the black slave was guaranteed by law in his privileged situation and this consciousness of the stability of slavery gave the owners a certain sense of concrete responsibility lacking to the encomenderos to whom Indians were subjected." Guillén, *Raíz y futuro,* p. 81.

similarly that the standard of living of the Indians on the *encomienda,* in this case in Chile, was "at a minimum level, using this concept in its strictest sense."[122]

Thus, in the geo–economically peripheral areas of the emerging world-economy, there were two primary activities: mines, principally for bullion; and agriculture, principally for certain foods. In the sixteenth century, Hispanic America provided primarily the former[123] while eastern Europe provided primarily the latter. In both cases, the technology was labor-intensive and the social system labor-exploitative. The surplus went overall disproportionately to supply the needs of the population of the core areas. The immediate profits of the enterprise were shared, as we shall see, between groups in the core areas, international trading groups, and local supervisory personnel (which include, for example, both aristocrats in Poland, and civil servants and *encomenderos* in Hispanic America). The mass of the population was engaged in coerced labor, a system defined, circumscribed, and enforced by the state and its judicial apparatus. Slaves were used to the extent that it was profitable to do so, and where such juridical extremism was too costly, the alternative of formally free but legally-coerced agricultural labor was employed on the cash-crop domains.[124]

In the core of the world-economy, in western Europe (including the Mediterranean Christian world), the situation was different in a number of respects. The population density was basically much higher (even in

[122]Alvaro Jara, "Salario en una economía caracterizada por los relaciones de dependencia personal," *Third International Conference of Economic History,* Munich 1965 (Paris: Mouton, 1968), 608.

Further evidence of the low standard of living of the Indian on the encomienda can be found in Guatemala where the product was indigo. In 1563, the Spanish Crown upheld a previous decision of the Audiencia to prohibit the employment of Indians on the grounds that it was "very harmful work." Robert S. Smith points out that this decree was ineffective:

"In 1583 colonial officials found that growers had devised a subterfuge: instead of hiring them for wages, the growers contracted with the Indians to haul out indigo plants at so much per load, paying them in clothing with only one tenth of what they should have received in money wages. . . . Seven years later the fiscal found that 'many mestizos, mulattoes and free Negroes and even slaves' (i.e., the laborers whom the government expected to do the work) were violating the law by hiring Indians to harvest and carry xiquilite [the plant that was the main source of indigo] at nominal wages." "Indigo Production and Trade in Colonial Guatemala," *Hispanic American Historical Review,* **XXXIX,** 2, May 1959, 187. Even slaves were hiring Indians—there is the measure!

[123]"[The] initial goals [of Spanish conquest show] a strong convergence towards the creation of mining economies in the different places of occupation and settlement. . . . What the Indians gave to Europe was fundamentally precious metals. Colonial products appeared relegated to a modest second place." Alvaro Jara, *Grandes voies maritimes dans le monde XV-XIXe siècles,* pp. 249–250. Jara points out that the tables showing volumes of sea traffic are very clear-cut in this regard: "Except for the decades 1591–1600 and 1621–1630, all the others between 1503 and 1660 seem to fit this formula: the greater the mining production, the greater the maritime traffic as the commerical counterpart [p. 266]."

[124]Max Weber makes a distinction between plantation and estate economies, a terminology frequently used. The main distinction seems to center on form of labor control and typical products. See *General Economic History* (New York: Free Press, 1950), 79–92. Plantations produce garden products (according to Weber), typically sugar cane, tobacco, coffee, cotton. Estates are used for stock-raising or wheat-growing or a combination of the two. I am not sure the distinction thus stated is useful, as the "estates" (as herein defined) found in eastern Europe were far more akin to the "plantations" of the Americas than to the "estates" of England, for example.

periods of demographic decline such as the fourteenth and fifteenth centuries).[125] The agriculture was hence more intensive.[126] In addition, part of the land was shifted from arable to pastoral use. The result was less coercion. In part, more skilled labor can insist on less juridical coercion. Or rather, the coercion has to be more indirect, via market mechanisms. In part, it was that in cattle breeding, it was always a temptation, especially in winter, to shift food from cattle to men. A manorial system was not able to deal with this problem effectively.[127] But the sixteenth century was a time of increased demand for meat, the demand for meat being elastic and expanding with a rising standard of living.[128] Also given the expansion of population, there was more demand for grain as well. The consequences

[125]However the density declined in southern Europe as the process of semiperipheralization, to be described later, occurred. Commenting on a paper of Marian Malowist relating to developments in eastern Europe at this time, Jaime Vicens Vives made this comparison with Catalonia: "In effect, we have noted, as a specialist in the evolution of peasant classes in a country quite different from 15th-century Poland, that is Catalonia, that if there is in both areas a very striking concordance in what we've called the 'second feudalism' this similarity cannot be explained by identical causes. Mr. Malowist, following his Polish precursors, [considers] as prime elements in the beginning of a new feudalization in the 15th and 16th centuries the development of Poland's Baltic commerce and the enlargement of internal markets—normal outcome of the growth of cities. In Catalonia, quite the contrary, the sources of the worsening of the juridicial status of the peasant population was the decadence of Mediterranean commerce on the one hand and the depopulation of the towns on the other. Thus, one arrives at the identical results starting from opposed facts." Comments made on the "Rapport de M. Malowist," p. 148.

Quite apart from the fact that I don't believe Vicens characterizes Malowist's position with total accuracy, I believe he misses the point. The causes of the peasant's new status in Poland and Catalonia are identical. It is only their starting-points that are different, Catalonia having been in the fourteenth century one of the relatively most advanced areas in Europe. The depopulation of Catalonia and the increase of Poland's population may have brought the resulting densities quite nearly in line with each other reflecting by the end of the "long" sixteenth century their not too different statuses in the European world-economy.

Similarly, when Pierre Jeannin points out that Baltic ports in fact increase their size and activity in the sixteenth century, cautioning us not to overstate the *decline* of the town in the periphery, we must acknowledge this to be so. See "Les relations économiques des villes de la Baltique avec Anvers

au XVIe siècle," *Vierteljahrschrift für Sozial- und Wirtschaftsgeschichte*, **XLIII**, 3, Sept. 1956, 196. But there are various things to bear in mind. (1) An increase in international trade of course leads to an increase in port activity. But what about administrative centers and foci of local trade? (2) An increase in overall population should normally have the consequence of an increase in the absolute size of towns, but what are the relative urban proportions? (3) Even a relative increase in the size of the urban population of the periphery may be (and undoubtedly was) a relative decline in relation to the degree of urbanization of western Europe.

[126]More intensive agriculture requires better terms for the peasant. See Ardant on how tithes discourage productivity (*Théorie sociologique de l'impôt*, **I**, p. 208), and how fixed taxes or rents encourage it (*Ibid.*, **I**, pp. 225–226).

[127]Witold Kula makes clear the theoretical dilemma: "[A] system which places on the serfs the major responsibility in the function of 'reproduction,' that is the care of the cattle, thereby creates the worst possible conditions for cattle raising. Negligence by peasants towards the animals, a source of profit more for the seignior than for them, is the constant worry of whoever runs a manor. The years of food shortage, generally years of low rainfall, place the peasant before the alternative of feeding the beasts or himself! The choice may easily be guessed. Finally the low productivity of the oxen made necessary having a large herd, which aggravated further the difficulties of supplying forage." *Théorie économique du système féodal: Pour un modèle de l'économie polonaise, 16e–18e siècles* (Paris: Mouton, 1970), 31–32. This consideration was not merely theoretical. Emmanuel Le Roy Ladurie shows that exactly this happened in Languedoc between 1515–1530. *Les paysans de Languedoc* (Paris: S.E.V.P.E.N., 1966), **I**, 323.

[128]See Kristof Glamann, *Fontana Economic History of Europe*, **II**, pp. 45–52. "The heyday of the cattle trade coincided with the golden age of the nobility [p. 50]."

were simple. Cattle-raising, which was profitable, required a different social organization of work. When it did not develop, for whatever reasons, pastoralism actually decreased.[129] Hence, Europe-wide, it became a matter of increased division of labor.

In the core area, towns flourished, industries were born, the merchants became a significant economic and political force. Agriculture to be sure remained throughout the sixteenth century the activity of the majority of the population. (Indeed this was true until the nineteenth century for northwest Europe and until the twentieth for southern Europe.) Nonetheless, the inclusion of eastern Europe and Hispanic America into a European world-economy in the sixteenth century not only provided capital (through booty and high-profit margins) but also liberated some labor in the core areas for specialization in other tasks. The occupational range of tasks in the core areas was a very complex one. It included a large remnant parallel to those in the periphery (for example, grain production). But the trend in the core was *toward* variety and specialization, while the trend in the periphery was toward monoculture.

The expansion of the sixteenth century was not only a geographical expansion. It was an economic expansion—a period of demographic growth, increased agricultural productivity, and the "first industrial revolution." It marked the establishment of *regular* trade between Europe and the rest of the inhabited world.[130] By the end of the century, the economy simply looked different and better.[131]

Thus far we have described the emergent forms of production and of labor control in the periphery and treated it in explicit and implicit contrast to the core areas. In fact, the core area structure is more complicated than we have indicated to this point. However before we treat this complexity we should look at the agricultural production of that third structural zone, the semiperiphery. We have not yet explicated the function of the semiperiphery for the workings of the world-system. Suffice it to say at this point that on a number of economic criteria (but not all), the semiperiphery represents a midway point on a continuum running from the

[129]As in Languedoc. See Le Roy Ladurie's description: "[T]he clearings diminishes land for grazing; the plantations (olives, chestnut, etc.), the terraces, and stone enclosures restrict the open fields with right of common. For all these reasons, stockbreeding reaches a plateau, then declines. In this ancient agriculture, which does not know fodder plants or which confines them to gardens, it is not possible simultaneously to develop animal and vegetable production. Their requirements are contradictory because they both seek the land which is still free but becoming daily rarer. For want of a *Mesta*, as in Spain, to defend the interests of the breeders, the development of cattle-breeding is soon sacrificed, in a traditional society undergoing expansion." *Les paysans de Languedoc*, **I**, p. 324.

[130]See J. H. Parry, "Transport and Trade Routes," in *Cambridge Economic History of Europe*, **IV**, E. E. Rich and C. H. Wilson, eds., *The Economy of Expanding Europe in the 16th and 17th Centuries* (London and New York: Cambridge Univ. Press, 1967), 191.

[131]See this comparison of Europe 1600 with Europe 1500: "First of all, an agricultural sector, still the principal activity, which is able to feed many more men than in 1500, and to feed them better; trade with the overseas worlds, a textile industry still greater than that of 1500, a mining and metallurgical industry far larger." Mauro, *Le XVIe siècle européen*, p. 257.

core to the periphery. This is, in particular, true of the complexity of economic institutions, the degree of economic reward (both in terms of average level and range), and most of all in the form of labor control.

The periphery (eastern Europe and Hispanic America) used forced labor (slavery and coerced cash-crop labor). The core, as we shall see, increasingly used free labor. The semiperiphery (former core areas turning in the direction of peripheral structures) developed an inbetween form, share-cropping, as a widespread alternative. To be sure, sharecropping was known in other areas. But it took primacy of place at this time only in the semiperiphery. The *mezzadria* in Italy and the *fâcherie* in Provence were already known from the thirteenth century on; *métayage* elsewhere in southern France from the fourteenth. And as economic difficulties of lords of the manor increased in the fourteenth and fifteenth centuries the domains were increasingly leased in this form not as an entity but in smaller units, capable of sustaining a family rather than a whole village. Duby notes that by the mid-fifteenth century "the large-scale cereal-producing enterprises that were still able to exist in western Europe disappeared. . . ." He calls this "one of the fundamental transformations of country life. . . ."[132]

Why did the transformation, however, take this particular form? That is, why, if a transformation was threatened, did not the seignior turn to the state to force the peasants to stay on the land, as in eastern Europe? And, on the other hand, why, if there were concessions, did it take the form of sharecropping rather than the transfer of land to small farmers who either bought the land outright or paid a fixed rent, the principal (not, of course, the only) solution in northwest Europe?

Dobb, in comparing western and eastern Europe in terms of the seigniorial reaction to the phenomena of desertion and depopulation, and considering western Europe the arena of "concession" and eastern Europe that of "renewed coercion," attributes the different reactions to the "strength of peasant resistance."[133] Ian Blanchard on the other hand agrees that the degree of peasant unrest is a factor but in a less direct

[132]Duby, *Rural Economy*, p. 325; see also p. 275. However in Castile the situation seems to have developed somewhat differently: "In the fourteenth and fifteenth centuries, the Castilian aristocracy reached a peak of power, an importance so over-whelming that it became the ruler of the State. The Castilian nobles did not adopt a defensive position as in the other Western kingdoms, but quite the contrary, they changed dynasties, took over the royal patrimony, and made the royal power an instrument of their ambitions. This phenomenon came about because the monarchy could not count on solid support from the cities. Many Castilian towns were on the side of aristocracy, and many more were subjugated by it." Vicens, an *Economic History of Spain*,

p. 245. Hence, argues Vicens, the sixteenth century saw the rise in Extramadura and Andalusia of great *latifundia*, which had been prepared for by the great land grants of the fourteenth and fifteenth centuries. See pages 247–248.

[133]And, Dobb adds, to the strength of peasant resistance, "the political and military power of local lords, rendering it easy or difficult as the case might be to overcome peasant resistance and forcibly to prevent the desertion of the manors, and the extent to which the royal power exerted its influence to strengthen seigneurial authority or on the contrary welcomed an opportunity of weakening the position of rival sectors of the nobility. . . ." *Studies*, pp. 51–52.

way. The crucial factor was labor availability. He argues that up to the 1520s there was a labor shortage in England and that legislators did indeed seek to coerce laborers to remain on the land while landowners reluctantly enclosed *faute de mieux.*[134] Thus coercion, Blanchard argues, was used in England as well, as long as there was depopulation. It was only when population was growing that the peasants erupted, demanding in effect land.

Whatever the case, the amount of peasant resistance explains little since we would want to know why peasants resisted more in England than in Poland—does Dobb really believe this?[135]—why lords were stronger or weaker, why kings strengthened seigniorial authority or weakened it. We are most likely to discover the reasons in the fact of the complementary divergence within a single world-economy, for which we suggested two explanations: the comparative strength of the towns at the beginning point of the divergence, and the degree of vacancy of land.

"Vacancy" of land can be restated in terms of a land/labor ratio. If there is plenty of land, one can make do with relatively inefficient means of production. One can engage in extensive agriculture. One can use slaves or coerced cash-crop laborers. Intensive agriculture requires free laborers. But why then sharecropping? Obviously because the situation is somewhere inbetween.

Let us note that from the peasant's point of view, sharecropping is perhaps to be preferred to coerced cash-crop labor, but not by too much. The net return is low, although in times of prosperity it may rise. The coercion via debt mechanisms is often as real as legal coercion. For H.K. Takahashi, *métayers* are "semi-serfs," working for "usurious landowners."[136] Bloch sees developments in France as a process of slipping back from the gradual liberation of the peasant from the seignior which had been taking place in the late Middle Ages:

> If—absurd hypothesis—the [French] Revolution had broken out in about 1480, it would have turned over the land, via the suppression of seigniorial receipts (*charges seigneuriales*) almost exclusively to a mass of small farmers. But, from 1480 to 1789, three centuries passed in which large estates were reconstituted.[137]

[134]"From the late 1520's onwards [however] the tenantry previously so silent about enclosures became vociferous in their denunciations of those who held land in pasture, thus preventing them acquiring new holdings which were needed to satisfy a growing population. This anger was often organized through legal channels but increasingly it became obvious that they would show no obedience to the law and would cast down the enclosures of land." Blanchard, *Economic History Review,* **XXIII,** p. 440.

[135]One possible explanation for a different degree of *effective* resistance is suggested by Braudel—differential density of population. In contrasting the settlements of low density in central Europe to those of high density in Italy ("village-cities") and the large centers of the Rhine, Meuse and Parisian Basin, Braudel says: "Now this low village density, in so many countries of central and eastern Europe, may it not be one of the essential causes of the fate of the peasantry? Vis-à-vis the seigniors, they found themselves all the more disarmed in that they lacked the elbow-to-elbow feeling of large communities." *Civilization matérielle,* p. 42.

[136]H. K. Takahashi, "The Transition from Feudalism to Capitalism: A contribution to the Sweezy–Dobb controversy," *Science and Society,* **XVI,** 4, Fall 1952, 324.

[137]Bloch, *Caractères originaux,* **I,** p. 154.

Why sharecropping however and not tenantry on the one hand or coerced cash-crop labor on the other? Although sharecropping had the disadvantage, compared to coerced cash-cropping, of greater difficulty in supervision, it had the advantage of encouraging the peasant's efforts to increased productivity, provided of course the peasant would continue to work for the seignior without legal compulsion.[138] In short, when labor is plentiful, sharecropping is probably more profitable than coerced cash-cropping.[139]

As for tenantry, no doubt by this logic it is more profitable still than cash-cropping. However there is a proviso. Tenants have fixed contracts and gain at moments of inflation, at least to the extent that the contracts are relatively long-term. Of course, the reverse is true when the market declines. Sharecropping thus is a mode of risk-minimization.[140] It follows that sharecropping is most likely to be considered in areas of specialized agriculture where the risks of variance outweigh the transactions costs.

But this was precisely a moment of high risk. Continued price inflation is very unsettling. Sharecropping seemed the remedy.[141] In some areas, peasants were lucky enough to have legal defenses which make the enforcement of sharecropping too expensive for the landowner, who then found straight rental preferable. Such an instance was England. Cheung suggests that the key was freehold tenure, known in England but not for example in France.[142]

[138]See Duby: "*Métayage* offered the masters one great advantage. It allowed them to profit from the hoped-for growth of demesne productivity, as well as from the rise in agricultural prices. . . . Even when the lord's participation was minimal, the contract assured him an important share in the net profits. [Presumably more than if he rented the land to the peasant.] For we must not forget that the *métayer* had to deduct seed and sometimes tithes from the portion which was left to him, and this was a heavy charge burdening the normally low yields of agriculture. Nevertheless the system presented inconveniences of which the lords were well aware. The wide fluctuations in crops necessitated close supervision." *Rural Economy,* pp. 275–276.

[139]As Duby says, the advantage of *métayage* to the landowner was that "cultivation costs were low, returns in marketable goods . . . very high [*Ibid.,* p. 280].

[140]Steven N. S. Cheung states this proposition theoretically: "The terms in a share contract, among other things, include the rental percentage, the ratio of nonland input to land, and the types of crop to be grown. These are mutually decided by the landowner and the tenant. For fixed-rent and wage contracts, however, given the market prices, one party alone can decide how much of the other party's resources he shall employ and what crops shall be grown. And since in a share contract the sharing of output is based on the *actual* yield, efforts must be made by the landowner to ascertain the harvest

yield. Thus negotiation and enforcement are mo¬e complex for a share contract than for a fixed-rent or a wage contract. . . .

"[I]f transaction cost is the only consideration then . . . share contracts will never be chosen. Why, then are the share contracts chosen? . . . Under a fixed-rent contract, the tenant bears most, if not all, of the risk [of factors exogenous to the production function causing high variance in yield]; under a wage contract, the landowner bears most, if not all the risk. Share tenancy may then be regarded as a device for risk sharing (or risk dispersion). . . ." *The Theory of Share Tenancy* (Chicago, Illinois: Univ. of Chicago Press, 1969), 67–68.

[141]"Brusquely, beginning in the 16th century, sharecropping, before that so unevenly distributed and even where it has been known in fact so rare, spread throughout France and held an even larger place there, at least until the 18th century. *Against monetary fluctuations, there is no surer remedy.* The Italian bourgeoisie, subtle financiers, were first to realize this. Had they not gone as far sometimes—for example, in Bologna beginning in 1376—to require by law this sort of contract of every citizen of the ruling city who rented out land to the inhabitants of the *contado* [surrounding countryside], who were dominated and submitted to pressure. French owners did not take long to make the same observation." Bloch, *Caractères originaux,* **I,** p. 152, Italics added.

[142]"Under a perpetual lease [which resulted from freehold wherein a lease for life was enforced by

Legal factors are not alone determining. For we must still explain the discrepancy between northern France which moved extensively toward lease arrangements and southern France where sharecropping was the pervasive mode. The law in both areas was substantially the same. Duby locates the key differential in the relative affluence of the farmer in the north as contrasted to "the depressed economic conditions" of the southern peasant "working on land whose productivity had probably not been increased by improvement in techniques as in the north. . . ."[143]

If, however, it was just a question of technology, we are only pushed one step back, to ask why technological advances made in one area were adopted in another area not that distant either geographically or culturally. Braudel suggests that soil conditions in Mediterranean Europe and northwest Europe were fundamentally different, the former being poorer.[144] Porchnev suggests that a further consideration is degree of involvement in the world-economy, the existence of large estates (hence the absence of sharecropping) being correlated with high involvement.[145]

May we not then consider sharecropping as a sort of second best? Unable to move all the way to large estates based either on enclosure and tenancy as in England or coerced cash-crop labor as in eastern Europe, the landed classes of southern France and northern Italy chose the halfway house[146]

---

law], the cost of enforcing a share contract may be so high as to make it undesirable, since tenancy dismissal is one effective device to insure against poor performance by sharecroppers." Cheung, *The Theory of Share Tenancy*, p. 34.

[143]Duby, *Rural Economy*, p. 327.

[144]Contrasting the situation of the two areas, Braudel says: "It was rare that a harvest [in the Mediterranean area] escaped all the successive dangers which threatened it. The yields were poor and, given the small area used for seed-beds, the Mediterranean was always at the edge of famine." *Civilisation matérielle*, I, p. 223.

Aldo de Maddalena does not agree: "In general, one must recognize that the productivity of arable land [in Italy] was rather low, except in exceptional circumstances. Braudel blames the climate for this low productivity of Mediterranean soil, but there must also be entered into the balance the deficiency of the technological apparatus, of the cultural system, of agrarian doctrine, of business capacity, of the availibility of capital, of the administrative and social structure, of the political and military vicissitudes in order to arrive at a more valid and historically justified view of the phenomenon." "Il mondo rurale italiano nel cinque e nel seicento," *Rivista storica italiana*, **LXXVI**, 2, giug. 1964, 423. No doubt one should take all these factors into account but running the book is seldom a helpful way of narrowing down plausible causal explanations. Note, however, the view of Sylvia Thrupp,

cited previously in footnote 52, on the *high* fertility of northern Italy in the Middle Ages.

[145]Boris Porchnev notes that it is true that large estates did not develop in France in this period the way they did in England: "[Such estates] are to be found nonetheless in feeble proportions, as an economic tendency still little developed, especially in the peripheral provinces where the proximity of the seas offer some advantageous commercial possibilities. The ports of Guyenne, Languedoc, Provence, Saintonge, Poitou, Normandy and Brittany facilitated the export of wine, of agricultural products, sometimes even wheat in contraband, even attempts to export livestock particularly sheep. In short the nobles attempted to taste the forbidden fruit of commerce." *Les soulèvements populaires en France de 1623 à 1648* (Paris: S.E.V.P.E.N., 1963), 289. Note, however, that Porchnev includes Languedoc and Provence in his list. We shall return to this question in a later chapter. For the moment, let us leave it that we are in the midst of a case of multiple causation.

[146]Marx saw sharecropping as just such a halfway house: "As a transition form from the original form of rent to capitalist rent, we may consider the métayer system, or share-cropping. . . . On the one hand, the farmer here lacks sufficient capital required for complete capitalist management. On the other hand, the share here appropriated by the landlord does not bear the pure form of rent. It may actually include interest on the capital advanced

of sharecropping, as a partial response to the creation of a capitalist world-economy, in the form of semicapitalist enterprises, appropriate indeed to semiperipheral areas.

If the semiperipheral areas remained semiperipheral and did not become the total satellites into which peripheral areas developed, it was not only because of the high land/labor ratio. It may also have been because the existence of a strong indigenous *bourgeoisie* has a particular impact on the development of *agricultural* production in times of distress. Duby points out that in areas where city merchants had been numerous and relatively powerful, many of the estates fell into the hands of these townsmen seeking protection against famine and the social status attached to land ownership, but not the trouble of actual farming. Giving out the land to sharecropping was a reasonable compromise.[147] How "reasonable" the compromise was from the point of view of the peasants is put into considerable doubt by G. E. de Falguerolles, since the orientation of these town bourgeois was toward short-run profit from their investment which had the effect of desolating the land over the following century.[148]

A second paradox, then, about the most "advanced" area. We already noted the strength of town workers keeping up the wage level, thus putting northern Italy at an industrial disadvantage vis-à-vis northwest Europe. Perhaps this same strength of workers accounted for maintaining disproportionate numbers of laborers in the rural areas by using guild restrictions to prevent their entry into urban employment, that is, in the sixteenth century period of demographic upsurge. This would have the result of weakening the bargaining position of the peasant. In any case, the "strength" of the town bourgeoisie seems to have led to a higher likelihood of sharecropping, and thus to the nonemergence of the yeoman farmer who would play such a large role in the economic advance of northwest Europe.

Let us now turn to those areas which would by 1640 be ensconced at the core of the European world-economy: England, the Netherlands, and

by him and an excess rent. . . . Rent no longer appears here as the normal form of surplus-value in general. On the one hand the share-cropper, whether he employs his own or another's labour, lays claim to a portion of the product not in his capacity as a labourer, but as possessor of part of the instruments of labour. On the other hand, the landlord claims his share not exclusively on the basis of his landownership, but also as lender of capital." *Capital*, **III**, ch. XLVII, sect, V, p. 803.

[147]"The contract of *métayage*, so widespread in the locality of Italian and French Mediterranean towns on lands made vacant by migration [in the period of fourteenth and fifteenth century demographic downturn] where the townsmen had been able to assume control, was in fact one form of cooperation between burgesses and peasants for the purpose of cultivating the arable and producing cereals." Duby, *Rural Economy*, pp. 356–357.

[148]"As it was practiced, sharecropping has the appearance of an essentially capitalist regime responding to the needs of bourgeois owners: Their ideal was to obtain from their lands a part of the revenue net and quit, convertible into money. They brought to the management their enterprises a mercantile outlook: they carefully entered into their *Livres de Raison* or *Livres de Recettes* the share of the harvest received, the sales of grain or livestock, pellmell with the interest on their loans [*le produit de leur usure*]. To these outsiders [*forains*], the interest in profit was the primary consideration; they were more or less ignorant of agricultural matters." G. E. de Falguerolles, "La décadence de l'économie agricole dans le Consulat de Lempaut aux XVIIe et XVIIIe siècles," *Annales du Midi*, **LIII**, 1941, 149.

to some extent northern France. These areas developed a combination of pasturage and arable production based on free or freer labor and units of relatively efficient size. As may be noted, Spain started down this path and then turned off it to become part of the semiperiphery. The reasons for this shift in economic role we shall expound at length in a later chapter.

In the crisis of the late Middle Ages, when a decline in population led to a lowered demand for agricultural products as well as higher wages for urban workers (and hence a better bargaining position for rural workers), the great demesnes declined in western Europe, as we have already seen. They could not become cash-crop estates as in sixteenth-century eastern Europe because there was no international market in a generally dismal economic scene. They had only two significant alternatives. On the one hand, they could convert feudal obligations into money rent,[149] which would reduce costs and increase income to the demesne owner, but involved a gradual transfer of control over the land. That is, it made possible the rise of the small-scale yeoman farmer, either as tenant on fixed rents or, if better off, as independent owner (who can be seen as someone who has, in the purchase of the land, paid a lump sum of rent for a number of years).[150] The alternative then open to the landlord was to convert his land to pasture: cattle or sheep. In the fifteenth century, both wool prices and meat prices had seemed to resist the effects of depression more, and in addition the costs in then scarce, hence expensive, labor were less.[151]

At this time, *both* England and Spain increased pasturage. With the expanding economy of the sixteenth century, wheat seemed to gain an advantage over wool,[152] but not over cattle which gave not only meat but tallow, leather, and dairy products, the consumption of all of which expanded

[149]["The liberation of serfs] was less given to them than sold to them." Marc Bloch, *Caractères originaux,* **I,** p. 111.

[150][Under a system of proprietorship of land parcels,], the price of land [represents] nothing more than capitalised rent. . . ." Karl Marx, *Capital,* **III,** ch. XLVII, sect. V, p. 805.

[151]See Slicher van Bath, *A.A.G.B.,* No. 12, 164–168. See Peter J. Bowden: "It was the profitablility of wool-growing as against corn production that was largely responsible for the spread of sheep-farming, especially in central England, between the mid-fifteenth and mid-sixteenth centuries. . . .

"As the output and export of cloth increased, wool prices rose. Taking the decade 1451–60 as base, the price of home-grown wool had approximately doubled by 1541–50. Grain prices remained comparatively stable during the late fifteenth century and showed no marked tendency to rise until after 1520, when prices in general moved upward." *The*

Wool Trade in Tudor and Stuart England (New York: Macmillan, 1962), 4–5.

[152]"By the mid-sixteenth century, however, the urge to switch from grain to wool was weakening. Land was becoming scarcer and labour more abundant. Corn prices, which had been rising since the 1520's, doubled in the 1540's, when the general price level moved sharply upward. Then, in 1557, the foreign market for English cloth collapsed and wool prices tumbled [Bowden, *ibid.,* p. 5]."

See Peter Ramsey: "Very broadly speaking then it might still pay to convert arable to pasture [in England] up to about 1550, provided that economies in labour could be made. To that extent the earlier commentators are confirmed. But after 1570 it probably paid better to reconvert from pasture to arable, provided the increase in labour costs did not offset the greater profit in selling grain." *Tudor Economic Problems* (London: Gollanc, 1968), 25.

with prosperity.[153] The most important thing to note about pasturage in the sixteenth century, especially livestock, was that it was becoming increasingly a regionally specialized activity. More cattle here, an advantage to large landowners, also meant less cattle elsewhere, which often meant a reduction in peasant consumption of meat and dairy products, a deterioration in his diet.[154] This overemphasis on livestock occurred in Spain, precisely. The two options—conversion of demesnes to leased land, and arable land to pasture—went hand in hand. For the latter made arable land all the scarcer, which made its rental value higher.[155] Furthermore, as arable land became scarcer, cultivation had to be more intensive, which meant that the quality of labor was very important, a further inducement to moving from labor services to money rent.[156]

The rise of sheep farming in the sixteenth century led to the great enclosures movement in England and Spain. But paradoxically it was not the large-scale proprietor who sought the enclosures but a new type, the small-scale independent proprietor.[157] It was of course the economic

---

[153]As Delumeau said of Rome: "To a city growing in population and wealth, it seemed [to the barons of the countryside] more advantageous to sell meat and cheese than wheat. Consequently, they systematically sabotaged all the efforts of the authorities to force them to limit their pasturage. This avidity for profit on the part of the nobility and the growing favor it accorded to stockbreeding clearly seems to have been accompanied by a veritable seigniorial reaction—a phenomenon that was not, furthermore, peculiar to the Roman countryside." Delumeau, *Vie économique,* **II**, pp. 567, 569.

Georges Duby links the expansion of stock-raising in France from the end of the thirteenth century on to "the growing demand for meat, leather, and wool originating in the cities." In turn, the growing importance of cattle (and wine) production "considerably accelerated the commercialization of the French countryside. . . ." "The French Countryside at the End of the 13th Century," in Rondo Cameron, ed., *Essays in French Economic History* (Homewood, Illinois: Irwin, Inc., 1970), p. 33.

[154]"[The] growing demand [Europe-wide] for cereals and wine deprived the country of meat, especially the peasants, and thus of an important element of their subsistence. The villages that had for a long time reserved their last pasturages for the butcher, ended by losing them all. . . .

"Regions where the relative insufficiency of population meant an inability to seek higher per capita production, as Aragon, abandoned the less fertile farms, developed an export production, and the

workers emigrated. . . . Thus, the disappearance of a rich source of nourishment went along with the impoverishment and subjection of the peasantry, stability in the rate of profit [*prix de revient*] and contributed to under-employment. . . ." José-Gentil da Silva, *En Espagne: développement économique, subsistence, déclin* (Paris: Mouton, 1965), 169–170.

[155]See Dobb, *Studies,* p. 58; Douglass C. North and Robert Paul Thomas, "An Economic Theory of the Growth of the Western World," *Economic History Review,* 2nd ser., **XXIII**, 1, Apr. 1970, 13.

[156]See Dobb, *ibid.,* p. 53.

[157]Julius Klein shows why this should be so: "The English enclosure movement and the similar process in Castile . . . synchronized to a surprising degree. In each case the episode had its beginnings in a stimulation of the sheep industry in the fourteenth century. . . . The exploitation of the confiscated monastic lands in England and the acquisition of the great properties of the military orders by the Crown in Castile contributed materially to the growth of the pastoral industry in both countries during the middle decades of the sixteenth century. Thereafter, however, in each of the two kingdoms there is apparent a gradual increase of enclosures, not so much for large-scale sheep-raising enterprises, as for the small copyholder in the case of England and for sedentary flocks and peasant agriculture in the case of Castile. In each country the high courts . . . protected the movement, and in each the motive to enclose the common lands

renewal of the sixteenth century that made possible the continued growth of these small-scale independent farmers.

For "sheep ate men," as the saying went, the rise of sheep farming thus creating the food shortages that had to be compensated both by more efficient arable production in England (the yeoman) and by Baltic grain (coerced cash-cropping).[158]

Furthermore, the increased enclosures made possible the growth in the rural areas of handicraft industries.[159] In Spain, however, the *Mesta* was too entrenched for the small-scale proprietor to make too much headway. And as we shall see later the imperial policies of Charles V gave some added strength to these large landowners. Instead of using its rural unemployed for industrial development, Spain would expel them and export them.

We must persist a little longer on this question of the development of western European agriculture and why it could not take the route of eastern Europe: large estates with coerced cash-crop labor. It was, in the end, because a capitalist world-economy was coming into existence. Paul Sweezy argues a sort of ecological continuum: "Near the centers of trade, the effect on feudal economy [of trade expansion] is strongly disintegrating; further away the effect tends to be just the opposite."[160] This is really

---

was supported by a desire to stimulate sedentary sheep raising. The ultimate effect in both was to promote small-scale agriculture. . . . In the peninsula the element which fought against the enclosure movement, and, in fact, successfully obstructed its progress for two centuries, was the large-scale migratory pastoral industry. In medieval and early Tudor England the anti-enclosure interests were very largely the agricultural classes." *The Mesta: A Study in Spanish Economic History, 1273–1836* (Cambridge, Massachusetts: Harvard Univ. Press, 1919), 314–315.

[158]"The cereal export trade from Prussia and Poland began at the end of the thirteenth century, and was followed in the fourteenth by that of the Baltic countries. Cereals were shipped to the Netherlands, northern Norway, and to the parts of England where there was a shortage of corn, such as the Fen district and the great sheep-grazing area." Slicher van Bath, *A.A.G.B.*, No. 12, 170.

[159]In explaining why these industries were found in some areas rather than in others, Joan Thirsk notes:

"The common factors seem to be these: a populous community of small farmers, often mainly freeholders . . . or customary tenants with a tenure almost as good as a freehold . . ., pursuing a pastoral economy. This may rest upon dairying in which case the farms are usually early enclosed, and manorial organization and cooperative farming, in consequence, is weak or non-existent. Or it may rest

upon breeding and rearing on generous pasture commons, where there is no practical incentive to enclose, where the arable land is meagre, and there again there is no strong framework of open fields of cooperative husbandry. . . . Underlying all this we may see a certain logic sometimes in the way these common factors are linked together. Some of the land best suited to pasture was not cleared until a comparatively late stage in local settlement history. It was likely to be immediately enclosed. It was likely to give rise to a community of independent farmers who recognized not the hamlet or the village, but the family, as the cooperative working unit. If the land was suitable for dairying, it had enough water to support a cloth industry too. In a less hospitable countryside, where there were wide moorlands or large fenland commons, and little suitable cornland, the husbandry was bound to consist in rearing and sheep-keeping. The commons attracted landless youths. The farming required less labour than a corn-growing farm and left men time to engage in a subsidiary occupation." "Industries in the Countryside," in F. J. Fisher, ed., *Essays in the Economic and Social History of Tudor and Stuart England* (London and New York: Cambridge Univ. Press, 1961), 86–87.

[160]Sweezy, *Science and Society*, **XIV**, p. 141. See also pp. 146–147. Joan Thirsk contributes some support for Sweezy's hypothesis: "But at the beginning of the sixteenth century, clear contrasts could still be observed at the extremities of the kingdom. Corn-

too simple a formulation, as Postan argues and Dobb agrees.[161] The Sweezy case is based on the alternatives for the peasant, the ability to escape to the city, the "civilizing proximity of urban life."[162] He neglects the possibility that in many peripheral regions, for example eastern Europe, the peasant had the alternative of frontier areas, often quite as attractive as cities. Indeed, it was precisely because the peasant used this alternative that juridical means were introduced in the sixteenth century to bind him to the land.

The difference was less in the peasant's alternatives, though this played a role, than in the landowner's alternatives. Where was he to draw the largest and most immediate profit? On the one hand, he could turn his land over to other uses (pasture land at a higher rate of profit or lease for money to small farmers—both of which meant dispensing with the feudal labor-service requirements) and using the new profit for investment in trade and industry and/or in aristocratic luxury. On the other hand, he could seek to obtain larger profits by intensifying production of staple cash-crops (especially grain) and then investing the new profits in trade (but not industry and/or aristocratic luxury).[163] The former alternative was more plausible in northwest Europe, the latter in eastern Europe, largely because the *slight* differential already established in production specialties meant that profit maximization was achieved, or at least thought

wall and Devon, Cumberland, Westmoreland, and Northumberland had many communities dispersed in lonely farmsteads, some still preserving vestiges of the clan spirit, still almost completely isolated from the commercial world. Corn-growing villages in East Anglia and east Kent, on the other hand, were deeply involved in large scale commercial dealings in food, and conducted their business seemingly without regard for any social obligation whether to clan, family, or manorial lord. Between the highland and the lowland zones [for example, the west Midlands], the contrasts were blurred." "The Farming Regions of England," in *The Agrarian History of England and Wales*, **IV,** Joan Thirsk, ed., *1500–1640* (London and New York: Cambridge Univ. Press, 1967), 15. For those who may feel that East Anglia is not exactly a point that close to the center, we must remember that it is its position in fact in the sixteenth century and not in the twentieth that is at issue. Here Thirsk observes: "East Anglia nowadays occupies a somewhat isolated geographical position off the main traffic ways between London and the north. In the sixteenth century, by contrast its rivers reaching into the heart of East Anglia, its long coastline, and its many ports, placed it in easy communication with the markets of London, north-eastern England, Scotland, the Netherlands, and the Baltic. Its farming, in consequence, developed early in the service of national and international markets, and specialization was

so far advanced that by the early seventeenth century, even in years of good harvest, many many districts were far from selfsufficient in corn.... [pp. 40–41]."

[161]"[I]n the more backward arts of [England], farthest from great markets, above all in the north-west, labour services were shed first, and the more progressive south-east retained them longest." M. Postan, "The Chronology of Labour Services," *Transactions of the Royal Historical Society,* 4th ser., **XX,** 1937, 171; Dobb, *Science and Society,* **XIV,** p. 161.

[162]Sweezy, *Science and Society,* **XIV,** p. 147.

[163]This should be qualified. The noble capitalist landowners of eastern Europe were of course interested in aristocratic luxury. Indeed, Jeannin goes so far as to say: "It is certain that, despite the limitations placed on purchases by the penury, passing or permanent, of the royal treasuries, the growth of sumptuary consumption constitutes one of the significant changes that characterized the evolution of aristocratic life in the North [of Europe, that is, in states bordering the Baltic] in the 16th century." *Vierteljahrschrift für Sozial- und Wirtschaftsgeschichte,* **XLIII,** p. 215. But note Jeannin refers nonetheless to penury as a limit. This is precisely the point. In an expanding economy, the absolute indulgence in luxury increased, but compared to the increase in western Europe, we can probably talk of a relative decline.

to be achieved, by doing more extensively and more efficiently what one already did best.[164] Hence, the state authorities encouraged enclosures for pasturing (and truck farming) in England, but the creation of large domains for wheat growing in eastern Europe.

As for why labor was contractual in northwest Europe and coerced in eastern Europe, it is insufficient to point to pasturage versus arable land use. For in that case, Hispanic America would have had contractual labor. Rather, demography plays the critical role, as we have already suggested. The western European alternative was one which assumed that there would be enough of a manpower pool at cheap enough rates to satisfy the land-owner's needs without costing too much.[165] In eastern Europe and Hispanic America, there was a shortage of labor by comparison with the amount of land it was profitable to exploit, given the existence of world-economy. And in the presence of such a shortage "the expansion of markets and the growth of production is as likely to lead to the increase of labour services as to their decline."[166] Indeed, in Hispanic America, the decline in population was the very fact which explained the rise of cattle and sheep raising, both of which became widespread in the sixteenth century, and which took the form of large-scale enterprises with an important compo-nent of forced labor because of the labor shortage.[167]

Finally, let us look at what the rise of money tenancy meant. Remember that in western Europe the conversion of feudal dues to money rent became widespread in the *late Middle Ages,* as we discussed in the last chapter, because of population decline. One must not think of this as an either/or proposition. Feudal dues could be paid in labor services, in kind, or in money. It was often to the landowner's advantage to switch back and forth.[168]

[164]Douglas C. North and Robert Paul Thomas in *Economic History Review,* **XXIII,** note that: "The enclosure taking place at this time occurred . . . in pastures producing raw wool and in areas suitable for truck farms. The former was in response to an expanding demand for raw wool and the second to increases in local demands for foodstuffs by the growing urban areas. The sixteenth-century en-closure movement was most extensive in the high-land regions of England because the returns to enclosures were higher there than in the arable regions, for two reasons. First, the areas suited to pasture had a lower population density than did the arable ones; hence, . . . fewer people had to reach agreement for the enclosure to occur. Second, and probably more important, the increase in the price of wool would have caused individuals holding land in common to use it inefficiently by each attempting to pasture more sheep. The cost to the individual of pasturing another sheep on the com-mon approached zero, but the cost to society of everyone doing so was positive. The common would tend to become overgrazed and the total output wool would actually decline. . . . Individuals with the power to enclose the common could avoid this occurence by enclosing areas and denying access to all others [p. 13]."

[165]Dobb calls such a manpower pool "proletarian or semiproletarian elements." *Science and Society,* **XIV,** p. 161.

[166]Postan, *Transactions of the Royal Historical Society,* **XX,** pp. 192–193.

[167]See François Chevalier, *Land and Society in Colo-nial Mexico* (Berkeley: Univ. of California Press, 1963).

[168]"The development of money rent is not always connected with the commutation of labor services. On a number of manors money rent arose as com-mutation of rent in kind. Finally, money rent could appear side by side with labor service, and rent in kind. Finally, money rent arose as a result of the leasing of a part of the demesne." Eugen A. Kos-minsky, *Past & Present,* No. 7, pp. 16–17. See Postan: "It has been tacitly assumed in this essay that rents and labour services stood in a complementary relationship to each other, and that an increase in one would, in normal circumstances, be accompanied by a decrease in the other." *Transactions of the Royal Historical Society,* **XX,** p. 191.

For this reason, the mere change in the *form* of feudal rent was not by itself critical. Indeed, Takahashi goes insofar as to argue that it is epiphenomenal,[169] but this seems to me to be quite overstating the issue. Even if it might be true for the thirteenth and fourteenth centuries to some extent, the rise of payment of dues in money terms certainly *evolved into* a meaningful difference by the sixteenth century, precisely because the "extra-economic" coercive forces were pressuring not the rural laborers but instead the landowners to go further than they intended.[170] Or at least they were pushing some landowners. At a time of expansion, there was competition for labor. The richest landowners could afford to buy the labor away from others. The smallest often had little choice but to settle for obtaining tenants on his land. It was those of inbetween size who may have held on the longest to the old feudal relationships.[171]

England and France had followed the same path in the late Middle Ages. In both there was manumission of serfdom, the rise of money tenancy, and correlatively the rise of wage labor. Yet a curious thing happened in the sixteenth century. England continued on this path. Eastern Europe moved toward the "second serfdom." Southern France moved toward sharecropping. In northern France, transformation seemed to stop short.

[169]"The change in the structure of feudal land property accompanying the decline of the manorial system brought a change in the form in rent: in England to money rent, in France and Germany to change in the nature of feudal rent. The peasants had previously contributed surplus labor directly in the form of work, and now paid it in realized forms—products or their money price. The change came to nothing more than this. . . . In both cases the feudal landlords, in virtue of their ownership, use 'extra-economic coercion' directly, without the intervention of the laws of commodity exchange, to take the surplus from the peasant producers *(tenanciers, Besitzer)* who actually occupy the land, the means of production." Takahashi, *Science and Society*, **XVI**, p. 327.

[170]Weber explains cogently why it was in the interest of a number of forces outside the manor to push this process towards a more complete transformation of the situation: "[T]he commercial interest of the newly established bourgeoisie of the towns . . . promoted the weakening or dissolution of the manor because it limited their own market opportunities. . . . Through the mere fact of the compulsory services and payments of the tenants, the manorial system set limits to the purchasing power of the rural population because it prevented the peasants from devoting their entire labor power to production for the market and from developing their purchasing power. . . . In addition, there was the interest on the part of the developing capitalism in the creation of a free labor market. . . . The desire of the new capitalists to acquire land gave them a

further interest antagonistic to the manorial system. . . . Finally, the fiscal interest of the state also took a hand, counting upon the dissolution of the manor to increase the taxpaying capacity of the farming country." *General Economic History*, p. 94.

[171]See Dobb: "It frequently happened that the smaller estates . . . were much less well supplied with serf-labour compared to their needs than was the case with the larger estates, especially those of the Church. Moreover, when 'enticements' or forcible kidnappings of serfs by one estate-owner from another occurred, it was the smaller estates that were most liable to suffer from the competition and the depredations of their richer and more powerful neighbors, and hence were most anxious to acquire protection from the law. . . . But sometimes . . . this had an opposite effect. If the amount of serf-labour that an estate could command fell below a certain crucial figure, its lord, if he found it worthwhile to cultivate the demesne at all, was of necessity forced to place reliance in the main on hired labour; and the question of the amount of compulsory services he could command from each of his serfs was a relatively little concern to him, at any rate of much less concern to him than to his richer neighbour. If hired labour was not available, the alternative open to him was not to increase or extend labour-services (since these would have been inadequate in any case), but to abandon demesne cultivation and instead to find such tenants for the land as he could to pay him a rent for its use." *Studies*, pp. 59–60.

As Bloch notes, "villages which had not by [the sixteenth century] been able to obtain their liberty found it harder and harder to do so."[172]

One way to look at this is as a limitation on the ability of the serf to free himself. Bloch regards it rather as a limitation on the ability of the seignior to force the serf into a tenancy arrangement.[173] Bloch explains this crucial French–English differential in terms of prior differences. France was more economically developed than England, in the sense that the money economy had spread earlier and more extensively. England was more politically "developed" than France, in the sense that it had stronger central institutions, deriving ultimately from the fact that royal power originated in England in a conquest situation whereas French kings had to slowly piece together their authority amidst true feudal dispersion. Let us see the logic of each of these arguments.

First, France was more centrally located to the currents of European trade and technology than England, and therefore its landed classes developed earlier, the process of conversion of feudal dues to money rents also occurring earlier.[174] But since the counterpressures to the breaking up of manors occurred more or less simultaneously in England and France, it follows that English manors still remained relatively more intact than French at the onset of the "long" sixteenth century. Therefore, Bloch implies, English landlords were relatively more free to take advantage of new commercialization possibilities of large domains than French landlords. The English moved to a system of wage labor and continued manumission. The French had to make the best of a bad situation and landlords sought to increase their incomes by renewed old-style pressures.

The second argument deals with the relationship of the king and the nobility as early as the *twelfth* century. The English had established a strong central control on the judiciary. The other side of this achievement, however, was that *within* the manor the lord, although he lost power over criminal offenses, obtained full authority to do whatever he wished about tenure. In the fourteenth and fifteenth centuries, the manorial courts

[172]Bloch, *Caractères originaux,* **I,** p. 117.

[173]"In east Germany beyond the Elbe, and in the Slavic countries east of there, the whole seigniorial system changed and made way for a new one. Feudal dues are no longer lucrative. No matter! The squire became himself a producer and merchant of wheat. In his hands are reassembled fields taken from the villagers, . . . the demesne devoured or bled the tenures. In England, events took another course. There too, it is true, direct development [by the squires] grew apace at the expense of peasant and communal land. Nevertheless, the squire remains largely a rentier. But most of his rents cease to be immutable. Henceforward small holdings would at most be given out for a limited term, more usually

at the pleasure of the seignior. Nothing simpler, at each renewal, than to adjust the rent to the economic circumstances of the moment. At the two ends of Europe, the fundamental trait is the same: the regime of perpetual tenures, which was largely responsible for the [thirteenth and fourteenth century feudal] crisis, was dispensed with.

Now, in France, in such a bald way, this was impossible [Bloch, *ibid.,* **I,** 131–132]."

[174]"[The] movement [in England] tending towards the diminution of manors had occurred much later [than in France]: end of the 13th–14th–15th, instead of 11th–12th–beginning of the 13th (roughly). A natural delay, since the seigniory had been created later." Marc Bloch, *Seigneurie française et manoir anglais,* p. 114.

downplayed copyhold in their interpretation of customary law. When royal justice finally was able to intervene in such questions toward the end of the fifteenth century, they discovered that "customary law" permitted variable rents.

In France, however, there was no central criminal justice. On the other hand, the lord of the manor never had exclusive authority over land law. Hence patrimoniality could not be so easily undermined. Who the true "owner" was became an obscure legal question. By the sixteenth century, there were jurists who were willing to argue the tenant could not be dislodged. Unable, therefore, to change the rents, the seignior had to reacquire the land—by judicial manipulation of documents, and by expanding via "rediscovery" the obligations of feudal dues.[175] Over the long run, this difference would be crucial.[176]

Hence, what Bloch seems to be arguing is that because the English legal system allowed more flexibility to the landlord, money tenancy and wage labor continued to expand, allowing both great pastoral estates and the yeoman farmer becoming gentry to flourish. It also would force more rural labor into urban areas to form the proletariat with which to industrialize. In France, paradoxically the very strength of the monarchy forced the seigniorial class to maintain less economically functional, more "feudal," forms of land tenure, which would hold France back.

Resolving the tenure issue had in turn great consequences for the role a country would play in the world-system. A system of estate management as in eastern Europe requires large amounts of supervisory personnel. Had English landlords moved in this direction, there might not have been sufficient personnel to man the many new administrative posts required in the emerging world-economy—commercial managers, eventually overseas personnel, etc. It is not that landowners ceded their personnel for these other uses, but that as these other uses expanded, there were fewer persons left for supervisory positions on estates. Tenancy was a way out.

[175]See Bloch, *Caractères originaux,* **I,** 132–139. A. D. Lublinskaya says of this analysis: "These explanations of Marc Bloch seem to me superficial." She does not however offer better in her article. "Préface à l'édition russe des *Caractères originaux de l'histoire rurale française,*" *Annales E.S.C.,* **XIV,** 1, janv.–mars 1959, 201.

Edouard Perroy goes even further along these lines than Bloch, because he argues that while England was shedding its feudal character in the late Middle Ages, it is precisely at this time that France is actually reinforcing hers, and with the concurrence, nay the very initiative, of the king. His argument runs as follows: France had been the country most affected by feudal decomposition in the early Middle Ages. Hence the king had virtually only the powers of a landowner, *primus inter pares.* The Capetian solution to this dilemma was to extend the seig-niory of the king to include all of France which became a vast feudal pyramid with the king as the only summit. Ergo, in the thirteenth century and afterward, the kings encouraged the transformation of allodial land into fiefs, thus bringing them under their ultimate authority. See Perroy, *Le Moyen Age,* pp. 370–371.

[176]We must run ahead of our story to indicate it: "In England, the fall of absolutism permitted, to the profit of the gentry, the spread of the celebrated 'enclosure' movement, the transformation of technical methods, but also, in practice, because of this transformation and of its effects, the ruin and dispossession of innumerable tenants. In France, by an analogous but inverse development, the victory of the absolute monarchy limited the extent of the 'feudal reaction.'" Bloch, *Caractères originaux,* **I,** p. 139.

Note then the overall picture. Northwest Europe is in the process of
dividing the use of her land for pastoral and arable products. This was
only possible as the widening market created an ever larger market for
the pastoral products,[177] and as the periphery of the world-economy provided cereal supplements for the core areas. The semiperiphery was
turning away from industry (a task increasingly confided to the core)
and *toward* relative self-sufficiency in agriculture. The agricultural
specialization of the core encouraged the monetization of rural work
relationships, as the work was more skilled and as landowners wished to
rid themselves of the burden of surplus agricultural workers. Wage labor
and money rents became the means of labor control. In this system, a
stratum of independent small-scale farmers could emerge and indeed
grow strong both on their agricultural products and on their links to the
new handicraft industries. Given the increase in population and the
decline in wages, it would then follow, as Marx said, that these yeomen
farmers "grew rich at the expense both of their laborers and their landlords."[178] They usurped (by enclosure) the lands of the former, arguing
publicly the need to guarantee the country's food supply[179] and then
hired them at low wages, while obtaining at fixed rentals more and more
land from the owners of large demesnes. We do not wish to overstate
the strength of this new yeoman class. It is enough to realize they
became a significant economic, and hence political, force. Their
economic strength lay in the fact that they had every incentive to be "entrepreneurial." They were seeking wealth and upward mobility: the
route to success lay through economic efficiency. But they were not yet
burdened down either by traditional obligations of largesse or status
obligations of luxury spending or town life.[180]

Obviously, such a redistribution of rural economic effort had a great
impact on the character of the urban areas. What was going on in the
towns? We know that the sixteenth century was a time of growing population in general and of growing town sizes, in absolute terms everywhere,

[177]The means by which the growing food-market
of London encouraged pastoral production in
further and further reaches of England and Wales
is described by F. J. Fisher, "The Development of
the London Food Market, 1540–1610," in E. M.
Carus-Wilson, ed., *Essays in Economic History*, **I**
(New York: St. Martin's, 1965), pp. 135–151.

[178]Marx, *Capital*, **I**, ch. XXXIX, p. 744.

[179]"[In England] the spread of the new industrialism gave strength to the copyholder's plea that the
substitution of small-scale farming for large-scale
grazing was the only solution to the country's food
problem." Klein, *The Mesta*, p. 344.

[180]Marc Bloch notes that there did emerge in

France in the sixteenth century the new social type
of "gentleman farmer," the domain owner who
supervised his own lands. "Nothing could be more
advantageous, if done in an intelligent manner, than
this supervision by the master himself. But it presumed residence. . . . But exile [from Paris], after
all, was a solution of desperation; furthermore,
many large landowners, nobles or bourgeois, had
neither the taste nor the free time to live on their
fields; not to speak of the fact that rich people usually owned many different fields, dispersed far and
wide, which made it possible for them to supervise
them all in person." *Caractères originaux*,
I, p. 149.

but relatively in core areas. We know it follows, logically and from empirical evidence, as Helleiner says, that "one has to assume that, in the [16th century], the pressure of population on its land resources was mounting."[181] In eastern Europe, some people moved into frontier lands. From the Iberian peninsula, some went to the Americas, and some were expelled (Jews, later Moriscos) to other areas of the Mediterranean. In western Europe generally, there was emigration to the towns and a growing vagabondage that was "endemic."[182] There was not only the rural exodus, both the enclosed and ejected rural laborer, and the migratory laborer who came down from the mountains to the plains for a few weeks at harvest time, the "true rural proletarians" for Braudel.[183] There was also the vagabondage "caused by the decline of feudal bodies of retainers and the disbanding of the swollen armies which had flocked to serve the kings against their vassals. . . ."[184]

What did all these wanderers do? They of course provided the unskilled labor for the new industries. In Marx's view, "the rapid rise of manufactures, particularly in England, absorbed them gradually."[185] And as we have seen, their availability was one of the conditions of the willingness of landlords to commute feudal services to rents.[186]

[181]Helleiner, *Cambridge Economic History of Europe,* **IV,** p. 24.

[182]Braudel and Spooner, *Relazoni del X Congresso Internazionale di Scienze Storiche,* **IV,** p. 242.

[183]Braudel, *La Méditerranée,* **I,** p. 67. "Subjected to terrible health and hygienic conditions, the peasant, here, had to live on very little. He had masters; what he produced was for his masters. Often newly arrived, a simple man torn from his mountain home, he was often duped by the proprietor or his agent. He was, in many ways, in a sort of colonial enclave, whatever his exact juridical situation was. . . . The plains belonged to the seignior."

[184]Karl Marx, *The German Ideology* (New York: International Publ., 1947), 51.

[185]*Ibid.,* 51–52.

[186]Dobb, *Studies,* p. 55. Dobb adds: "One has, indeed, the paradox that, provided only that this crucial level of productivity (relative to the price of hired labour) had been reached, hired labour might even have been *less* efficient than bond-labour, and its use might still have proved an advantage [p. 56]." He adds as a footnote: "The surplus available from hired labour did not need to be *larger* than that yielded by serf-labour (= the product of serf-labour when working for the lord), since, although we are assuming that hired labour is being substituted for serf-labour on the demesne, it is not being substituted for, but *added* to, serf-labour as a *source of surplus.* If we assume that the lord has com-

muted labour-services at an equivalent of what the surplus labour-time of serfs could produce when devoted to demesne cultivation, then the lord will gain from the change if the new hired labour produces any surplus at all above their wages, since he will now have this surplus as an addition to what he received as commuted dues from his serfs."

Furthermore, as Marc Bloch reminds us, "corvée-labor was not always absolutely free [to the landlord]. It was usual especially during 'boon-works' to feed the laborer [*tenancier*]. It therefore wasn't worth it if the price of food exceeded the worth of the labor. It may appear absurd to suggest that wages could be less than the cost of food for the wage-earner. But we must remember the poor quality of work. . . . [Furthermore] when services were not required of the peasant subject to the corvée, it meant the latter had bought them back; that is, a payment was demanded in their place. Thus we must place in one column the value of the replacement payment that might reasonably be expected, meaning as the result of sufficient social pressure, plus where relevant saving of the cost of the meals. In the other column, we shall place the price of the days of wage-labor which would take the place of corvée-labor. As the total of the one column exceeds or does not exceed the other, one would consider whether or not to dispense with corvées." *Seigneurie française,* pp. 116–117.

This picture of an expanding labor force, not producing food, is hard to reconcile, however, with another fact. Jones and Woolf argue that a precondition to industrial development, and one that was historically met for the first time in sixteenth century northwest Europe, is that, along with an increase in productivity and a wider market, there was "a breathing space from intense population pressure during which income rather than men might be multiplied. . . ."[187]

But what about the surplus population then that swelled the towns of the core states, that wandered the countryside as vagabonds? Well, for one thing, they kept dying off in large quantity. Some were hanged for being vagabonds.[188] Famines were frequent, especially given "the slowness and prohibitive price of transport, [and] the irregularity of harvests. . . ."[189] As Braudel and Spooner put it, an analysis of this economy "must take into account the 'youth' of this [vagabond] population whose life-span was on the average short because of famines and epidemics. . . ."[190]

This would then account for an otherwise puzzling phenomenon noted by Braudel: "The proletariat of the towns could not have maintained its size, still less have grown, were it not for constant waves of immigration."[191] It also helps to explain the puzzling circumstance noted by Phelps-Brown and Hopkins, that, despite the significant fall in wages of the workers, there was so relatively little social upheaval. They say: "Part of the answer may be that it was a fall from a high level [of the 15th century], so that great though it was it still left the wage-earner with a subsistence . . ."[192]

But this subsistence survival of the northwest European worker's wage level was only made possible by having a periphery from which to import wheat, having bullion to make the flow possible, and allowing part of the population to die off; which part would be a fascinating subject to pursue. Is it not probable that, already in the sixteenth century, there were systematic ethnic distinctions of rank within the working class in the various cities of Europe? For example, Kazimierz Tyminiecki notes precisely this phenomenon in the towns of sixteenth century East Elbia, where German

[187]Jones and Woolf, *Agrarian Change and Economic Development*, p. 4.

[188]Marx, *German Ideology*, 51.

[189]Braudel, *La Méditerranée*, **I**, p. 300.

[190]Braudel and Spooner, *Relazioni del X Congresso Internationale di Storiche*, **IV**, pp. 241–242.

[191]Braudel, *La Méditerranée*, **I**, p. 306. "These indispensable immigrants were often not men in distress or of mediocre quality. Often, they brought with them new techniques, no less indispensable than their persons to urban life. The Jews, forced to leave because of their religion and not their poverty, played an outstanding role in these transfers of techniques."

[192]See Phelps-Brown and Hopkins, *Economica*, **XXVI**, p. 294. The comparative differences in lifestyles of various classes of townsmen may not have been all that different from contemporary Europe. A suggestion of this may be gleaned from a 1559 study of 3,096 households (circa 12,000 persons) in Malaga. This study found a class division as follows:

> well-to-do [*razonables*], not necessarily rich, 10 per cent
>
> little people [*pequeños*], 70 per cent
>
> poor people [*pobres*], 20 percent

Would a twentieth century survey of Málaga, or even Paris, come up with something strikingly at variance with this? The survey is cited by Braudel, *La Méditerranée*, **I**, p. 413.

workers excluded Slavic migrants from higher occupations.[193] Not much research seems to have been done on the ethnic distribution of the urban working class of early modern Europe, but my guess would be that Tyminiecki's description might be shown to be typical of the whole of the world-economy. It is not only that, within this world-economy, towns were unevenly distributed, but that within the towns, ethnic groups were probably unevenly distributed. We must not forget here the concept of layers within layers.

If we must be careful to look at whom we mean by urban workers, we must be careful when we look at the upper classes. In medieval Europe, high status was held by warrior–landowners called nobles. For the most part, they were an occupationally homogeneous group, distinguished largely by rank which correlated roughly with size of domain and the number of vassals. To be sure, individuals and families moved up and down the rank scale. There were also a few towns in which emerged an urban patriciate. We have already discussed in the previous chapter some of the conceptual confusions of identity to which this gave rise.

But, in the sixteenth century, was the landowner–merchant aristocrat or bourgeois? It is clear that both generically and specifically this was unclear. The picture had become murky with the creation of a world-economy based on commerce and capitalist agriculture. Let us look successively at the international merchants and then the "industrialists," and see both their geographic distribution and their links to landowning classes.

In many ways the techniques of commercial gain used in the sixteenth century were merely an extension of the methods the towns learned to use vis-à-vis their immediate hinterland in the late Middle Ages. The problem of the towns collectively was to control their own market, that is, be able both to reduce the cost of items purchased from the countryside and to minimize the role of stranger merchants.[194] Two techniques were

---

[193]"In the part of Germany east of the Elbe, from Lusatia through Brandenburg to Mecklenburg—thus in area there despite a long domination by Germans (or Germanized princes) the Slavic element was still strong especially in the countryside—one sees that in this period, that is from the 14th century on, but especially in the 15th and first half of the 16th centuries, there typically came into existence in the towns restrictions on the admission of Slavs into the handicraft guilds. Thus, in addition to discriminations on the basis of nationality, we see others which are 'social' directed against the [Slavic] population. This is occasioned by the strong tendencies of the latter to emigrate to the towns." Kazimierz Tyminiecki, "Le servage en Pologne et dans les pays limitrophes au moyen âge," *La Pologne au Xe Congrès International des Sciences Historiques à Rome* (Warszawa: Académie Polonaise des Sciences, Institut d'Histoire, 1955), 25.

[194]In some ways one can think of the aristocrat in business as simply "stranger-merchant" from the point of view of the urban bourgeoisie. See Fritz Redlich's analysis: "[T]he bulk of restrictive regulations and codes of sanctions [against aristocrats in commerce] seem to have been issued and to have originated at a rather late date, namely by 1600. . . . Actually, it seems that the restrictions determined by occupations of younger sons rather than the activities of the heirs. . . . [I]n quite a few cases restrictions on noble business activities were issued to protect city merchants endangered by noble competition and not because these activities were considered inappropriate for noblemen. . . . [P]rohibitions seem to have generally pertained to retailing and handicrafts; they always left room for what we call entrepreneurial activities in agriculture, large-scale industry . . . and in many cases also in overseas trade." "European Aristocracy and Economic Development," *Explorations in Entrepreneurial History*, **VI**, 2, Dec. 1953, 83.

used. On the one hand, towns sought to obtain not only legal rights to tax market operations but also the right to regulate the trading operation (who should trade, when it should take place, what should be traded). Furthermore, they sought to restrict the possibilities of their countryside engaging in trade other than via their town. The result was what Dobb calls a sort of "urban colonialism."[195] Over time, these various mechanisms shifted their terms of trade in favor of the townsmen, in favor thus of the urban commercial classes against both the landowning and peasant classes.

But the profits in this, while important, were small by comparison with what might be earned by long-distance trade, especially colonial or semicolonial trade. Henri Sée estimates the profit margins of the early colonial commercial operations as being very high: "sometimes in excess of 200 or 300% from dealings that were little more than piracy."[196] There were really two separate aspects to this high profit ratio. One was the "monopsony" situation in the colonial area, that is, monopsony in the "purchase" of land and labor. This was arranged, as we have seen, by the use of legal force, whether in Hispanic America or in eastern Europe. The second was the effective lack of competition in the areas of sales of the primary products, western Europe. This lack of competition was the consequence, in part, of the lack of technological development, and in part of vertical linkage chains of merchandising.

[195]Dobb, *Studies,* p. 95. The move from "urban colonialism" to "national colonialism" might then be seen as a natural step, once technology had expanded the size of what Frederic Lane calls a "natural monopoly" of force: "In much of medieval Europe, governing more territory than one province brought disadvantage of scale. In contrast, by the seventeenth century it had become almost impossible for a government to maintain against outsiders its monopoly of even a single province unless its military establishment was strong enough to conquer a national kingdom. The size of the natural monopolies has changed, and there have been periods of competition and higher costs of protection while new natural monopolies in accord with new techniques were being established. In our age of atomic weapons there is perhaps no natural monopoly smaller than the whole world." "Economic Consequences of Organized Violence," in *Venice and History* (Baltimore, Maryland: Johns Hopkins Press, 1966), 415–416, fn. 4.

[196]Henri Sée, *Modern Capitalism* (New York: Adelphi Co., 1928), 41. Dobb similarly argues: "Internally the market was expanding [in England], not only through the growth of towns and the multiplication of urban markets, but also by the increased penetration of money economy into the

manor with the growth of hired labour and the leasing of demesne for a money-rent. Nevertheless it was foreign trade which provided the greater opportunities for rapid commercial advancement, and it was in this sphere that the most impressive fortunes were made." *Studies,* p. 129.

Lenin also argued the essential role of international trade in the development of national capitalism: "The need for a capitalist country to have a foreign market is not determined at all by the laws of the realization of the social product (and of surplus-value in particular) but, firstly, by the fact that capitalism arises only as a result of widely developed commodity *circulation,* which transcends the limitations of the state. It is therefore impossible to conceive a capitalist nation without foreign trade, nor is there any such nation." V. I. Lenin, *The Development of Capitalism in Russia* (Moscow: Foreign Languages Publishing House, 1956), 44.

It is as a result of this primacy of world trade that François Mauro can say that it is "commercial capitalism which distinguished Western Civilization between 1500 and 1800, between the Renaissance and the Industrial Revolution," "Towards an 'Intercontinental Model': European Overseas Expansion Between 1500–1800," *Economic History Review,* 2nd, ser., **XIV,** 1, 1961, 1–2.

To be sure, the technology of business transactions had seen some very important advances in the late thirteenth and early fourteenth centuries: deposit banking, the bill of exchange, brokers, branch offices of central commercial organizations. Chaunu estimates that these techniques enabled commercial capitalism to increase, "perhaps tenfold," its ability to skim surplus and thus have "the ships, the men, the means needed to feed the adventure of exploration and then of exploitation of new space, in close liaison with the state."[197] Nonetheless, the sum total of these commercial innovations was insufficient to make it possible for long-distance traders to enter the world market without substantial capital and usually some state assistance. Hence, not many could so enter, and those who were already in did not actively seek to alter this situation.[198]

Even more important were the vertical links. The sources of capital were limited. Let us remember, even the state apparatuses were large-scale borrowers. The profits of Portuguese sugar plantations based on slave labor, for example, went not merely to the Portuguese directly involved, but to persons in the more "advanced" European economies, who provided both initial capital and an industrial outlet.[199] It was not merely that northwest Europe could develop the factories, but that their vertical commercial links encouraged a financial dependence. Indeed it would not be extreme to talk of a system of international debt peonage, first perfected by Hanseatic merchants vis-à-vis Norwegian fishermen and furtrappers in the late Middle Ages[200] and later by the Germanic merchants of such towns as Riga, Reval, and Gdańsk vis-à-vis the east European hinterland. The technique was known elsewhere, being used by the merchants of Toulouse, the Genoese in the Iberian peninsula, and in parts of the wool trade of England

[197]Chaunu, *L'expansion européenne*, p. 311.

[198]"It was precisely the lack of development of the market—the inability of the producers to effect an exchange of their products on any more than a parochial scale—that gave to merchant capital its golden opportunity. . . . So long as these primitive conditions continued, so did the chances of exceptional gain for those who had the means to exploit them; and it was only natural that the perpetuation of such conditions, and not their removal, should become the conscious policy of merchant capital." Dobb, *Studies*, p. 89.

[199]"[The] system of sugar-cane plantations which existed [in São Tomé] was closely tied to large-scale international commerce in which first the great companies of Antwerp and then those of Amsterdam took part. In those great centers of economic life were established numerous sugar refineries functioning in the 16th century thanks to the increasing deliveries of molasses from São Tomé. We should observe that, despite the very active role of Portuguese merchants in the export of sugar from the island, the process of refining was not undertaken by Portugal whose economy was weak, but by the countries then thriving economically, which had important capital resources, skilled and free labour, that is, countries already on the road to development." Marian Malowist, "Les débuts du système des plantations dans la période des grandes découvertes," *Africana Bulletin*, No. 10, 1969, 29.

[200]"This was a system of purchasing goods by paying in advance for supplies yet to be delivered. . . . It is known that for 250 years the Hanseatic merchants in Bergen managed by means of this method to keep in their own hands almost the entire trade in fish and furs from northern Norway. The Hanseatic merchants made the fishermen in northern Norway directly dependent on them giving them payments in advance. At the same time this enabled them to eliminate for a long time the Norwegian burghers from this trade." Marian Malowist, "A Certain Trade Technique in the Baltic Countries in the Fifteenth to the Seventeenth Centuries," *Poland at the XIth International Congress of Historical Sciences* (Warsaw: Polish Academy of Sciences, The Institute of History, 1960), 103.

and Spain. What was the method? Very simple: it involved the purchase of goods in advance of their production, that is, payments in advance for supplies to be delivered in the future. This prevented sale on an open market. It allowed the merchants rather than the producers to decide the optimum moment for world resale. And since the money lent tended to be expended by the time of delivery of the goods, if not overspent, the producer was always tempted to perpetuate the arrangement. In theory forbidden by law, this system could only be applied by merchants who had the means and influence to be able to sustain the practice, that is "foreign merchants, or rich merchants who had easy access to foreign markets."[201] These merchants could thereby take the profits of the price revolution and multiply them. The way in which this system involved a vertical network of exploitation and profit making is clearly described by Malowist as it operated in Poland:

> In the sixteenth and beginning of the seventeenth centuries, when the Gdańsk merchants were paying less attention to the sea trade, they began to exert an increasing influence on agriculture in all parts of Poland. Towards the end of the sixteenth century when conditions for the export of grain were particularly favorable, agents of the Gdańsk merchants were regularly to be seen at the markets in the towns and villages of Poland, where they bought up grain.... [In] the seventeenth century, the rich merchants of Gdańsk, like the merchants of Riga, made advance payments not only to the lesser gentry, but even to the wealthy nobles of Poland and Lithuania.... This great flourishing of Gdańsk trade in the extensive hinterlands can be explained by the immense increase in the wealth of the Gdańsk merchants during the time of the revolution in prices.... The Gdańsk merchants received advance payments from the Dutch, and . . . the latter sometimes collected for that purpose certain sums from merchants in Antwerp.[202]

This system of international debt peonage enabled a cadre of international merchants to bypass (and thus eventually destroy) the indigenous merchant classes of eastern Europe (and to some extent those of southern Europe) and enter into direct links with landlord–entrepreneurs (nobility included) who were essentially capitalist farmers, producing the goods and keeping control of them until they reached the first major port area, after which they were taken in hand by some merchants of west European (or north Italian) nationality[203] who in turn worked through and with a burgeoning financial class centered in a few cities.

If the international merchants in the European world-economy were largely of certain nationalities, was this also true of "industrialists," and what was the relation of these two groups? Industrial production existed already in the Middle Ages, but it was scattered, small-scale, and mostly geared to a luxury market. It was only with the rise of a capitalist system

---

[201]*Ibid.*, p. 104.
[202]*Ibid.*, p. 114.
[203]See Dobb, *Studies*, p. 71.

within the framework of a world-economy that there could emerge industrial entrepreneurs.[204]

It was precisely in the areas of greater agricultural specialization that there was a thrust to industrialize, not only in moments of expansion but in moments of contraction as well. Marian Malowist talks to the conjuncture in these areas of the growth of a cloth industry and agricultural crisis of the fourteenth and fifteenth centuries.[205] Joan Thirsk notes how the rural thrust, the need to find alternate employment possibilities for ejected rural labor, continued to operate in sixteenth century England.[206]

This rural pressure however did not operate in the most "advanced" areas because the fact that many of these industries were then located in rural areas was a function not only of the rural search for employment, but of the urban rejection. Many of the centers of the medieval textile industry in Flanders and northern Italy had their capital invested in luxury

[204]"Before capitalist production, *i.e.*, in the Middle Ages, the system of petty industry obtained generally, based upon the private property of the laborers in their means of production; in the country, the agriculture of the small peasant, freeman, or serf; in the towns, the handicrafts organized in guilds. . . . To concentrate these scattered, limited means of production, to enlarge them, to turn them into the powerful levers of production of the present day—this was precisely the historic role of capitalist production and of its upholder, the bourgeoisie." Frederick Engels, *Socialism: Utopian and Scientific* (New York: International Publishers, 1953), 28.

[205]"[In] England, in the Low Countries, in southern Germany and in Italy, it is precisely in the fourteenth and fifteenth centuries . . . that we find a very marked development of a rural textile industry. The peasants engage in it on behalf of entrepreneurs living in towns, or sometimes also on their own account. It seems to me that this fact proves that agriculture did not suffice to give them a living. . . . In effect, while in Flanders, Brabant and Tuscany, we can observe a gradual decline in the production of luxury goods during this period, yet in Flanders itself, in Hainault, Holland, England, southern Germany and in parts of Italy, a new type of textile production grew up in the small towns and in the countryside. These textiles were not of the highest quality, but they were cheaper and therefore within the reach of the impoverished nobility and other less well-to-do consumers. . . . During the fourteenth and fifteenth centuries, both in industry and in long-distance trade, the role of articles in common use became more and more important as against that of luxury articles." M. Malowist, "The Economic and Social Development of the Baltic Countries from the 15th to the 17th Centuries," *Economic History Review*, 2nd ser., **XII**, 2, 1959, 178.

See Marx: "The original historical forms in which capital appears at first sporadically or *locally, side by side* with the old modes of production, but gradually bursting them asunder, makes up *manufacture* in the proper sense of the word (not yet the factory.) This arises, where there is mass-production for export—hence on the *basis of large-scale maritime and overland trade*, and in the centres of such trade, as in the Italian cities, Constantinople, the Flemish, Dutch cities, some Spanish ones such as Barcelona, etc. Manufacture does not initially capture the so-called *urban crafts*, but the *rural subsidiary occupations*, spinning and weaving, the sort of work which requires least craft skill, technical training. Apart from those great emporia, in which it finds the basis of an *export* market, and where production is, as it were *by its spontaneous nature*, directed towards exchange-value—i.e. manufactures directly connected with shipping, including shipbuilding itself, etc.—manufacture first establishes itself not in the cities but in the countryside, in villages lacking gilds, etc. The rural subsidiary occupations contain the broad basis of manufactures, whereas a high degree of progress in production is required in order to carry on the urban crafts as factory industries. Such branches of production as glassworks, metal factories, sawmills, etc., which from the start demand a greater concentration of labour-power, utilise more natural power, and demand both mass-production and a concentration of the means of production, etc. These also lend themselves to manufacture. Similary, paper-mills, etc." *Pre-capitalist Economic Formations*, p. 116.

[206]"One could reasonably postulate some association between the rise of population and pressure on the land in the sixteenth century, and the rise of the handknitting industry in the Yorkshire dales." Thirsk, *Essays in Economic and Social History of Tudor and Stuart England*, p. 88.

good production and were unable or unwilling to shift to the new market first made necessary by the monetary crisis of the fourteenth and fifteenth centuries and then made profitable by the creation of a world-economy in the sixteenth century. These entrepreneurs were not concerned in this case about frontiers.[207] One famous and key move of this kind was the flight of Flemish capitalists to England. What we must bear in mind is that at this stage the industries all had a shaky base. They rose and fell. They were like wanderers searching for a haven: "They resembled a thousand fires lighted at the same time, each fragile, in a vast field of dry grasses."[208] It is clear that the old advanced centers, the controllers of international trade, were not necessarily the centers of imagination and daring. It seems to bear out Henri Pirenne's belief in the noncontinuity of capitalist entrepreneurs.[209]

We are thus led to be prudent in the use of our terminology. Bourgeois and feudal classes, in an explanation which uses class categories to explain social change, should not be read, as it usually is, to mean "merchants" and "landowners." During the long period of the creation of the European world-economy, in the core countries of this world-economy, there were some merchants and some landowners who stood to gain from retaining those forms of production associated with "feudalism," namely ones in which peasant labor was in some way systematically and legally made to turn over the largest part of its product to the landowner (e.g., corvée, feudal rents, etc.). And there were some merchants and some landowners who stood to gain from the rise of new forms of industrial production, based on contractual labor. In the sixteenth century, this division often corresponded, as a first approximation, to big and small. Big merchants and big landowners profited more from the old feudal system; small (medium-size? rising?) ones from the new capitalist forms. But the big–small dichotomy should be used with caution and nuance and it only holds at this point of historical time. Theoretically, of course, it makes a lot of sense. New forms of social organization usually tend to have less appeal to those doing well under an existing system than to those who are energetic

[207]"When the industrial capitalists, yearning to have a cheap cloth to vend, tried to have such cloths produced in their towns, they found they were not allowed to do so. So they put out their work more and more to rural workmen. If that was forbidden by their city guilds and governments, they even moved their industry to other countries. The 'countries' on the Continent were not so very large." Robert L. Reynolds, *Europe Emerges* (Madison: Univ. of Wisconsin Press, 1967), 399.

[208]Braudel, *La Méditerranée,* **I**, p. 399.

[209]"I believe that, for each period into which our economic history may be divided, there is a distinct and separate class of capitalists. In other words, the group of capitalists of a given epoch does not spring from the capitalist group of the preceding epoch. At every change in economic organization we find a breach of continuity. It is as if the capitalists who have up to then been active recognize that they are incapable of adapting themselves to conditions which are evoked by needs hitherto unknown and which call for methods hitherto unemployed. They withdraw from the struggle and become an aristocracy, which if it again plays a part in the course of affairs, does so in a passive manner only." Henri Pirenne, *American Historical Review,* **XIX**, 3, Apr. 1914, 494–495.

and ambitious, but not yet *arrivé*. Empirically, it is complicated by other considerations.

Whatever their origins, this new class of "industrialists," some coming out of the yeoman farmer ranks and some reconverted merchants, were committed to what Vilar terms the essential characteristic of a modern economy: "the achievement of medium-sized profits in much larger markets: selling more selling in quantity, while earning less on a per-unit basis.[210] Part of the profit came from the wage-lag.[211] Part were windfall profits. Part were low real interest rates. Part were profits borrowed against the future in terms of noncalculated depreciation.[212] But profit there was. And the amount of profit not only created a political base for this class; it had an immediate impact on the overall economy. This was felt in many ways: as a stimulus to the production of raw materials and the mobilization of manpower, as a way of meeting a growing demand which became a mass demand. But in addition, it made possible the industry responsible for the creation of many external economies: roads, flood control devices, ports.[213]

It is clear, too, that the sixteenth century saw a remarkable shift of locus of the textile industry. During the late fifteenth and early sixteenth centuries, these industries expanded in the "old" centers: northern Italy, southern Germany, Lorraine, Franche-Comté, Spanish-Netherlands, and in England only in the southwest and only in woolen cloth. Then, new centers arose, principally in England and the northern Netherlands, in countries that had been, as Nef observed, "industrially backward at the beginning of the sixteenth century. . . ."[214]

We have sought to present the case in this chapter of the emergence of a new economic framework of action in the sixteenth century—the

---

[210]Pierre Vilar, in *Actes du Colloque de la Renaissance*, p. 50.

[211]Even J. D. Gould, a skeptic on this hypothesis, does recognize nonetheless that there was "a very sharp decline in the real income of the wage-earner" in this period. See "The Price Revolution Reconsidered," *Economic History Review*, 2nd ser., **XVII**, 2, 1964, 265. See also Dobb: "[The] remarkable gains of merchant capital in the fourteenth and fifteenth centuries, while the fruit of monopoly, were acquired by an exclusion of the mass of producers from the benefits of an expanding volume of trade rather than by any actual depression of the general standard of life. In other words, the lavish profits of the new trading class owed their source to a relative, rather than an absolute, reduction in the income of the producers. But in the second half of the sixteenth century (and probably also in the seventeenth, at least during the first half of it) there is evidence that this ceased to be the case." *Studies,*

pp. 119–120.

[212]For Gould, this factor was particularly important: "It is widely recognized today that in the mid-twentieth century, the impact of rising prices on industrial profits has come less from any lag of wages behind prices—in most cases there has been no such lag—than from the lag of capital costs behind them. . . . [P]art—an increasing part—of the *apparent* profit is unappropriated depreciation which will have to be made good somehow when the machine ultimately has to be replaced. The day of reckoning does finally come. But if the life of the machine or structure is a long one—and this way well have been the case with a very substantial part of the fixed capital of the Tudor and Stuart periods: waterwheels, salt pans, furnaces, and so on—then high *apparent* profit ratios may have been widespread in those centuries." *Ibid.,* p. 264.

[213]See Mauro, *Le XVIe siècle européen*, p. 298.

[214]Nef, *Conquest of Material World*, p. 116.

European world-economy based on capitalist methods. It involved a division of productive labor that can only be properly appreciated by taking into account the world-economy as a whole. The emergence of an industrial sector was important, but what made this possible was the transformation of agricultural activity from feudal to capitalist forms. Not all these capitalist "forms" were based on "free" labor—only those in the core of the economy. But the motivations of landlord and laborer in the non-"free" sector were as capitalist as those in the core.

We should not leave this theme without looking at the objections to this analysis. Ernesto Laclau has taken André Gunder Frank to task for arguing that sixteenth century Hispanic America had a capitalist economy. He argues that this is both incorrect and un-Marxist. Without diverting ourselves into a long *excursus* on Marxian exegetics, let me say simply that I think Laclau is right in terms of the letter of Marx's arguments but not in terms of its spirit. On the substance of the issue itself, Laclau's main argument is that Frank's definition of capitalism as production for profit for a market in which the profit does not go to the direct producer and feudalism as a closed-off subsistence economy are both conceptually wrong. He argues that Frank's definition, in omitting "relations of production" (that is, essentially whether or not labor is "free"), makes it possible not only to include sixteenth century Hispanic America but also "the slave on a Roman *latifundium* or the gleb serf of the European Middle Ages, at least in those cases—the overwhelming majority—where the lord assigned *part* [my italics] of the economic surplus extracted from the serf for sale.[215] He then suggests that, if Frank is right, "we would have to conclude that Elizabethan England or Renaissance France was ripe for socialism. . . ."[216] Finally he says far from feudalism being incompatible with capitalism, the expansion of the external market in Hispanic America served to "accentuate and consolidate [feudalism]."[217]

Laclau precisely beclouds the issue. First, the difference between the gleb serf of the Middle Ages and the slave or worker on an *encomienda* in sixteenth century Hispanic America, or a "serf" in Poland, was threefold: the difference between assigning "part" of the surplus to a market and assigning "most of the surplus;" the difference between production for a local market and a world market; the difference between the exploiting classes spending the profits, and being motivated to maximize them and partially reinvest them. As for Laclau's inference about Elizabethan England, it is absurd and polemical. As for involvement in a capitalist world market accentuating feudalism, precisely so, but "feudalism" of this new variety.

---

[215]Ernesto Laclau(h), "Feudalism & Capitalism in Latin America," *New Left Review,* No. 67, May–June 1971, 25.

[216]*Ibid.,* p. 30.
[217]*Ibid.*

The point is that the "relations of production" that define a system are the "relations of production" of the whole system, and the system at this point in time is the European world-economy. Free labor is indeed a defining feature of capitalism, but not free labor throughout the productive enterprises. Free labor is the form of labor control used for skilled work in core countries whereas coerced labor is used for less skilled work in peripheral areas. The combination thereof is the essence of capitalism. When labor is everywhere free, we shall have socialism.

But capitalism cannot flourish within the framework of a world-empire. This is one reason why it never emerged in Rome. The various advantages merchants had in the emergent world-economy were all politically easier to obtain than if they had sought them within the framework of a single state, whose rulers would have to respond to multiple interests and pressures.[218] That is why the secret of capitalism was in the establishment of the division of labor within the framework of a world-economy that was *not* an empire rather than within the framework of a single national state. In underdeveloped countries in the twentieth century, K. Berrill notes that "international trade is often much cheaper and easier than internal trade and . . . specialization between countries is often much easier and earlier than specialization between regions in a country."[219] This was also true in sixteenth-century Europe. We shall try to demonstrate how and why this worked in the course of this volume.

In summary, what were the economic accomplishments of the sixteenth century and how have we accounted for them? It was not a century of great technological advance, except for the introduction of coal as a fuel in England and northern France. A. Rupert Hall sees both industry and agriculture as "in the last phases of a series of changes, both technological and organizational" which had begun in the fourteenth century, with the "crisis." But, he notes, it was in the sixteenth century that there was a

[218]Talcott Parsons argues that the original development of industrialism had to be in the form of capitalism, that is a system in which there were "institutional restraints on the exercise of political power and which *independently* of the political structure would provide specific impetus to economic development." *Structure and Process in Modern Societies* (New York: Free Press, 1960), 101–102. The reason according to Parsons, is that: "Political influence as such . . . seems either to be oriented to relatively short-run 'constituency interests,' or to fall readily into traditional stereotyping. These seem to be the reasons Weber spoke of the 'economically irrational' influence of political interests [p. 107]."

This is plausible reasoning but does not seem to jell with the empirical fact that the state's role in capitalist development has been constant throughout modern history. Parsons has missed the essential geographical component of the structural differentiation, that economic activity took place within a world-economy, while the authority of political leaders, if not their power, was limited to arenas smaller than those encompassed by economic enterprise. It is this crucial structural disparity that gave the capitalists their essential leeway.

[219]K. Berrill, "International Trade and the Rate of Economic Growth," *Economic History Review*, 2nd ser., **XII**, 3, 1960, 352.

"diffusion of techniques from the core to the periphery of European civilization."[220]

Four things are striking about the sixteenth century. Europe expanded into the Americas. This may not have been determinative by itself, but it was important.[221] The crucial fact about the expansion was captured by Braudel: "the gold and silver of the New World enabled Europe to live above its means, to invest beyond its savings."[222]

To invest beyond its savings, and to increase its savings, by the price revolution and wage-lag. Whether or not the expansion of bullion was responsible for the expansion of production, and to whatever extent demographic expansion was the cause or consequence, the bullion itself was "merchandise, and a general expansion of trade underlay the 'prosperity' of the sixteenth century which was neither a game nor a mirage, not a monetary illusion."[223]

The third striking change was the pattern of rural labor—the rise of coerced cash-crop labor in the periphery and of the yeoman farmer in the core. Takahashi may exaggerate when he calls the yeoman farmer the "prime mover"[224] in the end of feudalism, but it is doubtful that one could have had a capitalist system without him. But also not without the coerced cash-crop labor.

Jean Néré attacks Dobb for putting exclusive emphasis on the availability of proletarian labor in explaining the rise of capitalism. He says one has to put this factor together with secular price movements.[225] Braudel and Spooner, on the other hand, caution against confusing accidental fluctua-

---

[220]A. Rupert Hall, "Scientific Method and the Progress of Techniques," *Cambridge Economic History of Europe,* **IV,** E. E. Rich and C. H. Wilson, eds., *The Economy of Expanding Europe in the 16th and 17th Centuries* (London and New York: Cambridge Univ. Press, 1967), 100.

[221]"The opening of a new frontier on the far shore of the Atlantic therfore created new opportunities, and a climate of thought which encouraged confidence in the possibilities of success. The opportunities existed; but so also did the individuals who were ready and able to seize them. . . . America may well have hastened the tempo of Europe's advance. It is even possible that the advance would not have occurred without America. But if this extreme proposition is accepted, it would still be advisable to remember the lapidary warning of Professor Braudel: "L'Amérique ne commande pas seule.' America is not in sole command." J. H. Elliott, *The Old World and the New, 1492–1650* (London and New York: Cambridge Univ. Press, 1970), 78.

[222]Braudel, in *Chapters,* p. 268.

[223]Braudel and Spooner, *Relazioni del X Congresso Internazionale di Scienze Storiche,* **IV,** p. 243.

[224]"The *prime mover* which has abolished the feudal order of production and property, and which brings about very naturally the formation of capitalist society, is to be found in the development of small and commodity production (petty bourgeoisie and independent peasants as commodity producers), and consequently in their economic 'polarization' between the industrial capitalists and the wage-earning labourers deprived of their land and obliged to sell their labours. This type of capitalistic evolution, we believe, must be classical and specifically characteristic of the economic history of western Europe." "On the 'Transition' from Feudalism to the Bourgeois Revolution," *Indian Journal of Economics,* **XXXV,** 140, 1955, 149–150.

[225]"Mr. Dobb . . . chooses as the clue in the maze (*fils conducteur*) of economic history the 'variations in available manpower'; that would surely be an interesting phenomenon to study, but our author . . . neglects almost entirely that other clue, the long-term movements of prices; . . . he does not consider the possibility of combining the two approaches." Jean Néré, "Le développement du capitalisme," *Revue historique,* **CCIII,** janv.–mars 1950, 68.

tions (the price revolution) for structural changes.[226] What is clear is that in the sixteenth century a "capitalist era"[227] emerges and that it takes the form of a world-economy. No doubt, "the fragility of this first unity of the world"[228] is a critical explanatory variable in the political evolution. But the fact is that this unity survives and, in the seventeenth and eighteenth centuries, did come to be consolidated.

One of the principal features of the European world-system of the sixteenth century is that there was no simple answer to the question of who was dominating whom? One might make a good case for the Low Countries exploiting Poland via Gdańsk, and certainly Spain exploiting its American possessions. The core dominated the periphery. But the core was so large. Did Genoese merchants and bankers use Spain or did Spanish imperialism absorb parts of Italy? Did Florence dominate Lyon, or France Lombardy, or both? How should one describe the true links between Antwerp (later Amsterdam) and England? Note that in all these cases we deal with a merchant city-state on the one hand and a larger nation-state on the other.

If we are to untangle the picture any further, we must look to the political side, the ways in which various groups sought to use the state structures to protect and advance their interests. It is to this question we now turn.

---

[226]"Every economic fluctuation, even when decisive, or violent, or creative, still remains an accident in a long-term, 'structural' history—the development of capitalism—which by its nature transcends accidents." Braudel and Spooner, *Cambridge Economic History of Europe,* **IV,** p. 450.

[227]"Although we come across the first beginning of capitalist production as early as the fourteenth and fifteenth centuries, in certain towns of the Mediterranean, the capitalistic era dates from the sixteenth century." Marx, *Capital,* **I,** ch. XXVI, p. 715.

[228]Braudel, in *Chapters,* p. 285.

3

THE ABSOLUTE MONARCHY
AND STATISM

Figure 4: "The Grand-Duke has the port of Livorno fortified," engraving by Jacques Callot from a collection called *The Life of Ferdinand I of the Medicis*. Ferdinand was Grand-Duke of Tuscany from 1587–1609. The engraving was made between 1614–1620.

It is evident that the rise of the absolute monarchy in western Europe is coordinate in time with the emergence of a European world-economy. But is it cause or consequence? A good case can be made for both. On the one hand, were it not for the expansion of commerce and the rise of capitalist agriculture, there would scarcely have been the economic base to finance the expanded bureaucratic state structures.[1] But on the other hand, the state structures were themselves a major economic underpinning of the new capitalist system (not to speak of being its political guarantee). As Braudel says, "Whether or not they wanted to be, [the states were] the biggest entrepreneurs of the century."[2] Furthermore, they were essential customers of the merchants.[3]

There are several different arguments about the role of the state in capitalist enterprise. One concerns its extent, a second, its economic impact, and a third, its class content. The third argument we shall discuss later. First, while there is much disagreement about the extent of state involvement in the world-economy of the nineteenth century, there seems to be widespread consensus that in the earlier periods of the modern world-system, beginning at least in the sixteenth century and lasting at least until the eighteenth, the states were central economic actors in the European world-economy.

But if most agree that the states did play this role, some feel it was an unnecessary and undesirable role. For example, Schumpeter, true to his belief in the long-range superior efficiency of private enterprise, denies that the state was good for business as purchaser of goods or credit. He says it is an "unpardonable [error] to think that in the absence of the extravagance of courts there would not have been equivalent goods from the peasants and the bourgeois from whom the corresponding means were taken."[4] Unpardonable it may be, but error perhaps not. Why is it not conceivable that, to meet tax demands, a peasant produces a surplus which he might otherwise either consume or not produce? Does Schumpeter really assume that in the sixteenth century the peasants of Europe were totally oriented to a commercial market?

As for the thesis that court expenditures were vital in the creation of credit, Schumpeter has two responses. One is that any benefit obtained in developing a "credit-engineering machine" must be weighed "against

[1]"The States, in the sixteenth century, come more and more to assume the role of large-scale collectors and redistributors of income; they seize via taxes, the sale of offices, rents, confiscations, an enormous part of the various 'national products.' This multiple seizure is effective since the budgets vary more or less with the state of the economy and follow the ups and downs of the price-level. The rise of the States thus follows the grain of economic life, is not an accident, or a disturbing force as Joseph A. Schumpeter a bit hastily considered it to be."

Braudel, La Méditerranée, I, p. 409.
[2]Ibid., I, pp. 409–410.
[3]"Without the profitable business made possible by loans to the State, the raising of taxes, the exploitation of royal domains, the expenditures for warfare and for the court, commercial capitalism would never have had such a spectacular rise in the first half of the sixteenth century." Hartung and Mousnier, Relazioni del X Congresso Internazionale di Scienze Storiche, IV, p. 44.
[4]Joseph A. Schumpeter, Business Cycles, I, p. 236.

all the destruction wrought and all the paralysis of economic activity spread, both by the methods of raising that revenue and by the uses it financed."[5] This involves a tremendous counterfactual argument, whose validity can only be assessed in terms of the entire argument of this book. The view expounded herein will be that the development of strong states in the core areas of the European world was an essential component of the development of modern capitalism. His second response is that the counterpart of loans to courts was economic privileges which were most probably economically unsound from the perspective of the interests of the larger community.[6] No doubt this is true, but to me this seems a description of the essence of capitalism, not an accidental distortion of its operations, and hence an assertion which in fact provides a good part of the refutation of Schumpeter's previous one.

We have already reviewed previously the various aspects of the economic crisis of the fourteenth and fifteenth centuries which contributed to the slow but steady growth of state bureaucracies. We have also mentioned the evolution of military technology which made obsolete the medieval knight and thereby strengthened the hand of central authorities who could control large numbers of infantrymen. The main political objective of the monarchs was the restoration of order, a prerequisite to economic resurgence. In Génicot's succinct summary, "by revealing the evil effects of a breakdown in authority, the troubled times established the case for centralization."[7]

But why should such political regimes come to the fore at this particular time? One classic response is to talk in terms of the centrifugal phenomena of new states, an argument often used about twentieth-century new states.[8]

---

[5]*Ibid.*

[6]"Lending to a court was, in spite of the exorbitant interest usually promised, very rarely a good business in itself. But precisely because such loans could, as a rule, not be repaid, they led to the acquisition of privileges and concessions in the field of commerce and industry which were the great business of the time. . . . The rise of the Fuggers to a position never again equalled by any financial house has . . . much to do with Charles V's embarassments [*Ibid.*, **I**, p. 236, fn. 1]."

[7]Génicot, *Cambridge Economic History of Europe*, **I**, p. 700. Joseph Strayer similarly argues that a causal link exists between the breakdown of order in the late Middle Ages and the new willingness of the aristocracy to "accept royal leadership" in the sixteenth century. He suspects the intervening variable may lie in a change in collective social psychology:

"It is difficult to decide what factors changed the behavior of the possessing classes. Some of them, especially the lesser landholders, had suffered as much from internal violence as had the poor, and like the poor, wanted peace and security. Some of them realized they could profit most fully from the

economic revival that was beginning by supporting stable governments. Some of them may have been impressed by the failure of most late fifteenth-century revolutions." *On the Medieval Origins of the Modern State* (Princeton, New Jersey: Princeton Univ. Press, 1970), 91.

[8]Mousnier says of sixteenth-century western Europe: "The necessity of a strong [central] power comes from the very composition of the nations [i.e., states]. They are a juxtaposition of territorial communities, provinces, countries (*pays*), municipalities, village communities, and corporative structures, such as the Orders, . . . the officer corps, the universities, the guilds. . . . The King *had to be* strong enough to arbitrate their conflicts and coordinate their efforts with a view to the common good. But their divisions give him the possibility of playing one against the other." *Les XVIe et XVIIe siècles*, p. 97. Italics added.

Had to be? Why so? A functional explanation seldom resolves the genetic problem, since not only are functional alternatives possible to envisage, but failure to meet the functional need is not only a possible contingency but often a very plausible one. Let us therefore momentarily withhold judgment on the "cause."

The initial thrust of the fifteenth century "restorers of order" came out of the "crisis of feudalism." The economic squeeze on the seigniors had led to increased exploitation of peasants and consequently to peasant rebellions. It had also led to internecine warfare among the nobility. The weakened nobility looked to the kings to preserve them from the threats of greater disorder still. The kings profited from the circumstances to enhance their own wealth and power vis-à-vis this very nobility. This was the price of their provision of security, what Frederic Lane calls their "protection rent" and which he reminds us were at that time both "a major source of the fortunes made in trade [and] a more important source of profits . . . than superiority in industrial technique or industrial organization."[9]

Of course, the king's advance was not merely a function of opportunity but of the pressures he was under himself. Eisenstadt argues that what he calls "bureaucratic politics" come into existence when "the political rulers cannot rely on the facilities available to them through their own resources (e.g., the king's domains), or through the unquestioning commitments of other groups. . . ."[10] But were commitments ever unquestioning? And as for the availability of resources, the fact that the kings' personal resources were insufficient for their objectives was a function of more ambitious objectives. We must then look to the pressures that led rulers to seek to *implement* more ambitious objectives.

One suggestion comes from Archibald Lewis, who ties it to the availability of land: "When . . . the sovereign has given out all the free land and none remains, it is necessary for him to begin to tax—taking back in another form the wealth he earlier showered out upon his people."[11] This need for national taxation did not immediately lead to "absolutism." Rather, the sovereign had to create parliaments to obtain the assistance of the nobility in the taxation process but only "until such time as the rulers felt powerful enough to dispense with such assistance."[12] Dobb has a different emphasis. He sees the pressure on the king as having come not from the shortage of land but from "labor scarcity." The growth of the state machinery served to promote "control of the labor market."[13]

It might follow from this analysis that if economic crisis led to greater power for the monarchs, the economic expansion of the sixteenth century

---

[9]See Lane, *Venice and History*, pp. 421–422.

[10]S. N. Eisenstadt, "Political Struggle in Bureaucratic Societies," *World Politics*, **IX**, 1, Oct. 1956, 17.

[11]Archibald Lewis, *Speculum*, **XXXIII**, p. 483.

[12]*Ibid.*, p. 483. See Edward Miller: "The attempt to establish general direct taxation was one of the principal influences behind the appearance from the thirteenth century onwards of representative assemblies bringing together the various groups of taxpayers in the persons of their proctors or delegates." *Fontana Economic History of Europe*, **I**, p. 14.

[13]Dobb, *Studies*, p. 24. Dobb contrasts "state intervention" and "freedom" as two modes of political organization within capitalist societies—a strangely liberal view for a Marxist. He explains their alternation in terms of labor scarcity. "[F]reedom flourishes most under Capitalism when, by reason of a superabundant proletariat, the mode of production is secure, whereas legal compulsion stands at a premium as soon as jobs compete for men and the mode of production grows less profitable as a source of income on capital and less stable [pp. 24–25]."

would have had the inverse effect. To a certain extent, as we shall see, this was true. The "first" sixteenth century was the era of imperial strivings, not of strong states, as we shall discuss in the next chapter. It was not until the "failure of empire," of which we shall speak then, that strong states once again came to the fore. And indeed it would only be the eighteenth century that historians would deem "the age of absolutism."[14]

In fact, however, despite fluctuations in the curve, we are faced with a secular increase in state power throughout the modern era. The capitalist world-economy seems to have required and facilitated this secular process of increased centralization and internal control, at least within the core states.

How did kings, who were the managers of the state machinery in the sixteenth century, strengthen themselves? They used four major mechanisms: bureaucratization, monopolization of force, creation of legitimacy, and homogenization of the subject population. We shall treat each in turn.

If the king grew stronger, it was unquestionably due to the fact that he acquired new machinery to use, a corps of permanent and dependent officials.[15] Of course, in this respect, Europe was just catching up with China. Hence we know that a bureaucratic state structure is by itself insufficient to demarcate the great changes of the sixteenth century, much less account for them. Nevertheless, the development of the state bureaucracy was crucial, because it was to alter fundamentally the rules of the political game, by ensuring that henceforth decisions of economic policy could not be easily made without going through the state structure. It meant that the energy of men of all strata had to turn in significant part to the conquest of the political kingdom. To be sure, we are still talking in this era of a relatively small bureaucracy, certainly by comparison with contemporary Europe.[16] But the difference of size and structure by com-

[14]See, for example, Max Beloff, *The Age of Absolutism, 1660–1815* (New York: Harper, 1962).

[15]"What then accounted for the difference between an *actual* absolutism in the 16th century and a *theoretical* absolutism in the middle ages, one which never became actual or only momentarily, noncontinuously, and intermittently?

"We must seek our answer in a new internal structural organ of the State, that is in the reinforcement and extension of and the power acquired by the corps of public servants, the 'officers' of the King (or of the Prince)—what we call today the 'bureaucracy'—which had come to the forefront of public life, and was involved in the daily activity of the State. Above all, as regards external affairs." Chabod, *Actes du Colloque*, pp. 63–64.

Edouard Perroy argues this process began in France as early as the thirteenth century: "The progress of the private authority of the king of France, both seigniorial and feudal, led to the development of the organs of [central] power. . . .

"[In] the last quarter of the thirteenth century, royal power, without ceasing to become ever

stronger, began to be transformed in its nature, under the influence of two factors. One was the idea of absolutism, that of public power [sovereignty]. . . . The other, equally important, was the pressure of the king's own men, whose numbers grew greatly with the growing complexity of administration and the ever expanded use of writing: a new class was coming into existence, that of the agents of power, of the men of the law and the pen. . . . At that moment, in effect, the corps of governmental personnel, collectively the depositary of an authority which was now capable of moving on its own steam, began to eclipse the royal personage. . . ." *Le Moyen Age*, pp. 372–373.

[16]"The spectacle of great political machineries may be a misleading image. Comparing those of the sixteenth with those of the fifteenth century, we see them inordinately increased in size. But it is still relative. If one thinks of contemporary times and the enormous mass of civil servants working for the State, the number of 'officers' in the sixteenth century is laughably small." Braudel, *La Méditerranée*, **II**, p. 37.

parison with the late Middle Ages represented nonetheless a qualitative jump.

How did a king acquire these men? He bought them. The problem of the king was not that he had no agents. There were persons who performed administrative and military functions in the realm, but they were not previously for the most part *dependent* on him, and hence were not bound to carry out his dispositions in the face of adverse pressure deriving from their own interests or from that of their peers and families. The king turned to persons, usually "of modest origin"[17] to become a paid, full-time staff. The major institution which made this possible has come to be known as the "venality of office." By contrast with bureaucracies based on a norm of financial disinterestedness and universalistic recruitment, no doubt these forms underline the *limited* power of the king, and the likelihood that state income would be diverted to increased payments to this venal bureaucracy. But by contrast with the preceding feudal system, venality made possible the relative supremacy of the state-system. As Hartung and Mousnier say, "Despite appearances, the venality of offices was most often favorable to the absolute monarch."[18]

The political choice was made by the king between realistic alternatives. In order to establish a rational bureaucracy, the state needed a sure source of prior funds other than that which the bureaucracy would bring in. K. W. Swart suggests that what monarchs lacked in the sixteenth century, unlike later governments, was the possibility to "issue loans without assigning a special part of their income as security for the interest."[19] They were caught in a cycle because in order to acquire this possibility they first had to create a stronger state machinery. Venality of office had the virtue of providing both immediate income (sale of office) and a staff. Of course this then went hand in hand with the development of a self-interested corporate group of venal officers.[20] To be sure, venality creates a "vicious circle" as Richard Ehrenberg points out, in which the increased bureaucracy eats up revenue and creates debts, leading to still larger fiscal needs by the state.[21] The trick was to transform the circle into an upward spiral wherein the bureaucracy was sufficiently efficient to squeeze out

---

[17]*Ibid.*, p. 29.

[18]"It is what permitted the Kings of Spain to bring the municipalities under their protection, what gave in France to Louis XII, Francis I and Henry II, Henry IV and Louis XIII, such a powerful means of influence over the Court and the companies. . . . It's only after the War of the Austrian Succession [1748] that venality . . . became unbearable. . . ." Hartung and Mousnier, *Relazioni del X Congresso*, **IV**, p. 48.

[19]K. W. Swart, *Sale of Offices in the Seventeenth Century* (The Hague: Nijhoff, 1949), 117.

[20]"As the rule of fiscality in monarchy grows, so does the importance of finance officials in the state. As venality develops, the finance officials multiply, organize, join together in associations which leads

to extending the scope of their authority with a view to assuring themselves further profits." G. Pagès, "Essai sur l'évolution des institutions administratives en France du commencement du XVIe siècle à la fin du XVIIe," *Revue d'histoire moderne,* n.s., No. 1, janv.–fevr., 1932, 26.

[21]"Excessive indebtedness on the part of the princes was made necessary by the conditions we have seen. It could not be borne without the system of farming out the taxes or the pledging of individual branches of revenue. This led to a frightful degeneration of the financial system, which was unavoidable while the circumstances lasted, which led to the repeated heaping up of debts." Richard Ehrenberg, *Capital and Finance in the Age of the Renaissance* (New York: Harcourt, 1928), 39.

of the population a surplus larger than the costs of maintaining the apparatus. Some states succeeded at this. Others did not. The crucial distinguishing factor would be their role in the world-economy.

The upward spiral operated something like this: The momentary advantages acquired by the king in the late Middle Ages because of the economic squeeze on the nobility created the funds that made it possible to begin to "buy" a bureaucracy. This in turn made it possible both to tax more and to borrow more. In those areas of the world-economy where economic transformation was proceeding in such a way as to ensure a disproportionate share of the world surplus, states found it easier to tax and to borrow, a sheer reflex of future-oriented confidence of money-possessing elements. The states used these increased revenues to increase their coercive power which in turn increased what might be termed "confidence in the coercive potential" of the state.

This made it possible for national debts to come into existence, that is, deficitary state budgets. National debts were unknown in the ancient world, and impossible in the Middle Ages because of the weakness of the central governments and the uncertainty of succession. It is only with the regime of Francis I in France in the sixteenth century that we first encounter this economic phenomenon.[22] For national debts can only exist when the state can force people to delay collecting them or at opportune moments refuse to pay them, while simultaneously forcing groups to lend, in specie or by various paper transactions, the current excess. It is part of the drive to ensure increasing revenues to the Crown. The Crown needed money with which to build up its state machinery, and had enough state machinery to obtain the money. The system employed was not yet mercantilism, a policy aimed at strengthening the long run tax base of the state, so much as "fiscalism," in Martin Wolfe's phrase,[23] a policy aimed at increasing the immediate income of the state.

[22]See Earl J. Hamilton, "Origin and Growth of the National Debt in Western Europe," *American Economic Review*, **XXXVII**, 2, May 1947, 118–130. This statement is true if we are speaking of presently existing states. Actually, as with most modern phenomena, there was a pretaste in the Renaissance Italian city-states. Marvin B. Becker traces the growth of a public debt in Florence from a "trifling sum" in 1303 to a sum in 1427 approximately equal to the total wealth of the Florentine populace. See "Economic Change and the Emerging Florentine Territorial State," *Studies in the Renaissance*, **XIII**, 1966, 7–9.

[23]Martin Wolfe, "Fiscal and Economic Policy in Renaissance France," *Third International Conference of Economic History*, Munich 1965 (Paris: Mouton, 1968), 687–689. See Fernand Braudel: "Beginning in the sixteenth century and with more éclat in this century of renewal, the States—at least those who would live, prosper, and especially resist the exhausting expenses of land and sea warfare—the

States dominate, deform economic life, subject it to a network of constraints; they capture it in their net. The temptation is great to explain everything by the desires and the weaknesses of the States, by their unstable games. But history is never one-sided. One can however defend the proposition, with solid arguments, that the part of economic life that was at that point most modern, that which we would readily designate as operating within the framework of large-scale merchant capitalism, was linked to these financial ups and downs of the State; stimulated and sought after by the State, it is progressively paralyzed by the latter's gluttony and the inevitable sterility of too heavy public expenses. This gluttony and this inefficacity—great forces of history—played a role in what would be the setback *(repli)* of the sixteenth century." "Le pacte de ricorsa au service du roi d'Espagne et de ses preteurs à la fin du XVIe siècle," in *Studi in onore di Armando Sapori* (Milano: Istituto Edit. Cisalpino, 1957), **II**, 1115.

At this point in time, nonetheless the *lack* of serious financial state machinery was still striking, "another sign of weakness," as Braudel calls it, of the sixteenth-century state, compared to later states.[24] Still, the weakness of the State as financial manipulator does not detract from the fact that national debts reflected the growing autonomous interests of the states as economic actors, as actors however with a special ability to pursue their economic ends.

Perhaps the most important use to which the surplus of money was put, once one deducted the cost of the administrative machinery used in collecting it, was in the creation of standing armies. Once again the way states got personnel initially was to buy them. The counterpart of "venal" bureaucrats was "mercenary" soldiers.

Who however was available to be purchased? Not just anyone, since being a mercenary was a dangerous albeit occasionally rewarding occupation. It was not an occupation generally speaking of choice. Those who could do better did so with alacrity. It was consequently an occupation whose recruitment was geographically and socially skewed, part and parcel of the new European division of labor.

The population growth in western Europe led as we have mentioned to the phenomenon of "vagabondage." There was a growth everywhere of a "lumpenproletariat." They were a threat to the not too well established order of the new states. Incorporating some of them into the armies served multiple functions. It provided employment to some, and used this group to suppress the others.[25] It gave the kings new weapons to control the lords, but also to sustain them. V. G. Kiernan has indicated how many of the mercenaries came from the "less-developed" corners of western Europe: from Gascony, Picardy, Brittany, Wales, Corsica, Sardinia, Dalmatia. "Altogether, a striking number of these recruiting-grounds lay in mountainous regions on the fringes of Europe, inhabited by alien peoples such as Celts or Basques."[26] And, it seems, above all, from Switzerland.[27]

[24]"[The] vast States are not yet in total contact with the mass of taxpayers, and therefore able to exploit them at will: hence the peculiar fiscal, and consequently financial, weaknesses. Except for [a few places in] Italy, at the tail end of the sixteenth century, the States still did not have either Treasuries or State Banks." Braudel, *La Méditerranée,* **II,** p. 39.

[25]Fritz Redlich points out that there were two sorts or mercenaries. There were to be sure the uprooted individuals—in the language of time, *fahrendes Volk,* or roving people. There were also in Switzerland and Germany a more "sedentary" variety who "remained rooted in their home communities." These were akin to a militia called up in emergencies. "The German Military Entrepriser and His Work Force," **I,** *Vierteljahrschrift für Sozial- und Wirtschaftsgeschichte,* Supp. No. 47, 1964, 115–117.
[26]V. G. Kiernan, "Foreign Mercenaries and Absolute Monarchy," *Past & Present,* No. 11, April 1957, 70.

[27]"In France, whose example was decisive for Europe, Louis XI inaugurated a system destined to survive down to the Revolution when, in 1474, he enlisted Swiss auxiliaries by arrangement with the Cantons. From now on Switzerland, conveniently close at hand, was to the French kings what Wales had been to the English [*Ibid.,* p. 72]."
Otton Laskowski attributes the popularity of Swiss mercenaries to their military competence. See "Infantry Tactics and Firing Power in the XVIth Century," *Teki Historyczne,* **IV,** 2, 1950, 106–115.
They were all the more required by France since at this time the French infantry was notoriously inferior. The explanation, according to Sir Charles Oman, was that "outside the standing force of Swiss, the units were perpetually being raised in a hurry, and disbanded when a crisis was over." *A History of the Art of War,* p. 45. This leads us to ask why the French infantry was disbanded at a more rapid rate than elsewhere. The answer is not clear, nor

Kiernan argues that this pattern of recruitment was not only directly responsible for controlling the social explosion of the sixteenth century;[28] it also had a second subtler impact, albeit one just as important, if we remember that, in our terms, we are dealing with a world-economy:

> The reservoirs of mercenary recruitment remained politically stagnant, compared with their neighbors, somewhat as Nepal and the Panjab, two great recruiting-grounds for the British army, long did. For Switzerland the three centuries of symbiosis with despotic France had evil consequences. Cantonal politics were corrupted by the fees received for licensing the export of soldiers, and rings of patricians increased their power at the expense of common people. . . . As Alfieri was to remark bitterly, these free-men of the hills became the chief watchdogs of tyranny. European history might have taken a different turn if the Swiss had still been as revolutionary a force in 1524, when the Peasants' War was fought, as fifty years earlier.[29]

The mercenaries were not even recruited directly by the state in most cases. The existing machinery did not permit it. Rather the state contracted with "military entrepreneurs," who sought profit. Redlich is dubious that this was an optimal means of capital accumulation since if their income was "extraordinarily high . . . typically their expenditures were tremendous."[30] But it is one more piece of evidence on how state building affected the rise of capitalism. In the short run at least, "in a society where there is chronic underemployment of resources, increased military expenditure has often stimulated more production of other kinds so that the amount of surplus rose in time of war."[31] But more than commerce and production was involved in the military enterprise. The system was credit-creating. For not only did princes borrow from bankers; so did the military entrepreneurs, whose capital was supplied by the large merchant bankers such as the Fuggers. This would remain true as late as the Thirty Years' War.[32]

is the fact sure. But, if true, it is one more indication of the uphill fight of the French monarchy to create a strong state.

[28]"European governments thus relied heavily on foreign mercenaries. One of the employments for which they were particularly well-suited was the suppression of rebellious subjects, and in the sixteenth century, that age of endemic revolution, they were often called upon for this purpose. 'Where are my Switzers?' was the cry of many a harassed monarch besides Claudius. . . . Rebellions headed by moneyed men could hire their own mercenaries. . . . However, in general, governments could outbid rebels at this game." Kiernan, *Past & Present,* No. 11, pp. 74–75.

There is a second sense in which the use of mercenaries contained social explosion. It limited the devastation of war. Oman points out that mercenaries quit when not paid. This had a direct impact on military tactics. Instead of frontal assault, a waiting-game was often more successful than press-

ing a military advantage. Military commanders seeing "signs of distress in the hostile camp" often simply let time pass because "a few more weeks of privations and bankruptcy would ruin the opponent." Oman, *A History of the Art of War,* p. 38.

[29]Kiernan, *Past & Present,* No. 11, p. 76.

[30]Redlich, *Vierteljahrschrift für Sozial- und Wirtschaftsgeschichte,* p. 401.

[31]Frederic Lane attributes this view to H. John Habakkuk. Lane adds this reservation: "But can it not be said that over the long run, other things being equal, a society that is able to attain a high level of employment of resources only by high military expenditure produces less surplus than if it were able to attain that same level of employment of resources with less military expenditures." *Venice & History,* p. 422, fn. 11. Of course, but the issue resides in the final "if."

[32]See Fritz Redlich, "Military Entrepreneurship and the Credit System in the 16th and 17th Centuries," *Kyklos,* **X,** 1957, 186–188.

Furthermore, it is not only that mercenary armies offered employment for the poor and entrepreneurial opportunities. Armies had to be fed. Typically, food merchants accompanied armies in the field, also serving as intermediaries for the booty.[33] Alan Everitt argues that army victualling was a major stimulus to regional grain specialization in Tudor England[34] and that it even stimulated the export trade.[35] This is all the more plausible if one takes into account that states also felt a responsibility to make sure that their growing bureaucracies had sufficient food as well.[36] The expansion of capitalism came thus to serve the short run needs of the state.

Here as with the civil bureaucracy the monarch was in a dilemma. The military entrepreneur was a necessary adjunct in the monarch's search for power. He also drained a goodly part of the surplus. No doubt the military entrepreneur was a more reliable agent of the prince than a noble vassal, but ultimately he too pursued his own interests primarily. Woe to the prince whose liquidity failed![37] The likelihood, however, of this happening was once again a direct function of the state's role in the world-economy.

Up to a point, in any case, the armies paid for themselves. For they made possible more taxes. Since the "weight of [these taxes] fell almost entirely on the people—especially those who lived in the country,"[38] the people chafed, and to the extent that they could, they rebelled.[39] The armies were then there to suppress these rebellions, to the extent that they could. The easiest form of rebellion, because the most difficult for the states to counteract, was banditry, which was of course the easier the

---

[33]See Redlich, *Vierteljahrschrift für Sozial- und Wirtschaftsgeschichte*, Suppl. No. 39, pp. 49–50.

[34]See Alan Everitt, "The Marketing of Agricultural Produce," in *The Agrarian History of England and Wales*, **IV**: Joan Thirsk, ed., *1500–1640* (London and New York: Cambridge Univ. Press, 1967), 521–522.

[35]"English farmers who in wartime increased their production or extended their acreage to meet the requirements of Tudor armies found themselves saddled, when peace was restored, with a considerable surplus. In all probability their wartime experience suggested the expedient of exploiting European markets, and their surplus was switched from the English soldier to the French or Flemish artisan [*Ibid.*, p. 524]."

[36]"The creation of specialized staffs of government employees—emphatically including standing armies—multiplied the number of hungry mouths for which the government had direct responsibility." Charles Tilly, "Food Supply and Public Order in Western Europe" (mimeo.), p. 20. See also pp. 36–40.

See C. S. L. Davies: "Few problems facing governments in a pre-industrial age could have been as

difficult as that of provisioning sufficient food for an army in the field." "Provisions for Armies, 1509–50: A Study in the Effectiveness of Early Tudor Governments," *Economic History Review*, 2nd ser., **XVII**, 2, 1964, 234.

[37]"Actually the war lord's worst risk was that the military enterpriser and, incidentally, also the labor force might try to get themselves paid at the expense of the political goals of their master. By the non-payment or belated payment of his debts (the usual accompaniment of military entrepreneurship and its foremost business risk), the war lord created for himself the risk of losing the war carried on for him by an unpaid enterpriser and labor force." Redlich, *Vierteljahrschrift für Sozial- und Wirtschaftsgeschichte*, p. 69.

[38]Génicot, *Cambridge Economic History of Europe*, **I**, p.700.

[39]Braudel notes that the first part of the sixteenth century was particularly lively, and that then it was rather quiet from 1550 to 1600. He comments: "It is therefore possible . . . that the solidity of the States at the time of Philip II explains this mutism, this popular discretion. The police were too tough. . . ." *La Méditerranée*, **II**, p. 80.

more mountainous the region.[40] The police of the state was still too thin to do too much about it, except in central areas, and this banditry often found a resonant chord in the opposition of some traditional seigniors to the new states.[41]

No doubt, as Delumeau puts it, "banditry was often the insurrection of the country against the city."[42] But who in the country and most importantly when? It is clear that peasant involvement in banditry seems to be highly correlated with moments of grain shortage.[43] Of course when a food riot occurred, the very poor were involved, but in banditry as a movement, especially in the Mediterranean area, it was not the very poor who made up the heart of the movement. It was more clearly the nascent yeoman farmers, who in the late sixteenth century, found in banditry their form of protest against the "refeudalization" that was occurring, against the semiperipheralization of their countries.[44] In such countries, it was particularly the small entrepreneurs, like the *massari* of southern Italy, who having fewer means of resistance to poor harvest years than larger landowners, feared a precipitous fall into the ranks of the rural poor, and hence employed banditry against these large landowners whom they saw as their immediate enemy.[45]

The other element involved in banditry was a part of the nobility, but again which ones? It seems to be those who were squeezed out by the economic upheaval. In our discussion of mercenaries, we pointed out that the growth of population along with various thrusts toward enclosure

[40]"Thus, when the sixteenth century comes to an end, the Mediterranean mountainside, everywhere overburdened by men and constraint, exploded in order to liberate itself. This diffuse warfare is confused with and blurs in our eyes with that form of disguised and interminable social warfare we call banditry, a vague word if there ever was one. In the Alps and in the Pyrenees, in the Apennines or the other mountain-ranges, Christian or Moslem, a common destiny may be sketched along these enormous mountainous wreaths, in the middle of which breathes the sea [Braudel, *ibid.*, p. 93]."

[41]"Behind the maritime pirates *(la course maritime)* were the towns, the city-states. Behind the highway robberies *(la course terrestre)*, was the continous assistance of seigniors who propped up the adventurers. The brigands often had at their head or behind them an authentic seignior. . . .

"Let us not oversimplify: widespread and of many varieties, brigandage was used by some nobles, but just as often directed against others. . . . For banditry is not only linked to the crisis of a certain element of the nobility. It is a mass, peasant-based movement [*Ibid.*, II, pp. 88–90]."

[42]Delumeau, *Vie économique*, II, p. 547.

[43]See *Ibid.*, II, pp. 543, 546–547, 608, 625.

[44]Rosario Villari expounds the impact of agricul-

tural involution on southern Italy: "The southern countryside, not touched by the waves of rural revolt which had accompanied the diffusion of the Protestant Reformation, reacted now to the ever more accentuated reimposition of feudal land dues and to the contemporary force of the economic and financial reorganization of the Church. The important fact is that those who participated in the movement were, more than the poor laborers, groups that played a role of management and social aggregation in the countryside.

"They were the agricultural entrepreneurs, the *massari*, semi-capitalist organizers of cereals production: forces in the countryside that had been able to profit throughout the secular phase of favorable conjuncture during the 16th century, reaping in part the fruit of the wage-depression and taking advantage indirectly of the financial crisis of the nobility and the development of the urban bourgeoisie. They are at that time wage-laborers, small or medium owners, agricultural entrepreneurs. With a physiognomy quite distinct from that of the wealthy bourgeosie, the *massari* had an organizational function of great importance in the primary production of the kingdom and in pasturage." *La rivolta antispagnola a Napoli: Le origini (1581–1647)* (Bari: Laterza, 1967), 61.

[45]*Ibid.*, pp. 61–62.

created the problem of vagabondage, and that the rise of mercenary armies served, among other purposes, to employ some of these "vagabonds" to hold the rest in line. Mercenary armies strengthened the princes. By the same token, they weakened the traditional nobility, not only by establishing forces strong enough to enforce the royal will, but also by creating an employment vacuum for the lesser nobility.[46] There was of course an alternative for impoverished knights in many areas. They could join the king's service. Furthermore, where the king was stronger, banditry was more difficult. But in areas where the prince was weak, his weakness made banditry more profitable and alternative service less available. It is in this sense that banditry implicitly was a demand for a stronger state rather than a flight into "traditional" resistance. It was a form of opposition, in some cases "the greatest force of opposition existing within the kingdom,"[47] but an opposition *within* the framework of the modern state.

It would hence be a serious error to see banditry as a form of traditional feudal opposition to state authority.[48] It was the consequence of the inadequate growth of state authority, the inability of the state to compensate for the dislocations caused by the economic and social turbulence, the unwillingness of the state to ensure some greater equalization of distribution in times of inflation, population growth, and food shortages. Banditry was in this sense created by the state itself, both by depriving some nobles of traditional rights (and hence sources of wealth) and some peasants of their produce to feed the new bureaucracies, and by creating in the state itself a larger concentration of wealth such that it became more tempting to try to seize part of it. Banditry was a symptom of the dislocations caused by the tremendous economic reallocations resulting from the creation of a European world-economy.

Political organisms are always more stable to the extent that they achieve even partial legitimacy. There is much mystification in the analyses of the process of legitimation caused by an almost exclusive look at the relationship of governments and the mass of the population. It is doubtful if very many governments in human history have been considered "legitimate" by the majority of those exploited, oppressed, and mistreated by their governments. The masses may be resigned to their fate, or sullenly restive,

[46]George Rusche and Otto Kirchheimer draw the consequences of this situation: "The cheap supply of mercenaries made the knights superfluous and cost them an important part of their income. Some suffered doubly, especially among the lower ranks, because the exhaustion of the soil and the growing misery of the peasants made it impossible for them to pay their rents. . . . Many of these hereditary, but landless, knights took to highway robbery just as their subjects were doing on a smaller scale. The main difference was that the destitute peasants had to rob openly, whereas the knights could conceal their aims under the pretext of legitimate warfare or of avenging the pauperized masses on the rich city merchants. . . . ." *Punishment and Social Structure* (New York: Russell & Russell, 1939), 13.

[47]Villari, *La rivolta antispagnola a Napoli,* p. 58.

[48]"Linking the phenomenon [of banditry] to the concept of feudal resistance to the state does not fit the facts of this historical situation. . . . The end of the sixteenth century is not a period of especially great anti-baronial pressure by the state; even in Rome the attempt by the Pope to recover the goods and rights usurped by the large landowners [*feudatari*] ended in 1581 with the definitive success of the usurpers [*Ibid.,* p. 60]."

or amazed at their temporary good fortune, or actively insubordinate. But governments tend to be endured, not appreciated or admired or loved or even supported. So it surely was in sixteenth-century Europe.

Legitimation does not concern the masses but the cadres. The question of political stability revolves around the extent to which the small group of managers of the state machinery is able to convince the larger group of central staff and regional potentates both that the regime was formed and functions on the basis of whatever consensual values these cadres can be made to believe exist and that it is in the interest of these cadres that this regime continue to function without major disturbance. When such circumstances obtain, we may call a regime "legitimate."

Legitimacy furthermore is not a once-and-for-all matter. It is a matter of constant compromise. In the sixteenth century, the ideology which arose as a means of legitimating the new authority of the monarchs was the divine right of kings, the system we have come to call absolute monarchy. Since absolutism was an ideology, we must beware of taking its claims at face value. It would be useful to examine therefore exactly what were the claims and how they corresponded to the realities of the social structure.

First, to what extent did "absolute" mean absolute? The theory that there were no human agencies that could, under most circumstances, make any legitimate claim of refusing to implement the proclaimed will of the monarch was not altogether new. However, it did get more widespread exposition and intellectual acceptance in this era than in earlier and later epochs. "Absolute" is a misnomer, however, both as to theory and as to fact. In theory, absolute did not mean unlimited, since as Hartung and Mousnier point out, it was "limited by divine law and natural law." They argue that "absolute" should not be read as "unlimited" but rather as "unsupervised" *(pas contrôlée)*. The monarchy was absolute by opposition to the past feudal scattering of power. "It did not signify despotism and tyranny."[49] Similarly, Maravall says that "in neither the initial nor subsequent phases of the modern state did 'absolute monarchy' mean unlimited monarchy. It was a relative absoluteness."[50] The key operational claim was that the monarch should not be limited by the constraints of law: *ab legibus solutus.*

Whatever the claims, the powers of the monarch were in fact quite limited, not only in theory but in reality. In most ways, the power of the king was far less than that of the executive of a twentieth-century liberal democracy, despite the institutional and moral constraints on the latter. For one thing, the state apparatus of the twentieth century has a degree of organizational capacity behind it that more than compensates for the increased constraints. To understand the real power of an "absolute" monarch, we must put it in the context of the political realities of the time and place.

[49]Hartung and Mousnier, *Relazioni del X Congresso*, **IV**, p. 8.

[50]José A. Maravall, "The Origins of the Modern State," *Cahiers d'histoire mondiale*, **VI**, 4, 1961, 800.

A monarch was absolute to the extent that he had a reasonable probability of prevailing against other forces within the state when policy confrontations occurred.[51] But even the strongest states in the sixteenth century were hard pressed to demonstrate clear predominance within their frontiers of the means of force, or command over the sources of wealth,[52] not to speak of primacy of the loyalty of their subjects.

The rise of the state as a social force, and absolutism as its ideology, should not be confused with the nation and nationalism. The creation of strong states within a world-system was a historical prerequisite to the rise of nationalism both within the strong states and in the periphery. Nationalism is the acceptance of the members of a state as members of a status-group, as citizens, with all the requirements of collective solidarity that implies. Absolutism is the assertion of the prime importance of the survival of the state as such. The former is by definition a mass sentiment; the latter by definition the sentiment of a small group of persons directly interested in the state machinery.

No doubt the proponents of a strong state over time would come to cultivate national sentiment as a solid reinforcement for their objectives. And to some extent they had something to work with in the sixteenth century already.[53] But this collective sentiment was usually primarily geared, to the extent it existed, to the person of the prince rather than to the collectivity as a whole.[54] The absolute monarch was a "heroic" figure,[55] the process of deification getting ever more intense as time went on. This

[51]Erik Molnar gives this careful definition: "[A]bsolutism is a political regime in which the power of the State is exercised essentially and effectively, by the sovereign over the whole of the territory, with the assistance of the military-bureaucratic organization which he has under his control. This definition includes as an essential criterion effective power which usually, when contested, prevails against adverse aspirations, as for example those formulated by a parliament or by a hereditary bureaucracy." "Les fondements économiques et sociaux de l'absolutisme," in *XIIe Congrès Internationale des Sciences Historiques: Rapports, IV: Méthodologie et histoire contemporaine* (Wien: Verlag Ferdinand Berger & Sohne, 1965), 155.

[52]"Nothing so clearly indicates the limits of royal power in the sixteenth century as the fact that governments were perennially in financial trouble, unable to tap the wealth of those most able to pay, and likely to stir up a costly revolt whenever they attempted to develop an adequate income." William J. Bouwsma, "Politics in the Age of the Renaissance," in *Chapters in Western Civilization,* 3rd ed. (New York: Columbia Univ. Press, 1961), **I,** 233.

[53]"There was no real national tradition in either the fifteenth or the sixteenth centuries; but there was a feeling of community which the kings were

able to turn to their own purposes, making their hold on power acceptable and something in which everyone freely collaborated." Maravall, *Cahiers d'histoire mondiale,* **VI,** p. 796.

[54]"[We should] avoid the temptation to interpret this new orientation of political thought [the idea of the State] as a consciousness of collective national solidarities. . . .

"We should note the fact that the jurists and the ideologists who progressively elaborated the idea of the State in the 16th century spoke much more often of the *Prince* (in the usage of Machiavelli) than of the people, of *authority* more than of *collectivity.*

"We ought therefore to reflect on this point of departure: the 'State' does not exist in itself. It is first of all essentially the affirmation of a new form of authority: the *public power of the sovereign.*" Georges de Lagarde, "Réflexions sur la cristallisation de la notion d'Etat au XVIe siècle," in Enrico Castelli, ed., *Umanesimo e scienza politica* (Milano: Dott. Carlo Marzorati, 1951), 247–248.

[55]"The vogue of Antiquity announces, in the sixteenth century, a new strength of Roman law and it adds to that the ancient idea of the 'hero,' of the demi-god, all-powerful and beneficent. . . . The hero is the model of the being to whom the peoples feel the need to deliver themselves." Mousnier, *Les XVI et XVII siècles,* pp. 96–97.

was the era in which the elaborate court ceremonial was developed, the better to remove the monarch from contact with the banal work (and incidentally the better to provide employment for court aristocrats, keeping them thereby close enough to be supervised and checked).

It was only in the late seventeenth and eighteenth centuries within the framework of mercantilism that nationalism would find its first real advocates amongst the bourgeoisie.[56] But in the sixteenth century, the interests of the bourgeoisie were not yet surely fixed on the state. Too large a number were more interested in open than in closed economies. And for state builders, premature nationalism risked its crystallization around too small an ethno-territorial entity. At an early point, statism could almost be said to be antinationalist, since the boundaries of "nationalist" sentiment were often narrower than the bounds of the monarch's state.[57] Only much later would the managers of the state machinery seek to create "integrated" states,[58] in which the dominant ethnic group would "assimilate" the outlying areas.

In the sixteenth century, a few states made substantial progress in centralizing power and achieving acceptance at least partially of the legitimacy of this centralization. It is not too difficult to outline the conditions under which this was likely to occur. Whenever the various cadres, the various groups who controlled resources, felt that their class interests were better served politically by attempting to persuade and influence the monarch than by seeking their political ends in alternative channels of action, then we can talk of a relatively effective monarchical system, a relatively "absolute" state.

"Absolute" conveys the wrong tone, the one of course kings hoped to convey. Absolutism was a rhetorical injunction, not a serious assertion. It might be perhaps wise to de-emphasize the concentration on the person of the king and simply talk of a strengthened state, or more "stateness."[59]

---

[56]"There is a place, at the antipodes of pure economics, for the very supple mixed formula: 'the market is the school in which the bourgeoisie first learns nationalism.' " Pierre Vilar, *La Catalogne dans l'Espagne moderne*, I (Paris: S.E.V.P.E.N., 1962), 34.

[57]"A good many of [the] people [of Western states], especially in or close to the capital, were coming to think of themselves as the king's own particular subjects, with something like the status of what would today be called a *Staatsvolk*. . . . A monarch struggling to bring over-mighty subjects under his control could bring against them the middle-classes, but he could also hope to achieve his purpose by expansion, outflanking the feudalism of the home province by mastering outlying ones." Kiernan, *Past & Present*, No. 31, p. 33.

[58][The] idea that a society should be integrated, that there should be, if possible, only one race, one language, one culture in a state, and that all or almost all people with political borders should have

a right to determine what should be done—all this is new, the result of 19th-century Western thinking." Wolfram Eberhard, *Conquerors and Rulers: Social Forces in Medieval China* (Leiden: Brill, 1965), 2nd rev. ed., 6.

[59]Charles Tilly measures "stateness" by "formal autonomy, differentiation from nongovernmental organizations, centralization, and internal coordination." From this it follows that "extreme stateness neither guarantees political stability nor assures power in the international arena. One might guess that an increase in stateness does ordinarily increase a government's command of the mobile resources within its subject population, does increase its capacity to free resources to objectives at a national or international scale." "Reflections on the History of European Statemaking," mimeographed draft of chapter 9 of Charles Tilly, ed., *The Building of States in Western Europe*, (Princeton, New Jersey: Princeton University Press), 18–19. In press.

We might better call the ideology "statism." Statism is a claim for increased power in the hands of the state machinery. In the sixteenth century, this meant power in the hands of the absolute monarch. It was a claim to power, the claim being part of the attempt to achieve it. Nobody, then or now, took it or should take it as a description of the real world of the time. This claim was validated up to a point in certain states, those that would make up the core of the European world-economy. It failed elsewhere, for reasons we shall elucidate later.

One of the major indications of success as well as one important mechanism in the process of centralizing power was the degree to which the population could be transformed, *by one means or another,* into a culturally homogeneous group. Once again it is less the masses that are relevant than the cadres in the broadest sense: the king, his bureaucracy and courtiers, the rural landowners (large and small), the merchants. In the sixteenth century, while core states are moving toward greater "ethnic" homogeneity among these strata, peripheral areas are moving precisely in the opposite direction.

Let us start by looking at the attitude of the state machinery toward the trader who belonged to a "minority" group. First, there were the Jews, a group which played a large role in trading activities throughout the Middle Ages. One of the things to note is that in both social and economic terms, there was "a steady deterioration of the Jewish status in the late Middle Ages."[60] On the one hand, as England, France, and Spain created stronger centralized structures, they began to expel the Jews: England in 1290, France at the close of the fourteenth century, Spain in 1492. But this phenomenon also occurred in Germany, where, if not expelled, the Jews were in many ways weakened in their role as trading groups. It was Jews who had conducted much of the international trade between western and eastern Europe along the northern transcontinental route between 800–1200 A.D., and were its mainstay.[61] During this period, in both regions, their legal status was reasonably favorable.[62] In the thirteenth

---

[60]Salo W. Baron, *A Social and Religious History of the Jews,* 2nd ed., **XI:** *Citizen or Alien Conjurer* (New York: Columbia Univ. Press, 1967a), 192.

[61]"At the end of the thirteenth century, the position of the Jews in international trade had weakened in Germany also as a result of a series of prohibitions directed against them. From that time onwards the entire trade with the east flowed along the later and better-known channels: the Italian-Mediterranean in the south and the Hanseatic in the north. The trans-continental route across Russia and Poland as it had functioned in earlier centuries ceased to figure in historical sources." J. Brutzkus, "Trade with Eastern Europe, 800–1200," *Economic History Review,* **XIII,** 1943, 41.

[62]Of Poland, Salo W. Baron states: "We know

very little about Jewish life during [the eleventh and twelfth centuries] but Jews evidently enjoyed full freedom of action and were subjected to few, if any, legal restrictions." *A Social and Religious History of the Jews,* 2nd ed., **III:** *Heirs of Rome and Persia* (Philadelphia: Jewish Publication Society of America, 1957a), 219. In Western Europe, the feudal system tended to be favorable to Jews by making them "a new group of royal vassals, somewhat akin to Christian nobles." Salo W. Baron, *A Social and Religious History of the Jews,* 2nd ed., **IV:** *Meeting of East & West* (Philadelphia: Jewish Publication Society of Ameria, 1957b), 50. This was true of Spain (see pp. 36–43), Carolingian France (see pp. 43–53), Germany (see pp. 64–75), England and Normandy (see pp. 75–86). Although feudalism

and fourteenth century, there is a general decline in both the legal status
and the economic role of the Jews *throughout* Europe.[63] However, by the
sixteenth century, we can speak of a geographical *imbalance:* their virtually
total absence in western Europe but, on the other hand, their presence
in *increased* numbers in eastern and parts of southern Europe, that is an
absence in the core and an increase in the periphery and semiperiphery.[64]

Although Jews played an ever increasing role in east Europe's economic
life, they were permitted only the role of merchant among professions
above the status of working-class. For them alone, the classic route of
entrepreneur to rentier was impossible.[65] Similarly in northern Italy, as
a result of the decline of the financial strength of the city-states, which
was due in part to their small size with consequent small tax base and
inability to protect their citizens outside the country,[66] the position of the
Jews began to improve somewhat, once again playing principally the role

"greatly complicated Jewish life in Western Europe
by both its anarchical diversity and its strengthening
of the Church's authority over Jews," it is also the
case that "the central and provincial organs of the
Church significantly contributed to Jewish security
by their continued insistence on basic toleration,
their strengthening of the royal power through
emphasis on the divine right of kings, their injunc-
tions to kings to rule justly, and their tireless prop-
agation of compacts aimed at establishing the 'divine
truce' for the more defenceless groups in the
population, including clerics and Jews [pp. 53–54]."
   [63]In the early Middle Ages, Jews had profited
from being "royal vassals." In the late Middle Ages,
these same kings became stronger. Yet the position
of the Jews began to decline. Baron comments:
"Since their respective princely masters derived ever
greater fiscal benefits from that relationship, it is
doubly astonishing that they failed to employ their
increasing power for more effective protection of
their Jewish 'serfs' [p. 198]." Baron finds the explanation in "the new type of nationalism gradually
taking shape in the late Middle Ages [p. 199]." In
addition, "the growing laicization of the medieval
societies intensified their ethno-religious intolerance
[p. 200]."
   [64]"Forced out from one country after another
[in the fourteenth and fifteenth centuries, . . . the
Jews] moved in increasing numbers to the opening
frontiers of east-central Europe and established
growing and ever more self-assertive communities
in Slavonic, Hungarian, and Lithuanian territories.
In many such endeavors they found their usefulness
to the respective societies as suppliers of cash and
credit and to the states as ready, often helpless,
objects of taxation was one of their greatest
economic assets." Salo W. Baron, *A Social and Religi-*

ous History of the Jews, 2nd ed., **XII:** *Economic Catalyst*
(New York: Columbia Univ. Press, 1967b), 30–31.
   Germany was a marginal area: "After the catastrophe of the Black Death, however, German Jewry,
decimated and impoverished, was forced more and
more to concentrate on money-lending. Though its
financial returns steadily diminished, it incurred
thereby the intense animosity of the population. . . .
The very rulers who, through their taxation, were
in many respects silent partners of the Jewish
bankers, now defended their wards less and less
vigorously. . . . Conditions went from bad to worse
in the stormy decades at the beginning of the sixteenth century, when social unrest and religious dissensions prepared the ground for the civil and religious wars [pp. 151–153]."
   [65]"It seems that the situation was different for
the numerous Jews in Poland, for whom the path
to landed property and social advancement was in
principle barred. In this case, we believe, investing
capital [in industrial and mining activities] was more
often engaged in." Marian Malowist, "L'évolution
industrielle en Pologne du XIVe au XVIIe siècle:
traits généraux," *Studi in onore di Armando Sapori*
(Milano: Istituto Edit. Cisalpino, 1957), **I,** 601.
   [66]"But how can we explain this fall [of the mercantile lead of the Italian city-states]? The elements
which contributed to it are the following: the class
struggle which flourished in the city-states, the bankruptcies through insolvency of royal debtors (bankruptcy of the Bardi Peruzzi), the absence of a large
state which would protect its citizens abroad; that
is, the fundamental cause is in the very structure
of the city-state which could not transform itself
into a large territorial State." Antonio Gramsci, *Il
Risorgimento* (Roma: Giulio Einaudi Ed., 1955), 9.

of merchants.[67] The Jewish issue, as it presented itself to rulers, was a dilemma of "fiscalism" versus nascent "mercantilism." On the one hand, these Jewish merchants were an important source of state revenue; on the other hand, non-Jewish merchants saw them as competitors and landowners as creditors, both groups often combining in pressure on the ruler to eliminate the Jews. The former consideration prevailed at first, as often as the kings were in a position to arrange it.[68] As the indigenous bourgeoisie grew stronger in the core states, intolerance to Jews made substantial legal progress.

The Jews were an easy target for their competitors because an ideological cause could be made of them. One could argue against their economic role on religious grounds. One way monarchs handled this in western Europe was to expel the Jews, but substitute another group which was less vulnerable on religious grounds although, from the point of view of the indigenous merchants, an equal competitor. For example, P. Elman describes how, when the English monarch was finally forced to expel the Jews in 1290, he welcomed Italian moneylenders in their place. Since the king often did not repay loans, "for practical purposes, the Italian loans may not have differed greatly from Jewish tallages."[69] Still, by the sixteenth century, the Italians were ousted from their role as entrepreneurs inside England,[70] if not in Spain,[71] but the Jews were ousting Poles in Poland.[72] How was this possible?

In western Europe, the increasingly diversified agricultural base along with the nascent industries strengthened the commercial bourgeoisie to the point where the king was obliged to take them politically into account. The other side of it was that they were able to serve as fiscal underpinning of the monarchy—as taxpayer, moneylender, and commercial partner—as well, if not better than foreign merchants. The "nationalist" reflex was thus natural.[73] In eastern Europe, however, the issue presented itself very differently. The monarchs were weaker, the merchants weaker, the agricultural producers stronger. The issue in eastern Europe in the sixteenth century, as in all other parts of the capitalist world system who came increasingly to specialize in the production of cash crops, was not the existence

[67]"So long as the North-Italian republics served as world centers of banking, Jews were effectively kept out of the homeland of these 'Lombards' whose financial resources so frequently exceeded their own even in the rest of Europe. After the financial crises of the thirteenth century, however, which led to the breakdown of [various] great firms . . . new opportunities opened up for Jews. . . .

"Italian principalities, too, before long appreciated the presence of Jews as an additional source of economic strength." Baron, *A Social and Religious History of the Jews*, **XII**, pp. 161, 163.

When the Jews of Spain and Sicily were expelled in 1492, "Italy was the only land in Christian Europe open to the refugees. . . ." Cecil Roth, *The History of the Jews of Italy* (Philadelphia: Jewish Publication Society of America, 1946), 178–179.

[68]"If the Jews had not been totally expendable in certain regions [of western Europe] . . . this was owing to a very large extent to the fiscal interests of the respective governments in the revenue they collected, directly or indirectly, through Jewish money lending via the growingly exhorbitant Jewish taxation." Baron, *A Social and Religious History of the Jews*, **XII**, p. 197.

See J. Lee Shneidman on thirteenth and fourteenth century Aragon: "Usually when one lends
money one expects the money to be returned. This
is not entirely true when one lends to the state.
While the kings frequently did repay a small loan,
the normal practice was to repay by reborrowing
or by making another loan from a different
individual to repay the first. Usually, the money
that the Jew loaned the state was lost, and he had
to recoup by the profits from tax collecting. Since
these profits became the source of further loans,
the monarchs were most anxious to insure that the
Jews recovered the value of the loan plus profit."
The Rise of the Aragonese-Catalan Empire, 1200–1350
(New York: New York Univ. Press, 1970), **II**, 433.

[69]P. Elman, "The Economic Causes of the Expulsion of the Jews in 1290," *Economic History Review*,
VII, 1, Nov. 1936, 151. Elman further argues that
it is *because* the Jews were "sucked dry" that the
Italians were asked to take their place.

[70]"By that time, . . . English overseas merchants
had joined forces with English townsmen and urban
xenophobia was broadening into economic
nationalism. In the late fourteenth century the
attempts of English cloth merchants to penetrate
the Baltic met with small welcome in the Hanse
towns. In these circumstances the privileges of the
Hansards in England (which included duties on
cloth lower even than those paid by denizens)
seemed grossly unjustified, and the English traders
demanded either reciprocity in the Baltic or the
curtailment of Hanseatic privileges in England. . . .
Meanwhile the Italians were the centre of a
similar controversy. . . . [The townsmen turned]
against the bullionist notions which were coming
into common currency. Their banking and
exchange operations were said to lead to an export
of gold and silver, and the character of their trade
[luxury 'trifles'] to a constant drain of bullion."
Edward Miller, "The Economic Policies of Governments: France and England," in *Cambridge Economic
History of Europe*, **III**: M. M. Postan, E. E. Rich, and
Edward Miller, eds., *Economic Organization and
Policies in the Middle Ages* (London and New York:
Cambridge Univ. Press, 1963), 330–331.

[71]1492 is the key date. Before that, Vicens notes:
"There was no urban bourgeoisie, as in the other
countries of the West. This gap was filled by a social
class outside the Christian religion: the Jews." *An
Economic History of Spain*, p. 248. After that, the
Genoese dominated: "The turning point in the history of Genoese merchants in Spain was the discovery of America and the subsequent opening of trading relations with the new continent. From then
on, their ascent to economic predominance in Spain
paralleled that nation's growing emergence as the
dominant power of the sixteenth-century world.
Fortune gave Spain two empires simultaneously, one

in the Old World, the other in the New. Spain's
unpreparedness for imperial responsibilities, particularly in the economic sphere, was the spring-
board for Genoese advancement." Ruth Pike, "The
Genoese in Seville and the Opening of the New
World," *Journal of Economic History*. XXII, 3, Sept.
1962, 348. See Chaunu, *Séville,* **VIII**, (1) 285–286.

See also Javier Ruíz Almansa: "Each of the three
racial groups (Christians, Jews, Moors) had taken
upon itself, in the social and economic structure
of the time, a determinate function. The elimination
created a vacuum difficult to fill and produced a
veritable organic upheaval of Spanish society. The
Genoese and Flemish merchants took over the functions previously performed by the Jews, but not
entirely. The handicraftsmen of southern France
fitted a large part of the gap left by the Moriscos.
. . ." "Las ideas y las estadísticas de población en
España en el siglo XVI," *Revista internacional de
sociología*, **I**, 1947, cited by Juan Reglá, "La expulsión de los moriscos y sus consecuencias," *Hispania,
revista española de historia*, **XIII**, No. 52, 1953, 445.

[72]"[In] Poland, which burst suddenly into modernity at the beginning of the fifteenth century, there
is a growing Jewish ascendancy, the result of
numbers, and almost a Jewish nation and state, all
of which will be swept away in the economic difficulties and pitiless repression of the seventeenth
century. . . ." Braudel, *La Méditerranée*, **II**, p. 137.

[73]"By the turn of the thirteenth and fourteenth
centuries, the great Italian houses . . . were
dominating the English wool exports and in some
years exercised a total monopoly of exports and
entire control of the royal Customs.

"From this position the Italians were eventually
ousted by syndicates of native merchants and finally
by the English Company of Staple. . . .

"By 1361 the English Company of Staple was in
possession of a virtual monopoly of 'wool exports' to
Northern Europe. . . .

"The monopoly suited . . . the wool merchants
. . . ; it suited the rising interest of the clothmakers
for it created wide discrepancies between wool prices
at home and abroad. Above all, it suited the king.
The custom and subsidy on the export of wool was
the best possible security which he could offer, and
a chartered company enjoying a monopoly of trade
was a much safer source of loans than the series
of firms and syndicates which had, one by one, gone
bankrupt in the early years of the Hundred Years'
War. . . . The only interest which suffered was that
of the wool-growers; and this may have been one
of the reasons why the production of wool declined."
M. M. Postan, "The Trade of Medieval Europe: The
North" in *Cambridge Economic History of Europe*, **II**: M.
M. Postan and E. E. Rich, eds., *Trade and Industry in
the Middle Ages* (London and New York: Cambridge
Univ. Press, 1952), 238.

or nonexistence of a commercial bourgeoisie. If there is a money economy, there must be people to serve as funnels for the complex exchange of goods and services which the use of money encourages. The issue was whether this commercial bourgeoisie was to be largely foreign or largely indigenous. If it were indigenous, it added an additional important factor in internal politics. If it were foreign, their interests were linked primarily to those of the emerging poles of development, what in time would be called metropoles.

Was not a critical reason for the "welcome" given to the Jews in eastern Europe in the sixteenth century the fact that the indigenous landowners (and perhaps also merchants in western Europe) preferred to have Jews as the indispensable local merchants in eastern Europe rather than an indigenous commercial bourgeoisie?[74] The latter, if it gained strength, would have a political base (totally absent for Jews) and might have sought to become a manufacturing bourgeoisie. The route they would doubtless have chosen would have involved reducing the "openness" of the national economy, which would threaten the symbiotic interests of the east European landowner–merchant. While we know that the early modern period was a time of *decline* for the indigenous bourgeoisie in eastern Europe,[75] "in the countryside, on the other hand, Jews played an increasing role as both the agents of the landlords and the traders and craftsmen in the small hamlets."[76] This illustrates a more general phenomenon of a world-economy. The class alliances *within* the political system of the state are a function of whether the ruling group is dominated primarily by those persons whose interest is tied to sale of primary products on a world market or by those whose interests are in commercial–industrial profits.

It is not the Jews alone who were the plaything of these transnational politico–economic alliances. Merchants in Catholic countries were often "Protestants." The central pan-European ideological controversy of the sixteenth and seventeenth centuries—Reformation versus Counter-Reformation—was inextricably intertwined with the creation both of the strong states and of the capitalist system. It is no accident that those

[74]Forced conversions occurred in Spain and Portugal. This was ideal for semi-peripheralization. The Jews were allowed to perform as Marranos. This allowed them to play a far more important role within the bourgeoisie than previously. When developments on the Iberian peninsula reached the point where it seemed desirable to squeeze out a local bourgeoisie, the coincidence between "bourgeois" and "new Christians" made the latter an easy target of persecution. See I. S. Revah, "L'hérésie marrane dans l'Europe catholique du 15e au 18e siècle," in Jacques Le Goff, *Hérésies et sociétés dans l'Europe préindustrielle, 11e-18e siècles* (Paris:

Mouton, 1968), esp. p. 333 with reference to Portugal.

[75]See Malowist, *Past & Present*, No. 13; Ferdo Gestrin. *Annales E.S.C.*, **XVII**, (1962).

[76]Salo W. Baron, personal letter, Nov. 16, 1970. See D. Stanley Eitzen: "The Jews were further disliked because of the work they did for the nobles and princes [in the 16th century]. They served as financial agents for the princes, leased and administered crown domains and estates of the gentry, and often worked as tax collectors." "Two Minorities: The Jews of Poland and the Chinese of the Philippines," *Jewish Journal of Sociology*, **X**, 2, Dec. 1968, 227.

parts of Europe which were re-agrarianized in the sixteenth century were also those parts of Europe in which the Counter-Reformation triumphed, while, for the most part, the industrializing countries remained Protestant. Germany, France, and "Belgium" were somewhere "in between," the long-term result being an ideological compromise. Germany divided between Protestants and Catholics. France and "Belgium" came to have few "Protestants" but developed an anticlerical, free-thinking tradition to which certain groups could adhere.

This is no accident, not because, following Weber, we think Protestant theology is somehow more consonant with capitalism than Catholic theology. No doubt one can make a case for this argument. On the other hand, it seems to be true in general that any complex system of ideas can be manipulated to serve any particular social or political objective. Surely Catholic theology, too, has proved its capacity to be adaptable to its social milieu. There is little reason at the abstract level of ideas why one couldn't have written a plausible book entitled "The Catholic Ethic and the Rise of Capitalism." And Calvinist theology could be taken to have anticapitalist implications.[77] The point I am making is a different one. By a series of intellectually accidental[78] historical developments, Protes-

[77]"Nonetheless, it is often regarded as axiomatic nowadays that Calvinism emerged as the religion which encouraged the strivings of the business man. In its cruder forms this doctrine asserts that Calvinism glorified acquisitive zeal, or, at the least, that it encouraged a belief that success in business might be regarded as a sign of being numbered amongst God's elect. Such a perversion of Calvinism is not unthinkable, though it is worth noting, not only that it would have been a perversion, but that it would have been a perversion particularly repulsive to strict Calvinists, as involving the sinful presumption of attempting to uncover the inscrutable workings of Providence. A more likely popular perversion of Calvinism would have been of quite a different nature. This would have been to let one's belief in Predestination lapse into fatalism, and lead to lethargy and lack of interest in one's work through a sense of powerlessness of individual efforts in the face of The Lord's will. Some years ago, the Commissioners appointed by the Carnegie Corporation to enquire into the 'Poor White' problem in South Africa seriously debated whether one factor causing a lack of gumption and of self-reliance amongst 'Poor Whites' was not this type of fatalism bred by a 'wrong Calvinism.' This forms an interesting commentary on the widely accepted belief in Calvinism as a stimulant to business enterprise. It suggests, very strongly indeed, that influences other than doctrinal ones determine the Calvinist's reaction to economic opportunities and stimuli." H. M. Robertson, "European Economic Developments in

the Sixteenth Century," *South African Journal of Economics,* **XVIII,** 1, Mar. 1950, 48.

[78]I am not seeking to deny that it may have been *easier* to use Calvinist theology to justify capitalist activity than Catholic theology. Not only does Weber think so, but some of his strongest critics think so too. For example, Christopher Hill argues: "Doctrines employing the motives of the heart, allowing social pressures to influence individual conduct more freely, flourish especially . . . in periods of rapid social change, and among those persons most exposed to its effect. Christianity arose in such a period; St. Augustine, on whose theology the reformers drew so heavily, also lived in an age when old standards were breaking down; and he too stressed inner motive rather than external action. . . . There appears to be a permanent tendency for established Churches to revert to ceremonial, and for opposition groups to stress the internal element." "Protestantism and the Rise of Capitalism," in F. J. Fisher, ed., *Essays in the Economic and Social History of Tudor and Stuart England* (London and New York: Cambridge Univ. Press, 1960), 34–35.

What I am arguing is that, given the social need, Catholicism could have been used to justify capitalism, and Protestantism need not have been. At the very most, I would agree with Hill's formulation: "But there is nothing in Protestantism which leads automatically to capitalism; its importance was rather that it undermined obstacles which the more rigid institutions and ceremonies of Catholicism imposed [p. 37]."

tantism became identified to a large extent in the period of the Reformation with the forces favoring the expansion of commercial capitalism within the framework of strong national states, and with the countries in which these forces were dominant. Thus when such forces lost out in Poland, or Spain, or "Italy," or Hungary, Protestantism declined too and often rapidly. The factors which favored the expansion of export agriculture favored the reassertion of Catholicism.

One must look at the Reformation as it developed. As Christopher Hill notes:

> The Church had long been a source of power, patronage and wealth to rulers of major powers like France and Spain. Those governments which broke with Rome in the early sixteenth century were on the fringes of catholic civilization, secondary powers whose rulers had not been strong enough to drive so hard a bargain with the Papacy—like England, Sweden, Denmark, Switzerland, Scotland.[79]

There was clearly at this point an element of the chafing of northern Europe against the economic weight of the more "advanced" Christian Mediterranean world.[80] But as we know, by the end of the extended sixteenth century, northwest Europe had become the core of the world-economy, eastern Europe the periphery, and southern Europe slipping fast in that direction.

P. C. Gordon-Walker seeks to tie the evolution of Protestantism—first Luther, then Calvin—to the two phases of the Price Revolution: 1520–1540/50—mild and limited to Germany and the Netherlands (Central European silver production); 1545 on for about a century (American silver). He argues that the paired phases are further linked to the successive structural needs of the new capitalist system:

> The social problem, presented by the Price Revolution, was really a problem with two parts. The first need was primary accumulation. . . . The second, subsequent, and really basic need was the acclimitisation of the classes of capitalist society into the new positions made necessary by the resources of primitive accumulation. . . .
> These two phases controlled the importance of various parts of Europe. From 1520–40 the leading areas were Spain (which inherited no strong middle class from the Middle Ages)[81] and Germany (which had a strong feudal bourgeoisie). From 1545–80, both Spain and Germany fell away, and the lead was taken by England, the Netherlands, and parts of France and Scotland. The parallelism between these areas and the areas of the Reformation is striking; as also the parallel

[79]Christopher Hill, *Reformation to the Industrial Revolution, 1530–1780*, Vol. II of the Pelican Economic History of Britain (London: Penguin Books, 1967), 34.

[80]"Then, in the 1520's, came the great revolt, the revolt of Luther. It was not a revolt within the old mature economy of Europe: it was a revolt of the 'underdeveloped,' 'colonial' areas of northern and central Europe, long taxed, frustrated and exploited

(as they felt) to sustain the high civilization of the Mediterranean and the Rhine." H. R. Trevor-Roper, "Religion, the Reformation, and Social Change," in *The European Witch-Craze of the Sixteenth and Seventeenth Centuries, and other Essays* (New York: Harper, 1969b), 32–33.

[81]See Baron, *A Social and Religious History of the Jews*, **XII**, p. 18.

in time between the first phase of the Price Revolution and Luther (both about 1520–40); and between the second phase and Calvin (both about 1545–80).[82]

One does not have to accept all the historical details to see that it is a relevant hypothesis.

What is more, we have further evidence on the close tie of religious and politico–economic conjunctures when we turn to the triumph of the Counter-Reformation in Poland. Stefan Czarnowski makes a careful analysis of why Poland shifted *back* to Catholicism from a Reformation that seemed to be gaining ground, and why it shifted with great rapidity. He notes a synchronization between the moment when the landed nobility *(noblesse territoriale)* took over political power in what he terms a "class dictatorship" and the moment of the Catholic offensive. In his analysis, he distinguishes between the aristocracy, the landed nobility, and the lesser *(petite)* nobility. He argues that it was in the ranks of the aristocracy (as well as the bourgeoisie) that the partisans of the Reformation were located. He sees the aristocracy as lusting after Church lands. The smaller landowners found it more difficult to fight the local curate, supported as he was by the still powerful Catholic episcopacy. So there was less advantage to them in embracing Protestantism and, hence they tended not to do so. Czarnowski and others point out that in Poland while it was the seigniors who favored Calvinism, the king and the bourgeoisie were inclined to Lutheranism.[83] This is quite a twist on the Weberian theme, but reminds us of the argument

[82]P. C. Gordon-Walker, *Economic History Review,* **VIII,** 1937, p. 14. "The concrete results of the Lutheran phase . . . were destruction of the Catholic hold upon the middle and lower classes, and sanction for the seizure of Catholic and feudal property. . . .

"[In the second stage] the chief problem now became class-acclimatisation. . . . The bourgeoisie had to exchange its subservience for the will to govern. . . . The working class had to exchange its loose, extensive labour for disciplined, regular and organized work. . . . Capitalist society . . . needed individualism to cloak the class-structure of society, which was nearer the surface than in feudalism. . . . The class-structure was both justified (from eternity) and obscured by the stress upon the individual's spiritual behavior as the sole criterion of social division; and that the correct social ethic and methods for its enforcement were ready-made for self-imposition amongst the Elect, and, if necessary, coercive imposition upon the Reprobate. . . .

"[As] class-acclimatisation which was the highest task of the Reformation was gradually accomplished, Protestants had to yield to other activities which became more important; above all, it had to give place to the secular state and to science [pp. 16–17, 18]."

[83]See Stefan Czarnowski, "La réaction catholique

en Pologne à la fin du XVIe siècle et au début du XVIIe siècle," *La Pologne au VIIe Congrès International des Sciences Historiques* (Société Polonaise d'Histoire, Varsovie: 1933), **II,** 300. See Thadée Grabowski: "The principal proponents of Lutheranism [between 1530 and 1555] were members of the clergy, bourgeois of German descent, and Polish students returning from Wittenberg and Königsberg, then centers of university education.

"The nobility were hardly involved at all. Lutheranism was too moderate for them and sustained . . . the royal power. . . . Being too dogmatic and monarchical, it displeased . . . the seigniors which were dreaming about a republic in the style of the ancient Roman republic." "La réforme religieuse en Occident et en Pologne," *La Pologne au Ve Congrès Internationale des Sciences Historiques,* Bruxelles, 1923 (Warsaw, 1924), 67–68.

Stanislaw Arnold however argues that this is not quite accurate: "It is certain that a part, but only a part, of the magnates became adepts of the Reform, especially of Calvinism. But Calvinism attracted particularly the most progressive elements of the middle nobility who were in power at this time in the country, especially in the Diet." "Les idées politiques et sociaux de la Renaissance en Pologne," *La Pologne au Xe Congrès International des Sciences Historiques à Rome* (Warszawa: Académie

of Erik Molnar who saw an alliance of the monarchy, lesser nobility, and bourgeoisie against the aristocracy. Czarnowski further argues that the "bourgeoisie" was in this case split. The "upper bourgeoisie" of the towns, especially of Cracow (an "old" commercial center), was allied to the aristocracy. He is speaking here of the town patriciate, those who from the end of the fifteenth century to about the middle of the sixteenth century "were part of that class of money-handlers and merchants which came into existence with the rise of nascent capitalism."[84] But Poland was not destined to take the path of England as a locus of the bourgeoisie of the European world-economy. The great crisis of 1557, of which we shall speak later, ruined not only financiers in Lyon, in Antwerp, in southern Germany, but the bankers of Cracow as well:

> [From] that moment on, the elan of the aristocracy and of Calvinism was weakened. . . . The goods which allowed the great commercialism of previous times to flourish: the silver of Olkusz, Hungarian copper, industrial products, continuously declined in value. The money with which the peasants paid their rent depreciated with a despairing rapidity. Meanwhile the international demand for Polish wheat, potassium, oak bark, skins, and horned beasts grew greater. The more that the producer of these latter goods could do without coins, use forced unpaid labor of serfs, and barter his products against those he needed, the better he resisted [the effects of the financial crisis]. This was precisely what the small and medium-sized landowners/nobility were able to do.[85]

This did not mean, notes Czarnowski, that there was no bourgeoisie in Poland. The Cracovian bourgeoisie may have been ruined, but they were replaced by Italians, Armenians, and Germans. In 1557, one international network fell and the Polish bourgeoisie–aristocracy who were tied into it fell with it. After that, another came into existence. The Poles who worked with it—the "nobility"—accepted Poland's new role in the world-economy. They gave their children to the Jesuits to educate, to keep them out of the influence of the old aristocracy: "Thus the Church of Poland ended by being, one might say, the religious expression of the nobility."[86] And

Polonaise des Sciences Institut d'Histoire, 1955), p. 160. Arnold criticizes Czarnowski specifically. See p. 159ff.

Fox and Tazibir however offer pictures close to those of Czarnowski and Grabowski. See P. Fox, "The Reformation in Poland," in *The Cambridge History of Poland*, I. W. F. Reddaway *et al.*, eds., *From the Origins to Sobieski (to 1696)* (London and New York: Cambridge Univ. Press, 1950) 329, 345–346; J. Tazbir, "The Commonwealth of the Gentry," in Aleksander Gieysztor *et al.*, *History of Poland* (Warszawa: PWN—Polish Scientific Publishers, 1968), 185–186.

[84]Czarnowski, p. 301.
[85]*Ibid.*, p. 304.
[86]*Ibid.*, p. 308. J. Umiński emphasizes the non-

Polish ingredients of Protestantism in Poland: "Lutheranism attracted chiefly the population of German descent inhabiting the Polish towns. . . . The so-called anti-Trinitarianism, which soon began to displace Calvinism among the nobility, was properly speaking not Polish. Polish anti-Trinitarianism was organized and directed mainly by foreigners." "The Counter-Reformation in Poland," in *The Cambridge History of Poland*, I, 412.

Janusz Tazbir points out the international implications of religious nationalism: "Catholicism marked Poland off from Protestant Sweden, Orthodox Russia and Mohammedan Turkey [p. 228]." Conversely, "the Papacy sought to realize, through Poland, not only its own political aims but often those of the Hapsburgs [p. 229]."

this nobility now triumphant could define Polish "national" sentiment as virtually indistinguishable from Catholic piety.

Thus it was that Poland became securely Catholic because she became definitively a peripheral area in the world-economy. The Counter-Reformation symbolized (not caused) the "social regression" that Protestants viewed it as being. But their pious shock was misplaced. For the social advance of northwestern Europe was made possible by the "regression" of eastern and southern Europe as well, of course, as by the domination of the Americas. The Counter-Reformation was directed not merely at Protestantism but at all the various forces of humanism we associate with the Renaissance. This is illustrated by the tensions between Venice and Rome in the sixteenth century. The controversy culminated in 1605 when Venetian actions in limiting certain rights of the Church led to an excommunication by Rome of the Venetian Senate. The Counter-Reformation was in Italy a Counter-Renaissance,[87] and its triumph there was a function of the transformation of northern Italy into a semiperipheral arena of the world-economy.

It is because the Church as a *transnational* institution was threatened by the emergence of an equally transnational economic system which found its *political* strength in the creation of strong *state* machineries of certain (core) states, a development which threatened the Church's position in these states, that it threw itself wholeheartedly into the opposition of modernity. But paradoxically, it was its very success in the peripheral countries that ensured the long-run success of the European world-economy. The ultimate abatement of the passions of the battle of the Reformation after 1648 may not have been because both sides were exhausted and there was a stalemate, but rather because the geographical division of Europe was the natural fulfilment of the underlying thrusts of the world-economy. As to the role of the Protestant ethic, I agree with C. H. Wilson:

> If Protestantism and the Protestant ethic seem to explain less of economic phenomena than they seemed at one time to do, it also appears there is, in the Reformation era, less to be explained. . . . Leadership in economic matters passed slowly from the Mediterranean to the north, and as the Italian cities declined, those of the Netherlands rose; but there was little in the way of business or industrial technique in use in northern economies that would have been unfamiliar to a Venetian merchant or a Florentine clothier of the fifteenth century.[88]

[87]"For behind the new heresies of Lutheranism and Calvinism lurked enemies potentially even more dangerous, of whose existence the Catholic authorities were well aware. And the Curia was in the long run probably less concerned to suppress Protestantism (a passing challenge) than to turn back the growing political particularism of the age, to centralize an ecclesiastical administration almost everywhere becoming increasingly federal and autonomous, to subordinate an assertive laity to clerical authority, to end the dangerous freedoms of ar-

tistic and intellectual culture, to reassert the validity of the objective, hierarchical and philosophic conception of reality that supported its claims to oversee the manifold activities of Christendom; in short, to bring to a halt all those processes that historians have come to associate with the age of the Renaissance." William J. Bouwsma, *Venice and the Defenses of Republican Liberty* (Berkeley: Univ. of California Press, 1968), 294.

[88]C. H. Wilson, "Trade, Society and the State," in *Cambridge Economic History of Europe*, **IV**, 490.

In the sixteenth century, some monarchs achieved great strength by means of venal bureaucracies, mercenary armies, the divine right of kings and religious uniformity *(cuius regio)*. Others failed. This is closely related, as we have suggested, to the role of the area in the division of labor within the world-economy. The different roles led to different class structures which led to different politics. This brings us to the classic question of the role of the state vis-à-vis the leading classes of the new capitalist era, the capitalist landlords and the capitalist merchants, sometimes not too helpfully abbreviated as aristocracy and bourgeoisie, since some aristocrats were capitalists and others not. Unfortunately, what role the state played, whose agent it was, the degree to which it could be thought to be a third force all are questions upon which no consensus exists. Pierre Vilar has well stated the basic underlying theoretical issue:

> A question of particular relevance is how feudal revenues were divided, by means of a system of "adjudications" and in other ways, between an idle aristocracy and an intermediary class of "merchant-cultivators" or similar types who transformed seigniorial revenues and held them ready for new types of investment; in other words how feudal revenues came to be mobilized for capitalist investment.[89]

One aspect of this is the degree to which the absolute state should be seen to be the last resort of a feudal aristocracy facing the "crisis" of feudalism, the reduction of seigniorial revenues, and the onslaught of other classes (the commercial bourgeoisie, the yeoman farmers, the agricultural laborers). One view is that of Takahashi, who sees absolutism as "nothing but a system of concentrated force for counteracting the crisis of feudalism arising out of this inevitable development [in the direction of the liberation and the independence of the peasants]."[90] This view is substantially shared by Christopher Hill,[91] V. G. Kiernan,[92] Erik Molnar,[93] and Boris Porchnev.[94]

A second point of view argues that the politics of the absolute monarchy is one upon which the aristocracy had a considerable, perhaps determining, influence, but one in which the monarch was more than a simple extension of the needs of this aristocracy. For example, Joseph Schumpeter argues:

[89]Vilar, *Past & Present*, No. 10, pp. 33–34.

[90]Takahashi, *Science and Society*, **XVI**, p. 334.

[91]"[The] absolute monarchy is a form of feudal state." Christopher Hill, "The Transition from Feudalism to Capitalism," *Science and Society*, **XVII**, 4, Fall 1953, 350.

[92]"Absolute monarchy in the West grew out of feudal monarchy of a particular sort." V. G. Kiernan, *Past & Present*, No. 31, p. 21.

[93]"All the forms of European absolutism have served the interests of the class of nobles or landowners and have expressed their political domination over the other classes of society, first of all over the peasantry, who were the most numerous class."

Erik Molnar, *XIIe Congrès International des Sciences Historiques: Rapports*, **IV**, p. 156.

[94]Porchnev seeks to explain the bourgeois origins of the bureaucracy as deriving precisely from the inherent contradictions of a feudal system where the indivisibility of political and economic phenomena mean that each noble pursues specific interests not necessarily in accord with those of the totality of his class. "There results a strange difficulty: the power structure of an aristocratic state [*état nobiliaire*] cannot be placed in the hands of aristocrats, for the taking of power by any specific group of aristocrats must inevitably provoke an overt struggle with the other elements of the seigniorial class." *Les soulèvements populaires*, p. 563.

> Thus the aristocracy [under the absolute monarchs] as a whole was still a powerful factor that had to be taken into account. Its submission to the crown was more in the nature of a settlement than a surrender. It resembled an election—a compulsory one, to be sure, of the king as the leader and executive organ of the nobility. . . .
>
> The reason [the nobles did not resist, even passively, the regime] was, in essence, because the king did what they wanted and placed the domestic resources of the state at their disposal. . . . It was a class rather than an individual that was actually master of the state.[95]

Braudel similarly insists that the conflict of king and aristocracy was a limited one, which included an effort by the king, on the one hand, to bring the nobility under his discipline, but, on the other hand, to protect its privileges against popular pressure.[96] The position of A. D. Lublinskaya seems very close to Braudel.[97] J. Hurstfield emphasizes the dilemma of the monarchies which "found it hard to rule without the nobility; but they found it equally difficult to rule with them."[98]

A third point of view, perhaps the most traditional one, is that of Roland Mousnier, in which the monarchy is viewed as an autonomous force, often allied with the bourgeoisie against the aristocracy, occasionally mediating the two.[99]

But is there a necessary conjuncture of these two propositions, that of the relatively autonomous role of the state machinery and that of seeing the class struggle as one between aristocracy and bourgeoisie? Molnar does not seem to think so. In the first place, he uses more categories. He talks of a feudal aristocracy to whom the monarch was in clear opposition. In addition, there was a "nobility" and a bourgeoisie, both potential allies.

[95]Joseph A. Schumpeter, "The Sociology of Imperialism," in *Social Classes, Imperialism* (New York: Meridian Books. 1955), 57–58.

[96]"In Christianity as in Islam, the nobility occupy the top position and they will not give it up. . . . Everywhere the State, a social as well as political revolution, but one just getting under way, has to struggle against these 'possessors of fiefs, masters of villages, fields, and roads, guardians of the immense rural population.' To struggle means to come to terms with them, to divide them and also to preserve them, for it is not possible to retain power in a society without the complicity of the ruling class. The modern State takes this weapon in hand; were it to break it, everything would have to be redone. And the recreation of a social order is not a small affair, all the more since no one thought seriously of this possibility in the sixteenth century." Braudel, *La Méditerranée*, **II**, p. 50 (cf. also p. 54).

[97]"In relation to both groups of the nobility the policy of absolutism aimed at defending their basic class interests, that is, their property. The absolute monarchy did not meet the openly reactionary demands of the *noblesse d'epée*, and in many cases

it directly opposed them—but this is still a long way from 'egalitarianism.' " A. D. Lublinskaya, *French Absolutism: The Crucial Phase, 1620–1629* (London and New York: Cambridge Univ. Press, 1968), 26.

[98]J. Hurstfield, "Social Structure, Office-Holding and Politics, Chiefly in Western Europe," *New Cambridge Modern History*, **III**: R. B. Wernham, ed., *The Counter-Reformation and the Price Revolution, 1559–1610* (London and New York: Cambridge Univ. Press, 1968), 130. He goes on: "But all over Western Europe the function of the aristocracy in society was inherently self-contradictory. As barons they had traditional ambitions and rivalries which frequently ran counter to the interests of the king's peace. But as hereditary officeholders—as many of them were—they were expected to enforce a legal system whose continuing strength depended upon the curbing of their own selfish powers."

[99]"[The] absolute monarchy results from the rivalry of two classes, the bourgeoisie and the nobility. . . .

"This class struggle is perhaps the principal factor in the development of absolute monarchies." Mousnier, *Les XVIe et XVIIe siècles*, pp. 97, 99.

The nobility seems to be smaller landowners and those more oriented to capitalist agriculture, but it is not entirely clear. He points out that while absolutism seemed to involve heavy taxation upon the peasantry, it is less clear how the money was distributed. On the one hand, the increased state budget was used to pay the tax collectors and the bureaucracy, pay off the state loans, and purchase military equipment, all of which benefited the bourgeoisie. But on the other hand, all the current expenses of the state—that is, the maintenance of court and army—were payments to the nobility. He sees this as a tactic of "maneuvering . . . between the nobility and the bourgeoisie."[100] Engels similarly points to the ways in which the state machinery comes to play, in some ways against its inner will, a mediating function, at least during "exceptional periods."[101]

One source of this unclarity about the relationship of monarch and aristocracy is the vagueness that exists about the composition of the nobility. No doubt family membership in the nobility varies over time; the situation is one of perpetual mobility in all societies with a nobility. But the sixteenth century was an era in which there was not only family mobility but occupational mobility. For example, the status of noble was presumably incompatible in Western feudalism with the occupation of entrepreneur. This was probably already a myth to a considerable extent in the municipalities of the late Middle Ages. By the sixteenth century, this was simply untrue in the whole of Europe, and in both urban and rural areas. Everywhere—in Italy, Hungary, Poland, East Elbia, Sweden, England—members of the nobility had become entrepreneurs.[102] This was so much the case that the nobility successfully sought to eliminate any formal impediments to this

[100]Molnar, *XIIe Congrès International des Sciences Historiques: Rapports,* **IV,** p. 163.

[101]"In possession of the public power and the right of taxation, the officers . . . present themselves as organs of society standing *above* society. . . .

"As the state arose from the need to keep class antagonisms in check, but also arose in the thick of the fight between the classes, it is normally the state of the most powerful, economically ruling class, which by its means becomes also the politically ruling class, and so acquires new means of holding down and exploiting the oppressed class. . . . Exceptional periods, however, occur when the warring classes are so nearly equal in forces that the state power, as apparent mediator, acquires for the moment a certain independence in relation to both. This applies to the absolute monarchy of the seventeenth and eighteenth centuries [but not the sixteenth?] which balances the nobility and the bourgeoisie against one another." Frederick Engels, *The Origins of the Family, Private Property and the State* (London: Lawrence Wishart, 1940), 195–196.

[102]In discussing the phenomenon of aristocrats in business in the fifteenth century in various Italian

cities, Paul Coles says: "The nobility were rehearsing the major role which they were to play in European business activity of the sixteenth century. . . ." "The Crisis of Renaissance Society: Genoa, 1448–1507," *Past & Present,* 11, April 1957, 19.

"[Toward the end of the fifteenth century there begins] a new tendency of Hungarian development [which] can be summed up economically as the growing participation of the seigniorial class in market-trading and later in the very production of these commodities [wine, cattle, wheat]." Zs. P. Pach, "En Hongrie au XVIe siècle: l'activité commerciale des seigneurs et leur production marchande," *Annales E.S.C.,* **XXI,** 6, nov.–déc. 1966, 1213.

"The participation of the nobility in the export trade of agricultural and livestock products, beginning at the end of the fifteenth century and increasing over time, constitutes another of those interesting phenomena linked to the development of direct exploitation of the land by the nobility. . . . The factor which facilitated this development [of nobles as importers of cloth and luxury goods] in the sixteenth century was the gradual suppression

occupational role wherever it existed, as happened in Spain.[103] Nor should we forget that, although in Protestant countries the Church was seeing its lands confiscated, the sixteenth century was an era of the Church as a capitalist agricultural entrepreneur, especially in Italy.[104]

The other side of this coin was that the successful bourgeois was constantly becoming a landowner and a noble, and thirty years later, it surely became difficult to draw clear lines separating the two. R. H. Tawney sees it as a normal process which was however much accelerated in the sixteenth century.[105] Both Braudel[106] and Postan[107] agree with the perception of

of customs duties in the largest towns, under the pressure of the nobility." Marian Malowist, *Studi in onore di Armando Sapori*, **I**, pp. 587–588.

"The range of the Junker's entrepreneurial activity widened during the sixteenth century with the assault on the industrial production and trading monopolies of the towns. . . . The emergence of the Junker as a trader, a smuggler, and an industrialist definitely smashed the traditional balance between town and countryside." Hans Rosenberg, *American Historical Review*, **XLIX**, p. 236.

Beginning with the late sixteenth century, most of the Roman countryside was in the hands of a dozen landowners. Their appellation was *mercanti di campagna*, merchants of the countryside. See Delumeau, *Vie économique*, **II**, p. 571.

The military entrepreneurs discussed previously were for the most part of noble origin. If not, this sort of entrepreneurial activity usually led to ennoblement. See Redlich, *Vierteljahrschrift für Sozial- und Wirtschaftsgeschichte*, Suppl. No. 47, pp. 411, 427–428.

See also Goran Ohlin, "Entrepreneurial Activities of the Swedish Aristocracy," *Explorations in Entrepreneurial History*, **VI**, 2, 1953, 147–162; Lawrence Stone, "The Nobility in Business, 1540–1640," *Explorations in Entrepreneurial History*, **X**, 2, Dec. 1957, 54–61.

[103]"To avoid any future difficulties, and to establish a uniform rule, a papal bull was obtained in 1622, which extended to all [Military] Orders the statute of Santiago, to the effect that the prohibition on commercial activity [for members of the Orders] applied not to large-scale entrepreneurs, but only to the small shopkeeper or common money-lender. . . . Trade was clearly a vital factor for Spain's continuance as an imperial power, and it could not be dismissed as vulgar money-making." L. P. Wright, "The Military Orders in Sixteenth and Seventeenth-Century Spanish Society," *Past & Present*, No. 43, May 1969, 66–67.

[104]"In the race for investment in land the Church and the non-profit associations [*gli enti morali*] (for the most part under the influence of the [Church]) found themselves in an advantageous position because they had entered it earlier than the laymen

and the 'private parties.' At the end of the 1500's half of the landed property of Milan was in their hands with well-known social and religious consequences." Bulferetti, *Archivio storico lombardo*, **IV**, pp. 21–22.

[105]"From a very early date the successful merchant has bought dignity and social consideration by investing his savings in an estate. The impecunious gentleman has restored a falling fortune of his house by commercial speculations, of which marriage into a commercial family, if not the least speculative, is not the least profitable. At the beginning of the sixteenth century both movements were going on simultaneously with a rapidity which was before unknown and which must be explained as the consequence of the great growth of all forms of commercial activity. The rise of great incomes drawn from trade had brought into existence a new order of businessmen whose enterprise was not confined to the seaport and privileged town, but flowed over into the purchase of landed estates, even before the secularization of monastic endowments made land speculation the mania of a whole generation." R. H. Tawney, *Agrarian Problems in the Sixteenth Century* (New York: Longmans, 1912), 187.

[106]"The bourgeoisie, in the sixteenth century, tied to the monarchy and in the service of the king, was always on the verge of disappearing. It risked not only ruin. Were it to become too rich, or fatigued by the hazards of merchant life, it bought offices, rents, titles or fiefs and allowed itself to be tempted by the life of the noble, with its prestige and its tranquil indolence. Service for the king led quite rapidly to ennoblement; by this path also, which does not leave out other paths, the bourgeoisie disappeared." Braudel, *La Méditerranée*, **II**, p. 68.

[107]"The propensity to retire into a life of *rentier* is not difficult to account for. The physical hazards of active trade abroad were not always matched by opportunities for enrichment, and the opportunity grew poorer as the foreign markets grew smaller. At the same time it is probable that capital was still sufficiently scarce to command a high rate of interest. . . . [This process] accounted only for one component of the new *bourgeoisie*, and there were other components as well. Above all, there were

a continuing pattern of transition from entrepreneur to rentier for those of non-noble status and see in it a search for long-run security. What is crucial, however, is to appreciate that despite this occupational mobility, the strength of the landowning class did not disintegrate. As Marc Bloch put it: "The seigniorial regime had not been undermined. Indeed it would soon take on a renewed vigor. Rather seigniorial property, to a large extent, changed hands."[108] It was the absolutism of the monarch which created the stability that permitted this large-scale shift of personnel and occupation without at the same time, at least at this point in time, undoing the basic hierarchical division of status and reward.

What then of the presumed key role of the state in assisting the commercial bourgeoisie to assert itself, to obtain its profits and keep them? The liaison was surely there, but it was a question of degree and timing, the mutual support of the early liaison developing into the stifling control of later years. It is no accident that the symbiotic relationship of merchant and king would come in the seventeenth and eighteenth centuries to seem one of direct opposition. Hartung and Mousnier see signs of this tension already in the sixteenth century.[109] Douglass C. North and Robert Paul Thomas, in seeking to outline the rise of various judicial and economic institutions which had the effect of encouraging entrepreneurial activity based on rising productivity as opposed to forms of commerce which merely redistributed income,[110] try to elucidate the conditions under which it made sense to have emphasized the institutional role of the state. They argue that alongside the economic distortions that state intervention brings to the market and hence to the likelihood of

the men who looked for and found security not outside but within occupations still largely commercial. They did so by trading in a smaller way, within well-organized and protected markets. . . . The bulk of the trade was in the hands of men of middling substance. And being middling they looked for safety and found it in cooperation, in combination, and more generally in numbers." M. M. Postan, in *Cambridge Economic History of Europe*, **II**, p. 218.

[108]Bloch, *Caractères originaux*, **I**, p. 129.

[109]"The liaison of capitalism and absolute monarchy was not always favorable to capitalism. It is certain that from the 60's of the 16th century, bankruptcies that affected all of Europe and state regimentation were by no means minor contributing factors to the slowing down of the progress of commercial capitalism on the continent. This slowing down was in the long run favorable on the other hand to the absolute monarchy. It prevented a too rapid growth of the bourgeoisie and helped to maintain a relative equilibrium of bourgeoisie and nobility, which is certainly one of the features of absolutism in western Europe." Hartung and Mousnier, *Relazioni del X Congresso Internazionale di Scienze Storiche*, **IV**, p. 45.

Christopher Hill makes a similar argument: "Monopolies were not bad in themselves: they were a form of protection for new industries in a backward country. The earliest monopolies were concerned with national defense—the Elizabethan Mines Royal aimed to make England independent of foreign copper for the manufacture of cannon. There were similar monopolies for saltpetre and gunpowder. But monopolies rapidly became noxious when they were used for fiscal purposes by governments hostile to capitalist development. In the seventeenth century monopolies were created, in order to be sold. . . ." *Reformation to the Industrial Revolution*, p. 96.

[110]They refer not only to economies of scale but to the reduction of transactions costs by means of "internalizing" externalities (via the reorganization of property rights), reducing costs of information (via brokerage), and reducing costs of risk (via joint stock-companies). See Douglass C. North and Robert Paul Thomas, *Economic History Review*, **XXIII**, pp. 5–7.

innovation, one must place the fact of "coercive power which permits government to undertake policies even though they may be strongly objected to by a part of the society."[111] This way of formulating the issue alerts us to seeing the functions of statism for capitalism in terms of a cost-benefit analysis. Whereas for the aristocracy the absolute monarchy represented a sort of last-ditch defense of privilege, for those deriving their income through the maximization of the economic efficiency of the firm the state machinery was sometimes extremely useful,[112] sometimes a major impediment.

We have now outlined the two main constituent elements of the modern world-system. On the one hand, the capitalist world-economy was built on a worldwide division of labor in which various zones of this economy (that which we have termed the core, the semiperiphery, and the periphery) were assigned specific economic roles, developed different class structures, used consequently different modes of labor control, and profited unequally from the workings of the system. On the other hand, political action occurred primarily within the framework of states which, as a consequence of their different roles in the world-economy were structured differently, the core states being the most centralized. We shall now review the entire sixteenth century in terms of a process, one in which certain areas *became* peripheral or semiperipheral or the core of this world-economy. We shall thereby try to give flesh and blood to what has risked thus far being abstract analysis. We shall also hopefully thereby demonstrate the unity of the whole *process*. The developments were not accidental but, rather, within a certain range of possible variation, structurally determined.

[111]*Ibid.*, p.8.

[112]Simon Kuznets puts his finger on the key element in the usefulness of the state for entrepreneurs: "The existence of sovereign government definitely implies the possibility of decision where conflicts that quite often bear directly and explicitly on major alternatives of economic growth may exist within the country and among the people." "The State as the Unit of Study of Economic Growth," *Journal of Economic History,* **XI**, 1, Winter 1951, 28.

4

FROM SEVILLE TO AMSTERDAM: THE FAILURE OF EMPIRE

Figure 5: "Massacre of the Innocents," oil painting by Pieter Brueghel, the Elder. It was painted about 1565 as a protest against Spanish atrocities in the Netherlands.

The European world-economy in creation was a great prize, and it is understandable that men should seek to control it. The route of imperial domination was the classical route, familiar to the men of the era. Many dreamed of the possibility. The Hapsburgs under Charles V made a valiant attempt to absorb all of Europe into itself. By 1557, the attempt had failed. And Spain steadily lost not only its political imperium but its economic centrality as well. Many cities aspired to be the hub of the European world-economy. Seville, Lisbon, Antwerp, Lyon, Genoa, and Hamburg all had aspirations if not claims. But in fact it would be Amsterdam, an unlikely candidate in 1450, which by 1600 had achieved preeminence. We turn now to this story of the failure of empire, entailing the decline of Spain and all of her allied city-states in favor of the successful rebels of Amsterdam.

The upward economic swing beginning circa 1450 created a buzzing prosperity first of all in all the old centers of trade, in what has been called the dorsal spine of Europe—Flanders, southern Germany, northern Italy—and, of course, as a result of the discoveries, Spain. It is striking how precisely these areas came to make up the Hapsburg empire under Charles V. In this expansion, the newest significant element was the sixteenth-century transatlantic trade of Spain, centering on Seville and her *Casa de Contratación de las Indias,* a trade which became so important that "all of European life and the life of the entire world, to the degree that there existed a world, could be said to have depended [on this traffic]. Seville and her accounts . . . should tell us the rhythm of the world."[1]

How did Spain come to play such a central role? After all, as we discussed in Chapter One, it was Portugal, not Spain, which took the lead in the fifteenth century overseas expansion of Europe. Furthermore, the fifteenth century was not a tranquil era in the history of Spain. Indeed, Jaime Vicens Vives says that "the word crisis sums up the history of Spain in the fifteenth century."[2]

The crisis was political (a period of rebellion and of internal warfare) and economic (the Europe-wide recession). Spain's reaction to the crisis in economic terms was to develop her sheep industry and to gain, as a result of low prices, a considerable share of the (reduced) world market.[3] The strength of the combine of wool producers in Spain, the *Mesta,* was

[1]Chaunu, *Séville,* **VIII,** (1), p. 14.

[2]Jaime Vicens Vives, *Approaches to the History of Spain,* 2nd ed. (Berkeley: Univ. of California Press, 1970), 76.

[3]"Without the crisis of the 14th and 15th centuries, without the attractiveness of the probably low prices of Castilian wool, without the well-known slowdown of the exports of English wool, without the active cloth industry of the Italian towns, the rise of sheepherding in Castile with its millions of wandering sheep would have been impossible, unthinkable." Braudel, *La Méditerranée,* **I,** p. 84.

such that attempts by potential Castilian bourgeois to have the king adopt protectionist policies in the fourteenth and fifteenth centuries all failed.[4] Even under the Catholic Monarchs, Ferdinand and Isabella, presumed partisans of industrial activity, Vicens finds that the industries mentioned produced "either luxury items or had only a local market."[5] Unlike England, Spain was not moving toward developing an important textile industry.[6] Ironically, it may have been the very fact of Castilian competition, combined with the depression of the late Middle Ages, that encouraged England to move on the road to industrial growth. The fact was, however, that Spain did not take this road.

But then, if the Spanish economy was structurally so weak, how do we explain the central *economic* position of Spain in the first half of the sixteenth century? Partly because the weaknesses were long-term, not short run, and partly because at some levels the political system was strong. Castile had a clear "national" task throughout the Middle Ages. On the one hand, there was the *Reconquista,* the gradual expulsion of the Moors from the Iberian peninsula, which culminated in the fall of Moslem Granada and the expulsion of the Jews from Spain, both in 1492, the year of Columbus. On the other hand, there was the drive to unify the Christian states of Hispania. This drive culminated in the union at the summit only, Aragon retaining a separate legislature, state budget, and socio–legal system.

Because Spain was built on a reconquest, feudalism as a *political* form was weak.[7] Consequently, as José Maravall states it, "having a political and social order which was not based on the feudal structure provided favorable

[4]"The fact that the cloth industry had attained considerable development in the 15th century is shown, in fact, by the proposal of the Cortes of 1348, held in Madrigal, requesting a ban on imports of foreign cloth and on exports of Castilian wool. This decidedly protectionist policy was not accepted by John II because of the firm intervention of the Mesta and those who were profiting from the wool trade: merchants, collectors, traders, and usurers. It was then that a violent struggle was begun by the great landowners to prevent the development of the Castilian bourgeoisie. This is the sense in which we must understand the agreement made by the Cortés of Toledo in 1462, when Henry IV fixed at one-third the proportion of the Mesta's total exports that could be retained by the Castilian cloth industry. This was a low proportion if there was any intention of keeping inside the country the wealth which was going abroad and making the fortune of so many aristocrats." Jaime Vicens Vives, *An Economic History of Spain,* pp. 259–260.

[5]*Ibid.,* p. 305.

[6]"Castile was basically an exporter of primary materials, wool, and not of cloth, and . . . one of the foundations of the mercantilist policy of the Catholic Monarchs was the encouragement of the merino wool of the *mesta* flocks. England, on the other hand, which also had a flourishing sheep industry, nine-tenths of whose fleece had traditionally been exported to Flanders, commenced already in the fourteenth century, as the flock began to grow in size, a policy of parallel industrial transformation of the primary materials." José Larraz, *La época del mercantilismo en Castilla (1500–1700)* (Madrid: Atlas, 1943), 20.

[7]Luis Vitale lists five reasons why feudalism was weaker in Spain than in other west European countries. They center around the impact of the Arab-Moslem conquests, the role of the Mesta, and the early role of the bourgeoisie. See *Latin America: Reform or Revolution?* pp. 34–36.

terrain for the development of 'state' forms."[8] A first-rate road system made political and economic liaison of the center and the periphery relatively easy.[9] Ferdinand and Isabella aided the *Mesta* to create a strong system of *national* markets.[10] They provided a system of individual mobility, albeit within a context of maintaining the values of rank and hierarchy.[11] They strengthened the bureaucracy, making of it one that was "rooted in the community . . . of which it is . . . 'pars rei publicae.' "[12] They nationalized, so to speak, the Catholic clergy.[13] Above all, they created "conditions in which Castile's existing economic potential could be amply realized."[14]

[8]Maravall, *Cahiers d'histoire mondiale,* **VI**, p. 791. This is not necessarily to say that the economic role of large landowners was weak. On the contrary Pierre Vilar argues on the basis of this fact that Spanish imperialism was "the highest stage of feudalism." "Le temps de Quichotte," *Europe,* **34**, No. 121–122, janv.–févr., 1956, 8.

However, we have already argued in the previous chapter why the emergence of such phenomena as *latifundia* should not be considered a "second feudalism" but rather "capitalist agriculture." See nonetheless Vilar: "In Spain, . . . or rather in *Castile,* the ruling classes engaged in the Conquista in the manner of the Reconquista: *in the feudal manner.* The occupation of lands, forcing men into submission, gathering up treasures, all this does not prepare one to 'invest' in the capitalist sense of this word. A nascent bourgeoisie could have done it. And from about 1480 to 1550, it did not hesitate to do it. However, because of its location on the money circuit, it first tried the unstable capitalism of ports and fairs. Furthermore, the 'productive forces' at its disposition—land, men, technical innovations—came quite quickly up against the law of diminishing returns on the plains of Castile. Thereupon, after 1550, it felt the sterilizing effect of monetary injections. One spends, one imports, one lends at interest. One produces little. Prices and wages jump up. Parasitism develops and enterprise wanes. It means poverty on the morrow [*Ibid.,* pp. 9–10]."

Vilar's discussion of the "unstable capitalism of ports and fairs" seems to refer to Marx's skepticism about the progressive quality of merchants' capital: "Yet its development . . . is incapable *by itself* of promoting and explaining the transition from one mode of production to another. . . . On the contrary, wherever merchants' capital still predominates we find backward conditions." *Capital,* **III**, Ch. XX, p. 327. Italics added.

[9]"It was 'truck transport' which permitted Castile to ensure links between the peripheral regions of the Peninsula which surrounded it and which often separated it from the sea. It is this phenomenon, not Castile by itself, which as [Ortega y Gasset] said, 'made Spain'. . . .[F]or is not the case of communication the first requirement for effective government? Castile . . . for all these reasons, became the center of gravity, the heart of Spain." Braudel, *La Méditerranée,* **I**, p. 49.

[10]"The special interest of Ferdinand and Isabella in restricting and regulating the *portazgos* [ancient tax levied by towns on goods and animals en route to market] on the flocks of the Mesta was due to the greatly increased importance of this organization as an instrument for the encouragement of internal communication. The nationalization of trade, the evolution from local and metropolitan to national markets, was a stage of economic advance the profound importance of which these enlightened sovereigns were the first in the peninsula to appreciate." Klein, *The Mesta,* p. 223.

[11]"The effect of Ferdinand and Isabella's policies was therefore to confirm and consolidate the importance of rank and hierarchy in Castilian society, but at the same time to offer opportunities of social advancement to many who would have had much less hope of acquiring a privileged status in earlier reigns. One of the keys to advancement was education, which might eventually lead to a place in the royal service. The other was wealth, particularly urban wealth, which made possible the alliance between the rich merchant families (including those of Jewish origin) and families of respectable aristocratic lineage." J. H. Elliott, *Imperial Spain, 1469–1716* (New York: Mentor, 1966), 113–114.

[12]Maravall, *Cahiers d'histoire mondiale,* **VI**, p. 805.

[13]"The Catholic Kings wanted no foreigners in the ecclesiastical positions in their kingdom, partly in order to preserve their privileges, but partly also in view of the little which foreigners knew about things in their kingdom [*Ibid.,* p. 86]."

[14]Elliott, *Imperial Spain,* p. 117. Elliott notes on the other hand a number of negative features about their reign. See pp. 123–127.

If the bullion flowed through Spain, if Castile could soar into the center
of the European sky, it was, says Pierre Vilar, "consequence as well as
cause."[15] But consequence of exactly what? Of in fact a long series of
facts centering around the economic role of metals: the weak bullion base
of the Mediterranean world, the previous centrality of the Sudan as supplier
of gold, the impact of Portuguese expansion on the northern African intermediaries of the Italian city-states, the role of the Genoese in Spain, and
the Genoese drive to find a non-Portuguese source of bullion (a drive
which only Spain was in a position to implement).

Let us trace this complex story. We have already spoken of the role
of bullion in medieval trade, and how Sudanic gold came to Europe via
North Africa to the Christian Mediterranean world. Suddenly in the middle
of the fifteenth century, the North African role diminished greatly. The
extent of this diminution seems to be a matter of some debate. Braudel
speaks of a collapse of the North African position.[16] Malowist acknowledges
reduction but calls it not catastrophic.[17] The sudden shortage of bullion

[15]Vilar, *Past & Present*, No. 10, p. 32. And, adds
Alvaro Jara, Spain soars ahead because it conquers
Hispanic America: "Spain was not insulated from
the framework of Europe; it received, in its turn,
the influence and reflection of the economic
necessities which came out of the latter's financial
centers and were communicated to her in one way
or another. Whether these were the needs of Spanish consumption (understanding consumption in
the general sense of provisions) or the requirements
of the military campaigns of the monarchy, the
Indian colonies formed a protective backdrop, without whose help it would be impossible to explain
Spanish predominance. Thus we do not need to
hesitate to speak of a coincidence of parallel interests
between the broad thrusts *(rasgos)* of the Spanish
conquest in America—based on private enterprise—and the needs of the metropolitan state-
machinery, which encouraged a form of conquest
that permitted it to amass prodigious treasures with
neither risk nor great outlay." "Estructuras de colonización y modalidades del tráfico en el Pacifico sur
hispano-americano," *Les grandes voies maritimes dans
le monde, XV-XIXe siècle, VII Colloque, Commission Internationale d'Histoire Maritime* (Paris: S.E.V.P.E.N.,
1965), 251.

[16]"From the last decade of the 15th century,
Sudanese gold begins no longer to arrive, at least
not in the same quantity, in the cities of North Africa. . . . [The] Mediterranean is suddenly deprived
of an important part of its supply of gold. . . .
Thereupon, the local prosperity of North Africa
falls like a house of cards. . . . What happened? . . .
Only this: in 1460, the Portuguese explorers
reached the approaches to the Gulf of Guinea. . . .
[B]eginning in 1482, São Jorge da Mina . . . is constructed. . . . This commences a veritable 'capture'
of Saharan economic traffic, a reversal of direction

and a diversion." Fernand Braudel, "Monnaies et
civilisation: de l'or du Soudan à l'argent
d'Amerique," *Annales E.S.C.*, I, 1, janv.-mars 1946,
12–13.

[17]"Much misunderstanding has arisen concerning
the influence of the Portuguese trading-posts *(comp-
toirs)* of Arguin (after 1448) and of São Jorge da
Mina (1482–1484) on the African gold commerce.
We must admit that the trading-post of Arguin to
some degree modified the direction of export of
Sudanese gold, without however damaging the
interests of the trans-Saharan countries and their
populations. . . . The Sudanese suppliers as well
as the Berber nomads occupied in this trade had,
upon the arrival of Europeans in Arguin, new purchasers of the mineral, but this in no way affected
their position in this trade. This was not true for the
traditional purchasers of the gold, that is to say, the
Maghrebians and the Egyptians who, it seems, were
to feel the effects of the appearance of European
competitors on the coasts of West Africa. . . .
At the present stage of research, we think rather
that the export of Sudanese gold to the Maghreb
and Egypt had perhaps lessened in fact, but that
this phenomenon was not of catastrophic proportions for the Arab world. It seems to us doubtful
as well that the decrease in the circulation of gold
at Ouardane can be attributed to the activity of
trading-post at the port of Mina, which was located
too far away. . . .
Whatever the case, at the end of the sixteenth
century and at the beginning of the seventeenth,
Djenné was still, according to the author of the
Tarikh es-Soudan, a great center of exchange of
Sahara salt for gold." Marian Malowist, "Le commerce d'or et d'esclaves au Soudan Occidental,"
Africana Bulletin, No. 4, 1966a, 56–59.

aggravated the Spanish state's financial burden, which had been rising steadily because of growing military and court expenses, by leading to a fall of value in the money of account, the *maravedi*.[18]

The financial crisis was serious, and it caused the Genoese of Spain to react, both because they were Spain's bankers and the purchasers of the gold. We have already spoken of Genoa's role in Spanish commerce. The Genoese were involved in many ways, not only as financiers.[19] But why could not the Genoese have gotten their gold via Portugal? Perhaps Portugal's strength, as the lead country in exploration, meant that its terms were not as advantageous for Genoa as those Spain would offer.[20] Perhaps also because its very strength led to a lack of imagination. Imagination is usually nothing but the search for middle run profits by those to whom short run channels are blocked. When channels are not blocked, imagination suffers. Portugal was already doing well enough with navigation down the African coast. It felt no pressure to set out on risky westward navigational ventures.[21] Chaunu eloquently argues the sensible proposition that it was not luck that accounts for Spain's discovery of America. She was the country best endowed in the context of the times "not only to seize opportunities that were offered, but to create them for herself."[22] England employed the Italian, John Cabot, but his second "English" expedition required *Spanish* support. It was not until the seventeenth century that France and England became countries of overseas exploration and not until the eighteenth that they really succeeded.[23]

Spain succeeded, however, in the sixteenth century in creating a vast empire in the Americas, one as large as the cost of maritime transport

[18]See Miguel Angel Ladero Quesada, "Les finances royales de Castille à la veille des temps modernes," *Annales E.S.C.*, **XXV**, mai-juin 1970, 784.

[19]The Genoese and other non-Spaniards played a large role not only in the search for bullion and in commerce in Spain, but in primary production in the Canary Islands. See Manuela Marrero, "Los italianos en la fundación de Tenerife hispánico," in *Studi in onore di Amintore Fanfani*, **V**: *Evi moderni e contemporaneo*. (Milano: Dott. A. Giuffrè-Ed., 1962), 329–337.

[20]"It is to the honor of Genoa, if honor there be, to have been the only one then to search for an anti-Portuguese solution," Braudel, *Annales E.S.C.*, **I**, p. 14.

[21]"The failure of Columbus in Portugal may be explained by the very advance of geographical knowledge of the milieux of government and commerce in the country. No one was willing to entrust money and human lives on the basis of such obviously erroneous hypotheses, if one was sensible and took into account especially the distances that had to be covered.

"Portugal moreover was too deeply committed to

the successful policy of African exploration, to the search via the Sudan of a direct maritime route to the Spice Islands, to take so thin a chance as the unlikely route proposed by Columbus." Chaunu, *Séville*, **VIII** (1), pp. 89–90.

[22]*Ibid.*, p. 235.

[23]"From the moment that one refuses to recognize that there has been a technological revolution between the early 16th century and the 18th century, that one refuses to admit that the role of Castile was logically favored by its position as the spearhead of the 'Reconquista,' at the intersection of the Mediterranean and the Ocean, at the intersection of the highpoint of the tradewinds to the north and the point of counterflow (*contreflux*) of the middle latitudes to the south, then one attributes to chance, that is to absurdity, the discovery of America by a Genoese navigator setting out from Palos, and, in the same spirit, the monopoly of Andalusia, once one neglects to consider the winds, the life of Andalusia in the 16th century, the long, and learned, effort of the southern Iberians of the peninsula, becomes the absurd fruit of an absurd caprice. . . ." Chaunu, *Séville*, **VIII** (1), pp. 236–237.

would permit.[24] It meant a lightning growth of transatlantic trade, the volume increasing eightfold between 1510 and 1550, and threefold again between 1550 and 1610.[25] The central focus of this trade was a state monopoly in Seville, which in many ways became the key bureaucratic structure of Spain.[26] The central item in the transatlantic trade was bullion. At first the Spaniards simply picked up the gold already mined by the Incas and used for ritual.[27] It was a bonanza. Just as this was running out, the Spaniards succeeded in discovering the method of silver amalgam which enabled them profitably to mine the silver which existed in such abundance, and which represented the truly significant inflow of bullion to Europe.[28]

The "lightning growth" of trade was accompanied by a spectacular political expansion in Europe as well. Upon the coronation of Charles V as Holy Roman Emperor in 1519, his domain in Europe included such varied and noncontiguous areas as Spain (including Aragon), the Netherlands, various parts of southern Germany (including Austria), Bohemia, Hungary, Franche-Comté, Milan, and Spain's Mediterranean possessions (Naples, Sicily, Sardinia, the Balaerics). For a moment, this empire, parallel in structure to the contemporaneous Ottoman Empire of Suleiman the Magnificent and the Moscovite Empire of Ivan the Terrible, seemed to be absorbing the political space of Europe. The nascent world-economy seemed as though it might become another imperium. Charles V was not alone in the attempt to absorb the European world-economy into his imperium. Francis I of France was trying to do the same thing,[29] and France had the advantages

[24]"Hispanic America attained its dimensions in less than half a century. The failure to conquer Araucanian Chile proves it. Colonial America, in order to grow and to survive, soon began to base itself on an efficient system of maritime commerce. The cost of transport demanded a large production of riches. It condemned the first America to the only systems capable of producing these riches immediately." Pierre Chaunu, *L'Amérique et les Amériques* (Paris: Lib. Armand Colin, 1964), 85–86.

[25]"How astonishing the dynamism of this first phase of expansion: We are truly in the presence here . . . of a structural break. This disparity is easily explained: 1504-1550, is this period not the transition from nothingness to being?" Chaunu, *Séville*, **VIII** (2), p. 51.

[26]"The Spanish State unable to free itself, in its oceanic policy, from the influence of the group of men in Andalusia who controlled the situation, sought with all its might to ensure a strict respect for a monopoly [that of Seville] which favored, among its other virtues, the efficacy of its control." Huguette and Pierre Chaunu, "Economie atlantique, économie-monde (1504-1650)" *Cahiers d'histoire mondiale*, **I**, 1, juil. 1953, 92.

[27]See Alvaro Jara, "La producción de metales pre-

ciosos en el Perú en el siglo XVI," *Boletín de la Universidad de Chile*, No. 44, nov. 1963, 60. See the Table on p. 63.

[28]"It is probable that without the use of the technique based on the properties of mercury, the whole European inflationary process would have been stopped and American mining would have entered a phase of stagnation and decadence." Alvaro Jara, "Economía minera e historia económica hispano-americana," in *Tres ensayos sobre economía minera hispano-americana* (Santiago, Chile: Centro de Investigaciones de Historia Americana, 1966), 37.

[29]"There is [in the sixteenth century] a French imperialism. First of all the French refused to acknowledge any dependence on the [Holy Roman] Emperor. 'The king is emperor in his kingdom.' Then Charles VIII went down to Italy [1494] to reach the Orient, lead a crusade, obtain some new titles in the Empire of Constantinople. He entered Naples, golden crown on his head, holding in his hands the imperial scepter and globe, everyone shouting: 'Most august Emperor.' Whereupon there was panic in Germany where they thought that he was desirous of the title of Emperor of the Germanic

of size and centrality.[30] But France had less resources for the attempt, and the election of Charles V over Francis I as Emperor was a great setback. Nonetheless France, located "in the heart"[31] of the Spanish Empire, was strong enough to make the story of the following 50 years one of virtual constant warfare between the two imperial giants, Hapsburg and Valois, a struggle that would result eventually in the exhaustion of both in 1557, and the end for a long while of dreams of imperium in Europe.

The long struggle of the two giants, France and Spain, was fought out in military terms principally on the Italian peninsula, first in the Franco-Spanish wars of 1494–1516, and then in the Hapsburg–Valois rivalry that continued until 1559.[32] The reason for the struggle over Italy, from the viewpoint of the empires, was clear. The northern Italian city-states had been in the late Middle Ages the centers of the most "advanced" economic activities, industrial, and commercial, on the European continent. If they no longer monopolized long-distance trade they were still strong in their accumulated capital and experience,[33] and an aspiring world-empire

Holy Roman Empire. This French imperialism, which took the form of attempts to dominate Italy and of the candidacy of Francis I in the [election of the] Holy [Roman] Empire of 1519, was replaced, after the election of Charles V by a defensive policy against the Hapsburgs." Mousnier, *Les XVe et XVIe siècles*, pp. 132–133.

Michel François similarly speaks of the "double heritage" of Francis I, on the one hand as a monarch whose authority had been created by the hard work of the political philosophers *(légistes)* and the men of government, and on the other hand as the heir to the imperial Italian enterprises of Charles VII and Louis XII which had "opened singularly enlarged perspectives for the French monarchy." "L'idée d' empire sous Charles-Quint," in *Charles Quint et son temps*, Colloques internationaux du C.N.R.S., Paris, 30 sept.-3 oct. 1958 (Paris: Ed. du C.N.R.S., 1959), 25.

[30]As of 1500, it could be said that: "England, Spain and Burgundy-Austria swung as it were in a kind of orbit around the first and greatest European power, France. . . . [T]he chief advantages of France were its size and central position. For Western Europe at the beginning of the modern period, France was the heartland. England, Spain, Italy and the German Empire lay arranged symmetrically about it, so that France commanded interior lines. And the heartland was also the most populous kingdom." Garrett Mattingly, *Renaissance Diplomacy*, pp. 129, 131.

[31]The expression is that of a sixteenth-century Spaniard, A. Pérez, in *L'art de gouverner. Discours adressé à Philippe II*, cited in Ruggiero Romano, "La pace di Cateau-Cambrésis e l'equilibrio europeo a metà del secolo XVI," *Rivista storica italiana*, **LXI**, 3, 1949, 527.

[32]See Oman, *A History of the Art of War*, p. 14, who comments on what a large percentage of the military struggle took place in Italy.

[33]R. S. Lopez suggests that the parallel to England after 1870 is apt, and adds: "If all this implied decadence, neither the Italians nor their new competitors fully realized it." "The Trade of Medieval Europe: The South" in *Cambridge Economic History of Europe*, **II**: M. M. Postan and E. E. Rich, eds., *Trade and Industry in the Middle Ages* (London and New York: Cambridge Univ. Press, 1952), 351.

Amintore Fanfani also observes the glory of Italy in the late Middle Ages and its decline in the fifteenth and sixteenth centuries: "The good fortune of Italy in the Middle Ages is linked to the fact that the ports on the Peninsula were the base of western trade to the Levant and of Levantine trade to the West; furthermore it is linked to the fact that the commercial links with the Levant were of a colonial nature while the links to the west were those of an exporter of industrial goods. It is not quite true that the Italians possessed their own colonies overseas and lacked them across the Alps, but in fact all or nearly all the Italians enjoyed the benefits of a purely economic colonization, not very apparent, hence rather greatly tolerated, but substantial, and therefore extremely fruitful. . . .

Beginning in the 14th century two facts began to perturb the situation on which was based Italian prosperity. . . . With the Turks who advanced, and the French and the English who liberated themselves, the perspectives of prosperity for the Italian economy were reduced, although throughout the sixteenth century, they managed not to be eliminated entirely." *Storia del lavoro in Italia dalla fine del secolo XV agli inizi del XVIII* (Milano: Dott. A. Giuffrè-Ed., 1959), 24–25.

needed to secure control over them. In the scattered political map of Italy,[34] only Lombardy had developed a relatively strong state machinery over a medium-sized area,[35] but one apparently still too small to survive politically.[36]

We are in fact speaking of a relatively small area, "a narrow urban quadrilateral, Venice, Milan, Genoa, Florence, with their discordances, their multiple rivalries, each city having a somewhat different weight. . . ."[37] The political problem for these city-states (as for those of Flanders) had long been to "[emancipate] themselves from feudal interference and [at the same time to keep] at bay the newer threat of more centralized political control offered by the new monarchies."[38] One of the ways they kept the monarchies at bay was to be linked to an empire.[39] So although Gino Luzzatto

[34]Why Italy was so disunited politically is not relevant to this analysis. The answer probably lies in the political developments of the early Middle Ages combined with the relative economic success in the late Middle Ages of some of the city-states. One classic explanation is that offered by Jacob Burckhardt: "The struggle between the Popes and the Hohenstaufen left Italy in a political condition which differed essentially from that of other countries of the West. While in France, Spain, and England the feudal system was so organized that, at the close of its existence, it was naturally transformed into a unified monarchy, and while in Germany it helped to maintain, at least outwardly, the unity of the empire, Italy had shaken it off almost entirely. The Emperors of the fourteenth century, even in the most favorable case, were no longer received and respected as feudal lords, but as possible leaders and supporters of powers already in existence; while the Papacy, with its creatures and allies, was strong enough to hinder national unity in the future, not strong enough to bring about that unity. Between the two lay a multitude of political units . . . whose existence was founded simply on their power to maintain it." *The Civilization of the Renaissance in Italy* (New York: Modern Library, 1954), 4.

See Wallace Ferguson: "The states of Renaissance Italy were necessarily different from those of the North, because the past history of Italy was so different, and that difference was partly the result of two purely political facts: first, the fact that from the tenth to the thirteenth century Italy was annexed to the German Holy Roman Empire, and, second, the fact that the Popes ruled a territorial state stretching right across the center of the peninsula." "Toward the Modern State," in Wallace Ferguson, ed., *Renaissance Studies*, **No. 2** (London, Ontario: Univ. of Western Ontario, 1963), 147–148.

[35]"What set Lombardy off from the rest of Italy in the 14th and 15th centuries was its political transformation. . . . [The] *signoria* [is] the fundamental 'innovation' underlying the vast economic changes in Lombardy in the period. . . . In more ways than one, the economic policies of the time in Lombardy, reaching out well beyond the policies of the commune, foreshadowed the mercantilism of England, not least in the treatment accorded the Church and its lands. . . .

"In what might be called their public works, their policies encouraging industry and trade, their improvements in agriculture, and in their population policies (material encouragements for large families, and for repatriation and migration to Lombardy), the Milanese dukes in many, perhaps all, significant ways anticipated the so-called mercantile states still in the offing." Douglas F. Dowd, "The Economic Expansion of Lombardy, 1300–1500: A Study in Political Stimuli to Economic Change," *Journal of Economic History,* **XXI**, 2, June 1961, 147, 160.

[36]For evidence that this phenomenon was more general than just Lombardy, see Mousnier, *Les XVIe et XVIIe siècles,* p. 93.

[37]Braudel, *La Méditerranée* **I**, p. 354.

[38]C. H. Wilson, *Cambridge Economic History of Europe,* **IV**, p. 492.

[39]Henri Pirenne points out the two-step process of emancipation of some of the towns: "A municipal republic did not, as a matter of fact, enjoy an absolute independence when it had thrown off its allegiance to its immediate lord. It only escaped the power of the count or bishop by putting itself under the direct power of the higher suzerain. The German town was only free in the sense that it exchanged the neighbouring and very active authority of its lord for the distant and very feeble authority of the Emperor." *Early Democracies in the Low Countries* (New York: Norton, 1971), 183.

The consequences for the creation of strong states were clear: "While in France and England the modern state found its chief adversaries in the great nobles, in the Low Countries it was the towns that hindered its progress [p. 187]."

describes what happened between 1530 and 1539 as Italy coming under the "domination direct or indirect of Spain over the largest part of the peninsula,"[40] and Paul Coles similarly says that "the dominant theme of international history in the first half of the sixteenth century was the struggle for Italy between French and Spanish imperialism,"[41] it is not clear that the city-states resisted this form of "domination" all that much. They may well have considered it their best alternative. We should remember that this was a world-economy and that the economic loci of activities and the "nationalities" of key economic groups were not related in any one to one fashion with the foci of political decision-making. Within such a framework, the linkup of the city-states and the empire was primarily a "marriage of interests."[42] Whereupon metaphor became reality. Ruth Pike points out that the greatest increase of Genoese in Seville occurs between 1503 and 1530 and that by the middle of the century they "largely controlled the American trade and exerted a powerful influence over the economic life of Seville."[43] However, as the Portuguese had done to an earlier wave of Genoese, the Spaniards dissolved them by absorption: "With naturalization came stability and assimilation, which in sixteenth-century Spain could only lead to the abandonment of trade by their descendants."[44]

In addition to controlling three of the four main Italian city-states (Venice remained outside its dominion), the empire of Charles V had two other economic pillars: the merchant-banking houses of southern Germany (in particular the Fuggers), and the great mart of the European world-economy of the "first" sixteenth century, Antwerp.

The situation of the merchant cities of southern Germany, on the other side of the Alps, was not really too different from those in northern Italy. R. S. Lopez, for example, notes that: "In the fifteenth century, the most rapidly advancing region lay in the towns of Southern Germany and Switzerland."[45] From 1460 to about 1500 or 1510 silver mining grew at a very rapid rate in central Europe, providing a further source of economic

---

[40]Gino Luzzatto, *Storia economica dell'età moderna e contemporanea*, Part I, *L'età moderna* (Padova: CEDAM, 1955), 116. He adds: "Venice alone remained independent in Italy, but she was immobilized by the ever more serious pressure of the Turks [p. 117]." Still, Domenico Sella feels that "Venice found her own luck in the crisis that struck the other cities of the Peninsula." *Annales E.S.C.*, **XII**, p. 36.

[41]Coles, *Past & Present*, No. 11, 41.

[42]"Sixteenth-century imperialism in Italy involved more than the initial military conquest. A measure of economic compensation for the forfeiture of political independence by the Italian republics was a necessity, rendered especially urgent in the case of Genoa, whose citizens were eager to repair losses caused by the contraction of Levantine trade. Compensation of this sort, Spain, through her possessions in the New World and later Flanders, was admirably fitted to provide. The history of relations between Spain and the Italian states in the sixteenth century is basically that of a marriage of interests, the Spanish crown battening politically upon Italy, Italian businessmen battening economically upon Spain [*Ibid.*, p. 41]." See his references in footnote 57, pp. 46–47.

[43]Ruth Pike, *Journal of Economic History*, **XXII**, p. 370.

[44]*Ibid.*, p. 351.

[45]Lopez, *Cambridge Economic History of Europe*, **II**, p. 349.

strength.[46] The sixteenth-century expansion of trade only seemed to reinforce the German role as a conduit of trade between northern Italy and Flanders.[47] At first not even the growth of Atlantic trade and the relative decline of Mediterranean trade seemed to affect their economic prosperity, especially once they were able to participate in the benefits of the Atlantic trade within the framework of the Hapsburg Empire.[48]

This was the era of the flourishing of those most spectacular of all modern merchant-capitalists, the Fuggers. The apogee of their strength, the era of Charles V, has sometimes been called the Age of the Fuggers. The Fuggers bought Charles' imperial throne for him.[49] They were the financial kingpins of his empire, his personal bankers par excellence. A contemporary chronicler, Clemens Sender, said of them:

> The names of Jakob Fugger and his nephews are known in all kingdoms and lands;
> yea, among the heathen, also. Emperors, Kings, Princes and Lords have sent to
> treat with him, the Pope has greeted him as his well beloved son and embraced
> him, and the Cardinals have risen up before him. All the merchants of the world
> have called him an enlightened man, and all the heathen have wondered because
> of him. He is the glory of all Germany.[50]

The Fuggers and Charles gave each other their power and their base. But this also meant that they rose and fell together. For, in reality, the activity of the Fuggers was "limited to the confines of the Empire of Charles, and was international only to the extent . . . that empire can be regarded as international. . . ."[51] When Charles and his successors could not pay, the Fuggers could not earn. In the end, the total loss of the Fuggers in unpaid debts of the Hapsburgs up to the middle of the seventeenth century "is certainly not put too high at 8 million Rhenish gulden."[52]

[46]See John U. Nef, "Silver Production in Central Europe, 1450–1618," *Journal of Political Economy*, **XLIX**, 4, Aug. 1941, 575–591. On the links between the role of the southern Germans in the new colonial worlds of Spain and Portugal and industrial operations in southern Germany, see Jacob Streider, "Origin and Evolution of Early European Capitalism," *Journal of Economic and Business History*, **II**, 1, Nov. 1929, 18.

[47]"Throughout most of the 16th century northern Italy and Flanders were the two chief areas of industrial and commercial activity in Europe, and contact between them was essential to the prosperity of both. . . . For all except very bulky goods, [the] overland routes had many advantages. . . . The flourishing trans-Alpine trade between northern Italy and southern Germany did not long survive the 16th century." Parry, *Cambridge Economic History of Europe*, **IV**, p. 185.

[48]Gerald Strauss says of the reaction of German merchants to the geographical reorientation of their

trade: "[They] had adjusted to this development by intensifying their ancient connections with these centers of European traffic [Antwerp and Lisbon]. For about half a century after 1500 the new commerce quickened the international trade of Nuremberg and Augsburg and other cities, and it more than compensated for the rapid decline of the transalpine carrying trade on which they had formerly depended." *Nuremberg in the Sixteenth Century* (New York: Wiley, 1966), 148. Parry, cited just above, seems to think there was not a "rapid decline" until a century later. Both authors agree however that, at least up to about 1550, commerce was flourishing in southern Germany. See also Streider, *Journal of Economic and Business History*, 14–15.

[49]See Richard Ehrenberg, *Capital and Finance*, pp. 74–79.

[50]Cited in *ibid.*, p. 83.

[51]Lublinskaya, *French Absolutism*, p. 8.

[52]Ehrenberg, *Capital and Finance*, p. 131.

But even more important than northern Italy or the Fuggers was
Antwerp, which "played in the economic life of the sixteenth century a
leading role."[53] J. A. van Houtte has traced the great difference between
Bruges in the fourteenth century, a "national" market center (that is,
primarily for Flanders) and Antwerp in the sixteenth century, an "international" market center, which linked the Mediterranean and Baltic
trades with the transcontinental trade via southern Germany.[54] Not only
did Antwerp coordinate much of the international trade of the Hapsburg
Empire, but it was also the linchpin by which both England and Portugal
were tied into the European world-economy.[55] It served among other things
as England's staple.[56] If it was able to play this role despite the fact that
Anglo–Italian trade, for example, would have been less expensive in transport costs had it transited via Hamburg, this was precisely because it offered
the multiple side advantages to merchants that only such an imperial mart
had available.[57]

In addition, at this time, Antwerp became the supreme money market
in Europe, "caused mainly by the increasing demand for short-term credit,

[53]Emile Coornaert, "La genèse du système
capitaliste: grande capitalisme et économie
traditionelle au XVIe siècle," *Annales d'histoire
économique et sociale*, **VIII**, 1936, 127.

[54]See J. A. van Houtte, "Bruges et. Anvers:
marchés 'nationaux' ou 'internationaux' du XIVe
au XVIe siècles," *Revue du Nord*, **XXXIV**, 1952,
89–108. Herman van der Wee (1963): "Antwerp's
emergence as Western Europe's commercial met-
ropolis and the growth of *transcontinental* trade centered on Central Germany were linked inseparably." *The Growth of the Antwerp Market and the European Economy* (The Hague: Nijhoff, 1963), **II**, 119.
He argues that this occurs c. 1493–1520 and that
the southern Germans consequently took "the commercial lead" in Antwerp during the first half of
the sixteenth century [p. 131]. See Pierre Jeannin:
"[T]he overland commerce of Antwerp in the
16th century attained an importance equal to,
if not superior to, that of maritime commerce."
Vierteljahrschrift für Sozial- und Wirtschaftsgeschichte,
XLIII, p. 198. See Ehrenberg, *Capital and Finance*,
pp. 112–113.

[55]"The cloth trade of England had a decisive
impact on the prosperity of Antwerp. Its curve coincided with that of the general development of the
Antwerp market. . . . Portuguese, Southern Germans, and Englishmen constituted the three pillars
of Antwerp's world commerce." J. A. van Houtte,
"Anvers aux XVe et XVIe siècles: expansion et
apogée," *Annales E.S.C.*, **XVI**, 2, mars–avr. 1961,
258, 260.
    See Philip de Vries: "[A]t the beginning of
the 16th century, England constituted . . . with the

Hapsburg countries of Burgundian heritage an
economic unity, of which Antwerp and Flanders
were the financial and industrial centers."
"L'animosité anglo-hollandaise au XVIIe siècle,"
Annales E.S.C., **V**, 1, janv.-mars 1950, 43.
    On the other hand imperial rivalry hurt Antwerp's
economic relations with France. "Quite naturally
Antwerp's trade with Lyon and particularly her
export of Portuguese spices suffered severely." Van
der Wee, *The Growth of the Antwerp Market and the
European Economy*, **II**, p. 144.

[56]Jan Craeybeckx defines the concept of a staple
thus: "Whoever interests himself more in reality
than in abstract distinctions will easily agree that
the staple was before anything else a market. Only
a market of some importance could claim to make
its 'staple' obligatory and force merchants to subject
themselves to its rules. . . . Privileges, which only
a few cities were able to offer, were not therefore
essential. Any city having a market or 'staple' (in
the narrow sense of the term) sufficiently to impose
its domination, de jure or de facto, on a more or
less extended region should be considered a staple."
"Quelques grands marchés de vins français dans
les anciens Pays-Bas et dans le Nord de la France
à la fin du Moyen Age et au XVIe siècle: Contribution à l'étude de la notion d'étape," *Studi in onore
di Armando Sapori*, **II**. (Milano: Istituto Edit. Cisalpino, 1957), 819.

[57]See Wilfred Brulez, "Les routes commerciales
d'Angleterre en Italie au XVIe siècle," *Studi in onore
di Amintore Fanfani*, **VI**: *Evo moderno* (Milano:
Dott. A. Giuffrè-Ed., 1962), 181–184.

chiefly occasioned by the Emperor Charles V's world policy. . . ."[58] Antwerp not only served as the securities exchange of the empire; the city itself as a collectivity became one of Charles's chief moneylenders.[59] Since empires had no firm tax base, they found it difficult to obtain the kind of credit modern states manufacture with relative ease. A sixteenth-century empire had credit to the extent that its sovereign did.[60] Thus he had to turn to the cities as "centers of public wealth"[61] to guarantee his loans. But cities too were limited in credit, and they in turn needed the guarantee of some large house such as the Fugger, as this account by Lonchay illustrates:

> The credit of the towns, as that of the provinces, as those of the receivers, was limited. That is why some financiers demanded the guarantee of a solvent commercial house, preferably that of a large bank, before agreeing to a loan to the government. Thus, in 1555, the merchants asked as a guarantee for a loan of 200,000 pounds letters of obligation from the states or the "responsion" of the Fugger. Maria of Hungary asked Ortel, the factor of that house to give his approval and promised to give him in exchange a counter-guarantee of income from taxes (*le produit des aides*).[62]

Thus Charles V, Castile, Antwerp, the Fuggers were all imbricated in a huge creation of credit laid upon credit, cards built upon cards, the lure of profits based on hope and optimism.

From the 1530s on, the growing trans-Atlantic trade gave Antwerp a new phase of expansion.[63] The combination of the two foci of commercial

---

[58]Van der Wee, *The Growth of the Antwerp Market and the European Economy*, **II**, p. 362. He argues that, despite a relative decline in the later years, "the Antwerp money market remained the strategic center of Hapsburg finances even in the early fifties [p. 206]."

Capital flowed by means of arbitrage between Antwerp, Venice, Lyon, Plaisance, Florence, Séville, and Rouen. See José-Gentil da Silva, "Trafics du Nord, marchés du 'Mezziogiorno,' finances génoises: recherches et documents sur la conjoncture à la fin du XVe siècle," *Revue du Nord*, **XLI**, 1959, 140.

[59]See Fernand Braudel, "Les emprunts de Charles-Quint sur la Place d'Anvers," *Charles Quint et son temps*, Colloques internationaux du C.N.R.S., Paris, 30 sept.-3 oct., 1958 (Paris: Ed. du C.N.R.S., 1959), 197–198.

[60]"Because of the development of wealth in general, States today enjoy almost unlimited credit. A nation, that is a productive nation, obtains money easily. . . .

"Public offerings, facility, rapidity are the characteristics of the loans obtained by modern states. It was different in the 16th century. Because of the rarity of capital, its dispersion, high finance

offered its services only at an onerous price to the borrower; the lack of its knowledge concerning the country's resources made it distrustful of the sovereign. It made no distinction between the Chief of State and the person of the prince, or if you wish, between a king and a private person." H. Lonchay, "Etude sur les emprunts des souverains belges au XVIe et au XVIIe siècles," *Académie Royale de Belgique, Bulletins de la Classe des Lettres et des Sciences Morales et Politiques et de la Classe des Beaux-Arts* (1907), 926, 928.

[61]*Ibid.*, p. 941.
[62]*Ibid.*, p. 943.
[63]"The new commercial expansion was very advantageous to the Netherlands. This was no coincidence. The Hispano-Netherlandish contacts had been given a solid dynastic union, backed by the increasing consumption of Spanish wool by the Netherlandish textile industry. The precious metals of the New World started to play a dominant role in Hapsburg world politics from the thirties onward. Since their financing was largely based on the Antwerp money market, this was a further important stimulus. In 1539 the Netherlandish economy was already so strongly linked with Spain via Antwerp that van der Molen wrote during the crisis,

expansion—the transcontinental trade in which southern German merchants were so central and the Atlantic trade of the Spanish (*cum Genoese*), both coming together in the Antwerp market which was also a money market created the atmosphere of "a feverish capitalistic boom."[64] This boom had its own dynamic which overwhelmed the politico-administrative framework of the Hapsburg putative world-empire. Beset by the incredible financial strains caused on the one hand by the social crisis that was raging in the Germanies and the military expenditures resulting from the desire to encompass the rest of Europe, either the empire had to go bankrupt or the capitalist forces. The latter turned out to be stronger. Let us review the two strains under which the empire operated.

In political terms, the years 1450–1500 were a time of "consolidation of the principalities" of Germany, a difficult task but one which succeeded in part. Geoffrey Barraclough writes: "The princes . . . raised Germany out of its inherited anarchy. . . ."[65] The consolidation was however too partial. When the Reformation and the Peasants' War of 1525 came along to perturb the new prosperity, the political divisions made it impossible to contain the turmoil, as other countries could do at this time.[66] The failure of the German "nation" has been variously explained. Napoleon once said that it was the failure of Charles V to put himself as the head of German Protestantism.[67] Engels has argued at length that it was the fear of Luther and the middle class of the revolutionary aspirations of the peasantry.[68] Tawney has pointed out the contrast with England where the peasants (that is, the yeomen) found significant allies among other classes and were considered sufficiently important "to make them an object of solicitude to statesmen who were concerned with national interests."[69]

What caused the social crisis with its politically self-defeating qualities, not too different in consequences from the outright subjection which large parts of Italy suffered? Probably the same factor: lack of *prior* political unity, that is, the absence of even an embryonic state machinery. "Germany" in the early sixteenth century is an excellent illustra-

---

caused by the devaluation: 'if large orders do not come soon from Italy or Spain, most of the Flemish clothiers will go bankrupt.' " Van der Wee, *The Growth of the Antwerp Market and the European Market*, II, p. 178.

[64]*Ibid.*, p. 317.

[65]Geoffrey Barraclough, *The Origins of Modern Germany* (Oxford: Blackwell, 1962), 352.

[66]Antwerp too suffered from great social tensions during the first half of the sixteenth century, that is during the era of Charles V, though here the main complaints seem to come from urban workers suffering the problems of the wage-lag which would not be overcome till 1561. See Charles Verlinden, "Crises économiques et sociales en Belgique à l'époque de Charles Quint," *Charles-Quint et son temps*, Colloques internationaux du C.N.R.S., Paris,

30 Sept.-3 Oct. 1958 (Paris: Ed du C.N.R.S., 1959), esp. p. 183. Antwerp however had no political upheaval at this time, a demonstration perhaps of Fanon's hypothesis that urban workers are less likely than peasants to resort to spontaneous uprisings. See Frantz Fanon, *The Wretched of the Earth* (New York: Grove Press, 1966), 85–117.

[67]Cited by A. J. P. Taylor, *The Course of German History* (London: Hamilton, 1945), 163. See Hurstfield: "The Protestant Reformation which might have unified Germany against the Pope divided Germany against the Emperor." *New Cambridge Modern History*, III, p. 130.

[68]Friedrich Engels, *The Peasant War in Germany*, in *The German Revolutions* (Chicago, Illinois: Univ. of Chicago Press, 1967), *passim*.

[69]Tawney, *Agrarian Problem*, p. 347.

tion of how deeply divisive "nationalist" sentiment can be if it precedes rather than grows within the framework of an administrative entity. Charles V could not lead German Protestantism because he was involved in an empire. German statesmen could not take into account the needs of the yeomen within the framework of national interests when no state existed within which to register whatever political compromise might be achieved. Men turned to the political arenas in which they might achieve their ends. These were the principalities and, since these were too small to be economically meaningful, they turned to their outside benefactors. The result was floundering and disaster.

The critical moment seems to have been in the early years of Charles V's rule. A. J. P. Taylor argues somewhat dramatically but not unpersuasively:

> The first years of Charles V were the moment of Goethe's phrase which, once lost, eternity will never give back. The moment for making a national middle-class Germany was lost in 1521 perhaps forever, certainly for centuries. By 1525, it was evident that the period of national awakening had passed, and there began from that moment a steady advance of absolutism and authoritarianism which continued uninterruptedly for more than 250 years. . . .[70]

In any case, the turmoil went on in a very acute form until the Treaty of Augsburg in 1555 and its solution of a divided Germany, based on *cuius regio eius religio*. Nor was the turmoil to end even then. In the early seventeenth century, Germany became the battleground of the Thirty Years War, and underwent severe regression, both demographically and economically.

The social turmoil of the Germanies was however only one problem for Charles V and not perhaps the greatest. It is surely insufficient to explain the collapse of his empire. Why then did it split apart? Why was it ultimately reduced essentially to Spain plus Hispanic America? And why did this latter Spain lose its preeminence and become part of the semiperiphery of Europe? Pierre Chaunu sees the rise of the economic importance of Hispanic America, its centrality to the economic life of the Hapsburg Empire, and indeed all of Europe, as "not the consequence but the cause of the partition of the states of Charles V."[71] J. H. Elliott and Ramón Carande similarly argue that the European imperialism of Charles V came to be

---

[70]Taylor, *The Course of German History*, p. 162.

[71]Pierre Chaunu, "Séville et la 'Belgique,' 1555–1648," *Revue du Nord*, **XLII**, 1960, 269. He adds: "Have we paid sufficient attention to the fact that this so-called division is in reality a multiplication? Have we realized to what extent the States of Philip II after 1560 were, despite the impressions given by historians too attentive to Europe only, immeasurably vaster than the empire of Charles V before 1540, that is before the fundamental changes caused by America. . . ?

"Once this perspective is accepted, the partition of 1555–1559 is placed in its true perspective. Charles V did not consider his son incapable of continuing in Europe the tasks he had begun. It seemed impossible to hold together states ever more vast, ever more numerous, extended beyond the seas, at the level of a world which measured in terms of the suffering, fatigues and time of men is far more nearly akin to a *cosmos* than to our very small planet of the 20th century. . . . It is under the impulsion of America at the end of the *conquista* that the empire of Charles V was split or more precisely that it was constituted around its axis of nourishment, the traffic between Seville and the Caribbean [pp. 270–271]."

unduly expensive for Spain, especially for Castile.[72] Indeed, Braudel argues that even the reduced empire (Spain and the Netherlands without central Europe) would turn out to be "too vast" in terms of its ability to keep its financial head above water, given the great price inflation.[73] The argument seems to be that the political extremities are a financial burden in moments of inflation that are greater than their value as income, especially perhaps in this early stage of capitalism.[74] Spain was an empire when what was needed in the sixteenth century was a medium-size state. The bureaucracy was inadequate because imperial Spain required a larger one than it could construct given its resources, human and financial. This is the fundamental cause of what historians have called the "slownesses" of the Spanish bureaucracy.[75]

Once again, the structural advantage of the world-economy as a system over a world-empire as a system seems to thrust itself upon us. For example, H. G. Koenigsberger describes Spain's inability to exploit its Sicilian

---

[72]"Charles V's imperialism, unlike that of his son, was essentially a Europe-based imperialism. Among the European territories of Charles it was the Netherlands and Italy which bore the brunt of the Imperial expenditure during the first half of the reign. But as each in turn began to be squeezed dry, Charles was compelled to look elsewhere for further sources of revenue. . . . [After 1540] the financial contributions of Spain—which meant essentially Castile—assumed a constantly increasing importance in relation to that of the Low Countries. . . .

"The Emperor's failure to extract larger contributions from the Crown of Aragon inevitably made him increasingly dependent on the fiscal resources of Castile, where the Cortes was far less powerful, and where there were a number of important sources of revenue outside the Cortes' control." Elliott, *Imperial Spain*, pp. 197, 199.

"Charles V, faced with the torment of penury, as perpetual as hell, knew that the economy was the servant of his designs, but did not have at his disposal a policy congruent with Spanish hegemony which he brought to its zenith. Neither he nor the Castilians began to perceive, even barely, the glimmerings of a national policy. His powers were not as great as his aspirations were elevated, and had he been able to conceive an adequate policy, which in the imperial sphere Gattinara proposed to him, it is doubtful that, given the situation, he could have implemented it. The multiple causes of these burdensome acts left Castile impoverished, despite the arrival, and swift transshipment, of the largest quantities of treasure of the modern economy." Ramon Carande, *Carlos V y sus banqueros: La vida económica en Castilla (1516–1556)*, 2a ed. corr. y aum. (Madrid: Sociedad de Estudios y Publicaciones, 1965), **I**, 140.

[73][I]n this storm of prices, were the Mediterranean states, or those close to the Mediterranean, more affected than the others, or were they not? An affirmative response seems to us probably correct, as far as Spain is concerned. Especially if one bears in mind the enormous expenses of warfare for this too vast empire." Braudel, *La Méditerranée*, **I**, p. 486.

[74]"Another movement can be seen within the Empire, . . . the isolation within Europe of Castile, whose prosperity would in the end be ruined by the 'treason' of the other members of the Empire and the multiplicity of burdens which, because of this isolation, were eventually to be hers.

One can note an analogous phenomenon in America, where the dynamic mining sectors of Mexico and Upper Peru finally go under, under the rapidly growing exigencies of a more and more financially deficient periphery. It is as though the edges, ready to detach themselves from the main body, become extremely heavy, as though the cost of imperial cohesion, as the economy shifts from expansion to long-term contraction, grows out of all proportion to the unit of cohesion and of domination, Castile in the one case, mining Mexico or Upper Peru in the other. This is true to such an extent that when, in the 18th century, the Italian and Flemish periphery detach themselves from Castile, this spurs an economic revival in the latter, discharging it of its burdens of imperial cohesion in which it ended by using itself up, profiting no one. . . .

For Castile, its Mediterranean extensions, dynamic elements in the first half of the 16th century, become gradually, by the beginning of the 17th century, passive elements for which one must pay, maintained by means of soldiers and money, always ready to rebel (as Aragon in 1640) whenever one asks of them an extra effort for the common defense." Chaunu, *Séville*, **VIII** (1), pp. 248–249.

[75]See Braudel, *La Méditerranée*, **I**, p. 343.

colony, attributing it to an absence of a political theory.[76] This seems to me to invert horse and chariot. Spain had no theory that encouraged her to establish a trade monopoly in Sicily because, bureaucratically, she was already spread too thin to exploit her empire properly. She devoted primary energy to maintaining an empire in the Americas, as well as conducting wars in the Netherlands and governing Hispania. To maintain her empire in America, she had to invest in a growing bureaucracy to keep the Spanish colonists and their allies among the Indian nobility under control.[77]

Could the Spanish empire have worked? Perhaps if it was structured differently. As Koenigsberger says: "Its fundamental weakness was . . . the narrowness of its tax base. Castile and the silver financed and defended the empire; the other dominions were, to a greater or lesser degree, onlookers."[78] Ferran Soldevila documents how the Castilians deliberately excluded even such a "close" group as the Catalans from the Hispano–American trade.[79] But if it were structured differently, it would not have been an empire, which is precisely our point. If the Catalans were incorporated into a single state with the Castilians, which they were not, and if Charles V's imperial ambitions had not both drained Castile and drew him into inevitable conflicts of interest with portions of his empire, conflicts that were self-defeating,[80] then Spain might indeed have had some chance

[76]"Since Sicily was an old established kingdom enjoying traditional commercial relations with her neighbours, it never occurred to Spanish statesmen to treat her like the American colonies. The absence of a developed Spanish theory of empire in Europe saved Sicily from the trade monopoly which Spain imposed on the colonists in the new world. Failing a genuine coordination of economic resources, such a trade monopoly would have been the only way in which a Spanish economic imperialism could have manifested itself. Sicily was unable to emancipate herself from the financial tutelage of Genoese bankers and from her commercial and industrial dependence on Florentine and Venetian manufacturers; but her citizens were, at least, able to sell the greater part of their wheat and silk to those who could supply them with finished goods." H. G. Koenigsberger, *The Government of Sicily Under Philip II of Spain* (London: Staples Press, 1951), 143.

[77]"From the 1570's onward it was evident that the operations of private enterprise and colonial administration would have to be modified to curb the unrestricted ruthlessness of Spaniards and their allies, the *caciques* of Amerindian nobility through whom they operated to obtain tribute and labor. For the efficient preservation, organization, and manipulation of Indian communities it was necessary to urbanize, Christianize, and incorporate them into the West European economy." Stanley J. and Barbara H. Stein, *The Colonial Heritage of Latin America* (London and New York: Oxford Univ. Press, 1970), 71.

[78]H. G. Koenigsberger, "The European Civil War," in *The Hapsburgs and Europe, 1516–1660* (Ithaca, New York: Cornell Univ. Press, 1971), 257.

[79]See Ferran Soldevila, "Barcelona demana a l'Emperador Carles V L'autorització per a comerciar directament amb America (1522)," in *Studi in onore di Amintore Fanfani,* **V**: *Evo moderno e contemporaneo* (Milano: Dott. A. Giuffrè-Ed.), 638–641.

[80]For example see Malowist: "Every disturbance in the delivery of grain and timber from the coast of the Baltic, that is, especially from Poland, produced a rise in the cost of living in Holland and the other provinces of the Low Countries and paralysed the foreign trade of Holland by preventing the exchange of goods with the countries of the Iberian peninsula, with Brittany, and with England. Thus the merchants of Amsterdam and the neighboring towns tried to maintain good relations with Danzig and Poland, and they opposed energetically Charles V's policy of hostility toward Denmark during the first half of the sixteenth century, a policy which caused the closing of the Sound and consequently rendered access to the Baltic impossible." *Economic History Review*, **XII**, p. 165.

Similarly the merchants of Antwerp were hurt by Charles V's attempts to keep a gold-silver fixed ratio, which led at various points to outflows of gold from the Netherlands to France. See Florence Edler, "The Effects of the Financial Measures of Charles V on the Commerce of Antwerp, 1539-42," *Revue belge de philogie et d'histoire,* **XVI**, 3–4, juil.–dec. 1937, 665–673.

of becoming a core state in the European world-economy. Instead, overextension merely exhausted Charles V and his successors.

In 1556 the empire split apart. Charles V abdicated. Philip II of Spain, son of Charles V, received the Netherlands, but the lands in central Europe became a separate realm. In 1557 Philip declared bankruptcy. Within the Spain–Netherlands, the center of political gravity then shifted back to Spain when Philip moved there in 1559. Thereupon came the Netherlands Revolution[81] which ended, some eighty years later after much ado and to and fro, in the division of the area into the northern, Calvinist, independent United Provinces (more or less contemporary Netherlands) and the southern, Catholic, so-called Spanish Netherlands (more or less contemporary Belgium). But this crisis was more than a Spanish crisis, or a Hapsburg imperial crisis. It was a turning point in the evolution of the European world-economy. For a crucial element in this revolution was the peace of Cateau–Cambrésis entered into by Spain and France in 1559. To understand the import of this treaty we first must look at the other aspirant to imperial rule, France.

No country illustrates better than France the dilemmas of western European states in the "first" sixteenth century. On the one hand, probably no European state emerged from the late Middle Ages with a relatively stronger monarchy.[82] We have already reviewed in a previous chapter Bloch's explanations of the differences between France, England, and eastern Europe in terms of the tenure arrangements as they emerged in the sixteenth century, based on the differing dynamics of their juridical structures in the late Middle Ages. While the English system permitted, as we saw, a legal redefinition of tenure to satisfy the new needs of landowners in the fourteenth to sixteenth centuries, these definitions were more frozen in France. Hence the nobility had to be politically more militant to retain their advantages. Thus whereas Bloch rightly points to the "decadence of seignorial justice"[83] in France by the sixteenth century, it is also true, as Rushton Coulbourn points out, that the political strength of

---

[81] For an account of its social content, and an assessment of its causes, see J. W. Smit, "The Netherlands Revolution," in Robert Forster and Jack P. Greene, eds., *Preconditions of Revolution in Early Modern Europe* (Baltimore, Maryland: Johns Hopkins Press, 1970), 19-54. The article contains a good brief bibliography.

[82] "It is in France that the bases for an absolute monarchy were best laid. . . . In effect, ever since the failure of the Estates-General of 1484, no claim to liberty, private or public, could be made against [the authority of] the king." Mousnier, *Les XVIe et XVIIe siècles*, p. 100.

See Eli F. Heckscher: "Geographically, [France] was a unified and compact kingdom as early as the first half of the 16th century, almost entirely free from enclaves and overlapping sovereign states. Her monarch had, perhaps, greater power over his country than anyone else in Europe and, finally, her statesmen had from early times followed a conscious economic policy in which tolls had a definite purpose to fulfill. . . . The persistence of feudal forms of organization really manifested itself only in the river and road tolls, *péages (pedagia)*, but in addition, the tolls of cities survived—here, just as in other countries, relics of the more or less autonomous city economy." *Mercantilism*, **I**, rev. ed. (London: Geo. Allen & Unwin, 1955), 78–79.

[83] Bloch, *Caractères originaux*, **I**, p. 107.

the nobility led to an economic structure which was less able to maneuver in the new world-economy.[84]

The consequences of the fact that there was not the relative merger of the nobility and the new merchant-gentry in France as in England were many. For the moment, let us concentrate on its implications for state policy in the world-system. Edward Miller points out that the political strength of trading interests was greater in England than in France. As a consequence, French trade policy was far more open in the late Middle Ages.[85] The end result was that, despite a stronger bureaucracy, France in the early sixteenth century had acquired fewer "powers of economic direction"[86] than England. The pressures of fiscalism in such a situation pushed the French monarch to imperial ambitions, a fortiori because the Hapsburgs also had them. They could have tried overseas expansion as did Spain, but they lacked the backing of international capital, that is

[84]"In the fifteenth century, the [French] nobility had shown the same tendency to merge with the *roturiers* [commoners] as their opposite numbers in England did, but in the sixteenth century the government sought deliberately to stop this, and succeeded in doing so by legislation barring commerce and certain other lucrative activities to noblemen. The trouble was that in France, as in most continental countries, the nobility had built up an immunity to taxation, and, if they went into trade, they carried their personal immunity with them, and the state lost some of its important new revenue. . . . [The] Crown in France remained sufficiently afraid of the nobility not to dare to take away their immunity. . . . Rushton Coulbourn, "A Comparative Study of Feudalism," Part Three of Rushton Coulbourn, ed., *Feudalism in History*, p. 316.

[85][Louis XI's] dominant intention was to make France once again a meeting-place of trade routes, in the light of his conviction that 'fairs and markets enrich the country' and that wealth would accrue from 'multiplying' traffic and merchandise within the kingdom. . . . In France, then, government support was only to a limited extent enlisted on the side of native trading interests and failed to establish those interests in a permanently organized form." Miller, *Cambridge Economic History of Europe*, **III**, pp. 334–335.

[86]*Ibid.*, p. 338. Joseph Strayer similarly argues that the French formula of greater centralization of administration masked far less uniformity of law, and hence far less possibility for a national economic policy: "For France as for England, the two essential areas of development were justice and finance. But the French kings had to build slowly, and their early institutions were far simpler and less formalized than those of England. . . .

"[The] series of annexations [by France in the twelfth and thirteenth centuries] posed serious questions for the French government. The relatively simple institutions which had been adequate to run a small royal domain would clearly have to be expanded and refined to deal with the greatly increased area and populations now subject to the king. The new provinces had their own institutions and customs which were often more sophisticated and specialized than those of the royal government. . . .

"The basic solution for these problems was discovered by Philip Augustus (1180–1223), the king who was the real founder of the French state. He allowed each province to keep its own customs and institutions but sent men out from Paris to fill all important provincial offices. Thus Norman courts continued to enforce Norman law, but the presiding officers were not Norman but royal agents drawn largely from the old royal domain. Provincial pride was placated, while the king kept effective control of his new possessions. . . .

"(By way of contrast, the English state, with its insistence on uniform institutions and laws, had great trouble in assimilating regions which had separate political traditions, such as the principalities of Wales or the petty kingdoms of Ireland.) But the emerging French state had to pay a heavy price for its flexibility. Local leaders were primarily concerned with the preservation of local customs and privileges; they distrusted the central government just as the central government distrusted them. They could not be used, to any great extent, in the work of local administration. In fact the basic rule of French administration was that no one should hold office in his native province." *On the Medieval Origins of the Modern State*, pp. 49–51.

northern Italian capital, for that.[87] The alternative was imperial expansion within Europe itself, directed precisely against northern Italy.

France had a competing international network of finance and trade, which centered on Lyon. In the early Middle Ages, the fairs of Champagne were for a while the great meeting point for the merchants of northern Italy and Flanders. They also served as an international financial center. Then in the late thirteenth, early fourteenth centuries, decline set in.[88] In the fifteenth century, the French monarchs carefully nurtured the growth of Lyon[89] and encouraged its links with Florence[90] who were the great bankers of the time.[91] By bringing together enormous amounts of capital in the early sixteenth century, both Lyon and Antwerp "reduced the power of the individual financiers within bearable limits [and thus] made it possible to raise large masses of capital at moderate rates. . . ."[92] Lyon was not quite the international center Antwerp was because the French kings sought simultaneously to make it "their financial arsenal."[93] Nor did Lyon ever match Antwerp as a commercial center. It was in short a second best.

Nonetheless, France tried. The Hapsburg and Valois empires both failed and fell together. Not only Spain but France also declared itself bankrupt in 1557. The Hapsburg however were first as if to emphasize their primacy

[87]"In the 15th and the 16th centuries, France failed twice on the seven seas of the world. . . . [F]ailure in the 15th century when the great discoveries were made without its sailors—or almost. Failure again in the 16th century when France . . . gives up in the struggle for routes, islands, coasts, and profits in the Atlantic, Africa, and America. . . .

"The overriding consideration, even before the Hundred Years' War, had been, ever since the Genoese galleys had made the successful liaison between the Mediterranean and the North Sea, the exclusion from the grand circuits of trade of the transcontinental routes and of the French economy. The Champagne fairs had lasted only a while. Now, without taking into consideration this collaboration of the general economy, I mean without in the 15th century the support of Venice or Genoa, without the complicity of Italian or Nordic international capital, how can one explain Lisbon or the seizure of Ceuta, or these roots that the Genoese were establishing in Andalusia, or much later the voyage of Magellan? Behind the Iberian good fortune there is this thrust of the 14th and 15th centuries, this complicity of international capitalism and its driving forces with Seville, Lisbon, later Antwerp, cities with linked destinies, whose linkages bypassed France. On top of all this . . . the dramas of the Hundred Years' War made everything worse. Made worse, but it did not create a crisis which had been set off already by the revolution in trade routes." Fernand Braudel, "La double faillite 'coloniale' de la France aux XVe et XVIe siècles," *Annales E.S.C.*, **IV**, 4, oct.–déc. 1949, 454. Perhaps it was not only the absence of external backing. Braudel concludes: "The colonial vocation calls into question the entire life, the whole structure of a country, to its very innards. Sixteenth-century France . . . is not ready for this *(ouverte aussi profondément)* [p. 456]."

[88]Robert-Henri Bauthier gives the following explanation: "In our opinion the causes of the decadence and decline of the fairs of Champagne are linked with the general transformation of the Western economy at the end of the 13th and the beginning of the 14th century. Important changes occurred in two essential areas: (1) Italian industrialization; and (2) the revolution in the market for precious metals. . . .

Since the main purpose of the fairs of Champagne was the provision of specie for the Italian purchases of French and Flemish draperies, their decadence became inevitable, for the drapery of all of northern France incurred the same crisis. . . .

The international economy rested traditionally on silver; at the end of the 13th century gold began to play a role, and the sudden variations in the ratio of the two metals completely disorganized the balance of the companies whose activity rested on foreign exchange and specie sales." "The Fairs of Champagne," in Cameron, ed., *Essays in French Economic History*, 62-63.

[89]See Ehrenberg, *Capital and Finance*, pp. 281–306.
[90]See *ibid.*, pp. 202–220.
[91]See *ibid.*, p. 193.
[92]*Ibid.*, p. 333.
[93]*Ibid.*, p. 307.

even in defeat. The two financial failures led very rapidly to the cessation of military fighting and the treaty of Cateau-Cambrésis in 1559, which was to change the political terms of reference of Europe for a hundred years. These bankruptcies thus were more than a financial readjustment. A whole world had come tumbling down.

What tumbled was not merely a particular state structure. It was more than the tragic abdication of Charles V amid the tears of his knights. What tumbled was the world-system. For a hundred years, Europe was enjoying a new prosperity. Men had tried to profit from it in the ways of old. But technological advance and the upsurge of capitalist elements had already progressed too far to make it possible to recreate political empires that would match the economic arenas. The year 1557 marked, if you will, the defeat of that attempt, and the establishment of a balance of power in Europe which would permit states which aimed at being nations (let us call them nation-states) to come into their own and to batten on the still flourishing world-economy.

Crises are symbolic turning points. As many historians have pointed out, many of the organizational features of the "first" sixteenth century do not disappear until much later: 1576, when the Spanish authority collapsed in the Netherlands, or 1588 with the defeat of the Armada, or 1598 with the Peace of Vervins (and the Edict of Nantes). It is not worth debating the most appropriate date, since a shift in organizational emphasis is always gradual, because the underlying structural factors move glacially.

But shift there was, and it is worth our while to spell out the implications this had for the European world-economy. Let us start with R. H. Tawney's description of the organizational emphasis of the "first" sixteenth century:

> In its economic organization the machinery of international trade had reached a state of efficiency not noticeably inferior to that of three centuries later. Before the most highly-organized economic systems of the age were ruined by the struggle between Spain and the Netherlands, and by the French wars of religion, there were perhaps ten to twelve commercial houses whose money-markets were the financial power-houses of European trade, and whose opinion and policy were decisive in determining financial conditions. In the Flemish, French, and Italian cities where it reached its zenith, and of which England was the pupil, the essence of the financial organization of the sixteenth century was internationalism, freedom for every capitalist to undertake every transaction within his means, a unity which had as its symptoms the movement of all the principal markets in sympathy with each other, and as its effect the mobilisation of immense resources at the strategic points of international finance. Its centre and symbol was the exchange at Antwerp, with its significant dedication, "*Ad usum mercatorum cujusque gentis ac linguae*," where, as Guicciardini said, every language under heaven could be heard, or the fairs at Lyons which formed, in the words of a Venetian, "the foundation of the pecuniary transactions of the whole of Italy and of a good part of Spain and of the Netherlands."[94]

Tawney says that this system collapsed because of ruinous wars. This is true, but the causal sequence is too immediate. We suggested in the last

[94]R. H. Tawney, "Introduction" to Thomas   Wilson, *A Discourse Upon Usury* (London: Bell & Sons, 1925), 62.

chapter that the efficient cause was the inability to make an imperial system viable given the economic thrusts of sixteenth-century Europe but its structural limitations, that is, the relatively low level of productivity and thinness of bureaucratic framework faced with an expanding economy based on scattered medium-size enterprise.

One crucial bottleneck became the growing financial demands of imperial state machineries and the consequent inflation of public credit which led to the imperial bankruptcies of mid-century. Charles V had run through states and their merchants as sources of finance: Naples, Sicily, Milan, Antwerp, Castile.[95] The classic exposition of this argument was made by Henri Hauser who argued that the European financial crisis of 1559 "probably hindered the evolution of commercial capitalism, and gave the impetus to the transformation of economic geography."[96] Hauser argues that the war between Spain and France that began in 1557 simply stretched the state credits too thin, led to defaults, and forced both states to make a hasty peace at Cateau-Cambrésis in 1559.

The consequences for the extended Hapsburg Empire were great. It led directly to the beginning of Spain's decline.[97] The crisis would lead to a definitive break of Antwerp and England, leaving the latter free to develop its new and winning economic alliance with Amsterdam.[98] In Antwerp itself, the boom which was based on the axis with Spain ended. "The bankruptcy of Philip II of 1557 brought the rupture which finally decided Antwerp's fate."[99]

Throughout Flanders, the crisis would lead to a reinforcement of Calvinist tendencies, especially among the skilled workers. In 1567, the Spanish sent the Duke of Alva to repress the new socio–political unrest but this simply resulted in the long run in an exodus of the Calvinist merchants and craftsmen to Protestant countries,[100] and by 1585 there was a collapse

[95]Braudel, *Charles Quint et son temps*, p. 199.

[96]Henri Hauser, "The European Financial Crisis of 1559," *Journal of European Business History*, **II**, 2, Feb. 1930, 241. For the description of the credit inflation, see pp. 242–250.

[97]"But it would make it impossible to realize the state of latent crisis from the very beginning of the reign of Philip II if we ignored the deceleration of the inflationary rhythm starting in the period 1560–65. It is no accident that the first bankruptcy of the State had already occurred in 1557 nor that the first great shift in Philip's policy occurred in 1568." Nadal, *Hispania*, **XIX**, p. 513. Nadal points out, contrary to Hamilton's assertion that the Spanish price-rise culminated at the end of the century, the data show a greater increase from 1501–1550 (107%) than from 1551–1600 (98%). See *ibid.*, pp. 511–512.

[98]"The crisis of 1557 had already affected the basis of Antwerp's position in the field of public finances disastrously. In later years the decline continued. Under Gresham's impulse the English Crown

detached itself completely from Antwerp's tutelage in the course of the sixties. . . .

"When in 1569 the Anglo-Netherlandish embargo led to a complete rupture, England felt strong enough to free herself from the commercial and financial influence of Antwerp. Hamburg received the latter's commercial, and London her financial legacy. Both places were assured of a brilliant future. Thus Antwerp lost for good the last basis of her first expansion." Van der Wee, *The Growth of the Antwerp Market and the European Economy*, **II**, pp. 222, 238.

[99]*Ibid.*, p. 207.

[100]See *ibid.*, pp. 232–236. See Parry: "The 'Spanish fury' of 1576 damaged Antwerp severely. Parma's siege and the capture of the city in 1585 resulted in the removal or bankruptcy of many business houses and the exile—mostly to Amsterdam—of thousands of Protestant artisans. . . . The seaborne trade which Antwerp had handled moved to Amsterdam." *Cambridge Economic History of Europe*, **IV**, p. 169.

of Flemish industry and commerce, which "were at a standstill for years."[101] The Netherlands revolt, combining social and political unrest consequent on this disaster, created a viable political base in the northern half of the Low Countries for its role as the center of world commerce beginning in the late sixteenth century.[102]

Southern Germany was hard hit too. Luzzatto points out that "the most severe blow came to them from first the insolvency then the bankruptcy of the Spanish crown which swept totally away the personal fortunes not only of the Fuggers but of the larger part of the great merchant-bankers of southern Germany."[103] As the situation worsened economically, the former commercial allies of southern Germany and northern Italy, began to invade each other's territory in competitive search of business, which was a mutually destructive affair.[104]

The political consequences of this collapse for the Germanies were enormous. What Barraclough calls the "revolutionary ferment of Protestantism which, in reaction against the decline of the empire . . ., was strongly national in character"[105] swept Germany. But, as we have already mentioned, Charles V's involvement in his empire meant that he could not invest his political fortunes in German unification, no more than he could take the perspective of a Spanish nationalist. The compromise of *cuius regio* entrenched the German principalities, undermined the German bourgeoisie, and put off all hope of unification for centuries. Germany would come to be largely divided into a Lutheran north and northeast, the latter at least economically part of the eastern European periphery, and a wealthier, Catholic southwest (including parts of the Rhine country). As A. J. P. Taylor says: "Both developments were a retreat from the flourishing days of the Renaissance, which had embraced all Germany. . . ."[106] Even

[101]Van der Wee, *The Growth of the Antwerp Market and the European Economy,* **II,** p. 183. Two recent writers assert however that the decline of Antwerp is exaggerated and that it remained relatively strong for a long time to come. See Jan Craeybeckx, "Les industries d'exportation dans les villes flamandes an XVIe siècle, particulièrement à Gand et à Bruges," *Studi in onore di Amintore Fanfani,* **IV:** *Evo moderno* (Milano: Dott. A. Giuffrè-Ed., 1962), 415. Nonetheless, Craeybeckx admits that Antwerp's new post-1585 enterprises "did not, of course, prevent the slipping of the center of gravity of international commerce towards Amsterdam and London [p. 416]."

Jean A. van Houtte is even stronger. He calls the picture of decline "gravely deformed." "Déclin et survivance d'Anvers (1550–1700)," *Studi in onore di Amintore Fanfani,* **V:** *Evi moderno e contemporaneo*

(Milano: Dott. A. Giuffrè-Ed., 1962), 706. He points out that if wartime blockade hurt Antwerp's sea trade, it did not affect her overland trade. See *ibid.,* 720. He asserts that throughout the seventeenth century, Antwerp's merchant classes would remain "not of negligible importance [p. 722]."

[102]See Verlinden in *Charles Quint et son temps.* Jaime Vicens Vives in the discussion following the paper argues that the same thing held true in Catalonia. See *ibid.,* p. 187. See J. W. Smit: "In summary, we cannot fail to be impressed by the socioeconomic situation as a precondition of the Netherlands revolution." [*Preconditions of Revolution,* p. 43].

[103]Luzzatto, *Storia economica,* p. 151.

[104]See Strauss, *Nuremberg in the Sixteenth Century,* p. 150.

[105]Barraclough, *Origins of Modern Germany,* p. 370.

[106]Taylor, *Course of German History,* p. 20.

in the relatively wealthier southwest, there would come to be a reversion to handicraft industries by the seventeenth century.[107] Taylor may exaggerate the extent of Germany's prosperity and economic leadership in the early sixteenth century, but he is undoubtedly correct in noting the dramatic collapse of nascent economic development.[108]

The effort of Charles V. to dominate politically the European world-economy thus redounded negatively upon Spain and upon the Germanies, upon the cities of Flanders and of northern Italy, and upon the merchant houses which linked their fate to empire. The construction of an empire had seemed a reasonable thing to attempt, even a possible one. But it was not.

We have already told in large part the story of the Spanish colonial enterprise in the Americas. It would be best simply to describe here the situation as a phenomenon internal to the Spanish empire, in order to measure the impact of Spanish decline upon the Americas. Spain had established colonies in the Caribbean and some of the littoral surrounding it (contemporary Mexico, Guatemala, and Colombia) as well as in Peru and Chile. These colonies were conceived as economic complements not only of Europe as a whole, but of Spain in particular.[109] Spain did not have the administrative energy to create a large bureaucracy in the Americas. Therefore they used the old expedient of empires, the cooptation of local chieftains into the political system as intermediary agents of the Crown and the Spanish settlers.[110]

[107] R. Ludloff describes German developments thus: "technical advances and a decided progress toward capitalist organization in the sixteenth century, a check—due in part to the growing exactions of the feudal power of the territorial lords and a reversion to petty methods of production in the seventeenth century." "Industrial Development in 16th–17th Century Germany," *Past & Present*, No. 12, Nov. 1957, 58.

[108] "Germany was at this time the life-line of European commerce, and her towns towered above all others in prosperity. Indeed the national monarchies in other countries sprang even more from resistance to the German commercial supremacy than from resistance to the Empire. . . .

"Every trading community experiences its ups and downs attendant on the world market; but no trading community in modern Europe has ever experienced such a profound and lasting disaster as did the German middle class just at the moment when their financial power was at its greatest and their national consensus fully asserted—just at the moment, indeed, when they might have expected to become the dominating political force, as they were already the dominating economic force in

central Europe." Taylor, *The Course of German History*, pp. 17–18.

[109] "The settlers imported from Spain the goods they needed to maintain their Spanish mode of life in an American environment. They developed, to pay for these imports, a ranching, plantation and mining economy, producing goods for sale in Europe. For their plantations they required slaves, and so created a market for a whole new trade with West Africa. Finally, in the middle of the century they stumbled upon the richest silver mines in the world, which enabled them to pay for still more imports, and which nourished trade with Europe by supplying the specie necessary for the purchase of eastern products." Parry, *Cambridge Economic History of Europe*, **IV**, p. 199.

[110] "Within the various indigenous societies, the end of the supremacy of the authorities of pre-Columbian times led on the one hand to a growth in the abuses of power by traditional chiefs (caciques, curacas) over the mass of the population, and on the other hand to a self-serving collaboration of these chiefs with the settlers, especially the encomenderos. . . .

Just like England, France, Belgium, etc., in Africa or Asia in the 19th century, the Spanish state in

Nor did Spain have the energy to control entirely its own settlers. To keep their political loyalty, it made many economic concessions. One of these was to forbid Indians independent bases of economic power by barring them from raising cattle, the one activity in which they might have been able to compete effectively in the new capitalist economy.[111] Furthermore, not only were the Indians barred from this profitable activity, but its very success weakened them economically, for sheep ate men, in middle America just as in England.[112] The settlers were nonetheless dependent on continued Spanish support, not so much against Indian and African slave rebellions, as against English and other intrusions into their trade and hence their profit margins.[113] Hence, though they were occasionally unhappy with the Crown and its bureaucracy, they did not organize as an autonomous force. Besides, the settlers, many of humble origin, profited from the fact that the colonies were export economies.[114]

Indeed, as often happens, in imperial structures, subimperialisms grew up—layers within layers. We can speak of the ways in which Mexico (that is, the Spaniards in Mexico) "colonized" Peru. Mexico had a far larger population. There was a constant disparity in price levels throughout the sixteenth and seventeenth centuries. Mexico exported manufactures, luxuries, and slaves to Peru and received in return specie and mercury.[115]

16th century America adjusted the ancient territorial subdivisions of indigenous societies, displaced the centers of population, and claimed to recognize only one hierarchy of chiefs, that which was appointed *(investie)* and controlled by it. In the 16th as in the 19th centuries, colonial authority thus was led to make compromises, but the chiefs, whether traditional or new, were in the end only the instruments of its tax-gathering." Charles Verlinden, "L'état et l'administration des communautés indigènes dans l'empire espagnole d'Amérique," *International Congress of Historical Sciences.* Stockholm 1960. *Résumés des communications.* (Göteborg: Almquist & Wiksell, 1960), 133.

[111]See Wolf, *Sons of the Shaking Earth,* pp. 182–183.

[112]See *ibid.,* pp. 197–198.

[113]See E. E. Rich's description of the economics of the slave-trade: "It was almost an inevitable feature of dependence on slave-labour that the demand should never be fully and cheaply met, for the labour-force is the most easily expended factor in a slave-owning system. . . . In such circumstances it is not surprising that smuggled and connived shipments should be numerous and attractive. . . . In general it was assumed that such shipments would seriously invade a real property of Portugal when they went to the African coast to get slaves, but that in taking them to sell in the Spanish possessions they would be merely evading a formal veto; Portugal was the serious barrier to free trade rather than Spain. So far did this approach to the slave

trade carry sixteenth-century merchants that a powerful group of English merchants saw the possibility of setting up an Anglo-Spanish partnership for the trade in such terms as would satisfy the settlers' need for slaves, the Spanish government's desire for economic strength and control, and the English merchants' desire for the profits entailed. . . . John Hawkins began to trade in slaves to the West Indies in the hope that he might establish a regular commercial cooperation between England and Spain." *Cambridge Economic History of Europe,* **IV,** pp. 325–326. We must ask ourselves why the Spanish authorities were not receptive to Hawkins' projects which seemed aimed primarily at Portuguese merchants. Was it not possibly because English intrusion seemed in the long run more dangerous for Crown and settler, and the Crown saw this proposal as an opening wedge?

[114]"From the very beginning of its colonial existence [sixteenth century], Chile has had an export economy. . . . Quite typically, Chile began her existence as an exporter of gold. But the mines . . . were not rich and did not last very long. . . . Yet, untypically among Spanish mainland colonies, though perhaps not unlike Guatemala, even at that time, Chile exported a product of her land: tallow from her livestock." André Gunder Frank, *Capitalism and Underdevelopment in Latin America,* p. 29.

[115]See Woodrow Borah, *Early Colonial Trade and Navigation Between Mexico and Peru,* Ibero-Americana: **38** (Berkeley: Univ. of California Press, 1954), 81–82, 86–88.

When the Philippines entered the Spanish trading sphere, the Spaniard in Mexico became the middleman between Manila and Lima, cutting out the Spanish Manileños.[116] This re-export of Chinese wares via Manila from Mexico to Peru became the mainstay of the intercolonial trade.[117] The Spanish Crown tried unsuccessfully to break Mexico's role, as it was cutting into the profits of Castile.[118] "No one will contest," says Chaunu, "that during the 16th century Mexico behaved towards Peru as a metropole towards its colony."[119]

One of the effects of political overextension in Europe combined with economic contraction in the "second" sixteenth century was that there was an increased emigration of Spaniards to America.[120] It provided a job outlet for Spaniards who needed it and an immediate source of income for the Spanish state, since positions in the American colonial bureaucracy were sold.[121] On the other hand, the growing population of Spaniards living off the land in America in the face of economic contraction, along with the disastrous demographic decline of the Indians under early Spanish rule, combined to create a "century of depression" in Hispanic America[122]

---

[116]See William C. Schurz, "Mexico, Peru, and the Manila Galleon," *Hispanic American Historical Review*, **I**, 4, Nov. 1918, 391.

[117]See Borah, *Early Colonial Trade*, p. 121.

[118]See *ibid.*, pp. 118–120, 124–127.

[119]Pierre Chaunu, "Pour une histoire économique de l'Amérique espagnole coloniale," *Revue historique*, **LXXX**, 216, oct.–déc. 1956, 218.

[120]The extent of the emigration is explored by Jorge Nadal in *La población española (siglos XVI a XX)* (Barcelona: Ed. Ariel, 1966), 73–80. There was to be sure overpopulation. "[The] image [of an overpopulated Castile] is inseparable from that of Spanish grandeur," affirms José-Gentil da Silva. "Villages castillans et types de production au XVIe siècle," *Annales E.S.C.*, **XVIII**, 4, juil.-août 1963, 735. Is emigration thus to be linked to decline? Perhaps, but not in a simple correlation.

[121]"[C]olonial office-holding . . . furnished opportunities to Spaniards of all ranks and income for employment and enrichment denied them by the contracting metropolitan economy. Moreover, the augmented colonial administration tables of organization gave the Spanish monarchy the chance to sell colonial offices to eager placemen who in turn found other Spaniards ready to advance loans to newly-appointed administrators bound for their positions of control over submissive Amerindian masses." Stein & Stein, *The Colonial Heritage of Latin America*, pp. 71–72. Swart underlines the fact that Spain extended venality to its colonies, which France did not, a sign of the *burden* of colonies at this time. See Swart, *The Sale of Offices*, p. 41.

[122]"All of the data available point to the conclusion that only in the best years after 1576–1579 through much of the seventeenth century were the white inhabitants able to secure easily sufficient food to feed themselves and the servants and workmen directly dependent upon them. Factors other than the labor supply were probably operative in this period; the unexplained drop in numbers of livestock at the end of the 16th century and in the early decades of the 17th century can hardly have been due to lack of herdsmen alone; but labor supply was probably the most important factor present in a continuing shortage of foodstuffs and other items of urban supply. . . . In mining, the evidence also points unmistakeably to a severe and continuing shortage of labor owing to the shrinkage in Indian population. . . .

"The economic difficulties besetting the cities of New Spain . . . were almost certainly paralleled by similar developments in the major Spanish colonies in the New World. . . . Fewer economic opportunities and a worsening of living conditions in Spain meant that numbers of Spaniards migrated to the colony, where, bad though the economic conditions may have been, food was still more abundant throughout the late 16th and most of the 17th centuries than in Spain. Because of the nature of colonial society, these immigrants meant little if any addition to the labor force in New Spain, but rather an increase in the number of people to be fed. . . . Through their coincidence in time, the economic and demographic crises of Spain and her colony . . . interacted to the disadvantage of both." Borah, *New Spain*, pp. 25–26, 29. See Alvaro Jara on the crisis of the end of the century in Chile in *Guerre et société en Chili: essai de sociologie coloniale*, pp. 105–119.

and as a result gradually to give rise to the system of haciendas based on debt peonage.[123] But the hacienda was oriented to a smaller economic world than the plantation,[124] one of relative self-sufficiency of a settler elite.[125] Spain itself found the developing system of lessening economic benefit to her and of increasing political difficulty. It would be easy later for other European states to obtain the economic benefits of Hispanic America while Spain continued to bear its imperial political costs.[126]

[123]"One may conclude that the rise of the hacienda was essentially a development rather than a struggle. The evolution of the great estate responded to such realities as the size of cities and Spanish populations, the degree of acculturation among the Indians, and the nature of Spanish society in early modern times . . . wherever it might appear that the Crown or the Church became a prime mover in its development, one will find on close examination that deeper forces were at work. Crown policy has been credited with the destruction of the encomienda, but natural developments in the colonies had doomed the institution. On the one hand, the fortunes arising from commerce and mining were not directly dependent upon the encomienda; on the other hand, the sheer growth of Spanish society produced newly powerful families who began to carve out estates of their own, undermining the inflexible encomienda system." James Lockhart, "Encomienda and Hacienda: The Evolution of the Great Estate in the Spanish Indies," *Hispanic American Historical Review,* **XLIX,** 3, Aug. 1969, 428.

[124]The Steins distinguish between hacienda and plantation in this manner: "[The hacienda is an] estate of large dimensions raising grains or cattle [whose] products were consumed locally at the mining centers or large urban areas such as Mexico City and Lima. Amerinds constituted the labor force, dependent, relatively immobile, constrained by a special form of wage labor, debt peonage. . . . Unlike the hacienda, the plantation was an independent economic unit created to produce staples for external, that is, European consumption." *The Colonial Heritage of Latin America,* p. 40.

[125]"By the early 1590's, the formation of Spanish-owned estates apparently reached a point at which, provided they could secure enough labor, their production could meet the food requirements of the Spanish cities. This is not to say that the cities were freed of all reliance upon Indian production, but rather that in a pinch they could squeeze through upon food produced by the farms owned and controlled directly by their own vecinos." Borah, *New Spain,* p. 33.

See Huguette and Pierre Chaunu who note that exports from Spain to the Americas shift from being composed principally in the sixteenth century of primary goods destined for the settlers to manufactured goods in the seventeenth century, goods manufactured in Italy or northern Europe and transshipped by Spain. They ask: "How can we explain

this major shift? By the fact that Spanish colonization, as it developed, became more the master of its natural conditions. One example, among others: the successful planting of wine-grapes on the Pacific coast, in the dry oasis of Peru, despite the somewhat platonic interdictions which the Andalusian aristocracy obtained from a complacent government. And not less by the further fact that the Spaniards of later generations, born in the Indies amidst the Indians, no longer held the same culinary prejudices towards local food that their fathers felt, when transplanted from one universe to another. Finally and especially, because of the economic folly of transporting, at enormous cost, products of low value, by definition untransportable over the long distances between Spain and America, a folly that was no longer made possible by the very high returns of the silver mines of the New-World. When these returns lessened for a host of reasons (exhaustion of the most accessible lodes, scarcity of manpower in the mining areas, increased price for mercury necessary for the amalgam, and especially the reduced purchasing price of silver as a result of the price revolution of the 16th century), silver was exported less to Europe and served rather to create in America a better equilibrated and more diverse economy." *Cahiers d'histoire mondiale,* **I,** pp. 99–100.

[126]"The imperialism of Philip II's reign had been based on a Spanish-Atlantic economy, in that it was financed out of the resources of America and of a Castile which had itself received regular injections of silver from the silver-mines of the New World. . . .

"From the 1590's . . . the economies of Spain and of its American possessions began to move apart [that is, became competing rather than complementary economies], while Dutch and English interlopers were squeezing themselves into a widening gap." Elliott, *Imperial Spain,* pp. 285, 287. This is another way of saying that Spain was becoming part of the semiperiphery of the European world-economy.

André Gunder Frank notes the degree to which the economic surplus generated in Chile in the sixteenth century was spent on luxury goods which could be seen as equivalent to a "drain on Chile's foreign exchange and domestic resources," one not necessarily to the advantage of Spain. *Capitalism and Underdevelopment in Latin America,* p. 33.

Hence, in the post-1557 era, Spain not only lost the central European parts of her empire and after a long struggle the northern Netherlands. She was losing some of the benefits of her remaining colonies. Furthermore, the very fact that the Americas had become such an important source of revenue for Spain, as much as 10% of the total, led to Spain's slowing down the process of expansion in order to consolidate the gains already won.[127] But the slowdown turned out to be more than temporary.

The decline of Spain has been one of the great topics of modern European historiography. The cause, in our terms, seems to be that Spain did not erect (probably because she could not erect) the kind of state machinery which would enable the dominant classes in Spain to profit from the creation of a European world-economy, despite the central geographical-economic position of Spain in this world-economy in the sixteenth century. This indicates that the "core" areas need not be those that are most "central," either in geographical terms or in terms of trade movements.

Spain already suffered from some underlying faults of economic structure as she entered the sixteenth century. First, as we previously mentioned, the relative organized strength of the migratory sheepherders was an important barrier to the rise of a yeomanry, because they were able to retain their prerogatives against enclosures of arable land. In England, sheep raising was less migratory and more compatible with an enclosures system which permitted the slow rise of copyhold.[128] Second, there was the lack of a significant industrial sector, and such as there was (cloth and silk industries in Castile) would collapse in the crisis of 1590.[129] Vicens attributes this a bit mystically to "Castile's failure to comprehend the capitalist world."[130] In any case, his empirical description of what happened after

[127]"It was natural that Philip [II] should wish, in the interests of security, to hold up further conquest until existing provinces could be peopled with industrious Spaniards and settled Indians, and administered by methodical and obedient civil servants. Above all, the discouragement of expansion arose from recognition of the growing importance of the Indies as a source of royal revenue. . . . At the time of Philip II's accession his income from the Indies was nearly 10 per cent of his total revenue and was increasing. In the light of Philip's vast debts and enormous commitments in Europe, it inevitably became a major aim of royal policy to increase the Indies revenue more and more rapidly; to concentrate Spanish capital and ingenuity and Indian labour upon silver-mining and other revenue-producing activities; and to insist upon the development of existing and profitable provinces, rather than allow the dissipation of energy in distant and speculative new *entradas*." J. H. Parry, *New Cambridge Modern History*, **III**, pp. 510–511.

[128]"[The large Spanish cities in the sixteenth century] were already noting a fundamental truth in agrarian economy which, most unfortunately for Castile, was not to be fully appreciated until two disastrous centuries had elapsed. The fact was that arable and pastoral life could very well be combined, and that the two were by no means hostile and mutually exclusive." Klein, *The Mesta*, pp. 327–328.

[129]"From the 16th to the 17th century, the Netherlands, England, France imported from Spain primary materials: olive oil, dyes, wool, while Spain received in exchange, their manufactures, but also cereals. The international specialization defined thereby eliminated Spanish industry from obtaining lasting investment. Only small artisanal enterprise remained to struggle for its existence." Da Silva, *En Espagne*, pp. 177–178.

[130]Vicens Vives, *Approaches*, p. 98. Ramón Carande is perhaps more relevant when he points out that, throughout the sixteenth century, Spanish cloth production was steadily declining in quality. See *Carlos V*, **I**, pp. 191–192. See Elliott, *Imperial Spain*, p. 193.

the crisis indicates that the pattern of expenditure represents at least an intervening variable of decline:

> Precisely those who did possess money (aristocrats, gentry in Andalusia and Extremadura, and retired government officials) petrified it in construction (churches, palaces, and monasteries) or sanctified it in works of art. But none of them succumbed to the temptation to engage in industry, or even simply in commerce.[131]

A similar shift in investment pattern affected the Catalan bourgeoisie who were far more oriented to the new capitalist economy. Braudel notes their increasing shift away from commerce to investment in cultivable land. "Is this not one of the aspects of the economic drama of Barcelona? The bourgeoisie of Barcelona began to place its money in land rather than continuing to risk it in maritime enterprise."[132] Does this not cause us to reflect: How is it that in a center of the most important empire in Europe at this time its bourgeoisie is turning from overseas investment to grain growing, instead of building up their industrial base?[133] There is another puzzle. Many writers make statements similar to Vilar: "For the metals which enriched Spain parasitically . . . flowed out into those countries *where its purchasing power was greatest.*"[134] Or Vicens: "True, Castile did rely upon the injection of precious metals from America at critical moments in the struggle with the rest of Europe."[135]

Surely one factor here was the continued key financial role of foreigners: Genoese, Dutch, Portuguese Jews, French.[136] Another was the unwilling-

[131]Vicens Vives, *Approaches*, p. 99.

[132]Braudel, *La Méditerranée*, **I**, p. 63.

[133]Spain was increasingly turning to agricultural crops which were suitable to estate-production. One major such instance was wine which became "work of wage-earning peasants, rural laborers." Da Silva, *En Espagne*, p. 159. In addition, the wage-levels of these laborers were being further depressed by the influx of French migrants (p. 113). See Nadal, *La población española*, pp. 80–88.

Conversely, it was losing out in fisheries as a producer while remaining in the consumption-market. H. A. Innis spells out the implications of this: "The decline of the Spanish fishery [in Newfoundland] is the reverse side of the opening of the Spanish market to France, England and New England fisheries. It ushered in the trade which for centuries meant to England the development of Newfoundland, the continuation of a nursery for seamen, the consumption of British manufactured goods, and the means of drawing Spanish specie. It is probably not too much to say that in the sixteenth and seventeenth centuries the cornerstone of the British Empire had been truly laid in Spanish trade. Protestant England's consumption of cod declined with

the changing standard of living but Catholic Spain presented a steady and increasing market. The toast of Newfoundland fishermen, 'To the Pope and ten shillings,' is a toast which all good citizens of the British Empire will join." "The Rise and Fall of the Spanish Fishery in Newfoundland," *Proceedings and Transactions of the Royal Society of Canada*, 3rd ser., **XXV**, Section II, 1931, 167.

[134]Vilar, *Past & Present*, No. 10, p. 32 (fn. 88).

[135]Vicens Vives, *Approaches*, p. 97.

[136]"The principal beneficiaries of this crisis were the foreigners—the hated Genoese ('white Moors' as an irate Catalan called them), the Portuguese Jews and the heretical Dutch. Foreign bankers ran the Crown's finances; foreign merchants had secured a strangehold over the Castilian economy, and their tentacles were wrapping themselves round Seville's lucrative American trade." John Elliott, *Past & Present*, No. 20, p. 69.

"The profound scorn for terrestrial matters, the ideal of an ecumenical mission for Spain, definitively interred any program for the economic recovery of Castile. Genoese bankers monopolized the profits from the exploitation of American mines; Genoese outfitters controlled the provisioning of the fleets.

ness of Charles V to take a Spanish *nationalist* perspective and adopt a mercantilist policy[137] before the Castilian bourgeoisie was overwhelmed by the impact of rising prices, luxury expenditure of the aristocracy, and the inflationary and antiprotectionist effects of the Emperor's borrowings,[138] all of which were tied to Spain's involvement in the pan-European Hapsburg

Meanwhile, Italian, Flemish, and French merchants seized control of the colonial trade by means of the fairs at Medina del Campo and the embarkations from Seville and Cádiz. Far from reacting, the monarchy became more and more involved in dangerous financial disorders that tied it to the capitalist machinery on the far side of the Pyrenees; at first this tie was indispensable, then ruinous, and finally sterile. . . . We find no capital invested in the country either to increase the productivity of the agricultural soil or to form commercial companies to exploit the oceanic world—not even to exploit the slave trade, which was left in the hands of the Portuguese and the French." Vicens Vives, *Approaches*, pp. 97–98.

Ramón Carande makes it very clear that this dependence of sixteenth-century Spain on foreign bankers is a direct consequence of the expulsion of the Jews: "Before the 16th century, foreign bankers were not present in Castile and Aragon, as they were in England and France, for example. Not that there had not been for a long time, throughout the 13th, 14th, and 15th centuries, exotic merchants in these kingdoms. . . . Nevertheless, our kings, those of Castile and of Aragon, did not need bankers foreign to the kingdom. The Abrahams, Isaacs, and Samuels sufficed. The Jews in the economic sphere, and especially in the field of credit, did not find throughout the Middle Ages, within the country, competitors capable of displacing them. The Jews were simultaneously the treasurers and the moneylenders to the kings." *El crédito de Castilla en el precio de la política imperial*, discurso leído ante la Real Academia de la Historia (Madrid, 1949), 24. See Klein, *The Mesta*, p. 38.

[137]Elliott, *Imperial Spain*, p. 196. This is also the thrust of Ramón Carande's chapter entitled, "The mercantilist crossroads." *Carlos V*, **I**, ch. vii. See therein: "In the pursuit of his objectives, Charles V made of Spain, as he himself admitted, his larder. He wrote these words to Ferdinand: 'I can only sustain myself because of my kingdoms in Spain;' but he did not therefore institute any scheme of national unification. The various territories were so many provinces having incompatible interests, as in classical times. Although not involved in the empire as a whole, their collective economic interests were dependent on the decision-making of the emperor and hence did not receive the needed attention within the national market [p. 159]."

Luis Vitale argues that Spanish policy was not

"mercantilist" but "exchangist" [*cambiaria*]. *Pensamiento crítico*, No. 27, p. 23. Indeed he argues that the roots of Spain's decline were in her failure to adopt a protectionist policy. "Paradoxically, Spain converted herself into the principal impetus for industry in the enemy countries of England and France [p. 24]."

[138]See Elliott, *Imperial Spain*, pp. 192–193. Klein indicates the way in which the emperor's borrowing impinged upon his ability to adjudicate internal Spanish conflicts. In the early sixteenth century, the privileges of the Mesta, having led to rising prices for food, were combatted in the Cortes by various interests who wished to encourage more arable farming: "Charles himself was in a somewhat trying position with reference to the whole pasturage problem. In the first place he proposed, naturally, to exploit the Mesta and its industry as his grandparents had done—which meant unrestricted pasturage. His policy in this direction was encouraged also by the fact that in 1525 he had farmed out to his creditors, the Fuggers, the very valuable pasture lands of the *maestrazgos* or grand masterships of the military orders; and to permit any considerable inroads of cultivation upon these lands might lead to embarrassing queries from his bankers. On the other hand, as his financial necessities had increased, special subsidies or *servicios* had to be requested from the Cortes. In order to secure these sums he was compelled to grant licenses for the enclosure of public lands to several larger cities whose influence was needed to carry the vote of the subsidies through the Cortes. . . .

"Charles was not long, however, in making his decision, for his plans and ambitions were not of the type that could wait patiently upon the development of a whole new industry. He must have funds at once, and one of the most exploitable resources available in his Spanish realms was the long established and now most flourishing pastoral industry, which was at just that time more prosperous than it had ever been before, or indeed was ever to be again. . . . Forest conservation and arable land were both to be subordinated to the interests of pasturage." Klein, *The Mesta*, pp. 327–328.

And if this were not enough, the decline in silver imports after 1590 led the Spanish government to attempt to recoup its losses by a disastrous policy of overtaxing the remaining Spanish bourgeoisie. See Elliott, *Past & Present*, No. 20, p. 71.

empire. The results of these two factors, the large role of non-Spanish financial interests within Spain and the unwillingness (or inability) of the government to take appropriate protective measures, led to an inversion of Spain's economic role.[139]

Instead of moving against foreign merchants, Spain pursued the path of expelling Spanish non-Catholics, a self-destructive course. Spain's international position as the leading opponent of the forces of Protestantism in Europe and of Islam in the Mediterranean, led, once having suffered the defeat of the Great Armada in 1588,[140] to follow through on the logical internal conclusions of international policy. Having expelled Jews in 1492, Moors in 1502 and 1525, and having persecuted *marranos* and "Erasmians" throughout the sixteenth century, Spain expelled the last pseudo-religious minority, the so-called *Moriscos* in 1609.[141] The Moriscos numbered 300,000 and were mostly agricultural workers, disproportionately located in Valencia and Andalusia.[142] The explusion of the Moriscos tore at the internal social structure of Spain. It originated as a consequence in part of the economic setbacks of the first decade of the seventeenth century,[143] in part as a result of the declining international situation of Spain.[144] It was a move aimed at the landed aristocracy of the *latifundias* by the bourgeois elements of Spain, a last effort as it were to break the hold of this class not geared to capitalist growth.[145] But the aristocracy saved itself by finding a compensation for its lost income in a refusal to

[139]"Philip II seems to me to have regularly found himself in the position of a 19th-century South American government, rich in its production and its mines, or in its plantations, but disarmed all the more vis-à-vis international finance. The government was free to become angry, even to strike out, but then it was forced to submit, to turn over its resources, its command posts, to be 'understanding.' " Braudel, *La Méditerranée*, **I**, p. 464.

[140]"For some time it had been apparent that Spain was losing its battle against the forces of international Protestantism. . . . If any one year marks the division between the triumphant Spain of the first two Hapsburgs and the defeatist, disillusioned Spain of their successors, the year is 1588." Elliott. *Imperial Spain*, pp. 282–283.

[141]"Morisco is the term for Muslims living in Christian territory who were forced to accept Christian baptism or leave Spain, from 1502 in Castile and from 1525 in Aragon. Most complied, minimally, but retained the Arabic language and old customs." Footnote written by Joan Connelly Ullman in Vicens Vives, *Approaches*, p. 31.

[142]See Vicens Vives, *Approaches*, pp. 102–103. Vicens bases his figures on the work of Henri Lapeyre, *Géographie de l'Espagne morisque* (Paris: S.E.V.P.E.N., 1959).

[143]"[In] the course of the early years of the 17th century [in Spain, there occurred a] reversal of the

principal trend of prices in 1601-1604, [and a] reversal of the principal trend [of] the overall volume of trade between the Spanish Atlantic areas and Hispano-America in 1608-1609. The precise location in time of the expulsion of the Moriscos [1609] owe much to this Spanish modality of conjuncture." Pierre Chaunu, "Minorités et conjoncture: L'expulsion des Morèsques en 1609," *Revue historique*, **CCXXV**, 1, janv.–mars 1961, 93.

[144]Juan Reglá points out that in the 16th century, Moriscos were considered a potential "fifth column" and that fears of Ottoman advance redounded on the treatment of the Moriscos. See "La cuestión morisca y la conyuntura internaciónal en tiempos de Felipe II," *Estudios de historia moderna*, **III**, 1953, 222–228.

[145]See Juan Reglá "La expulsión de los moriscos y sus consecuencias," *Hispania, revista española de historia*, **XIII**, No. 51, 1953, 222. Klein however, sees it as being in part a defense of pastoral against arable production interests: "[It] may be said that it appears not unlikely that the Mesta used its influence with the monarchs to secure the expulsion of the Moriscos in 1609. The records of its litigations against individual enclosures of pasturage for arable purposes show, during the last years of the reign of Philip II, a surprisingly large number of Morisco defendants. Although a considerable part of the Moriscos were peddlers, traders and

pay its loans owed to the bourgeoisie, a move in which the state supported them.[146] Pierre Vilar sums up the result by saying: "Instead of hurting the feudal economy, it thus boomeranged on their creditors: well-to-do yeomen (*laboureurs riches*), and bourgeois."[147] The net result was twofold. On the one hand, "the expulsion of the Moriscos had the consequence of disequilibrating for more than a century the Iberian peninsula. Decided in Castile, it broke the back of Valencia and Aragon."[148] On the other hand, it deepened the economic difficulties still more[149] and sent Spain looking for ever more ephemeral scapegoats of its decline.[150]

Meanwhile, the government found itself ever more indebted abroad, ever more prone to meet budgetary crisis by debt repudiation (1557, 1575, 1596, 1607, 1627, 1647) and finally "unable to raise more money and therefore unable to go on fighting."[151] And at home, the "fantastically expensive foreign policies of Charles V and his dependence on credit to finance them" had the consequence, argues J. H. Elliott, not only of establishing "the dominance of foreign bankers over the country's sources of wealth" but also of ensuring that "within Castile the brunt of the burden was borne by those classes which were least capable of bearing it."[152] The resulting dilemma of Spain was captured as early as 1600 by a lawyer-theologian named Martin González de Cellorigo: "Thus it is, that if there is no gold or silver bullion in Spain, it is because there is; the cause of her poverty is her wealth."[153]

mendicants, by far the greater number were peasant agriculturists. Their expulsion . . . was . . . unquestionably one of the severest losses ever known in Spanish agrarian history." *The Mesta*, p. 338. See Jorge Nadal: "The motives for this persecution can be reduced to two: on the one hand, the Moor minority, ideologically unbudgeable, emerged better in economic terms than the Christian minority from the growing economic difficulties; on the other hand, the Muslim vassals, more docile than their opponents, favored the interests of the feudal aristocracy." *La población española*, p. 63.

[146]See Juan Reglá, *Hispania, revista espanol de historia*, **XIII**, No. 52, 1953, 446.

[147]Vilar, *Europe*, **34**, p. 6.

[148]Chaunu, *Revue historique*, **CCXXV**, p. 97. See Juan Reglá, "La expulsión de los moriscos y sus consecuencias en la economia valenciana," *Studi in onore di Amintore Fanfani*, **V**: *Evi moderni e contemporaneo* (Milano: Dott. A. Giuffrè-Ed., 1962), 525–545. J. H. Elliott, if he is somewhat reserved on the negative economic impact on Spain overall of the explusion of the Moriscos, concedes that: "At least for Valencia, then, the expulsion of the Moriscos was an economic disaster." "The Spanish Peninsula, 1598–1648," *New Cambridge Modern History*, **IV**: J. P. Cooper, ed., *The Decline of Spain and the Thirty Years' War. 1609–48/59* (London and New York: Cambridge Univ. Press, 1970), 455.

[149]"It is probable that one of the immediate consequences of the expulsion of the Moriscos was that

the volume of trade of the *Carrera* in the period 1614-1622 was unable to match that of the record period 1605-1613. . . ." Chaunu, *Revue historique*, **CCXXV**, p. 93.

[150]"Have we paid sufficient attention to . . . the extent of [object-]transfer which occurs in the course of the conjunctural deterioration of seventeenth century Spain, when the useful Morisco scapegoat was suddenly lacking, to Jews or those accused of being Jews?" Chaunu, *ibid.*, p. 94.

[151]G. N. Clark, *The Seventeenth Century* (London and New York: Oxford Univ. Press (Clarendon), 1929), 42.

[152]Elliott, *Imperial Spain*, p. 204.

[153]Cited by Vilar, *Europe*, **34**, p. 10. H. G. Koenigsberger makes the same point in more modern language: "Thus, to the amazement of foreigners, all the silver from Peru could not make Spain a rich country. American treasure helped to pay for the emperor's wars and made the fortunes of Genoese bankers, but far too little of it was invested in production so as to overcome the country's economic backwardness. As Charles V's empire became more and more a Spanish empire, the economic weakness of Spain became an ever more serious handicap in her struggle with her west-European rivals." "The Empire of Charles V in Europe," in the *New Cambridge Modern History*, **II**: G. R. Elton, ed., *The Reformation, 1520–1559* (London and New York: Cambridge Univ. Press, 1958), 322–323.

The growing economic difficulties of Spain combined with the inability to create a strong state machinery led to extensive brigandage with which the state was not coping well.[154] The "slowness" of the bureaucracy got worse, not better, as these very difficulties created a structural rigidity in which "Spanish kings were able to go on and on, and rule with a minimum of change and reform."[155] And despite the decline in state income, the state maintained, perhaps even increased, the high level of luxury expenditures of a parasitical court bureaucracy.

The crowning blow may have been demographic (which enters, when it does, as an intervening variable, as we have argued). If in the "first" sixteenth century, Spain's population (or at least that of Castile) was large and growing,[156] this ceased to be true in the "second" sixteenth century for multiple reasons: emigration to the Americas, military deaths, famine and plague in 1599–1600 in Andalusia and Castile, and, as we have seen, expulsion of the Moriscos in 1609. It was not therefore that Spain was somehow less entrepreneurial than other parts of Europe.[157] It is that, for reasons we have adduced, the state machinery was not adequately and properly constructed, and hence that "adverse circumstances proved too strong," in Elliott's phrase,[158] and that Spain demonstrated a "hypersensitivity . . . to the phenomenon of secular contraction," in Chaunu's phrase.[159] In any case, Spain did not become the premier power of Europe. On the contrary, she was destined to become first semiperipheral and then peripheral, until in the twentieth century she tried slowly to begin to move back upward. Nor had Spain declined alone. She had brought down in her wake all those parts of Europe that had been linked to her ascension: northern Italy, southern Germany, Antwerp, Cracow, Portugal. With the exception of Portugal, all of these were essentially city-states servicing both the Hapsburg (and Spanish) empires as well as the world-economy as a whole. Their prosperity did not long survive the restructuring of the world-system in the "second" sixteenth century.

The new system was to be the one that has predominated ever since,

[154]Da Silva attributes the rise of brigandage to the fact that "the extreme tensions of sales prices and the market placed the peasants at the mercy of local seignoirs. . . ." *En Espagne*, p. 161. Juan Reglá considers it to be one of the byproducts of the French crisis: "Futhermore, the French crisis projected into Catalonia and Aragon copious surges of Gascon emigrants who engaged in banditry with great vigor." *Hispania*, **XIII**, p. 233. No doubt it's a bit much to place it all on the Gascons. But Enrique Serraíma notes that in 1582, the situation in the Pyrenees becomes calamitous because the Huguenots and the indigenous mountain bandits "make common cause." "Hugonotes y bandidos en el Pirineo catalán," *Estudios de historia moderna*, **IV**, 1954, 211.

[155]V. G. Kiernan, *Past & Present*, No. 31, p. 37.
[156]"Spain's great imperial successes of the sixteenth century had been achieved primarily by the courage and vitality of the surplus population of an overcrowded Castile. Figures for the population of sixteenth-century Spain are scanty and unreliable, but it could probably now be generally agreed that Castile's population increased during much of the century, as it increased elsewhere in Europe, with the fastest rate of increase in the 1530's." Elliott, *Past & Present*, No. 20, p. 57.
[157]See Elliott's arguments in *Imperial Spain*, pp. 194–195.
[158]*Ibid.*, p. 195.
[159]Chaunu, *Séville*, **VIII**, (1), p. 244.

a capitalist world-economy whose core-states were to be intertwined in a state of constant economic and military tension, competing for the privilege of exploiting (and weakening the state machineries of) peripheral areas, and permitting certain entities to play a specialized, intermediary role as semiperipheral powers.

The core-states themselves had drawn a salutary financial lesson from the economic catastrophes of the Hapsburg and Valois empires. They were determined not to get caught out again in a financial maze out of their control. First, they sought to create the kind of import controls which would enable them to maintain a favorable balance of trade, a concept which came into currency at this time. [160] But the states did more than worry about the balance of trade. They worried also about the gross national product, though they did not call it that, and about the share of the state in the GNP and their control over it. The result was that, by the end of the "second" sixteenth century, as Carl Friedrich points out, "the state itself had become the source of credit, rather than the financial houses which had hitherto loaned funds."[161]

Thus began a period of turning inward. Overall, the following period may perhaps be considered, as R. B. Wernham does, "one of the most brutal and bigoted in the history of modern Europe,"[162] but the conflicts at first were more within than between states. Between the states, there reigned for the moment a relative calm, born of weariness—"a bickering and still explosive co-existence."[163]

This political turning inward of the state—that is, statism, because it was not necessarily nationalism—was intimately linked to the nature of economic development. It is important to start by remembering comparative demography. France in 1600 was estimated at 16 million population, the

[160]"The financial collapse of all the great powers under the strain of war in the late 1550's and the consequent peace of Cateau-Cambrésis had impressed all governments with the need for amassing a war-chest in bullion." Lawrence Stone, "Elizabethan Overseas Trade," *Economic History Review*, 2nd ser., **II**, 1, 1949, 35. Stone cites the new French guiding principle: "Les choses desquelles les hommes se peuvent passe ne doibvent estre jugées nécessaires." ("The things men can do without should not be thought to be necessary.")

[161]Carl J. Friedrich, *The Age of the Baroque* (New York: Harper, 1952), 8.

[162]"Introduction," *New Cambridge Modern History*, **III**: R. B. Wernham, ed., *The Counter-Reformation and the Price Revolution, 1559–1610* (London and New York: Cambridge Univ. Press, 1968), 1.

[163]"So the great conflicts that had torn Europe during the first half of the sixteenth century died away as the combatants one by one sank down exhausted. In the east the long struggle between Christians and Moslem Turks slowly cooled into a bickering and still explosive co-existence. In the centre, in the Holy Roman Empire, the Augsburg settlement of 1555 consecrated a triple balance, precarious but generally treasured, between Lutheran princes, Catholic princes, and a Hapsburg emperor whose power (such as it was) rested more and more upon the far eastern frontiers of the empire, in the Austrian duchies and Bohemia. In the west the settlement of Cateau-Cambrésis in April 1559 recognised a rough and unstable balance between the French monarchy and the Spanish branch of the house of Hapsburg, the two leviathans that still towered over all the other powers and whose long quarrel was now rather suspended than ended. Each of these conflicts, as it died away, thus left behind it its own particular political system and after 1559 each of these systems went more and more its own way in growing isolation from the rest." *Ibid.*, p. 2.

largest in Europe, although the various German principalities added up
to 20 million. Spain and Portugal (united after 1580) were about 10 million,
England and Wales 4.5 million. Densities are in quite a different order.
The areas with the traditional merchant–industrial city-states headed the
list: Italy with 114 per square miles and the Low Countries with 104.
France had 88 and England and Wales 78. Spain (and Portugal) had only
44.[164]

The meaning of both absolute figures and densities is ambiguous. Numbers meant strength in war and industry. They also meant people to rule
and mouths to feed. The optimal size is far from clear, as our previous
discussion already indicated. For the "second" sixteenth century, Frank C.
Spooner registers skepticism about the economic benefits of expanding
population. He speaks of "diminishing returns."[165] At first after Cateau-
Cambrésis, "the economic activity of western Europe enjoyed a period
of prolonged ease and recuperation."[166] This was the period of silver inflation which undercut German mining, appreciated gold, and stimulated
Europe's economy.[167] One consequence of the silver inflation was that,
as Tawney observes, "by the latter part of the sixteenth century, agriculture,
industry and foreign trade were largely dependent on credit."[168] A second
consequence is that it definitely shifted the economic center of gravity
from central Europe to the new Atlantic trade to the west. Spooner says
of the Treaty of Cateau-Cambrésis that it "was not so much the closing
of a period as an opening on the future," and he adds: "The path of
the future lay . . . across the Atlantic and the seven seas of the world."[169]

Economically, the most striking event of this time was however not located
in the Atlantic but to the north. Astrid Friis argues it was rather "the
exceptional expansion of the sea trade in the Netherlands and England
coeval with a rapid rise in the imports of Baltic goods, especially grain, into
other parts of Europe."[170] In her view, crises in bullion, credit and finance

[164]These figures are to be found in Frank C. Spooner, "The Economy of Europe, 1559–1609" in *New Cambridge Modern History*, **III**: R. B. Wernham, ed., *The Counter Reformation and The Price Revolution, 1559–1610* (London and New York: Cambridge Univ. Press, 1968), 33. See Braudel, *La Méditerranée*, **I**, pp. 361–362; Cipolla, *Guns and Sails*, p. 86 (fn).

[165]"Yet changes in population were not always as favourable to economic development as may at first be imagined. More men brought more vagabonds and bandits to live on the fringe of society and the law; they also raised the demand for employment, which created another difficult problem. In short, the growth of population implied a whole series of advantages, mixed with burdens and inconveniences. It is possible . . . that at a given moment human production follows the laws of diminishing returns, a process of deterioration. . . . Europe at the end of the sixteenth century had become relatively overpopulated, more especially in the western

countries, the most dense and the most wealthy. A technological revolution such as the Industrial Revolution might have saved the situation but this came two centuries later. In other words, it is possible that the level of production could not reach the required capacity, and was insufficient for the population. In effect, supply did not respond to the increasing demand." Spooner, *New Cambridge Modern History*, **III**, p. 34.

[166]*Ibid.*, p. 14.

[167]See *ibid.*, p. 26.

[168]Tawney, *A Discourse Upon Usury*, p. 86.

[169]Frank C. Spooner, "The Hapsburg-Valois Struggle," *New Cambridge Modern History*. **II**: G. R. Elton, ed., *The Reformation 1520–1559* (London and New York: Cambridge Univ. Press, 1958), 358.

[170]Astrid Friis, "An Inquiry into the Relations between Economic and Financial Factors in the Sixteenth and Seventeenth Centuries," *Scandinavian Economic History Review*, **I**, 2, 1953, 193. See also pp. 209–213.

are not the motor of economic (and political) change, but its consequence.[171] In this case, she says, it was the grain penury that was the immediate cause of the strain on the money market.[172] One of the outcomes of this was to strengthen enormously the hand of Amsterdam which was already at that time the pivot of the Baltic grain market and which, thereby, was able to remain more solvent than Antwerp and other cities of the southern provinces.

Thus we go from Seville to Amsterdam. The story of the "second" sixteenth century is the story of how Amsterdam picked up the threads of the dissolving Hapsburg Empire, creating a framework of smooth operation for the world-economy that would enable England and France to begin to emerge as strong states, eventually to have strong "national economies."

These developments were for the most part the consequence of the fact that the first expansionist phase of the European world-economy was drawing to its close in this period. It was the moment when the "great tide began to ebb, as if its rise lacked the requisite momentum to overcome the obstacles and impediments which it itself had raised."[173] We shall turn now to the responses of the traditional centers of population and finance, the Low Countries and northern Italy. Then, in the next chapter we shall deal both with the emergence of England not only as the third political power of Europe (alongside France and Spain) but as the one most rapidly advancing in the industrial sphere, and with the ways in which France, in making the shift from an imperial to a statist orientation, was constrained from obtaining the full benefits of the organizational shift.

How important were the Low Countries at this time? Lucien Febvre, in his introduction to Chaunu's *magnum opus* on the Atlantic trade, suggests—no, affirms—that the trade to and from the Netherlands pales in comparison:

> From the point of view of an economic history seen from on high, from the point of view of world and cultural history on a grand scale, what is there in common between this coastal trade of bulk goods, useful, but in no ways precious, going from North to South and from South to North . . . this coastal trade of foodstuffs, the barter, the modest purchases, the short-haul transport to which it gave rise—and, considering only the trade going from America to Europe, the contribution of precious metals in quantities theretofore unknown, which was to revive both the economy and the polity, the "grand policies" of European powers and, thus, to

[171]Addressing herself specifically to Hauser's thesis about the crises of 1557–1559, she asserts: "[T]he root of evil development is rather to be found in the prevailing economic conditions than in the financial policy. Not that I shall bestow any praise on the latter. Probably a breakdown in the finances of the Netherlands-Spain could not have been avoided in the long run. But certainly the ability of the inhabitants to pay taxes and to advance loans by which the income from taxes could be anticipated was an important factor in the financial system of the ruler of the Netherlands. . . .

"W. R. Scott who . . . has concerned himself much with the depressions of early modern times, especially in England, says that among simultaneous factors that may have speeded them bad harvests, plagues, and interruptions of commerce by war are too marked to be ignored. Precisely these three factors can be traced in the Netherlands in the fateful year 1557." *Ibid.*, p. 195.
[172]See *ibid.*, pp. 213–217.
[173]Spooner, *New Cambridge Modern History,* **III,** p. 42.

precipitate and accelerate social upheavals of incalculable scope: enrichment of
a merchant and financial bourgeoisie rising, as did the Fuggers and so many others,
to princely rank; progressive decadence of a nobility which maintains its status
and its brilliance only by exploiting parasitically the benefits acquired by the creators
of wealth; the long supremacy in Europe of the Hapsburgs, masters of the overseas
gold and silver: Beside so many great things, what is the importance of this local
trade *(trafic casanier)*, this potluck trade of the Sound and its barges, dragging pru-
dently their fat stomachs under foggy skies?[174]

What indeed? This is the question. Even if Febvre's facts were totally correct—and there seems reason to believe that he has seriously underestimated
the northern trade[175]—we should hesitate before accepting the intimidating
flourish of Febvre's prose. For this potluck local trade carried raw materials
for the new industries and food for the townsmen.[176] As we have seen,
it ensconced and codified a new European division of labor. Precious metals
after all must be used to buy real goods, and as we have also seen, the
precious metals may not have done too much more for Spain than pass
through its ledgers.

Nor was it only a question of the *economic* centrality of the trade which
revolved around the Low Countries. It was also a question of specialization
in the new skills required to run a financial and commercial focus of the
world-economy. It was the command of such skills that enabled the Dutch
to seize control of the world spice trade from the Portuguese as we move
from the "first" to the "second" sixteenth century.[177]

[174]Lucien Febvre, "Préface" to Huguette & Pierre Chaunu, *Séville et l'Atlantique (1504–1650)*, I: *Introduction méthodologique* (Paris: Lib. Armand Colin, 1955), xiii.

[175]See Jan Craeybackx's review of the book by Emile Coornaert, *Les français et le commerce internationale à Anvers (fin du XVe–XVIe siècles)* in which he remarks that Coornaert's book "provides abundant proof that the traffic between the various parts of the old continent was far more than a small-scale daily grind *(train-train quotidien)* as described by Lucien Febvre in his preface to the first volume of the work, a remarkable work, by H. and P. Chaunu on *Séville et l'Atlantique*. The statement must be considerably revised when we realize that merely the arrivals of wine from Middlebourg often equalled, even exceeded, at least in tonnage if not in value, the annual volume of traffic between Spain and the New World." "Les français et Anvers au XVIe siècle," *Annales E.S.C.*, **XVII**, 3, mai–juin 1962, 543.

[176]See the description by Aksel E. Christensen: "The Baltic exports . . . beside the corn practically exclusively consisted of raw materials and auxiliary materials for the Dutch and South-Western European industry. Among the industries which it supported ship-building was the most prominent. . . . Hemp was the raw material for rope-making, a distinct auxiliary industry for ship-building and the

fishery (fishing-nets), while flax i.a. was the basis of the other auxiliary industry, the making of sail. [Also pitch, tar, and metals for ship-building]. . . .

"Indeed, the Baltic trade was the 'mother' and 'soul' of Dutch commerce, not only the earliest and still the most important wholesale trade, but also the fundamental basis for the prosperity and growth of the mercantile marine." *Dutch Trade to the Baltic about 1600* (Copenhagen: Munksgaard, 1941), 365–366. See J. G. van Dillen, "Amsterdam's Role in Seventeenth-Century Dutch Politics and its Economic Background," in J. S. Bromley and E. H. Kossman, eds., *Britain and the Netherlands*, **II** (Groningen: Wolters, 1964), esp. pp. 133–135.

[177]"A new world-economy was . . . created [in the second half of the fifteenth century], an economy in which Lisbon and the *Casa de Contratación* controlled the spice-trade of the world and directed the fleet of spice-ships to their entrepôt at Goa and then to the anchorages of the Tagus. Portuguese administration and financial techniques proved inadequate for such lucrative burdens, [and] the Dutch proved their capacity as interlopers. . . . [T]he spice trade under Dutch control formed an invaluable adjunct to their trade to the Baltic and to northwestern Europe. The new and expanded trade in spices and eastern produce was geared into a trade system which spread throughout

The importance of the Low Countries for intra-European trade is of course nothing new. As S. T. Bindoff reminds us, "from the eleventh to the seventeenth century the Netherlands . . . were one of the nodal points of European trade. . . ."[178] We have noted the key role of Antwerp in the "first" sixteenth century.[179] Antwerp fell in 1559,[180] and the important thing to note is that the succession was by no means obvious. As we know, Amsterdam stepped into the breach, but Lawrence Stone argues that one way to read this fact is to see it as the failure of England as much as the success of the Dutch, a failure that would "retard" England's ascendancy in the world-system.[181]

Amsterdam's success then was politically as well as economically important. But what was the political framework that made this success possible? The last five decades of the sixteenth century mark not only the rise of Amsterdam but the so-called Netherlands Revolution, whose boundaries in time and space are as amorphous (or rather as contested) as its social content.

To begin with, was it a revolution? And if it was a revolution, was it

---

Europe and, indeed, across the Atlantic." E. E. Rich, "Preface," in *Cambridge Economic History of Europe,* **IV**: E. E. Rich and C. H. Wilson, eds., *The Economy of Expanding Europe in the 16th and 17th Centuries* (London and New York: Cambridge Univ. Press, 1967), xii.

See also E. E. Rich again: "The Dutch, meanwhile, had reaped the advantages of the trade of the New World without finding it necessary to participate actively in voyaging and trading either to the east or to the west. Much of their energy was absorbed in their religious disputes and in the long struggle with Spain; and they were able by virtue of their geographical position and of their commercial acumen to make their country, and their great city of Antwerp, the entrepôt for the spices of the East and the bourse for the treasures of America. The North Sea herring trade, too, brought them into profitable commercial touch with Portugal and the Mediterranean, and their Baltic trade in timbers, flax, tar and furs made them indispensable to the other states of western Europe, in particular to England." "Expansion as a Concern of All Europe," *New Cambridge Modern History,* **I**: G. R. Potter, ed., *The Renaissance, 1493–1520* (London and New York: Cambridge Univ. Press, 1957), 468.

[178]S. T. Bindoff, "Economic Change: The Greatness of Antwerp," *New Cambridge Modern History,* **II**: G. R. Elton, ed., *The Reformation, 1520–1559* (London and New York: Cambridge Univ. Press, 1958), 51.

[179]Hanseatic trade to France and later to the Iberian peninsula passed via Bruges as early as the thirteenth century. By the sixteenth century, Antwerp could not be bypassed. In general, by this time, Hanseatic ships survived more as transporters

than as merchants in the Atlantic trade. See Pierre Jeannin, "Anvers et la Baltique au XVIe siècle," *Revue du Nord,* **XXXVII,** avr.-juin 1955, 107–109. Jeannin notes that "the Antwerp milieu acted as a dissolvant on Hanseatic traditions and institutions [p. 97]."

[180]Not everyone agrees. Frank J. Smolar, Jr. argues that its decline is exaggerated in "Resiliency of Enterprise: Economic Causes and Recovery in the Spanish Netherlands in the Early Seventeenth Century," in Charles H. Carter, ed., *From the Renaissance to the Counter-Reformation* (New York: Random House, 1965), 247–268. The detailed argument is on pp. 251–252, and he concludes: "Indications of inherent economic strength and potential for extensive recovery are strong; the evidence for it is large, and largely unexploited [p. 253]."

[181]"England succeeded in reorganizaing her commerce in such a way as adequately to compensate for the shattering blow of the collapse of Antwerp. But she failed—indeed she hardly tried—to take on the mantle of Elijah. The unique opportunity that was offered in the period between the fall of Antwerp and the rise of Amsterdam was let slip. There are indications that in the critical period of English economic history, she did in fact succeed in taking over from Germany the leadership in mining and industrial techniques. But she lost the race for supremacy in commerce and shipping to the more enterprising, more efficient and better organized Dutch. It is not too much to suggest that this failure to profit by the collapse of Antwerp retarded the rise of England to a position of world greatness by at least a century." Stone, *Economic History Review,* **II**, p. 54.

a national revolution or a bourgeois revolution? And is there any difference between these two concepts? I shall not now begin a long excursus on the concept of revolution. We are not yet ready in the logic of this work to treat that question. I should like merely to underline at this point that it seems to me this question is no more ambiguous (and to be sure no more clear) in the case of the Netherlands "Revolution" than in the case of any other of the great "revolutions" of the modern era.

The historical literature reveals one very great schism in interpretation. Some consider the Revolution essentially the story of the "Dutch" nation—that is, of the northern Netherlanders, Calvinists, struggling for liberty and independence against the Spanish crown, the latter aided and abetted by the "Belgian" (southern Netherlander) Catholics. Others consider it essentially a revolt of the all-Netherlands ("Burgundian") nation, supported by persons from all religious groups, which succeeded in liberating only half a nation. J. W. Smit ends a survey of the historiography with this very sensible comment:

> These problems, however, can only be resolved if we stop treating the Revolt as a *bloc* and if we become aware that there were a number of revolts, representing the interests and the ideals of various social, economical and ideological groups: revolts which sometimes run parallel, sometimes conflict with one another, and at other times coalesce into a single movement.[182]

From the point of view of the world-system as it was developing we must ask why it was the Netherlands and in the Netherlands alone that a complex national-social revolution occurs in the "second" sixteenth century, an era of relative quiet and social order elsewhere (except, most importantly, for France) and how it was that the revolt was largely successful.[183]

During the era of Charles V, Netherlands internal politics was not remarkably different from the politics of other parts of Europe. The nobility was in an ambivalent relationship to its prince, fearing his growing political and economic power, seeing him as a protector of their interests both against the bourgeoisie and popular revolt, finding service for the prince a financial salvation for the "younger sons" or distressed peers, ultimately siding with the prince.[184] Then, suddenly, we get a situation in which "the

---

[182]J. W. Smit, "The Present Position of Studies Regarding the Revolt of the Netherlands," in Bromley & Kossmann, eds., *Britain and the Netherlands* (Groningen: Wolters, 1964), **I**, 28.

[183]"The political development that . . . took place [in the late sixteenth century], combined with the dramatic rise of an economy conducted by a merchant class led by the regent families, explains to a large extent the remarkable position which they came to hold in Holland in the seventeenth century." D. J. Roorda, "The Ruling Classes in Holland in the Seventeenth Century," in Bromley & Kossman,

eds., *Britain and the Netherlands* (Groningen: Wolters, 1964), **II**, 112–113.

[184]"The nobility had the option to seek the prince's help against their common bourgeois enemy or to ally with the bourgeoisie against the prince, who was no less prone to want to curtail the power of the nobles. During the reign of Charles V the nobility seemed to have opted for the prince. The higher nobility rose rapidly in the emperor's service, while the lower nobility was content either with lesser administrative functions or with service in the army." J. W. Smit, *Preconditions of Revolution*, p. 31.

frustrated prosperous bourgeois of the booming towns joined the desperate declassed craftsmen and thriving or declining nobles, and local riots coalesced into a general revolution."[185] How come?

I think the key to the *outbreak* of revolution is not in the social discontent of artisans and urban workers, nor in the bourgeoisie who were doubtless to be the great beneficiaries of the revolution, but in the fact that large parts of the "Netherlands" nobility were suddenly afraid that the prince was not *their* agent, that his policies would in the short and medium run threaten their interests significantly and that it was outside their political possibility to persuade him to make alterations in his policy, since his political arena (the Spanish empire) was so much larger than one which, if established, they might control.[186] In short, they had a reflex of "nationalist" opposition.[187]

Let us look at some of the evidence. The nobility there, as elsewhere, was in increasing debt. Furthermore, the Emperor was steadily cutting into their sources of current income.[188] When Philip II came to power, he discovered sudden resistance to his fund raising.[189] The last years of Charles V were trying ones—great financial demands of the Emperor combined with a decline in real income of the nobility caused by the price inflation. The bankruptcies and the economic difficulties resulting from the peace treaty of Cateau-Cambrésis made the situation suddenly worse.[190]

Then, on top of the economic grievances, Philip II obtained Rome's permission in 1559 to create new bishoprics. The move was intended to rationalize political and linguistic boundaries, increase the number of

[185]*Ibid.*, p. 41.

[186]"Are not great revolutions due to the conjunction of prosperous classes who want to become revolutionary, and wretched classes who are obliged to do so, whereas revolutions of pure poverty are actually short-lived?" Comments by Pierre Vilar in *Charles-Quint et son temps*, p. 188.

[187]"In the sixteenth century, almost for the first time, opposition movements became nation-wide and included classes, or elements of classes, ranging from princes of the blood to unemployed artisans." H. G. Koenigsberger, "The Organization of Revolutionary Parties in France and the Netherlands During the Sixteenth Century," *The Journal of Modern History*, **XXVII**, 4, Dec. 1955, 336.

[188]"The central government and the hated lawyers were, moreover, steadily encroaching on their remaining seigneurial rights. In 1520, a proclamation prohibited the levying of new tithes and sought to abolish feudal rights existing for less than 40 years. In 1531, the Crown forbade lords to exact gifts or new services from their tenants. The decline of income from the exercise of the rights of jurisdiction has already been mentioned." H. G. Koenigsberger, "Property and the Price Revolution (Hainault, 1474–1573)," *Economic History Review*, 2nd ser., **IX**, 1, 1956, 14.

See Smit: "But it is difficult to determine whether such hostility was inspired primarily by concern to preserve their economic standing or by the desire to maintain their social status. The higher nobility still received considerable income, but its relative economic position, like that (to a lesser extent) of the lower nobility, seems to have been declining because of conspicuous spending. Obviously, economic pressures were only one of the nobility's many grievances, but they constituted a major incentive to revolution in a class which felt beleaguered on all sides." *Preconditions of Revolution*, pp. 41–42."

[189]See Pieter Geyl, *The Revolt of the Netherlands (1559–1609)* (London: Williams & Norgate, 1932), 69–70.

[190]"If the decline in the real income of the lower nobility was, in fact, due to rising prices, then it was probably not spread evenly throughout the first three quarters of the sixteenth century but concentrated in the 15 or 20 years before the outbreak of the great revolt, the years after 1550, when prices rose much more rapidly than before. Thus, if there was a crisis, it was a comparatively sharp and sudden one, aggravated by demobilization from the *bandes d'ordonnances*, the aristocratic Netherlands cavalry, after the treaty of Cateau-Cambrésis, in 1559." Koenigsberger, *Economic History Review*, **IX**, p. 14.

bishoprics, and require that bishops be technically skilled (that is, theologians rather than sons of great lords). For good measure, the plan required that the funds to endow the new bishoprics were to be taken from the revenues of certain historic and hitherto financially independent abbeys, the new bishops replacing the abbots in the various political assemblies. No doubt, as Pieter Geyl remarks tersely it showed Philip to be a "diligent" state builder.[191] Still, "it is not to be wondered at that there arose a storm of opposition to a plan which involved such a strengthening of the King's authority at a moment when his designs were viewed with mistrust on all sides."[192]

In the other direction, the nobility sought to transform the Council of State into "an exclusively aristocratic executive body."[193] Philip refused but compromised by withdrawing Spanish troops, leaving his government in the Netherlands with only forces supplied by the local nobility and the urban centers to maintain order. If one adds to this picture the general grievances of the lower classes and middle bourgeoisie brought on by the recession of the 1560s[194] and the general weakness of the Church under attack now for forty years, a revolt became possible:

> Religiously indifferent mobs attacked prisons, the hated symbols of oppression, and freed Protestants. Toleration became the general slogan and in conjunction with the demand for a free Estates-General, became the core of the opposition's political program. For some time these slogans worked as perfect generalized beliefs of a national, or interprovincial, scope; they were simple principles and above all were socially neutral.[195]

We must not forget that this is shortly after the peace of Cateau-Cambrésis, that this peace permitted the sessions of the Council of Trent to resume, and thus for the Counter-Reformation to become institutionalized.[196] Hence Catholicism and the Spanish Crown were more closely identified than previously.

The "Revolution" went through a number of phases: the first uprising (in both north and south) and its suppression (1566–1572); the second uprising (more "Protestant") of only Holland and Zeeland in the north (1572–1576) ending in the Pacification of Ghent; a radical uprising in Flanders in the south (1577–1579); a division of the country into two from 1579 on (United Provinces in the north, a loyalist regime in the south); an attempted reunification in 1598; conclusion of a lasting truce in 1609.

Over this period, what should be noticed is that the conflict—amorphous

[191]"It was a striking instance of what the monarch could do in the way of state building, and exhibits Philip as a diligent worker in the tradition of his house." Geyl, *The Revolt of the Netherlands*, p. 71.
[192]*Ibid.*, p. 72.
[193]Smit, *Preconditions of Revolution*, p. 47.
[194]See *ibid.*, pp. 42–43.
[195]*Ibid.*, p. 48.

[196]"The peace between France and Spain was the political foundation upon which rested the Trentine reorganization of Catholicism. A fact of especial transcendence, not only for one people alone, but for all of Christianity." Manuel Fernandez Alvarez, "La Paz de Cateau-Cambrésis," *Hispania, revista española de historia*, **XIX,** No. 77, oct.-dic., 1959, 544.

and multisided in the beginning—took on an increasingly clear form as the struggle of the Protestant, or rather "Protestantized," north for national independence of the north with a regime in the latter consonant with the needs of the commercial bourgeoisie, whose strength on a worldwide scale grew throughout the struggle and subsequently in the seventeenth century. Once started, there probably was very little that Spain, given "the failure of empire," could do to stop it,[197] especially given, as we shall see, the new European balance of power. Indeed, the constraints on Spain are clearly indicated by the fact that virtually every major political turning point in the Spanish–Netherlands relationship from 1557 to 1648 was immediately preceded by a financial crisis in Spain.[198]

Though the Netherlands Revolution was a "nationalist" movement, it involved a religious component from the beginning. While the nobility sought in the beginning to monopolize the form and nature of the quarrel with the King, the Calvinist community broke through their prescribed passive role into a frenzy known as the Breaking of the Images which swept the country, north and south. Geyl describes the authorities as "paralyzed with fright" and the Calvinist leaders themselves showing "surprise and discomfiture."[199] It was religion that added the note of

[197]Koenigsberger comes to the defense of Philip II: "Philip II has been almost universally condemned for sending Alva to the Netherlands. But have not these judgments been based largely on the historian's hindsight? Could a strong sixteenth-century ruler have acted differently when faced with the double opposition of the high nobility (albeit a constitutional opposition) and a revolutionary religious movement with a military organization (albeit in its infancy)? In France and in Scotland the Calvinists had built up their formidable organizations because of the weakness of the French and Scottish governments. It was a commonplace of sixteenth century statecraft that rebellion should be crushed in its infancy. Moreover, this policy very nearly succeeded. It failed because it was, perhaps, already too late, even in 1567, and because Alva did not command the sea power to crush the Water Beggars. Undoubtedly, Philip misunderstood the complexity of the situation, and Alva proved to be the wrong choice for his purposes. But that also was not so obvious as it became later; for Alva had behaved with considerable tact in the war against Pope Paul IV. Yet, . . . even Alva's cruelty did not raise a spontaneous outburst of rebellion from an oppressed people; the revolt of 1572 became possible only through the action of the highly organized and ruthless Water Beggars and their equally highly organized 'fifth column' in the Holland and Zeeland towns." *Journal of Modern History,* **XXVII**, p. 341.

[198]The link of internal developments in Spain to the ups and downs of the Netherlands Revolution is neatly spelled out by H. Lonchay: "Not only did

these [Spanish financial] crises interest the exchanges of Antwerp, London, and Amsterdam, but they had an impact on the events of [Belgium] which has not been noticed. That of 1557 explains why, despite the victories of Saint-Quentin and Gravelines, Philip II was in such a hurry to conclude peace with France. That of 1575 makes us understand the Spanish Fury and all the excesses of the foreign soldiers so long deprived of their pay. The transaction of 1596 precedes the handing-over of the Low Countries to the archdukes, which Philip II decided upon only because he thought it easier to establish peace thereby in the Low Countries than by the use of force. The decrees of 1607–1608 give us the reason why Philip III resigned himself to signing the truce of Twelve Years, so wounding to his pride. That of 1647 was certainly not irrelevant to the sudden willingness of Philip IV to recognize definitively the independence of the United Provinces. Thus the fate of Belgium was tied to that of Spain and often one cannot understand the political history of the one without knowing the financial situation of the other." *Académie Royale de Belgique,* pp. 994–995.

[199]Geyl adds: "In any case it was a truly Calvinistic work, fierce and honest, restrained by no respect for art and beauty, striving to purge the land for God's elect from the devilish ornaments of idolatry, and to pull down at one blow a past of a thousand years. Nor did the deed once done lack dour approbation from the side of the intellectual leaders of Calvinism." Geyl, *The Revolt of the Netherlands,* p. 93.

ideological passion to the Revolution and enabled I. Shöffer to compare the Breaking of the Images to the storming of the Bastille and the street riots in Petrograd in March 1917.[200]

Though this phase quickly passed, the strength of the Calvinists as a revolutionary party, as sixteenth-century Jacobins in the analogy of H. G. Koenigsberger,[201] meant that they had the stamina to persist when others fell by the wayside, to use a policy of "terrorizing the population,"[202] and to be able "to mobilize the mob at strategic moments."[203] When in the Pacification of Ghent, the authorities tried to solve the conflict by religious partition, they merely entrenched the Reformed party in Holland and Zeeland and reinforced the identification of the political and religious cause,[204] which led eventually to the "Protestantization" of areas under Protestant control. The division of the country in 1579 led to a consolidation on each side and thus to a lasting religious polarization.[205] The actual lines of administrative division were the result of geo–military factors. The southern Netherlands was open country where Spanish cavalry could prevail. The northern part was covered with waterways and other barriers to cavalry movement. It was, in short, ideal guerilla country.[206] In the

[200]See I. Schöffer, "The Dutch Revolution Anatomized: Some Comments," *Comparative Studies in Society and History,* **III,** 4, July 1961, 471.

[201]See Koenigsberger, *Journal of Modern History,* **XXVII,** p. 335. Gordon Griffiths suggests similarly that the Dutch Revolution may be seen to be analogous to the French Revolution in terms of the categories developed by Crane Brinton. See "The Revolutionary Character of the Revolution of the Netherlands," *Comparative Studies in Society and History,* **II,** 4, July 1960, 452–472.

[202]Koenigsberger, *Journal of Modern History,* **XXVII,** p. 342.

[203]*Ibid.,* p. 343.

[204]See Geyl, *The Revolt of the Netherlands,* p. 161.

[205]Pieter Geyl argues: "The true explanation, then, of the division of the Netherlands into a Protestant North and a Catholic South is the exact opposite of the current one. It is not because the South was Catholic and the North Protestant that the rebellion failed here and succeeded there: it is because the rivers enabled the rebellion to entrench itself in the North, while Spain recovered the provinces situated on the wrong side of the strategic barrier, that in course of time there sprang into existence this dual system of the Protestant Northern Republic and the Catholic Southern Netherlands, or Protestant Holland and Catholic Belgium." *Debates with Historians* (New York: Meridian, 1958), 209. See Henri Lapeyre, *Les monarchies européennes du XVIe siècle,* Collection Nouvelle Clio 39 (Paris: Presses Universitaires de France, 1967), 188–189.

Thus, administrative separatism leads to religious polarization. Furthermore it was not that Calvinists became capitalists but that capitalists became Calvin-

ists. H. R. Trevor-Roper makes the case: "If the great Calvinist entrepreneurs of the mid-seventeenth century were not united by Calvinist piety, or even by its supposed social expression, what did unite them? If we look attentively at them we soon find certain obvious facts. First, whether good or bad Calvinists, the majority of them were not native of the country in which they worked. Neither Holland nor Scotland nor Geneva nor the Palatinate—the four obvious Calvinist societies—produced their own entrepreneurs. The compulsory Calvinist teaching with which the natives of those communities were indoctrinated had no such effect. Almost all the great entrepreneurs were immigrants. Secondly, the majority of these immigrants were Netherlanders. . . . Moreover, when we look closer still, we discover that these Netherlanders came generally from a particular class within the Dutch Republic. Even there they were, or their fathers had been, immigrants. Either they were 'Flemings' —that is, immigrants from the southern provinces now under Spanish rule—or they were Liégeois, from the Catholic prince-bishopric of Liège." *The European Witch-Craze,* pp. 15–16.

[206]"Belgium (to use a modern term) was for the most part a 'cavalry country' fit for great battles in the open, from Gemblours to Waterloo. 'The Cockpit of Europe' is a region that can be lost and won in the field. Not so Holland (to use again a modern word) which is for the greater part of its extent so cut up by arms of the sea, rivers, canals, and marshes, that it is hard to find within its borders room to set a large army in formal array." Oman, *A History of the Art of War,* p. 541.

course of time, those to the north *became* Protestant, those to the south *became* Catholic.

Hence it is not that, as many have already argued, Protestantism is particularly consonant with social change—no more with nationalism than with capitalism. It is rather, as Sir Lewis Namier is quoted, "religion is a sixteenth-century word for nationalism."[207] Protestantism served to unify the northern Netherlands. We noted in the previous chapter how and why Catholicism became linked with Polish national sentiment. And Catholicism did the same thing for Ireland.[208] Wherever a religion was not firmly linked to the national cause, it did not prove capable of surviving, as Calvinism in France.[209]

What was going on was that, in the maelstrom of conflicting interests, new organizational structures could only be built by strange and unstable alliances. Men sought to secure these alliances. H. G. Koenigsberger captures the point precisely:

> Religion was the binding force that held together the different interests of the different classes and provided them with an organization and a propaganda machine capable of creating the first genuinely national and international parties in modern European history; for these parties never embraced more than a minority of each of their constituent classes. Moreover it was through religion that they could appeal to the lowest classes and the mob to vent the anger of their poverty and the despair of their unemployment in barbarous massacres and fanatical looting. Social and

[207]Cited in Christopher Hill, *Reformation to the Industrial Revolution*, p. 23. In a personal communication, Hill states that "Namier made the remark on one of several discussion evenings which undergraduates of [Balliol] College had with him in 1934 when he was delivering the Ford Lectures in Oxford." See F. Chabod: "If there are sentiments which play a role in the life of the state in the 16th century, they are religious in nature rather than national or patriotic. In the case of France, this applies to internal politics only, as foreign policy was early on unbound from ideology. But in the case of the Hapsburgs, did this not also apply to foreign policy?" *Actes du Colloque*, p. 620.

[208]"Catholicism in Ireland, like Protestantism in the Netherlands, had drawn new strength from its identification with a national cause. Although Irish society was infinitely less sophisticated than that of the Netherlands, its struggle against English domination was characterized by many of the same features as the Dutch struggle against the domination of Spain. In both societies a religious cause enhanced, and was enhanced by, a sense of national identity. In both, the affiliation of national leaders to an international religious movement provided new opportunities for securing international assistance." J. H. Elliott, *Europe Divided, 1559–1598* (New York: Harper, 1968), 302.

[209]"There was . . . one essential difference between the régimes in France and the Netherlands

which profoundly affected the respective characters of their political opposition. Catherine [of France] herself was half foreign, but she headed a royal government which remained a symbol of national unity in a divided country. Margaret, as the daughter of Charles V and a Flemish woman, was a Netherlander by birth; but she headed a royal government that was increasingly regarded as alien. This proved in the long run to be a fact of incalculable importance, for it allowed the opposition to appear—as it could never convincingly appear in the France of the 1560's—as the defender of national traditions against foreign innovations." Elliot, *ibid.*, p. 126.

If we ask why Calvinism was not revolutionary in England under Elizabeth as it was in the Netherlands and France at this time, once again the position of the royal authority made a difference: "To begin with, England had already expended much of her nationalist spirit against the Papacy under Henry VIII's quarrels with the Roman Church. . . . In England, the question of foreign influence after Queen Mary was never a serious problem again until Charles II's reign. But even more important in the English situation was the absence after 1588 of a Catholic sovereign, who, as in France and Holland, served as a constant reminder of the Roman Antichrist." Leo F. Solt, "Revolutionary Calvinist Parties in England Under Elizabeth I and Charles I," *Church History*, **XXVII**, 3, Sept., 1958, 235.

economic discontent were fertile ground for recruitment by either side, and popular democratic tyranny appeared both in Calvinist Ghent and Catholic Paris.[210]

If religion then serves as a national cement, it tells us little about the social content of the resulting state structures. J. W. Smit argues that the Netherlands Revolution was essentially, despite the ambiguities, a bourgeois revolution, bringing the bourgeoisie to power, and the partition of the Netherlands and the resulting state boundaries are a measure of the degree of its strength in the face of its enemies.[211]

To be sure, the nobility were involved at various places and times, particularly in the beginning, but they were frightened away from the nationalist cause by the recurring undercurrents of social radicalism.[212] But if radical social movements had a sufficient base in the lumpenproletariat of the towns born of economic expansion *cum* recession, as exemplified by the brief control of Ghent by Jan van Hembyze from 1577–1579,[213]

---

[210]Koenigsberger, *Journal of Modern History,* **XXVII,** pp. 350–351. See Robert M. Kingdon on Calvinism as a transnational movement: "[T]he revolts of the sixteenth century cannot be viewed solely as chapters in separate national histories; they must be considered as in part at least the work of a revolutionary international religious organization—the Calvinist Church." "The Political Resistance of the Calvinists in France and the Low Countries," *Church History,* **XXVII,** 3, Sept. 1958, 233.

[211]"After all, in spite of the qualifications we must make, the new republic became the first real capitalist and bourgeois nation with a strongly marked, very mercantile national identity. The key to an [interpretation of the contradictory facts] resides, I think, in the fact that the revolution succeeded in only part of the Netherlands. I would like to defend the proposition that the Netherlands Revolution was indeed, among many other things, an innovative, progressive, societal revolution. But the mercantile bourgeois class . . . was too weak to establish its government in all of the Netherlands; . . . It could found a state in its own image only in Holland, where the market economy, already in an advanced stage of development, was swollen by southern capital, people, and skills, and where it had no major opposition from rival social groups." Smit, *Preconditions of Revolution,* pp. 52–53. See T. Wittman: "[T]he war of independence of 1566–1605 against Spain constituted a coherent process and entirely fulfills the criteria of a bourgeois revolution. The anti-feudal struggles of the urban and peasant masses blended into their resistance to Spanish oppression and to the Catholic Church; and these mass movements brought to the fore of the Estates-General a leadership which, especially after the formation of the Union of Utrecht, and

despite all its limits and contradictions, expressed the social aspirations of the bourgeoisie." "Quelques problèmes relatifs à la dictature révolutionnaire des grandes villes de Flandres, 1577–1579," *Studia historica,* No. 40 (Academicae Scientarum Hungaricae), 1960, 3–4.

[212]"Whenever there was a serious threat of social revolution—from the breaking of the images in 1566, to the aggressive democratic dictatorship of the Ghent Calvinists, in the late 1570's—the Hainault nobility closed their ranks and united for the preservation of the social *status quo,* even if this meant submission to the rule of Spain." H. G. Koenigsberger, *Economic History Review,* **IX,** p. 15.
"In the long run, not even religion was able to reconcile the nobility with democratic dictatorships, and one side or the other was driven into alliance with the formerly common enemy. The result was, in every case, the breakup of the revolutionary party and the defeat of the popular movement." H. G. Koenigsberger, *Journal of Modern History,* **XXVII,** p. 351.

[213]See Wittmann: "The corporations. . . were not at all behind the leftward thrust of the revolution; they were rather its beneficiaries, and even, more than once, its fetters. In the big Flemish towns the conditions for radicalization existed: pauperization and accelerated social differentiation provoked by the decomposition of the feudal regime in a situation in which the factors making for a rapid transition to capitalist production did not yet exist. The plebeian masses formed out of the ranks of ruined masters, journeymen, apprentices, petty merchants and various elements of the lumpenproletariat reflected in their political behavior, albeit only instinctively, this stage of evolution." *Studia historica,* p. 16. Wittmann adds in a footnote: "With regard to the enormous growth of the lumpenproletariat

they were rapidly isolated and destroyed themselves by losing sight of the national theme and turning against the bourgeoisie, and hence, paradoxically, toward alliance with the king's forces.[214]

Thus, slowly, emerged a confederation of town governments who quickly shed any "democratic" trimmings but who also were free from the economic burdens which their participation in the old Spanish system inflicted.[215] The merchants created for themselves a loose confederation without the administrative apparatus of most other states. Many have termed this a weakness but Smit is closer to the point when he reminds us that the state machinery of the Dutch Republic "permitted the achievement of a higher degree of economic integration than any of the monarchies of Europe. The bourgeoisie of Holland had carried through exactly the degree of reform it needed to promote economic expansion and yet feel free from overcentralization."[216] Thus, the Netherlands Revolution may never have started without the defection of many nobles from the established order. It may never have gotten a second wind without the radical currents from below. But in the end it was the bourgeoisie who held firm to the reins and emerged the beneficiaries of the new social order.

Why, however, the Netherlands and not elsewhere? We said that the "second" sixteenth century was the era of turning inward, the rejection of the imperial ideal in favor of seeking to create the strong state. There was still, however, during part of this period one arena in which all the

---

in the 16th century, . . . Engels made some pertinent remarks in *The Peasant War in Germany*. . . . In analyzing mass movements in the Middle Ages, Marxist historians have not yet given this factor a close examination [p. 16]."

Smit comments on the religious views of these lumpenproletarians as follows: "At the same time we must ask ourselves how far indifference towards dogmatic religion had spread among the masses too: how far the people who had been the iconoclasts of 1566 and the revolutionary unemployed of 1572 were a floating group of indifferents, rather than *future* recruits than at that moment the vanguard of Protestantism or Catholicism. The answer to the question whether the Revolt was Calvinist in character or purely political, modern or conservative, depends largely on the examination of the social and ideological structure of the population." *Britain and the Netherlands*, I, p. 24.

[214]"Nowhere was the revolution carried so far as in Ghent." Koenigsberger, *Journal of Modern History*, **XXVII**, p. 344. See also Wittman: "Nevertheless there existed neither the objective condition, a revolutionary bourgeoisie guided by its own interests, nor the subjective condition, a more consequential policy on the part of Hembyze and his supporters. Lacking these the radicalization led to its own negation when in 1583, after the 'French Fury,' Hembyze, who had totally undermined the author-

ity of the Orangists, placed himself at the head of the forces of Ghent against William of Orange and appealed for help to the Spaniards. The treason of Hembyze does not raise a moral issue—contrary to the way in which it has been usually treated heretofore by historians. It is rather a process that may be found in all precocious bourgeois revolutions. In England, also, at the time of the Protectorate of Cromwell, some Levellers, once their party had collapsed, established relations with the royalists and the Spaniards, just as Hembyze and Dalthenus had done. " *Studia historica*, p. 36.

[215]"Thus the patricians of the Republic were not kept in check from below. However, it is still more noticeable that the Revolt also caused nearly every restraint from above to disappear. In the first half of the sixteenth century, the central administration had backed the local patricians against any coalition of ambitious men of prominence and discontented small citizens in their towns. The central administration had also seen to it that the regents should not exercise power outside their own towns. After the Revolt, on the other hand, the urban magistracies came to be in practice completely independent. They ruled without anybody's interference, all but unbridled." Roorda, *Britain and the Netherlands*, **II**, pp. 114–115.

[216]Smit, *Preconditions of Revolution*, p. 52.

great powers intervened, one arena of general entanglement. It was the Netherlands. One way to interpret the Netherlands Revolution is to see it as the effort of the local dominant groups to achieve the same exclusion of outsiders from political interference, the same control of self, that Spain, France, and England at least were striving to enjoy.

Another way to interpret it is to say that because after 1559, Spain, France, and England balanced each other off, the Netherlanders had the social space to assert their identity and throw off the Spanish yoke. This was particularly true after the defeat of the Spanish Armada in 1588.[217] It was not that any of these countries stood for the independence of the Netherlands. Spain did not want to lose part of her dominions. France, although it wanted to weaken Spain, vacillated because of the implications for the internal religious struggle in France. England wanted to get Spain out but not let France in, and preferred therefore Netherlands autonomy under nominal Spanish sovereignty.[218] The point however is that this conflict within the world-system, this weakening of Spanish world dominance, made it possible for the bourgeoisie of the United Provinces to maneuver to maximize *its* interests. By 1596, they could enter as equals in a treaty with France and England, when only shortly before they had offered themselves as subjects to the one or the other. As Geyl comments: "Once more the mutual jealousies of France and England where the Low Countries were concerned proved a benefit."[219]

The significance of the Netherlands Revolution is not that it established a model of national liberation. Despite the romantic liberal historiography of the nineteenth century, the Dutch example did not serve as a generator of ideological currents. The importance lies in the economic impact on the European world-economy. The Netherlands Revolution liberated a force that could sustain the world-system as a system over some difficult years of adjustment, until the English (and the French) were ready to take the steps necessary for its definitive consolidation.

Let us recall the prior economic history of Amsterdam and other towns of the northern Netherlands. The Dutch had been playing an increasing role in Baltic trade.[220] They gained a footing in the late Middle Ages and

[217]See Geyl, *The Revolt of the Netherlands,* pp. 217–219.

[218]On France, see G. N. Clark, "The Birth of the Dutch Republic," *Proceedings of the British Academy,* 1946, 191. On England, see R. B. Wernham, "English Policy and the Revolt of the Netherlands," in Bromley and Kossman, eds., *Britain and the Netherlands,* (Groningen: Wolters, 1964), **I,** 30–31.

[219]Geyl, *The Revolt of the Netherlands,* p. 225.

[220]"[I]n the course of the fifteenth century, the fishing and shipbuilding towns of the provinces of Zeeland and Holland prospered slowly but irresistibly, extended their coasting trade farther and farther east until they became most dangerous rivals of the Hanse in just those Prussian quarters upon which rested the chief economic strength of

the League." Carl Brinkmann, "The Hanseatic League: A Survey of Recent Literature," *Journal of Economic and Business History,* **II,** 4, Aug. 1930, 591.

At the same time, Holland was gaining a large share of Scotland's overseas trade, about one-half of the tonnage toward 1560. The statistics are not that strong: "In any event the number, or even the aggregate tonnage, of vessels following the different trade routes would be an imperfect guide to the real significance of the trade between Scotland and the Low Countries because, apart from coal and salt, the goods entering that trade were of relatively high value as compared, for example, with the Norwegian trade [of Scotland]." S. G. E. Lythe, *The Economy of Scotland in its European Setting, 1550–1625* (Edinburgh: Oliver & Boyd, 1960), 245.

by the early sixteenth century were replacing the Hanseatic cities. Their total Baltic trade was on a rising curve in the sixteenth century, reaching a point, in about 1560, when they controlled about 70% of the trade. Although the Revolutionary period interfered somewhat with the level of Baltic trade, the Dutch recouped their temporary decline by 1630.[221]

The effect of the Revolution was not only to ensure the economic decline of Flanders but to strengthen the north in personnel because of the migration of many Flemish bourgeois north. "If Holland and Zeeland flourished, it was partly because they fed on the best vital forces of Flanders and Brabant."[222] Furthermore, the principle of religious toleration proclaimed by the United Provinces in 1579 led to the arrival of Sephardic Jews beginning in 1597. "Bringing their riches and business acumen to supplement the prosperity of the mercantile states of the north, such an emigration became by definition a European phenomenon."[223]

As soon as the political struggle within the Netherlands seemed to stabilize, the Dutch surged forward from being merely a center of Baltic trade to being a center of world trade.[224] Furthermore, the new trade increased rather than decreased the importance of the Baltic trade, which the Dutch themselves called the "mother trade." After all, eastern Europe supplied both the grain to feed Dutch cities and the naval supplies essential

---

[221]"An analysis of the ship figures in the Dutch trade to the Baltic leads to the preliminary conclusion that neither the revolt against Spain nor the great expansion to the new far routes during the years before and after 1600 involved a lasting decline in the Dutch command of the Baltic trade." Christensen, *Dutch Trade*, p. 90.

Oscar Albert Johnsen shows that the Norwegians took advantage of the 1572 Dutch uprising against the Spanish to inaugurate "direct and regular commercial relations entre the countries of the King of Spain. . . ." However, after the end of the Twelve Years Truce in 1621, the Dutch fleet was strong enough to attack the Norwegians: "[T]his piracy and these confiscations practically ruined our navigation in the Mediterranean entirely." "Les relations commerciales entre la Norvège et l'Espagne dans les temps modernes," *Revue historique*, 55e année, fasc. 1, sept.-déc. 1930, 78. Johnsen admits it was not merely Holland's naval strength that undid Norway but their commercial strength. See p. 80.

As Pierre Jeannin says: "One can debate the exact moment when Dutch commerce won out over the Hanse, but in about 1600 the triumph was complete." *Vierteljahrschrift für Sozial- und Wirtschaftsgeschichte*, **XLIII**, pp. 193–194.

[222]Geyl, *Revolt of the Netherlands*, p. 239.

[223]Spooner, *New Cambridge Modern History*, **III**, p. 31. Braudel goes further: "As the secular regression

of 1350–1450 pushed the Jewish merchants towards Italy and its sheltered economy, the crisis of 1600–1650 finds them in the shelter again, this time of the North Sea. The Protestant world saved them by preferring them and they, conversely, saved the Protestant world by preferring them. After all, as Werner Sombart remarked, Genoa was as well placed as Hamburg or Amsterdam in terms of the maritime routes which went to America, India, or China." *La Méditerranée*, **II**, p. 151.

[224]"During [the] brief period between 1590 and 1600 the Dutch . . . created a *completely new trading system*. Although still in their swaddling clothes the routes of Dutch colonial and Levantine trade . . . had at once been established. The new trade, principally the Indian trade, at once became the centre of interest both of the reigning institutions, of the leading merchants, and of the whole contemporary public." Christensen, *Dutch Trade*, p. 19.

Violet Barbour suggests that the rapidity of Amsterdam's rise was visible to contemporaries: "Foreigners observed Amsterdam's rise to supremacy in world trade with surprise not unmixed with resentment. Suddenly, as it seems, the city was there." *Capitalism in Amsterdam in the Seventeenth Century* (Ann Arbor, Michigan: Ann Arbor Paperbacks, 1963), 17. See Da Silva, *Revue du Nord*, **XLI**, p. 143, who dates the Dutch supremacy very exactly between 1597 and 1598.

to Dutch fishing interests and shipbuilding.[225] Shipbuilding in turn was a key to Dutch success elsewhere.[226]

This illustrates once again the cumulating quality of economic advantage. Because the Dutch had an edge in Baltic trade, they became the staple market for timber. Because they were the staple market for timber, they reduced shipbuiding costs and were technologically innovative. And in turn they were thus still better able to compete in the Baltic trade. Because of this edge, they could finance still further expansion.[227] On this basis Amsterdam became a threefold center of the European economy: commodity market, shipping center, and capital market, and it became "difficult to say which aspect of her greatness was most substantial, or to dissociate one from dependence on the other two."[228] This process of cumulating advantage works most in an expansionist stage of economic development before the leading area suffers the disadvantages of out-of-date equipment and relatively fixed high labor costs.

There was another reason for the ability of the Dutch to prosper. Braudel

[225]Christensen, *Dutch Trade*, p. 424. See Barbour: "The mainspring of the city's new wealth, as of her earlier modest eminence, seems to have been the trade in grain and naval supplies, and the carriage, storage, and marketing of these and other heavy goods. Circumstances—famine, war, and the altered technique of warfare which called for more and bigger guns, sea adventure which called for more, bigger, and better-armed ships—greatly increased the demand for goods and services which Amsterdam was equipped to supply." *Capitalism in Amsterdam*, p. 26. She also talks of Amsterdam's role in marine insurance after 1592 (pp. 33–35) and in the supply of arms and munitions after 1609 (pp. 35–42).

[226]"Amsterdam being the staple market for timber, shipbuilding in Holland was cheaper than elsewhere. Whereas the English clung to large and armed merchantmen, the Dutch about 1595 began to build a new type of ship called the flyboat [*fluyt*], a light but practicable ship, long, narrow and speedy, employed to carry a ponderous and clumsy cargo. The flyboat was easy to work with a small crew. The low freightage explains why other seafaring nations could hardly compete with Dutch shipping to the Baltic, Norway and Muscovy." J. G. van Dillen, *Britain and the Netherlands*, **II**, p. 136. See Violet Barbour, "Dutch and English Merchant Shipping in the Seventeenth Century," in Carus-Wilson, ed., *Essays in Economic History* (New York: St. Martin's, 1965), **I**, 227–253.

There is a brief description of the technical advantages of the Dutch *fluyt* in J. H. Parry, *The Age of Reconnaissance* (New York: Mentor Books, 1963), p. 83. Herbert Heaton argues that the superiority of Dutch shipbuilding is explained by financial and economic considerations: "(1) Raw materials were bought in bulk for cash at low prices; . . . (2) In constructing the vessels there was some standardization of design, parts, and building methods. . . . (3) The builder was able to borrow money at a much lower rate than his foreign rival." *Economic History of Europe*, rev. ed. (New York: Harper, 1948), 275.

[227]"Grain provided cargoes and paid freights to keep Amsterdam's merchant marine moving, and so made possible cheap transport of commodities less ship-filling in bulk. . . . As late as 1666 it was estimated that three-fourths of capital active on the Amsterdam bourse was engaged in the Baltic trade." Barbour, *Capitalism in Amsterdam*, p. 27.

[228]Barbour, *ibid.*, p. 18. André-E. Sayous spells out the advantage of Amsterdam's role as a financial center: "On the other hand, Amsterdam improved its techniques: it became easier to spread sea risks among groups of capitalists and to obtain credit in modern forms. Marine insurance developed thanks to the participation of many persons dividing the dangers and taking a more exact reading of their extent in fixing the rates; . . . As for credits, if the methods did not improve, at least the amounts lent for merchandise increased; and the letter of exchange was utilized not only in transferring payments from one place to another, but as true anticipatory credit: it still however did not serve for arbitrage following the demands of the market." "Le rôle d'Amsterdam dans l'histoire du capitalisme commercial et financier," *Revue historique*, **CLXXXIII**, 2, oct.–déc. 1938, 263. See also pp. 276–277. For Sayous, the key factors in Amsterdam's rise are, in fact, the "new forms of grouping capital and of speculation [p. 279]."

poses the question of why, after 1588, the English did not come to dominate the seas, as they would eventually. He finds it in the Dutch economic ties with Spain, relatively unbroken despite the political turmoil.[229] Could not England have created the same link with Spain's American treasure? Not yet, England was still too much of a threat to Spain to be permitted this kind of relationship.[230] And Spain was still strong enough to resist England. The Empire may have failed, but control of the European world-economy still depended on access to Spain's colonial wealth. Holland, albeit in revolt against Spain, was still part of her. And in any case, Holland was no political threat, unlike France and England.

Holland thus profited by being a small country. And she profited by being a "financially sound" state.[231] She offered the merchants who would use her arena maximum advantages. Her route to riches was not that of the incipient mercantilism of other states[232]—essential for long-run advantage but not for maximizing short-run profit by the mercantile and financial classes. Her route was the route of free trade.[233] Or rather this was her route in the "second" sixteenth century when she predominated on the seas. When Amsterdam was still struggling for a place in the commercial sun, she had been protectionist in policy.[234]

From the point of view of the European world-economy as a whole,

[229]"Only one explanation is plausible: Holland, thanks to its location next to the Catholic Low Countries and by its insistence in forcing the doors of Spain, remained more than [England] linked to the [Iberian] peninsula and to its American treasures without which it could not feed its own commerce. . . . Between Spain and Holland, there is the link of money, reinforced by the peace of 1609 to 1621, broken as is the entire fortune of Spain about the middle of the seventeenth century, at the moment when—is it pure coincidence?—the wheel begins to turn against Holland." Braudel, *La Méditerranée*, **I**, pp. 572–573.

Barbour lays emphasis on Amsterdam's control of grain: "It is possible that the rise of Amsterdam as a bullion market owed much to war trade with Spain, and something to war loot. Thus in 1595, and in several subsequent years down to 1630, the Spanish government was obliged to authorize export of the precious metals in return for grain imports." *Capitalism in Amsterdam*, p. 49. And once again, we find advantage to cumulative: "But direct remissions of silver from the bar of Cadiz to Holland were only part of the story. There was also indirect remission from countries whose nationals had shared in the treasure discharged at Cadiz—remissions payments for services of commodity purchases, attracted by speculative possibilities, or merely in quest of security and freedom of disposition [pp. 50–51]."

[230]See Braudel, *La Méditerranée*, **I**, p. 209.

[231]Friedrich, *The Age of the Baroque*, p. 8.

[232]As José Larraz (1943) says, if there was a Dutch mercantilism, it "was a rather liberal version of mercantilism." *La época del mercantilismo*, p. 186.

[233]"The Dutch were in favor of the widest possible open trade everywhere; the English preferred a tightly restricted trade, especially between England and its colonies, but also between outside countries and England." Robert Reynolds, *Europe Emerges* (Madison: Univ. of Wisconsin Press, 1967), 442.

See also Barbour: "Freedom to export the monetary metals, rare elsewhere in the seventeenth century, helped to stabilize exchange rates in Amsterdam and so encouraged the circulation of bills of exchange as negotiable instruments of credit, the discounting and sale of which became a lively business in the city." *Capitalism in Amsterdam*, p. 53.

[234]"An essential condition for Amsterdam's imposing role as the commodity exchange of western Europe appear to have been provided by the protectionist line, followed in its maritime policy during the second half of the fifteenth century. In accordance with this, all shipmasters arriving from the Baltic who were citizens of Amsterdam were required to call at the city. The same applied to Amsterdam citizens co-owning a vessel with a non-citizen skipper. This rule, which is a navigation law in embryo, was aimed against Lübeck and against the direct traffic from the Baltic to Flanders, especially Bruges." Glamann, *Fontana Economic History of Europe*, **II**, p. 35.

with its era of expansion coming to an end, Dutch world trade becme a sort of precious vital fluid which kept the machine going while various countries were concentrating on reorganizing their internal political and economic machinery. Conversely, however, the success of the Netherlands policy was dependent on the fact that neither England nor France had yet pushed their mercantilist tendencies to the point where they truly cut into the market for Dutch merchants operating on free trade assumptions.[235] This may be because the Dutch still were too strong because of their relative control of the money market by their continuing Spanish links.[236]

If Amsterdam succeeded Seville, if the northern Netherlands became the commercial and financial center of the European world-economy in the "second" sixteenth century, how may we describe what happened to the city-states of northern Italy, particularly Venice and Genoa which seemed to expand, rather than diminish, their commercial and financial roles at precisely this time? What we may say is that this expansion was short-lived and masked a process of decline hidden beneath the glitter so that, by the end of the "second" sixteenth century, these areas were relegated to the semiperiphery of the European world-economy.

The true forward surge of Amsterdam did not occur until 1590. Between the crisis of 1557 and 1590 came the Netherlands Revolution. The Netherlands role in world commerce was necessarily less during that period. As a result, Genoa picked up some of the functions formerly played by Antwerp and, in banking, by the Fuggers.[237] Curiously, England which had most to lose by the fall of Antwerp, because it threatened to deprive England

[235]"Large purchases, liberal credit, and cheap transport combined to keep Amsterdam prices on a level with those prevailing in places of origin. In 1606 a member of the House of Commons maintained that the Dutch could sell English cloth dressed in the Netherlands and re-exported thence, more cheaply than the English trading companies could do." Barbour, *Capitalism in Amsterdam*, p. 95.

[236]For example, see Barbour on Dutch foreign investment and its strength: "[In the seventeenth century] for the most part foreign goods seeking credit for purchases, or short-term advances, addressed themselves to private capital in Amsterdam. . . .

"In a succession of wars between the northern crowns for supremacy in the Baltic, Dutch capital, like Dutch shipping, fought on both sides. . . .

"England and France offered less virgin soil to foreign capitalism than the countries of the North, the commercial and industrial aptitudes of their own middle classes being vigorous and competitive, and finding aggressive support for their respective goods. But in both countries Dutch capital was at work." *Ibid.*, pp. 105, 111, 119. See Braudel in footnote 229 above.

[237]"[T]he century of the Genoese bankers from 1557 to 1627 which, in the clock of grand capitalism,

fits in between the brief century of the Fuggers and that of the mixed capitalism of Amsterdam. . . . It is clear that the fortune of the Genoese did not suddenly come into existence by the wave of a magic wand in 1557, in the wake of the strange bankruptcy of the Spanish State, and did not disappear overnight in 1627, on the occasion of the fifth or sixth Spanish bankruptcy. . . . Genoa remained for a long time yet one of the pivots of international finance." Braudel, *La Méditerranée*, **I**, pp. 454–455.

See also Elliott: "Genoese bankers moved in alongside the Fuggers as creditors of Charles V, and, as the influence of the Fuggers declined after the royal bankruptcy of 1557, so that of the Genoese grew." *Europe Divided*, pp. 59–60.

And Spooner: "After about 1570 the heyday of the Genoese began, opening a century when they took over the running from the Fuggers, whose financial pre-eminence declined with the fading prosperity of the German mines after 1530." *New Cambridge Modern History*, **III**, p. 27.

Venice also played a key financial role at this time: "Venice had become in the long economic expansion of the sixteenth century a decisive relay-point in the international circulation of bills of exchange. . . . Since 1587, Venice had had a deposit bank, the *Banco della Piazza di Rialto*. By the decree of

of access to American bullion,[238] engaged in impetuous short run military seizures of treasure that led the Spaniards to ship the bullion through Genoa.[239] Genoa's strength thus partly derived from the turmoil of the Netherlands, partly from its total devotion to the primacy of economic considerations,[240] partly from their continuing close ties with the Spanish monarchy and commercial system,[241] ties whose origins we spelled out previously.

As for Venice, whereas the "first" sixteenth century was an era of the decline of Mediterranean trade (the impact of the Turkish conquest of Constantinople and Egypt, and the new Portuguese sea routes to the east), the "second" sixteenth century saw a great revival of its trade, especially in the eastern Mediterranean.[242] This revival had already begun about

1593, the Senate stipulated that bills of exchange should be settled by entries in its ledgers. As a result, a great instrument in international transactions was thus created. In effect, the Republic had a double monetary system: [the *moneta corrente* and the *moneta di banco*]." Frank C. Spooner, "Venice and the Levant: An Aspect of Monetary History (1610–1614)," in *Studi in Onore di Amintore Fanfani*, **V:** *Evi moderno e contemporaneo* (Milano: Dott. A. Giuffrè-Ed., 1962), 646–647.

[238]"A policy of entente between Philip II and Elizabeth had been possible, as long as the queen and the English merchants were permitted, via their borrowing on the exchange of Antwerp, to participate in the American goldmine (*pactole*). However, precisely that order, that equilibrium was jeopardized by the crisis of 1566 and the threatening landing of the Duke of Alva into the Netherlands in 1567. . . . Everything henceforward changed in the enormous sector of the Atlantic." Braudel, *La Méditerannée*, **I,** p. 438.

[239]"In the financial realm, . . . Antwerp began to lose its position in the center beginning in 1568, when Elizabeth of England confiscated the treasure found aboard a fleet of Spanish galleys which had taken refuge in the port of Plymouth. . . . The English Channel was no longer safe; hence the Genoese bankers decided to change the itinerary of the precious metals by having them pass through Genoa and the fairs of Besançon. Thus, the latter town became towards the end of the 16th century the leading banking place in western Europe and the distribution center of the arrivals of silver which continued to flow in from the New World. From a banking point of view, it was therefore not Amsterdam which reaped the succession of Antwerp; . . . Amsterdam did not become the world center of precious metals until 1640. . . ." Raymond de Roover, "Anvers comme marché monétaire au XVIe siècle," *Revue Belge de philologie et d'histoire*, **XXXI,** 4, 1953, 1044–1045. See Braudel: "[B]eginning in 1580, the true distribution center of the white metal, as much and

more than Spain itself, was the great cities of Italy. They derived from this role enormous benefits, on condition of exporting to the Levant, something both easy and profitable, a part of the overabundant silver coins of Spain." *La Méditerranée*, **I,** pp. 450–451.

[240]"I think it unnecessary to insist upon the well-known fact that Genoa was a monetary market exceptionally free from the intrusion of any non-commercial element. There never existed for example any noticeable ecclesiastical pressure on financial activity." Carlo M. Cipolla, *Economia internazionale*, **V,** p. 256.

[241]Lonchay demonstrates that the real interest rate charged the Spanish crown by Italian bankers was from 16–20%. See *Académie Royale de Belgique*, pp. 950–951. H. G. Koenigsberger says that: "More than any other state, Genoa had staked her fortunes on that of the Spanish monarchy. . . . As long as Peru sent her silver to Seville, the Genoese plutocracy flourished." "Western Europe and the Power of Spain," *New Cambridge Modern History*, **III:** R. B. Wernham, ed., *The Counter-Reformation and the Price Revolution, 1559–1610* (London and New York: Cambridge Univ. Press, 1968), 257.

[242]"Thanks to the convergence of several different forces, towards the middle of the sixteenth century, the markets of Levant were well furnished in oriental merchandise and Venice recovered her previous commercial prosperity. But the depression had been profound during the first half of the century." Vitorino Magahlães-Godinho, "Le repli vénitien et égyptien et la route du Cap, 1496–1533," in *Eventail de l'histoire vivante: hommage à Lucien Febvre*, Vol. **II** (Paris: Lib. Armand Colin, 1953), 300. See Frederic C. Lane, "The Mediterranean Spice Trade: Its Revival in the Sixteenth Century," in *Venice and History*, (Baltimore, Maryland: Johns Hopkins Press, 1966), 581–590, and his earlier article, "Venetian Shipping During the Commercial Revolution," in *Venice and History*, 13–24; see also E. E. Rich, *New Cambridge Modern History*, **I,** esp. p. 447.

1540 and was due in part to Portuguese inability to control the Indian Ocean trade,[243] in part to some competitive advantages of Venice over Portugal,[244] and in part to Portuguese weakness in Europe[245] as well as Spain's crisis in the Netherlands.[246]

But the revival of northern Italy could not last. Neither its agricultural nor its industrial base were sound, unlike the northern Netherlands and a fortiori England, and by the seventeenth century, we talk of the decline of Italy.

The weakness of the agricultural base was multifold, given the growth of population in the sixteenth century, particularly accentuated in the period 1580–1620.[247] We have already mentioned the relative difficulty of soil conditions. It is true that, during the "first" sixteenth century, as profits from trade declined, there was a shift of investment to agriculture, particularly wheat.[248] This was especially true of monastic orders which were not permitted to engage in urban commerce. This trend was accentuated, particularly in the Terraferma around Venice[249] between 1570

[243]"It is probable that Mediterranean commerce, tied to Arab intermediaries, was able to keep for itself, by offering higher prices, the products of higher quality. The Portuguese probably overdid it by holding to extremely low purchase prices in Asia. . . . Mediterranean commerce to the Orient, having lost none of its interest for the intermediaries, could only be stopped by force, which meant overseeing the points of origin. The Portuguese succeeded in doing this on several occasions. . . . But the rigor of their surveillance lasted but a limited time, and then relaxed of its own accord." Braudel, *La Méditerranée,* **I**, pp. 459–496.

[244]"At the beginning of the 16th century, the Mediterranean Spanish trade passed through a severe crisis, in consequence of the opening of a direct Portuguese trade with India by way of the Cape of Good Hope. . . . The Portuguese monopoly, however, proved short-lived. Formidable though they were at sea, the Portuguese could not hope, with a few warships operating from widely-scattered bases, to suppress permanently a whole flourishing commerce which supplied Egypt and the Turkish empire as well as European customers. . . . The Indian Ocean Spanish trade—or the greater part of it—soon reentered its old channels; with it revived the Mediterranean trade in Venetian ships. In straight competition over price and quality the advantages were by no means all on the side of the Portuguese ocean trade. The costs and risks of the Cape route were great, and tended to increase; and the Portuguese had no goods to offer which could make a profitable outward freight. They bought spices with bullion, and the proceeds of the homeward passage had to cover the costs of the outward passage also. . . . There may also have been a difference in quality of spices, Portuguese spices tending 'to spoil and to lose their aroma on the long sea voyage.'" J. H. Parry, *Cam-*

bridge Economic History of Europe, **IV**, pp. 164–165.

[245]See S. T. Bindoff on the impact of the discontinuance of the Portuguese royal factory as a permanent institution in 1549. "Whatever the reasons for this step, or its immediate consequences, it symbolised the passing of an age." *New Cambridge Modern History,* **II**, p. 68.

[246]See J. B. Harrison, "Colonial Development and International Rivalries Outside Europe, II: Asia and Africa." *New Cambridge Modern History,* **III**: R. B. Wernham, ed., *The Counter Reformation and the Price Revolution, 1559–1610.* (London and New York: Cambridge Univ. Press, 1968), 533–534.

[247]For example, Carlo M. Cipolla notes that in Milan between 1580 and 1610–1620, "there was an intensive demographic expansion." *Mouvements monétaires dans l'Etat de Milan (1580–1700)* (Paris: Lib. Armand Colin, 1952), 31. An analogous expansion is noted for Florence, with 1619-20 being the point of downturn, in Ruggiero Romano, "A Florence au XVIe siècle: industries textiles et conjoncture," *Annales E.S.C.,* **VII**, 7, oct.-déc. 1952, 508–512.

[248]"Wheat, by itself, established the overwhelming superiority of agricultural production over all other [economic activities in the 16th century]. Agriculture is the prime industry of the Mediterranean, although wheat represents but one part of agricultural income." Braudel, *La Méditerranée,* **I**, p. 385.

[249]"The fundamental reason [for this shift] must surely be what profits the Venetians hoped to make from the land. . . . An early incentive was probably the example of the profits made by the great monasteries through land reclamation, already in the fifteenth century. . . .

The crucial period of change to landed activities would seem to be between about 1570 and 1630, when Venetian possession increased by probably 35%." S. J. Woolf, "Venice and the Terraferma:

and 1630, as local investors responded to the rise in agricultural prices and the decline in industrial profits.

Nevertheless, despite increased production, there was famine. Part of the explanation lies in a factor which, from the point of view of the social system, is accidental and external: a sudden increase of rain and cold in the last decades of the sixteenth century which led to the increase of swampland, and hence of malaria.[250] The latter was particularly serious since Italy was already suffering from its increase as a result of the extension of land cultivation in the process of internal colonization.[251] Still one would have thought that a region having so much bullion would have imported wheat. This seems to have happened to some degree, enough to spread the effects of the famine by creating shortages elsewhere,[252] but not apparently enough to maintain an agricultural base for industrial production. Why not? One can speculate that the new large agricultural producers (such as the monasteries) did not lend their political weight to expanded grain imports.[253] There was of course the cost factor. Baltic grain was

Problems of the Change from Commercial to Landed Activities," in Brian Pullan, ed., *Crisis and Change in the Venetian Economy in the Sixteenth and Seventeenth Centuries* (London: Methuen, 1968), 194–195.

See Bouwsma: "Throughout, Italian ownership of land by the church had been expanding in the period of the Counter-Reformation; and special conditions had carried this tendency further in Venetian territory than elsewhere. Ecclesiastical corporations had participated enthusiastically with their special accumulations of capital in the great reclamation projects of the age." *Venice and the Defenses*, p. 343.

[250]Braudel concludes his account of the relationship of the rains and recession with this comment: "The whole of the social drama of hunger, which dominated the century in its closing years, has perhaps its true origin in this unsettling, perhaps a rather slight one, of the atmospheric conditions. This hypothesis is put forward at the extreme limit of our prudence, but it had to be stated." *La Méditerranée*, I, p. 248.

[251]"One cannot escape anywhere the impression of a recrudescence of the evil [of malaria] in the 16th century. Perhaps because man engaged at that time in the development of his old enemy, the lowlands. The whole 16th century, even the 15th century, was a quest for additional land. Where was one more likely to find it than in the humid and loose-soiled plains? But nothing is more harmful than the stirring of infested land. . . . The internal colonization which went on everywhere in the Mediterranean in the 16th century involved a high cost. . . . It was particularly high in Italy. If the latter missed out on the conquest of faroff lands, remaining outside that great movement, is it not, among other reasons, because she was occupied with the conquest at home of the entire area that could be cultivated by the technology then available from

the flooded plains to the tops of the mountains?" Braudel, *La Méditerranée*, I, 59. See P. J. Jones, "Per la storia agraria italiana nel medio evo: lineamenti e problemi," *Rivista storica italiana*, **LXXVI**, 2, giugno 1964, 307–308.

[252]"The food situation in the Mediterranean area would in all probability have been much more serious if the flow of precious metals from America had not provided means of payment for the large purchases of grain. Thus the climate fluctuation became one of the factors which helped to spread the effects of the influx of precious metals all over Europe. The expansion of commerce and shipping which had been going on since the middle of the fifteenth century must also have helped to mitigate the effects of the crop failures. Nevertheless, the climatic changes did a great deal to weaken the Mediterranean countries in relation to the rising nations on the Atlantic and North Seas." Utterström, *Scandinavian Economic History Review*, **III**, p. 44.

[253]"[B]efore as after the [food] crisis [of 1591], the Mediterranean lived essentially from the products of its own agriculture. Nothing occurs comparable to what develops in the Low Countries in the case of Amsterdam or to what will take place even more extensively, but much later, in the England of free-exchange. The urban universes do not give over to anyone else the task of supplying them with provisions." Braudel, *La Méditerranée*, I, p. 387.

Nonetheless the import of grain did increase. It was in fact Braudel who, along with Romano, pointed out the role wheat played in the expansion of Leghorn: "[I]s not the rise of Leghorn linked to its increasing role as a wheat port? The great famine of 1591 and the influx of wheat from the north . . . mark, we believe, the major turning-point." Fernand Braudel and Ruggiero Romano, *Navires et marchandises à l'entrée du Port de Livourne (1547–1611)* (Paris: Lib. Armand Colin, 1951), 22.

far, and Egyptian and Syrian grain was often unavailable, either because
they too were suffering shortages or because of a state of war with the
Turks.[254]

Furthermore, to the extent that they were importing grain, it was under
the worst bargaining conditions possible and via their commercial rival,
the Dutch. For Amsterdam controlled the Baltic stocks and could dole
them out at its pleasure.[255] This conjunctural advantage of Holland over
northern Italy could then be transformed into something more permanent
because of the linkages created by the world-economy. Spooner notes the
role of the new sophisticated credit techniques—endorsement of bills of
exchange, *patto di ricorsa* (a form of short-term credit), and public banks—all
of which were emerging just at this point. This credit system was international, and, as northern Italy began to decline, the locus of these activities was
shifted without ado.[256] For the merchant financiers saved themselves, in
Genoa as elsewhere, without too much worry about geographical loyalties.

But industry? Was not northern Italy an industrial center, and indeed
one that was infused with new life, especially in Venice? J. H. Elliott mentions
new investment between 1560 and 1600, and a moment of "opulent splen-

---

[254]How important this cutoff of the Levant as a
source of grain is is indicated by J. H. Parry's description of the situation in the fifteenth century: "In
the West, more populous and less productive, the
situation was more difficult. Florence, Genoa,
Venice, Ragusa, Naples, and the cities of the east
coast of Spain—these last mostly set in country producing wine, or oil, or wool—all were importers
of grain by sea, since their local supplies were
inadequate or unreliable, and local land transport
was costly. The principal western sources were
Apulia and Sicily, both controlled politically by the
rulers of Aragon, who were regular importers; but
the western Mediterranean as a whole was rarely
self-sufficient in grain, and the importing cities also
had constant recourse to the cheap and plentiful
grain of the Levant. Venice, particularly, relied
upon eastern grain; its Aegean colonies were a useful source of supply, and the republic also regularly
imported grain from Egypt. There existed in the
eastern Mediterranean therefore, a specialized,
complicated, and necessarily flexible sea-borne
trade in grain. The ships, Venetian, Genoese, Rag-
usan, were large, were designed to carry their bulky
cargo, and usually carried nothing else." *The Age of
Reconaissance*, p. 53.

[255]"In the Mediterranean, conditions were different: because of the danger constantly threatening
from the Algerian corsairs, large and armed ships
were indispensable in that area. . . . Nevertheless,
Amsterdam succeeded in capturing part of the
Mediterranean trade, owing to her large stocks of

grain. Many years of the late sixteenth and the first
half of the seventeenth century happened to be
times of shortage of grain in Italy and Spain,
whereas the Amsterdam warehouses were well
stocked with Polish and East Prussian rye and wheat,
so that the Dutch merchants could make large
profit." Van Dillen, *Britain and the Netherlands*, **II**,
p. 136.

See Parry, *Cambridge Economic History of Europe*,
IV, pp. 158–159. Parry adds one further consideration for the cause of the grain-shortage in the
Mediterranean: "The massive scale of Turco-
Spanish hostilities in the 1570's, and the association
of Venice with Spain, also dislocated the normal
trade in grain and at the same time increased the
demand for victualling navies, armies and garrisons
[p. 159]."

[256]"In another respect, the extent of credit was
intimately linked with the network of trade, with
the associations of merchants, in ports, markets and
fairs all over Europe. The activity of the merchant
financiers of Genoa was an outstanding example.
Established in Italy, the traditional focus of Europe,
and involved in the great Atlantic venture of Spain,
with agents all over the continent, they were the
channels through which the shift in emphasis was
effected in the international economy from the
south to the north of Europe and the Atlantic. Thus
they prepared the way for the extraordinary success
of Holland." Spooner, *New Cambridge Modern History*,
III, p. 31.

dour."[257] The opulence however did not last. From being one of the most advanced industrial areas in Europe in 1600, northern Italy became a depressed agricultural region by 1670. We have already suggested that the prosperity was deceiving. Domenico Sella says of Venice's economic prosperity in the late sixteenth century that it could not "conceal the fact that the base on which it rested was somewhat narrower than in the past and that, accordingly, her economy had become somewhat more vulnerable."[258] There are two main considerations here. One is the loss of France and England as customers becauses of the rise of their own textile industries. Hence the market was now confined more or less to northern Italy and Germany. The second is that sea transport was now more and more in the hands of non-Venetian ships. As Carlo Cipolla puts it: "The whole economic structure of the country was too dependent upon its ability to sell abroad a high proportion of the manufactured articles and the services that it could offer.[259]

What does it mean to be *too* dependent on sales of manufactured goods? After all, the secret of the success of core areas of a world-economy is that they exchange their manufactures for the raw materials of peripheral areas. But that simple picture leaves out of account two factors: politico–economic ability to keep down prices of raw materials imports (which we argued was more possible for the Netherlands than for northern Italy), and ability to compete in the markets of *core* countries with the manufactured products of other core countries.

The story here was quite simple. While the Dutch could undersell the English in England, the Italians by contrast were probably outpriced[260]

---

[257]"At a time when other parts of Europe were devoting more of their attention and resources to maritime trade, Venice chose to move in exactly the opposite direction. The Venetian fleet began to decline in the years after 1560. . . . But, this maritime retreat coincided with a great shift of Venetian capital from seafaring to the mainland. Here it was used, not for trade, but for the acquisition of land and the building up of a large-scale textile industry capable of competing successfully with the North Italian and Netherlands textile industries, both of which suffered from the European wars. This policy, at least in the short run, yielded rich rewards. For the rest of the century, . . . [Venice] basked in an opulent splendour which made it seem as if the days of its former glory had miraculously returned." Elliott, *Europe Divided*, pp. 58–59.

[258]Domenico Sella, "Crisis and Transformation in Venetian Trade," in Brian Pullan, ed., *Crisis and Change in the Venetian Economy in the Sixteenth and Seventeenth Centuries* (London: Metheun, 1968), 90.

[259]Carlo M. Cipolla, "The Decline of Italy: The Case of a Fully Matured Economy," *Economic History Review*, **V**, 2, 1952, 180–181. This is true not only of Venice but of Milan as well. See Cipolla, *Mouvements monétaires*, pp. 33–34. The details of this decline of Venice are admirably spelled out in the symposium covering the period 1620–1720: *Aspetti e cause della decadenza economica veneziana nel secolo XVII. Atti del Convergno (27 giugno–2 luglio 1957)* (Venezia-Roma: Istituto per la Collaborazione Culturale, 1961).

[260]E. J. Hobsbawm is somewhat reserved on the validity of this argument about Italian over-pricing. See "The Crisis of the Seventeenth Century," in Trevor Aston, ed., *Crisis in Europe, 1560–1660* (London: Routledge & Kegan Paul, 1965), 19. Barry Supple however gives some confirming evidence of Cipolla's hypothesis in *Commercial Crisis and Change in England, 1600–1642* (London and New York: Cambridge Univ. Press, 1959), 159–160. See also Ruggiero Romano's explanation of the decline of Venetian shipbuilding, especially after 1570: "[The policy of loans for construction] could not counter-

and old-fashioned.[261] The Italian guilds kept the labor costs up. State taxation was comparatively high. The Italians produced for the quality market. Others came along with lighter and more colorful cloths—less durable, of inferior quality, but cheaper. The secret of modern industrial success was revealing itself early. When the Thirty Years War interfered with the German market as well, disaster followed: decline in production of textiles; disinvestment of capital; migration of industries to the rural areas to escape guild labor costs and the tax collector. Since the industries were noncompetitive, they died out.[262]

Could northern Italy at least have played the role of the northern Netherlands? Possibly, but there was probably not room for them both, and Holland was better suited for the task for a host of reasons than Venice or Milan or Genoa. Nor could Italy follow the path of England and France, for

balance the high prices charged by the Venetian arsenals, high in comparison with those of naval construction elsewhere, especially in northern Europe." "La marine marchande vénitienne au XVIe siècle," in M. Mollat *et al.*, eds., *Les sources de l'histoire maritime en Europe, du Moyen Age au XVIIIe siècle,* Actes du IVe Colloque International d'Histoire Maritime (Paris: S.E.V.P.E.N., 1962), 46.

[261]"The success of Northern cloth was due to two factors: they cost less and their quality, perhaps less estimable than that of Venetian products, responded more to the new exigencies of fashion." Sella, *Annales E.S.C.,* **XII,** p. 39.

One should remember that *quality* work in the sixteenth century mean *more,* not less, industrialized work. In an era in which factory work is associated with production for the masses as well as mass production, and artisanship survives as a mode of fine craftsmanship for a specialized market, it requires a leap of imagination to realize that the opposite was true before the industrial era. Then it was that factories, that is, assemblages of workers cooperating together in one place under direct supervision, were used only in those rare cases where quality was of the essence as in some luxury items or where accuracy was highly valued for reasons of safety, or where there was some other problem necessitating a large measure of control. Such was the case, for example, of rope (cordage) production in sixteenth-century Venice, where the Senate worried about "the security of our galleys and ships and similarly of our sailors and capital." The Senate did not trust such an enterprise to private hands, moreover. The statement of the Senate is cited by Frederic Lane in "The Rope Factory and Hemp Trade in the Fifteenth and Sixteenth Centuries," in *Venice and History,* (Baltimore, Maryland: Johns Hopkins Press, 1966), 270.

[262]"When a country is in the unfortunate position in which Italy found itself at the beginning of the seventeenth century, sooner or later a number of

forces, either natural or induced, come into operation to bring about a readjustment. The steps necessary to correct the disequilibrium may be varied: the development of new types of production, the search for new markets, the discouragement of certain types of consumption, the lowering of the relation between the domestic price level and the world price level, and so on. If a country is able to develop new types of production or exploit new markets, it can, broadly speaking, maintain both its level of employment and its standard of living. Otherwise it must naturally acquiesce in a drastic reduction in its standard of living and very probably, in its level of employment." Cipolla, *Economic History Review,* **V,** pp. 186–187.

E. J. Hobsbawm doubts whether it was possible for northern Italy to do otherwise than it did: "The decline of Italy . . . illustrates the weaknesses of 'capitalism' parasitic on a feudal world. Thus sixteenth-century Italians probably controlled the greatest agglomerations of capital, but misinvested them flagrantly. They immobilized them in buildings and squandered them in foreign lending during the price-revolution (which naturally favored debtors) or diverted them from manufacturing activities to various forms of immobile investment. . . . Yet Italian investors, who had long been aware that too large cathedrals hurt business, were acting quite sensibly. The experience of centuries had shown that the highest profits were not to be got in technical progress or even in production. . . . If they spent vast amounts of capital non-productively, it may simply have been because there was no more room to invest in progressively on any scale within the limits of the 'capitalist sector'. . . . [T]he general boom of the later sixteenth century . . . and the suddenly expanded demands of the great absolute monarchies which relied on private contractors, and the unprecedented luxury of their aristocracies, postponed the evil day." *Crisis in Europe,* pp. 18–19.

one thing for lack of political unity.[263] When the plague hit Italy in 1630,[264] it reduced the pressure on food supply, but it also drove wages up still higher. It served as a last straw. Northern Italy thus completed the transition from core to semiperiphery. We already noted previously that Spain had been making the same transition at this time. No doubt northern Italy never fell as far as some other Mediterranean areas like southern Italy[265] and Sicily,[266] but this was to be a small consolation in the centuries ahead. R. S. Lopez in recounting all the things that went wrong for the Christian Mediterranean since 1450, concludes sadly: "Obviously the primacy of the Mediterranean peoples could not survive so many adversities."[267]

[263]Amintore Fanfani makes this the first, though not the only, explanation for the decline: "In Italy there was no other possibility than seeking refuge in agriculture, and on the other hand they could not succeed in slowing down the decadence because of the lack of three things: (1) lack of a large unitary market or of a strong tendency towards unification; (2) the absence of Italy from the great movement of European oceanic expansion; (3) lack of an important economic program adequate to the real needs of the Italian economy." *Storia del lavoro,* p. 48.

[264]The severity of the plague is indicated by its impact on population: "The pandemics of 1630 and 1657 cancelled the gains of the period 1580–1629 and 1631–55 and brought back the Italian population to the level of about 11 million." Carlo M. Cipolla, "Four Centuries of Italian Demographic Development," in D. V. Glass & D. E. C. Eversley, eds., *Population in History* (London: Arnold, 1965), 573.

[265]"The sale of land [and consequently the rise of feudal capitalism] took place throughout the [Italian] peninsula, from Piedmont . . . to Sicily. . . ." Bulferitti, *Archivio storico lombardo,* **IV,** p. 21, fn. 30. Villari describes the process for southern Italy of what he calls the "commercialization of feudal lands [*feudo*]." *La rivolta antispagnola a Napoli,* p. 164. The sale of such lands by the state facilitated the rise of new groups who were ennobled. "It was a complex movement of expansion and consolidation of feudal domains to which the higher bour-geoisie gave a strong impulse and which coincided with a very energetic affirmation of the economic and social power of the traditional nobility [p. 192]." One consequence was the "feudalization of towns [p. 168]" which was strongly but ineffectively resisted. The style of life in the towns changed: "One of the most visible consequences of feudal expansion was the increase in the consumption of luxury and unproductive goods, with the construction of palaces, chapels, villas, gardens in the urban centers of the province of a new phase of its urban development [pp. 193–194]."

[266]"Seriously under-industrialized, with most of its banks and credit controlled by foreigners, with the profits of its export trade enriching Genoese, Venetian, and Catalan merchants, and with an agricultural system which combined the disadvantages of the feudal economy with those of a modern credit system, Sicily remained a poor country and was never able to catch up on the lead which the North of Italy had gained in the later Middle Ages." Koenigsberger, *The Government of Sicily,* p. 82.

[267]Lopez, *Cambridge Economic History of Europe,* **II,** p. 353. Braudel writes of an "ebb [*reflux*] of the economy" throughout the Mediterranean beginning in the 1620's. "L'économie de la Méditerranée au XVIIe siècle," *Les Cahiers de Tunisie,* **IV,** 14, 2e trimestre, 1954, 195. Emmanuel Le Roy Ladurie speaks of this "leper of decline [*décroissance*] which afflicts [from 1620 on] the Italians, the Castilians, and the Hispano-Americans." *Paysans,* p. 636.

l'Blond excul

Bellange fec.

5

THE STRONG CORE STATES: CLASS-FORMATION AND INTERNATIONAL COMMERCE

Figure 6: "Two Beggars Fighting," etching by Jacques Bellange, official painter, engraver, and decorator of the Court of Lorraine at Nancy from 1602 to 1616. The etching was made between 1612–1617 (Washington, D.C.: National Gallery of Art, Rosenwald Collection).

One of the persisting themes of the history of the modern world is the seesaw between "nationalism" and "internationalism." I do not refer to the ideological seesaw, though it of course exists, but to the organizational one. At some points in time the major economic and political institutions are geared to operating in the international arena and feel that local interests are tied in some immediate way to developments elsewhere in the world. At other points of time, the social actors tend to engage their efforts locally, tend to see the reinforcement of state boundaries as primary, and move toward a relative indifference about events beyond them. These are of course only *tendencies* and not all actors are bound to observe the dominant tendency, nor is consistency obligatory or likely for the actors.

I should stress that I am talking of an organizational tendency, not a structural one. The issue is not whether the world-economy is more or less integrated, whether the trends are inflationary or deflationary, whether property rights are more or less concentrated. These structural variables underpin the organizational options but the correlation between the two is long run, not middle run. Organizational options are political choices, are decisions men make about the forms which are most likely to support their interests.

In the "second" sixteenth century, after the peace of Cateau-Cambrésis, the economic balance would swing. Northwest Europe became the economic heartland of the European world-economy. It is now time to look at what gave England and France such fundamental strength. Since the rise of the industrial sector is an important element in this picture, let us see what kind of industrial transformation was going on and how it was that England especially seemed to benefit from it so greatly.

The most important aspect of the industrial transformation of the "second" sixteenth century is not in the novelty of its technology (although there was some), nor in its social organization. The factory and mass production were still essentially unknown. Nor did the overall level of industrial production of the European world-economy rise that much. Domenico Sella reminds us that despite all the economic development of the "long" sixteenth century, "Europe's industrial sector as it stood in 1700 bore far greater resemblance to its medieval antecedent than to its nineteenth century successor."[1]

The key change was in the geographical distribution of industry. Up to about 1550, there were nodes of industrial activity in various parts of Europe. The "industrial backbone of Europe ran . . . from Flanders to

[1]Domenico Sella, "European Industries, 1500–1700." *Fontana Economic History of Europe*, **II**, 5, 1970. 5. Ruggiero Romano asserts that there were very few "real" industries in the sixteenth century, only: "essentially textile products, mineral extraction industries, and naval construction. All the remaining productive activity was in essence based on the work of the individual artisans." *Revista storica italiana*, **LXXIV**, p. 500.

Tuscany,"² but there was some industry everywhere. From about 1550, industrial activity began to concentrate in certain states of "northwest" Europe and decline in other European states. It is striking the extent to which this decline hit one area after another of the territories that made up Charles V's empire.³

As industry drastically declined in some areas, it seemed to divide itself into two varieties in the remaining areas of Europe. John Nef distinguishes between northern Italy, France and Switzerland on the one hand and the "north" of Europe (England, the Dutch Republic, Sweden, Denmark, and Scotland) on the other. According to Nef:

> In the [former] there was a notable growth in the products of the artistic and the luxury industries, a fresh development of art and artisanry, but only a slight increase in the output of the heavy industries, and consequently no remarkable change in the volume of output. In the [latter] there was an expansion of the heavy industries, and consequently of output, for which there had been no precedent.⁴

Sella draws his geographical lines a bit differently. He includes Flanders and southern Germany along with northern Italy among the areas of decline, for which as we have seen he has good reason. He makes no mention of Switzerland. He distinguishes rather between Sweden and France which show some gains and England and the Dutch Republic where the gains achieved were "far more remarkable"⁵ and in each of which was established "a broad spectrum of industrial activities."⁶

²Sella, *Fontana Economic History of Europe*, **II**, 5, p. 64.

³"[T]here was a marked decline in the volume of output, a diminution in the scale of industrial enterprise, and a shrinkage in the relative importance of industry . . . [in] a large part of Europe, the Imperial and the Spanish dominions, including Franche-Comté and the southern Netherlands—all territory which had been nominally united for a generation under the Emperor Charles V. . . ." John U. Nef, *War and Human Progress* (New York: Norton, 1963) 6. Nef gives dates for the decline in each of the parts of the former Hapsburg imperial complex on pp. 6–7.

⁴*Ibid.*, p. 6.

⁵Sella, *Fontana Economic History of Europe*, **II**, 5, p. 65.

⁶*Ibid.*, p. 66. See Heaton, *Economic History of Europe*, pp. 314–319. The picture Eli F. Heckscher draws of Sweden in what he calls the "maturity of the medieval economy," a period between 1520 and 1600, tends to confirm Sella: "What is remarkable about the Swedish economy in the sixteenth century is not that at length there was a change, but that the change was so late in coming. Sweden remained essentially medieval throughout the period. Isolated as it was politically, economically, and intellectually, the country still looked to the past rather than to

the future. The tasks performed by the government were still so minor that neither rulers nor taxpayers felt hampered by the continued existence of natural economy. Since the government did not defray any substantial expenses abroad, it had no need to acquire foreign currencies through exports. The way of life of the population at large remained so unchanged that, except for salt, import trade was of little general concern." *An Economic History of Sweden* (Cambridge, Massachusetts: Harvard Univ. Press, 1954), 77–78.

François Mauro insists on the phenomenon of key industries to explain the leading role of England and Holland: "[I]t was . . . the mining and metallurgical industries which played a role in the commercial revolution analogous to that which the steel industry plays in the contemporary Third World. Alongside the merchant class appeared the class of industrialists. The great fortune of England and the Netherlands was to have both of them: the one aiding the other, the one furnishing machines, other the consumption products for the mass of the workers. Antwerp-Liège-Hondschoote: that is the triangle of Belgian success in the 16th century. London-Newcastle, that is the axis of the British pre-industrial revolution under the reign of Elizabeth." *Le XVIe siècle européen*, pp. 298–299.

Both authors agree however on the great rise of England. This is all the more startling when we recall that many describe the relation of medieval England to the European continent as "colonial,"[7] and that Nef contends that as late as 1547 England was "industrially in a backwater compared with most continental countries, including France." Yet, because of England's industrial expansion, particularly between 1575 and 1620, "the positions of the two countries [came to be] reversed. . . ."[8]

The late Middle Ages saw a major shift in the composition and hence destination of England's export trade. She started out as a supplier of raw materials—cereals, wool, and to a lesser extent metals and leather. By the sixteenth century, the export of these items had declined relatively, and in the case of cereals absolutely, and cloth had become the major export of England.

Cereals (in particular wheat) played a diminishing role from the fourteenth century on. This was due, partly, to the fact that eastern Europe began to export grain and came to absorb a very large part of the international grain market. This may have served to dampen any tendency to expand English production unduly.[9] Instead, as we also know, England moved toward the breakup of the demesnes, a factor usually explained by demographic decline, fall in the price level (especially of cereals), and high cost of living. To be sure, the growth of the London market in the fifteenth and sixteenth centuries led to a new demand for wheat,[10] but

---

[7]Postan, *Cambridge Economic History of Europe*, II, p. 233. Elsewhere, however, Postan manifests greater reluctance to see the relations of England to Italy in the Middle Ages as parallel to twentieth century colonialism's cycle of borrowing techniques and capital, followed by expulsion of the colonial ruler. He argues that the difference lies in the gradualness of English growth, whose cause is found primarily in population expansion and other domestic factors, combined perhaps with a little borrowing and foreign investment. He argues here that the rule of Italians was "very secondary and relatively unimportant when set against the picture of national economy as a whole. Indeed it may well be that where the impact of the Italians was most effective was not in their direct investment nor in their lessons of higher technique, but in the part they played in helping the kings to unsettle the economic life of the country. Royal taxation and royal finance extracted from landowning and landworking classes large amounts of wealth previously immobilized and decanted it into the hands of merchants, financiers, contractors to the armies, and war profiteers. In this way some of the wealth of the country which would otherwise have been hoarded was made available for commerce and industry." "Italy and the Economic Development of England in the Middle Ages," *Journal of Economic History*, **XI**, 4, Fall 1951, 345.

[8]John U. Nef, *Industry and Government in France and England, 1540–1640* (Ithaca: Great Seal Books, 1957), 1.

[9]"Throughout the earlier Middle Ages, but more especially in the 13th century, England was an exporter of foodstuffs, including grain. Later still, another and much more important source of grain appeared. As a result of German colonization of the Slavic lands beyond the Elbe vast new agricultural resources were opened up, and from the end of the 13th century onward East German and Polish rye flowed to the west. By the beginning of the 14th century Baltic grain began to contribute to the Flemish food supplies, and by the time it ousted English grain from the Scandinavian markets." Postan, *Cambridge Economic History of Europe*, **II**, p. 121.

See A. R. Myers: "Until the sixteenth century English exports, except for cloth, consisted mostly of raw materials—metals, wheat and other foodstuffs, wool, and leather—and by the fourteenth century English exporters of some of these commodities, especially wheat, were facing the increasingly powerful competition of the newly-colonized lands of East Germany." *England in the Late Middle Ages*, Volume IV of the Pelican History of England (London: Penguin Books, 1952), 57.

[10]See F. J. Fisher, *Essays in Economic History*, **II**, pp. 197–207.

by that time the English demesnes were broken up and the grain was supplied in part from abroad.[11] Ireland and Norway became economic "colonies" of England although England was still a "colony" of the continent.[12] This was the period too of the legal incorporation of Wales into the English Crown which provided England with an internal colony, devoted at this time in particular to raising cattle.[13]

The wool export trade was "already steadily declining"[14] in the fifteenth century, because of Spanish competition, the rise of textile exports, and the absorption of the wool by the cloth industry in England itself. In particular, the export taxes on wool, used as a fiscal device by the state, "acted as a tariff shelter for the nascent English cloth industry."[15] By 1614, the export of wool was formally prohibited, at which time England attempted to regulate Ireland's trade in wool, turning Ireland into an exporter of wool but not cloth, and only to England.[16]

The English textile industry had two features very important for the emergent world-economy. It was more and more a *rural* industry in England, and it involved England in a search for widespread export markets.

We have referred, in a previous chapter, to the theory of Marian Malowist that in England, as in some other parts of Europe, the recession of the fourteenth and fifteenth centuries, which had caused a sharp reduction in agricultural income, led to the creation of rural textile industries to supplement income. From the point of view of the capitalists, rural industries also had the virtue of avoiding the high wages imposed by city guilds[17] and taking advantage of the cheaper water power to run fulling

[11]See M. M. Postan, "The Economic and Political Relations of England and the Hanse (1400 to 1475)" in Eileen E. Power and M. M. Postan, eds., *Studies in English Trade in the Fifteenth Century* (New York: Barnes & Noble, 1966), esp. 139–141. See N. S. B. Gras: "In the Tudor period, there occurred a change of the greatest importance. . . . London had broken the continuity of its early independence of foreign corn. . . . The growth of London had created a large demand which in turn gave rise to an organized import trade. . . . All this is the more interesting when it is realized that there was a great increase in general corn exportation in the sixteenth century." *The Evolution of the English Corn Market* (Cambridge: Harvard Univ. Press, 1915), 101–102. See Marian Malowist, "Histoire sociale: époque contemporaire," in *IXe Congrès International des Sciences Historiques.* I: *Rapports* (Paris: Lib. Armand Colin, 1950), 310.

But cf. van Dillen: "[In the seventeenth century,] England was self-supporting but the Netherlands were not. That is why originally the grain imported was chiefly destined for the Netherlands." *Britain and the Netherlands,* II, p. 134. See also Alan Everitt in *Agrarian History,* IV, pp. 524–527.

[12]G. N. Clark, *The Wealth of England from 1496 to 1760* (London: Oxford Univ. Press, 1946), 27–28. But Norway was also exporting primary products to Scotland, Denmark, and the Netherlands, which decreased her dependence on England. See Lythe, *The Economy of Scotland,* p. 147.

[13]"The administrative changes in Wales during the Tudor period favored the development of the cattle trade by putting down disorder in the Marches." Caroline Skeel, "The Cattle Trade Between Wales and England From the Fifteenth to the Nineteenth Centuries," *Transactions of the Royal Historical Society,* 4th Ser., IX, 1926, 138.

[14]Eileen E. Power, "The Wool Trade in the Fifteenth Century," in Eileen E. Power and M. M. Postan, eds., *Studies in the English Trade in the Fifteenth Century* (New York: Barnes & Noble, 1966), 39.

[15]Myers, *England in the Late Middle Ages,* p. 132.

[16]See P. J. Bowden, *The Wood Trade in Tudor & Stuart England* (London: Macmillan, 1962), pp. 203–212.

[17]See Postan, *Cambridge Economic History of Europe,* II, p. 244. See Ramsey, *Tudor Economic Problems,* p. 101.

mills.[18] These rural industries produced textiles "not of the highest quality but. . . .cheaper and therefore within the reach of the impoverished nobility and other less well-to-do customers."[19] This expansion of the rural textile industry in England more than compensated for any decline in the urban centers.[20] But in time of economic contraction, the internal market was far too small to sustain the industry. "Hence, this industry had to look for markets abroad. This . . . it did not fail to do in England and Holland from the second half of the fourteenth century on."[21]

Thus, textiles became the hub of English export trade, a shift from the thirteenth century when grain export played a larger role, and this within the context of what Postan calls "precocious mercantilism."[22] One aspect of this was the squeezing out of alien merchants, the Italians in particular, a process that was carried out in the fifteenth century,[23] not to be sure without difficulty.[24] It was even harder to squeeze out the Hanseatic merchants, but that too was accomplished by the sixteenth century.[25]

The cloth trade created great difficulties for England. The need to sell in many markets meant that England was subject to more loss as a result of competition and political difficulty than from the relatively sheltered

[18]"The rapidly expanding use of fulling-mills from the late twelfth century onward achieved by water-power what had so far been done by hand or foot. Running water to work the mills was found in the Cotswolds, the Pennines, and the Lake District and by the beginning of the fourteenth century the cloth industry was already moving to these districts. Worsted cloth, made particularly in East Anglia, did not need fulling, and was therefore not so dependent on waterpower, but even worsted manufacture tended to move into the villages, because of the restrictive policy of the town crafts. Their attempts to keep up the price of their wares hastened their decay, for the unorganized village cloth-workers were willing to take lower wages. . . . The development of the rural cloth industry in late medieval England was thus due rather to this advance in technique and organization than (as is sometimes alleged) to Edward III's invitation to Flemish weavers to settle in England." Myers, *England in the Middle Ages*, p. 56.

[19]M. Malowist, *Economic History Review*, **XII**, p. 178.

[20]"The decline of the [cloth] industry in the thirteenth century in what had been its most flourishing urban centres is as striking as its expansion in rural regions during the same period, but it is the urban side of the matter which had hitherto attracted the attention of historians, and from it they have falsely deduced a decline in the industry as a whole." E. M. Carus-Wilson, "An Industrial Revolution of the Thirteenth Century," *Economic History Review*, **XI**,

1941, 59. See Edward Miller: "Output [of the English textile industry] increased rapidly during the fourteenth century in what many scholars have considered to be an age of economic contraction." "The Fortunes of the English Textile Industry During the Thirteenth Century," *Economic History Review*, 2nd ser., **XVIII**, 1, Aug., 1965, 39–60.

[21]Malowist, *Economic History*, p. 179. See Postan: "As long as English exports consisted mainly of wool, there was no need for English merchants to go far afield in search for market and customers. Wool was a raw material of industry; its customers were foreign cloth manufacturers; and the only cloth manufacturing centres were not only highly localized but also situated near at hand, mainly in the Low Countries. On the other hand, finished cloth had to be sold to potential customers, and in the main centers of potential consumption, or in other words, to men and women all over continental Europe and beyond." *Cambridge Economic History of Europe*, **II**, p. 245.

[22]Postan, in Power and Postan, eds., *Studies in English Trade*, p. 103; cf. Clark, *Wealth of England*, pp. 39–40.

[23]See Alwyn A. Ruddock, *Italian Merchants and Shipping in Southampton, 1270–1600* (Southampton: University College, 1951), *passim.*

[24]See Jacques Heers, "Les Génois en Angleterre: la crise de 1458–1466," in *Studi in onore di Armando Sapori* (Milano: Instituto Edit. Cisalpino, 1957), **II**, 812, 824.

[25]See Postan, *Studies in English Trade*, p. 101.

wool trade.[26] In fact, the cloth industry received a number of setbacks in the fifteenth century because of its exposed position. Both Postan and S. T. Bindoff see these setbacks as the major explanation of the creation of the new commercial organization of overseas traders, the Fellowship of Merchant Adventurers of London, formally created in 1486 and monopolizing the export links with Antwerp.[27] But what the English lost in breadth of market, they made up in quantity. Furthermore, they were pressed to rationalization and efficiency since, as Bindoff notes, "the new situation meant not only an increased demand for cloth, especially for the particular lines favoured by the foreign buyer, but—what was more important—a demand for more cloth to be delivered at an overseas market at a particular time."[28] In addition, the English side was more unified than the Netherlands side which was beset by intercity competition, and hence the Merchant Adventurers could engage in a "calculated avoidance of any commitment to a sole use of one of the towns,"[29] remaining thereby in an economically advantageous bargaining position.

There is one further positive aspect to England's trade position. Her taxation was less oppressive than that of some of the older centers of commerce (Flanders, northern Italy) and her technical organization was

[26]"An outstanding difference between the trade in wool and that in cloth in the fifteenth century lay in the conditions under which each commodity was marketed. Except for Italian shipments, wool was sold to continental buyers by Englishmen at Calais, a mart in English possession, and professedly cherished by the government. In contrast, cloth, sold on the continent by aliens as extensively as by Englishmen, was marketed in regions extending from Prussia round the western coast of Europe to Italy. This outspread and unprotected market-area was more exposed to disturbance than was the concentrated and sheltered wool market at Calais with its supplementary Italian trade. The larger markets for English cloth were the Baltic regions, especially Prussia and Poland, the Low Countries and the lower Rhine, finally northern France and Guienne. It happened that, during the period 1448-76, not only was Guienne lost to England, but the markets of the Baltic and of the Low Countries were unsettled through political dissensions. The conditions of the three market areas should therefore be noted in assessing responsibilities for the decline in the cloth trade." H. L. Gray, "English Foreign Trade from 1446 to 1482," in Eileen E. Power & M. M. Postan, eds., *Studies in English Trade in the Fifteenth Century* (New York: Barnes & Noble, 1966), 25.

[27]"By the middle of the fifteenth century, the English cloth merchants had been excluded from all their more distant outposts. The Scandinavian market had been lost at the turn of the century. Connexions with Prussia, and, through that country, with the whole of central and eastern Europe were finally lopped off by the successive Anglo-Hanseatic conflicts in the 30's and 50's. The concentration of Eng-

lish trade in the Netherlands, the specialization of English industry on unfinished cloth, the rise of the company and of the monopoly of the Merchant Advanturers—all these familiar features of English trade at the close of the Middle Ages could be traced to the break-up of England's medieval empire at the end of the Hundred Years' War." Postan, *Economic History Review*, **XII**, 1942, 3. See also Postan in Power & Postan, eds., *Studies in English Trade*, p. 153.

"But it is undoubtedly the English who hold price of place among the Antwerp 'nations' of this time, and the choice of Antwerp as the 'mart town' for English cloth ranks second only to the establishment of the spice-staple as the reason why merchants were drawn there from all over Europe. It was in the face of many discouragements that the English cloth trade had struggled to acquire an entrepôt in the Netherlands during the fifteenth century. The persistence which it displayed, and which was to be so amply rewarded, was a virtue born of necessity, for it was their failure to maintain themselves elsewhere along the coast of Europe which drove so many English merchants to try their fortunes in the Netherlands; there is much to be said for the view that the rise of the English cloth-trade to Antwerp, like the rise of the Merchant Adventurers' Company which came to dominate it, was a function not of growth but of the contraction of English overseas trade as a whole." S. T. Bindoff, *New Cambridge Modern History*, **II**, pp. 53–54.

[28]S. T. Bindoff, *Tudor England*, Vol. V of The Pelican History of England (London: Penguin Books, 1950), 20.

[29]Bindoff, *New Cambridge Modern History*, **II**, p. 54.

up-to-date and hence more economical, thus giving her competitive advantages as early as the beginning of the "first" sixteenth century.[30] So it was that in the beginning of the "second" sixteenth century, England had a flourishing export trade, two-thirds of it going to Antwerp, the other third to France and the Iberian peninsula. Its net deficit with France was covered by the bullion resulting from its favorable balance with the Hapsburg areas. At the beginning of the Elizabethan era, England's overseas trade could already be described in glowing terms.[31]

England had political as well as economic advantages as the "second" sixteenth century began. It could be argued that England internally was exceptionally unified and from a relatively early period.[32] We shall not review here the reasons for this, which we discussed to some extent previously, except to notice that the explanations fall into two main camps: The form of medieval social structure was said to have lent itself particularly well to the development of a strong monarchy,[33] and the natural geography of insular England posed fewer obstacles to the centralizing thrust of the monarch than areas on the continent.[34]

[30]"In the case of either international trade or internal transactions, the costs of packing, transport, unloading, legal proceedings, and taxation added up to but a small part of the cost price. This is a fact worthwhile underlining; this western commerce, in the 15th century, was subject to more favorable conditions than that of Genoa, which maintained a far heavier tax policy. In any case certain commercial techniques (transports or accessory operations) were sufficiently advanced to permit relatively low prices. Whether it is a question of expensive goods like English cloth or a cheap product like alum, these costs stayed low: a mark of a more modern economy. . . .

"Conditions of credit are also very important. In London, one obtained money easily, without excessive formalities and without having to utilize more or less under-the-table methods." Heers, *Studi in onore di Armando Sapori*, **II**, p. 832.

[31]"England's overseas trade . . . consisted of bartering a single product, cloth—the result of what, for the age, was a truly gigantic industrialization, involving a great agrarian revolution and a change in the whole pattern of internal economy—in return for a number of articles, many of which [England] was climatically unable to produce, together with a range of industrial finished products of every kind to serve the growing needs of the civilized and luxury-loving upper and middle classes. England clothed the Northern European peasant and in return absorbed a great proportion of the products contrived by Europe's technical skills and imported from the East and South by Europe's merchant marine. The balance of trade hung entirely upon the capacity of Europe to handle, transport, and purchase the cloth of which England was an almost unlimited purveyor." Lawrence Stone, *Economic His-*

tory Review, **II**, p. 39.

[32]See Strayer, *On the Medieval Origins of the Modern State*, pp. 44–45. Eli F. Heckscher notes that England had a unified coinage under Henry II in the second half of the twelfth century, whereas France only achieved this in 1262. *Mercantilism*, **I**, p. 119.

[33]For example, Marc Bloch: "[The conquest of William] had taken place at the very moment when the transformation of economic and intellectual conditions throughout the West began to favor the struggle against disintegration. It is significant that almost from the very first this monarchy, born of a successful war, seems to have had at its disposal at an early date an educated personnel and bureaucratic machinery. . . .

"Although [should it not read because?] in certain respects no state was more completely feudal, the feudalism was of such kind as ultimately to enhance the prestige of the crown. In this country where every piece of land was a tenement, the king was literally the lord of all the lords. Nowhere was the system of military fiefs more methodically applied." *Feudal Society*, pp. 429–430.

[34]For example, Hecksher: "One of the two main causes of [difficulties in creating a centralized state in the Middle Ages] was the existing condition of communication facilities, in particular land communication, which, under primitive technical conditions, always offered greater difficulties before the great inventions than inland waterways or coastwise traffic. A country such as England, with its remarkably long coast line in proportion to its land area, had, for this reason, far greater possibilities of achieving political union than continental states, and of these none was worse than Germany." *Mercantilism*, **I**, p. 36. See Clark, *The Wealth of England*, pp. 4–5, 44–45.

Given such explanations, let us see in what ways did the Tudor monarchs make the most of these "natural" opportunities, and thus explain England's ability to pursue its tentative industrial advantages in the "second" sixteenth century.

One factor was what is sometimes called the Henrician or Tudor "administrative revolution" which G. R. Elton put forward as having occurred between 1530–1542 under the genius of that "most radical of modernizers,"[35] Thomas Cromwell. Elton argues that this period was one of real change, one which saw the creation of the modern sovereign state: "The Tudor state was a national monarchy to a degree new in England, and while the apparent emphasis lay on the monarch the real stress was already on its national character."[36] The administrative revolution was a concomitant of the greater coordination required by emerging capitalist interests. If England were to be a coherent entity within the framework of the world-economy, it could no longer be several somewhat separate economies.[37]

Elton sees a series of new procedures instituted—a new mode of managing finances, the centralization of administration under the principal secretary, the organization of the privy council as a sphere of coordination, the rationalization of the king's household—each of which involved a reorganization "in the direction of greater definition, of specialization, of bureaucratic order."[38] Elton's work has given rise to one of those endless controversies in which historians debate, without the aid of quantitative data, the degree to which some "differences" add up to a qualitative jump.[39]

Was the Henrician Reformation really new or not? Was the administrative change truly revolutionary, or was it simply one more step in a process going on continuously from the fourteenth to the seventeenth centuries? Christopher Hill seems to me to hold a sensibly balanced view of what was going on:

> Throughout the Middle Ages [the] see-saw continued: more "bureaucratic" government under baronial control when the king was weak or a minor; "Household" government under the king's personal control when he was strong. But in the

[35]The phrase is that of H. R. Trevor-Roper, to be found in "England's Modernizer: Thomas Cromwell" in *Historical Essays* (New York: Harper, 1966), 74.

[36]G. R. Elton, *The Tudor Revolution in Government* (London and New York: Cambridge Univ. Press, 1953), 4.

[37]"[D]ifferent regions of England (and to some extent even different towns) had in . . . the fourteenth and fifteenth centuries their different economic histories, in the same way as the economic development of different nations of Europe in the nineteenth century, is rightly treated as largely separate stories. . . . In this respect the appearance of capitalism is itself a powerful coordinating

influence." Dobb, *Studies*, p. 21.

[38]Elton, *Tudor Revolution*, p. 415. Also, the "fundamental change [was] the change from a bureaucracy trained in the church or the king's household to a bureaucracy trained in a minister's household and then employed in the service of the state [p. 308]."

[39]See Penry Williams and G. L. Harriss, "A Revolution in Tudor History?" *Past & Present*, **25,** July 1963, 3–58; G. R. Elton, "The Tudor Revolution: A Reply," *Past & Present*, **29,** Dec. 1964, 26–49; G. L. Harriss and Penry Williams, "A Revolution in Tudor History?" *Past & Present*, **31,** July 1965, 87–96; G. R. Elton, "A Revolution in Tudor History?" *Past & Present*, **32,** Dec. 1965, 103–109.

sixteenth century this cycle was broken. Departments "went out of court" without the king's losing control over them. . . .[40]

This period of administrative strengthening of the state was at the same time, as Hill also reminds us, "the only period in English history since 1066 when the country had no overseas possessions (except Ireland)."[41] So the administrative talent could all be focused inward. The results are very straightforward and very important.

England was able to develop a strong capital city as a cultural and economic unifying force.[42] And England was able to maintain internal peace at a time of turmoil on the continent, without a standing army, which accounts in part for its industrial advance.[43] Why should England have escaped

[40]Hill, *Reformation to Industrial Revolution*, p. 28. This is better as a summary, I think, than Elton's somewhat more extreme version: "The reforms of the 1530's, the bureaucratization of government, succeeded in obtaining that continuity which marks modern government and prevents real anarchy even in the days of civil war." *Tudor Revolution*, p. 417.

[41]Hill, *ibid.*, p. 25.

[42]"The sixteenth century saw the integration of English towns into a single national unit, to an extent that was not paralleled on the continent. . . . The significant expansion of London, and its growing power as a unifying force, may be dated to the post-Reformation era. . . . Taking advantage of the establishment of law, order, and internal police, the ending of private war in Wales and the North, the elimination of franchises and the slow improvement of communications, merchants from the City gradually broke down the privileges of the local corporations. At the same time Protestant preachers, financed from London, worked to bring the dark corners of the kingdom to a real understanding of the religion accepted by the capital." Hill, *ibid.*, pp. 25–27.

The exceptional position of England compared to the continent is stressed also by Heckscher: "In no other country was the task of establishing a unified toll system relatively so easy as in England, and two factors were in the main responsible for this. The first, as in all other spheres, was the united and unbroken strength of the English monarchy, and the second was the overwhelming importance of sea transport, making land routes and inland waterways far less important than was the case in such compact geographical blocks as Germany and France. . . .

"England occupied a unique position not only through the insignificance of her road and river tolls. She was also able to evolve a national customs system, entirely independent of the municipal tolls and completely in the hands of the state, the customs

being neither modified by numerous exemptions nor normally farmed. . . .

"It was, moreover, characteristic that not only were the customs in the hands of the state, but they showed a precocious distinction between foreign and domestic trade." *Mercantilism*, pp. 46, 51, 52.

See Gino Luzzatto, *L'età moderna* (Padova: CEDAM), p. 14.

Barry Supple formulates the question of economic integration more conservatively: "We cannot yet speak of a national market for the factors of production or for most consumer goods. But regional specialization and trade were sufficiently far advanced to create an economic balance which would be alarmingly susceptible to commercial disturbance." *Commercial Crisis*. p. 3. On the growth of the London market as a stimulus to national economic development, see two articles by F. J. Fisher: "The Development of the London Food Market, 1540–1640," in Carus-Wilson, ed., **I**, 135–51; "The Development of London as a Centre of Conspicuous Consumption in the 16th and 17th Centuries," in Carus-Wilson, ed., **II**, 197–207.

[43]"At the transition from medieval to modern times the English people were in arrears, culturally, as compared with the rest of west and central Europe, including west and south Germany; whether that epoch is to be dated from the close of the fifteenth century or from any earlier period, and whether this comparison is to be made in industrial and material civilisation or in immaterial terms of intellectual achievement and the arts of life. But during the succeeding century the English community had made such gains that by its close they stood (perhaps doubtfully) abreast of their Continental neighbours. This British gain was both absolute and relative, and was due both to an accelerated advance in the Island territory, although the retardation is more visible on the Continent during the seventeenth century than even towards the close of the sixteenth century. . . .

"Elizabethan England had the differential advan-

the religious wars of the continent when it could be argued, as R. B. Wernham does, that in the period following the treaty of Cateau-Cambrésis, "the internal instability of the British Isles [caused largely by the uncertainty of the English succession] made them . . . the danger area and focal point in the rivalries of Western Europe."[44] Mainly it was this very rivalry and the relative exhaustion of the French and Spanish empires (which we already spelled out) combined with the boldness of the Act of Supremacy of 1559 in establishing England as an Anglican state[45] that "made possible the emergence of a third great power in western Europe and the eventual supersession of the twin imperialisms of Hapsburg and Valois by a multiple balance of powers.."[46]

Relative internal peace and no standing army also meant a lower need for taxation and of a bureaucracy swollen beyond its efficient size by the sale of offices.[47] The expansion of central power was by means of a more efficient bureaucracy more than through a much larger (and more burdensome) one. It was also made possible by the economic position of the monarch himself, England's greatest landowner.[48] But as greatest landowner in a relatively isolated and unified national economy whose strength was to be built on the new industries, where lay the interests of the king? No doubt the king's interests were ambiguous, since as landowner the king sought to maximize his income from his lands, and as king he sought to maximize his income from the landowners.[49] One way to try to solve

tage given it in the matter of enterprise that the rest of Christendom was presently involved in destructive wars, which, fortunately for the English industrial community, fell with exceptional severity on the most capable of their industrial and commercial rivals." Thorstein Veblen, *Imperial Germany and the Industrial Revolution* (Ann Arbor, Michigan: Ann Arbor Paperbacks, 1966), 92, 98.

[44]R. B. Wernham, "The British Question 1559–69," *New Cambridge Modern History,* **III**: R. B. Wernham, ed., *The Counter-Reformation and the Price Revolution, 1559–1610* (London and New York: Cambridge Univ. Press, 1968), 209.

[45] See *ibid.,* 212.

[46]*Ibid.,* 233.

[47]See Hurstfield on the general problem for all Europe, including England: "Then governments of sixteenth-century Europe found themselves faced with relatively slender resources against ever-mounting commitments. . . . [They] were faced with a situation in which the middle classes could not, or would not, carry the major share of the costs of national government. But if the middle classes proved uncooperative, the monarchies themselves, in relations to the middle classes, were ambiguous to a degree.. . . [Thus there resulted] a widespread series of attempts . . . throughout Europe to tax the economy by subterfuge; to use existing commercial and industrial processes as a fiscal sponge. They

necessarily involved the distortion of the economy; and this was proceeding on a massive scale. The best manifestation is the widespread sale of office." J. Hurstfield, *New Cambridge Modern History,* **III**, pp. 139–140.

But see Christopher Hill on England: "The Tudor peace, and the lack of a standing army in England, meant that taxation was relatively light by the standards of the continent. . . . [T]he small sums contributed in their turn to the failure of England to evolve a bureaucracy of comparable strength to that, say, of France." *Reformation to Industrial Revolution,* p. 101.

[48]"The fundamental fact in the restoration of royal power was the restoration of royal wealth; in order to be the most powerful man in the kingdom the king had to be the richest. In effect this meant towards the end of the fifteenth century, that he had to be the greatest landowner." Elton, *Tudor Revolution,* p. 25.

[49]"The period of absolutism was inaugurated by the dissolution of the monasteries, which economically refloated the ruling class and recruited it from below by endowing new families. For some time before this the landlords had been seeking to reconstruct their economic power by means of enclosures and rent-raising, but such measures provoked peasant discontent and made necessary a strong central government to reinforce politically the economic

the dilemma was for the Crown to try to reduce its role as a landlord. But then the monarchy had to find a substitute source of income. Toward this end, in 1610, the Crown offered Parliament the "Great Contract"—an exchange of its feudal rights for an annual allowance.[50] This proposal failed because of disagreement about the size of the annual amount. As the amount of income from royal rent was then diminishing, this failure was to contribute to the political strains of the era.

Internal instability and internal peace, an administrative revolution but a relatively small bureaucracy, a national network of markets and the king as a great landowner—a curious combination, leading to G. E. Aylmer's "paradox and truism that early Stuart England was at one and the same time a 'much-governed' country and a country with very little government."[51] This paradox is in fact the secret of England's relative success. To understand it, we must turn to a central debate of modern English historiography: the nature of the English upper classes in the century preceding the English Revolution, and the role of the much disputed "gentry."

Going through the literature of this debate, what J. H. Hexter has called "the storm over the gentry"[52] gives one the sensation of watching a fast and seemingly endless pingpong volley, where each play is brilliantly riposted ad infinitum. It requires distraction rather than concentration to realize that there are two debates intertwined: one over the substantive issues of English history in the "second" sixteenth century, and the other over the fundamental lines of battle in modern social science. Armed with this insight, it then requires concentration to notice that some people are in fact switching sides very fast in the middle of the debate, thus creating the illusion of a single straightforward ball game.

If the debate is difficult to unravel, it is because the story itself is so complex. Let us start by seeing what is thought to have happened in terms of landownership.

Frank C. Spooner argues that the profound economic crisis that shook Europe from about 1540 to 1560 "was particularly severe in the case of England. . . ."[53] This was no doubt one of the factors that led to the

---

and social power of the landlords. However, this led the absolute monarchy into the dilemma which it never solved and which caused its downfall. If it gave the landlords a free hand it was faced with peasant revolts which might overthrow the ruling class; if it restrained the landlords and protected the peasants it was confronted by a revolt in the ruling class which might endanger the monarchy." Brian Manning, "The Nobles, the People, and the Constitution," *Past & Present*, **9**, Apr. 1956, 48.

[50]See Gordon Batho, "Landlords in England. A. The Crown," in *The Argarian History of Englnd and Wales*, Joan Thirsk, ed., **IV**: *1500–1640* (London

and New York: Cambridge Univ. Press, 1967), 273.

[51]G. E. Aylmer, *The King's Servants* (New York: Columbia Univ. Press, 1961), 7.

[52] J. H. Hexter, "The Myth of the Middle Class in Tudor England," *Reappraisals in History* (New York: Harper, 1963), 117–162.

[53]Spooner, *New Cambridge Modern History*, **III**, p. 15. Lawrence Stone says that from 1540 there was "a period of three cycles of increasingly dizzy booms and abysmal slumps, ending in fiscal collapse in 1553." "State Control in Sixteenth-Century England," *Economic History Review*, **XVII**, 1, 1947, 106.

official proclamation of the Reformation which made possible the confiscation of the monasteries and of other church properties. The Crown then sold most of this land, both to provide immediate income and as a means of political consolidation, giving the purchasers what Christopher Hill calls "a vested interest in Protestantism."[54] This political decision dramatically expanded the amount of land available on the market, which accelerated the whole process of extension of capitalist modes of operation in a way and to a degree that no other European country (except possibly the northern Netherlands) was experiencing at that time.[55] The lands once sold were sold again (and often a number of times over). Where did this all lead to over the next 75 years? This seems to be one of the cornerstones of the debate.

There seems to be relatively little debate about two arguments that R. H. Tawney put forward in his initial essays. One argument was "that the tendency of an active land-market was, on the whole, to increase the number of medium-sized properties, while diminishing that of the largest."[56] Note however that this does not necessarily say anything about who, peers or "gentry," own these "medium-sized" properties.[57] The second point that Tawney makes is that this land shift resulted in "a more business-like agriculture."[58] Again, relatively little argument here.

But what was the social classification of those who controlled the land? There is the storm. It is far more than a semantic issue but semantics plays its role, as everyone proceeds to give varying meanings to aristocracy, gentry (upper gentry, lower gentry, mere gentry, gentlemen), and yeomen. It is no accident that the scholars debate furiously here, because the whole point is that this period in English history is not only a moment of economic change and great individual social mobility, but of the change of categories. Not only are we unsure how to designate the meaningful social groupings; the men of the time also were.[59] To point however to the fluidity of a

[54]Christopher Hill, "Some Social Consequences of the Henrician Revolution," in *Puritanism and Revolution* (New York: Schocken Books, 1958), 44. Marc Bloch asserts that "the dissolution of the monasteries (1536–1539) hastened the fusion of classes. The Crown gave or sold the largest part. All the classes, nobility, gentry (many of whom had served the monks as administrators or farmed their lands), merchants (London syndicates of merchants), were beneficiaries." *Seigneurie française*, p. 122.

[55]See Clark, *Wealth of England*, pp. 64–65. Lawrence Stone argues that, in addition, the exigencies of the family system led to considerable sales by the nobility of their land. See *The Crisis of the Aristocracy, 1558–1641,* abr. ed. (London: Oxford Univ. Press, 1967), 76–88.

[56]R. H. Tawney, "The Rise of the Gentry, 1558-1640," in E. M. Carus-Wilson, ed., *Essays in Economic History* (New York: St. Martin's, 1965), **I**, 202.

[57]This is particularly the point of one of Tawney's severest critics, J. P. Cooper, who suggests that many peers owned medium-sized estates and many laymen held more than ten manors. See "The Counting of Manors," *Economic History Review,* 2nd. ser., **VIII**, 3, 1958, 381–383.

[58]Tawney, *Essays in Economic History,* **I**, p. 189.

[59]"One cannot, without being misleading, envisage the beginnings of modern society in rigorous 'class' terms, especially if one insists on restricting the notion of class to the Marxist tripartite classification. At a given moment, the wage-workers may act against their masters, after which they may, on the contrary, act with their masters against the oppression of commercial capital or the government; the peasants might very well rise up at one and the same time against the maneuvers of the king to diminish the power of *their* nobles, and against the attempts of the nobles to increase the rate of feudal

concept in a given epoch is not to point to its uselessness. It should urge the scholar on to skeptical boldness.

To untangle the threads, we must start by following the terms of discourse. Let us go successively through aristocracy, gentry, and yeomen. But as we do it, let us remember that "economic changes were hurrying the more enterprising among [those who controlled the land, whatever their designation,] into novel methods of estate management. . . . They stood to gain much if they adapted their farming to meet the new commercial conditions. They stood to lose much if they were so conservative as to adhere to the old methods."[60] It seems fairly clear that there was no across-the-board correlation of social status and adaptability to the demands of capitalist agriculture. Lawrence Stone paints a picture of the aristocracy as guilty of "incompetent management" on large estates and with a "spreading taste for conspicuous waste," such that "the gap between income and expenditure grew from a tiny crack to a vast chasm."[61] In addition, the aristocracy had to bear the high costs of litigation and public service, for "the Tudors operated through an unpaid bureaucracy."[62] But their efforts to increase income were to no avail: they traded away long leases for quick cash returns; they overborrowed; they depended on state favors until the state could or would give no more. All to no avail:

> The process of attrition of the economic resources of the aristocracy . . . was one that continued without interruption throughout the Elizabethan period. . . . By 1603, it would seem as if the whole hierarchic structure of Tudor society was on the verge of imminent dissolution.[63]

Yet it is this same author who, a few years later, sings the imagination and enterprise of these same aristocrats in this same Elizabethan era:

dues. At the level of the country as a whole, the peasants never succeeded in establishing a real solidarity; and, on the contrary, one often finds city-dwellers their oppressors. Every person belonged to several social groups: his family, his guild (*corps de métier*), his town or village, his county—called "country" in the 16th century—his country in the modern sense of the term, and his economic class. Most often, doubtless, he defined himself in terms that were a combination of these diverse social memberships. One spoke of the 'cloth workers of Norfolk' rather than of the cloth workers as a whole, or of men of Norfolk as a whole. The notion that individuals had of themselves, of their memberships and their allegiances, depended simply on the circumstances of the moment. The question of knowing what was the 'fundamental' allegiance of an individual is a question to which there is no answer, not only because the data are difficult to evaluate, but also because these choices are rarely made in the abstract rather than in relation to particular circumstances." C. S. L. Davies, "Les révoltes

populaires en Angleterre (1500–1700)," *Annales E.S.C.*, 24, **I,** janv.-févr. 1969, 59–60. What Davies says about the mode and complexities of self-designation of social affiliation is of course true, but in no way contradicts a Marxist model of classes. Marx allowed for precisely the same considerations. Davies is useful, however, in reminding us that at this time, for many, class memberships were regional rather than national.

[60]Tawney, *The Agrarian Problem*, p. 195.

[61]Lawrence Stone, "The Anatomy of the Elizabethan Aristocracy," *Economic History Review*, **XVIII,** 1 & 2, 1948, 3–4.

[62]*Ibid.*, p. 15.

[63]*Ibid.*, pp. 37–38. See Tawney: "The materials for generalisation have hardly yet been put together; but to say that many noble families—though not they alone—encountered, in the two generations before the Civil War, a financial crisis is probably not an overstatement." *Essays in Economic History*, **I,** p. 181.

[I]n this period the peerage fulfilled a role that no other class, neither the gentry nor the merchants, was able or willing to rival. . . . The importance of the aristocracy at this period is due rather to their willingness to encourage and finance new ventures, which were regarded as risky and therefore failed to secure the backing of more cautious social groups. Since large-scale mining and metallurgical industries were still novelties in the Tudor period they took the lead in their expansion. Since oceanic trade and exploration were novelties they again played a prominent part.[64]

Nor was this initiative, it seems, absent on their demesnes:

[T]he older nobility showed a surprising readiness . . . to develop new resources on their own estates. . . . The economic and social decline of the peerage relative to the gentry between 1558 and 1642 is certainly not due to any lack of entrepreneurial initiative.[65]

It is hard to reconcile the two portraits by Stone. Since Stone's statistics on the degree of financial crisis of the aristocracy have been subject to so much attack, and since he has partially but not wholly retreated,[66] we may well ask with H. R. Trevor-Roper:

If "over two-thirds of the English aristocracy were in 1600, not merely living above their means but poised on the brink of financial ruin," . . . how are we to explain the fact that they not merely recovered from this imminent ruin, but survived the far greater crisis of the next sixty years? Their extravagance did not diminish in those years. . . . How did they do it?[67]

Trevor-Roper's explanation is that the predicament of the aristocracy, "though genuine, was nothing like so serious as Mr. Stone, with his swollen figures, supposes," that they "clung" to their lands, and that the rise in value of land after 1600, did "more than King James did, or any king could do," to sustain their fortunes.[68] It turns out, however, that Stone does not disagree. Although he dates it from 1620, he says that:

[64]Lawrence Stone, "The Nobility in Business, 1540–1640," *Explorations in Entrepreneurial History,* **X**, 2, Dec. 1957, 61.

[65]*Ibid.,* p. 60.

[66]See H. R. Trevor-Roper, "The Elizabethan Aristocracy: An Anatomy Anatomized," *Economic History Review,* 2nd ser, **III**, 3, 1951, 279–298, and reply: "But Mr. Trevor-Roper is probably correct in accusing me of exaggerating the long-term gravity of the crisis of the 1590's." Lawrence Stone, "The Elizabethan Aristocracy—A Restatement," *Economic History Review,* 2nd ser., **IV**, 1, 2, & 3, 1951–52, 311. In the concluding section, Stone says: "[Trevor-Roper's] denial that a majority of the Elizabethan aristocracy was in full economic decline seems to be contradicted by the evidence ... [p. 320]." See also Cooper, *Encounter,* **XI**, p. 388; Lawrence

Stone, "Letter to the Editor," *Encounter,* **XI**, 1, July 1958, 73; J. H. Hexter, "Letter to the Editor," *Encounter,* **XI**, 2, Aug., 1958, 76.

[67]Trevor-Roper, *Economic History Review,* **III**, pp. 290–291.

[68]*Ibid.,* 291–292. P. J. Bowden gives a further explanation of why the decline was less serious than some suppose: "Even under such circumstances as these, however, it did not necessarily follow that the landlord was bound to suffer a decline in real income. The assumption made earlier, that rent was the landlord's only source of revenue, does not, in fact, represent the true position. Landlords' receipts in the sixteenth and seventeenth centuries came from a variety of sources. Most landlords probably engaged in direct farming to fill the needs of the household, if not for the market. ... (*cont.*)

Even the most incompetent [member of the landed classes] could not fail to profit from the massive rise in average rents in the early seventeenth century, and thereafter the levelling off of prices reduced the importance of inefficient estate management.[69]

As for J. H. Hexter who attacks both Stone and Tawney on the one hand and Trevor-Roper on the other, he argues:

> Around the 1580's the land market began to boom, and it seems to have continued to boom for the next half century. . . . [O]n the whole a general increase in land values is likely to be most profitable in gross to the men who have the most land to profit from, that is, to the very segment of the landed class which both Tawney and Trevor-Roper have consigned to economic debility.[70]

Aside, however, from a quibble about dates, the position Hexter takes on this item is *not* at variance with Stone and Trevor-Roper. Finally, let us turn to a fourth point of view, differing in many ways from the three others, that of Christopher Hill. On this question, he says:

> So for a section of the aristocracy the Reformation brought economic loss, though not for the class as a whole. We should be careful not to see anything "anti-feudal" in this process [of land transfers]. Indeed, in a sense the dissolution [of the monasteries] led to an intensification of feudalism, since it multiplied tenures in chief. . . . The ecclesiastical property which passed to [the monarchy] was soon dissipated. . . . In the short run, then, the Reformation strengthened the position of the lay landed ruling class as a whole, though it weakened some of those members of it hitherto powerful.[71]

If then there turns out to be less argument about the aristocracy than it seemed on first glance, can we say the same about the gentry who were the original focus of the debate? Gentry is of course a much vaguer term. Cooper spells out some of the difficulties:

> The peerage is a group of individuals enjoying a legally defined status which belongs . . . to only one male member of each family. Thus the younger sons of peers

"Apart from rent income and the proceeds of direct-farming, . . . by far the most important source of receipts for the majority of landlords was timber." "Agricultural Prices, Farm Profits, and Rents," in *The Agrarian History of England and Wales*, Joan Thirsk, ed., **IV:** *1500–1640* (London and New York: Cambridge Univ. Press, 1967), 675, 677. Bowden asserts that because some rents were fixed and others were not, the real consequences were two: "The range of rents, as between different holdings [widened];" and "the differential between rates for poorer and better qualities of land [narrowed] [pp. 689, 693]."

[69]Stone, *The Crisis of the Aristocracy*, p. 94.

[70]J. H. Hexter, "The Storm Over the Gentry," in *Reappraisals in History* (New York: Harper, 1963),

133. If one were to believe Hexter, there may once have been two sides to this controversy—Tawney and Trevor-Roper—but he, Hexter, has more correctly perceived that both the contestants were "pseudo-Marxians," against which he placed his own "Whig interpretation." It is all the more curious, then, to discover upon close inspection that Hexter's arguments can in fact be dissected into three categories—one in fact pro-Tawney (and "worse," in accord with Christopher Hill), a second pro-Trevor-Roper, and a third different from both. It is not at all sure that the third of these slices is the largest. Furthermore, as the citation demonstrates, Hexter sometimes invents nonreal differences.

[71]Hill, *Puritanism and Revolution*, pp. 36–37.

and their descendants will appear as gentry in Professor Tawney's classification. Great landowners, whenever they could afford it, were usually more generous to their sons in cash or land than is sometimes supposed. . . . Such provision certainly influenced the distribution of property. . . . [T]he gentry were not only, like the peerage, recruited from below, they were also recruited from above. . . . Furthermore, the groups are non-compatible in another respect: the peerage is a group strictly defined by legal status, while the gentry is not definable in any such fashion. It is a classification by wealth and to some extent by mode of life. . . . Although peerages were sold after 1603, entry to the peerage was never by a simple test of wealth and style of life.[72]

Who then are the gentry? The gentry are not yet peers, and are more than "yeomen," the latter a term as difficult to define as gentry. But then we discover that included among "gentry" are not only younger sons of peers, but various categories such as knights, esquires, and gentlemen. This should make it clear what is happening. In the hierarchical order of feudal society a large number of categories evolved which prescribed rank, duties, privileges, and honors. The ranks were constantly evolving, the family continuity of course unstable, the income correlates of rank varying. The expansion of capitalist agriculture was reflected in the stratification system by a new category of "landowner" (which to be sure might be subdivided by size of holding). Gentry emerged as a term covering capitalist landowners. The other terms did not disappear. But the "gentry" was a group label which expanded slowly to absorb and obliterate other terms. In the Elizabethan period, there were still "aristocrats" and "yeomen" in addition to "gentry" at the very least. In the twentieth century, there are only really "farmers." We get nowhere if we reify "gentry" be defining it either as it was defined at a certain moment in time or as we determine the social reality to have been at that moment in time. The whole point about "gentry" is not only that it was a class in formation but a concept in formation. It was, however, a case of new wine in old bottles. F. J. Fisher seems to me to put it exactly right: "The effect of the economic changes of the new sixteenth and seventeenth centuries was less to create new categories of men than to offer the existing categories new opportunities and to inspire them with a new spirit."[73]

[72]Cooper, *Economic History Review,* **VIII,** p. 381. Hexter wishes too to distinguish between the peerage and the aristocracy, counting younger sons of peers as "aristocrats" and not "gentry." *Reappraisals in History,* p. 127.

[73]F. J. Fisher, "The Sixteenth and Seventeenth Centuries: The Dark Ages in English Economic History?" *Economica,* n.s., **XXIV,** 93, 1957, 17. Fisher also reminds us, however, that the old meaning of the categories were not yet bereft of social consequences: "And if land by itself was not a sufficient passport to social bliss, gentility was not out of reach. At first sight it is true, the status-system

of the sixteenth and seventeenth centuries does not seem highly favourable to the rising man. As I understand it that system, at least in its cruder manifestations, was essentially biological. It was based upon a colour bar; though the relevant colour was that of the blood rather than of the skin. A man's status depended less on his own distinction than of the possession of an ancestor who had been distinguished before him. And the more remote that ancestor, and hence presumably the less of his blood which flowed through an Elizabethan's veins, the higher the status of that Elizabethan was. One of the most pathetic stories of the sixteenth century

Christopher Hill, by contrast, seems to me to add to the confusion in this formulation of the problem:

> We must surely start from the fact that "the gentry" were not an economic class. They were a social and legal class; economically they were divided. The inflationary century before 1640 was a great watershed, in which, in all sections of the community, economic divisions were taking place. Some yeomen were thriving to gentility; others were being submerged. Some peers were accumulating vast estates; others were on the verge of bankruptcy. It is easy to argue that "the gentry" were either "rising" or "declining" if we take samples of the class; for some families were doing the one and others the other.[74]

Though the empirical description of the social facts seems to me faultless, the theorizing seems to me to miss the point, precisely the Marxist point. "The mark of the gentry," says Julian Cornwall, "was the ownership of land."[75] The term gentry was *coming* to cover a group of men all in the same relationship to the means of production: owners of unentailed land producing for the market. The clarity of this process was confused by the fact that men still valued the social perquisites of an older legal category[76] but it was the common *economic* thrust that was the dominant unifying theme of this category in the sixteenth century and later. Within an economic class, some can be more wealthy than others, more successful than others in the market. Variation in income does not demonstrate that a group is not a class.

What light does this then throw on the now classic debate on the gentry? Tawney's essential point was that the gentry were a group with a style of life better adapted to survival in the age of inflation than the spendthrift peerage and the fly-by-night speculators. "Compared with the adventurers who dealt in properties they had never seen, the local gentry was a settled population confronting mere marauders."[77] Their advantage over their French counterparts was that they were "kept few and tough by the ruthlessness of the English family system, which sacrificed the individual to the institution.[78] They were politically far stronger than their Dutch counterparts, "wholly severed from their rural roots"[79] because they "combined

is that, I think, of the efforts of Lord Burleigh—a man of distinction by any rational criteria—to prove his descent from a Welsh princeling who probably never existed and who, if he did exist, was probably hardly distinguishable from the sheep of his native hills [pp. 13–14]."

[74]Christopher Hill, "Recent Interpretations of the Civil War," in *Puritanism and Revolution* (New York: Schocken Books, 1958), 8.

[75]Julian Cornwall, "The Early Tudor Gentry," *Economic History Review*, 2nd ser., **XVII**, 3, 1965, 470. He adds: "They were in fact the chief landowning class, far outstripping the peerage who in any case were few in number at this time."

[76]Tawney incidentally argues that the gentry, or rather at this point in the argument the squirearchy, held "a position determined, not by legal distinction, but by common estimation. . . ." *Essays in Economic History*, **I**, p. 174.

[77]*Ibid.*, p. 197.

[78]*Ibid.*, p. 174.

[79]*Ibid.*, p. 175. This assessment of the Dutch situation is contradicted in a recent doctoral dissertation, a brief summary of which has been published, and which argues that the rural sector was every bit as important in the Dutch economy of the time as it was in the English. See Jan de Vries, "The Role of the Rural Sector in the Development of the Dutch Economy: 1500–1700," *Journal of Economic History*, **XXXI**, 1, Mar. 1971, 266–268.

the local and popular attachments essential for a representative role with
the aristocratic aroma of *nobiles minores,* and played each card in turn with
tactful, but remorseless, realism."[80] Hence they epitomize the process of
succession of elites which Pirenne argues was the essence of the social
history of capitalism.[81] The outcome was that "political institutions [were
not in] accord with economic realities," which led inexorably to an English
Revolution led by the "rising" gentry and caused by "impersonal forces
too strong for both [Parliament and ruler to control]."[82]

The basis of Trevor-Roper's attack, as is well-known, aside from challenging Tawney's statistics and coding operations,[83] was to suggest that the
basic model of the political arena was off base:

> I have already suggested that office rather than land was the basis of many un-
> doubtedly "rising" families. I would now go further. Instead of the distinction between
> "old" and "new" landlords, between peers and gentry, I would suggest as the signifi-
> cant distinction of Tudor and Stuart landed society, the distinction between "court"
> and "country," between the officeholders and the mere landlords. . . .
> What fortunes were made by the officials of Henry VIII who carried out the
> nationalization of monastic property! Naturally the best bargains went to them
> and to their local agents, the office-holding gentry in the counties. . . .
> But what of the mere gentry who had no such positions? As each prize came
> more valuable it moved farther away from their reach.[84]

Hence, the English Civil War can be seen, at least in part, as the rebellion
of the overtaxed "mere" gentry against a Renaissance court.

Finally J. H. Hexter insists that there is a "third group of English landlords."[85] He says a look at the Parliamentary opposition to the Stuarts
shows they are drawn not from the "power-hungry rural middle class"
of Tawney, for they are "rich country gentry" (is that really so different
from Tawney?); nor are they the "angry hard-pressed yokels" of Trevor-
Roper, for they were an "unusually well-educated group of men" (is that
really incompatible with Trevor-Roper?)[86]

[80]Tawney, *Essays in Economic History,* **I,** p. 175.

[81]"Professor Pirenne, in a well-known essay, has argued that the capitalists of each successive era are normally recruited, not from those of the preceding one, but from individuals of humble origin, who fight their way upwards; form in time a new plutocracy; relapse, having done so, into dignified torpor; and in their turn are superseded. There are periods when somewhat the same alternation of progression and stagnation can be observed in the history of the landed classes. The three generations before Harrington wrote were one of them." R. H. Tawney, "Harrington's Interpretation of His Age," *Proceedings of the British Academy,* 1941, 218.

[82]*Ibid.,* p. 207.

[83]See H. R. Trevor-Roper, "The Gentry, 1540–1640," *Economic History Review,* Supplement

1, 1953, 4–24. For the continuation of this part of the debate, see R. H. Tawney, "Postcript," in E. M. Carus-Wilson, ed., *Essays in Economic History* (New York: St. Martin's, 1965), **I,** 206–214; Cooper, *Economic History Review,* **VIII,** pp. 377–81; Hexter, *Reappraisals in History,* pp. 124–129; Hill, "Recent Interpretations," p. 9.

[84]Trevor-Roper, *Economic History Review,* pp. 26, 27, 30.

[85]Hexter, *Reappraisals in History,* p. 131.

[86]*Ibid.,* pp. 135–136. At another point Hexter, who is never at a loss for images but dislikes statistics, says of early Stuart England: "Into the vacuum caused by the temporary incapacity of the magnates poured the country gentry—not the brisk hard-bitten small gentry of Professor Tawney, nor yet the mouldy flea-bitten mere gentry of Professor

However if we follow Hexter's positive assertions, we shall in fact be led to a fairly clear picture of the social role of the gentry, though not to the one he apparently thinks he leads us. He says at one point in his critique: "We are still left with the problem that started Tawney on his quest. . . . Why at this particular historical juncture did the 'country' find its leadership in social strata beneath the top? Why among the gentry rather than among the nobility?"[87] Hexter's answer is essentially that the political rise of the gentry is to be explained by the growing military power of the king and concurrent decline of the military power of the territorial magnates. "Consequently the gentry of the Tudor period acted with greater independence than their predecessors in the days of Lancaster and York. . . ."[88] As many have observed, who ever said otherwise? And as Stone pointedly remarks: "Mr. Hexter's deus ex machina to explain the rise to political power of the gentry is altogether too superficial: he says that the aristocracy lost military control. Of course; but why did this happen?"[89] We are thus returned to those central variables we have been discussing (as have Tawney and Trevor-Roper): the growth of a bureaucratic state machinery and the development of capitalist agriculture—and the link between the two.[90]

Hexter next takes off against "the myth of the middle class." But here he is really challenging nineteenth-century liberalism and not the "unconscious" Marxism which he suggests underlies so much of modern economic history.[91] In fact his own analysis is not in reality so far away from that of Tawney and Trevor-Roper. The Tudors, he says, were not promiddle class, except for "a small inner coterie of Tudor merchant-bankers," a group of "Court-bound capitalists."[92]

Trevor-Roper—but the rich, well-educated knights and squires who sat in the Parliaments of James I and Charles I [p. 148]." See Cooper's comment on Hexter's attitude toward statistics: "Finally, as against Professor Hexter, I believe if there had been more careful study of accounts and rentals in the first instance and less counting of manors, the controversy need never have taken its present form. In fairness to Mr. Stone I should add that, since his first incursion into the subject, he has devoted a great deal of time to such studies. I imagine that Mr. Stone and I can at least agree on the necessity for continuing such studies, instead of abandoning them, as Professor Hexter suggests." "Letter to the Editor," *Encounter*, **XI**, 3, Sept. 1958, 74.

[87]Hexter, *Reappraisals in History*, p. 142.

[88]*Ibid.*, p. 147.

[89]Lawrence Stone, *Encounter*, p. 74.

[90]"If we can no longer accept unreservedly Professor Tawney's thesis that the gentry rose at the expense of the peerage between 1540 and 1640, or that the Jacobean peerage differed markedly in its estate management from the Elizabethan, there

is no gainsaying the rise within the landed class of certain families, or that many of these families, especially in the early Stuart period, owed their improved status to the profits of office, profession, or trade rather than to the yields of their lands." Gordon Batho, "Landlords in England. B. Noblemen, Gentlemen, and Yeomen," in *The Agrarian History of England and Wales*, **IV**: Joan Thirsk, ed., *1500–1640* (London and New York: Cambridge Univ. Press, 1967), 285. But, adds Batho: "The importance of office-holding and of political influence in raising some families in the social hierarchy must not, however, be exaggerated. While large incomes were enjoyed by the fortunate few, the majority of household and central government posts were poorly paid and did not permit of large gains apart from the official fees, even in Stuart times [p. 289]."

[91]J. H. Hexter, "A New Framework for Social History," *Reappraisals*, p. 14.

[92]J. H. Hexter, *Reappraisals in History*, pp. 103, 105.

Tudor policy was really very consistent:

> [It] was usually quite tender of vested interests. It protected old ones and created new
> ones in the emergent forms of enterprise. . . . It was not the policy of the Tudors
> either to stand mulishly athwart the path of change, or to allow it free rein, but to
> guide it, to bring it as they said to some rule conformable with good order.[93]

And, for good measure, Hexter adds, "the Tudors regarded the middle class as the milch herd of the commonwealth."[94]

But it was precisely Lawrence Stone who emphasized the degree to which the Tudors exercised economic control, favored a handful of entrepreneurs, but not the bourgeois classes as a whole, and placed the strengthening of the state's military power at a premium,[95] and it is the essence of Trevor-Roper's argument that the gentry rebelled against being a milch herd.

Finally, says Hexter, it is not the case that the capitalist spirit only emerged in the sixteenth century for it had long been in existence, nor that "the sixteenth-century landowners waited for the example and inspiration of town merchants"[96] to engage in capitalist agriculture. Precisely so. But then we are back to the picture of an emerging capitalist class recruited from varying social backgrounds.[97]

Why should this be strange? It was, as we have seen, happening throughout the European world-economy.[98] No doubt, there were varying political expressions of different subgroups within the "gentry." Barrington Moore for example has a suggestion about the political opposition of Trevor-

[93]*Ibid.*, p. 109.

[94]*Ibid.*, p. 110.

[95]"The first half of the sixteenth century was a period of tentative but ever more numerous experiments in economic control, but there is no evidence for an increase in commercial freedom. . . .

"Security, not prosperity, was the main object of Tudor economic rule. . . .

"But the paradox of Tudor administration and perhaps the ultimate cause of the collapse of the whole system is to be found in the extent to which its programme of the paternalist state, or social justice and conservatism was sacrificed to the implementation of the more pressing needs of planned autarky and opportunist war finance. All Tudor governments were the most resolute theoretical opponents of those social changes and those new bourgeois classes from which they are supposed to have derived most support." Stone, *Economic History Review*, **XVIII**, pp. 109, 111, 115.

[96]Hexter, *Reappraisals in History*, p. 91; cf. also pp. 83–84.

[97]It may be the case, as Christopher Hill suggests, that: "In the inflationary century, it seems to have been farmers, yeomen, lesser landlords, which first developed the bourgeois qualities necessary to success—thrift, industry, readiness to rack rents and watch markets, moderate consumption and reinvestment of profits. Peers and greater gentlemen with traditional standards of expenditure to maintain were slower to adapt themselves, and continued to spend sums for which their rent-rolls gave no justification. Such men became increasingly dependent on the court for economic survival." *Reformation to Industrial Revolution*, pp. 65–66. But it is at most a question of degree.

[98]See Zs. S. Pach's specific comparison of Hungary and England: "[Landowners as merchants] are not an original phenomenon if we compare [Hungary] to the developments in England in this period, where an analogous process was taking place. We are thinking of the 'new nobility,' of the English 'gentry' who essentially received in rent-form what had been due to them as feudal dues. They engaged in the sale of wool, of wheat, and of other goods and, having expropriated the small peasants and farmers, entered into the direct exploitation of their property characteristics of the bourgeoisie." *Annales E.S.C.*, **XXI**, p. 1230.

Roper's "declining gentry" which makes that phenomenon totally compatible with the political opposition of Tawney's "rising gentry." He quotes Tawney: "There are plenty of gentry who stagnate or go downhill. It would be easy to find noble landlords who move with the times, and make the most of their properties."[99] Moore then says of those who "stagnated":

> These "growlers and grumblers" may have supplied a portion of the radical element behind Cromwell and the Puritan Revolution, though this impetus had its main origins farther down the social scale. Thus, under the impact of commerce and some industry, English society was breaking apart from the top downward in a way that allowed pockets of radical discontent produced by the same forces to burst temporarily into the limelight. . . . In this process, as the old order breaks up, sections of society that had been losing out due to long-run economic trends come to the surface and do much of the violent "dirty work" of destroying the *ancien régime,* thus clearing the road for a new set of institutions. In England the main dirty work of this type was the symbolic act of beheading Charles I.[100]

Probably Hexter is right in suggesting there were three types of landlords—"rising," "declining," and others. And it's very plausible that political opposition tends to correlate with the first two types more than with the third. In an explanation of the politics of the early Stuart era these details are crucial.[101] In assessing the trends of social change, it is far more important to see the rise of the gentry not as an economic force nor as a political entity but as a social category.

Concentration on detail, while it often lays bare the vacuousness of weak generalization, can also obscure secular change. Lawrence Stone, after making just such a detailed analysis of the complexities of social mobility in England at this time, points out that the form of this analysis tended to drop from view two important shifts of English society:

> The first was a polarization of society into rich and poor: the upper classes became relatively more numerous, and their real incomes rose; the poor became relatively more numerous and their real incomes fell. The second a greater equality among the upper classes: firstly the wealth and power of the greater gentry increased relative to that of the aristocracy; and secondly members of the trades and professions rose in wealth, number and social status relative to the landed classes.[102]

J. Hurstfield makes a similar point with emphasis on its impact on the politics of the "second" sixteenth century:

> In England the aristocracy never became a caste and the landed gentry never became a lesser nobility. Hence the middle and upper classes stood in much closer relation to each other than they did to the monarchy; and, in times of crisis, had much more in common with each other than they had with the Crown.[103]

[99]Tawney, *Essays in Economic History,* **I,** p. 186.
[100]Barrington Moore, Jr., *Social Origins of Dictatorship and Democracy* (Boston: Beacon Press, 1966), 16.
[101]In this connection, Christopher Hill is absolutely right: "[W]e should stop generalizing about the gentry," *Puritanism and Revolution,* p. 27.
[102]Lawrence Stone, "Social Mobility in England, 1500–1700," *Past & Present,* **33,** April 1966, 28–29.
[103]Hurstfield, *New Cambridge Modern History,* **III,** p. 148.

Stone and Hurstfield are both demonstrating the crucial point here: the process of emergence of a new class category within which the "old" distinction of aristocrat–gentry was losing its significance. As Perez Zagorin sums up the situation, the general tendency of the long sixteenth century in England, "was to give to men . . . in a position to deploy capital in agriculture, trade, and industry . . . the command of social life."[104] And this combined class gained at the expense of the peasantry.[105] The English situation is a good illustration of Lattimore's generalization: "[I]n any gradually changing society it is always those who rule that hang onto the best of what is left of the old order, and at the same time take the best of what is offered by the new, [leading in time to] a considerable diversification. . . ."[106]

If the "gentry" were simply the name for the capitalist farmers as they became a class, what are yeomen? Yeomen is a term just like gentry, a pre-existing socio–legal term whose content was evolving in the sixteenth century. Mildred Campbell, in her book on the English yeomen, sifts through the various uses of the word and its relation to such terms as farmer, gentleman, freeholder, husbandman, and laborer, noting acerbically: "There is nothing, one may say at the outset, as explicit as the distinction just discarded."[107] Her conclusion is that

> yeomen status viewed in terms of its relationship to other groups in the social structure assumes a fairly definite character. They were a substantial rural middle class whose chief concern was with the land and agricultural interests, a group who lived "in the temperate zone betwixt greatness and want," serving England, as it was given a "middle people" . . . in condition between the gentry and the peasantry to serve.[108]

[104]Perez Zagorin, "The Social Interpretation of the English Revolution," *Journal of Economic History,* **XIX,** 3, Sept. 1959, 388. He adds: "The class whose formation is the present focus of interest was being continuously recruited, and it naturally comprised diverse elements as to status, wealth, and source of income. But despite these and other differences, its members were species of the same genus. They constituted a single economic class, for what they had in common was the possession of capital that they employed for the end of profit and further accumulation [p. 389]."

[105]"Between 1500 and 1700 the end result of great activity in land transfer seems to have been something like a net movement of a quarter of the land across the social boundaries, sometimes by an owner crossing a boundary and taking his land with him, sometimes by land crossing the boundary on change of ownership. The gainers in this process were the great landowners and the gentry, the losers the institutional holders, crown and church, and the peasants, probably in roughly equal proportions. . . .

"In the sixteenth century the structure of land-ownership responded to the pressures of the market, the growing demand for agricultural produce, with a trend away from subsistence farming and towards more commercial farming, and this had its effect upon the peasant element; not only did it create the situation in which many manorial lords exploited their legal rights to the utmost but also it offered the opportunities for the fortunate and enterprising yeoman to prosper. But the structure also responded to the pressures of the competitive world of status, and the drive of newly-made mercantile wealth to find security in land. Status needed new defences, in expenditure rather than in numerous bodies of retainers and followers, and this was another source of pressure on the peasants' position." F. M. L. Thompson, "The Social Distribution of Landed Property in England since the Sixteenth Century," *Economic History Review,* 2nd ed., **XIX,** 3, 1966, 515.

[106]Owen Lattimore, *Inner Asian Frontiers of China,* p. 123.

[107]Mildred Campbell, *The English Yeoman Under Elizabeth and the Early Stuarts* (New Haven, Connecticut: Yale Univ. Press, 1942), 25.

[108]*Ibid.,* p. 61.

To appreciate the role of this group we must return to a theme discussed in a previous chapter, the evolution of the tenure system in English agriculture. Marx in his discussion of the genesis of capitalist ground rent makes a crucial point which is often overlooked in the exegesis of his views:

> [A]s soon as rent assumes the form of money-rent, and thereby the relationship between rent-paying peasant and landlord becomes a relationship fixed by contract —a development which is only possible generally when the *world*-market, commerce and manufacture have reached a certain relatively high level—the leasing of land to capitalists inevitably also makes its appearance. The latter hitherto stood beyond the rural limits and now carry over to the country-side and agriculture the capital acquired in the cities and with it the capitalist mode of operation developed—i.e., creating a product as a mere commodity and solely as a means of appropriating surplus-value. This form can become the general rule *only in those countries which dominate the world-market* in the period of transition from the feudal to the capitalist mode of production.[109]

The relevance of Marx's point is that the process of transformation in the land tenure system is not unique to England, as is obvious. But as England (and the Dutch Republic) become more and more the core territories of the European world-economy in the "second" sixteenth century (and even more in the late seventeenth and eighteenth centuries), the process goes further and faster in these areas precisely because they are the core. It is crucial that resources be used more efficiently in order to benefit from the central trading and financial position in the world-economy. In England, it paid the landed classes to move to a system of fully alienable land just as it paid the landed classes in Poland (and even say in southern France) to restrain moves in this direction.

To make land fully alienable, to have production for commodity sale as the overriding consideration of agriculture, one has to eliminate not only various kinds of feudal tenure systems. One has to eliminate also the peasant farmer, for the peasant may hold on to the land and engage in marginal kinds of production activities for considerations that do not maximize short-run profitability. How was in fact such elimination accomplished?

H. John Habakkuk points out that there are three ways of expropriating peasants: chasing them from their tenures and incorporating their land into the domain; forcing them to yield life tenures for limited rentals; whittling away at the communal rights of the peasants. He argues that in

---

[109]Marx, *Capital,* **III,** chap. XLVII, Sect. IV, p. 799. Italics added. He adds: "This appearance of capital as an independent and leading force in agriculture does not take place all at once and generally, but gradually and in particular lines of production. It encompasses at first, not agriculture proper, but such branches of production as cattle-breeding, especially sheep-raising, whose principal product, wool, offers at the early stages constant excess of market-price over price of production during the rise of industry, and this does not level out until later. Thus in England during the 16th century [p. 801]."

the "second" sixteenth century only those peasants who were tenants for a limited term or for life without right or renewal were effectively subject to such forms of expropriation, and he estimates that this added up to only about 35% of the peasantry.[110] As for the sale of lands, the picture is far from one-sided:

> During [this] period . . . there were certainly lords (*seigneurs*) who bought land from the peasants; there were also some peasants who accumulated so much goods that they were elevated to the rank of gentry. In both cases, the result was a diminution of peasant property. But there were also peasants who bought the great domains when they were put on sale, or who obtained copyhold lease. The net result of these transactions is not known. But it is altogether possible that those acquisitions added up to a gain rather than a loss for the peasantry; whereas, on the one hand, the lords expropriated the peasants, on the other the peasants, in acquiring goods nibbled at the domains of the lords.[111]

The full capitalization of agriculture was yet to come in England. In the sixteenth century, the yeoman still had his role to play. The increasing commercialization of agriculture at this time offered the small landowner not only "dangers" but "opportunities." Campbell, who waxes a bit romantic, sees the yeomen as rather heroic:

> Scheming landlords and land-hungry neighbors were ever ready to take advantage of a man's misfortunes. Though prices in the main steadily went up, there were sometimes fluctuations that came without warning and in uncertain sequence. Other evils added to the insecurity of the times. Uncontrolled epidemics were a constant dread. Loss by fire was common, and insurance of any kind practically

[110]See H. John Habakkuk, "La disparition du paysan anglais," *Annales E.S.C.,* **XX,** 4, juil.–août 1965, 652–654. Tawney points out how the legal situation worked to permit this situation: "If economic causes made a new system of farming profitable, it is none the less true that legal causes decided by whom the profits should be enjoyed. . . . [M]any customary tenants practiced sheep-farming upon a considerable scale, and it is not easy to discover any economic reason why the cheap wool required for the development of the cloth-manufacturing industry should not have been supplied by the very peasants in whose cottages it was carded and spun and woven. The decisive factor . . . was the fact that the tenure of the vast majority of small cultivators left them free to be squeezed by exorbitant fines, and to be evicted when the lives for which most of them held their copies came to an end. It was their misfortune that the protection given by the courts since the fifteenth century to copyholders did not extend to more than the enforcement of existing manorial customs. . . . Living, as they did, with the marks of villein tenure still upon them, the small cultivators of our period were fettered by the remaining remnants of the legal rightlessness of the Middle Ages, without enjoying the practical security given by medieval custom, and

felt the bitter breadth of modern commercialism, undefended by the protection of the all-inclusive modern state which alone can make it tolerable." *Agrarian Problems,* pp. 406–408. (Note that Tawney speaks of "the vast majority of small cultivators." He did not look into this empirical question, however, as closely as Habakkuk.)

The ambiguities of the tenure system was in addition a major factor in the rise of a lawyer class in the towns. As more land became de facto alienable, a more exact definition of individual rights was sought. For the small cultivator, one alternative to forced sales or other undesirable changes in his tenure was to defend himself against the semilegal incursions into his rights by hiring lawyers.

"In addition to private merchants and their factors and servants, a small but powerful élite of professional men emerged in the sixteenth century. Every provincial town of any size had its corps of notaries, lawyers, and scriveners; boroughs of the size of Northampton or Maidstone might have half-a-dozen such men, often styling themselves 'gentlemen' and descended from minor landed families. . . ." Everitt, *Agrarian History,* **IV,** p. 555.

[111]Habakkuk, *Annales E.S.C.,* **XX,** p. 657.

unknown. Either a man must have savings in hand for such rainy days or else go in debt. . . .

But when it is a case of sink or swim, unless the odds are too great against a man he usually tries to swim. . . . And despite the uncertain conditions depicted above, more than ever before in the history of English landholding the little man who had industry and an abundance of enterprise was getting his opportunity. Those who could weather the storms found in the higher prices and better market opportunities for profit that urged them on to still greater effort. Gain begets the desire for more gain.[112]

If the yeomen was not the direct beneficiary of the dissolution of the monasteries, he might eventually get a piece of the pie.[113]

As many have pointed out, there were two kinds of enclosure going on in that era: enclosure of large domains for pasture, and small land consolidation for more efficient tillage. It is in this latter process that the yeomen played the central role, a role all the more important because it had important social consequences in terms of increasing food supply

[112]Campbell, *English Yeomen*, pp. 68–69. Eric Wolf is more hard-nosed in his analysis of the conditions under which peasants become oriented to increased production for the market: "The perennial problem of the peasantry thus consists in balancing the demands of the external world against the peasants' need to provision their households. Yet in meeting this root problem peasants may follow two diametrically opposed strategies. The first of these is to increase production; the second, to curtail consumption.

"If a peasant follows the first strategy, he must step up the output of labor upon his own holding, in order to raise its productivity and to increase the amount of produce with which to enter the market. His ability to do so depends largely on how easy it is for him to mobilize the needed factors of production—land, labor, capital (whether in the form of savings, ready cash, or credit)—and, of course, the general conditions of the market. . . .

"First, [this strategy] becomes possible when traditional liens on the peasants' funds of rents have weakened—a condition likely to occur when the power structure through which funds have been siphoned off to traditional overlords has become ineffective. Second, we may expect to find this phenomenon where it has become possible for the peasant to escape the demands placed on him to underwrite with ceremonial expenditures the traditional social ties with his fellows. If he can refuse to commit his surplus to ceremonial outlays, he can use the funds so released to support his economic ascent. The two changes frequently go together. As the overarching power structure weakens, many traditional social ties also lose their particular sanctions. The peasant community, under such circumstances, may see the rise of wealthy peasants who shoulder aside their less fortunate fellows and move

into the power vacuum left by the retreating superior holders of power. In the course of their rise, they frequently violate traditional expectations of how social relations are to be conducted and symbolized—frequently they use their newly won power to enrich themselves at the cost of their neighbors. Such men were the rising *yeomen* of sixteenth century England, the rich peasants of China, the *kulaki* or 'fists' of pre-revolutionary Russia." *Peasants*, pp. 15–16.

[113]"Probably few yeomen in the earlier years after the dissolution profited by the release of monastic lands; for this property went at first to large landholders as gifts and in payment of services, or was purchased. But large quantities of it came early into the hands of speculators and so on the market, where after division and redivision it was by the late sixteenth century being brought within reach of the small buyer." Campbell, *English Yeomen*, pp. 70–71.

Joyce Youings cautions against overstatement: "A great deal of the monastic land was resold by the original grantees, some of it changing hands many times, but the market was not so brisk, nor the speculation so rife, as many writers have suggested. . . . Not all these changes of landownership were clear sales. Releases of parts of property between partners to a grant have been ignored, but some of the 'resales' clearly may have been simply releases by agents to their principals." "Landlords in England. C. The Church," in *The Agrarian History of England, and Wales*, Joan Thirsk, ed., **IV:** *1500–1640* (London and New York: Cambridge Univ. Press, 1967), 349–350. Furthermore she points out that: "For the majority of laymen, whether gentlemen or yeomen farmers, quicker profits were to be made by leasing than by buying monastic lands [p. 348]."

without incurring the kind of political opposition which pasturage enclosures encountered.[114] Part of the improvements came from other factors that increased efficiency of labor. Thirsk attributes it to:

> the use of more intensive rotations, accompanied by heavier manuring; the use of improved varieties of grain; and, probably most important of all, the impressive increase in the total acreage of land under the plough as a result of the reclamation of waste and the conversion of pasture. . . . Heavier manuring of the arable, of course, was made possible by keeping larger numbers of animals, which resulted in a great increase in the supply of meat and wool and other animal products. Heavier rates of stocking were made possible by the improvement of pastures and meadows by fertilizers, by the improved supply of spring grazing, through the watering of meadows in the west country, the growing of tares elsewhere, and by the increased supply of summer grazing through the use of bogs and the reclamation of coastal marshland and fen. *Thus improvements in arable and pastoral husbandry went hand in hand,* each helping the other, and *both serving to promote the specialization and interdependence of regions.*[115]

The inclusion of Wales in the English division of labor at this time aided this process of agricultural improvement. For one thing, the imposition of English legal forms, particularly primogeniture, led to great uncertainty about the land tenure system. This was propitious for the creation of large domains in Wales. "From one end of Wales to the other it was a time of estate-building and the laying of family fortunes."[116] This was particularly true in the "anglicized lowlands" which showed "marked inequality in the size of holdings. . . ."[117] I would suspect the landlords were disproportionately English. The degree of agricultural improvement brought about by enclosures in Wales seem to have been greater than in England. Wales had still been suffering until that time from "predatory techniques."[118] This meant, however, even greater displacements of population, who migrated to England, there most probably to become part of the lumpenproletariat, and many of them ending up as mercenaries as we have already mentioned.

---

[114]"But usually the yeomen were among the land nibblers who were relatively free from opprobrium among their contemporaries, and for the most part among later writers. The fact also that the small inclosures were usually for benefit of tillage rather than conversion to pasture helped the men who made them to escape much of the abuse heaped upon those who assisted in the process of depopulation." Campbell, *English Yeomen*, p. 91.

[115]Joan Thirsk, "Farming Techniques," in *Agrarian History of England and Wales,* **IV:** Joan Thirsk, ed., *1500–1640* (London and New York: Cambridge Univ. Press, 1967), 199. Italics added. Within England, however, as opposed to between England and Wales, it is less sure there was too great a regional specialization. At least E. J. Buckatzsch shows in his study of tax assessments that "the pat-

tern of geographical distribution of wealth in England . . . remained essentially unchanged from the end of the thirteenth century to the end of the seventeenth century, [only changing] fundamentally during the eighteenth century." "The Geographical Distribution of Wealth in England, 1086–1843," *Economic History Review,* **III,** 2, 1950, 195.

[116]Frank Emery, "The Farming Regions of Wales," in *The Agrarian History of England and Wales,* Joan Thirsk, ed., **IV:** *1500–1640* (London and New York: Cambridge Univ. Press, 1967), 124.

[117]*Ibid.,* p. 152.

[118]T. Jones Pierce, "Landlords in Wales. A. The Nobility & Gentry," in *The Agrarian History of England and Wales,* Joan Thirsk, ed., **IV:** *1500–1640* (London and New York: Cambridge Univ. Press, 1967), 380.

Campbell says that the age was an age of "land hunger."[119] "[A]mong the land hungry none were more avaricious than the yeomen."[120] It obviously paid off by the evidence we have from rural housing in England from 1570 to 1640, the period of "The Great Rebuilding," the work, according to W. G. Hoskins, of "the bigger husbandmen, the yeomen, and the lesser gentry, all largely of the same social origin in medieval centuries."[121] Lawrence Stone cites this same fact, however, as further evidence of the "rise of the gentry,"[122] an indication once again of the fluidity of the designations we are using. Are not these yeomen simply the less well-capitalized version of the gentry who are capitalist farmers?[123]

This becomes clearer if we see who in fact loses out in the process of enclosures (of both varieties). As the enclosures proceeded—whether the large-scale enclosures of sheepherders or the small-scale enclosures of improving yeomen—a number of men who formerly lived on and off the land were forced to leave it, and others were reduced to the status of landless rural laborers working for wages.[124] This has long been considered to be a central element in the creation of the labor surplus that

[119]Campbell, *English Yeomen*, p. 65.

[120]*Ibid.*, p. 72.

[121]W. G. Hoskins, "The Rebuilding of Rural England, 1570–1640." *Past & Present*, No. 4, Nov. 1953, 30.

[122]Stone, *Past & Present*, No. 33, p. 26.

[123]Peter Laslett sees the key division in *class* between gentlemen (nobles plus gentry) and the others (yeomen plus common laborers.) See *The World We Have Lost* (New York: Scribner's, 1965), chap. 2, esp. 26–27. But in this same chapter he reproduces Gregory King's schema (pp. 32–33) for 1688 which draws the line, more correctly in my view, between, in King's terminology, those who 'increase' the wealth of the kingdom (nobles, gentry, merchants, freeholders, artisans) and those who 'decrease' it (laborers, cottagers, common soldiers, vagrants). (That is, I hold King's line of division to be correct, not his characterization of the nature of work on each side of the line.) Laslett does acknowledge that yeoman "was the status name of the most successful of those who worked the land," and observes that it "became sentimentalized very early [p. 43]." But he seems to be stuck with the gentry's preference to exclude those who were not 'idle' rather than the analyst's observation of their economic and political interests.

"From Elizabethan times onwards there are plenty of domestic inventories to show the style of life of the lesser gentry; it was of course indistinguishable from that of the wealthier yeoman." M. W. Barley, "Rural Housing in England," in *The Agrarian History of England and Wales*, Joan Thirsk, ed., **IV**: *1500–1640* (London and New York: Cambridge Univ. Press, 1967), 713.

See Gordon Batho: "But there was no sharp difference between the lesser gentry and the richer yeomen. . . . In fact, the [legal] definition [of a yeoman] was virtually meaningless, for many a yeoman in Tudor and early Stuart times, like Latimer's father, had no land of his own, but was a copyholder or leaseholder. In innumerable wills and legal documents of the age a man is described in one place as a yeoman and in another as a gentleman, or a man describes himself as a gentleman but is described by others as a yeoman. For it was not gentility of birth or degree of wealth which distinguished the classes. Many of the younger sons of the lesser gentry became yeomen; many gentry were newly risen from the yeomanry or, with the aid of business and professional profits, from humbler origins still. Few gentry could have traced their ancestry back for three centuries, as some yeomen families like the Reddaways of Devon could." *Agrarian History*, **IV**, p. 301.

[124]The point is that the squeeze was on one way or the other: "To sum up: a substantial number of small farmers were dangerously placed in Tudor England. They were liable to dispossession in those counties where the incentive to enclose was strong, and this was true of the Midlands at the beginning and end of the 16th century. Where enclosure was not the rule, they were liable to rack-renting, arbitrary fines, and the invasion of their rights of pasture on the commons. . . . [I]nsecurity was very general, and the copyholders, who formed (as contemporaries agreed) the backbone of agrarian England, could expect only partial and intermittent protection from Tudor governments." Ramsey, *Tudor Economic Problems*, p. 36.

is a critical element in the "commercialising of English life."[125] This shift occurred between 1540 and 1640. In the economic squeeze, some small men gained but many more lost.[126] Indeed, the very process of fulfilling the liberation of the peasant from the constraints of feudalism may have served as an additional mode of impoverishment. Alexander Savine, in his article on the remains of feudal villeinage in Tudor England, notes the paradox "that for the bondman of the sixteenth century his personal dependence upon the lord became most burdensome at the moment he got his freedom."[127] The paradox is very simple to unravel. Manumission was not free. It was bought. Indeed, it must have bought high, because Savine notes:

> Manumission of bondmen was regarded as a regular source of seigniorial income. . . . The enfranchisement of the last bondsmen was a paying policy. The thing was done so openly in the sixteenth century that Elizabethan courtiers could receive as a special sign a favour from the sovereign a commission to enfranchise a definite number of villein families on the Crown manors; that is to say, they were enabled to repair their fortunes with the payments for enfranchisement.[128]

Villeins no longer gave work-week service to the lord on the demesne.[129] Rather, the "personal dependence of the bondman became a mere pretext for extortion."[130] Thus, in the process, no doubt, many became landless paupers.

We find further evidence of this pauperization in the virtual disappearance of the husbandman category. On the one hand, some husbandmen were "rising to be yeomen and the distinctions between husbandmen and yeomen were being blurred."[131] And on the other hand, the poorer husbandman was getting to be worse off than many rural laborers who were cottagers, and needed to engage in part-time wage labor to make ends

[125]"From a wider point of view the agrarian changes of the sixteenth century may be regarded as a long step in the commercialising of English life. The growth of the textile industries is closely connected with the development of pasture farming, and it was the export of woollen cloth, that 'prodigy of trade' which first brought England conspicuously into world-commerce, and was the motive for more than one of those early expeditions to discover new markets, out of which grew plantations, colonies, empire. . . . The displacement of a considerable number of families from the soil accelerated, if it did not initiate, the transition from the medieval wage problem, which consisted in the scarcity of labour, to the modern wage problem, which consists in its abundance." Tawney, *Agrarian Problems*, p. 3. See Joan Thirsk, "Enclosing & Engrossing," in *The Agrarian History of England and Wales.* Joan Thirsk, ed., IV: *1500–1640* (London and New York:

Cambridge Univ. Press, 1967), 210; Bowden, *Agrarian History*, **IV**, p. 598.

[126]"A small minority of farmworkers was still possessed of relatively extensive holdings or common-rights and was able to profit by the new commercial openings of the age, working their way up, in a generation or two, into the yeomanry. The middle and lower ranks of cottagers, however, were losing their modest property-rights and sinking to the level of a landless proletariat." Alan Everitt, "Social Mobility in Early Modern England," *Past & Present*, **33**, Apr. 1966, 57.

[127]Alexander Savine, "Bondmen Under the Tudors," *Transactions of the Royal Historical Society*, n.s., **XVII**, 1903, 268.

[128]*Ibid.*, pp. 270–271.

[129]See *Ibid.*, p. 275.

[130]*Ibid.*, p. 276.

[131]Batho, *Agrarian History*, **IV**, p. 303.

meet.[132] Might not husbandmen spasmodically employed have thought it desirable to become laborers regularly employed?

In any case, both these categories of farmworkers were those vulnerable to enclosure and encroachment on their commons' right. Encroachment, in particular, led to abandonment of villages and migration.[133] Everitt points out that the growing distinction between the peasant–yeomen and the "poor squatters and wanderers, virtually landless, often lately evicted from elsewhere" was a phenomenon to be observed particularly in the more recently-settled forest areas of the countryside[134] and that "it was from this latter group, in consequence of their semi-vagrant origins, that the growing army of seasonal workers was largely recruited, called into being by the needs of commercial farming."[135]

Thus arose the crucial political problem of begging and vagabondage, a notorious feature of Elizabethan England.[136] Frank Aydelotte sees three separate factors combining to explain the upsurge of vagabondage in Elizabethan times: enclosures to be sure and most importantly; but also Tudor peace and hence the disbanding of enormous bands of retainers kept by nobles; and also the dissolution of the monasteries and the disappearance of their role as dispensers of charity. Aydelotte's view of these vagabonds, which cannot be far different from that of the rulers of the day, is to see them as a *social* problem:

> Far from being either an impotent or a harmless class, the vagabonds of the sixteenth century represented much of the solid strength of medieval England. Many of them came from good stock, but in the economic scheme of modern England they found no useful place. They had brains to plan villany and audacity to execute it. Their ranks contained political, religious and social malcontents and agitators. Hence it was that they were a danger as well as a pest in the England of Elizabeth. The vagabonds were menace enough to cause the lawmakers, from Henry VII onwards, to give their best thought to a remedy, both by framing statutes and

---

[132]"[T]here was sometimes no sharp distinction between the better-off labourer working his own holding and supplementing his income with seasonal wage-work, and the poor husbandman whose holding was insufficient to support his family and who turned to occasional wage-work to augment his resources. All that can be said is that the employment of the former tended to be regular, and of the latter spasmodic." Everitt, "Farm Labourers," in *The Agrarian History of England and Wales*, Joan Thirsk, ed., **IV:** *1500–1640* (London and New York: Cambridge Univ. Press, 1967), 397.

[133]See *ibid.*, p. 409.

[134]One of the attractions of the forest areas was the availability of by-employments (forest & woodland crafts; spinning & weaving of flax, hemp, or wool). See Everitt, *Agrarian History*, **IV**, pp. 425–429; Thirsk, *Agrarian History*, **IV**, pp. 109–10.

[135]Everitt, *Past & Present*, No. 33, p. 58.

[136]"Begging and vagabondage in England did not begin in the sixteenth century. . . . Nevertheless there is abundant evidence that in the sixteenth century the numbers of rogues and vagabonds were larger in proportion to the population than they have ever been before or since. . . ." Frank Aydelotte, *Elizabethan Rogues and Vagabonds*, Volume I of Oxford Historical and Literary Studies (London and New York: Oxford Univ. Press (Clarendon), 1913), 3.

"The unruly vagrants and the fearsome beggar bands, familiar to students of Elizabethan England, had their counterpart in the 'idill lymmaris and harlottis falslie calling thame selffis egiptianis,' who roamed Scotland, extorting food and money, robbing and threatening and bringing panic to isolated farms and clachans." Lythe, *The Economy of Scotland*, p. 29.

providing for their execution, until the problem was finally solved, as far as legislation
could solve it, by the admirable poor laws of 1572, 1597, and 1601.[137]

Admirable? Perhaps, although doubtless not in the simple sense Aydelotte
wants us to admire them.

These laws do however throw light on the role the state machinery was
playing. First let us note that "social welfare" legislation, previously
unknown in Europe, appears on the scene in *many* places at this time.
Furthermore, it is not even a matter of simultaneous invention, but of
conscious cultural diffusion.[138] Second, the relationship of such legislation
to economic transformation is ambiguous. It was to be sure a response
to a social crisis brought on by economic change, a means of averting
political rebellion.[139] But its economic meaning was not one of straightforward support for the capitalist classes. It was a form of political stabilization
whose effect was as constraining to the employers as to the laborers, perhaps
even more.[140] This policy of monarchical constraint on the free play of
capitalism in the sixteenth century is in marked contrast with the collaboration of the state to intervene in the process of the great and definitive
enclosures of the eighteenth century.[141]

The Tudors and early Stuarts are often thought to have "failed," because
the ultimate outcome of their policy was the English Revolution. But
perhaps the English Revolution should be viewed as a measure of the
"success" of the Tudor–Stuart monarchs, in that they held off rebellion
so long. Let us look at the reactions of sixteenth-century English peasants
under stress. Many chose vagabondage. Another possibility was peasant
rebellion, and rebellions there were, to be sure. But it should be noticed
that there were fewer in England at this time than earlier, and fewer

---

[137]Aydelotte, *Elizabethan Rogues and Vagabonds*, p.
17.

[138]See Robert M. Kingdom, "Social Welfare in Calvin's Europe," *American Historical Review*, **LXXVI**,
1, Feb. 1971, 50–51.

[139]"Most of the anti-inclosure legislation of the
sixteenth century coincides with periods of dearth.
Complaints of dearth are audible at the time of the
risings of 1536, 1548-9, and 1596." Edwin F. Gay,
"The Midland Revolt and the Inquisitions of
Depopulation of 1607," *Transactions of the Royal Historical Society*, n.s., **XVIII**, 1904, 213, fn. 2.

[140]G. N. Clark, in describing the Tudor economic
code which can be gleaned from the Statute of
Artificers (or Apprentices), the tariff, the laws to
encourage shipbuilding, the Acts against enclosures,
and the poor law, has this to say: "The new Legislation accepted and even furthered money economy:
it carried forward the limiting of trade, or paying
wages in kind. But the general tendency of these
enactments was conservative: they aimed at providing an adequate supply of labour first for agriculture, then for the simpler crafts, and at restricting

entry into the occupations of higher social standing
and into those which were thought to be carried
on in unsuitable places. . . .

"The Elizabethan code thus aimed at stabilizing
the existing class structure, the location of industry
and the flow of labour supply by granting privileges
and by putting hindrances in the way of mobility
and freedom of contract; but it was not the product
of a simple doctrinaire economic policy; it reconciled
or effected a compromise between conflicting interests." *Wealth of England*, pp. 84, 86.

[141]"England withstood without great damage the
calamity of the [sixteenth-century] enclosures only
because the Tudors and the early Stuarts used the
power of the Crown to slow down the process of
economic improvement until it became socially
bearable—employing the power of the central government to relieve the victims of the transformation,
and attempting to canalize the process of change
so as to make its course less devastating." Karl
Polanyi, *The Great Transformation* (Boston: Beacon
Press, 1944), 38.

at this time in England than in France or elsewhere on the continent.

Each of these contrasts is worth looking at. R. H. Hilton argues that the sixteenth-century enclosures had a "pre-history." The process of leaving the land goes back to the thirteenth century. There was of course the phenomenon of depopulation, but Hilton feels that poverty was a more basic explanation for the rural exodus.[142] Then came the inflationary, "long" sixteenth century. Whereas in eastern Europe the landlords forced the laborers back onto the land because the expanded cash-crop production required it, England took a route of pasturage (which required less labor) and increased efficiency of arable production (which required less labor). Far from wanting to farm estates directly, large landowners sought tenants, and preferred "capitalist farmers" as tenants to "peasants."[143] Since this was to the disadvantage of many in the rural areas, why did the peasants not resist more than they did? Hilton argues that they were too weak to resist.[144] Further confirmation is to be found in the observation by C. S. L. Davies that there was relatively *more* peasant resistance in the "first" sixteenth century than in the "second," whereas if harshness of conditions were sufficient to explain peasant outbreaks, the opposite would have occurred. It is only after 1590 that rent rises surge ahead of price increases. Davies gives two kinds of explanations for this. On the one hand, the concept of variable rent was relatively new and therefore outrageous in the "first" sixteenth century, whereas by the "second," the peasants were habituated to this concept.[145] And second, and perhaps more importantly, the "yeomen" were not negatively affected by the enclosures.[146]

Let us now turn to a comparison of the lot of the "yeomen" in England and France at this same period. Here Davies notices that it was the burden of taxation which led most directly to rebellion against the central authority, and that this burden was less in England than in France because of the

[142]"[L]apses of holdings into the lord's hands were not simply due to the failure of the population to replace itself naturally.... Poverty ...—not the lack of land but lack of equipment and money reserves—may have been a factor [in the surrender of holdings], not incompatible with a drift to towns or to country industry." Rodney H. Hilton, "A Study in the Pre-History of English Enclosure in the Fifteenth Century," *Studi in onore di Armando Sapori* (Milano: Istituto Edit. Cisalpino, 1957), I, 678–679.

[143]"The demesne could be rented to large-scale capitalist farmers, who would draw the largest part of their income from the products of the land, and not from their own property. For the landlords, this method was, from every point of view, preferable. The capitalist farmer had a larger capital base than the peasant, and he was not tempted, as was the peasant, to give greater care to his own farm, at the expense of the land he rented from the landlord. One sees why therefore the landlord

preferred to give limited leases to a small number of capitalist farmers than to a large number of peasants." Habakkuk, *Annales E.S.C.*, **XX**, p. 650.

[144]"English peasant communities in the thirteenth and fourteenth centuries had been capable of great resistance, even successful resistance to attacks on their conditions by the landlords. If they allowed themselves to be evicted in the fifteenth and sixteenth centuries it was because economic and social changes had destroyed the cohesion that had been their strength in the past." Hilton, *Studi in onore di Armando Sapori*, p. 685.

[145]See C. S. L. Davies, *Annales E.S.C.*, **XXIV**, p. 35.

[146]However, "this was not at all the case obviously with those who had to live by their wages nor with those small tenantholders who had to supplement their means with additional wages from industrial or agricultural work. The latter lost heavily during this period." *Ibid.*, pp. 36–37.

smaller size of the state, the relatively less venal and hence less extractive bureaucracy, and the institutional weakness of the regions which reduced the weight of state machinery as well as eliminating foci of rebellion.[147]

Finally, let us look at one last contrast, peasant revolts in sixteenth-century England and those of the eighteenth century. Tawney points out that this is a contrast between their "prevalence . . . in the middle of the sixteenth century" and their "comparative rarity two hundred years later," although the same potential cause, the enclosures, was there.[148] Tawney argues that the agrarian disturbances of the sixteenth century "mark the transition from the feudal revolts of the fifteenth century, based on the union of all classes in a locality against the central government, to those in which one class stands against another through the opposition of economic interests."[149]

What then is it we are saying? It seems that the sixteenth century, particularly the period between 1540–1640, is a period of class *formation*, a capitalist agricultural class (whose wealthier members are called "gentry" and whose lesser members are called "yeomen"). The social process of land consolidation in England at this time is one of increasing income to this class as a whole including to the lesser members of it, while it involves the beginnings of the creation of a proletariat, most of whom was still not firmly settled in the towns but rather were "vagabonds," seasonal wage workers with subsistence plots, and lumpenproletariat in the towns.

The state machinery was not a coherent strong independent force but a battleground of two conflicting trends—those persons of high traditional status who were at best partially adapting to the new economic possibilities, and those rising elements (whatever their background in terms of traditional status and whatever their relative wealth in the present) who pushed toward the full commercialization of economic life.

While both these elements sought and from time to time received the assistance of the state, neither was sure that it stood to profit from a greatly strengthened state machinery, largely because both sides feared that the other side would dominate the state bureaucracy. A policy of "social welfare" served the interests of preserving order and interfering with the full play of market forces. It eased the transition, and thus had advantages for all the forces in play.

England's position in the world-economy precisely made this balancing game possible. It was sheltered from too much outside interference by the struggle of the two great military powers: Spain and France. It was

---

[147]See *ibid.*, pp. 54–55. See Tawney, *Agrarian Problems*, pp. 340–342.

[148]*Ibid.*, p. 321.

[149]*Ibid.*, p. 322.

unencumbered by imperial obligations.[150] It was free therefore to pursue its economic specialization, especially with the assistance of eastern Europe's raw materials, fed to it in part by its commercial alliance with the Dutch Republic, which also wanted shelter from the military giants, and which "paid the costs" of keeping the world trade machinery operating. The English state machinery was just strong enough to fend off baneful outside influences, but still weak enough not to give too great an edge either to "traditionalist" elements or to the new parasites of the state bureaucracy, so that neither the one nor the other were able to eat up totally the surplus of the most productive forces. In short, it was a question of optimal position: relative political insulation while having the economic advantages of the world-economy, a relative balance of forces internally which maximized internal peace, but minimized the errors of an overbearing state machinery.

How come, then, one might properly ask, the English Revolution? It might be said now that we are arguing that the proof of the "success" of England during this era is that the English Revolution occurred when it did—neither earlier nor later—and that the forces of modern capitalism emerged clearly triumphant, despite their presumed "defeat" and a presumed "Restoration" of the old. To appreciate this issue of timing, we should look at three related phenomena: the politics of alliance in this era, the patterns of migration, and the so-called commercial crisis of the early Stuart era. This will enable us to talk about the "real issues" that were the background to the English Revolution.

H. R. Trevor-Roper insists that the essential conflict is that of court and country. If this is his key point, then he has won, because this presumed opponents—for example, Stone and Hill[151]—have conceded the case. The issue however is not there. It is what political game was the Court playing, how was this game related to the social and economic transformation going on, and in what ways was it consequence and cause of England's role in the European world-economy.

The state-machinery, the Court, was at one and the same time a protagonist of the drama and a mediating agency, a vector of different forces. This was true of all the so-called absolute monarchies. They balanced forces; they served as power brokers; they effected compromises. But one of the

---

[150]"The end of the Middle Ages in England was marked by contraction rather than expansion: withdrawal from the long dream of conquest in France, and, what is particularly significant, a marked shrinkage of area of English control, of English language and civilization, in Ireland. Gaeldom came once more lapping like lake water up to the walls of the towns—Dublin, Waterford, Cork, Galway, last outposts of earlier Anglo-Irish. In the early fifteenth century, with Owen Glendower's rebellion, Wales achieved a temporary quasi independence; though it was defeated and crushed, Wales remained resentfully aloof, unabsorbed. Nor was any real progress made with the integration of Cornwall or the Scottish Borders, where they 'knew no king but a Percy,' into the fabric of the state." A. L. Rowse, "Tudor Expansion: The Transition from Medieval to Modern History," *William and Mary Quarterly*, 3rd ser., **XIV**, 3, July 1957, 312.

[151]Stone, *Encounter*, **XI**, p. 73; Hill, *Puritanism and Revolution*, p. 28.

outcomes they hoped for was to strengthen themselves, to become absolute in deed rather than merely in theory and in aspiration.

Given the ambiguity of its role and its objectives, the Court was ambivalent about the onsurge of capitalist elements. On the one hand, the Crown courted the "bourgeoisie," that is to say, the conglomerate of landed capitalist proprietors and well-to-do farmers, professional men (lawyers, divines, and medical practitioners), the wealthier merchants.[152] "Haunted by the fear of feudal revolts,"[153] as Tawney puts it, the State saw in them allies for its own ends. But the Court, when all is said and done, was dominated by the aristocracy, the king first among them—old aristocrats, men newly come to the titles and valuing them all the more for it, others in the service of the king aspiring to the peerage—and the Court could not be sanguine about the undermining of the hierarchical status system of which it was the apex. Nor was it sanguine. It cherished this system, reinforced it, elaborated it, paid for it. The Renaissance Court outshone all others that Europe had known.

Its need for money and political allies led the Court to further commerce and commercialization. Its need for stability and deference led it to be uneasy about the aggressive successes of the new class. To the extent that it was competent, the Court sought to apply a slow brake to an accelerating process of capitalist transformation while at the same time increasing the political centrality of state institutions. This was no different in Tudor England than in Valois France or Hapsburg Spain. What was different was both the historical background and the international position in the sixteenth century which made the new English capitalist class both relatively stronger and more able to absorb within it very large elements of the old aristocracy.

Many writers note that, about 1590–1600, there was a critical moment in the politics of England. Tawney writes:

> Few rulers have acted more remorselessly than the early Tudors on the maxim that the foundations of power are economic. They had made the augmentation of the royal demesne, and the protection of the peasant cultivator, two of the keystones of the New Monarchy. By the later years of Elizabeth, the former policy was crumbling badly, and the latter, always unpopular with the larger landowners, was encountering an ever more tenacious opposition.[154]

Over time the weight of the Crown's decisions was leaning toward the capitalist farmers, as opposed to the aristocracy as such.[155] The latter, in order to survive, became more and more like "rising gentry" and hence,

[152]See Tawney, *Essays in Economic History,* **I,** p. 176.
[153] Tawney, *Proceedings of the British Academy,* p. 211.

[154]*Ibid.,* p. 216. See Tawney, *Essays in Economic History,* **I,** pp. 176–177.
[155]See Stone, *Crisis of the Aristocracy,* pp. 124, 133.

from the point of view of the peasantry, more and more exploitative.[156] Hence the ties grew thinner between lord and peasant, and the latter were no longer likely to respond to regional vertical appeals of loyalty in national conflicts.[157] The Crown bureaucracy itself however was becoming overblown and "wasteful," a process which had its natural limits, as Trevor-Roper argues.[158] Then, agree Stone and Trevor-Roper, by 1590, overexpenditure led to cutback. Peace in Europe (the interval between 1598 and 1618) reduced the costs for all the states.[159] In England, the sale of titles by James I increased the income[160] and crisis was thereby averted. Crisis averted but extravagance increased, because of the logic of the Crown's dual-stranded policy.[161]

A century of Tudor rule may not have caused a sharp decline in the ownership of land by peers as Tawney originally thought. It seems in the end that all that happened is that the royal demesne was partially parceled out to non-peer capitalist farmers.[162] The beneficiaries of Tudor rule were doubtless both peers and non-peers who were able to master the new economy.[163] Tudor juggling kept them on top of the situation. But the "long" sixteenth century was nearing its end. And the strains of its contradictions would be felt under the early Stuarts. This is the point which Trevor-Roper makes:

> Even in the 1590's, even a far less expensive, more efficient bureaucracy had been saved only by peace: how could this much more outrageous system [of the Stuarts and other European monarchs of this time] survive if the long prosperity of the sixteenth century, or the saving peace of the seventeenth, should fail?
>
> In fact, in the 1620's they both failed at once. In 1618 a political crisis in Prague had set the European powers in motion. . . . Meanwhile the European economy . . . was suddenly struck by a great depression, the universal "decay of trade" of 1620.[164]

[156]See Tawney, *Agrarian Problems*, 191–192. Tawney concludes: "The brilliant age which begins with Elizabeth gleams against the background of social squalor and misery. . . . [A]ll that the peasants know is that his land-agents are harsher [p. 193]."

[157]See *ibid.*, p. 229.

[158]"A booming economy can carry many anomalies, many abuses. It could even carry—provided it went on booming—the incredibly wasteful, ornamental, parasitic Renaissance court and Churches. Provided it went on booming—But how long would it boom? Already, by 1590, the cracks are beginning to appear." H. R. Trevor-Roper. "The General Crisis of the Seventeenth Century," in *The European Witch-Craze of the 16th and 17th Centuries and Other Essays* (New York: Harper, 1969a), 68–69.

[159]See *ibid.*, p. 69.

[160]See Stone, *Economic History Review*, **XVIII**, p. 39.

[161]When Elizabeth sought to respond to the economic crisis of the 1590s, the aristocracy itself was menaced. See Stone, *Crisis of the Aristocracy*, pp. 124, 133. Not yet ready to eliminate "the buttress which only an aristocracy can offer it" (Tawney, *Proceedings of the British Academy*, p. 212), the Crown renewed and expanded its extravagance. See Trevor-Roper, *The European Witch-Craze*, p. 69.

[162]See R. W. K. Hinton, "Letter to the Editor," *Encounter*, **XI**, 1, July 1958, 74–75.

[163]See H. R. Trevor-Roper, "Letter to the Editor," *Encounter*, **XI**, 1, July 1958, 73–74. Even if it is true that, as J. P. Cooper argues, "there is still no good evidence that the total landed wealth of the peerage was less [in 1642 than in 1559]." (*Encounter*, **XI**, p. 74) it is likely that the land shifted toward peers who were oriented to the capitalist market.

[164]Trevor-Roper, *The European Witch-Craze*, p. 70.

So we are once more back to the workings of the world-system. England's reaction to the so-called "crisis of the seventeenth century" was somewhat different from that of others. This is why she could enter the era of mercantilism with so much greater strength. One aspect of this strength was the high degree of commercialization of her agriculture, a process we have been describing. The other side was her "industrialization."

John Nef argues that England underwent an "early industrial revolution" in the period 1540–1640, and that by comparison France did not.[165] He asserts there were three main developments in England. A number of industries previously known on the Continent but not in England were introduced (paper and gunpowder mills, cannon foundries, alum and copperas factories, sugar refineries, saltpeter works, brass making). New techniques were imported from the Continent, especially in mining and metallurgy. Finally, the English made their own positive contribution to technology, especially in connection with the substitution of coal for wood.[166] Furthermore, Nef argues that "capital investment along with technical inventive ingenuity, was being oriented as never before in the direction of production for the sake of *quantity*."[167] If, however, one asks of Nef, why this sudden shift of England from being an industrial "backwater" to being relatively advanced, Nef offers principally a geographical explanation. The large internal market, a prerequisite for industrial concentration, was made possible "by the facilities for cheap water transport which Great Britain, by virtue of her insular position and good harbors, enjoyed to a greater degree than any foreign country except Holland."[168] No doubt this is true, but since the geography was the same in earlier centuries, we are left uncertain as to why the sudden spurt.

What does seem to be clear is that there was a spurt: in industrial technology, in degree of industrialization, and correlatively in population. K. W. Taylor, in observing the doubling of the English population under Tudor rule, offers two explanations: domestic peace and the new geography of world trade which changed England's location in the "world" and hence ended the concentration of its population in the south and east. "Like

---

[165]See John U. Nef, "A Comparison of Industrial Growth in France and England from 1540 to 1640," in *The Conquest of the Material World* (Chicago, Illinois: Univ. of Chicago Press, 1964), 144–212. See however, the reservations of P. J. Bowden on this hypothesis in *Agrarian History*, **IV**, pp. 608–609. A more sympathetic appraisal of Nef's theses from a French source is to be found in Gaston Zeller, "Industry in France Before Colbert," in Rondo Cameron, ed., *Essays in French Economic History* (Homewood, Illinois: Irwin, Inc., 1970) 128–139.

[166]The production of coal in Newcastle went from 30,000 tons annually in 1563–64 to 500,000 in 1658–59. See Braudel, *Civilisation matérielle*, p. 281.

[167]John U. Nef, "The Progress of Technology and

Growth of Large-Scale Industry in Great Britain, 1540–1640," in *Conquest of the Material World* (Chicago, Illinois: Univ. of Chicago Press, 1964), 136.

[168]*Ibid.*, p. 142. See Nef again: "England owed her increasing economic independence and power most of all to the phenomenal expansion of coastwise trade and of trade by land and river. That expansion was made possible by the vigorous exploitation of the natural resources and markets within the island of Great Britain, so rich in minerals and good soil and so well provided with harbors that made possible shipment of commodities by water at relatively low costs to every port in the British Isles." *War and Human Progress*, p. 111.

a potted plant, long left undisturbed on a window-sill and then transferred to an open garden, the economy of England threw out new leaves and branches."[169] Taylor's geographical explanation, because it speaks of England's position relative to the world-economy as opposed to Nef's argument of internal geographic advantages, is more satisfying since it deals with an element that precisely changed in the sixteenth century. Furthermore, if we remember the new importance of the Baltic as well as of the Atlantic trade, the argument is further strengthened. Still by itself, it is not enough to explain the discrepancy with France. Perhaps we shall have to look to factors within France that prevented her from taking as much advantage of the new geography as did England.

Let us further note that England's doubling of population was selective, because it involved not only demographic growth but quality immigration and helpful emigration. On the one hand, there is the oft-noted influx of continental artisans—Flemish clothiers, German metallurgists, etc.—whose arrival is usually attributed to the upheavals of the religious wars. But, if they went to England, it is because, as G. N. Clark argues, England had become "the place where capital and management could earn a better remuneration."[170] Let us however remember that the end of the Elizabethan era was a moment of economic and social strain—too great expenditures of the court, plus population growth combined with enclosures and hence the rise of vagabondage. As F. J. Fisher reminds us, contemporaries thought of Elizabethan England "as a country in which population pressure was gradually reducing many to poverty and possibly diminishing the national income per head."[171]

There are two ways to handle the problem of surplus population within a country: remove them from the cities (that is, geographically segregate them), or remove them from the country altogether. In Tudor–Stuart England, both were tried. On the one hand, the poor laws, the "laws against the poor" as Braudel calls them,[172] pushed them to the rural areas to exist in a borderline fashion. On the other hand, it is just at this time that England begins to think of overseas colonization—to Ireland first from about 1590, then to North America and the West Indies. In the case of external emigration, the temptation for the emigrants was social mobility.[173]

[169]K. W. Taylor, "Some Aspects of Population History," *Canadian Journal of Economics and Political Science*, **XVI**, Aug. 1950, 308.

[170]Clark, *Wealth of England*, p. 51. See Edward Taube, "German Craftsmen in England During the Tudor Period," *Journal of Economic History*, **IV**, 14, Feb. 1939, 167–168. A description of the varied ways in which the Flemish immigrants "altered patterns of English life in both basic and trivial matters" is to be found in John J. Murray, "The Cultural Impact of the Flemish Low Countries on Sixteenth and Seventeenth Century England," *American Historical Review*, **LXII**, 4, July 1957, 853ff. This is also the period of the first major Welsh immigration into England. See Bindoff, *Tudor England*, p. 24.

[171]Fisher, *Economica*, **XXIV**, p. 16.

[172]Braudel, *Civilisation matérielle*, p. 56, G. N. Clark notes: "From the year of the Spanish Armada the Crown tried to stop the expansion of London, first by Acts of Parliament, then by proclamations, commissions, and judicial proceedings." *Wealth of England*, p. 94.

[173]See Stone, *Past & Present*, No. 33, pp. 32–33.

Malowist suggests we look to an explanation of the second wave of European expansion which begins in the end of the sixteenth century—that of England, Holland, and to a lesser extent, France—not only in the commercial factors often cited, but in the need to dispense with surplus population. He notes that many see demographic expansion as a stimulus of economic expansion, but he reminds us that there is an optimal point. "Difficult economic situations and certain social situations unfavorable to economic progress seem therefore to create conditions which favor emigration, even the most risky."[174] Once again, only optima can be considered in a country "prematurely overpopulated."[175] Like England, France exported its population, to Spain in the sixteenth and seventeenth centuries (to replace the expelled Moriscos), later to the "islands" of America, and killed many off in the persecutions of the Protestants.[176] By the end of the eighteenth century, to be sure, France's population was once more balanced.[177] But it took far longer to arrive at this balance than England. And it was only at a price of internal warfare which strengthened some of the wrong forces and expelled some of the right ones—wrong and right, that is, from the point of view of industrial transformation. These pluses of English development become clear in the outcome of the European economic crisis of the 1620s. Before however we deal with that, we must look at what happened in France between Cateau-Cambrésis and the crisis.

For Frank C. Spooner, "the decade 1550–1560 is decisive [for France]."[178] It is marked by a sudden gold shortage which turns France's attention to African exploration and leads to a development of the western maritime regions. It marks the rise of Paris as a financial center (as against Lyon which definitively declines by 1580).[179] Furthermore, it is marked by the outbreak of the religious civil wars which were to preoccupy France for the rest of the century. This double development (of the maritime regions and Paris) and the religious wars are not unconnected.

The inflation affected the income of the nobility, particularly the lesser nobility who lived on fixed rents. But the peasants did not benefit, as

---

[174]Malowist, *Annales E.S.C.*, **XVII**, p. 929.

[175]Braudel, *Civilisation matérielle*, p. 37. Lublinskaya notes that this was argued by A. de Montchrétien as early as 1615. See *French Absolutism*, p. 132.

[176]Note however that Pierre Goubert argues that French population grew steadily during the sixteenth century despite the religious wars. "Recent Theories and Research in French Population between 1500 and 1700," in D.V. Glass and D.E.C. Eversley, eds., *Population in History* (London: Arnold, 1965), 465.

[177]The great epidemic of 1628–1633 no doubt helped in this respect. See J. Meuvret,

"Demographic Crisis in France from the Sixteenth to the Eighteenth Century," in D.V. Glass and D.E.C. Eversley, eds., *Population in History* (London: Arnold, 1965). 509. The plague raged also in Germany and Italy.

[178]Frank C. Spooner, "A la côte de Guinée sous pavillon français (1559–1561)." *Studi in onore di Armando Sapori* (Milano: Istituto Edit. Cisalpino, 1957), **II**, 1001.

[179]See Braudel, *La Méditerranée*, **I**, 449. See Emile Coornaert, "Les échanges de la France avec l'Allemagne et les pays du Nord au XVIe siècle," *Revue d'histoire économique et sociale*, **XXXV**, 3, 1959, 244.

might normally be expected, because of the devastations wrought by civil war. One major consequence was the vastly increased importance of the state machinery not only because of the vast expansion of tax farming that occurred at this time, but also because nobles who wished to survive economically sought financial refuge in attaching themselves to the court.[180]

France at this time was faced with one major problem in seeking to reorient itself to the new European world after Cateau-Cambrésis. It was neither fish nor fowl, no longer empire, but not quite a nation-state. It was geared half to land transport, half to sea transport. Its state machinery was at once too strong and too weak.

There are two arenas in which this ambiguity of option can be seen most clearly. One is in the arena of trade, the other is in politics and religion. The facts of the economic trading zones did not mesh with the political boundaries. This was to some extent true everywhere in Europe of course (and to some extent always true), but it was particularly glaring for France, especially if one compared France with what is the case for her great economic rivals-to-be: England and the northern Netherlands. Emile Coornaert describes the situation at the beginning of the sixteenth century in this way:

> In the region which, in rapid outline, runs from Paris and the bend of the Loire to the Mediterranean, France was part of an economic zone which still was heavily under the influence of the Italians, the principal men of affairs, masters of commercial techniques, since the last of the Middle Ages in all of western Europe. Thanks especially to them, this zone was the most developed from the point of view of organization and modes of work. In France, the pole and, at the same time, the port of exit in this part of the country was Lyon, which put it in contact with the south and centre of the continent and contributed rather actively to its links with the north-west. The latter which included the north of France and the French maritime front of the Ponant, the Low Countries, England, and the Rhenish fringe of the Empire constituted another zone. Its pole was Antwerp, which controlled contacts with northern Europe and, in large part, with Germany. From the point of view of techniques, it was on the way to reaching the level of the Southern European zone.[181]

This economic split meant that France was further from having a *national* economy than England, far closer in this regard to Spain. But whereas Spain's problem was that Spain was part of a larger Hapsburg Empire which, at least under Charles V, she did not really control, France's problem was that, after 1557, she was attracted in at least three different directions. The political heart of the country—roughly the northeast and including the capital—was attracted to a continental land mass, the economy

[180]See Henri Hauser, "The Characteristic Features of French Economic History from the Middle of the Sixteenth Century to the Middle of the Eighteenth Century," *Economic History Review*, **IV**, 3, Oct. 1933, 261–262.

[181]Coornaert, *Revue d'histoire économique et sociale*, **XXXV**, p. 242.

that had been dominant in the "first" sixteenth century, that is, linked to Antwerp even after her decline.[182] The northwest and west of France was attracted to the new European world-economy and its Atlantic and Baltic trades.[183] The south of France was developing the system of *métayage* we previously discussed, part of the general movement of the Christian Mediterranean toward primary production, toward export-oriented, capitalist agriculture.[184]

For Henri Hauser this motley assortment of activities and orientations adds up to a "happy condition in which [France] could dispense with her neighbours while they could not do without her."[185] He even wishes to call this "autarchy." To me, it seems quite the opposite, a situation in which France is the sum of centrifugal economic forces. It is in order to counter this fractionation that the controllers of the state machinery move so strikingly to reinforce it, to create Europe's strongest state, what will become under Louis XIV the very model, for contemporaries and for history, of the absolute monarchy.

One of the critical sources of the economic dilemma of France arises out of a change in the technological substratum of the European world-economy. To appreciate its importance, we must first dissect some conflict-

[182]"That Antwerp continued powerfully to attract the French, long after 1550, is explained by the economic splintering *(morcellement)* of France, a country whose industrial equipment was furthermore still largely insufficient." Jan Craeybeckx, "Les français et Anvers au XVIe siècle," *Annales E.S.C.,* **XVII,** 3, mai-juin 1962, 548. Indeed, Nef argues, of increasing insufficiency: "[The] fifty years of rapid, growth in English industry [1550–1600] were in France a period of retrogression. . . ." *Conquest of the Material World,* 1964a, p. 146.

[183]See J. H. Parry, "Colonial Developments and International Rivalry Outside Europe, I. America," *New Cambridge Modern History,* **III:** R. B. Wernham, ed., *The Counter-Reformation and the Price Revolution, 1559–1610* (London and New York: Cambridge Univ. Press, 1968), 530. H. A. Innis notes that: "In the first half of the sixteenth century, the fishing fleets in the New World had belonged chiefly to France. . . ." *The Cod Fisheries* (New Haven: Yale Univ. Press, 1940), 49. Both Channel and Biscay ports were involved. The trade was so extensive that they could support "production of a surplus of dry fish for the English market."

Similarly, Jeannin notes: "In the French maritime expeditions to the Baltic, the primary role is . . . surely that of Dieppe. . . . The French ships that crossed the Sound in the 16th century are overwhelmingly from Normandy, and among Normans, the people of Dieppe are dominant. *Vierteljahrschrift für Sozial- und Wirtschaftsgeschichte,* **XLIII,** p. 329.

The extensive French trade with Scotland had two segments: a Normandy trade in which manufactures and services were exported, and a Biscay trade in which salt and wine were exported. See Lythe, *The Economy of Scotland,* pp. 172–182. The former trade was very like that the Low Countries had with Scotland at the time. "Both [north France and the Low Countries] had their own distinctive vegetable products, both had a relatively high level of industrial technique, both served as entrepôts for exotic goods from further afield [pp. 174–175]."

[184]"As it was practiced, *métayage* appeared to be an essentially capitalist mode of production, meeting the needs of the bourgeois proprietors. . . ." G. E. de Falguerolles, "La décadence de l'économie agricole dans le Consulat de Lempaut aux XVIIe et XVIIIe siècles," *Annales du Midi,* **LIII,** 1941, 149. De Falguerolles argues that the origin of this system is to be found in the debts accumulated by the small landholders as a consequence of the rise in royal taxation and the price inflation of the late sixteenth century. See pp. 142–146. He sees the system as putting an enormous burden on the land, by requiring it to make possible: (1) payments of taxes by wheat exports; (2) rent payments to the bourgeoisie (sharing of grain, vegetables, animal products, bricks, fall harvest, first tree harvest); (3) allowing men and cattle to subsist. The combination of the three burdens led by the eighteenth century to catastrophe: "exhaustion of the land, ruin of the bourgeoisie, misery of the rural population [p. 167]."

[185]Hauser, *Economic History Review,* **IV,** p. 260.

ing evidence on the relative costs of sea and land transport in pre-industrial Europe. On the one hand, there are the frequent and seemingly obvious statements that in pre-industrial Europe, "land transport was still extremely expensive and the nations which had the best command of sea-borne trade secured the fastest economic growth."[186] Furthermore, as Kristof Glamann suggests, the theory of widening circles as a result of economic intercourse particularly applies to maritime trade. Indeed, he says, "international trade [via water routes] is in many cases cheaper and easier to establish than domestic trade."[187] On the other hand, Wilfrid Brulez points out:

> In the 16th century, . . . land transport retained a primordial role. This fact is indisputable for the trade between the Low Countries and Italy: although they had Antwerp, a first-rate maritime outlet and what's more a world center, the Low Countries undertook the overwhelming majority of their commercial relations with Italy by land route. [Shipments by sea] occurred between the two countries, but their importance remained minimal.[188]

The situation seemed to be different by the seventeenth century. What had happened? Very simple. It seems that, although there was technological advance in both land and sea transport at this time, the rate of improvement was different, such that it came to be the case that "for very heavy and bulky goods water transport was the most economical under all circumstances [with the exception of live cattle]."[189] The development of the Dutch *fluyt* referred to previously was probably of central importance in this regard. Conversely, in the sixteenth century, land remained a cheaper, more efficient, and safer means of transport for men, for light and expensive manufactures, and for precious metals.[190]

What is the significance of this for France? We presented the politics of the "first" sixteenth century as revolving around the attempts by Spain and France to transform the European world-economy into a world-empire. Despite the Atlantic explorations, these attempts were primarily oriented to land routes. Indeed, this may be a supplementary reason for their failure. The politics of the "second" sixteenth century was oriented to the creation of coherent nation-states obtaining politico–commercial advantages within the framework of a nonimperial world-economy. These attempts were primarily oriented to the maximum utilization of sea routes (external and

[186]K. Berrill, *Economic History Review*, 2d ser., **XII**, 3, p. 357.

[187]Glamann, Fontana Economic History of Europe, **II**, p. 7.

[188]Wilfrid Brulez, *Studi in onore di Amintore Fanfani*, **IV**, 125. Furthermore, Brulez adds, it seems to be the same factors which account for the majority of English-Italian trade going overland at this time: "Certainly textiles, which were the heart of Anglo-Italian trade, never used the sea route except secondarily, and continued, through-out the century, to be transported overland [p. 126]."

[189]Glamann, *Fontana Economic History of Europe*, **II**, p. 31.

[190]See Jacques Heers, "Rivalité ou collaboration de la terre de l'eau? Position générale des problèmes," *Les grandes voies maritimes dans le monde, XVe–XIXe siècles*, VIIe Colloque, Commission Internationale d'Histoire Maritime (Paris: S.E.V.P. E.N., 1965), 47–50.

internal). The natural geographic advantages of the northern Netherlands and England served them well here. The politics of France was a tension, often inexplicit, between those who were land-oriented and those who were sea-oriented.[191] The critical difference between France, on the one hand, and England and the United Provinces, on the other, was that in the latter cases, to be sea-oriented and to wish to construct a strong polity and national economy were compatible options, whereas for France, because of its geography, these options were somewhat contradictory.

The first strong hint we have of this comes in the religious controversies and civil wars that racked France from the death of Francis II in 1560 to the truce enshrined in the Edict of Nantes in 1598.

Let us just look briefly at some of the class and geographic coordinates of the religious struggle. As long as France was primarily oriented to a struggle with the Hapsburg empire and counted on Lyon as their contestant for chief international trading center, religious toleration was possible.[192] After Cateau-Cambrésis the international financial need for religious toleration disappeared. At the same time, the prosperity of Lyon declined, both because of its lessened importance as a financial center and because it was a major battleground of the Wars of Religion.[193] The wars had brought together many disparate forces whose politics often became detached from their original motivations, as usually happens in the heat of extended political turmoil. Nonetheless, it should be possible for us to disentangle some of the strands. Hurstfield's account of the origins of the civil wars in the

[191]See this discussion by A. L. Rowse of how the French state failed to serve the interests of the sea-oriented groups in the mid-sixteenth century: "In the 1550's French interlopers were increasingly active in the West Indies. But by the truce of 1556 France accepted Philip II's demand for prohibition of the trade, except by special licence from him—which was not readily forthcoming, we may suppose. The French sea-captains refused to accept this, but they were without the support of their government. Contrast England under Elizabeth: the fact that England was Protestant was an inestimable advantage; it gave us a free hand, and we were no longer hampered and held back as the French were. By the definitive treaty of Cateau-Cambrésis (1559), Henry II, in the interests of Catholic unity, renounced all French enterprise in South America. . . . What France lost by the miserable (and orthodox) Valois! The torch passed to the hands of Admiral Coligny, the Huguenot leader, the true and far-seeing exponent of the interests of France." *The Elizabethans and America* (New York: Macmillan, 1959), 7–8. Rowse's Protestant passions are no doubt to be discounted. But the description of the internal conflict of different groups in France, and their consequences for France's role in world-

economy seem to me sound. The point about Protestantism, as we already discussed when treating of its decline in Poland, is that those with interests in the new thrust of nation-states operating within a world-economy tended to find cognitive consonance in being Protestants, thus symbolizing an opposition to the imperial power and *Weltanschauung* of the Hapsburgs, which was especially closely linked to the Counter-Reformation after Cateau-Cambrésis.

[192]"In 1552, to cover the expenses of the 'German journey,' the King, or rather Tournon, applied not only to the Italians but to two Augsburgers, the Zangmeister brothers, and to Georg Weikman of Ulm, all three established at Lyon. The king took these agents of German anti-imperialist finance under his protection, guaranteed their religious liberty, and promised them secrecy." Henri Hauser, *Journal of European Business History*, **II**, p. 247.

[193]"In France the crisis of St. Quentin was followed almost immediately by the outbreak of the wars of religion. Now the city of Lyon was particularly exposed on account of its geographical position. It was occupied, besieged, and sacked in turn by Catholics and Huguenots, and threatened by all the enemies of France, with the Duke of Savoy in the first line." Hauser, *ibid.*, p. 255.

New Cambridge Modern History runs as follows:

> In France during this period the tension between monarchy and nobility flared up into a long and bloody struggle. It is, of course, well known that the French civil wars derived from powerful secular no less than religious causes. . . . The Calvinist movement in France had first, in the mid-sixteenth century, taken hold upon the merchant and the artisan; and its early martyrs—as in Marian England—came from the humblest stock. But by the time the civil wars began in 1562 the nobility, both high and provincial, had joined in and indeed taken over control. Contemporaries in France recognized the importance of distinguishing between the wings of the movement describing the one group as "Huguenots of religion," and the other group as "Huguenots of state." These latter stood for much more than religious dissent. They represented the long-standing hostility of the ruling families of provincial France to the power of Paris; to the crown and its ally, the Catholic church; and above all, to the Guises, the family most closely identified with that church and most bitterly opposed to the aims and interests of those provincial and often decaying noble houses. (The traditional use of the expression "provincial nobility" in part confuses the issue: most of its members would be regarded in England as belonging not to the nobility but to knightly and gentry families.)[194]

Hurstfield thus draws a picture of France close to that Trevor-Roper draws of England, of the Country versus the Court. And such a picture evokes all the unclarity that the English analogy does—were nobility (or gentry) "rising" or "declining?" In whose interests did the state in practice operate? Let us put next to Hurstfield the picture as drawn by Koenigsberger in the same volume of the *Cambridge History:*

> After the bankruptcy of 1557, Henry II squeezed another seven million livres in extraordinary taxes out of his unfortunate subjects. Nevertheless, the limit had been reached. There were *peasant* revolts in *Normandy* and *Languedoc*. The nobles, though exempt from taxation, had spent their incomes and mortgaged or sold their estates in the king's service on the heavy ransoms demanded of noble prisoners after the disaster of St. Quentin (1557). . . .
>
> In the towns, the *small artisans* and *shopkeepers* had been hit by heavy taxation and by the periodic collapse of rural purchasing power that followed bad harvests such as that of 1557. The *journeymen* saw food prices rising faster than wages and found that the growing influence and rigidity of the *guilds* blocked the advance of the majority to mastership. . . .
>
> After 1559 the *nobility joined the movement in large numbers, especially in the south.* . . .
>
> It was only [in 1573] that Huguenot organization reached its full development, in a broad arc stretching from *Dauphiné* through *Provence* and *Languedoc* to *Béarn* and *Guienne*. As in the Netherlands, the successful revolution tended to become *localised*, both by an alliance with provincial feeling against an interfering central government and by the hopes of the military situation.[195]

[194]Hurstfield, *New Cambridge Modern History,* **III**, p. 131.
[195]H. G. Koenigsberger, "Western Europe and the Power of Spain," *New Cambridge Modern History,* **III**: R. B. Wernham, ed., *The Counter-Reformation and the Price Revolution, 1559–1610* (London and New York: Cambridge Univ. Press, 1968), 281–282,

290. Italics added. Note that Koenigsberger speaks of the growing influence of the guilds. John U. Nef makes the following comparison: "But during the late sixteenth and early seventeenth centuries the gild system was beginning to break down in England, at the very time it was being strengthened and extended in France." *Industry and Government,* p. 25.

In reaction to this, Catholic local unions arose, also emphasizing their regional identity and claims to (traditional) provincial autonomy. Paris localists sided with the Catholic League.[196] Furthermore, both camps were linked to outside forces, the Huguenots to England and the Protestant princes of Germany, the Catholics to Rome and the rulers of Spain and Savoy. "Thus, all revolutionary movements of the period were linked to powers and interests outside their national boundaries."[197]

King Henry III, attempting to arbitrate the struggle, in the end dealt blows to and alienated both camps. In a sense, it was a brilliant tactical coup to seek to de-escalate the conflict by recognizing the Protestant pretender, Henry of Navarre (Henry IV), as his successor, provided he became a Catholic. It was then that Henry IV issued his famous: "Paris vaut une messe." Note that it was Paris, not France, and it was Navarre who said it.

Henry IV switched camps which was easy enough since his motivation was different from that of his mass base. The nobility then by and large withdrew from the conflict and became Catholicized. This defused the religious content of the conflict and hence weakened the strength of the political opposition.[198] It also frustrated the lower classes who turned to angry but relatively ineffectual *jacqueries*.[199] In the end, the Huguenots were more strongly regionally based than ever. They had lost their congregations in the north and east and remained strong in the south.[200]

One of the underlying tensions clearly was regional. On the one hand, Normandy and Brittany were pulling away; on the other hand, so was the whole of the south whose separatism had remained latent since its defeat in the thirteenth century. The reasons for the pulls were in both

[196]See Koenigsberger, *New Cambridge Modern History*, **III**, pp. 302–303.

[197]*Ibid.*, p. 292.

[198]"Religion was the binding force that held together the divergent interests of the different classes and provided them with an organisation and a propaganda machine capable of forming the first genuinely national and international parties in modern European history; for these parties never embraced more than a minority of each of their constituent classes. It was through religion that they could appeal to the lowest classes and the mob to vent the anger of their poverty and the despair of their unemployment in fanatical looting and in barbarous massacres." Koenigsberger, *New Cambridge Modern History*, **III**, pp. 306–307.

[199]"When the parties lost their revolutionary impetus and their preaching its social content, they rapidly lost the support of the lower classes. The devastations caused by the wars of the League and the increasing misery of the French peasants produced a growing number of peasant movements directed against the seigneurs and their rents, against the clergy and their tithes, and against the

tax collectors and their *taille;* but they took no account of religion or the political parties. These *jacqueries* culminated in the movement of the Croquants in central and southern France in 1594-5. They fought a pitched battle against a league of seigneurs, formed for the sole purpose of defeating them. This and many similar outbursts in the seventeenth century throw a sombre light on the rural society and the tax system of France; but they remained without political effect until the revolution of 1789." *Ibid.*, p. 307.

The *jacqueries* are not hard to explain in view of what Le Roy Ladurie describes as the "double pauperization" suffered by the lowest levels of the peasantry of Languedoc in the years 1550–1590: "that which afflicted the small landowners, whose number was increased by the division of lands, without the real income per unit showing a true increase to compensate for the diminution of the size of lots; and that which afflicted the wage-workers, as the result of the fall of real wages." *Paysans du Languedoc*, **I**, p. 317.

[200]See Koenigsberger. *New Cambridge Modern History*, **III**, p. 314.

cases that the creation of a strong national economy served to limit rather than expand profit opportunities for the local notables: the bourgeoisie of the maritime west who sought to use their money to break into the Atlantic–Baltic trade rather than construct a state bureaucracy and army; the landed capitalists of the south who sought a free international market. The partisans of the center were not anticapitalist in orientation. They had essentially a middle-range orientation: first strengthen the state and commercial possibilities will follow.

As in England, the monarchy was caught in the contradiction of wishing to create a national economy based on new forces that could compete successfully in the new world-economy and being the apex of a system of status and privilege based on socially conservative forces. Wishing not to choose rashly, the king—in France as in England—felt more comfortable in his aristocratic penchant than in a role as the harbinger of the new. What was different however was that in England the nascent capitalist elements, both rural and urban, felt they stood to gain from a stronger national economy. France however had merchant elements who felt they were being sacrificed to a remote Paris, and capitalist agriculture in the south whose structure and hence needs were nearer to those of landowners in peripheral countries like Poland (who needed an open economy before all else) than to landowners in England within whose domains the new cottage industries were growing up. In England, there was a sense in which the king could count on his opponents to restrain themselves since his "national" stance was in their "short-run" interests. The king in France could not, and had to use sterner means to hold the country together: hence civil war in the second half of the sixteenth century, and bureaucratic centralism, which was to come in the first half of the seventeenth century.

The price however was heavy. The Wars of Religion would facilitate the rise of absolutism, to be sure. But as Mousnier adds: "Unlike in England, the development of trade, of industry and of the bourgeoisie was retarded (freiné)."[201] Nor had the price been yet fully paid. The era of Louis XIII and Richelieu was to see a further cost exacted. In order, however, to assess this price, we must now shift back to the general situation of the world-economy.

The "long" sixteenth century was now drawing to an end. And, so say most historians, the evidence is that there was a crisis. Crisis or crises? For there was an economic recession in the 1590s, an even bigger one

---

[201]Mousnier, *Les XVIe et XVIIe siècles,* p. 103. The negative economic effect of the Wars of Religion had a cumulative effect, because as H. M. Robertson argues, "where economic conditions took an unfavorable turn, the use of the state as a protective agency for existing but threatened interests became common practice." In Germany the multiplicity of authorities meant shrinking markets and let to the reemergence of the guilds and urban monopoly. "In France, also, the power of the gilds had been considerably strengthened by the end of the century, through the ordinances of 1581 and 1597." "European Economic Developments in the Sixteenth Century," *South African Journal of Economics,* **XVIII,** 1, 1950, 46.

in the 1620s, and what some see as a coup de grâce around 1650. We shall not dwell too long on the debate of dates—whether the ideal cutting point for the story is 1622 or 1640 or 1650. Spooner indeed argues that one of the key phenomena to notice about this "culminating point and watershed" of the long sixteenth century was that the turning point "was spread over a fairly wide period of time."[202] We have chosen 1640 as the terminal date for a variety of reasons, and do not pledge even so not to transgress this boundary. The main point is nonetheless that, virtually without exception, historians accept the idea that there was some kind of critical turning-point somewhere around this time.[203]

Of what did it consist? First, a price reversal, the end of the price inflation which had sustained the economic expansion of the European world-economy. The price trend did not reverse itself all at once. It is crucial to the understanding of this period and to the subsequent development of the world-economy to see that, in general, the reversal occurred earlier in the south than in the north, earlier in the west than in the east, and earlier in areas on the sea than inland in the continent.[204] There was a gap, and of not a few years.

Trouble began in Spain shortly after the defeat of the Spanish Armada. Trade still had however its ups and downs. Chaunu's data show 1608 as the highpoint of the Spanish Atlantic trade. Then a sort of plateau until 1622, which Chaunu attributes to the economically relieving qualities of temporary peace,[205] followed by the definitive downturn. The military–political defeat of the Armada merely however punctured a balloon, stretched thin by the exhaustion of the resource base of Spanish prosperity. Spanish exploitation of the Americas had been of a particularly destructive variety, a sort of primitive hunting and gathering carried out by advanced technology.[206] In the process, Spain exhausted the land and

[202]Frank C. Spooner, "The European Economy 1609–50," *New Cambridge Modern History,* **IV**: J. P. Cooper, ed., *The Decline of Spain and the Thirty Years' War, 1609–48/59* (London and New York: Cambridge Univ. Press, 1970), 69.

[203]Except perhaps René Baehrel, who goes against the current and designates a price phrase as running from 1594 to 1689, in which 1628-55 is simply the intermediate period. See *Une croissance: la Basse-Provence rurale (fin XVIe siècle-1789)* (Paris: S.E.V.P.E.N., 1961), 50–57.

[204]See Pierre Chaunu, "Le renversement de la tendance majeure des prix et des activités au XVIIe siècle," *Studi in onore di Amintore Fanfani,* **IV**: *Evo moderno* (Milano: Dott A. Giuffrè-Ed., 1962), 231.

[205]"Peace is perhaps the principal secret of this very paradoxical sustenance of the traffic beyond 1608-12 up to 1619-22, of these slightly more than ten years which separate by a long hesitation the clear end of the phase of ascendancy of a prosperity that was no more and the clear beginning point of the phase of descent for the Spanish Atlantic."

Pierre Chaunu, *Séville et l'Atlantique (1504–1650),* Vol. **VIII** (2 bis): *La conjoncture (1593–1650)* (Paris: S.E.V.P.E.N., 1959), 889. See also pp. 1404–1405.

[206]"All of America in the 16th century had been thought of as a gigantic field in which to pick produce *(champ de ceuillette).* The gathering, either by a simple transfer into commercial circuits of potential riches hoarded by centuries of sterile labor, or by scratching of surface lodes or of those soils closest to routes of transport, was only possible through an intermediary, only thanks to the cushion of Indian humanity. But the first use of the Indians, to this end, had been destructive of men without any care to conserve them, used as riches that one does not intend to restore. Hence rapid exhaustion of the area sown in forty years, of the entire surface in seventy years. To the point that the great plantations of the 17th century had to make use entirely of imported labor." Chaunu, *ibid.,* pp. 1422–1423.

its men. Furthermore, Spain not only used up Indian labor; she used up, in other ways, as we have seen, her own labor.[207]

One very important consequence was the fall in bullion import. For example, bullion annually imported on the average into Seville from the Americas in the period 1641–1650 was 39% of that imported in the period 1591–1600 in the case of silver and only 8% in the case of gold. The output of bullion had fallen "victim to the relentless law of diminishing marginal returns and declining profits."[208] Since however trade did not suddenly diminish—indeed it was still expanding—devaluation was inevitable.

Here for the first time the existence of a single world-economy of uneven national development made a crucial difference. The countries of northwest Europe devalued far less than those of southern, central, and eastern Europe.[209] These are of course bullion prices. René Baehrel has a very brilliant excursus in which he demonstrates that shifts in bullion prices bear no necessary relationship to shifts in prices and that men make their real economic decisions primarily in terms of the latter.[210] It is significant, however, that he does this in a book devoted to discussing the economy of the seventeenth and eighteenth centuries. A. D. Lublinskaya makes the point that what distinguishes the seventeenth from the sixteenth century is precisely the fact that, after 1615 for the first time, there is "an *independent* movement of prices, *not* dependent on the influx of gold and silver."[211] She asserts that this fact defines the end of the "price revolution." Ruggiero Romano insists that there occurs a sudden aggravation of devaluation in the years 1619–1622: "What matters is the intensity of the phenomenon. . . ."[212] There was such an abundance of money in 1619 that the interest fell to 1.2%, "the absolute minimum interest rate for the whole period 1522–1625."[213]

From the general depression, only Holland and to some extent (to what extent we shall soon see) England escape.[214] Indeed Romano argues that Holland not only escapes, but that plus or minus 1590–*1670* are a period of Dutch agricultural *expansion*.[215]

[207]See *ibid.*, pp. 1423–1425.

[208]Spooner, *New Cambridge Modern History*, **IV**, p. 79.

[209]Spooner makes this crystal clear in *ibid.*, Table II (p. 86) and Map I (p. 87). England and Holland are the most resistent to devaluation, Poland, Genoa, and Spain the least. France is only very slightly better than Spain.

[210]See Baehrel, *Une Croissance*, pp. 2–20; also René Baehrel, "Economie et histoire à propos des prix," in *Eventail de l'histoire vivante: hommage à Lucien Febvre* (Paris: Lib. Armand Colin, 1953) **I**, 287–310. Baehrel concludes this article: "Pay attention to 'social screens,' Marc Bloch recommended. Must we also speak of 'economic screens?' Lucien Febvre taught me once that Luther's objec-

tion to the indulgences was that they provided a false security.' Can we say as much about bullion-prices? [p. 310]"

[211]Lublinskaya, *French Absolutism*, p. 15.

[212]Romano, *Rivista storica italiana*, **LXXIV**, p. 522.

[213]*Ibid.*, p. 525. Romano draws his figures from Cipolla, "Note sulle storia del saggio d'interesse," Table III. I believe Romano has copied Cipolla's figure wrong. It should be 1.1%.

[214]See Ruggiero Romano, "Encore la crise de 1619–22," *Annales E.S.C.*, **XIX**, 1, janv.–févr. 1964, 33.

[215]See Romano, *Rivista storica italiana*, **LXXIV**, p. 516. Glamann incidentally indicates why this eventu-ally ends. He notes that the role of Baltic grain in

Why should northwest Europe have been relatively so insulated against the winds of ill fortune? Chaunu has an explanation which is rather complex. In the sixteenth century, prices in northwest Europe rose less sharply than those in Spain because of the time lag in the arrival of bullion. Northwest Europe however always obtained part of its bullion in contraband. The proportion of contraband bullion rose as time went on. Hence the inflationary impact of the contraband bullion was rising in percentage of total impact just as Spanish prices were beginning to drop. "The prices of northern Europe, by a lesser receptivity to depressive factors, tend thus to come closer to the Spanish price-levels."[216] This seems a bit farfetched, since it depends for its plausibility on assuming that there was no significant decline in the absolute as opposed to relative supply of contraband bullion, which, it can be inferred from Spooner's figures, was probably not the case.

Pierre Jeannin seems nearer the mark in analyzing the resistance of northwest Europe to depressive forces as deriving from advantages this region had within the world-economy.[217] He cites geographic location (on the Atlantic at a crossroads between the breadbaskets and forests of the northeast and the countries in need of their exports); industrial aptitudes (rooted in the past, as Dutch and English textiles; or in economic potential released by the extension of the international economy, as Swedish iron). Furthermore, the very expansion of productive forces in the north meant a continued rise in population at the very moment of demographic decline in the Mediterranean region. Pierre Chaunu estimates that between 1620 and 1650 the population of the Empire went from 20 to 7 million, Italy declining by 2 million between 1600 and 1650. *Relatively* sheltered from the demographic decline were England and, this time, France.[218]

As a geopolitical phenomenon, this meant the end of the Spanish Atlantic and the establishment of a European Atlantic.[219] The war whose resumption in 1624 marks in fact a crushing blow to the Spanish economy began with the Dutch attack on the Portuguese colony of Brazil, Portugal at

Europe declines in significance *after 1650,* and hence the Dutch economic role declines, because of the rise of a new self-sufficiency in grain in southern and western Europe. *Fontana Economic History of Europe,* **II,** p. 42. This in turn may be explained in part by a reduction in population (perhaps) and in larger part by the increase of both the productivity and extent of arable land, which for southern Europe was part of its peripheralization. Furthermore in the contraction of the European world-economy of 1650–1750, England found it profitable to maintain its own high trade balances by taking back some of the international trade in grains she had yielded in more profitable eras to peripheral areas.

[216]Chaunu, *Séville,* **VIII** (2 bis). p. 90.

[217]"The 'prosperity' enjoyed by the north-west is not a form of grace bestowed by one does not know which mysterious power; it results from internal causes, among which a summary inventory distinguishes quickly between structural and conjunctural elements." Pierre Jeannin, "Les comptes du Sund comme source pour la construction d'indices généraux de l'activité économique en Europe (XVIe-XVIIe siècles)," *Revue historique,* **CCXXXI,** avr.–juin 1964, p. 325.

[218]See Pierre Chaunu, "Réflexions sur le tournant des années 1630–1650," *Cahiers d'histoire,* **XII,** 3, 1967, 259–260.

[219]See Lublinskaya, *French Absolutism,* p. 52.

the time belonging to the Spanish crown.[220] In terms of the Asian trade, and especially pepper, between 1590 and 1600, the Dutch and English invaded what was hitherto a Portuguese–Spanish monopoly, which accounts for a collapse in spice prices.[221] One can well understand how it was that the men of that era developed a mercantilist perspective that led them to feel that "the sum of prosperity in the world was constant, and the aim of commercial policy . . . was to secure for each individual nation the largest possible slice of the cake."[222]

But it was not in fact constant. On the one hand, one could argue that the end of the sixteenth century meant for all of Europe "collapse of profit, the flight of rent, economic stagnation."[223] But one must be specific. Romano insists that the sixteenth century was "just like the 12th and 13th centuries, a century of large *agricultural* profits."[224] It is the decline of the *easy* agricultural profits that is going to explain the increased role of large-scale capitalist agriculture based on ever more coerced and lowly-paid agricultural labor in the late seventeenth and eighteenth century. Romano's comments are apt:

> These vast phenomena, which Fernand Braudel has called on the one hand "faillite," "trahison de la bourgeoisie," and on the other hand "réaction seigneuriale," do not seem to be, on closer inspection, two separate and distinct types, but only one: almost the very same people, or at least, the descendants of one family who *betrayed* their bourgeois origins (and above all their bourgeois functions), and entered the system of the *réaction seigneuriale*, a phenomenon which when dealing with the Italian case I have called "refeudalization."[225]

But once again, as Romano observes, Holland and to a lesser extent England are exceptions.

We must not however get ahead of our story. It is crucial to understanding the subsequent era to look closely at how England and France coped with the closing convulsions of the "long" sixteenth century. The consolidation of the European world-economy which was to occur in the seventeenth and eighteenth centuries would center around the competition of England and France for primacy. But in a sense the crucial cards were dealt in the period 1600–1640.

[220]See Chaunu, *Séville*, **VIII** (2 bis), 1535–1537 for the impact on the Spanish economy.

[221]See H. Kellenbenz, "Autour de 1600: le commerce de poivre des Fuggers et le marché internationale de poivre," *Annales E.S.C.*, **XI**, 1, janv.–mars 1956, esp. 23, 27.

[222]Glamann, *Fontana Economic History of Europe*, **II**, p. 5. Is this so wrong even from the perspective of today? H. M. Robertson's view is: "In the 19th century there was, perhaps, a tendency to minimise or even to neglect the costs of economic progress; at present there is, perhaps, a tendency to pay them an exaggerated respect. In the 16th century these costs were so much to the fore as to make it appear that almost axiomatic that one man's or one country's gains was another's loss; that greater activity here meant less employment there; that, as the Dutch proverb succinctly puts it, *De éen man zijn brood is de ander zijn dood.*" *South African Journal of Economics*, **XVIII**, p. 46.

[223]Chaunu, *Cahiers d'histoire*, **XII**, p. 264.

[224]Romano, *Annales E.S.C.*, **XIX**, p. 33. Italics added.

[225]Romano, *Rivista storica italiana*, **LXXIV**, pp. 511–512. For Holland as an exception, see p. 512; for England as a more limited exception, see pp. 517, 519.

When G. N. Clark seeks to explain the "remarkable" advance of industry in England in the "second" sixteenth century, he suggests that the root lay in international commerce. And when he analyzes England's international commerce in this period, he finds three main contrasts between the end of the period and the beginning: (1) although England's international trade expanded absolutely, it declined in relation to internal industry in providing for consumption needs; (2) although Amsterdam succeeded Antwerp as the pivot of the European world-economy, England's relationship to the Netherlands shifted from one of dependence and complementarity to one of rivalry; (3) England's external trade became far more diversified within Europe, and England began systematic trade with Russia, the Levant, the Indian Ocean area, and the Americas.[226]

Before the end of Elizabeth's reign, however, these changes had not yet occurred to a noticeable degree. Nor did they develop in so smooth a fashion as Clark implies. For these changes upset the delicate social and political equilibrium that the Tudors had attempted with so much skill to create and laid bare the conflicting interests that were to tear the English political system apart. Let us take each of these changes in turn.

It is no doubt true that international trade declined as a proportion of the gross national product, and that this might be interpreted as a sign of England's long-term economic health. But this misses the point that the very process of internal industrialization made England's social structure more, not less, dependent on the vagaries of the world market. Barry Supple points out that, unlike in the period after the Industrial Revolution, fixed capital played a small role in the industrial economy and hence fluctuations in the national economy were not caused by excess capacity nor were they intensified by fluctuations of a capital goods industry. Fluctuations in credit also were a lesser factor than later. Hence the prosperity of the home market was largely a function of harvest fluctuations (induced by climate variations) and "overseas demand which was frequently the strategic determinant of alterations in internal activity."[227] And such alterations were politically critical precisely because of England's industrial development:

> Cloth production was sufficiently far advanced to have ceased, in the main, to be a by-employment for a predominantly agrarian population. Hence for the government and for the community at large the existence of the textile industry meant the perennial threat of an outbreak of distress and disorder among a landless, and even propertyless, class. The situation had helped produce the Elizabethan Poor Law and made generations of statesmen wary of encouraging industrial growth.[228]

[226]See Clark, *Wealth of England,* pp. 103–107.
[227]Supple, *Commercial Crisis,* p. 9.
[228]Supple, *ibid.,* 6–7. See Astrid Friis, *Alderman*

Cockayne's Project and the Cloth Trade (Copenhagen: Levin & Munksgaard, 1927), 22.

What might England then do to assure economic, hence political, stability? One solution Supple indicates: It was to draw back still further. F. J. Fisher observes that "Bacon looked back on the reign of Elizabeth as a critical period during which England had been dangerously dependent on foreign grain. . . ."[229] Over time, this is the path of deindustrialization which northern Italy took. Another solution might be to push outward and overcome the supply squeeze by obtaining additional sources of supply and the demand squeeze by securing new markets.[230] This is the path on which the northern Netherlands was embarking. To try one or the other solution meant making critical options in terms of England's internal social structure. These were precisely the decisions that the Tudors spent all their energy avoiding. The result was a halfway house. Lawrence Stone's examination of the volume of Elizabethan overseas trade leads him to conclude that the "famous expansion of trade in the reign of Elizabeth appears to be a pious myth."[231]

If then we turn to degree to which England had liberated itself from Dutch economic tutelage by 1600, we find to be sure that the process of growing control by the English commercial bourgeoisie over English internal trade had been more or less completed by such acts as abolishing Hanseatic privileges first in 1552 and definitively in 1598.[232] This was to the advantage of closed monopolies like the Merchant Adventurers.[233] The interest of such groups lay largely in the uneasy equilibrium of the halfway house.

When, under the Stuarts, other merchants obtained the legal rights to make a more forthright challenge of the Dutch role in industrial finishing of textiles—the so-called Alderman Cockayne's Project[234]—they failed. For Supple this failure demonstrated that

[229]F. J. Fisher, "Tawney's Century," in Fisher, ed., *Essays in the Economic and Social History of Tudor and Stuart England* (London and New York: Cambridge Univ. Press, 1961), 4–5.

[230]Fisher outlines the squeeze as follows: "In primary production, the obstacles to expansion lay mainly . in the field of supply and arose largely from the limitations of contemporary techniques. . . .

"[I]n the sixteenth and seventeenth centuries, as in the Middle Ages, men looked to the land not only for their food but also for their drink, for their fuel, and for such basic, industrial materials as timber, wool, hides, skins, and tallow. . . . Under such circumstances economic and demographic expansion tended to place upon the land a strain that in later ages and under different circumstances, they were to place upon the balance of payments. . . .

"In secondary production, by contrast, the obstacle to expansion seems to have lain in the field of

demand rather than in that of supply. . . . In most industries, the main factor of production was labour and labour was both plentiful and cheap. . . . The labourer and cottager, irregularly employed and miserably paid, were poor customers." *Ibid.*, pp. 3, 4, 6.

[231]Stone, *Economic History Review*, **II**, p. 50.

[232]"In a symbolic way this latter event of 1598 was a sign that England was moving from the periphery towards the centre of a new trading system." W. E. Minchinton, "Introduction," *The Growth of English Overseas Trade in the Seventeenth and Eighteenth Centuries* (London: Methuen, 1969), 3. "Was moving . . . towards," but not yet there —that is the point!

[233]See Rich, *New Cambridge Modern History*, **I**, pp. 461–462.

[234]The standard account is to be found in Friis, *Alderman Cockayne's Project*, p. 22.

the international division of labour by which the Dutch dyed and dressed England's semi-manufactured textiles was not an arbitrary phenomenon sustained by artificial survivals of company regulation. On the contrary, by the early seventeenth century it reflected economic realities against which England might tilt only at her peril.[235]

Hence, Elizabethan constraint in hesitating to expand outwardly may not have been so unwise.[236] The Tudors had been thereby postponing internal social conflict until they had strengthened the political autonomy of the state machinery from outsiders, so that England would have the strength to tolerate the explosive but inevitable readjustment of political and social forces.

Finally, to what extent was the Elizabethan era one of diversification overseas? To be sure, it was at this time that the English ships returned to the Baltic and began to make voyages to the Mediterranean, to Russia, to Africa. And this was the time of the constitution of the first chartered companies. But we must be careful not to exaggerate. On the one hand, eastern Europe was still more closely linked with the economies of France and Spain (via Amsterdam) than with England[237] and, on the other hand, it is the trade with France and the rebel Dutch provinces that is still fundamental to England in the period of Elizabeth.[238]

The realities of the English commercial scene are both cause and consequence of the policies of the Tudor monarchs. They were straddling a fence.[239] The international economic crisis of the period 1590–1640 made this fence-straddling increasingly impossible, and hence the political stability of the monarchy and the monopolies it sheltered increasingly tenuous. Stability is not always everyone's *summum bonum*. To some it was "irksome."[240] By 1604, the chafing of those merchants who sought to pursue the possibilities of commercial expansion found expression in various free trade bills pushed in Parliament. The immediate impetus was probably the peace with Spain which had opened changed trade perspectives as peace is wont to do, both by eliminating certain obstructions to trade, and by dint of the unemployment, so to speak, of the previously flourishing band of privateers.[241]

For the next decade, things looked bright for the English cloth industry

---

[235]Supple, *Commercial Crisis*, pp. 49–50.

[236]Stone himself admits: "It is very significant of the new pattern of English economy that the two great consumer markets for which the expanding production catered were the military needs of the State and the basic essentials of life for the poorer classes." *Economic History Review*, **XVII**, p. 108.

[237]See R. W. K. Hinton, *The Eastland Trade and the Common Weal in the Seventeenth Century* (London and New York: Cambridge Univ. Press, 1959), ix–x.

[238]See Stone, *Economic History Review*, **XVII**, p. 51.

[239]"Stability depended on restricting the growth of capitalism, and that was the economic policy of the absolute monarchy. . . . [At the same time,] the military and strategic requirements of the absolute monarchy led it to foster in some degree the emergence of industrial capitalism." Manning, *Past & Present*, No. 9, p. 49.

[240]"By the end of the sixteenth century, the stability that had seemed so desirable a generation earlier had been found irksome; as conditions for trade expansion once more came into being the feeling against such expansion declined; and the uprooting of these vested interests that had grown behind the restrictions of the great depression become one of the major tasks of the seventeenth century." Fisher, in Carus-Wilson, ed., *Essays in Economic History*, **I**, p. 172.

[241]See Friis, *Alderman Cockayne's Project*, pp. 149–150.

which reached an export peak in 1614. But it was to be, in Supple's phrase, "a transitory Indian summer."[242] It was followed by an "unrivalled" economic depression, which "ensured a permanent restriction of the overseas market for old draperies."[243] What caused this sudden downfall? Actually it was not so sudden, but rather as R. W. K. Hinton says, "a sudden worsening of a situation that had been deteriorating for some time."[244] What happened was that the devaluation of continental currencies by reference to England created highly unfavorable terms of trade which "priced the [English] cloth out of [their north and central European] markets."[245] This led to an outflow of bullion which was made worse by the need for foreign grain as a result of bad harvests in 1621 and 1622.[246] The dramatic loss of bullion "was of great significance in an unsophisticated economy dependent on steady supplies of a secure metallic coinage."[247]

J. D. Gould argues that England now paid the price of having "wasted" her international price advantage of 1550–1600 "in a scramble for privileges." Consequently, now that the price advantage had been reversed, "England was left saddled with a rigid, ologopolistic, high-cost economy, ill-fitted to cope with a competitor [the Dutch] who throve on low costs, adaptability, and up-to-dateness."[248] The Dutch were now able to break into England's own import trade,[249] and textile exports to Germany and eastern Europe were hit by both Dutch and local competition.[250]

Both the merchants and the government were alarmed. The merchants reacted by demanding more protection, such as limiting the rights of non-English to import the goods into England, increased mandatory use of English shipping, the freedom to re-export Baltic grain which both enlarge

[242]Supple, *Commercial Crisis,* p. 29.

[243]*Ibid.,* p. 52.

[244]Hinton, *The Eastland Trade,* p. 20. See Supple: "For it is well to remember that the full impact of the depression can only be explained by reference to the harm derived from the Cockayne project, the growth of rival industries, the financial burdens of English cloth, the disturbances provoked by continental warfare, and the widespread pre-existing difficulties for English merchants. These meant that the economy, once any untoward event took place, would experience yet another of those periods of extreme economic decline which are perpetual historical rivals for the appelation 'the Great Depression.'" *Commercial Crisis,* p. 64.

[245]Supple, *ibid.,* p. 80.

[246]See *ibid.,* pp. 89–96.

[247]*Ibid.,* p. 162.

[248]J. D. Gould, "The Trade Depression of the Early 1620's," *Economic History Review,* 2nd ser., **VII,** 1, 1954, 87.

[249]See Hinton, *Eastland Trade,* pp. 18–19. Also see his account of a particular empirical study: "The years 1611 to 1618 were the only years of our period when both England and the United Provinces were

at peace, and when, therefore, their ships and merchants competed in this respect on equal terms. It is apparent that in competition on equal terms the Dutch were rapidly establishing absolute commercial mastery, doubtless mainly through their notoriously low freight rates. The year 1615 is the first year we see in the Boston [Lincs.] port books. . . . [W]e find that in 1615–18 the value of all dry goods (i.e., except wine) imported from the United Provinces was greater than the value of all dry goods imported from all other places together, whereas the reverse is true at every other time. Similarly in the same period more ships came into Boston every year from the United Provinces than from all other places together, which is not true of any other year in the series except 1628, a year of very small trade. . . . [These facts] lend colour to the contemporary explanation of the depression of 1620, that it was attributable in large measure to the effect of the Dutch entrepôt on English import trades." "Dutch Entrepôt Trade at Boston, Lincs., 1600–40," *Economic History Review,* 2nd ser., **IV,** 3, Apr. 1957, 470.

[250]Hinton, *Eastland Trade,* p. 45.

the cloth trade and bring in bullion for the grain.[251] The government
had quite a different perspective. First, the agricultural interests well represented in parliament were pushing for a ban on the *import* of corn,
because of their need for protection against low prices.[252] Second, the government concentrated on how to reconcile its needs "to alleviate local
destitution, in order to prevent riots and tumults, and to revive commerce,
in order to maintain economic stability and power."[253] To do the first,
the government was tempted by the solution of governments of twentieth-
century underdeveloped countries, the creation of employment. But, like
today, such a solution is not easy.[254] Rather than provide new protection,
the government moved in the direction of loosening monopolies, to see
if that would revive commerce and industry.[255] But they could not go
very far in this direction because the arrangement of privileged companies
had too many advantages for the government. It secured the loyalty of
a quasi-public bureaucracy which performed consular and customs functions, was a source of income via loans and taxation, and even substituted
for the navy as a protective device in international commerce.[256] "The
patents and monopolies, the cloaking of selfish aims beneath verbose
platitudes, were an integral part of the fabric of Stuart government."[257]
If the government moved at all in the direction of antimonopolism, it
was in fact only under the pressure of parliament, "vociferously representative of the outports and the lesser gentry."[258]

Nor was England in luck as far as the gods were involved. The trade
revival of 1623–1624 was set back by the plague of 1625 as well as by
a poor harvest. The resumption of war with Spain, so harmful to Spain
as we have seen, was no aid to England. The renewed need for grain
led to another balance of payments crisis.[259] Thus the traditional heart
of English industry came to find itself "in the middle of an extended
history of decline, painful adaptation, and widespread redundancy."[260]
Crown interference did not solve the problem; it only aggravated the situation by creating a "crisis of mercantile confidence."[261]

It was apparently not so easy for the English textile industry to cut
costs. It was partly that the merchants were too closely imbricated in the
state-machinery for the Crown to be able to force the industrialists to

---

[251]See *ibid.*, pp. 28, 31–32.

[252]See *ibid.*, p. 29.

[253]Supple, *Commercial Crisis,* p. 64.

[254]"In attempting, with varying degrees of success,
to find some means of persuading traders to continue buying cloth at a time when they claimed they
were unable profitably to sell it abroad, the [Privy
Council] found itself in a hornets' nest of controversial issues." *Ibid.,* p. 237.

[255]See *ibid.*, pp. 68–69.

[256]See *ibid.*, pp. 242–243.

[257]*Ibid.*, p. 227.

[258]*Ibid.*, p. 71.

[259]See *ibid.*, pp. 99–102. See W. B. Stephens: "Less
predictable from literary evidence is that the later
'twenties were to many outports the real years of
crisis while the setback suffered in the early 'twenties
was limited, short, and followed by something of
a boom." "The Cloth Exports of the Provincial Ports,
1600–1640." *Economic History Review,* 2nd ser., **XXII,**
2, Aug. 1969. 241.

[260]Supple, *Commercial Crisis,* p. 119.

[261]*Ibid.*, p. 125.

run a leaner shop.[262] Also it must have been that the workers were relatively strong enough to withstand the introduction of significant wage cuts.[263] The only solution, therefore, other than de-industrialization, was to circumvent the vested interests by the development of new industries. It was here in fact that England found its commercial salvation, in the so-called "new draperies,"[264] which saw a remarkable rise as an export item precisely as the "old draperies" fell.[265]

[262]"The government, from the start, was presented with a hopeless task. Were legal requirements to be enforced, then costs would rise to such an extent as to augur wholesale unemployment. If a change in production methods was the result of economic depression, as most often seems to have been the case, then it was no answer to the latter to attempt to restrain the former. Given contemporary industrial techniques there might have been some cases where English cloth was losing ground abroad primarily because it was corrupt. But there seem to have been many more instances where the causal process was reversed; and in this case, since false manufacture was only a limited and hopeless form of cutting costs, the answers to England's problems lay in other directions." *Ibid.* p. 147.

[263]"Where unskilled labour was inexpensive and abundant, low-quality goods could be manufactured at a low cost. This was especially likely to apply where widespread poverty typified a region in which the production of textiles provided only a by-employment for the labourers concerned. Labour in an employ not expected to produce the wherewithal of total subsistence is normally cheaper than that in a full-time occupation. This was the reason adduced by Adam Smith to explain the historical cheapness of coarse, relative to fine, cloths. In the early seventeenth century economic conditions in eastern Europe approximated to this situation, and this meant that that area was eminently suited to the effective production of cheap cloth if the quality expectations of market demand were lowered." *Ibid.*, p. 140.

[264]The varieties of cloth were multiple. There seem to have been (a) woollens: warm and heavy; that is, broadcloth; relied for strength on felting qualities of wool; used curly short-staple fibers; often the yarn was carded, that is converted into a maze; the wool was fulled, that is, soaped and beaten in damp state to make it warmer, more opaque and durable; monotonous in design; suitable for colder climates; (b) "newer types" of cloths (but still basically woollens): narrower and cheaper; includes kersies, dozens, straits; early shift in direction of new southern markets; (c) worsteds proper: spun from combed, long-staple wool; relied on strength of warp and weft; lighter than broadcloth and used less wool per yard; not fulled; well suited

to non-tropical Mediterranean climate; (d) "new draperies" or "stuffs": basically a variant of worsteds; lightest of all; wide variety of patterns; occasionally fulled; sometimes silk, linen, or cotton constituted the weft: includes bayes, sayes, serges, perpetuanas, stammetts, tammies, rashes, fustians, and many others. See Bowden, *Wool Trade*, pp. 41–43; Friis, *Alderman Cockayne's Project*, p. 2; Supple, *Commercial Crisis*, p. 5; D. C. Coleman, "An Innovation and its Diffusion: The 'New Draperies,'" *Economic History Review*, 2nd ser., **XXII**, 3, Dec. 1969, 418–423.

[265]The cause of this rise has been attributed by P. J. Bowden to technological, rather than commercial, factors. He argues: Pasturage had a far greater influence than temperature upon the fineness of the fleece and the length of its staple. The more nutriment which a sheep received the larger it became. The staple of the wool was no exception and like every other part of the animal, increased in length and bulk as a result of better feeding. . . . The enclosures for sheep-farming made life easier, both for the farmers and his sheep. As Lord Ernle has already stated, 'as enclosures multiplied, sheep were fed better, and the fleece increased in weight and length though it lost something of the fineness of its quality.' Thus throughout the sixteenth and seventeenth centuries there was a gradual diminution in the supply of fine, short wool grown in England and an increase in the supply of longer and coarser wool." "Wool Supply and the Woollen Industry," *Economic History Review*, 2nd ser., **XI**, 1, 1956, 45–46. Supple replies that Bowden "fails to take into account either the expansion of continental industry, against which an inferior product had to be measured, or the remarkable growth in European wool supplies, upon which continental industrialization was based. Further, competition was at its keenest not *directly* in the high-quality market, but in the market for relatively coarser textiles—which presumably expanded to the extent that inferior goods produced abroad were being substituted for the traditional English broadcloth. It was a series of radical changes in the market and in alternative supplies, not solely a deterioration in the English industry, which had such unfortunate repercussions for the old draperies." *Commercial Crisis*, p. 143.

There was a second solution to the dilemma of high prices: England developed a re-export trade. And it was this aspect of England's commercial policy that stimulated the two most striking new features of the seventeenth century: the interest in colonial expansion, and the Anglo–Dutch rivalry. Both trends would crystallize after the Civil War but both were in evidence before it.[266]

New products required new markets. And it was Spain and the Mediterranean area in general that provided the most important new arena of English export,[267] an area relatively free from the constrictions of the old English monopolies.[268] The Spanish market in particular was attractive because of "internal inflation and colonial purchases."[269] England was beginning to eat off the carrion of the Spanish Empire. And as Italian industry declined, English exports partially filled the gap.[270]

As for colonization, we must remember that for a long time it was not necessary for England (France, or Holland) to engage in direct colonial enterprises. The Treaty of Cateau-Cambrésis, no doubt as a sign in part of weariness with imperial expansion, included the extraordinary clause which read: "West of the prime meridian and south of the Tropic of Cancer . . . violence done by either party to the other side shall not be regarded as in contravention of the treaties."[271] This concept, popularly known as "No peace beyond the line," was reaffirmed at Vervins in 1598. It allowed, to be sure, the freedom to create new settlements, but also the freedom to plunder. And for fifty-odd years plunder was far more profitable than settlement would have been.[272] Colonization, by contrast,

[266]See F. J. Fisher, "London's Export Trade in the Early Seventeenth Century," *Economic History Review*, 2nd ser., **III**, 2, 1950, 159—161.

[267]"The growing strength of the English economy in the half century or so before the Civil War is nowhere more clearly expressed than in its relations with the Mediterranean. In this period English industry solved technical problems which had hitherto held it back, and flooded the markets of the eastern and western Mediterranean with woollen goods, incidentally reducing Turkey and Italy to the role of suppliers of industrial raw materials." Ralph Davis, "England and the Mediterranean, 1570–1670," in F. J. Fisher, ed. *Essays in the Economic and Social History of Tudor and Stuart England* (London and New York: Cambridge Univ. Press, 1961), 117.

[268]See Fisher, *Economic History Review*, **III**, p. 336. See Bowden: "The [old woollen fabrics] were best fitted for wear in northern, central and eastern Europe, whilst the [new worsted fabrics] were admirably suited for the warm, but non-tropical, Mediterranean. It was England's fortune that she possessed a quasi-monopoly of long-staple wool. . . ." *Economic History Review*, **IX**, p. 57. Monopoly

now in the sense of absence of competition, not in the sense of legal restrictions of entry. By the mid-seventeenth century, long-staple wool was grown in Ireland, and by the end of the century, it was grown in limited amounts in Holland, Zeeland and Flanders. (See p. 53, fn. 3.)

[269]Fisher, *Economic History Review*, **III**, p. 155.

[270]See Charles Wilson, "Cloth Production and International Competition in the 17th Century," *Economic History Review*, 2nd ser., **XIII**, 2, 1960, 212.

[271]Cited in Rich, *New Cambridge Modern History*, **I**, p. 467.

[272]"The [New World Spanish] colonists—avid for slaves and manufactured goods of all kinds, with a good deal of specie at their disposal, yet confined in law to dealing with a rapacious and inefficient monopoly—offered a perfect interlopers' market, with considerable risk to enter." Parry, *New Cambridge Modern History*, **III**, pp. 516–517.

John Maynard Keynes was one of the first to recognize the importance of privateering in the process of capital accumulation in England. He reproached an earlier generation of historians for neglecting this major source of bullion: "It is characteristic of our historians that, for example, the *Cambridge*

seemed a dubious venture. It was assumed that the Spaniards had already gotten the good spots and "even the mercurial Elizabethans—and most certainly the queen herself—were aware of the hopelessness of prospecting at random over a vast continent."[273] Besides, England had Ireland as an outlet for homestead emigrants.[274]

These attitudes changed in the period after 1600. England consolidated her links with Scotland by the union of the two thrones in the person of James I. The colonization of Ireland took on a new seriousness, both for England and for Scotland.[275] Ireland became integrated into the British division of labor. Her woods were used up to supply England with timber.[276] She would become in the course of the next 100 years the site of a major iron industry controlled by Englishmen.[277] And England would begin to create settlements in North America. Parry ascribes the change to the decline of Spanish prestige, and to the search for raw materials—cheap food, especially fish,[278] and strategic supplies (timber, hemp and pitch) whose Baltic sources might be cut off in wartime. In addition, they would be a new market for manufactures and a place to export paupers.[279] All true no doubt but, except for the consideration of Spain's military strength, all would have been largely true a century earlier. Is not the new scramble for colonies by the three powers of northwest Europe merely a sign of

Modern History should make no mention of these economic factors as moulding the Elizabethan Age and making possible its greatness." *Treatise on Money,* **II,** p. 156, fn. 1.

Webb designates the process, "hit[ting] a windfall once removed." That is: "Instead of taking the gold and silver from its source as the Spaniards had done, they took it by short shrift after the Spaniards had acquired it. . . ." *The Great Frontier,* p. 196.

[273]Parry, *New Cambridge Modern History,* **III,** p. 524.

[274]See *ibid.,* p. 526. Even in Ireland, England's attitude was relaxed at this time. Ireland traded extensively with Spain. If the English were unhappy and suspicious, they did not seek to repress the trade. "England under Elizabeth was, in this matter at least, easier-going than in later years. Nor were Irish Catholics subject to economic disabilities." Cyril Falls, *Elizabeth's Irish Wars* (London: Methuen, 1950), 20.

[275]See Lythe, *The Economy of Scotland,* pp. 63–70. A corresponding Scottish attempt to establish settlements in Nova Scotia at this time failed because "after 1603 Scotland no longer had an independent foreign policy, she had not yet acquired the wholehearted goodwill of England and, in Nova Scotia, she fell foul of France, the one other nation which might have championed her ambitions [p. 75]."

[276]In 1600 Ireland was covered for one-eighth of its territory by woodlands. They had all virtually disappeared by 1700. Quick profits were forthcoming from the sale of timber for tanning of leather,

shipbuilding, pipe and barrel-stave making and iron smelting. Timber was also cut down for domestic purposes (building materials, firewood). In addition to economic motives, there was the military consideration of eliminating bogs and woods in which Irish resisters could not be pursued by English horsemen. See Eileen McCracken, "The Woodlands of Ireland circa 1600," *Irish Historical Studies,* **XI,** 44, Sept. 1959, 273, 287, 289.

[277]"It has been generally assumed that the rise of the English-controlled iron industry in Ireland coincided with a shortage of fuel in England. It now seems probable that the cost of fuel rather than the shortage of fuel was the difficulty that beset the English industry. . . .

By the end of the sixteenth century fuel and labor were the dearest items in the cost of running an English works. . . . During the same period in Ireland it was much cheaper. . . ." *Ibid.,* p. 295.

[278]In the period 1550–1600, the English had begun to displace the Spanish in the fisheries of North America. This was all the more true after 1580 when Denmark began to enforce a system of licence fees to fish in Icelandic waters. By the end of the century, England was established on the Avalon peninsula. It was not until 1600–1650, however, that England was securely ensconced in Newfoundland and New England and could capture the Spanish market. See Innis, *The Cod Fisheries,* pp. 30–81.

[279]See Parry, *New Cambridge Modern History,* **III,** p. 527.

their competitiveness? Was it not largely a pre-emptive colonization, especially in the wake of Spain's decline?

The impact of these international economic convulsions forced a political crisis in England. I think Perez Zagorin has caught quite accurately the nature of the conflict:

> [T]he genesis of the English revolution is not to be found in a class struggle—for the leading sections of both sides in the Civil War included many who were drawn from the same economic class, whose development had been steadily proceeding during the preceding century. It is to be found, rather, in a conflict within this class among England's governing groups.[280]

And this internecine warfare within the governing class was not merely forced by the exigencies of international economic arena but made possible by prior elimination of two great dangers to the English political system, as Stone asserts: "The ring [had been] cleared of interference by the poor or by the Spaniard. . . ."[281]

There are two somewhat silly arguments relating to the onset of the Civil War. One is whether it was or was not inevitable. To Tawney's assertion that "the fall of the monarchy was hastened by the measures taken by the Tudors to preserve it,"[282] Trevor-Roper asserts that the main problem was a wasteful administration, which could have been reformed by Parliament. "For, of course, monarchy itself was no obstacle. It is absurd to say that such a policy was impossible without revolution."[283]

We shall see shortly the consequences for France of the administrative reforms Trevor-Roper retrospectively recommends to the Long Parliament. But "inevitability" is a pointless game to play. If one element had been different, of course the results would have been different. But if one, why not two, three? The reality is that the Civil War did in fact occur and the task of the student is to explain it.

The other silly question is whether or not the "real" issues dividing England were not beliefs about liberty and religion. Mr. Hexter insists that these were the issues and affects some surprise that so many of his

[280]Zagorin, *Journal of Economic History,* **XIX,** pp. 391–392. This argument is very similar to that originally put forward by Tawney: "It was primarily a struggle between economies of different types, which corresponded more closely with regional peculiarities than with social divisions." *Essays in Economic History,* I, p. 186.

[281]Stone, *Economic History Review,* **XVII,** p. 120. Surely it is only in such an ambiance of relative security that we can find the curious picture of chartered companies turning on their benefactor, the state. See Robert Ashton's explanation: "[I]t is difficult to avoid the conclusion that many of the companies had reached a stage in their development, when they were inclined to take a large measure

of government support for granted, and to be more conscious of those of their aims which remained unfulfilled than of the substantial gains which were actually achieved. Given such an attitude of mind, apparent breaches of privilege were all the more likely to assume a disproportionate importance in the eyes of the concessionnaires." "Charles I and the City," in Fisher, ed., 151. Had the social structure been under real attack from within or without, it is hard to imagine that the chartered companies would have thus indulged themselves.

[282]Tawney, *Proceedings of the British Academy,* p. 212.

[283]Trevor-Roper, *The European Witch-Craze,* pp. 86–87.

partners and antagonists in the controversy agree (Hinton, Stone, Pocock, Hill, Trevor-Roper speaking for himself and Tawney.) He welcomes them to his "Whiggish" company.[284] J. G. A. Pocock at least takes umbrage, insisting he is a "post-Marxist" rather than a "neo-Whig."[285] But it is a silly argument because of course the protagonists of the Civil War expressed many of their divisions in ideological terms revolving around political freedom and religious perspectives. And of course they meant it. And of course the outcome of the Civil War was to have consequences for the normative system governing English political life.

To dissect the ideological coordinates of a political and social conflict is however never meaningful unless one can root that analysis in the social relations prevailing at the time and thereby comprehend the implication of ideological demands for these relationships. The debate is *really* about the totality of these relationships, about whether they should remain as they are or change in some specific direction.

The English Civil War was a complex conflict, as all major social upheavals are. *One* major thrust of it was that between those who emphasized the role of the monarchy, who hoped thereby to hold on to a slipping system of privilege and deference,[286] whose fears of social revolution outweighed other considerations, who were somewhat paralyzed before the forced choices of the world-economy, and those, on the other hand, who gave primacy to the continued commercialization of agriculture, who welcomed some change in social patterns, who saw little virtue in the extravagance of the Court, who were oriented to maximizing England's advantage in the world-economy.

Let us turn to France, where things were the same, but most importantly were not the same. Davis Bitton says of the years 1560–1640 that they were "a crucial phase of the transition from the French nobility of the late Middle Ages to the French nobility of the Old Regime."[287] So were they in England. But what a different transition was made in France. In the great debate between Boris Porchnev and Roland Mousnier—which we shall get to in a moment—Porchnev argues in essence that what happened in France in this era was that "the venality of offices brought about not the 'embourgeoisement' of power, but the 'feudalization' of the bourgeoisie."[288] To which Mousnier replies: "There was no such thing as a 'feudal-absolutist' order. To the extent that there was a tendency toward absolutism, it was involved in a struggle against the feudal order. What remained of the feudal order tended to paralyze absolutism."[289] Although I think the debate is partially semantic, and that for the rest Porchnev

[284]Hexter, *Encounter*, **XI**, p. 76.

[285]J. G. A. Pocock, "Letter to the Editor," *Encounter*, **XI**, 4, Oct., 1958, 70.

[286]See Stone, *Crisis of the Aristocracy*, pp. 349–351.

[287]Bitton, *The French Nobility in Crisis* (Stanford, California: Stanford Univ. Press, 1969), 1.

[288]Boris Porchnev, *Les soulèvements populaires en France de 1623 à 1648* (Paris: S.E.V.P.E.N., 1963), 577.

[289]Roland Mousnier, ed., *Lettres et mémoires addressés au Chancelier Séguier (1633–1649)*, Vol. I (Paris: Presses Universitaires de France, 1964), 82–83.

had the better of the argument, what might be said is that Mousnier is closer to the truth if one applies his reasoning to explain England and that of Porchnev to explain France. That is to say, schematically and in an oversimplified fashion, one might assert that in England the aristocracy lost in the short run and gained in the long by transforming itself into bourgeois capitalists, while in France the aristocracy gained in the short run and lost in the long run by forcing the bourgeoisie to abandon its proper function and thus to some extent contribute to economic stagnation. Why this should have been so, we are arguing, is essentially a function of their differing relationship to the world-economy.

But first let us review once again to what extent this is a fair description of the French social system. For reasons we have already outlined, the French state in 1600 was stronger than the English state. This meant that the bureaucracy was "for the bourgeoisie the main means of rising in the social hierarchy,"[290] much more so than in England. In turn this venality led to a greater direct interest of the bourgeoisie in the French monarchy.[291] This leads Mousnier to argue that there was a relatively open class situation in France at this time.[292] But Mousnier himself shows how difficult was the ascent. He points out that for a *roturier* to make it up to the status of *maître des requêtes* required normally four generations.[293] I think in fact Porchnev catches the class situation with more subtlety. It is less that there is very much interclass mobility than that there exist strata of people for whom the sentiments of class attachment vary according to the concrete situation. The most significant such stratum is the bureaucracy of bourgeois origin, the *noblesse de robe:*

> At the moment that a worker, who has retained his links to his village, loses his job in the factory, he becomes once again a peasant. In the same fashion, when one sought to take back from the *officiers* their property rights and privileges, that is to say deprive them of their status as privileged nobility, they automatically fell back virtually into their original status as bourgeois. . . . [The] *officiers* negatively affected by [the decisions of] Mazarin felt themselves to be bourgeois and, at the beginning of the Fronde, their attitude was the same as that of the whole of the bourgeois class.[294]

It is precisely because of the relative ease of acquiring formal aristocratic status in France (true in England under the Stuarts, too, but less so) that there arose in the sixteenth century that "ambiguity of noble status" of which the French aristocracy complained and which led to their "intense,

---

[290]Roland Mousnier, *La vénalité des offices sous Henri IV et Louis XIII.* (Rouen: Ed. Maugard, n.d., ca. 1945, 58.) See also pp. 518–532.

[291]See G. Pagès, "La venalité des offices dans l'ancienne France," *Revue historique,* **CLXIX,** 3, 1932, 493–494.

[292]"If there remained the maintenance of distance between the hierarchy of classes, sometimes even class struggle, there was no clear-cut separation of classes. The passage from one of the other occurred by minute graduations via multiple and nuanced relationships," Mousnier, *Vénalité,* p. 532.

[293]See Mousnier, *Lettres et mémoires,* **I,** pp. 168–169.

[294]Porchnev, *Les soulèvements populaires,* p. 578.

obsessive concern with honorific privileges,"[295] and also to the very great emphasis on strict rules of behavior and the theory of *dérogeance*.[296]

The traditional description of the absolute monarchy as being in alliance with the bourgeoisie against the nobility always ran up against the fact that the so-called classic regime of the absolute monarchy of Louis XIV was also the prime example of the reassertion of the seigniorial privilege. Marc Bloch solved this dilemma by arguing that the seigniorial reassertion was the more fundamental of the two antipathetic phenomena, and that without the absolute monarchy, this tendency would have had full force. In other words, one could say that "the victory of the absolute monarchy limited the extent of the 'feudal reaction.' "[297]

A. D. Lublinskaya essentially agrees,[298] drawing this picture of France in the "second" sixteenth century. After 1559, the role of foreign bankers declined in France, both because of the decline of Italy and Germany and the religious wars. These wars however prevented the French commercial bourgeoisie from filling the gap. In order to obtain funds, therefore, the French government created a system of tax farming. Eventually the tax farmers became fused into the state's financial machinery. "Tax farming was a profitable business. It was on this fact that the government founded its system of forced loans from the chief tax-farmers, turning the latter into its creditors."[299] Hence the intimate links between "financiers" and the state, so much so that their own survival depended on the strength of the state, provided that the "strong government which they wanted . . . remained strongly in need of credit from them."[300] Although it was perhaps not true that the monarchy imposed no taxes on the nobility,[301] it was the very dependence on the venal *officiers* that made this most difficult since, Lublinskaya asserts, tax reform necessarily would have involved the cash outlay of repurchasing the offices, which was far too expensive.[302] Anything which increased state indebtedness reinforced the position of these *officiers*. In particular, "war was very profitable to the financiers."[303]

That some of the reasoning here is very ad hoc can be seen by quick reference to England where "fiscal feudalism" or revenue farming by

[295]Bitton, *The French Nobility in Crisis*, p. 100.

[296]See *ibid.*, pp. 70–76.

[297]Bloch, *Caractères originaux*, I, p. 139.

[298]"The main line of the policy of the absolute monarchy followed a direction favorable to the bourgeoisie, which badly needed a strong central authority, able to defend its economic interests beyond the frontiers of France as well as within them." Lublinskaya, *French Absolutism*, p. 330.

[299]*Ibid.*, p. 240.

[300]*Ibid.*, p. 271.

[301]"It would be totally inexact to imagine the nobility to be completely protected from the fiscal pressures imposed on the country by the governments

of Louis XIII and the Regency." Pierre Deyon, "A propos des rapports entre la noblesse et la monarchie absolue pendant la première moitié du XVIIe siècle," *Revue historique*, **CCXXXI**, avr.-juin 1964, 342.

[302]See Lublinskaya, *French Absolutism*, p. 226. Corrado Vivanti adds that such a move would have been politically as well as financially dangerous for the state, since it would have "brought about a coalition of the entire Third Estate against the absolute monarchy." "Le rivolte popolari in Francia prima della Fronde e la crisi del secolo XVII," *Rivista storica italiana*, **LXXVI**, 4, dic. 1964, 966.

[303]Lublinskaya, *French Absolutism*, p. 271.

syndicates of businessmen became common practices under Elizabeth and the early Stuarts,[304] with no religious wars to explain it and no large-scale growth of a venal bureaucracy subsequent upon it. Furthermore, to the extent that tax profiteering was constrained, this was the result of administrative reform whose immediate motivation was the exigencies of war finance and the need to reduce significantly the cut of the fiscal intermediaries between state and taxpayer.[305]

No matter, however. There was a more fundamental attack on this line of reasoning launched by Boris Porchnev. Porchnev unleashes a full-scale assault on the argument that "venality was a form of the political supremacy of the bourgeois,"[306] a theory he attributes to Pagès and then Mousnier. Porchnev wishes to argue that seventeenth century France was "in its main features, still a feudal society characterized by the predominance of feudal relations of production and feudal forms of economy."[307]

Porchnev argues that capitalist forms exist but that the bourgeoisie "participated in the political power of the feudal state only to the degree that it did not act as a class of capitalist society."[308] The bourgeoisie sought titles for reasons of vanity and cupidity and also adopted an aristocratic life style. In addition, they were induced to abandon true bourgeois economic activities because of the fiscal advantages of using money as credit capital rather than as industrial or agricultural capital.[309]

Hence when peasant uprisings occurred in the period 1623–1648 (to which we shall come in a moment), the bourgeoisie vacillated. On the one hand, they too were unhappy about high taxes. On the other hand, they identified with the interests of the aristocracy and feared the plebeians. Some revolted; some fled the country; and others came to terms with the state by purchasing offices and putting their money into credit operations.[310]

If one asks how come that England and Holland produced a nobility that was *"embourgeoisée"* but France did not, the answer is that "in France, feudalism had a perfection and a classical vitality which prevent any *embourgeoisement* of the nobility."[311] It was not that France was more backward, but that "the qualitative particularities of the French economy made impossible a grouping of classes that would have permitted a bourgeois semi-revolution on the English model."[312] The lucidity of Porchnev's arguments flounders at this crucial comparison where he has to fall back on unexplained perfections, undefined particularities, and the conceptual vagueness of "semi-revolution."

---

[304]See J. Hurstfield, "The Profits of Fiscal Feudalism, 1541–1602," *Economic History Review*, 2nd ser., **VIII**, 1, 1955, 53–61; Robert Ashton, "Revenue Farming under the Early Stuarts," *Economic History Review*, 2nd ser., **VIII**, 3, 1956, 310–322.

[305]See Hurstfield, *Economic History Review*, **VIII**, p. 60.

[306]Porchnev, *Les soulèvements populaires*, p. 39.
[307]*Ibid.*, p. 43.
[308]*Ibid.*, p. 545.
[309]See *ibid.*, pp. 545–561.
[310]See *ibid.*, pp. 282–285, 446.
[311]*Ibid.*, p. 580.
[312]*Ibid.*, pp. 580–581.

It is just at this point in the argument that Corrado Vivanti offers a helping hand to Porchnev. Agreeing completely with Porchnev's rejection of Mousnier's arguments that the Fronde was an isolated element in French history, he suggests that Porchnev has not followed the logic of his own argument to the end, but instead gets bogged down in denouncing the bourgeoisie for betraying the revolution. They could do no other, for they "did not yet form a social group sufficiently strong and autonomous" to do otherwise.[313] Vivanti poses this hypothesis in the form of a question:

> To what extent can the "feudal reaction" or "restoration" and the very "betrayal of the bourgeoisie" in the 17th century be said to lay the base—in a different fashion from what one may find elsewhere, in analogous conditions of crisis—for that capital accumulation which the [French] economy of the 16th century had not succeeded in creating?[314]

That is to say, given "those objective obstacles which finally precluded the Third Estate from engaging in autonomous action in the political and social arenas,"[315] was this path not second best? If it did not permit France the degree of development which England would come to have, it nonetheless prevented France from descending to the role of a semiperipheral state like Spain and Italy. Even southern France, which went down the road of sharecropping, did not regress economically to the extent of neighboring Mediterranean areas. Le Roy Ladurie insists that one can say of southern France (and Catalonia), unlike northern Italy and Castile, that the state of the economy "is becalmed and restrained, is modified and grows heavy, but it does not yet turn around. . . . The drama of Languedoc is not the fall, but the inelasticity, the rigidity of agricultural production; not regression [*décroissance*] but absence of marked growth."[316] It would happen to southern France eventually, but 50 years later than to other areas.

Lucien Goldmann makes a parallel critique of the theory of the alliance of the absolute monarchy and the bourgeoisie. He argues that, on the contrary, the basic alliance was between the monarchy and the nobility, with, however, the monarchy safeguarding its flank by creating a new bourgeoisie. Then, however, Goldmann argues, precisely to keep this bourgeoisie bourgeois and not pseudo-aristocratic, the monarchy introduced the reform of the *paulette* in the early seventeenth century.[317] The *paulette* by instituting in effect a tax on offices kept the bureaucracy venal and

---

[313]Corrado vivanti, *Rivista storica italiana*, **LXXVI,** p. 966.

[314]*Ibid.*, p. 965.

[315]*Ibid.*, p. 965.

[316]Le Roy Ladurie, *Paysans*, pp. 636–637.

[317]The *paulette* was named after the financier Paulet who conceived of it. Before the decree of 1604 which installed the *paulette*, offices could be sold by one person to another, but not passed on to heirs, because if an official died less than 40 days after his resignation, the transaction was invalidated. The decree of 1604 made it possible to leave an office to one's heirs, provided that the official paid at the beginning of each year a tax *(the paulette)* worth one-sixtieth of the value of the office. See Swart, *The Sale of Offices*, pp. 9–10.

hence kept the bourgeoisie bourgeois,[318] and thus also dependent on the monarchy.[319]

Goldmann's explanation centers on distinguishing between two varieties of state officials: an older one made up of *notables* and the *noblesse de robe,* the *officiers* and members of the *Cours souverains* and *parlements,* and a newer one, who were the *commissaires* and *Conseillers d'Etat,* and who served as *intendants* and *maîtres de requêtes.* Goldmann sees the latter as displacing the former "in the first half of the seventeenth century, and especially from 1620 to 1650."[320] Goldmann analyzes the impetus behind this new system as an attempt of the monarchy "to regain ground after the coming to power of Henry IV in 1598,"[321] ground that had been lost during the religious wars.

Since the *officiers* had been a great aid to the monarchy during the religious wars and hence expected that their power and importance would grow not fall, they were upset both by the *paulette*[322] and the rise of the *commissaires.* The tension between *officiers* and *commissaires* grew, reaching a high point around 1637–1638. This Goldmann links up with the rise of Jansenism among the *officiers,* an ideology that "insisted upon the essential vanity of the world and upon the fact that salvation could be found only in solitude and withdrawal."[323]

While Goldmann's portrait of the monarchy is close to that of Porchnev, his portrait of the bourgeoisie is closer to that of Mousnier, who avows "feeling an extreme repugnance to considering the 17th century as a 'feudal' epoch, since it was rather one in which 'commercial capitalism' has profoundly penetrated the country"[324]—the whole of the country and not just the towns. The monopolies were not a break in the rise of capitalism but "a condition of its development at this stage."[325] But Mousnier is most outraged at the assimilation of the *officiers* to nobility. He reacts with the flair of a true aristocrat.

> An *officier* of some importance is judicially a noble. A noble, but not a gentleman nor a seignior *(un féodal).* Porchnev never makes the distinction. Would we call the

[318]"The government of the limited monarchy depended upon the *officiers* and the *Cours souverains,* and therefore presupposed a close understanding between the King and the Third Estate. The government of the absolute monarchy depended upon the *Conseils* and the *Intendants,* and therefore presupposed a balance of power between the different classes, between the nobility on the one side and the *officiers* and the Third Estate on the other. The development of absolute monarchy thus involved . . . a policy of alliance between the Crown and the nobles. This brought with it the risk that the aristocracy would find its way into the apparatus of government in the same way as the bourgeoisie had done when the king was allied with the Third Estate. The Crown therefore had first of all to see that this apparatus remained above all social classes,

and secondly, to ensure that the *offices* remained the exclusive province of the middle class." Lucien Goldmann, *The Hidden God* (New York: Humanities Press, 1964), 127–128. Ergo, the *paulette.*

[319]See *ibid.,* p. 120.

[320]*Ibid.,* p. 141.

[321]*Ibid.,* p. 106.

[322]Upset, that is, at first. Once they lost their early hopes of power and influence, they saw the beneficial side of the *paulette.* See Goldmann, *The Hidden God,* p. 129.

[323]*Ibid.,* p. 120.

[324]Roland Mousnier, "Recherches sur les soulèvement populaires en France avant la Fronde," *Revue d'histoire moderne et contemporaine,* **V,** 1958, 107.

[325]*Ibid.,* p. 108.

Venetian nobility, those great merchants, a feudal corps? In France, the public insisted on the distinctions. An *officier*, ennobled by his office, remained a bourgeois. People deplored the fact that the true nobility, that of gentlemen, was without employ by the state and public office was the prerogative of those who were called ironically the "gentlemen of pen and ink." Bourgeois, that is what one still was, whether *officier* or *commissaire*, even seated on the *fleur de lys* and wearing the purple of office, even rigged out in a title of knight, even baron, even president of Parliament or member of the Royal Council.[326]

Mousnier concludes by denying that either he or Pagès had ever suggested that the bourgeoisie controlled the monarchy. "It is the monarchy which subjected all the classes in reconstructing the state. But in this work it was aided by the bourgeoisie. . . ."[327]

It is important to notice that in this debate a number of issues have gotten scrambled together. One is the nature of the system. Another is the nature of the relations between the classes. A third is the role of the monarchy. We have already explained in a previous chapter why we believe the term "feudalism" with respect to agricultural production at this time (market-oriented cash crops, even if based on coerced or semicoerced labor) is confusing and unhelpful to analysis. To insist that France is primarily involved in a capitalist world-economy at this time does not necessarily entail arguing, however, that the bourgeoise wielded substantial political power. Obviously it did not. In eastern Europe, the aristocrats were capitalist farmers and the indigenous commercial bourgeoisie was on its way to extinction. Nor does it speak necessarily to the particular role the monarchy played in France as opposed to other states in this world-economy. J. H. M. Salmon observes that "like the debate over the gentry and aristocracy in England, the controversy [concerning early seventeenth-century France] is concerned with the character of early modern society and government."[328] Precisely!

Mousnier is probably more right than Porchnev in seeing the monarchy as an institution which, far from clearly dominating the situation, was struggling to assert its political preeminence, even in France. But Porchnev is more right than Mousnier in seeing that one of the developments that most clearly distinguishes France from England is the comparative political

---

[326]*Ibid.*, p. 110. Corrado Vivanti responds to Mousnier: "Besides when Mousnier, seeking to show the extreme consequences and abuses of such terminology, asks: 'would we call the Venetian nobility, those great merchants, a feudal corps?,' by analogy there jumps to mind the famous lines of verse: 'You who are a king in Sardinia and but a bourgeois in Pisa.' ['voi che re siete in Sardegna/ed in Pisa cittadini'] and one is led at the very least to reply that, in effect, the Venetian patriciate also engaged in the takeover of feudal domains in the Eastern [i.e. Byzantine, later Ottoman] Empire and in the Terraferma." *Rivista storica italiana,* **LXXVI**, p. 969.

[327]Mousnier, *Revue d'histoire moderne et contemporaine,* **V,** p. 110.

[328]J. H. M. Salmon, "Venality of Office and Popular Sedition in Seventeenth Century France," *Past & Present,* No. 37, July 1967, 43. Almost the same language is used by Minna Prestwick in a review of Porchnev's book and of one by Robert Mandrou: "Thus what began as a controversy on the nature of the risings in seventeenth century France has moved on into a debate about the structure of society and the character of government. . . ." *English Historical Review,* **CCCXX,** July 1966, 572.

success in France of the old aristocracy whose short-run interests were not conducive to the long-run ability of France maximally to profit from the division of labor in the world-economy.

Let us now turn to the closing "crisis" of the "long" sixteenth century and see exactly what impact this had on the French political arena. We start with the fact that the fall of prices in France in the period 1600–1610 was in fact economically favorable to France and its bourgeoisie.[329] Even Porchnev admits that it would be too much to argue that industrial capitalists were of no significance in France. He accepts the fact that "the evolution of capitalism continued on its path, but at a slower pace."[330]

The problem was in large part in foreign trade, the importance of which to national economies we argued previously when discussing England's reaction to the commercial crisis. Although France between 1600–1610 had somewhat recouped the losses occasioned by the disruptions of the religious wars, another great decline set in after 1610, this time largely the consequence of Dutch and to some extent English competition. And what made the Dutch and even the English able to outprice the French in this period was that, at a moment of a contracting world market, the accumulated edge of industrial capital and technology of the prior 50–60 years was critical:

> France lagged behind her competitors in respect of all the important indices. The division of labour in French manufactories was at a lower level; the shortage of skilled workers did not allow the entrepreneurs to establish an adequate hierarchy of wage-levels. State subsidies, which were absolutely necessary at that time, were casual and sporadic, and small in amount, while accumulation of money was not on a large enough scale; France was excluded from that direct plundering of colonies which nourished primitive accumulation in Holland and Spain, and industry in England as well.
>
> The consequences of this was that French industrial products were comparatively expensive. As a result, the French commercial and industrial bourgeoisie was unable to compete successfully with the Dutch and the English in its own home market, and to some extent also in foreign markets. It was obliged to use its capital in other ways. . . . French shipbuilding and navigation, and therefore also French trans-oceanic trade, was behind English and Dutch, technically and economically. . . .
>
> For all these reasons, the French bourgeoisie was very interested indeed in increased protection, and the government of France endeavored to meet its needs in this respect.[331]

[329]"The low prices did not affect industry adversely. In France, for instance, the first decade of the seventeenth century was a period of boom in manufacture, craft production and agriculture, a period in which the State debt was reduced, the State budget was balanced, and so on. The profits of merchants and manufacturers increased, and they succeeded in becoming considerably richer in these years." Lublinskaya, *French Absolutism*, p. 13.

[330]Porchnev, *Les soulèvements populaires*, p. 560.

[331]Lublinskaya, *French Absolutism*, pp. 144–145. Zeller points out that the whole system of *manufactures royales* which flourished in sixteenth century France, especially under Henry IV, was based on the desire to prevent precious metals from leaving the country. Thus, the king encouraged the establishment of *luxury* industries, in order to avoid importing them. *Essays in French Economic History*, pp. 130–131.

The consequences were serious in the contractions

This then fitted France into the world-economy at a middle layer. While the French were able to exploit to some extent Spain and Germany, the English and Dutch could exploit the French market as well as that of Spain.[332]

The relative strength of the French state machinery compared to England and the United Provinces did not necessarily serve it well in regard to this dilemma. Had the French monarchs of the time been unreservedly committed to the development of industry and the interests of the bourgeoisie, no doubt France might have overtaken the after all not so great lead that the other two countries had. But the French monarchs were ambivalent. Their intrusion was not always conducive to maximizing national commercial interest in the world-economy. Indeed, Nef attributes one of England's secrets of success not to a difference of royal intent but to the fact that the French were more efficient in their interference with bourgeois enterprise.[333] Similarly, Nef argues, England's comparative isolation from European wars in this period meant less emphasis on the "habits of obedience of the royal authority"[334] than in France. The ability of the French monarch to tax combined with the ability of the nobility to be exempted from taxation meant a heavier burden not only on the populace, but on the bourgeoisie as well.

Finally, we must not miss the link between achieved position in the world-economy as of say 1610 and future position. The French difficulties in competing with the Dutch and the English in their home markets encouraged them to concentrate in the production of those goods in which they had some historical edge and a relatively larger home market than other

of the early seventeenth century. "[T]he deflation was particularly difficult for the French economy. The products that France exported did not provide striking profit margins. Its exports rested mainly on the differences between French and Spanish prices. From the day the influx of precious metals slowed down, that difference shrank.

"From another viewpoint, the deflationary period was marked by a notable attempt at economic rationalization in countries that had resolutely set out in the direction of capitalistic production: the United Provinces and England. Capitalistic production meant an attempt to take advantage of the accumulation of money to maximize profits in a market with adequate monetary means.

"It is easy to understand, in comparison, why French manufacturing efforts, from Henry IV to Louis XIV, were but a series of more or less successful attempts to develop luxury industries aimed at limiting imports. In spite of all, the country as a whole remained in that state of monetary poverty observed by Desmarets but which Colbert, as early as 1670, had recognized when he admitted to the king 'the general difficulty' experienced by the farmers and receivers-general of taxes in 'drawing money from the provinces' and when he concluded that there was even less of it 'in public commerce.'" Jean Meuvret, "Monetary Circulation and the Economic Utilization of Money in 16th- and 17-Century France," in Rondo Cameron, ed., *Essays in French Economic History* (Homewood, Illinois: Irwin, Inc., 1970), 148–149.

[332]See Lublinskaya, *French Absolutism*, p. 328.

[333]"But the great difference between ⌊France and England⌋ was not in the nature of the [industrial] laws; it was in their enforcement. In France the officials were so vigorous about enforcing the laws that craftsmen sometimes tried to massacre them for their zeal. In England the officials were so lax that workmen sometimes struck in an effort to remind them of their duty.... [M]ost of the regulations were of a kind that interfered with the progress of capitalist industrial enterprise...." Nef, *Industry and Government*, p.56.

[334]*Ibid.*, p. 98.

European countries—luxury products, especially silks.[335] But the cheaper goods for the wider markets would in the long run provide a surer industrial base.

The Thirty Years' War placed great pressures on the French. As the military expenses rose and the armies expanded, so did the size of the state bureaucracy and, as cause and consequence, the degree of taxation, both directly by the state and de facto in addition by means of the depredations of the troops in the countryside.[336] The impact of war on the price of Baltic grain and hence on food prices in general we have already mentioned. This was all considerably aggravated by the great epidemics that raged between 1628 and 1633, and especially in 1630–1631. Whether poor harvests led to the spread of disease, or disease led to a grain shortage, the two occurred together and hit France badly.[337]

Given this analysis, it is easy to see why peasant uprisings should have been so extensive in France at this time. Not only were state exactions of the peasantry rising but the nobility was having difficulty getting its rents and dues from the peasants because of their economic squeeze.[338] No doubt this meant in many instances that the nobles and the peasants of an area were simultaneously upset with the monarchy, and that to some extent "the sense of loyalty and mutual obligation [between seignior and peasant] did persist"[339] in early seventeenth-century France, but it would be an error to push this idea too far, as some are inclined to do. For surely it is not only present-day analysts but peasants of the time who could perceive that, after the Wars of Religion, the seignior, as Salmon puts it, "whether of the old *noblesse* or the new, was less a companion in peasant misery than its partial cause."[340] It was after all precisely the

[335]See Sella, *Fontana Economic History of Europe*, II, p. 26.

[336]Both Porchnev and Mousnier agree. See Porchnev, *Les soulèvements populaires*, pp. 458–463. See Roland Mousnier, *Peasant Uprisings in Seventeenth-Century France, Russia, and China* (New York: Harper, 1970), 306–311.

"The war, coinciding as it did with the long years of economic depression, made demands on the financial resources and administrative machinery of these states [of western and northern Europe] which forced their governments both to extend their administrative competence and to increase taxation. But while these two policies were logically complementary, they proved to be politically incompatible. The bureaucratic machinery for the extension of royal power either did not exist at all, or where it did, was inefficient and ill-controlled. The greater the financial pressure, the more central governments were thrown back on the voluntary cooperation of the privileged classes and corporations. . . .

"In theory the French monarchy was absolute. Its legislative and executive authority and its almost unfettered powers of taxation were generally accepted throughout the country. In practice, however, the monarchy was limited by the virtually untouchable immunities of classes, corporations, and individuals, and by the lack of effective central control over the large and heterogeneous bodies of royal officials. As everywhere else, the production of war demanded both greater centralization and made it more difficult to carry this out." H. G. Koenigsberger, *The Hapsburgs and Europe*, pp. 279–280.

[337]See J. Meuvret, *Population in History*, esp. 511–512. "In France the tax burden went from 43 to 80 million pounds from 1623 to 1640. The price of wheat, however, went down markedly beginning in the period 1638–40. This conjunction of fiscal increase and economic regression explains the great revolts of the end of Richelieu's ministry." Ardant, *Impôt*, II, p. 754.

[338]See Porchnev, *Les soulèvements populaires*, p. 119.

[339]Elizabeth S. Teall, "The Seigneur of Renaissance France," *Journal of Modern History*, XXXVII, 2, June 1965, 150.

[340]Salmon, *Past & Present*, No. 37, p. 43.

political doing of the nobility that accounts for the slow progress of economic development.[341] At the same time, the partial industrialization of France ensured that such discontent spread from rural to urban areas, the two being linked by the growing numbers of persons, a sort of lumpenproletariat without fixed employment, who moved back and forth and whose margin of existence was too small to endure much aggravation of crisis.[342]

Robert Mandrou contributes to this debate by asking us to consider the popular uprisings of 1623–1648 in the context of the ongoing history of France which saw such uprisings both earlier and later. He reminds us that the various taxes "must be seen as the signs of a greatly deteriorated economic situation and not simply as the only or most immediate cause of the revolts."[343] Mandrou then urges us back to a most fruitful route. He asks us to be:

> attentive to localizations, to cartography: the West, Normandy, Guyenne, the Center (Marché, Berry, Bourbonnais), this is the area most often affected, the most stimulated by these chain-reactions of troubles. May we see in this a consequence of the greater participation of these provinces that face the break in the rise of the "long 16th-century": the ebb of the years 1620-1680 leading to a more evident depression here than in the areas that are more continental, more undeveloped (*fruste*)? But are not these zones of rural and urban agitation of the 17th century also the provinces in which the religious wars were the most ardent in the preceding century?[344]

This is indeed a precious clue and one that fits very well into our overall hypothesis, furthermore one on which both Mousnier and Porchnev agree. Mousnier says:

> The study of each uprising cannot be separated from research on the local economies and social structures. Why did the rural uprisings occur principally in the West, the Center, and the Southwest? Would it not be possible to classify towns according to the degree of development of capitalism therein and to examine whether it does not correlate with some constants in the revolts?[345]

Porchnev notes that the uprisings of 1623–1648 were preceded by three series in the sixteenth century. The first two were those of 1520–1550,

---

[341]"France remained a land of poor peasants overlaid by a class of rentier lords; she remained a poor and poorly developed country relying on traditional economic methods. The trends which began in the period of peace before the outbreak of the religious wars did not mature, whereas in England they underwent a straightforward development." Friedrich Lütge, "Economic Change: Agriculture," *New Cambridge Modern History*, **II**: G. B. Elton, ed., *The Reformation 1520–1559* (London and New York: Cambridge Univ. Press, 1958), p. 47.

[342]See Porchnev, *Les soulèvements populaires*, pp. 268–275. Porchnev borrows the term "plebeians"

from Engel's *Peasant War in Germany* to describe these townsmen. He says: "Plebeians do not yet constitute the pre-proletariat, but a disparate mass, which has roots in different groups of feudal society, and which, little by little, is fusing together to become a true unity [p. 269]."

[343]Robert Mandrou, "Les soulèvements populaires et la société française du XVIIe siècle,' *Annales E.S.C.*, **XIV**, 4, oct.-déc. 1959, 760.

[344]*Ibid.*, p. 761.

[345]Mousnier, *Revue d'histoire moderne et contemporaine*, **V**, p. 112.

linked to the Reformation, and those of 1570–1590, during which the popular movements "placed their hopes in the Catholic League of which they declared themselves to be partisans." Then, from 1590–1600, there was a last wave which had now become non-religious in format.[346] Indeed, Porchnev argues further that the popular disgust with the religious wars led to the desanctification of authority, which in turn accounts for the great need felt to reassert state authority in the early seventeenth century.[347]

This argument of Porchnev raises once again some questions about the meaning of religious movements and affiliations in early modern Europe, their links to the assertion of national entities and conversely to religious centrifugal forces. We have earlier spoken of Koenigsberger's treatment of the Huguenots as a French national revolutionary movement.[348] It is certainly within the realm of reasonable speculation that the Huguenots might have consolidated in the south and west of France in a manner parallel to the consolidation of the Calvinists in the north of the Netherlands, which could have resulted in a partition as in the Netherlands. This was certainly a fear at the time.[349] Within the framework of such a perspective, it is not surprising that the Huguenots at one point called upon Catholic Spain for aid. The liquidation of the Huguenots was then part and parcel of the drive to maintain the integrity of France as a state,[350] and Mousnier points out the role that the venality of office played after 1620 in buying off the Calvinist cadres.[351]

That the regionalism was more fundamental than the religious schism is clearly indicated in the way in which southern France, the Occitania of old, switched from being a Huguenot stronghold. Henri Espieux speaks of the Reformation finding its strongholds "both in Occitania and in the fringes of the ancient Roman Gaul of the 6th century, while Catholicism is essentially northern. . . ."[352] But, he notes, when Henry of Navarre

[346]"Towards the end of the 16th century, convinced of the uselessness of the banners of the Reformation and Catholicism to defend their interests, the popular masses rejectred any religious cover for their class struggle, after having undergone all the various political and confessional disillusionments. It is in part for this reason that, at the end of the 16th century, when the French popular masses spoke simply and frankly in terms of the language of class that the French feudal classes hastened to 'put an end to the internecine religious wars,' and, forgetting their quarrel, rallied to the monarchy of Henry IV." Porchnev, *Les soulèvements populaires,* p. 47. See also pp. 280–281.

[347]See *ibid.,* pp. 572–573.

[348]See Koenigsberger, *Journal of Modern History,* **XXVII,** pp. 338–340.

[349]See Lublinskaya, *French Absolutism,* p. 166.

[350]Georges Duby and Robert Mandrou speak of "the Catholics who are defending the political unity of the kingdom." *Histoire de la civilisation française,*

Vol. I: *Le Moyen Age et le XVIe siècle* (Paris: Lib. Armand Colin, 1958), 341. See Victor-L. Tapié "[T]he France of the Regency and the first years of Louis XIII . . . was a prey. . . . Several provinces of France remained the object of territorial contestation. . . .

"[A]t that time, no state was strong enough or rich enough to create around itself a shield (*concours*) of peace and economic progress, but a resolute State could safeguard the conditions of its territorial independence and permit 'its natural resources the possibility of bearing their own fruition. Richelieu's merit was in seeing this, and that of Louis XIII was to understand that his minister served him well." *La France de Louis XIII et de Richelieu* (Paris: Flammarion, 1952), 524–526.

[351]See Mousnier, *Vénalité,* pp. 601–602.

[352]Henri Espeiux. *Histoire de l'Occitanie* (Nîmes: Le Centre Culturel Occitan. Collection Cap-e-Cap, 1970), 155.

becomes king "to the detriment of the Occitan cause," then "by a singular turnabout, Occitania became sympathetic to the League *(ligeuse)*—the only way remaining to it to pursue its difference. . . ."[353] Finally, Espieux argues, the Occitans embraced Jansenism in the same "non-conformist spirit," a cause that "contributed to the maintenance of their rebellious attitude *(humeur frondeuse)*."[354] Espieux sees this rebelliousness as Occitania's method of resisting the integration into France imposed upon it in the sixteenth century, achieved and reinforced by the fiscal burdens it was made to bear, and made more unpalatable still by the economic decline of Marseilles and Bordeaux in the "second" sixteenth century, not only with regard to Paris, but even in relation to Barcelona and Genoa—once again layers within layers.[355]

Porchnev's description of the uprising in Normandy in 1639 records similar themes. As he traces the story, peasants in Normandy had a heavier seigniorial burden in the fourteenth and fifteenth centuries than elsewhere in France. Because of this fact as well as the destructions of the Hundred Years' War, peasants fled, thus creating an acute labor shortage, which led to the relatively rapid decline of perpetual leases in favor of term leases more favorable to the peasantry. The price revolution, and France's emerging role in the world-economy, led to a setback for the peasant proprietors—higher rents, smaller plots, the partial return to a natural economy, in short, a brake on capitalist development.[356] At a time when the English yeoman farmer was benefiting from the enclosures of arable land, his Norman equivalent was losing out. As for the bourgeoisie, Porchnev points to the division between its two segments: the magistrates, tied to local interests, and hence playing with rebellion; and the financiers, firmly tied to the state and hence bent on sustaining the local aristocracy.[357] The rebellion can be seen as discontent with the politics of the center which was depriving the Norman peasant proprietor (and local bourgeois) of the benefits of fuller participation in the new world-economy.

In the west as in Occitania, the monarchy was being viewed as pursuing a French "national" perspective that was economically regressive. In the name of the traditional, the outer provinces were demanding more not less economic progress.[358] It was no accident then that the Normandy uprising of 1639 was followed by uprisings in Provence, Bretagne, Languedoc, and Poitou.[359] Nor was it an accident that the immediate background of the Normandy uprising was the monarch's unwillingness to relieve the tax burden of Normandy in the wake of the economic difficulties following

[353]*Ibid.,* p. 159.
[354]*Ibid.,* p. 161.
[355]See *ibid.,* pp. 146–154.
[356]See Porchnev, *Les soulèvements populaires,* pp. 402–403, 418–419.
[357]See *ibid.,* p. 578.

[358]A 20th-century example of this phenomenon is described by Jeanne Favret in "Le traditionalisme par excès de modernité," *European Journal of Sociology,* **VIII,** 1, 1967, 71–93.
[359]See Porchnev, *Les soulèvements populaires,* p. 470.

upon the epidemic of 1632–1633 because: "His Majesty being burdened by too heavy expenses cannot relieve his people as he would wish."[360] This he could not do, because the money was being spent on creating the French national entity.

Suppose—great historical game—that France had been a differently shaped geographical entity, covering only the north and west of France with Rouen as the capital. Suppose Occitania had been a separate state from the thirteenth century on. Might not such a truncated France have found that the national interests of the central state machinery and the commercial interests of the bourgeoisie were somewhat more in harmony one with the other? Might not such a France, seemingly weaker, have been able to do what England did—respond to the emerging world-economy by creating an industrial base? Perhaps.

But such a France did not exist. The France that did exist was, as we said, neither fish nor fowl, and rent by religio-regional strife. The pressure toward a one-religion state was as powerful in sixteenth-century Europe as the pressure toward a one-party state in twentieth-century Africa, and for the same reason, the need to combat centrifugal forces. But the price was heavy. For France the price was coming to terms with the aristocracy largely on its terms—the *"réaction seigneuriale,"* the *"féodalisation"* of the bourgeoisie. There was to be no civil war in the seventeenth century, only the *Fronde.* The bourgeois revolution would come in 1789, at another epoch, for another purpose, and in some ways too late. In the seventeenth century, the French administrative bourgeoisie, the *noblesse de robe,* was constrained to remember that it could not afford the luxury of pursuing its narrow interests too far since, if it did, the integrity of the state and hence the economic foundation of this administrative bourgeoisie was threatened.

The differing roles (roles, not intents) of the monarchies in England and France was in the end a critical factor. One way to look at this is to define the political struggle as one in which the monarchies of the era were trying to erode the privileges of all non-state groups and to observe, as Cooper does, that by and large they succeeded better against the towns (and hence segments of the bourgeoisie) than against the landed classes.[361] Braudel speaks of the towns being "held in check" or "disciplined" by the monarchies.[362] In this view, the landed classes were seeking to use the state to aid them to stay out in front in the swift currents of economic expansion. In this perspective, the Frondeurs, though they lost, won, whereas the English aristocracy, though there was a Restoration, lost. In the end, Braudel argues, English primacy in the world would be that of London, "which constructed England to its requirements *(à sa guise)* after the peaceful revolution of 1688."[363]

[360]*Ibid.*, p. 425.

[361]J. P. Cooper, "General Introduction," *New Cambridge Modern History,* **IV**: J. P. Cooper, ed., *The Decline of Spain and the Thirty Years' War.*

1609–48/59 (London and New York: Cambridge Univ. Press, 1970) 15.

[362]Braudel, *Civilisation matérielle,* p. 399.

[363]*Ibid.*, p. 396.

In the vacillation between the demands of the bourgeoisie and the aristocracy, the monarchies of both England and France moved ever closer to the demands of the aristocracy. The difference was that in England the interests of the commercial bourgeoisie were linked with a strong center, whereas in France to some extent they were linked to the national periphery. This difference was a consequence of geographical considerations within the framework of the European world-economy.

One consequence was that, in order to hold an intrinsically more rambunctious bourgeoisie in check, the French monarchy had both to strengthen itself and to buy them off by the venality of office, which in turn diverted them from industrial investment. In England, the aristocracy to survive had to learn the ways of and partially fuse with the bourgeoisie. In France, the pressure was on the bourgeoisie to survive. In France and England, the center won out against the periphery. But in England, this meant furthering the cause of the national bourgeoisie, whereas in France it was a setback for the bourgeoisie.

The English Civil War occurred at the last possible moment. The resurgence of the landed classes in the next 150 years was to be great everywhere, even in England. But there at least the bourgeoisie had won *droit de cité*. And the landed classes meant less the aristocracy and more the gentry who were in the end *bons bourgeois*. In France, the bourgeoisie was far too weak in the seventeenth century to produce a Cromwell. It would not be until 1789 that they would find their interests consonant with those of the state as state. By then, the world-economy had evolved and it would be too late for France to achieve primacy within it.

Nº 4. INT JORNAEL VAN C. ducß. FOLY. 31.

6

THE EUROPEAN WORLD-ECONOMY: PERIPHERY VERSUS EXTERNAL ARENA

Figure 7: "The (Dutch) fleet off Mozambique, and the capture of a (Portuguese) carrack near Goa," an illustration from the "Journal of Observations of an East Indian Voyage by Cornelis Claeszoon of Purmerent, steersman of the ship Bantam, which sailed in the service of the mighty Lords of the United Company," published in 1651.

The boundaries of an entity defined in political terms are relatively easy to ascertain. If we want to know the territory covered by the Chinese empire in the year 1600, we need to consult some archives which tell us of the juridical claims as of that date. To be sure, there will always be marginal regions, where sovereignty is contested by two rival state structures, or one in which the imperial authority can scarcely be perceived as existing de facto which may lead us to consider the claim to be juridical fiction. But the criteria are fairly straightforward: The combination of asserted authority with some measure (however gross) of effective authority (however thin) will generally give us what we need.

But what shall we say of the boundaries of a social system not defined in political terms, of a "world-economy" such as we have been dealing with here. By saying that in the sixteenth century there was a *European* world-economy, we indicate that the boundaries are less than the earth as a whole. But how much less? We cannot simply include in it any part of the world with which "Europe" traded. In 1600 Portugal traded with the central African kingdom of Monomotapa as well as with Japan. Yet it would be prima facie hard to argue that either Monomotapa or Japan were part of the European world-economy at that time. And yet we argue that Brazil (or at least areas of the coast of Brazil) and the Azores were part of the European world-economy. There was a transit trade across Russia between western Europe and Persia.[1] Yet we argue that Persia was certainly outside this world-economy and so even was Russia. Russia outside, but Poland inside. Hungary inside, but the Ottoman Empire outside. On what basis are these distinctions determined?

It is not a question of the simple volume of trade or its composition. Celso Furtado says:

> Apart from gold and silver, little that could be produced in the Americas during the first century of colonization was marketable in Europe. Unlike the East Indies, which produced articles of great value per unit of weight, such as spices, silks and muslins, the Americas produced nothing that could become the basis of a lucrative trade.[2]

Nonetheless, the Americas inside, and the East Indies outside, or at least so we contend.

We shall denote this distinction as one between the periphery of a world-economy and its external arena. The periphery of a world-economy is

[1]For a summary of this trade, see H. Kellenbenz, "Landverkehr, Fluss- und Seeschiffahrt im Europäischen Handel," in *Les grandes voies maritimes dans le monde, XVe-XIXe siècles*, VII Colloque, Commission Internationale d'Histoire Maritime (Paris: S.E.V.P.E.N., 1965), 132-137.

[2]Celso Furtado, *Economic Development of Latin America*,**II**.

that geographical sector of it wherein production is primarily of lower-ranking goods (that is, goods whose labor is less well rewarded) but which is an integral part of the overall system of the division of labor, because the commodities involved are essential for daily use. The external arena of a world-economy consists of those other world-systems with which a given world-economy has some kind of trade relationship, based primarily on the exchange of preciosities, what was sometimes called the "rich trades." We shall try to demonstrate this distinction primarily by analyzing the differences between Russia and various parts of eastern Europe and those between the Indian Ocean area and Hispanic America *in the sixteenth century*.

At first glance, both Russia and eastern Europe seem to have great similarities. They both seem to experience the rise of large domains engaged in cash-crop production and based on coerced labor. Indeed, as Braudel points out, this occurs also in the Ottoman Empire at this time.[3] In both areas, the coercion of the peasants is primarily the result of actions by the state authorities. In both areas, the landlord class seems to emerge from this era greatly strengthened and the bourgeoisie weakened. Furthermore, both areas seem to be affected by the Price Revolution and to conform to its general parameters with reasonable faithfulness. Yet a closer look will reveal some differences.[4]

We shall treat the differences between Russia's relations with western Europe and eastern Europe's relations with western Europe as coming under three principal headings: (a) a difference in the nature of the trade, (b) a difference in the strength and role of the state machinery, and (c) as a consequence of the two prior points, a difference in the strength and role of the indigenous urban bourgeoisie.

The great prerevolutionary Russian historian, V. O. Kluchevsky, constructed his history of Russia on the assumption that "the principal fundamental factor in Russian history has been migration or colonisation, and

[3]"If the historians speak, for the West between the 16th and 18th centuries, of a 'refeudalization,' . . . an analogous phenomenon takes place in Turkey. . . . The pioneering work of Busch-Zantner pointed out . . . these *tschiftliks*, demesnes created in his opinion as part of a process of improvement and in grain-growing regions. Ömer Lutfi Barkan and his students . . . have observed this growth of modern property to the benefit of the sultans and pashas whom we know to have been involved in the grain 'boom;' . . . they reserved for themselves the sale of wheat to western buyers, which they forbade to the 'people.' We can guess at the extent of the transformation. Turkey is living, as is western Europe, in the era of the price 'revolution' and the agricultural revolution that came as a result, there as elsewhere, of demographic growth." Braudel, *La Méditerranée*, I, p. 537.

[4]The essence of our position was stated by J.H.

Elliott. He recognizes that "several of the features of life in the marchlands of Europe [i.e., eastern Europe] repeated themselves on Russian soil." By this he is referring to the fact that in both areas there developed at this time large demesnes producing for the market with coerced cash-crop labor. Nonetheless, says Elliott: "The serf society of Muscovy, however, remained a world on its own, threatening to its neighbours because of its growing military power, but still economically unrelated to the European world. On the other hand, Poland, Silesia, Brandenburg and Prussia were being inexorably drawn into the orbit of West European life. . . ." *Europe Divided*, p. 47. See George Vernadsky: "Geopolitically speaking, the Russian background is not European but Eurasian. Medieval Russia is not so much Eastern Europe as it is Western Eurasia." "Feudalism in Russia," *Speculum*, **XIV**, p. 306.

. . . all other factors have been more or less inseparably connected therewith."[5] To the extent that this is true, it is a phenomenon of the sixteenth century when, just as the rest of Europe, Russia "entered upon a new era of economic growth. . . ."[6] It is commonly asserted that the conquest of the Volga khanate of Kazan in 1552 followed by that of Astrakhan in 1556 was a turning point.[7] In the following century Russia colonized the forest-steppe zone to the south, along the Don to the Azov Sea and along the Volga to the Caspian. It also pushed a large part of the way across Siberia. At that same time, the Ukrainians (then under Polish rule) advanced along the Dnieper, all of which'would become part of Russia in 1654. The expansion southward and eastward by Russia was an important event in modern world history and it is important to note that the direction of the expansion is a function of the strength of the regimes in the regions surrounding Russia. As George Vernadsky reminds us, it was at "the very time when the Russians were checked and thrown back in the west [that] they started advancing in the east toward Siberia."[8]

Hence, in the case of Russia, Western traders were faced with a country far more immense than Poland or Bohemia or Mecklenburg, and one that was itself clearly an imperial structure. Whereas the external trade of Poland was almost exclusively with western Europe, Russia traded *both* westward and eastward and, as Jerome Blum says, the "Eastern trade was probably of more importance to Russia than her commerce with the West."[9]

It is not only that the trade eastward was larger in volume but that it was of such a nature and volume that it tended to create a world-economy, or as some writers put it, working in a slightly different theoretical framework, a national market. A. G. Mankov points to the crucial role of grain production, a concept with which we are already familiar: "One cannot speak of the effective development of commercial relations within feudal society before the time when cereals become merchandise—which

[5]V. O. Kluchevsky, *A History of Russia*, **I**, (London: Dent, 1911), 2.

[6]Jerome Blum, *Lord and Peasant in Russia from the Ninth to the Nineteenth Century* (Princeton, New Jersey: Princeton Univ. Press, 1961), 120. He adds: "Among the most conspicuous evidences of this were the increases in area and population of the realm. Russia, like the Atlantic states of West Europe, embarked in the sixteenth century upon an ambitious program of colonial expansion. The collapse of Mongol power, and the emergence of the unified Russian state under the leadership of Moscow, offered the opportunity for seemingly limitless territorial acquisition in the vast Eurasian land mass that lay beyond Muscovy's borders."

[7]"The conquest of Kazan was a tremendous military victory and a great political achievement. From the religious point of view, it was understood as a triumph of Christianity over Islam." George Ver-

nadsky, *The Tsardom of Muscovy, 1547–1682*, Vol. V of *A History of Russia* (New Haven, Connecticut: Yale Univ. Press, 1969), Part 1, 58.

"The fall of Kazan suddenly eliminated the barrier of the progression of the Slavs to the East." Roger Portal, *Les Slaves* (Paris: Lib. Armand Colin, 1965), 110.

[8]Vernadsky, *Tsardom*, **V**, 1, p. 175.

[9]Blum, *Lord and Peasant*, p. 128. See M. V. Fechner, *Torgovlya russkogo gosudarstva so stranani voctoka v XVI veke*, who is cited by M. Mollat *et al* as saying that the Russian trade with the East, by river and caravan, was "much more important" than its trade with the West ("always overestimated."). *Relazioni del X Congresso Internationale di Scienze Storiche*, **III**, p. 780. Mollat *et al.* themselves hesitate to take a position on relative volume "without figures."

testifies to a certain level of differentiation between agriculture and crafts
(métiers)."[10] Let us therefore examine the phenomenon of expanding wheat
production, known both in Poland and in Russia in the 15th and 16th
centuries. Poland, as we have already argued, is by the sixteenth century
integrated into the European world-economy, on whose markets wheat is
sold, and for whose markets wheat is grown. As Braudel and Spooner put
it: "The dominating feature of the end of the [sixteenth] century is clearly
the fact that Polish wheat is now absorbed into the general pool of European
prices."[11] This was crucial both for Poland and for the rest of Europe,
for which Poland had become at that time "the greatest exporter of
cereals."[12]

The rise of a Polish wheat-exporting economy meant, as we have seen,
the rise of large domains with coerced cash-crop labor. It meant also the
rise of the political strength of the *nobility,* whose economic interest in
removing obstacles to trade matched that of western European merchants.
Their combined efforts maintained Poland as an open economy.[13] How
dependent the prosperity of the Polish nobility was on this open trade
was clearly illustrated by the economic difficulties provoked by the blockade
of the Vistula by Gustavus Adolphus of Sweden between 1626–1629, who
sought thereby to "cut the nerve" of Poland.[14] The fact that "cereal export
via the Baltic ports had rapidly taken on [in Poland] proportions such
that it dominated the entire economic structure of the country"[15] is used
by Jerzy Topolski then to explain the devastating effects of seventeenth-
century regression in Poland, effects that varied in different parts of Poland

[10]A. G. Mankov, *Le mouvement des prix dans l'état russe au XVIe siècle* (Paris: S.E.V.P.E.N., 1957), 28.

[11]Braudel and Spooner, *Cambridge Economic History of Europe,* **IV,** p. 398.

[12]Stanislas Hoszowski, "L'Europe centrale dans la révolution des prix: XVIe et XVIIe siècles," *Annales E.S.C.,* **XVI,** 3, mai–juin 1961, 446.

[13]"The economic policy of the nobility found however its fullest expression in the famous parliamentary decree of 1565, forbidding Polish merchants to export Polish products and import foreign goods, and officially encouraging foreign merchants to enter Poland. To be sure this law remained a dead letter. Nonetheless it is an eloquent illustration of the tendencies in those days of the Polish nobility in political and economic policy, and, we believe, the tendencies of the nobility of other Baltic countries, with the exception of Sweden. We may consider that what characterizes the attitude of the nobility of that time vis-à-vis the trade and industry of the bourgeoisie was a *sui generis* anti-mercantilism." Marian Malowist, "Über die Frage des Handelspolitik des Adels in den Ostseeländern im 15, und 16. Jahrhundert," *Hansische Geschichtsblätter,* 75Jh., 1957, 39.

[14]"The export of Polish cereals found itself thereupon to be prohibited. Gustavus Adolphus understood perfectly the importance of this deed for the Polish nobility. 'Occupato hoc flumine [the Vistula],' he said to the envoy of Bethlen Gabor, 'praecluso etiam portu Dantiscano et omni maris Baltici aditu prohibito, ipse iam nervus rei gerendae Poloniae incisus est.' He was right. Stopping the export of wheat led to a fall of prices within the country, felt both by the nobility and the peasants, the principal taxpayers of Poland. Raising the taxes became all the more difficult as the expenses of the state rose because of the necessity of paying for the calling up of the troops. It was only due to the efforts of the king and his entourage that Poland could fight, for all of three years and despite financial difficulties, this war which required so much effort." Wladyslaw Czalpinski, "Le problème baltique aux XVIe et XVIIe siècles," *International Congress of Historical Sciences,* Stockholm, 1960. *Rapports,* **IV:** *Histoire moderne* (Göteborg: Almqvist & Wiksell, 1960), 41.

[15]Jerzy Topolski, "La régression économique en Pologne," *Acta poloniae historica,* **VII,** 1962, 46.

according to the degree to which the local economy was export-oriented.[16]

It may be objected that the value of the wheat involved is rather small as a proportion of the total product of the European world-economy, but Boris Porchnev replies that "it is not the quantities of merchandise exported (not too great in point of fact) which ought to be the object of the attention of scholars, but rather the rate of profit which was shared between the merchant middlemen and the landed proprietors exploiting the labor of the serfs."[17] And Stanislaw Hoszowski points out that in the overall inflation of the sixteenth century, not only did Polish prices start to rise even before those of western and central Europe, before the impact of American treasure on prices,[18] but also, within Poland, it was the "landed proprietors who obtain(ed) the maximum benefit of [the rise in prices] while peasants and the townsmen only los(t) by it."[19] The counterpart of this economic squeeze of the peasants was the frequency of peasant revolts.[20]

Let us now compare the role of wheat production in Russia at this time. Let us start with Mankov's assertion about sixteenth-century Russia: "one can speak at this time only of an internal cereals market."[21] That is, although almost no wheat is exported, "there existed already, in the sixteenth-century, a link between local markets, sometimes very far apart from each other."[22] Thus capitalist agriculture emerged at this time, and in similar forms, both in Poland (and other countries of eastern Europe) on the one hand, and Russia on the other. But whereas the former produced for an expanding west European market, in Russia, "seigniors produced for the expanding domestic market."[23] Indeed, in the sixteenth century, "special permission was required of the tsar to ship [grain] out of the country."[24] The specialization of the sixteenth-century European world-economy was being replicated in smaller form within the Russian world-economy. The core of the Russian world-economy was exporting manufactured goods (metal wares, textile products, leather goods, weapons, and armor) in return for luxury goods, cotton cloth, horses, and sheep.[25] In addition, they *re*exported Western

[16]See *ibid.*, pp. 47–48.

[17]Boris Porchnev, "Les rapports politiques de l'Europe Occidentale et de l'Europe Orientale à l'époque des la Guerre des Trente Ans," *XIe Congrès International des Sciences Historiques*, Stockholm, 1960. *Rapports*, **IV**: *Histoire moderne* (Göteborg: Almqvist & Wiksell, 1960), 137.

[18]See Hoszowski, *Annales E.S.C.*, **XVI**, p. 446.

[19]*Ibid.*, p. 453.

[20]See S. Pascu, V. V. Mavrodin, Boris Porchnev, and I. G. Anteleva, "Mouvements paysans dans le centre et le Sudest de l'Europe du XVe au XXe siècles," *XIIe Congrès International des Sciences Historiques, Rapports*, **IV**: *Méthodologie et histoire contemporaine* (Wein: Verlag Ferdinand Berger & Söhne, 1965), 21–35.

[21]Mankov, *Le mouvement des prix.* p. 28.

[22]*Ibid.*, p. 38. See discussion on pp. 38–43.

[23]Blum, *Lord and Peasant,* p. 205.

[24]*Ibid.*, p. 128.

[25]See *ibid.*, 128–129. See R. H. Hilton and R. E. F. Smith: "It should be noted, incidentally, that the development in the sixteenth century of regional trade in a wide range of goods with Iran, Turkey, the Nagai Horde and the Uzbek khanates was particularly important. While Russia has sometimes been regarded as a semi-colonial supplier of raw materials to the West at this time, to the Orient Russia was a supplier of manufactured goods as well as of raw materials." "Introduction" to R. E. F. Smith, *The Enserfment of the Russian Peasantry* (London and New York: Cambridge Univ. Press, 1968), 27.

manufactured goods eastward, "though this activity was apparently not of much significance in the sixteenth century."[26] Russia was feeling the happy effects of being the focal point of an economic community: "Furs, salts, hides, and other wares streamed into the older regions from the colonies, creating new wealth and stimulating commercial and industrial activity."[27]

But what about Russian trade with the West? Did it not parallel Polish trade? We must be careful not to read back into the sixteenth century phenomena of the eighteenth and nineteenth centuries, by which time a separate Russian world-economy had indeed disappeared and Russia had become one more peripheral area of the European world-economy.[28]

It is true, on first glance, that what was happening in the sixteenth century was that "in her trade with the West, Russia exchanged raw materials and semi-finished goods for manufactured wares."[29] Russia exported various raw materials used for naval stores (flax, hemp, grease, wax) plus furs and imported luxury articles and metal goods (including munitions). But in neither direction does it seem the trade was critical. For western Europe, not until the seventeenth century could it be said that Russia was important as a "reservoir of grain and forest products."[30] T. S. Willan sees Russia's chief value for England, the western country with which Russia traded most in the sixteenth century, "as a source of essential materials for the navy." But he adds:

> It is a little difficult to say whether the trade was equally valuable for the Russians. Their equivalent for the naval stores exported to England was perhaps the arms and munitions which the company was alleged to be sending to Russia, especially in the "fifties" and the "sixties."[31]

"Especially in the 'fifties' and the 'sixties' "—we shall return to that observation. A. Attman suggests that the crucial import was not the metal goods but rather silver in form of bullion and of art objects. He offers as verification of this hypothesis the extraordinary accumulation of silver in the churches, monasteries and palaces as well as important finds of metal bars.[32] If one remembers that a major export was that of furs, "then the livery of dignity and wealth,"[33] one of the so-called "rich trades," we can consider the major portion of Russian–Western trade in the sixteenth century to be an exchange of preciosities, a method of consuming surplus rather than produc-

[26]Blum, *Lord and Peasant,* p. 129.

[27]*Ibid.,* p. 122.

[28]"From the time of Ivan the Great at the close of the fifteenth century, we can easily trace the growing connexions of Russia with western Europe . . . . In this respect Peter the Great's reign brings no sudden change. But it remains true that the impression on the minds of people outside—and no doubt also within—Russia was henceforward very different." Geoffrey Barraclough, *History in a Changing World* (Oxford: Blackwell, 1957), 192–193.

[29]Blum, *Lord and Peasant,* p. 128.

[30]Malowist, *Economic History Review,* **XII,** p. 180.

[31]T. S. Willan, "Trade Between England and Russia in the Second Half of the Sixteenth Century," *English Historical Review,* **LXIII,** No. 247, July 1948, 320.

[32]Cited in Mollat *et al., Relazioni del X Congresso Internazionale de Scienze Storiche,* **III,** p. 782.

[33]Parry, *Cambridge Economic History of Europe,* **IV,** p. 167.

ing it, hence dispensable at moments of contraction, and consequently not central to the functioning of the economic system. This is not to say it was unimportant. Middlemen profited by it. No doubt the state obtained some customs revenue from it. No doubt also it reinforced the system of social prestige accumulation. The point however is that if a blockade had occured equivalent to that of Gustavus Adolphus of the Vistula in 1626, the impact on Russia's internal economy would have been far less than on Poland's.

We have been using Poland as our example of a country in the periphery of the European world-economy (as opposed to being in the external arena). But Poland was in many ways an extreme case. Would there be any difference if we looked at other countries in the periphery? The answer is there would be some but it does not seem crucial.

For example, in both Bohemia and Hungary, the "forced labor" of the "serfs" was not always exclusively in the form of the *corveé* but sometimes in the form of "forced wage labor."[34] Josef Válka notes that this intermediate form of labor service in Bohemia is linked with the fact that agricultural production is diversified and directed to an internal market.[35] Josef Petrán similarly points out in various of the smaller territories of central Europe (Bohemia, Silesia, Saxony, Austria), there was less of a tendency for the growth of large estates and he suggests that we are witnessing the birth of specialization not only between agriculture and industry but within agriculture itself, where however "naturally the specialization could not be complete."[36] Malowist points out that agricultural specialization in Denmark parallels that of eastern Europe, for, during the sixteenth century, the Danish and Holstein nobility "developed an economy based on the labour of serfs, as well as on the trade of agricultural and dairy products, and also on the product of their serfs, whose chances of engaging in commerce were limited to a minimum."[37] But he says that this social process of aristocratic appropriation "which can be seen most clearly in Poland, Brandenburg, Pomerania, Mecklenburg and Livonia, showed itself *more feebly* in Denmark."[38]

What we can say about these examples is that they show the texture of the European division of labor to be getting more complex already

---

[34]"[The Czech seigniory in the sixteenth century] utilizes, in fact, not only the *corvée*, but also wage-labor and forced wage-labor. . . . There existed therefore wage-labor. But it is a form of wage-labor heavily overlain with feudal relations: wage-labor on the lord's domain becomes simply one more obligation for the serfs." Josef Válka, "La structure économique de la seigneurie tchèque au XVIe siècle," *Deuxième Conférence Internationale d'Histoire Economique*, **II**: *Middle Ages and Modern Times* (Paris: Mouton, 1965), 214–215.

"Wage-labor was combined with the *corvée*, but always, despite everything, under a feudal regime and by constraint. Thus, the new tendencies of Hungarian agriculture in the 16th century were characterized by the extension of seigniorial domains, at the expense of peasant holdings, by the extension of seigniorial market production, and by the recourse to forms of wage-labor." Zs. S. Pach, *Annales E.S.C.*, **XXI**, p. 1229.

[35]See Válka, *Deuxième Conférence Internationale*, **II**, pp. 212–213.

[36]Josef Petrán, *Deuxième Conférence Internationale d'Histoire Economique*, **II**, p. 222.

[37]Malowist, *Economic History Review*, **XII**, p. 180.

[38]*Ibid.*, p. 188. Italics added.

in the sixteenth century. However, the meaning of a low export ratio for
Bohemia, a small country surrounded by the rest of the European world-
economy and a similar low ratio for Russia, a large empire on the edge
of the European world-economy, must have been quite different. Bohemia's
freedom of political action was ultimately far smaller and hence her
economic dependence ultimately far greater. This is a case where the analyst
must look at absolutes for minima and proportions for maxima.[39] Bohemia
had less give in case of a trade cutoff than Russia. Therefore its economic
activities had to be developed more consciously within the framework of
the needs of the European world-economy.

Let us now return to the remark of Willan about the 1550s and 1560s.
It should be obvious from our exposition thus far that the line between
periphery and external arena is fluid, both in the sense that it is hard
for an analyst to fix it and in the sense that it shifts easily. One way to
look at the history of Russia in this period is to see it as reacting to a
tentative attempt of Europe to include it within the world-economy. This
attempt failed then because Europe's technology and economy was not
yet sufficiently strong. Eventually, in a later era, it would succeed. Robert
Reynolds states this process somewhat ethnocentrically:

> As far as we can tell, it was the English who opened a gateway and detonated
> Russian expansion. . . . England's opening of the [northern] route [in 1553] gave
> Russia a tremendous market for furs, which stimulated the Cossacks on the frontier
> and the Stroganovs with their capital and managerial talent to push as fast as pos-
> sible to the eastward and the northward. Each year they took up new sections for
> the fur trade, exactly as the French and English furtraders, and then the Americans,
> pushed farther and farther to the west in North America. With the great market
> for fur, the possibility was opened to buy fine textiles, metal goods, and other
> things from western Europe.[40]

How did this English thrust into the Russian world fit in with the latter's
internal political developments? It is to this picture we must now turn,
to see how Russia reacted to "bringing it into Europe" and how this reaction
further differentiated Russia from eastern Europe. Malowist notes that
the grain grown in central Russia was sold in the north and northeast of
European Russia and in Siberia.[41] Thus the development of Russian wheat
production "had facilitated the colonization and conquest" of its own very
rich territories of the north and east which in turn "furnished immense
riches, first of all for the treasure of the Czars, and later, for the merchants."[42]

To appreciate the role of the Russian state, we should recapitulate what
we argued in the previous chapter about the role of the state in the core

[39]See for example Malowist: "The great importance of foreign manufactures did not hinder the
development of Russian industry in the same way
as in the Baltic countries, because of the immense
area of the country, even though, at first, Russian
industry had been little developed." *Economic History
Review*, **XII**, p. 189.

[40]Reynolds, *Europe Emerges*, pp. 450, 453.

[41]See Malowist, *Past & Present*, No. 13, pp. 35–36.

[42]Malowist, *Economic History Review*, **XII**, p. 189.

states of western Europe, proceed to look at the role of the state in the peripheral states of eastern Europe, and then compare both with the role of the state in Russia. We presented the absolute monarchy as a structure in which the king and his entourage aspired to political primacy with the direct assistance of a patrimonial and venal bureaucracy and mercenary standing armies. On the one hand, the king sought the assistance of favored segments of the urban commercial bourgeoisie who supplied him with money and some political counterweight to the centrifugal tendencies of the old nobility. On the other hand, the king was the pinnacle of the system of traditional social status and was ultimately the protector of the nobility against the corrosive effects of the developing capitalist system.[43]

In terms therefore of the two social strata, the old nobility and the commercial urban bourgeoisie, the absolute monarchy was for each a lesser evil, and its strength grew on the basis of their lack of alternatives. For it served them both well by creating the possibility of enabling the country as an entity to get a disproportionate share of the surplus product of the entire European world-economy. In the sixteenth century, we can speak at most of state "fiscalism" or "precocious mercantilism." From about 1650 on, the Western states engaged in a full-scale mercantilist policy designed to strengthen their relative position in the world-economy even further.

While the sixteenth century was a period of the rise of state power in western Europe, it was an era of decline for state power in eastern Europe, both cause and consequence of the latter's economic position. This is a further instance of the cumulative impact of social changes. As the landed aristocracy of Poland grew stronger through its profitable role in international trade and the indigenous bourgeoisie grew weak, the tax base of the state frittered away which meant that the king could not afford to maintain an adequate army.[44] The magnates then needed to assure

---

[43]Joseph A. Schumpeter catches the inner contradictions of the absolute monarchy very acutely: "The king, the court, the army, the church and the bureaucracy lived to an increasing extent on revenue created by the capitalist process, even purely feudal sources of income being swelled in consequence of contemporaneous capitalist developments. To an increasing extent also, domestic and foreign policies and institutional changes were shaped to suit and propel that development. *As far as that goes,* the feudal elements in the structure of the so-called absolute monarchy come in only under the heading of atavisms which in fact is the diagnosis one would adopt at first sight.

"Looking more closely, however, we realize that those elements meant more than that. The steel frame of that structure still consisted of the human material of feudal society and this material still behaved according to precapitalist patterns. It filled the offices of state, officered the army, devised policies—it functioned as a *classe dirigente* and,

though taking account of bourgeois interests, it took care to distance itself from the bourgeoisie. The centerpiece, the king, was king by the grace of God, and the root of his position was feudal. . . , however much he availed himself of the economic possibilities offered by capitalism. All this was more than atavism. It was an active symbiosis of two social strata, one of which no doubt supported the other economically but was in turn supported by the other politically." *Capitalism, Socialism and Democracy* (London: Allen & Unwin, 1943), 136.

[44]"What [Poland] lacked in the sixteenth century was not a lively spirit, of which there was much evidence, but a large and active monetary economy. If the Polish state was so profoundly fragile, and the king existed 'more to be repressive than to exercise power,' the explanation is to be found in the social and political order of the 'Republic,' as well as in the impossibility of accumulating significant resources in silver and hence of having a modern army." Braudel, *La Méditerranée,* I, p. 184.

their own protection, but this in turn made for the possibility of private wars.⁴⁵ Some of these private armies equalled in size that of the Crown.⁴⁶ The king became an elected king, and the central legislature, the *Seym,* began to turn over much of its authority to local diets.

From this point on, disintegration of the state machinery proceeded apace. Janusz Tazbir shows how one step led to the next:

> From 1613 decisions concerning taxation were, as a rule, transferred to the local diets. This decentralization of the fiscal system led to a situation in which some districts had to pay bigger taxes than others. The chaos was further deepened when the local diets were entrusted with the voting of taxes even for the defense of the State (1640). All this was bound to result in a decline of the revenues of the treasury which, in turn, rendered payments to the army virtually impossible.
>
> The soldiers, who [were] owed arrears of pay, organized military leagues or confederations which ravaged the country constituting dangerous centres of political ferment.⁴⁷

In western Europe, royal property grew at the expense of church property, even in Catholic Spain, but not in Poland. During the first impact of the Reformation some parochial Church lands were confiscated by Protestant gentry, but even then the bulk of major Church property was untouched. Then the Counter-Reformation triumphed for reasons we have already elucidated. However because of the very weakness of the State, royal property declined.⁴⁸

Similar processes were occurring elsewhere in eastern Europe. Most people today associate the state of Prussia with two phenomena: the strong state and a strong Junker class. The sixteenth century precisely saw the rise of a strong Junker class in the areas that would later constitute Prussia. But it was also a century in which the state grew weaker, not stronger.

For one thing, the system of estates based on tiny cottage holdings and

⁴⁵"The reformating [sic!] aspirations of the Court induced the magnates to seek a further weakening of the administration. The gradual restriction of the royal prerogative was coupled with the growth of the privileges of the great nobles, especially the magnates of the eastern marches, who had at their disposal their own armed forces, great wealth and numerous clients among the dependent local gentry. Thus, the individual magnates had everything that the reigning monarch was refused—abundant financial resources, a strong army and the support of a political party. . . . Already at the beginning of the seventeenth century, individual magnates' families were engaged in private wars against one another, devastating the country and devouring its resources." Janusz Tazbir, *History of Poland,* p. 209.
⁴⁶See *ibid.,* p. 224.
⁴⁷*Ibid.,* p. 225.

⁴⁸"In marked contrast to ecclesiastical, particularly monastic estates, royal property in the modern period continued to shrink. The Statute of King Alexander (1504) had restricted the royal right to give, sell, or mortgage royal domains, but chronic scarcity of money compelled his successor, Sigismund I (1506-1548), to continue the policy of his brother although on a somewhat smaller scale. Royal estates were the chief security of towns. In Western Europe, where money was lent mostly by merchants and bankers, creditors used to take over as security royal revenue—customs or taxes. In Poland, however, noble creditors as well as a few rich merchants-bankers made the most of the opportunity to secure royal estates." Antoni Maczak, "The Social Distribution of Landed Property in Poland from the Sixteenth to the Eighteenth Centuries," *Third International Conference of Economic History* (Paris: Mouton, 1968), I, 456–457.

corvée[49] which grew up in east Elbia at this time and was called *Gutsherrschaft,* replacing the older feudal form called *Gutswirtschaft,* differed from the older form most markedly, as the very name would indicate, in the internal system of authority. In the new system, as Friedrich Lütge puts it, "the estate [was] something like a small political unit within the State: its inhabitants [were] only indirectly subjects of the territorial prince."[50] Second, as in Poland, the Hohenzollerns were using their crown estates and even the former church lands[51] as security for loans, a process which steadily undermined their strength. These measures, taken *in extremis* by the Crown, were extremely beneficial to the Junker class.[52]

This process of decline of princely power in Germany continued throughout the sixteenth century and reached a low point in 1648 with the Peace of Westphalia, which concluded the Thirty Years' War, a peace which A. J. P. Taylor argues was "not the cause of German decline and weakness, but rather the result. . . ." Although peace was "imposed" by foreign

[49]"Gutsherrschaft involved the gradual elimination of the old manorial tenantry and the creation of numerous tiny cottage-holdings. . . ." Helleiner, *Cambridge Economic History of Europe,* **IV,** p. 26.

[50]Lütge, *New Cambridge Modern History,* **II,** p. 36. Similar language is used by J. Siemenski about Poland: "In short [in the sixteenth century] the large landed estates became petty States ruled by their lords and squires who decided on the levies imposed on the peasantry (in the form of services and use of monopolies) and on the scope of the peasants' self-government. . . ." "Constitutional Conditions in the Fifteenth and Sixteenth Centuries," *Cambridge History of Poland,* **I:** W. F. Reddaway *et al.* eds., *From the Origins to Sobieski (to 1696)* (London and New York: Cambridge Univ. Press, 1950), 427.

[51]Not even the confiscation of church lands helps, unless the economic base of the area is strong enough to supply an adequate tax base: "Exactly as in England, the dissolution of the monasteries [in east Elbia] did not make the rulers independent of the votes of credit granted by the Estates. The princes' growing needs of money and the quickly rising prices forced them to sell or pawn many of the monastic estates to noblemen. . . . Thus, contrary to a widely held opinion, the princes' power was not strengthened by the Reformation, but it continued to decline," F. L. Carsten. *Origin of Prussia* (London and New York: Oxford Univ. Press (Clarendon), 1954), 166.

[52]"The payment of debts in form of land, especially demesnes, was obviously most profitable to the lender in the era of the Price Revolution. The prevalent system of credit creation through the pledge of crown estates and the turning over of their management as security to the creditor based the contraction and repayment of loans on a combination of money economy and natural economy. From the landlord's viewpoint the demand for 'public' credit opened up the chance of making capital reproduce itself at an exceptionally high rate through the medium of speculative investments in land. The cash received by the borrower usually was far below the real capital value of the pawned assets. The margin tended to widen on account of the continuous upward trend of the price of land and of agricultural commodities. The creditor, therefore, was indemnified with an exorbitant and flexible economic rent which, while in possession of the security, could be further increased by more efficient utilization or ruthless exploitation. Only the persistence of acute fiscal maladjustment and the restricted character of the capital market, which in consequence of the economic decline of the cities and burgesses had been increasingly subject to the influence of the large landowners and the higher government officials, forced the Hohenzollerns to resort again and again to this method." Rosenberg, *American Historical Review,* Part 1, **XLIX,** p. 22.

The same decline of princely power in favor of the landed nobility can be found in the Spanish kingdom of Naples, thus giving further evidence of the close link between emergent economic role and political structure. There, the landlords turned towards grain production, especially in the early 17th century. They maintained and increased their parliamentary prerogatives, effectively reduced the scope of power of the Spanish viceroy, maintained control of the bureaucracy by placing their own people in its high posts, retaining venality only for the lesser posts, and maintained absolute supremacy in the military organization of the state. See Villari, *La rivolta antispagnola,* pp. 3–5, 14, 17, 24–25, 28.

powers, without their intervention matters would have been still worse. "The only alternative in 1648 was not less foreign interference but more—the continuance of the war until most of Germany was actually partitioned between Sweden, France, and the Habsburgs."[53]

The position of Sweden is worth brief attention, as the evolution of Sweden's state machinery approached the model of western Europe rather than that of the periphery, although it was economically very under-developed at this time. It was strong, not because its commerce and industry was strong, although iron production grew steadily beginning in 1540;[54] it was paradoxically rather that its agriculture was weak, and its aristocrats wished to take hold of the profits of other lands for want of being able to create them on their own. Or, so at least, Malowist argues:

> [I]t would be worth our while to go over certain aspects of Swedish domination of the Baltic. In fact, the beginnings of Swedish expansion, modest at first, are also to be found in the 15th century. Furthermore, Sweden in the 15th and 16th centuries was economically a very backward country, not only by comparison with western Europe, but even by comparison with east Germany or Poland. . . . Thus it should be noted that there was nothing in the situation of the Swedish merchants which can explain Sweden's aggression against its neighbors, since these merchants made infinitesimal profit out of Sweden's conquests and even, on occasion, sought to oppose the policy of conquest, considering it to be rather a source of ever-increasing taxation.
>
> On the contrary, the group which strongly supported expansion was the aristocracy, the nobility, unable to increase its income, rather small at that time, at the expense of a peasantry that was strong and well-organized. And it was precisely to the great lords and the nobility that the conquests and the administration of conquered territories brought important sources of new revenue.[55]

And if we ask why the peasantry was so strong, may it not be precisely the fact that Sweden at that time was endowed with "an agriculture which could barely supply its own needs," and hence its only real source of immediate wealth was to be "something of a parasite living on the weakness of her neighbours, a consequence of the enormous growth in the power of the nobility."[56]

Sweden as a mild deviant case thus illustrates the process well. As a peripheral state with a weak bourgeoisie, it was an arena in which the political power of the aristocracy grew with the economic expansion of the sixteenth century. But the growth of wheat was hindered by the climatic downturn of the time which affected negatively in particular the Scandinavian countries.[57] The nobility hence needed conquest and for that they

---

[53]Taylor, *Course of German History,* p. 23.

[54]See Frank C. Spooner, *New Cambridge Modern History,* **IV,** p. 97.

[55]Malowist, *Annales E.S.C.,* **XVIII,** p. 926.

[56]Malowist, *Economic History Review,* **XII,** p. 189.

[57]"It seems therefore that the case of the Nordic countries must be considered a special one: a too severe winter cold there is extremely harmful to the cultivation of grains, and a series of rigorous winters can have serious consequences, while it would be practically harmless or even beneficial in France." Le Roy Ladurie, *Histoire du climat.* p. 281

needed a strong, not a weak, state. Once they had the strong state, they would be able in the seventeenth and eighteenth centuries to use mercantilism as a lever of industrial advance, and hence be spared the fate of Poland.

We are now ready to look at Russia. One key piece of evidence for the hypothesis that Russia was *not* part of the European world-economy is precisely the growth of the absolute monarchy in Russia in a manner that bears substantial parallels to developments in western Europe and is strikingly different from eastern Europe.

What are the facts? The rise of coerced cash-crop labor in sixteenth-century Russia was the product of state intervention in the economy, directly linked to the creation of military benefices called *pomestia*, used to reward supporters of the tsar. In a sense, there is some parallel here to the *encomiendas* in Hispanic America. Unlike in Hispanic America, however, the system of coerced labor could not be as suddenly introduced because land first had to be expropriated from the old nobility (the *boyars*) and the monasteries. Nor was there any equivalent to the *cacique* as an intermediary, except insofar as the Russian Orthodox priest might be considered to play an analogous role in some areas. Rather, legislative enforcement of "serfdom" came at the end of a process in which the "refeudalization" had been set in motion by a process of growing peasant debt. V. O. Kluchevsky describes how this worked:

> [T]he landlord's loan gave rise to relations wherein the seigniorial peasant had to choose between a definite term of insolvent peasanthood and an indefinite term of slavery [that is, working off the debt in the form of personal labor]. Yet this restriction was not [a] police attachment to the place of domicile . . . but a mere industrial dependence, through debt, upon an individual (i.e. upon the landowner) under the general civil law of the country. Thus the close of the sixteenth century saw the peasant's right of removal expire of itself, and without any abrogation by law. . . .
>
> [The] peasant, when bargaining with the landowner for a plot and a loan, of himself, and in perpetuity, renounced (through his tenancy-contract) the right of ever, or by any means whatsoever, terminating the obligations which by that contract he assumed.[58]

Voluntary enserfment, however, became insufficient in Russia when the military successes of Ivan the Terrible in the middle of the sixteenth century led to the incorporation of large vacant lands in the southeast of what is today European Russia. To keep the peasant population from running away to these new lands, which meant for the holders of *pomestia* losing their manpower and thereby for the government its taxpayers, "restrictions on peasant liberty to move were introduced."[59] As Alexander Gerschenkron

[58]Kluchevsky, *A History of Russia*, **II**, pp. 233, 241.
[59]Marc Szeftel, "Aspects of Feudalism in Russian History," in Rushton Coulbourn, ed., *Feudalism in History* (Princeton, New Jersey: Princeton Univ. Press., 1956), 176.

remarks, "the process of enserfment is almost inconceivable without the power of the state. How else could it be achieved in a country so open towards the vast empty space in the south and the east as was the great Russian plain?"[60] The active role of the state machinery was hence very closely linked with the fact that Russia was involved in a conquest operation.

So of course was Spain. But Spain, because of the bullion, the Italian creditors, and the Hapsburg links, was and remained intimately linked with the European world-economy. Russia sought to create its own world-economy. Nonetheless the original process of Russian state creation had some parallels to that of Spain. Spain was created as the result of a *reconquista* of its territory by a Christian crusade against Moslem conquerers from North Africa. Russia was created as a process of overthrowing the "Tartar yoke," of reconquering its territory by a Christian crusade against Moslem (or Islamized) invaders from Central Asia. Muscovy's role paralleled that of Castile and the élan of a common struggle greatly aided Muscovy's triumph.[61]

As part of the price of getting the assistance of the traditional warrior class, the *boyars,* in this reconquest, the Muscovy tsars had to concede to them a claim to perpetual primacy according to a rank order early in historical time.[62] This system, known as *mestnichestvo,* was one of those important traditions created by the process of change. In order to balance off this new strength of the aristocracy, Ivan III in the late fifteenth century created a new system of nonallodial fiefs called *pomestia* which were granted as a prebend in return for military service. The *pomestia* were created out of conquered frontier lands, from land confiscated from monasteries and errant *boyars,* and also from free peasant land.[63]

For lack of a Reformation, however, the Church was able to fight back and the existence of two kinds of land tenure, *pomestia* and the old manorial form known as *votchina,* gave the monasteries a great opening, as owners of *votchini* began to sell or donate their lands to the Church, especially

[60]Alexander Gerschenkron, "Review article: Lord and Peasant in Russia from the Ninth to the Nineteenth Century," *Journal of Economic History,* **XXIV,** 1, Mar. 1964, 56.

[61]"Such were the new phenomena prominent in Moscow's absorption of Rus from the middle of the fifteenth century onwards. First the local communities began openly to turn to Moscow, either of their own accord, or at the instance of their respective governments; which caused the Muscovite unification of the country to acquire a different character and a faster rate of progress. That is to say, it ceased to be a matter of seizure or of private negotiation, and became a *national,* a *religious* movement." Kluchevsky, *A History of Russia,* **II,** p. 8.

[62]See *ibid.,* **II,** p. 44.

[63]"The transformation entailed more than just a curtailment of the hereditary allodial estate *(votchina)* and emergence of the temporary land holding *(pomestye)* which was predicated upon performance of service to the state on the part of the holder. In the course of the process considerable areas of formerly 'black' [that is, free] peasant lands were reassigned by the state to its servants. This eminently political process is quite incomprehensible save within the framework of the expanding state and its growing needs." Alexander Gerschenkron, "An Economic History of Russia," *Journal of Economic History,* **XII,** 2, Spring 1952, 131. On the fiscal origins of the system, cf. Ardant, *Impôt,* **II,** pp. 1089–1097.

after 1550, in return for life tenancies. There were religious justifications to be sure, but the key factor seems to be socio–political.[64]

It was the creation of new forms of tenure, the *pomestia*, not based on traditional reciprocal feudal obligations and often in frontier areas, combined with the fact of territorial expansion and hence the ready availability of land, that led the government down the path of making peasant work and residence obligations increasingly compulsory throughout the sixteenth century, beginning with the Code of 1497 and culminating in the Assembly Code of 1649.[65] Without such restrictions, the peasants would have refused service. The political strength of the Church meant that the state was unable to stem this drain of land out of the taxation system. The only alternative was to increase the taxes on the remaining land, further squeezing the peasants.[66] Since, in addition, peasants were offered more favorable terms on monastic lands, increased taxation served as a further impetus to peasant emigration.

This is the background to the question of "the fifties and the sixties." The reign of Ivan IV (the Terrible) from 1547–1584 was a critical period in Russian history, for Ivan by a single-minded concentration on the objective of increasing state authority crystallized the form of internal social structure that Russia was to know for several centuries to come, while trying to establish the autonomy of the Russian state from the European world-economy. As we shall see, he was successful in the latter goal in the short run. Or to put it another way, he held off the wolves at the door long enough to make it certain that when Russia would later be absorbed into the world-economy, it came in as a semiperipheral state (like seventeenth and eighteenth century Spain) rather than as a peripheral state (like Poland).

Within Russia, the main weapon of the tsar in increasing state power was by the creation of a patrimonial state machinery (as in western Europe),

[64] "Land acquisitions by the monasteries reached their zenith during the political and economic crises of the latter part of the sixteenth century. Many votchinniks, to preclude the loss of their land through economic disaster or royal confiscation, gave their property to monasteries in return for life tenancies of all or part of the land they donated, or of some other land owned by the monastery. Thereby the erstwhile proprietor was able to live out his life peacefully under the protection of the monastery, enjoy the income from his property, and escape the perils that beset the votchinnik class during Ivan the Terrible's reign." Blum, *Lord and Peasant*, pp. 191–192.

[65] See *ibid.*, pp. 247–268. Hilton and Smith date its onset from 1460 (see *Enserfment* pp. 18–19, 42–46, 73–75), but agree it became definitive in 1649 (see pp. 25, 141–152).

[66] "The connection between the question of monas-terial *votchini* and the fortunes of the peasantry was a dual one. On the one hand, the fact that it was from the stock of fiscal, court and service lands that monasterial *votchini* were formed, and that all attempts to arrest the leakage of those lands to the monasteries, and to restore them to the exchequer and to service, proved futile compelled the Government to make good on peasant labor (through increased taxation) what it lost on monasterial ownership; while, on the other hand, the fact that the leasehold lands of the monasteries constituted a perpetual menace to the revenue-producing possibilities of fiscal and service estates (owing to the easy leasehold terms of the former luring peasantry from the latter) obliged the Government to attempt to lessen the evil by imposing restrictions upon the peasant's right of migration." Kluchevsky, *A History of Russia*, **II**, 197. For the general plight of the peasantry, cf. Blum, *Lord and Peasant*, pp. 219–246.

linked in the case of Russia even more than in the case of France and England to the redistribution of land rights. One key reform was the abolition of the *kormlenie* system of regional administration, a system of tax-farming prebends, and replacing it with a bureaucracy paid partly in cash and partly by the grant of land.[67] This reform not only created a central bureaucracy; it created at the same time its tax base.[68] This was combined with the creation of local government institutions firmly in the hands of local gentry whose rise was favored by and part of the expansion of the tsar's authority.[69] It was at this time (1556) that military service was firmly linked to the holding of *pomestia,* thus giving the tsar an assurance of a relatively loyal standing army.[70] The growing of *pomestia* and hence the growing complexity of supervising the operations of the system led to the creation of a central land office in Moscow for the *pomestia.*[71]

Meanwhile, externally Ivan IV was pursuing a policy of expansion not only toward the frontier lands in the south (at the time, the Crimea) but in the west toward the Baltic, the so-called Livonian war which dragged on for twenty-five years (1558–1583). Its object was to establish Russia as a Baltic power. It was a long and essentially inconclusive war.[72] Had it been more conclusive, Russia might have been definitively drawn into the European world-system at that time.

One can understand why expansion westward tempted the tsar in his capacity as entrepreneur. Unlike the rulers of the various countries of eastern Europe, the tsar was in a position to profit directly from the expansion of trade because of the already stronger state machinery. In Poland it was the aristocracy which managed to gain a monopolistic control on the export trade; in Russia it was the tsar. He reserved these rights for himself and those he favored.[73] Thus foreign trade was of interest to the

[67]See *ibid.,* pp. 142–143. The word *kormlenie* is translated as a "living" by R. E. F. Smith, *The Enserfment of the Russian Peasantry* (London and New York: Cambridge Univ. Press, 1968), 156.

[68]It was in the regime of Ivan the Terrible that Russia first saw the establishment of a system of direct taxation by the state. See A. Miller, "Considérations sur les institutions financières de l'état moscovite au XVIe et XVIIe siècles," *Revue internationale de sociologie,* **XL,** 7-8, juil.-août 1932, 374–378. Miller shows clearly how this was linked to the abolition of the *kormlenie:* "Since the population no longer had to make payments to the 'kormlenshchiki,' one substituted for them a series of taxes which henceforth were raised for the benefit of the central government [p. 378]."

[69]See Vernadsky, *Tsardom,* **I,** pp. 84–85.

[70]See *ibid.,* pp. 85–86.

[71]"It became necessary to introduce standardization and bureaucratization into the serving relationship to ensure its proper functioning. . . . The

movement toward uniformity was especially evident in the normalization of the size of the holdings turned over to the pomeshchiks." Blum, *Lord and Peasant,* p. 179.

[72]See Vernadsky, *Tsardom,* **I,** pp. 87–174.

[73]"Tsar Ivan IV was considered, in the opinion of foreigners, one of the richest feudal lords in Europe. . . . The very profitable royal-trade monopolies applied to foreign trade relied exclusively on the manorial economy of the Tsar himself and his entourage." Peter I. Lyashchenko, *History of the National Economy of Russia to the 1917 Revolution* (New York: Macmillan, 1949), 213–214.

This may explain why Ivan IV at first seemed so favorable to the development of commercial links with England. Indeed, Inna Lubimenko argues that he wanted it far more than Elizabeth, and that it was England's reserve which led to Ivan's strong reaction. See *Les relations commerciales et politiques de l'Angleterre avec la Russie avant Pierre le Grand* (Paris: Lib. Ancienne Honoré Champion, 1933), 40–53.

tsar not only as a source of customs revenue but as an outlet for the very large amount of goods delivered to him in kind by his peasants. As the city served the medieval feudal lord, so Ivan IV sought to use all of Europe. Since the enterprise was vast, he found it convenient and profitable to enlist the cooperation of a commercial bourgeoisie (both foreign and indigenous) to handle the merchandise. When Polish aristocrats eliminated Polish commercial middlemen, they thereby escaped paying certain taxes on their goods. Thus the state lost revenue and the Polish bourgeoisie declined. When the landlord is the sovereign, any taxes dispensed or saved are simply bookkeeping transactions. Ergo, in Russia, there were no great financial advantages in making the individuals who supervised the transfer of goods members of the firm's staff as opposed to independent entrepreneurs. Since they were the latter to start with, it was easier to let them remain that.

Hence, in Russia as in western Europe, the indigenous commercial bourgeoisie survived, and the state machinery was strengthened at the same time.[74] Had Tsar Ivan IV succeeded, it is not certain that the Russian merchants would have fared quite as well as they anticipated. We shall never know, since when the Livonian war ended in stalemate externally, all that had really been accomplished was to bring to a head an internal social and economic crisis within Russia.

In the intrinsically unstable political arenas of the time, lack of continuous success by a state in the international area led to open clashes of interest at home which always bore the risk of disintegration of the state. To counteract this inner turbulence, Ivan IV resorted to strong police measures—the notorious *Oprichnina* for which he earned the title of "the Terrible." It essentially involved the creation of a special palace guard, with the aid of which the tsar drastically purged his enemies, especially among the aristocracy. The weapons were two: death and confiscation of property, the latter enabling the tsar to redistribute land to those whose loyalty he hoped to keep.

It was politically successful in that it ended the fear of *coup d'état*. But, in the opinion of many, it backfired. Blum for example says:

> The shock of the *Oprichnina*, together with the steady drain of the long and unsuccessful Livonian War . . . upon the country's resources, deranged the social and economic structure of the realm. . . . The confiscation of the great landed complexes and their subdivisions into pomestia did violence to the agricultural system

---

[74]"It is thus clear that maritime trade not only favored capital accumulation in Russia, but strengthened those forces whose interest lay in the unity of the country and the might of its state. . . . [The increasingly numerous and wealthy merchants were] interested both in free trade within the country and political and commercial expansion abroad; for such expansion would enable [them] to make contact with the West via Lithuania and the Baltic, and would throw open the wealth of Siberia, and perhaps of the Middle and Far East." Malowist, *Past & Present*, No. 13, pp. 38–39.

upon which the nation's economy was based, setting back techniques, cutting down on production, and creating new tensions between seigniors and peasants.[75]

Blum also blames the heavy taxation combined with plagues, crop failure, and invasions for mass flights of peasants.[76] A sharp and sudden inflation between 1575 and 1590 reflected these happenings and accentuated them. A. G. Mankov, on the basis of his study of Russian price movements in the sixteenth century, is willing to go so far as "to see in the crisis of the years 1580–1590 a generalized crisis of the national economy,"[77] a view he asserts he shares with Soviet historical writing generally.[78]

Vernadsky argues in a similar vein that the Livonian War was a dreadful error, because Russia had no choice but to continue fighting on the Crimean front and hence by opting to fight in Livonia, Russia was opting for a two-front war, a policy with disastrous results.[79] This seems to me to miss the crucial point that Russia may equally well have had no choice in Livonia.

[75]Blum, *Lord and Peasant,* pp. 146–147. Blum also speaks of "a calamitous drop in production in the 1570's and 1580's." Jerome Blum, "Prices in Russia in the Sixteenth Century," *Journal of Economic History,* **XVI,** 2, June 1956, 196. See Lyashchenko: "The transition from the old form of the large, feudal, self-contained economy to the new form of the serf-operated *pomestye,* rooted in the drive for a maximum exploitation of labor, could not fail to produce a rather protracted general decline in the whole national economy of the Moscow state of the sixteenth century. . . .

"Through their immunities the *votchini* had so many privileges for attaching the peasants to their land that they could easily gather to themselves large labor forces and bring about the gradual enslavement of the peasants. . . . The average *pomestye* economy could not be operated by *kholop* ['villein'—see Smith, p. 162] labor, little of which was owned, to say nothing of its poor quality, particularly under conditions of a money economy. But neither was it able to base its production entirely on economically dependent peasant labor, since the economic strength of the *pomestye* economy was often not very great. The necessary organization of labor of the *pomestye* could be achieved only by extra-economic compulsion, 'binding' the labor power to the *pomestye* by enslaving the toilers not only through indebtedness, loans, duration, and so forth, but also through the recognition of the *pomeshchik*'s 'right' to the compulsory labor of the peasant. . . .

"The ruin of the peasantry and the increase of economic pressure on the part of the *pomeshchik* forced the peasants to reduce their arable land [having reached "more than 95% by the middle of the sixteenth century," it declined "in the central province . . . to 31.6 percent and in the Novgorod province to a mere 6.9 percent" by the 1580s] and

to seek salvation in running away from the enslaved to the 'free' lands. As a result, a decline not only of the *pomestye* itself, but also of the peasant economy connected with it, became evident during the sixteenth century." *National Economy of Russia,* pp. 191–193.

[76]See Blum, *Lord and Peasant,* pp. 158–159.

[77]Mankov, *Le mouvement des prix,* p. 126. The French text reads 1570–1580, but a contextual reading seems to indicate that this is a typographical error, which I therefore have corrected.

[78]"The situation changed brusquely in the course of the following decade [1580–1590], in connection with the economic crisis well-known to have occurred at that time. Soviet historical literature gives a primordial role to this crisis. Its causes, its nature, and its geographical scope have been amply developed. The hypertension of all the forces of the national economy during the painful Livonian War, its unfavorable outcome, the ruin and abandonment of entire regions where the agricultural economy had just previously been very developed, the creation at this moment of the 'Oprichnina,' which dislocated the landholdings of the boyars and the princes, the forced reallocation of land and the 'scattering of the little people.' . . . The decadence of agriculture and the ruin of the peasants who lived on the reserved territories led in particular to the reduction of the cereals market. Demand rose sharply for want of cereals, and prices increased." Mankov, *ibid.,* p. 36.

Mankov, incidentally, is sure that Russia is more or less part of Europe's price revolution. Jerome Blum offers this caution: "There may well have been [an analogous price rise in Russia] but [Mankov's] data do not prove it. . . ." *Journal of Economic History,* **XVI,** p. 185.

[79]See Vernadsky, *Tsardom,* **I,** pp. 94–95.

Vernadsky views the Livonian War as a failure, one in which the Russians were "lucky to be able to conclude an armistice with Sweden on August 5, 1583, even though the terms of it were highly unfavorable."[80] Perhaps, alternatively, we could think of it as a gigantic success. Russia was *not* pulled into the European world-economy. Her bourgeoisie and her monarch were spared, at least for the moment, the fate of their Polish counterparts.

This is not entirely fanciful. Boris Porchnev analyzes the grand pattern of international relations in Europe in the sixteenth century as one in which the opponents of the Hapsburg–Catholic objective of creating a single imperial system sought to encourage the creation of an eastern barrier of states—Sweden, Poland (later Poland-Lithuania), and the Ottoman Empire, "directed primarily against central Europe" but which also became "a barrier isolating, from the rest of Europe, Russia which was becoming ever stronger."[81]

As Catholicism regained ground in Poland, however, the state of Poland-Lithuania became an ally of Spain. When, in the years following Ivan IV, the Russian state was rent by internal quarrels culminating in the so-called "Time of Troubles" (1610– 1613), Poland, secretly supported by the Hapsburgs and, for separate motives, Sweden, engaged in an "attempt to dismember and subjugate Russia,"[82] an attempt which failed. Furthermore, Vernadsky asserts there was also English interest at this time in establishing "a protectorship over all or part of Russia."[83] No doubt a major contributing factor to the failure was the existence of the sharp divisions of the Thirty Years' War which constantly diverted Russia's immediate enemies into more pressing tasks.

But Russia was coming ever nearer to absorption by Europe. Ivan IV's "disastrous" policies delayed this. See Kluchevsky's description of what was happening at the end of the "long" sixteenth century:

> We see England and Holland helping [Tsar] Michael [1613-45] to become reconciled to his enemies, Poland and Sweden, for the reason that Muscovy was a valuable market for the former, and also a convenient road to the East—to Persia, and even to India. Again, we see the French King proposing to conclude an alliance with Michael, in order to meet the commercial interests of France in the East, where she was the rival both of England and of the Dutch. . . . The Empire of Tsar Michael was *weaker* than the Empire of Tsar Ivan [IV] and Theodor [1584- 98], *but far less isolated* in Europe.[84]

Should not the "but" read "and therefore?" What Ivan had been seeking

---

[80]*Ibid.*, p. 166. He adds: "Thus ended the Livonian War which had lasted for a quarter of a century, required many hardships and sacrifices on the part of the Russian people, and, together with the after effects of the oprichnina, plunged Russia into a deep socioeconomic crisis."

[81]Porchnev, *International Congress of Historical Sciences*, 1960, **IV**, p. 140.
[82]*Ibid.*, p. 142.
[83]Vernadsky, *Tsardom*, **I**, p. 291.
[84]Kluchevsky, *A History of Russia*, **III**, p. 128. Italics added.

was the creation of a Russian Empire, not a piece of the European pie. That was to be the objective at a later time of Peter the Great.

The third great difference between Russia and eastern Europe was, as we have indicated, the direct consequence of the different structure and direction of commerce and the differing strengths of the state machinery. In Russia the cities and the indigenous bourgeoisie survived the "long" sixteenth century whereas in eastern Europe they very largely did not. And the land, although for the most part in the same large estate form as developed in eastern Europe, was in Russia in the hands of "new men," sometimes called "gentry," sometimes "lesser nobility" (we have already seen how little relevant this distinction is). These were men descended not from the old *boyar* class, but drawn from two groups, the *dvoriane* (a sort of court nobility) and the so-called "sons of boyars" who were in earlier epochs minor and outlying aristocrats. Those boyars who survived were largely "non-royal kinsmen of the tsar."[85] Thus, especially after the Time of Troubles, when Tsar Michael was able to carry through to their logical conclusion the policies of Ivan IV, a new class of magnates emerged.[86] Eventually the new aristocracy took over all the formal appurtenances of the old. *Mestnichestvo* was abolished in 1682. The *pomestia* became de facto transferable by sale and inheritance, thus vitiating the distinction from the *votchini*.[87] The Code of Laws of 1649 lessened considerably the distinction between the two forms of property[88] and in 1731 the two forms would be legally merged.[89]

The rise of "new men"of course occurred everywhere—certainly in western Europe as we have seen, in many ways in eastern Europe as well. But Blum catches the essential point:

[85]"The magnates of the seventeenth century were predominantly new men. Just nine of the twenty-three wealthiest men in the tsar's service at the middle of the century were descendants of old princely families. The rest were non-royal kinsmen of the tsar (whose family was of Moscow boyar origin) and other members of the untitled serving class, including men who came from the lesser gentry." Blum, *Lord and Peasant*, p. 212. See Malowist, *Economic History Review*, **XII**, p. 189; Lublinskaya, *French Absolutism*, p. 60.

[86]"But as a class the gentry shared in the victory of absolutism. Loyal instruments of the tsars in the fight against the great nobility, leaders in the national revival in the Time of Troubles [first years of the seventeenth century], and the electors of [Tsar] Michael [1613], they were rewarded by being made the ruling class in place of the *kniazhata* [princes] and boyars. Those members of the old aristocracy who had managed to retain part of their power fought in vain against this conquest by the gentry of the highest posts in the state. They tried

to prevent it by insisting upon the now hopelessly antiquated *mestnichestvo* system, but the claims of genealogy could no longer withstand the will of the tsar. Appointments and promotions were made at the order of the throne, and were based on merit and probably more often on favoritism, but not on lineage. Finally, in 1682, the long obsolete *mestnichestvo* system was abolished." Blum, *Lord and Peasant*, p. 151.

[87]"In the seventeenth century *boiar* and *pomeshchik* became nearly indistinguishable, the land of both became heritable and bore no necessary relationship to service actually done." C. M. Foust, "Russian Expansion to the East Through the Eighteenth Century" *Journal of Economic History*, **XXI**, 4, Dec. 1961, 470. "[In 1731] another imperial ukase ordered that henceforth the pomestye was to be known as a votchina." Blum, *Lord and Peasant*, p. 185.

[88]See Vernadsky, *Tsardom*, **I**, pp. 394–411.

[89]See Vernadsky, *Speculum*, **XIV**, pp. 321–322.

The Russian experience . . . differed in one important respect from the rest of Eastern Europe (and resembled that in the West). In the other Eastern lands the ascent of the lesser nobility was made possible by the decline in the powers of the sovereigns. In Russia the gentry owed its rise to the increase in the tsar's power. It was the tail of the kite of the new absolutism.[90]

Finally, the contrast between eastern Europe and Russia is clear in the urban areas. Towns declined more in eastern Europe, the indigenous urban bourgeoisie declined more and native industry declined more. It was to be sure a relative matter. Russia in comparison to *western* Europe may be considered to have declined, relatively if not absolutely. And the decline was not total in eastern Europe. Yet the evidence seems to indicate a qualitative gap between eastern Europe and Russia.

The difference may have been less in the "first" sixteenth century.[91] But as the landed proprietors engaged more and more in direct trade, they pursued openly "antiurban" activities in eastern Europe.[92] With the rise of "kinglets" in Poland and *Gutsherrschaft* in east Elbia, the prince as landowner found little in his own immediate needs to make him

[90]Blum, *Lord and Peasant*, p. 151. Note incidentally how Blum slips into using the term "gentry" as synonymous with "lesser nobility." See Tazbir on the relation of the Polish gentry with the monarchy: "This gave rise in 1537 to the 'Hen's War,' when the open display of opposition by the gentry gathered near Lwów in preparation for an armed expedition forced the King, Queen Bona and the magnates around them to accept a compromise. At the root of the gentry's success lay also the consolidation of their economic position. This was the result of the development of estates worked by serf labour, the size of which grew at the expense of the peasants who were removed from their holdings and given either smaller or less productive plots of lands." *History of Poland*, p. 176.

[91]Tazbir, for example, argues of Poland: "The economic prosperity of the towns could not be thwarted by the laws of the Seym which exempted all goods purchased by the gentry and those manufactured on their estates from taxation. Identical laws in other countries did not have any adverse effects on the situation of the townspeople. There existed also in Poland, at the time, numerous mixed burgher-gentry companies which were faring quite well. The law of 1565, which barred the burghers from trading in grain and forbade Polish merchants to sell Polish goods abroad and import foreign goods to Poland, placed the big towns in a rather advantageous position as they thus became the only intermediary in this trade. Foreign merchants were only allowed to display their goods there. Moreover, the law of 1565 never went into effect. Nor could the

ban on the purchase of land by the burghers, which was enacted several times by the Seym, hinder the development of towns. On the contrary, it favoured investment of capital derived from trade in manufacturing enterprises." *History of Poland*, pp. 177–178.

But then he notes as well: "At the turn of the sixteenth century Polish towns began to feel the effects of the steady development of the manorial farm economy based on serf labour. . . . A different kind of town were those founded at the turn of the sixteenth century on the lands of the magnates' latifundia. . . . These townships being the property of the local lords were naturally subjected by them to increased exploitation. The supremacy of the nobility had made itself felt also in other urban centres. . . . The adverse effects on Polish towns and handicrafts of the political supremacy of the gentry and of the expansion of farm economy based on serf labour were to become evident only in later years, but the first signs of an economic crisis had been apparent already in the first half of the seventeenth century [pp. 226–227]."

[92]"[The] decline of the cities was much accelerated by the anti-urban policies followed by the East German, Livonian, Polish and Bohemian nobility. . . . One of their primary aims was to break urban monopolies of foreign and domestic trade. They were also determined to put an end to the cities' practice of receiving runaway peasants. . . ." Jerome Blum, *American Historical Review*, **LXII**, p. 834.

sympathetic to townsmen.[93] And as the towns declined the nobility grew still stronger.[94] In Russia, Kluchevsky might speak of the "extraordinarily slow and painful growth of Russian towns and town industries during the sixteenth and seventeenth centuries,"[95] but at least it was growth not decline. Blum is more positive. He says:

> The new importance of exchange in economic life [in the 16th century] was signalized by the reemergence of the city as a center of industry and commerce and as a market for farm goods and other wares produced in Russia and in foreign lands. Old towns were revivified, new ones established, and some rural settlements (as Novgorod land registers show) began to abandon agriculture for trade and industry.[96]

Along with the strength of the towns went the strength of the indigenous commercial bourgeoisie. The local aristocracies not only took over the export trade from the local merchants, "depress[ing] them into the role of agents"[97] but shared the import trade with a *foreign* bourgeoisie.[98] The

[93]"The Reformation had another consequence [in east Elbia]: outside Prussia, the rulers became the owners of large domains, so that their interests as landlords henceforth coincided with those of the nobility and were opposed to those of the towns in matters of commerce." Carsten, *The Origins of Prussia*, p. 166.

[94]"Above all, it was the long-lasting decline and the subjugation of the eastern towns which eliminated all resistance to the rise of the nobility. . . .

"The subjugation and the decline of the towns fundamentally changed the medieval balance of society and made way for the rule of one class over another. In Prussia, the same result was achieved by the cession of all important towns to Poland in 1466 [except Königsberg]." *Ibid*, pp. 116, 147.

[95]Kluchevsky, *A History of Russia*, **II**, p. 145.

[96]Blum, *Lord and Peasant*, p. 23.

[97]Malowist, *Economic History Review*, **XII**, p. 186. See Carsten: "Until the sixteenth century the corn exports of Brandenburg were handled by the towns and their burghers who benefited considerably from this trade. When the nobility became more interested in producing corn for the market it began to invade the sphere of urban enterprise [p. 170]."

See Ferdo Gestrin: "The Slovenian bourgeoisie evolved in an opposite sense to what might be expected given the general process. More than to non-agricultural production, it remained tied to commerce, especially to transit trade, but they were defeated in this arena by the double competition of the peasants and the lords. That is why throughout the [sixteenth] century . . . they never ceased to decline slowly despite some passing improvements in their situation." "Economie et société en

Slovénie au XVIe siècle," *Annales E.S.C.*, **XVII**, p. 687.

See Hoszowski: "[The Polish gentry] wanted not only an income from the produce of their land, but also from trade in these products. For this reason they managed, by appropriate Seym legislation, to secure freedom of transit on the Vistula and its tribuaries, then freedom from customs duties on agricultural and forest products being exported abroad from their own demesnes, as well as from having to pay customs dues on all goods imported from abroad for use on their own estates and farms. In actual practice, the feudal class extended this customs privilege, and without paying customs dues they exported grain, cattle, and other farm products bought from the peasants in the villages or at the country markets. They also brought some foreign commodities into the country along the Vistula without paying customs dues, and then sold these goods to the people living on their estates. In this way, the gentry gathered into their own hands the trade in agricultural products, timber and forest products, ousting the burghers from this trade, and severely cutting down the town merchants' opportunities to take a profit on imported goods." *Poland at the XIth International Congress*, p. 127.

[98]"The economic policy of the nobles of the Baltic countries also contributed in great measure to the decline of the towns. This policy consisted in intensifying the export of foodstuffs and primary products and favoring the import of manufactures by giving strong support to foreign trade in their own territories. This course of action was intended to assure the abundance of foreign goods and to keep their prices down." Malowist, *Economic History*

indigenous bourgeoisie of one country was the foreign bourgeoisie of another. German merchants who could find no place in the economies of east Elbia were more than welcome in Poland, and were appropriately grateful politically.[99] Indeed one might speculate as to whether the later recuperative power of the German bourgeoisie is not due to the fact that they survived in places like Poland and Slovenia. In Russia, on the contrary, though indigenous merchants ran into competition from large landholders, including the monasteries, and most especially the tsar himself, they nonetheless survived.[100] One factor that helped was that the leading merchants, known as *gosti*, were allowed to play the double role of agents of the tsar, both commercial and fiscal, and merchants on their own account.[101] Eventually then they could break away from their connections with the tsar, even became effective rivals to him. And in the end, "private enterprise did carry, in point of fact, a large share of the Russian expansion to the Pacific, though rarely supported by the state, but rather competitive with it."[102]

As for the handicrafts industries, these seemed to decline everywhere, largely because the absence of tariff barriers allowed the ever more economical products of western European industry to outsell the local products.[103] To the extent that local industries survived, as for example

---

Review. XII, p. 188. Malowist calls this policy "anti-mercantilism."

"A primary characteristic of Poland's export trade was that it was dominated by the gentry as far as the whole country was concerned . . . whereas imports from abroad came largely to be in the hands of foreign merchants." Hoszowski, *Poland at the XIth International Congress*, p. 129.

"More fearful than competition in the rural areas for the commercial bourgeoisie and urban prosperity was the arrival of foreign capital [from Italy and southern Germany]." Gestrin, *Annales E.S.C.*, **XVII**, p. 680.

[99]"The townspeople of Gdańsk were well aware of the economic advantages to be derived from political union with Poland, and therefore, in spite of their German origin and use of the German language, among the majority of the patricians, merchants and tradesmen of Gdańsk there was a strong leaning towards Poland. . . . [The people of Gdańsk] were anxious to maintain their union with Poland, which was the source of their prosperity." Hoszowski, *Poland at the XIth International Congress*, p. 141.

[100]"Unlike Western Europe where trade was predominantly a middle-class occupation, persons from all levels of Russian society engaged in commerce. . . . The Tsar himself, like his ancient forebears, the princes of Kiev, was the single most important businessman in the entire empire. . . . Nor did the tsars limit themselves to dealing in the

products of their own holdings. They maintained monopolies on many articles. . . . Sometimes the tsar, through his commercial agents and officials, engrossed the entire output of a commodity, raised its price, and then compelled merchants to buy." Blum, *Lord and Peasant*, p. 129.

[101]"Besides trading on their own account, [the *gosti*] were the tsar's business agents, being chosen for this function from among the most successful traders in the realm. They also were given responsibility for gathering certain taxes and were required to turn in a sum fixed by the government. In return for these duties they were accorded a special status akin to that of the serving nobility. Among the merchants the Stroganovs were the most famous. Of peasant origin, they began their rise in the latter part of the fourteenth century in the salt trade. As time went on they expanded their activities to other industrial and commercial enterprises. They became great landowners in the colonial north and played the leading role in the commercial exploitation of the riches of Siberia." *Ibid.*, pp. 130–131.

[102]Foust, *Journal of Economic History*, **XXI**, p. 475.

[103]"These active commercial relations of the Netherlands, as well as of other Western states, with the Baltic countries, lead us to note in passing that if the wealth of Polish nobles, for example, was closely linked to the export of wheat to Holland, conversely the free import of Western merchandise selling at lower cost and of higher quality (especially the Dutch and English cloths) contributed to the

lace in Czechia, it was by serving as rural cottage industries for merchant houses outside their area.[104] Still and all, this made some difference as it encouraged a diversification of agriculture and prepared the way for the later industrial development of Bohemia.[105] In Russia, however, because it was its own world-economy, some of the accumulated capital went into industrial development.[106] Even in the case of the most important export industry of the European world-economy, textiles, where one would have thought the Russian industry would have collapsed before the competition, the local industry retained most of the mass market and even a part of the quality market.[107]

ruin of the national industry. Along the same lines the ever greater monopolistic tendencies of the Dutch fleet gradually led to the ruin of the fleets of the Baltic towns, including that of Gdańsk, Poland's chief port. . . .

"Drawing great profits from their privileged economic position in the Baltic, the Netherlands, England, and early on France took more and more of a serious interest in what went on in this part of Europe. First of all, these states wished to preserve their trade from the inconveniences of war. That is why one can note new efforts at mediation in conflicts [in 1617, 1629, 1635]. . . ." Czalpinski, *XIe Congrès International des Sciences Historiques, Rapports,* **IV,** p. 37.

[104]"From the second half of the sixteenth century on, there begin to be concluded collective contracts between the German commercial houses of Nuremberg and of other cities on the one hand and Czech lace corporations on the other hand, which involved a pledge by the corporations to deliver specified quantities of lace having a determinate level of quality, at prices fixed in the contract.

"After the Thirty Years' War, it seems to be the case that the form of collective delivery by corporations to commercial houses could no longer ensure, under the new conditions of the time, a sufficient quantity, or merchandise for the overseas exports. One had to develop new forms of production and commerce. This was to be the system called putting-out *(Verlagssystem),* whose beginning may be found already in the 16th century, but whose full development only came about in the second half of the 17th and the 18th centuries." A. Klíma and J. Macůrek, "La question de la transition du féodalisme au capitalisme en Europe centrale (16e-18e siècles)," *International Congress of Historical Sciences,* Stockholm, 1960, *Rapports,* **IV:** *Histoire moderne* (Göteborg, Almqvist & Wiksell, 1960), 87.

[105]"A special characteristic marked out the large Czech estate of the 16th and early 17th centuries. There too one sees the development of grain production and of primary agriculture, but at the same time, they went on to the processing of agricultural

products, for example beer from grain, and other beginnings of industrial production. It was especially the brewery which gave to the large Czech estates, as distinguished from the large estate of neighboring Germany, Poland, and northern Hungary (that is, Slovakia), its special features. . . . Another distinguishing trait of Czech agricultural production as compared to neighboring countries, particularly in the sixteenth century, was the development of fish-breeding in ponds. . . . Furthermore, the large feudal estate sought in the Czech lands to penetrate also into industrial production. In the 16th and 17th centuries, they were particularly involved with the search for metallic minerals, with mining, and with iron-production." *Ibid.,* pp. 99–100.

[106]"The conditions for capital accumulation in the hands of a native class of merchants were therefore much more favorable in Russia than in Poland, an advantage which was even greater, because the Russian nobility, which underwent serious, very serious crises in the sixteenth and early seventeenth centuries, took no great part in large-scale trade.

"Again, it seems that the capital accumulated locally was used for productive purposes to a much greater extent than in Poland. Its investment accelerated the tempo of colonization in the economically backward regions of Russia and along its northern and south-eastern frontier. It certainly helped to increase the quantity of products essential both for the country's internal needs and its foreign trade. Merchants, moreover, invested heavily in certain industries, such as salt-mining and the iron-industry of the Urals, which was to prove of considerable importance for the equipment of the Russian armies. The quantity of commodities essential to the country's population as a whole therefore grew; even large numbers of peasants were drawn into the web of the commodity economy." Malowist, *Past & Present,* No. 13, p. 39.

[107]"Our conclusion therefore is that, among woollen cloths, it is the linsey-woolsey and the *svitka* cloths which were the most common in the 16th century; this is corroborated by the testimony of the foreign

We could make a similar analysis of why the Ottoman Empire was not part of the European world-economy.[108] It is perhaps more to the point to turn our attention to the issue of the Portuguese Indian Ocean trade and how that differed from the Spanish Atlantic trade.

We must begin by dispensing with the myth of the role of the Turks in the rise of the Portuguese Indian Ocean trade. Far from the rise of the Ottoman Empire having led to a closure of the eastern Mediterranean to western Europe and hence having motivated Portugal's search for the Cape route to Asia, it is now generally recognized both that Portugal's overseas explorations predated the rise of the Ottomans and that the decline of the eastern Mediterranean spice trade predated Portugal's entry into it. Indeed, A. H. Lybyer precisely attributes the Levant's "decline" not to cultural resistances to modern technology, but to the structural diversion of trade and hence its noninclusion in the expanding European world-economy.

> [The Turks] were not active agents in deliberately obstructing the routes. They did not by their notorious indifference and conservatism greatly, if at all on the whole, increase the difficulties of the oriental traffic. Nor did they make the discovery of new routes imperative. On the contrary, they lost by the discovery of a new and superior route. Had there been no way around Africa the whole story of the Levant since 1500 might have been very different. In the first place, the Mameluke sultans might have found in their uninterrupted trade sufficient financial support to enable them to resist successfully the attack of the Turks in 1516. But if the Turks had conquered Egypt while the full steam of oriental trade still ran through it, they must either have been deprived far sooner than was actually the case of the control of these routes, or they would have had to accomodate themselves to the great and increasing trade through their dominions. In the latter case they might have been forced into adopting modern ways, and into adding to their wonderful capacity for territorial unification a parallel scheme of organizing their trade. . . . The shifting of the trade-routes was done, not by the Turks, but in their despite and to their disadvantage.[109]

visitor, Barberini. He emphasizes, not without arrogance, that Russians do not know to manufacture cloths and they import from abroad, for us: 'All the same, in the Russian countryside, they make ordinary cloth for the use of the lower classes, principally rural, of the population. These are the linsey-woolsey cloths; they distinguish between better, average, and poorer quality, and they are sold in the village marketplaces.'

"A second group, considerably less important, included the quality cloths, used by the highest classes of the population, as well as the Tsar's court. These were principally imported cloths: Flemish (from Bruges, Ypres, Brabant), and later English. But this category included also cloths made in Russia. Novgorod, in particular, was noted for its high quality cloth." Mankov, *Le mouvement des prix*, p. 102.

[108]Two articles which discuss the Ottoman Empire of the sixteenth century in relation to Europe are Bernard Lewis, "Some Reflections of the Decline of the Ottoman Empire," *Studia islamica*, **XI**, 1958, 111–127, and Ömer Lutfi Barkan, " 'La Méditerranée' de Fernand Braudel vue d'Istamboul," *Annales E.S.C.*, **IX**, 2, avr.-juin 1954, 189–200.

See the comment by Otto Brunner: "In its close link between political power, long-distance commerce and the luxury-trade, Byzantium stood undoubtedly far closer to the Russian type [of economy] than to the Western European [type]." "Europäisches und Russisches Bürgertum," *Vierteljahrschrift für Sozial- und Wirtschaftsgeschichte*, **XL**, 1, 1953, 15.

[109]A. H. Lybyer, "The Ottoman Turks and the Routes of Oriental Trade," *English Historical Review*, **CXX**, Oct. 1915, 588.

We have, in an earlier chapter, sought to explain the complex of forces within Portugal (and Spain) which led to the explorations of the fifteenth century and the overseas trade and empires of the sixteenth. It is striking when one reflects upon how the economic motivations of the Iberian expansion pointed heavily to Atlantic areas (the Western Hemisphere, though they did not know it, and West Africa) but not to Asia, even though the ideology of the explorations set great stock on the search for a route to the Indies. For example, when Vitorino Magalhães-Godinho makes a long list of the factors which dominated the early phase of Portuguese expansion (from the lack of gold, to the grain shortage, to land and slaves for sugar production, to the need for fishing areas), there is no mention of pepper or spices or drugs, of silks or porcelain or precious stones, in short, of all that the Portuguese would in fact import from Asia in the sixteenth century.[110] But in the last quarter of the fifteenth century Portuguese interest in the spice trade awakened,[111] and the search for Prester John became linked to this interest in the mind of King John II, "for [the] kingdom [of Prester John] would serve him as a way-station on the route to India, from whence Portuguese captains would bring back those riches heretofore distributed by Venice."[112] And the gold of West Africa plus the pepper and spices of Asia would in fact make up more than half the revenue of the Portuguese state by 1506 with the portion of the Asian trade growing thereafter, constituting thus the "underpinning of the imperial economy."[113]

Vasco de Gama came, saw, and conquered far more and far faster than Julius Caesar. It is indeed extraordinary that, in a very few years, Portuguese ships comletely dominated the extensive trade of the Indian Ocean. What was the structure of this enterprise and how did it come to be so quickly established?

The answer to the latter is relatively easy: the technological superiority of the gunned ship that had been developed in Atlantic Europe in the two prior centuries, and to which a crucial technological innovation—the cutting of ports for guns in the actual hulls of the ships as opposed to the superstructure—had been achieved in 1501.[114] Was this technological advantage enough to explain Portuguese success, or must we add thereto the belief that Portugal "went to Asia in a spirit of determination to succeed, which was stronger than the will of the Asiatic peoples to resist," as George

[110]Godinho, *L'économie de l'empire portugaise,* pp. 40–41. For one thing, Europe seemed to be well provided with spices via the Levant (see p. 537) and Godinho doubts that at that time the Portuguese had more than fleeting and romantic interest in spices: "Did [Henry] or other Portuguese of his time truly orient their activities towards these countries of marvels [in the Orient]? It hardly seems so; why should Portuguese commerce have been interested at that time in trying to divert to its profit the spice routes? [p. 548]"

[111]See *ibid.,* pp. 43, 550–551.

[112]*Ibid.,* p. 551.

[113]*Ibid.,* p. 831. See Table on p. 830.

[114]"The [cutting of ports] was of very great importance. It gave the bigger ships the possibility of increasing their armament vastly. Mounting the guns on the main deck not only made it possible to mount

B. Sansom insists?[115] Perhaps, although I tend to feel that cultural qualities, such as a spirit of collective psychology, are the product of very specific social structural conjunctures and do not long outlive their base.

In any case from about 1509 when the Portuguese defeated the Egyptian fleet at Diú, the Portuguese navy held "uncontested hegemony"[116] in the Indian Ocean. In addition, during the sixteenth century (but only until 1570 for the Straits of Malacca) Portuguese traders were to be found not only there but in the China Sea, on the coasts of Africa east and west, in the south Atlantic, in Newfoundland, and of course in Europe. "Thus, present everywhere, a Portuguese economy."[117]

The Portuguese system of control in Asia was basically very simple: a fleet of two squadrons (one to block the Red Sea and one to patrol the western coast of India), a Governor-General at Goa and seven fortresses on the periphery.[118] For commercial purposes they maintained a series of trading posts *(feitoria)* and established three great intermediate markets: Malacca, Calicut, and Ormuz, and a subsidiary stop at Aden.[119] The greatest of them was Malacca which became a giant store house and entrepôt, located there almost obligatorily because the monsoons forced the sailing ships coming from points east to unload there.[120] This structure was evolved by Portugal's leading figure on the scene, Affonso Albuquerque, who worked it out as a solution to the military dilemmas of the enterprise.[121]

---

many more, but it also made possible the use of much bigger pieces without imperilling the stability of the vessel. . . .

"When the sailing vessels of Atlantic Europe arrived [into the Indian Ocean], hardly anything could resist them. As Albuquerque proudly wrote to his King in 1513, 'at the rumour of our coming the (native) ships all vanished and even the birds ceased to skim over the water.' This was not rhetorical prose. Within fifteen years after their first arrival in Indian waters the Portuguese had completely destroyed the naval power of the Arabs and the King could justifiably style himself 'Lord of the Conquest, Navigation and Commerce of Ethiopia. Arabia, Persia and India.' " Carlo M. Cipolla, *Guns and Sails*, pp. 82, 137.

For a detailed description of Portuguese ships in this era, see François Mauro, "Types de navires et constructions navales dans l'Atlantique portugais aux XVIe et XVIIe siècles," *Revue d'histoire moderne et contemporaine*, **VI**, juil.-août 1959, 185–193.

[115]Cited approvingly by C. R. Boxer who gives this reason for doubting the sufficiency of the technological explanation: "The monopoly was not, however, so all-embracing as it sounds. Apart from the fact that the Portuguese never had enough warships of their own to enforce it in all times and places, the corrupt colonial officials were easily bribed, and native shipping was often freighted by

(or in the name of) Portuguese merchants." "The Portuguese in the East, 1500–1800," in H. V. Livermore, ed., *Portugal and Brazil, an Introduction* (London and New York: Oxford Univ. Press (Clarendon) 1953). 193.

[116]Godinho, *L'économie de l'empire portugais*, p. 18.

[117]*Ibid.*, p. 19.

[118]See *ibid.*, p. 574.

[119]See *ibid.*, pp. 591, 595.

[120]See *ibid.*, p. 594.

[121]"As European rivals with equal maritime power challenged the Portuguese claims, the defence of the vast trade which had been won demanded close organization, and the garrison posts needed troops who would stand up to European attack and who could hold on when naval support was lacking. The Portuguese answer was worked out in thesis form by their Governor, Affonso Albuquerque, who developed a plan for a series of independent forts and for channeling trade through the entrepôt of Goa on the Malabar coast and to Europe through the sole port of Lisbon, who concentrated his defensive system on the vulnerable area of the Persian Gulf and the Gulf of Aden, and who advocated a solution to the manpower question by the evolution of a half-breed population." Rich, *Cambridge Economic History of Europe*, **IV**, pp. 204–205.

By and large the trade was in the hands of the state,[122] and when Portugal's role began to wane in the latter part of the sixteenth century, the private sector pulled out of the reduced trade entirely because of the increased risk.[123]

In a few small areas, the Portuguese exercised direct sovereignty. In several areas, such as Cochin or Ceylon, the local ruler was under Portuguese "protection." But in most places, the Portuguese made no pretense at political rule, instead "circulating and trading in conformity with the laws, usages, and customs of the states in which they found themselves."[124] As Donald F. Lach puts it, the Europeans at that time were "mainly interested in those countries where effective unity and central authority help(ed) to provide stable conditions for trade and a favorable climate for evangelizing."[125]

To appreciate why we do not consider the Indian Ocean trading area to be part of the European world-economy despite the fact that it was so completely dominated by a European power, we must look successively at the meaning of this dominance for the Asian countries affected, its meaning for Europe, and how it compares with those parts of the Americas under Iberian rule.

There seems little doubt that a major element in Portugal's lightning ascendancy first in the Indian Ocean then in the China Sea, was the "vacuum in sea-borne trade," as Trevor-Roper calls it, that existed at this time in both areas: "The vast trade of Asia—of which the long-distance trade with Europe was but a fragment—lay open to the first comers. The Portuguese came and took it; and while the vacuum lasted—until Europe overtook them or Asia resisted them—it was their monopoly."[126] The vacuum was not economic but political, for it is central to the understanding of the situation that the Portuguese did not create the trade. They took over a pre-existing trade network, in the hands at that point of time of Moslem merchants (Arabs and Gujeratis) in the Indian Ocean and *Wako* pirates

[122]"The most extensive overseas commerce carried on by the state was Portugal's trade with Indian and the intermediate ports on the Africa coast—a trade which broke entirely new ground. From its earliest days and until 1577, this colonial trade was carried on and to the extent that the legal forms regulating the trade were adhered to, it was undertaken entirely on the king's account, at his own risk, and in his own ships, and licences to private merchants for the Indian trade were given only in exceptional cases, though somewhat more frequently in the African trade." Heckscher, *Mercantilism*, I, p. 341.

[123]"However, from the end of the 16th century, misfortune fell upon the Cape route, whose traffic declined considerably. Now the English and the Dutch brought large cargos of pepper and other spices and drugs to Europe. That is the essential reason why, beginning in 1597, trade came back

into the hands of the state: private entrepreneurs no longer dared take the risk of forming companies for the 'harvest' of the returning merchandise ['la ferme de *trazida*']. . . . The Dutch engaged in their early operations with certainty as to their profit from both trade and the seizure of Portuguese ships; their ships traveled, there and back, in no fear of attack, which was not true for the Portuguese. Private entrepreneurs therefore did not wish to invest their capital; putting together only small sums, most of the capital being invested by the state, was not sufficient to constitute a company." Godinho, *L'économie de l'empire portugais*, pp. 696–697.

[124]*Ibid.*, p. 656.

[125]Donald F. Lach, *Asia in the Making of Europe*, Vol. I: *The Century of Discovery* (Chicago, Illinois: Univ. of Chicago Press, 1965), Book II, 827–828.

[126]H. R. Trevor-Roper, *Historical Essays*, p. 120.

in the China Sea.[127] The ouster of the Moslem traders, which comes first in time, was "by brute force and not by peaceful competition."[128] It was primarily due to politico–naval superiority.[129]

The great import from Asia to Lisbon was pepper, or pepper and spices. Already at the end of the fifteenth century before Portugal was in the picture, Europe probably consumed a quarter of Asia's production;[130] and, to meet the increased demand of Europe, Asian production doubled over the course of the century.[131] In return, what Asia principally got from Europe was bullion, silver and gold.[132] The silver came largely from the Americas and Japan.[133] The gold seems largely to have come at first from West Africa,[134] then from southeast Africa, Sumatra and China.[135]

[127]On the ouster of the Moslems in the Indian Ocean, see Godinho, *L'économie de l'empire portugais,* p. 630; C. R. Boxer, *The Portuguese Seaborne Empire,* pp. 45–48. On the Portuguese as replacements for the *Wako* pirates, see Trevor-Roper, *Historical Essays,* p. 120, which in turn is based on C. R. Boxer, *The Christian Century in Japan,* and Sansom, *A History of Japan,* **II,** p. 268.

[128]Boxer, *Portuguese Seaborne Empire,* p. 46.

[129]"Fortunately for the Portuguese, at the time of their appearance in Asian waters the empires of Egypt, Persia, and Vijayanagar had no armed shipping in the Indian Ocean, if indeed they possessed any ships at all, and Chinese ships were officially confined to navigation along the China coast by imperial decree." Boxer, in Livermore, *Portugal and Brazil,* pp. 189–190.

[130]See Godinho, *L'économie de l'empire portugais,* p. 596.

[131]See ibid., pp. 581–582, 591; Boxer, *Portuguese Seaborne Empire,* p. 59.

[132]Pepper was the principal commodity imported from the East, and silver bullion was the principal export to 'Golden Goa'. . . . For most of the second half of the sixteenth century the Malabar pepper traders refused to accept payment in anything but gold. . . ." Boxer, *Portuguese Seaborne Empire,* pp. 52, 60.

It should be noted that Chaunu feels that this trade was a good bargain for Europe: "120 to 150,000 tons of spices were bought, almost without merchandise in return, for 150 tons of gold, which the weight of domination had seized from the feeble African societies, and a quantity of specie difficult to calculate, but not at all comparable to the 6000 tons of equivalent silver which remained to be made up." *Conquête et exploitation des nouveaux mondes (XVIe siècle),* Collection Nouvelle Clio 26 bis (Paris: Presses Universitaires de France, 1969), p. 323.

[133]"[It] is the trade with America which alone permitted Europe to develop its Asian trade. For without the silver of the New World, spices, pepper, silk, precious stones, later China porcelain, all these precious luxuries could not have been acquired by the West." Chaunu, *Séville,* **I,** pp. 13–14.

"Trade with the West reached a turning point in the period after the opening of the Mexican-Peruvian silver mines, for their yield flowed in considerable portion to China in exchange for silk, porcelain, and tea." Max Weber, *Religion of China,* p. 5. Weber points out that silver depreciated in relation to gold in China at this time, going from 4 : 1 in 1368 to 8 : 1 in 1574 to 10 : 1 in 1635 to 20 : 1 in 1737.

"Next to China the principal country with which Portugal traded was Japan. The prosperity of Macao [in the sixteenth century] was in a great measure owing to the export of bullion from that country." Chang, *Sino-Portuguese Trade,* p. 117. It was Portugal's ability to control the trade between China and Japan that gave her some of the bullion with which to trade in southeast Asia and India.

"The sudden increase in the production of gold and silver, particularly of silver, after the sixteenth century, was closely connected with new developments in foreign trade.

"The development of trade with Japan by Portuguese ships and the consequent increase of profits were in fact a result of the intermediary trade consisting of the exchange of Japanese silver for Chinese raw silk and other commodities.

"It was the main purpose of the trade licenced by Hideyoshi to secure Chinese commodities in a third country because of the Ming policy of forbidding landings of foreign ships, especially of Japanese ships, on the mainland. Japanese foreign trade enjoyed a brilliant period of development, and it was in this period that the production of precious metals in Japan reached its most flourishing peak." A. Kobata, "The Production and Uses of Gold and Silver in 16th and 17th Century Japan," *Economic History Review,* 2nd ser., **XVIII,** 2, Oct. 1965, 245–246.

[134]See Chaunu, *Conquête,* p. 316.

[135]See Boxer, *Portuguese Seaborne Empire,* p. 60.

Given Europe's passionate hoarding of bullion, it is strange indeed that this kind of formal imbalance of payments should persist for so long. But if Europe wanted Asia's offerings, it seems that this was the price they had to pay. This points to one fundamental sense in which Asia was not part of the European world-economy at this time, since from 1500 to 1800 Europe's relations with Asian states "were ordinarily conducted within a framework and on terms established by the Asian nations. Except for those who lived in a few colonial footholds, the Europeans were all there on sufferance."[136] And this despite Europe's military superiority. For we must remember that this military superiority was only a *naval* superiority.[137]

From an Asian point of view, the Portuguese traders differed in one fundamental respect from those that had preceded them historically. The buyers were "not merchants—private entrepreneurs—but a formidable naval power, acting, in the name of a foreign state, on behalf of its merchants and itself."[138] This meant that trade relations—indeed prices—were fixed by treaties recognized under international law. But states had to deal with states. And it took the Portuguese a while to accustom themselves to the high level of state dignity they encountered.[139] Initially, the Portuguese were willing to make the enormous profits that seizures would bring, but after 10 short years, they realized this was a very shortsighted policy.[140] They turned instead to becoming the arbiters of and intermediaries for *intra*-Asian trade, the profits from which they used to capitalize the Cape route trade, bringing both spices *and* bullion to Portugal. It was, as Godinho says, a "grandiose dream," an "enterprise beyond her possibilities *(démesurée)*."[141] They sacrificed the bullion (and more) for the spices, but they did achieve a "centralized intra-Asian trade," and that was "something quite new in Asia."[142] Translated into terms of the European world-economy, the Portuguese role as middlemen meant that "a good deal of European imports derived from invisible exports of shipping and commercial services."[143] The degree to which intra-Asian trade was central to the economics of Portuguese involvement in Asia is highlighted by the fact

[136]Lach, *Asia in the Making of Europe*, Book I, p. xii. See Braudel: "In the 16th and following centuries, in the vast Asiatic area which produced spices, drugs, and silk, there circulated therefore precious coins of gold and especially of silver [minted in the Mediterranean]. . . . [T]he great discoveries might turn routes and prices topsy turvy; they could change nothing of the fundamental reality [of a payments deficit.]" *La Méditerranée*, I, p. 422.

[137]"Although the Europeans traveled with seeming ease along the maritime routes of Asia, they penetrated the main continental states infrequently and with difficulty. And, in the sixteenth century,

they were never in a position to force their will upon the imperial rulers of India or China; the great political and cultural capitals of the Asiatic continent in no way felt threatened by their arms." Lach, *Asia in the Making of Europe*, Book I, p. xii.

[138]Godinho, *L'économie de l'empire portugais*, p. 619.

[139]See the marvelous story of Vasco da Gama's faux pas upon first meeting the king of Calicut in Godinho, *ibid.*, pp. 588–590.

[140]See *ibid.*, pp. 627–629.

[141]*Ibid.*, pp. 630–631.

[142]Meilink-Roelofsz, *Asian Trade*, p. 119.

[143]Cipolla, *Guns, and Sails*, p. 136.

that it was only after 75 years, in 1578, that the first nonstop express ship *(une 'carrière' de droiture)* went from Lisbon to Malacca.[144]

Thus, for Asia, Portuguese traders meant two things: Asian traders had to deal with a state as the agent for traders, and *intra*-Asian trade was rationalized. Yet J. C. van Leur does not think this adds up to enough to warrant the designation of social change:

> The Portuguese colonial regime . . . did not introduce a single new economic element into the commerce of Southern Asia. . . . The Portuguese regime only introduced a non-intensive drain on the existing structure of shipping and trade. The next period [that of the Dutch] would in its time organize a new system of foreign trade and foreign shipping, it would call into life trenchant colonial relationships, and it would create new economic forms in Europe—not perhaps as a direct result but rather as a parallel development bolstered by the system. . . .
>
> The international Asian character of trade was maintained, while the political independence of the Oriental states remained practically uninfringed upon by European influence. The great intra-Asian trade route retained its full significance.[145]

The literature tends to support van Leur's assessment.[146] The Portuguese arrived and found a flourishing world-economy. They organized it a little better and took some goods home as a reward for their efforts. The social organization of the economy as well as the political superstructures remained largely untouched. The major change occurs in the production of pepper, the only spice which "gave rise to mass production."[147] But

---

[144]See Godinho, *L'économie de l'empire portugais,* p. 655.

[145]J. C. Van Leur, *Indonesian Trade and Society* (The Hague: Hoeve Ltd., 1955), 118–119, 165. Even Meilink-Roelofsz, who in general is reserved about van Leur's analysis, sees a major change occurring only as of the seventeenth century: "The present study only proposes to show that as early as the first half of the seventeenth century. . . . European ascendancy was beginning to manifest itself, even though—let it be readily admitted—this was not so yet everywhere or in every respect." *Asian Trade,* pp. 10–11.

[146]"The Portuguese couldn't have succeeded, in fifteen years, to control half the trading in the Indian Ocean had they not incorporated and went beyond a thousand-year-old experience, had they not been able largely to build upon what already existed. Their routes superimposed a new hierarchy; they diverted the most important currents of trade. But essentially, they left intact a thousand years of communications and exchanges. The Portuguese revolution is rapid because it is restricted to the summit." Chaunu, *Conquête,* p. 177.

"The presence of the Portuguese in India was scarcely felt except by a few individuals in a few places. . . . [I]t is probable that had the Portuguese

abandoned their Indian empire at the end of the sixteenth century they would have left even less trace than did the Greeks, Scythians, and Parthians —perhaps some coins, some mutilated words in the language of the bazaars, some dwindling communities of mixed blood, and some fading traditions of foreign warriors and priests." George B. Sansom, *The Western World and Japan* (New York: Knopf, 1950), 87.

"Malacca as a vital nexus of trade continues, even after its capture by the Portuguese, to follow long-established commercial practices." Lach, *Asia in the Making of Europe,* Book II, p. 829.

"Only their navies enabled the Portuguese to hold their own, and even then their position was a precarious one. On land warfare, their superior armament was of little avail, being in fact less suited than the native weapons to fighting on tropical terrain. The Europeans, moreover, were confronted with greatly superior numbers of natives who were familiar with the countryside and accustomed to the climate. Thus throughout the entire sixteenth century Portuguese influence remained confined to a small area around the settlements on the coast." Meilink-Roelofsz, *Asian Trade,* p. 124.

[147]Godinho, *L'economie de l'empire portugais,* p. 577.

the technology of pepper is so simple that it required very little labor to expand production by more extensive production, for pepper has an important quality: "Once planted, it does not need to be cared for."[148] Hence, a century of Portuguese dominance meant for most of Asia principally that Portuguese rather than Arabs made the profit. The Indian historian K. M. Pannikkar sums up this perspective by saying:

> It made no difference to Indian rulers whether their merchants sold their goods to the Portuguese or to the Arabs. In fact, the Portuguese had an advantage in that they were able to sell to Indian rulers arms and equipment that they required. So far as the Indian merchants were concerned, very soon they worked out a system of permits by which they were able to carry on their trade without the competition of Arab merchants, and in that sense the Portuguese monopoly may be said to have helped them.[149]

This is why despite the fact that "the enterprises of the Portuguese kings . . . combined monopolies of protection, of transportation, and of products transported,"[150] Charles Boxer can call Portuguese maritime dominance an "inherently brittle superstructure."[151] Asia, or even Indian Ocean border regions, did not become part of the European world-economy in the sixteenth century. Asia was an external arena with which Europe traded, on somewhat unequal terms to be sure. That is to say, elements of monopoly imposed by force intruded on the market operations. There was, in Chaunu's phrase, a "thalassocratic *Conquista*"[152] by Portugal. But Asia's inner life remained basically unchanged by the contact. Surely it would be hard to argue that Asian primary production was an integral part of this time of the European division of labor.

Further evidence can be found if we look at the impact of Portuguese Asian trade on Europe. Europe did not conquer Asia in the sixteenth century because she could not. Her military advantage was only at sea.[153] On land she was still retreating in the face of Ottoman attack,[154] and this military balance would only change with the Industrial Revolution.[155]

---

[148]*Ibid.*, p. 578.

[149]K. M. Pannikar, *Asia and Western Dominance*, p. 53.

[150]Frederic C. Lane, *Venice and History*, pp. 426–427.

[151]Boxer, *Portuguese Seaborne Empire*, p. 57.

[152]Chaunu, *Conquête*, p. 205. See C. R. Boxer: "The old Portuguese colonial empire was essentially a thalassocracy, a maritime and commercial empire, whether mainly concerned with the spice of the East, the slaves of West Africa, or the sugar, tobacco and gold of Brazil. It was, however, a seaborne empire cast in a military and ecclesiastical mould." *Race Relations in the Portuguese Colonial Empire, 1415–1825* (London and New York: Oxford Univ. Press (Clarendon), 1963). 2.

[153]"The relative advantage of Europeans was upon the seas. On land they remained for a long time highly vulnerable. . . . [The] Europeans were unable to produce an effective mobile field artillery until the fourth decade of the seventeenth century. . . .

"Europeans generally felt that any attempt to extend their control over Asian hinterlands had no chance of success. . . .

"As late as 1689 the forces of the East India Company were completely routed on land in India." Cipolla, *Guns, and Sails*, pp. 138, 141, 145.

[154]"While Europe was boldly expanding overseas and was aggressively imposing her predominance over the continents of Asia, Africa and the Americas, on her eastern border she was spiritly retreating under the pressure of Turkish forces." *Ibid.*, p. 140.

[155]"The Europeans' effective conquest or control of vast hinterlands came later as one of the byproducts of the Industrial Revolution." *Ibid.*, p. 146.

What Asia provided for Europe at this time was luxuries. Now luxuries are important and not to be sneered at, but they take second place to food (grain, cattle, fish, sugar) and the manpower needed to raise them. They took second place also to bullion, not hoarded bullion but bullion as money (although it was only magic that bullion could be used as money, the magic lying in the possibility of its eventual use as a commodity, if need be). Compared to food and even to bullion, a world-economy can adjust relatively easily to the shifts in luxury supply.

Pepper, it may be argued, was not quite a luxury, nor even spices, for they were essential to the preservation of food and as medicine.[156] Once again, it was a matter of degree. The food that was preserved was largely meat, not quite a luxury but not quite destined either for those on subsistence diets. Likewise the medicines.[157] Of course, as Chaunu argues, with a rising standard of living in Europe and a changing balance of power in the world, pepper was becoming less of a luxury. The question, I suppose, is how much less:

> When does [pepper] first appear in West? Traditionally one points to several turning-points [jalons]. The first of them are the contacts between East and West in the 12th and 13th centuries in the Mediterranean, at the time of the Crusades. To tell the truth, two factors must be taken into account. The rise of the consumption of pepper must certainly be tied to the increase in the 14th and 15th centuries of meat consumption, a phenomenon that has been clearly established. Much more lasting however the development of consumption-patterns involving far-off and costly products seems to me inseparable from the shift in the power-situation from the 12th and 13th centuries. The spices procured *in the conditions of the 13th* [century] constituted a luxury. To get them required developing that power which would permit Western Christianity to develop slowly its potential [*le lent décollement de ses moyens*]. This power allowed the West to come to have one after the other those various stimulants to the taste-buds and the nervous system that Latin Christianity had been less clever in producing than Oriental civilizations.[158]

In any case, to the extent that pepper was not a luxury but a seminecessity, it was precisely the *malaguette* of West Africa, not Asian products, which was the most important in *quantity*, if not in price.[159]

---

[156]"We find it difficult, nowadays, to imagine the importance of spices in the 16th century. . . . Yet, when sugar was all but unknown, when neither refrigeration nor winter stock-feed was available to provide anything but spiced or salted meat in winter, when there were few vegetables to add vitamins and variety to the diet, and when spices or other Eastern drugs formed the main *materia medica*, they held a really important place in Europe's commerce." Robertson, *South African Journal of Economics*, **XVIII**, p. 42. It is not true, however, as we have seen, that sugar was virtually unknown at this time. It was being grown extensively on Mediterranean and Atlantic islands, and was being introduced into Brazil and later the Caribbean.

[157]One should however bear in mind the hierarchy of importance. Pepper was relatively more important than the spices. Chaunu observes: "Pepper was not considered, in 16th-century trade, a spice. Pepper, this infantry of the palace and of the conservation of meat, did not have the prestige of spices in the narrower meaning of the term, nor of drugs." *Conquête*, p. 200.

[158]*Ibid.*, pp. 316–317. Italics added.

[159]"The African spice trade represented for Portugal a volume of traffic noticeably higher than any of the Asiatic spices other than pepper and ginger, and often greater than their sum total. By itself, malaguette almost constantly exceeded ginger. Of course, the price of the grains only was a fraction

There is of course no question that the Asian trade was *profitable* to
Portugal. That after all was the point of it. Godinho spends 25 pages
evaluating this. One example, perhaps spectacular, will suffice. The
merchandise which returned was evaluated in 1512 by Albuquerque as
eight times the worth in Portuguese currency of that sent out.[160] It is easy
to see therefore why pepper was "the most notable speculative commodity
of the [sixteenth and seventeenth centuries], attracting the attention of
the greatest merchants and capitalists of the age."[161] The divisibility and
durability of pepper, as well as its profit margin, "rendered it an excellent
object for speculation."[162]

This speculation was not simply that of the capitalists as individual entrepreneurs. It was preeminently that of the Portuguese state which sought
"to increase national wealth by the use of military power," in the formulation
of Frederic Lane.[163] We shall consider below the costs of this policy. It
is pertinent however at this point to insert Lane's evaluation of this collective "speculation":

> In the long run of fifty or a hundred years, a more peaceful policy, fostering
> a greater development of the Eastern trade, might have made the nation richer.
> Although the conquest of India increased Portuguese national income for a time,
> it was followed by a decrease later in the productivity of the nation's labor. It
> does not therefore supply a clear case of success in using armed force to increase
> the nation's prosperity.[164]

But could Portugal have pursued a "more peaceful policy?" This is doubtful,
partly as Lane himself suggests, because of the kind of capital and labor
that existed in Portugal in 1500.[165]

Nonetheless, the discussion on profitability makes clear the limitations
to profit by trade in an external arena. The profits, when all is said and

---

of the price of the Oriental spices: in March 1506,
a quintal cost 8 *cruzados*, while that of pepper sold
for 22, of cinnamon for 32 and 33, and of ginger
for 18 to 19. Despite its low price, the total value
of the malaguette often equalled, sometimes was
greater than, that of each of the other spices, pepper
and ginger excepted: for 200 quintals of grains at
8 *cruzados* (and as of 1506, 11) were equal in value
to 500 of cinnamon at 32 *cruzados* or of 840 of ginger
at 19 *cruzados*." Godinho, *L'économie de l'empire portugais*, p. 547. See pp. 539–542 for the botanical
descriptions and geographic locations of the West
African products.

[160]The evaluation can be found in *ibid.*, pp.
683–709. The example is on p. 699.

[161]Glamann, *European Trade*, p. 52.

[162]*Ibid.*, p. 53.

[163]Frederic C. Lane, "National Wealth and Protection Costs," in *Venice and History* (Baltimore, Maryland: Johns Hopkins Press, 1966), 376.

[164]*Ibid.*, p. 381.

[165]"The activity in which the Portuguese then displayed superiority over other nations was not
shrewd trading but bold adventuring both in navigation and in war. Because of the military and religious
traditions of the Portuguese and their class structure, the crusading policy pursued in India may
well have stimulated energies which obtained more
wealth than the Portuguese could have gained by
less bellicose means. A Venetian of 1500 was likely
to believe that the Portuguese could gain more by
a more peaceful policy because such might have
been the case had the Portuguese ruling class been
similar in character to the Venetian in 1500. At that
date many Venetian nobles had become wedded
to peaceful trade or to the management of country
estates. They were no longer, as they had been three
or four hundred years earlier when bullying Byzantium, equally efficient either as merchants or as sea
raiders." *Ibid.*, pp. 395–396.

done, are those of plunder. And plunder is over time self-defeating, whereas exploitation within the framework of a single world-economy is self-reinforcing.

Perhaps this will be clearer if we now seek to compare systematically Iberia in Asia and Iberia in the Americas. A word should be said first about the relations of Portugal and Spain. The papal bull, *Inter Coetera,* in its second version of June 1493 drew a famous line, supposedly allocating various parts of the non-European world to the care of Portugal and Spain for the purposes of evangelization.[166] For the Atlantic regions, this came to mean that Portugal's sovereignty was recognized over Brazil and the Atlantic non-Caribbean islands but that of Spain over the bulk of the continent. Presumably Asia was "allotted" to Portugal. But Magellan convinced Charles V to reinterpret the map, it being difficult in the sixteenth century to estimate longitudes, and he laid claim on behalf of the Spanish Crown to the Philippines in 1520,[167] which however was not in fact occupied until 1564. Indeed it is only when Portugal begins to falter as a source of pepper supply because of the revival of Venice's role that Spain sends her expedition to the Philippines in search of pepper, there and in China.[168]

Thus we have a largely Hispanic role in the Americas with a Portuguese corner, and a largely Portuguese role in Asia with a Spanish corner. It is striking how *Iberian* policy was roughly similar in both areas. For in the sixteenth century, Iberia establishes *colonies* in the Americas, but *trading-posts* in Asia.[169]

We have already written of Spanish policy in the Americas and Portuguese policy in Asia. It is noteworthy that each sought to generalize from its dominant experience to the other area but, realizing its error, each came to adapt itself to the requirements of the area. The Portuguese sought to limit their involvement in Brazil to an entrepôt arrangement, but were forced to colonize it as a preemptive measure as of 1530.[170] Similarly the

[166]The story is complex because of diplomatic intrigues. See Samuel Eliot Morison, *Admiral of the Ocean Sea* (Boston: Little Brown, 1942), 367–374; Chaunu, *Conquête*, pp. 251–254.

[167]See Pierre Chaunu, "Le galion de Manille," *Annales E.S.C.*, **VI**, 4, oct.-déc. 1951, 449.

[168]See *ibid.*, pp. 450–451.

[169]Spain originally intended to establish trading-posts, not colonies, in the Americas. It was only the absence of the kind of political economy that would have permitted such a relationship that drew Spain on to colonization. Luis Aznar describes this development: "Neither the rudimentary gold placers nor the slave traffic nor the capitation . . . brought in enough to equal the expenses of the first three expeditions undertaken by Columbus in the 15th century and to pay the salaries of the first settlers. News of the misfortune in Hispaniola quickly spread and led to discredit in the circles of the court. . . .

"[The Court changed its policy and thus] in this manner, what began as a feudal enterprise, became in the beginning of the sixteenth century an organic system of government, prototype of what the colonizing countries would establish in the course of the first two centuries of the modern era." "Las etapas iniciales de la legislación sobre indios," *Cuadernos americanos*, **VII**, 5, sept.-oct. 1948, 177–178.

[170]"[D]uring the first half of the sixteenth century the Portuguese considered the discovery of Brazil (1500) as a matter of secondary importance. In fact, efforts to consolidate control over the seaboard of what is now Brazil, roughly between the present ports of Santos and Recife, were largely a reflex action taken to prevent France and England from establishing competitive coastal enclaves for the export of Brazilian dyewood used in the manufacture of woollens in the Low Countries and England. Only the fear of competition led to sustained occupa-

Spaniards sought to utilize an *encomienda* system in the Philippines, but the international commerce was insufficient to sustain the costs and they reverted to the Portuguese pattern. "The trade of Manila thus settled down to a straight exchange of silver from New Spain against Chinese wares."[171]

The reasons for the two different policies seem to be, as we have already hinted, twofold. On the one hand, the rewards of American colonization were in some sense greater. On the other hand, the difficulties of colonizing Asia were much greater. The combination of the two meant that the Americas became the *periphery* of the European world-economy in the sixteenth century while Asia remained an *external arena*.

By rewards we do not mean short-run profit, although even here the Americas seem to do better than Asia by about 50%,[172] but long-run profits in terms of opportunity costs. The Asian trade was an *import trade*, especially that part of it which bypassed the Levant.[173] Indeed one of the reasons Spain eventually gave up the Manila Galleon was precisely opposition at

---

tion in the latter half of the century and the establishment of a plantation economy." Stanley J. Stein and Barbara H. Stein, *The Colonial Heritage of Latin America*, p. 22; Chaunu, *Conquête*, p. 222.

See this analysis of Portugal's attitude toward Brazil at this point in time: "The absence of treasures which could be easily plundered lessened Portugal's interest in Brazil in the early years, particularly as her trade with the East Indies was then at its height. To attract private capital for her American colony, the Portuguese Crown divided it into twelve hereditary captaincies (*donatários*), who took over many of the royal privileges. The want of any economic base, except in the region where the cultivation of sugar cane had been introduced, led to the collapse of this experiment. The Crown had to assume direct responsibility for the cost of defending vast territories which long remained of little economic value. Although formally modelled on Portuguese feudal institutions, the system of hereditary captaincies should be seen as an endeavour to attract private capital for the task of commercial expansion directed by the Crown, comparable to the trading corporations set up in England and Holland during the latter half of the sixteenth century." Celso Furtado, *Economic Development of Latin America*, pp. 9–10, fn. 2.

[171]Harrison, *New Cambridge Modern History*, **III**, p. 554.

[172]"We have nonetheless for the 16th century order of magnitude. . . . If Lisbon, with the Far East, is worth 1, Brazil is worth between .05 and .1, and Seville 1.5. At the beginning of the 17th century, Seville is worth more or less one and a half times Lisbon." Chaunu, *Conquête*, p. 269.

This tells us nothing however about the importance of this trade to Europe as a whole. "It is dif-

ficult to measure the share of Seville and Lisbon, that is the share of the monopoly, the share of the southwest quarter of the Iberian peninsula, because the monopoly is easier to measure than the European world on which it rests. The differences in the possibilities of measurement in relation to the evaluation of the importance of the American trade dominated by Seville and the Asiatic trade dominated by Lisbon do not result from some intrinsic inability to measure monopolies but far more from our temporary inability to measure the rest [that is, what is not part of the monopoly.]" *Ibid.*, p. 273.

[173]"While most imports from overseas were paid for by the export of bullion and coin—the East Indian trade was decidedly an import trade with the principal object of satisfying a European demand rather than of finding markets for European products—imports via the Levant presented a rather different face. The worlds of Araby and the Indies coveted a number of articles from the countries of the Mediterranean. Copper was a metal in particular demand and was despatched eastwards from central Europe via Venice. Coral from the fisheries off the Tunisian coast was exported eastwards, some of it by the French Compagnie du Corail that operated from Marseilles in the second half of the sixteenth century. Fabrics, quicksilver and saffron, together with opium from Egypt, entered into the stream of goods exchanged between the Mediterranean countries, the Levant and the Indies. This circumstance undoubtedly explains also why the caravan trade did not come to a standstill when the Portuguese found the sea route to the Indies and tried to redirect pepper transport." Glamann, *Fontana Economic History of Europe*, pp. 56–57.

home to the bullion drain it represented.[174] To be sure, this is not, as we have indicated, without some exceptions. It seems for example that Indian teak forests were to some extent incorporated into the European world-economy as suppliers of timber for ships built in dockyards at Goa.[175]

But this is minor compared to the harvest of bullion, wood, leather and sugar from the New World, which evolved during the century from a gathering technique to a stable form of production using cheap labor and European supervision,[176] and thus *transformed* the social structure of the areas involved, incorporating them into the European world-economy.[177]

It is only when Europe had no choice, could not get a product within the framework of its own world-economy that it went to the outside arena to get it at higher cost. Take for example silk. Woodrow Borah has described the reasons for the collapse of Mexican raw silk production in the late sixteenth century.[178] It is just then, as Chaunu points out, that we have

---

[174]"The greatest adversary of the Manila galleon was without a doubt the Spanish administration itself. In the eyes of the merchants of Seville, whose complaints easily reached the Councils of the King, in the eyes of the bullionist orthodoxy of the Court, the galleon trade was the worst of all the trades with the Far East; its deficit was made up for by the export of precious metals." Chaunu, *Annales E.S.C.,* **VI,** p. 458.

Another reason to oppose this outflow of bullion was that it increasingly did not even pass through Lisbon and Seville: "By the Cape route, the [silver] *reales* flowed out over the whole of the Orient. Thanks to them, the China trade—porcelain, raw silk and silk fabrics, gold—won out over other trades, and led to frequenting Japan, outlet for the silk, source of silver. The depth of desire of China for the white metal on the one hand and the development of Spanish America on the other, led to the creation of a direct route from Acapulco to Manila, which aroused the hostility of Goa and of Lisbon and brought them both closer to Seville, equally hurt by it." Godinho, *L'économie de l'empire portugais,* p. 833.

The Spanish case makes a striking contrast nonetheless with that of England. In the early seventeenth century, the English East India Company similarly came under attack for the efflux of silver which accompanied its trade and which many deemed responsible for the trade depressions of the time. "To this the stock answer was that, since the Company's re-exports to the Continent and the Middle East exceeded in value the treasure sent to the Indies, the whole question was inseparable from the country's balance of payments as a whole." K.M. Chaudhuri, "The East India Company and the

Export of Treasure in the Early 17th Century," *Economic History Review,* **XVI,** 1, Aug. 1963, 25. The Company was of course perfectly right. "Europe" was losing bullion, but not England. It was Spain's inability to place herself at the nexus of interregional trade in Europe, as had England at that time, that made the difference.

[175]See Boxer, *Portuguese Seaborne Empire,* pp. 56–57; also Godinho, *L'économie de l'empire portugais,* p. 683.

[176]See Chaunu, *Conquête,* pp. 290–296, 300–311.

[177]See Boxer's description of the impact of sugar on the Brazilian social structure. *Portuguese Seaborne Empire,* pp. 84–105. As for the mining operations, see Alvaro Jara: "It is unquestionable that in many regions of the Americas mining had a tremendous power to reorganize, even undermine, the structure that the people had had in the pre-colonial era. The new concentration of the indigenous population produced by the creation of mining centers —and we are not thinking only of Potosí but of many other centers of silver, gold, and mercury production—created probably for the first time the social phenomenon of those floating and dispossessed masses, uprooted of everything, without a future or any security for the morrow, grouped in pseudo-urban zones, in which the conception of the city had no significance for them as such, at least insofar as urban life might entail an increase in their former standard of life." Jara, *Tres ensayos sobre economía minera hispano-americana,* p. 28.

[178]Woodrow Borah points out that silk was originally raised because it was "compact and easily moved by carrier or mule, promised low transportation costs, a sure outlet in the colony or in Spain, and large profits." *Silk-raising in Colonial Mexico,*

"the apogee of the Galleon trade, the massive, brusque and ephemeral arrival of Chinese silk on the Indies market."[179] Of course, when the Spaniards have no more American silver to offer the Chinese, they cannot buy the silk and the Manila Galleon trade collapses about 1640.[180]

As a general rule, the geographical bounds of a world-economy are a matter of equilibrium. The dynamics of forces at the core may lead to an expansionist pressure (as we saw happened in Europe in the fifteenth century). The system expands outward until it reaches the point where the loss is greater than the gain. One factor is of course distance, a function of the state of the technology. Early on, we mentioned the concept of a sixty-day world. There are many ways of estimating time. Compare Chaunu's description of time from Iberia to the Americas, and time from Iberia to Asia. Of the first he says: "Outward passage one month, return six weeks, round trip including loadings and unloadings, in an annual cycle including everything between the winter dead periods."[181] Of the other he says:

> At the point of maximum distance—let us say the Seville-Manila axis as of 1565—the universe born of the long transformation of the 15th and 16th centuries is a five-year universe. That is, five years is the average time necessary for a round trip from Spain to the Philippines.[182]

Clearly the difference was considerable.

But the resistance of distance was compounded by the resistance of establibed authority. The Americas were easily conquered. Even the structured states, like the Aztecs and the Incas, were no match for European arms. Asia was another matter altogether. Neither Portugal, nor even its seventeenth-century successors, were able to summon the firepower to make significant land conquests. For lack of this, they could not establish a system, as in the Americas or eastern Europe, where a little force permits a large expropriation of surplus. On the contrary, it required a lot of force (the Portuguese against their maritime rivals) to achieve the acquisition of a lesser amount of surplus (because the local rulers could insist on a far larger percentage). One way to look at this is to estimate the profitability of alternative uses of force. Frederic Lane conceptualizes it thus:

Ibero-Americana: **20** (Berkeley: Univ. of California Press, 1943), 15. Borah offers three explanations of this decline: decline in Indian population because of maltreatment; overtaxation and exploitation of Indians which led to their withdrawal and destruction by them of the mulberry groves; cut in profits because of the additional supply to the world market from the Philippines. See his long discussion of these causes of decline on pp. 85–101.

[179]Chaunu, *Annales E.S.C.,* **VI,** p. 462 (fn. 1). Although Borah seems at one point to indicate that the rise of the Philippine trade was one of the causes

of the decline of Mexican silk, at another point he suggests that the inverse is true, thus supporting Chaunu: "In contrast, development of the Philippine trade coincided with the decay of Mexican silk-raising; large-scale importations of Chinese silks began in 1579, and about that time domestic silk culture began to decline." Borah, *Silk-raising,* p. 90.

[180]See Chaunu, *Annales E.S.C.,* **VI,** pp. 460–461.

[181]Chaunu, *Conquète,* p. 290.

[182]*Ibid.,* p. 277. A long discussion of distance-time is to be found on pp. 277–290.

I venture to propose as a hypothesis that the [colonial] enterprises which used force to plunder and to prevent the trade of rivals [for example, the Portuguese in Asia] were in general subject to diminishing returns, but that many enterprises using force to create protection [against the destruction or seizure of its capital and the disruption of its labor force], including many that imposed forced labor [for example, the Portuguese in Brazil], enjoyed the advantage of increasing returns.[183]

Handling oneself in the periphery and in the external arena are different skills. It is only in the periphery that the economically more powerful group is able to reinforce its position by cultural domination as well. The Portuguese understood this far better than the Spanish. The latter took Christian evangelization as a greater priority than did the Portuguese, who were more sensitive to the limits of their power in this great Christian–Moslem encounter in sixteenth-century Asia. Chaunu points out that the Spanish put great effort into stopping Moslem penetration of the Philippines. They succeeded to some extent, but they paid an economic price: "This deep-seated hostility to Islam, this inability to make deals with the Moslem princelets of the Moluccas, is this not the true explanation, far more than Portuguese hostility, why the Spaniards in the Philippines could not make a success of the spice trade?"[184] Compare this with the Portuguese decision in the Kongo where first they played with evangelization, colonization, even cash-crop agriculture, then later realized the costs were too high and retreated to an entrepôt relationship in which they sought primarily slaves and ivory.[185]

In Asia, the Portuguese dominance of the Indian Ocean and the Straits of Malacca faced increasing challenge as the "long" sixteenth century went on—from the Arabs *cum* Venice (the old Levant route), from the rising stars of northwest Europe (England and Holland), and from resurgent indigenous forces in Asia.

In an earlier chapter, we already treated the revival of the Eastern Mediterranean in the "second" sixteenth century. Thus, let us merely briefly review the matter here. To cut off the Levant required a costly blockade. The core of the matter was that the "Portugal was not rich enough to maintain this vast network, its fortresses, its costly squadrons, its func-

[183]Lane, *Venice and History*, p. 28.

[184]Chaunu, *Annales, E.S.C.*, **VI**, p. 455 (fn. 2).

[185]Alfredo Margarido notes: "[T]he 'pagan' Congo refused the imprint of Catholicism and resisted the exigencies of a colonial economy *(économie de traite)*. The Portuguese were obliged to dismantle the kingdom, in order to create there the indispensable *surplus* needed to pursue their colonization policy in South America." "L'ancien royaume du Congo," *Annales E.S.C.*, **XXV**, 6, nov.-déc. 1970, 1725.

Boxer also says that what he calls the "promising experiment" broke down after the death of King Dom Affonso I in 1543 "partly because of Portugal's growing commitments in Asia and South America, but mainly owing to the spread and intensification of the slave-trade." *Race Relations*, p. 20. See also Boxer, *Portuguese Seaborne Empires*, pp. 97–103; Georges Balandier, *Daily Life in the Kingdom of the Kongo* (New York: Pantheon, 1968).

tionaries.[186] By the 1530s, the Turks were once again able to land in the Persian Gulf, and from that point on the Portuguese share of the trade declines.[187] By 1560, Alexandria was exporting as much spices to Europe as in the late fifteenth century,[188] though, to be sure, it was proportionately less. The Portuguese furthermore were unwilling or unable to lower their prices to meet Venetian competition.[189] And of course we are only referring to the pepper trade, since the trade in drugs seems at no point to have become a Portuguese monopoly.[190] Indeed Portuguese decline is to be measured by the fact that eventually, after 1580, they sought for a cut in the Venetian trade itself.[191] The decline of Portugal was therefore very real. Godinho warns us not to go to the other extreme and see a rosy pic-

[186]Braudel, *La Méditerranée*, **I**, p. 496. Another factor in this high profit trade was corruption: "For some decades after 1500 the Portuguese put serious obstacles in the way of the Red Sea trade and forced the prices of spices at Alexandria up above the fifteenth-century level. Later the Portuguese officials in India became so inefficient, or so easily corrupted, that they no longer placed costly obstacles in the way of trade through the Red Sea and the Persian Gulf." Frederic C. Lane, *Venice and History*, p. 33.

[187]See Lybyer, *English Historical Review*, **XXX**, p. 586.

[188]Lane, *Venice and History*, p. 31.

[189]Godinho cites a sixteenth-century Venetian merchant, Cesare de Fedrici: "The pepper that goes to Lisbon is not as good as that which comes through the straits of Mecca [presumably the Red Sea]; because the envoy of the King of Portugal many years ago made a contract with the King of Cochin in the name of the King of Portugal, and fixed the price of pepper, with the consequence that the price could neither rise nor fall. Thus the price is very low, such that the peasants give it over very reluctantly, and it is unripe and dirty. Since the Arab merchants pay better, they are given better pepper, better treated." *L'économie de l'empire portugais*, pp. 638–639.

Godinho insists that losses on the Cape route are *not* an explanation of Portuguese decline: "In conclusion: in the course of 136 years, the losses add up for the outward voyage to less than 11%, and for the return voyage to less than 15%. When, in 1558, in drawing up a sort of budget for the spice trade, there was included an item for an annual loss of one out of five ships (20%) on the return trip, the calculation was very generous. The Italian Sassetti, who was acquainted with the Mediterranean, and who had had the experience of having been forced to return to his port of departure the preceding year, wrote from Cochin that it was less dangerous to go from Lisbon to India than from Barcelona to Genoa [p. 671]."

It may be asked, as Guy Chaussinaud-Nogaret does in a review of Godinho's book, why it was that the Portuguese at this time never developed great private companies, as did later the English and the Dutch, that might have been able to use more efficient commercial methods to outbid their European competitors. (The attempt to create such a company in 1628 failed.) "Why did Portugal, which seemed to have been at the forefront of the great movement which saw the coming into being of modern commercial capitalism, find itself at the beginning of the 17th century incapable of following the northern [European] models [by then in existence]? Does not part of the answer lie in the role of international capitalism in Lisbon, what Virginia Rau has called 'cosmopolitan speculation' ['*agiotage*']? Which brings us back to the question of who were the great beneficiaries of the spice trade. Apparently not the country which held the monopoly: the 'king of pepper' saw his finances eaten away by the enormity of the required investments." "L'or, le poivre, le Portugal et l'économie mondiale," *Annales E.S.C.*, **XXV**, 6, nov.-déc. 1970, 1595. See, in the light of this comment, Furtado's view, already recorded in footnote 170.

The one attempt of the Portuguese to establish such a private company was virtually at the initiative of the state. Founded in 1628, it was dissolved by 1633. See Da Silva, *En Espagne*, pp. 140–141.

[190]See Godinho, *L'économie de l'empire portugais*, pp. 596-616. He says that Portuguese actions in the Indian Ocean, even at their high point of efficacity, "had almost no impact on the drug supply [p. 616]."

[191]See *ibid.*, p. 771. Since the Turks forbade subjects of the King of Spain (which included the Portuguese after 1580) to trade in their dominions, Portuguese merchants assumed French, English, or Venetian names.

ture for Venice in its upswing,[192] a view we have already had occasion to expound. For Venice could not pick up all that Portugal dropped.

An even more effective rival was northwest Europe. We should not forget that when the Crowns of Spain and France both declared bankruptcy in 1557, the Portuguese Crown followed suit in 1560. We shall not review the reasons for the rise of Holland and England. But we should take note of one crucial factor in the spice trade, which is that there were in fact *two* spice trades, often called "the Asian contract," and "the European contract." That is to say, there were profits on the spices brought from Asia to Lisbon (or Venice or later Amsterdam) and there were profits on these same spices as they were resold to their ultimate European consumers, who were principally to be found in northern Europe.[193]

The Portuguese did not have the network to sell the pepper in Europe, especially after the decline of Antwerp, with whom they had had close relations. Chaunu says of Portugal in 1585:

> Cut off from the North, the king of Spain, who rules in Lisbon since 1580, offers in vain the contract of Europe. Italy is not strong enough [*n'est pas du taille*]. No one in Spain can dream of it. He must substitute for Antwerp all the strength of German capitalism, that of the Welsers and the Fuggers.
> How can it be said more clearly? The contract of Europe in the end takes priority over the contract of Asia.[194]

But the Welsers and the Fuggers, in turn, are not strong enough to stand up to the English and the Dutch.[195] And the rise of the Dutch is in fact the final blow to Venice because Amsterdam, "more efficient than [Lisbon], breaks the neck of the old Mediterranean commerce."[196]

The Dutch (and English) not only had advantages in Europe. Their naval superiority in the Indian Ocean had an extra financial advantage. They could make profits not only from the trade but from plundering

---

[192]See *ibid.*, p. 714. Also Godinho says of the initial Venetian difficulties in 1502: "The crisis was not caused by the Portuguese voyages, because it precedes them. . . . That is to say that the establishment of the Indies route and the action undertaken against Red Sea commerce were taken against a body with extremely sensitive open wounds which, outlasting the immediate cause of the outbreak of crisis, transformed it into a lasting depression [p. 729]."

[193]See H. Kellenbenz, *Annales E.S.C.*, **XI**, p. 8.

[194]Chaunu, *Conquête*, p. 358.

[195]"Hamburg enjoys only briefly its primacy in the international spice trade. The 1590's were of great importance in the enlargement of colonial trade. The Dutch and the English sought successfully to enlarge their participation in the world spice market." Kellenbenz, *Annales E.S.C.*, **XI**, p. 23.

The Dutch network in Europe was also used to

horn in on the Brazilian sugar trade at this time: "Brazil was the chief source of the sugar consumed in Europe. Most of the trade in sugar and slaves between Brazil and Portugal or between west Africa and Brazil was still in the hands of Portuguese merchants and contractors, many of them of Jewish origin; but the export of sugar from Portugal to the rest of Europe was handled by Dutchmen, and Dutch skippers also plied a clandestine trade with the Brazilian ports. The local Portuguese connived at this trade, and resisted the attempts of the Spanish bureaucracy to prevent it. Merchants in Portugal, also, lent their names to Dutch commercial enterprises, on a commission basis, during the periods when Dutch trade to Iberian ports was officially forbidden." Parry, *Age of Reconnaissance*, p. 277.

[196]Chaunu, *Séville*, **I**, p. 13.

Portuguese ships as well.[197] Even so, the Dutch (and English) did not yet intrude a new element on the Asian scene. They continued the Portuguese role of middlemen.[198]

This brings us then to what is happening in Asia. As the Portuguese collapse, some control is recovered by Asian rulers. For example, from 1570 on in the Straits of Malacca, the Javanese take over the spice trade, at least until the intrusion of the Dutch in 1596.[199] For a while the Portuguese compensated for this by their new monopoly of carrying trade between China and Japan.[200] But as the Japanese came to overcome internal anarchy, they no longer needed the Portuguese. Originally the Ming Emperors had forbidden the Japanese to trade because of anger at the *Wako* pirates. Once the *Wako* were under control, direct trading was once again possible. Furthermore, now the Dutch and English came on the scene with no kind words for Spain(–Portugal). The Japanese grew uncomfortable with the Jesuits, and it was possible now for Japan to withdraw from the world, especially since indigenous manufacturers were eliminating the need for Chinese silk.[201]

---

[197]See Godinho, *L'économie de l'empire portugais*, pp. 696–697. But Godinho provides prudential warning against the importance of this very factor, at least from a Portuguese perspective, on p. 671.

The Dutch and English begin to move into the Americas as well at this time. When Spain caused a blockade of Dutch shipping in the Iberian Peninsula in 1595, the Dutch suffered an acute shortage of salt, an Iberian export product. Hermann Kellenbenz underlines the fact that salt, "was very important for the [Dutch] herring industry. . . ." "Spanien, die nördlichen Niederlande und die Skandinavisch-baltische Raum in der Weltwirtschaft und Politik um 1600," *Vierteljahrschrift für die Sozial- und Wirtschaftsgeschichte*, **XLI**, 4, 1954, 293.

The Dutch discovered that salt was available on the peninsula of Araya on the Caribbean shores of South America. They began to exploit it, and the returning ships engaged in smuggling and raiding for good measure. The result was serious for Spain: "For Spain herself, first of all, it meant that her restrictive European salt policy [political pressure on the northern Netherland 'rebels'] had proved a fiasco. She lost outright the sales price and the duties she formerly obtained through disposing of Peninsular salt to the Dutch. Now the latter received American salt cost-free and tax-free, which they estimated to be worth one million florins a year." Engel Sluiter, "Dutch-Spanish Rivalry in the Caribbean Area, 1594-1609," *Hispanic American Historical Review*, **XXVIII**, 2, May 1948, 181.

Spain sought to oust the Dutch and succeeded in doing so temporarily, but only at the cost of manning a large armada and reopening the Iberian Peninsula to the Dutch by the Truce of 1609. It was in a sense too late to undo the damage. "For Spain, the large-scale intrusion of the Dutch in the Caribbean, which was synchronized with their heavy maritime-commercial pressure in the Far East, West Africa, Brazil, Guiana, and the Peninsula itself, was one more factor to complicate Iberian defense of the tropical colonial world. . . . Spain temporarily mended her fences in the Caribbean and, to a certain extent, elsewhere, but at what price! Thrown sharply on the defensive there and everywhere in the colonial world by the Dutch in this period, she so exhausted herself in protecting the vital tropical zone that she had no energy left to assert her exclusive claims in still unoccupied areas upon the fringes of her empire. Only when seen in this context does it become intelligible, for example, why England was able to found and to maintain Virginia, her first slender outpost in America, without interference from the Spaniards, who were solidly based in the Caribbean and in Florida." Sluiter, *Hispanic American Historical Review*, **XXVIII**, pp. 195–196.

[198]See Cipolla, *Guns, and Sails*, p. 136. See Chaudhuri: "Both the English and the Dutch found participation in the 'country trade' of Asia extremely lucrative, and their normal pattern of trade was to invest their silver in purchasing piece goods in India which were then exchanged for the spices of the East Indies. *Economic History Review*, **XVI**, p. 26.

[199]See Godinho, *L'économie de l'empire portugais*, pp. 814–817.

[200]See Boxer, *Portuguese Seaborne Empire*, p. 63.

[201]See Trevor-Roper, *Historical Essays*, pp. 120–123.

It is perhaps the case that Japan's withdrawal was occasioned by the evangelistic overaggressiveness of the Christian Church, as C. R. Boxer asserts.[202] One has to take seriously an hypothesis which comes from Boxer, whose breadth of knowledge and historical judgment command respect. However, there is little concrete empirical evidence presented by him to back up this judgment. Might they not have withdrawn in any case, given their growing internal strength and the thinness of the links they had to any world-economy?

Portuguese citizens themselves drew the lesson of the decline of the entrepôt boom. They began to cut themselves off from the home country, and adjust to survival in Asia. They became, in economic terms, largely Asians of European extraction, though less so in political terms and doubtless not at all in cultural terms. J. B. Harrison describes the ever-increasing military and political autonomy of the *Estado da India* in the course of the sixteenth century, a process that went along with the growing importance for the Portuguese of the intra-Asian trade.[203] With the growing conflict of interests between the Portuguese at home and in India,

> the Portuguese encrust themselves into the worlds of the Orient, installing themselves everywhere as *casados* [literally, those who maintain a household], fit themselves into local or regional interests, give themselves over to local or inter-regional operations.[204]

When Spain absorbs Portugal in 1580, this accentuates the process further. The local Portuguese do not wish to cut the Castilians into their market, and the King of Spain has not got the strength to force them.[205] But this means that instead of edging into the status of a peripheral area,

[202]"But for the introduction, growth, and forcible suppression of militant Christianity in the 16th and 17th centuries, it seems probable that Tokugawa Japan would not have retired into its isolationist shell. This in turn implies that Japan's overseas expansion in that period would not have proved abortive. The Japanese, whether peacefully or otherwise, would have established themselves in the Philippines, Indo-China, and in parts of Indonesia by the turn of the 17th century; and they would, in all probability, have been able to share in the fruits of Europe's industrial revolution, for several decades before they actually did." C. R. Boxer, *The Christian Century in Japan*, p. vii. It is always difficult to deal with "what if" analyses. But it seems to me one can interpret the subsequent sequence quite differently. Could one not argue that only because Japan went into its shell so effectively at that time was it able to emerge in the 19th century in a form strong enough to resist playing a peripheral role in the world-system, and hence to industrialize rapidly.

A similar point of view to Boxer on the motive

for seclusion is expressed by Eijiro Honjo: "[E]vils attending the spread of Roman Catholicism in Japan caused the Tokugawa shogunate to adopt the seclusion policy. . . ." "Facts and Ideas of Japan's Oversea Development Prior to the Meiji Restoration," *Kyoto University Economic Review,* **XVII**, 1, Jan. 1942, 1.

[203]See Harrison, *New Cambridge Modern History,* **III**, pp. 538–543. Godinho says of the captaincy of the Moluccas about 1570 that it was "practically independent." *L'économie de l'empire portugais,* p. 812.

[204]Godinho, *L'économie de l'empire portugais,* p. 783.

[205]"The first move of the panic-stricken Portuguese inhabitants at Macao [when they learned in 1582 of the 1580 union of Portugal and Spain] was to place the colony beyond the reach of Spanish Governors. For if the Portuguese at Macao were to be reduced to the status of ordinary Spanish subjects and if the Port of Macao then would be open to Spaniards as might be expected, the Portuguese 'monopoly' of the China trade

a century of Iberian involvement pushed Asia further away. It would not be until a century or so later that Europe would be strong enough to begin to incorporate these regions.

would immediately come to an end and their loss would be beyond repair." Chang, *Sino-Portuguese Trade*, p. 100.

A compromise was reached. The Portuguese of Macao were granted a semi-independent status, swearing allegiance to the Spanish Crown but flying the Portuguese flag and obtaining from the Chinese the status of a second-class mandarinate. Chang is clear on the motives of the Spanish for accepting this compromise: "The Castilian king . . . fearing interference with the internal affairs of Macao might lead to defiance or even open revolt, acquiesced in its nominal allegiance." *Ibid.*, p. 101.

7

THEORETICAL REPRISE

Figure 8: "Richmond Palace," or "The Thames at Richmond," an oil painting of the first quarter of the seventeenth century, done by David Vinckenboons (1578–1629), a Flemish artist who migrated to England and painted on Royal Commissions in the time of both James I and Charles I.

Theorizing is not an activity separate from the analysis of empirical data. Analyses can only be made in terms of theoretical schema and propositions. On the other hand, analyses of events or processes must include as a starting point a whole series of specific values of certain of the variables, on the basis of which one can explain how the final outcomes were arrived at. In order to convey the historical explanation with clarity, it is often the case that one has to assume or glide over the exposition of the formal interrelations between variables.

Consequently, it often makes sense to review the material a second time more briefly and abstractly at the conclusion. No doubt this should be useful to the reader. But it is even more important for the author, in forcing a degree of rigor in the analysis whose absence might readily pass unnoticed amidst the complexity of detail. The empirical material treated thus far has surely been complex—indeed, far more complex than it was possible to portray. Hence, I propose to review what I have been arguing in this book.

In order to describe the origins and initial workings of a world system, I have had to argue a certain conception of a world-system. A world-system is a social system, one that has boundaries, structures, member groups, rules of legitimation, and coherence. Its life is made up of the conflicting forces which hold it together by tension, and tear it apart as each group seeks eternally to remold it to its advantage. It has the characteristics of an organism, in that it has a life-span over which its characteristics change in some respects and remain stable in others. One can define its structures as being at different times strong or weak in terms of the internal logic of its functioning.

What characterizes a social system in my view is the fact that life within it is largely self-contained, and that the dynamics of its development are largely internal. The reader may feel that the use of the term "largely" is a case of academic weaseling. I admit I cannot quantify it. Probably no one ever will be able to do so, as the definition is based on a counterfactual hypothesis: If the system, for any reason, were to be cut off from all external forces (which virtually never happens), the definition implies that the system would continue to function substantially in the same manner. Again, of course, substantially is difficult to convert into hard operational criteria. Nonetheless the point is an important one, and key to many parts of the empirical analyses of this book. Perhaps we should think of self-containment as a theoretical absolute, a sort of social vacuum, rarely visible and even more implausible to create artificially, but still and all a socially-real asymptote, the distance from which is somehow measurable.

Using such a criterion, it is contended here that most entities usually described as social systems—"tribes," communities, nation-states—are not in fact total systems. Indeed, on the contrary, we are arguing that the only real social systems are, on the one hand, those relatively small, highly autonomous subsistence economies not part of some regular tribute-demanding system and, on the other hand, world-systems. These latter are to be sure distinguished from the former because they are relatively large; that is, they are in common parlance "worlds." More precisely, however, they are defined by the fact that their self-containment as an economic-material entity is based on extensive division of labor and that they contain within them a multiplicity of cultures.

It is further argued that thus far there have only existed two varieties of such world-systems: world-empires, in which there is a single political system over most of the area, however attenuated the degree of its effective control; and those systems in which such a single political system does not exist over all, or virtually all, of the space. For convenience and for want of a better term, we are using the term "world-economy" to describe the latter.

Finally, we have argued that prior to the modern era, world-economies were highly unstable structures which tended either to be converted into empires or to disintegrate. It is the peculiarity of the modern world-system that a world-economy has survived for 500 years and yet has not come to be transformed into a world-empire—a peculiarity that is the secret of its strength.

This peculiarity is the political side of the form of economic organization called capitalism. Capitalism has been able to flourish precisely because the world-economy has had within its bounds not one but a multiplicity of political systems.

I am not here arguing the classic case of capitalist ideology that capitalism is a system based on the noninterference of the state in economic affairs. Quite the contrary! Capitalism is based on the constant absorption of economic loss by political entities, while economic gain is distributed to "private" hands. What I am arguing rather is that capitalism as an economic mode is based on the fact that the economic factors operate within an arena larger than that which any political entity can totally control. This gives capitalists a freedom of maneuver that is structurally based. It has made possible the constant economic expansion of the world-system, albeit a very skewed distribution of its rewards. The only alternative world-system that could maintain a high level of productivity and change the system of distribution would involve the reintegration of the levels of political and economic decision-making. This would constitute a third possible form of world-system, a socialist world government. This is not a form that presently exists, and it was not even remotely conceivable in the sixteenth century.

The historical reasons why the European world-economy came into existence in the sixteenth century and resisted attempts to transform it into an empire have been expounded at length. We shall not review them here. It should however be noted that the size of a world-economy is a function of the state of technology, and in particular of the possibilities of transport and communication within its bounds. Since this is a constantly changing phenomenon, not always for the better, the boundaries of a world-economy are ever fluid.

We have defined a world-system as one in which there is extensive division of labor. This division is not merely functional—that is, occupational—but geographical. That is to say, the range of economic tasks is not evenly distributed throughout the world-system. In part this is the consequence of ecological considerations, to be sure. But for the most part, it is a function of the social organization of work, one which magnifies and legitimizes the ability of some groups within the system to exploit the labor of others, that is, to receive a larger share of the surplus.

While, in an empire, the political structure tends to link culture with occupation, in a world-economy the political structure tends to link culture with spatial location. The reason is that in a world-economy the first point of political pressure available to groups is the local (national) state structure. Cultural homogenization tends to serve the interests of key groups and the pressures build up to create cultural-national identities.

This is particularly the case in the advantaged areas of the world-economy—what we have called the core-states. In such states, the creation of a strong state machinery coupled with a national culture, a phenomenon often referred to as integration, serves both as a mechanism to protect disparities that have arisen within the world-system, and as an ideological mask and justification for the maintenance of these disparities.

World-economies then are divided into core-states and peripheral areas. I do not say peripheral *states* because one characteristic of a peripheral area is that the indigenous state is weak, ranging from its nonexistence (that is, a colonial situation) to one with a low degree of autonomy (that is, a neo-colonial situation).

There are also semiperipheral areas which are in between the core and the periphery on a series of dimensions, such as the complexity of economic activities, strength of the state machinery, cultural integrity, etc. Some of these areas had been core-areas of earlier versions of a given world-economy. Some had been peripheral areas that were later promoted, so to speak, as a result of the changing geopolitics of an expanding world-economy.

The semiperiphery, however, is not an artifice of statistical cutting points, nor is it a residual category. The semiperiphery is a necessary structural element in a world-economy. These areas play a role parallel to that played, *mutatis mutandis,* by middle trading groups in an empire. They are collection points of vital skills that are often politically unpopular. These middle areas (like middle groups in an empire) partially deflect the political pressures which groups primarily located in peripheral areas might otherwise direct against core-states and the groups which operate within and through their state machineries. On the other hand, the interests primarily located in the semiperiphery are located outside the political arena of the core-states, and find it difficult to pursue the ends in political coalitions that might be open to them were they in the same political arena.

The division of a world-economy involves a hierarchy of occupational tasks, in which tasks requiring higher levels of skill and greater capitalization are reserved for higher-ranking areas. Since a capitalist world-economy essentially rewards accumulated capital, including human capital, at a higher rate than "raw" labor power, the geographical maldistribution of these occupational skills involves a strong trend toward self-maintenance. The forces of the marketplace reinforce them rather than undermine them. And the absence of a central political mechanism for the world-economy makes it very difficult to intrude counteracting forces to the maldistribution of rewards.

Hence, the ongoing process of a world-economy tends to expand the economic and social gaps among its varying areas in the very process of its development. One factor that tends to mask this fact is that the process of development of a world-economy brings about technological advances which make it possible to expand the boundaries of a world-economy. In this case, particular regions of the world may change their structural role in the world-economy, to their advantage, even though the disparity of reward between different sectors of the world-economy as a whole may be simultaneously widening. It is in order to observe this crucial phenomenon clearly that we have insisted on the distinction between a peripheral area of a given world-economy and the external arena of the world-economy. The external arena of one century often becomes the periphery of the next—or its semiperiphery. But then too core-states can become semiperipheral and semiperipheral ones peripheral.

While the advantages of the core-states have not ceased to expand throughout the history of the modern world-system, the ability of a particular state to remain in the core sector is not beyond challenge. The hounds are ever to the hares for the position of top dog. Indeed, it may well be that in this kind of system it is not structurally possible to avoid, over a long period of historical time, a circulation of the elites in the sense that the particular country that is dominant at a given time tends to be replaced in this role sooner or later by another country.

We have insisted that the modern world-economy is, and only can be, a capitalist world-economy. It is for this reason that we have rejected the appellation of "feudalism" for the various forms of capitalist agriculture based on coerced labor which grow up in a world-economy. Furthermore, although this has not been discussed in this volume, it is for this same reason that we will, in future volumes, regard with great circumspection and prudence the claim that there exist in the twentieth century socialist national economies within the framework of the world-economy (as opposed to socialist movements controlling certain state-machineries within the world-economy).

If world-systems are the only real social systems (other than truly isolated subsistence economies), then it must follow that the emergence, consolidation, and political roles of classes and status groups must be appreciated as elements of this *world*-system. And in turn it follows that one of the key elements in analyzing a class or a status-group is not only the state of its self-consciousness but the geographical scope of its self-definition.

Classes always exist potentially *(an sich)*. The issue is under what conditions they become class-conscious *(für sich)*, that is, operate as a group in the politico-economic arenas and even to some extent as a cultural entity. Such self-consciousness is a function of conflict situations. But for upper strata open conflict, and hence overt consciousness, is always *faute de mieux*. To the extent that class boundaries are not made explicit, to that extent it is more likely that privileges be maintained.

Since in conflict situations, multiple factions tend to reduce to two by virtue of the forging of alliances, it is by definition not possible to have three or more (conscious) classes. There obviously can be a multitude of occupational interest groups which may organize themselves to operate within the social structure. But such groups are really one variety of status-groups, and indeed often overlap heavily with other kinds of status-groups such as those defined by ethnic, linguistic, or religious criteria.

To say that there cannot be three or more classes is not however to say that there are always two. There may be none, though this is rare and transitional. There may be one, and this is most common. There may be two, and this is most explosive.

We say there may be only one class, although we have also said that classes only actually exist in conflict situations, and conflicts presume two sides. There is no contradiction here. For a conflict may be defined as being between one class, which conceives of itself as the universal class, and all the other strata. This has in fact been the usual situation in the modern world-system. The capitalist class (the *bourgeoisie)* has claimed to be the universal class and sought to organize political life to pursue its objectives against two opponents. On the one hand, there were those who spoke for the maintenance of traditional rank distinctions despite the fact that these ranks might have lost their original correlation with economic function. Such elements preferred to define the social structure as a non-class structure. It was to counter this ideology that the bourgeoisie came to operate as a class conscious of itself.

But the bourgeoisie had another opponent, the workers. Whenever the workers became conscious of themselves as a class, which was not too frequently in the sixteenth century, they defined the situation as a polarized two-class situation. In such circumstances, the bourgeoisie found itself in a deep tactical dilemma. To the extent that they maintained their own *class*-consciousness, they abetted by this fact workers' class-consciousness, and thereby risked undermining their own political position. To the extent that, in order to deal with this problem, they muted their class-consciousness, they risked weakening their position vis-à-vis the tenants of traditional high rank.

The process of the crystallization of class-consciousness of a bourgeoisie, thinking of itself as a universal class, drawing its members from all social ranks, has been illustrated in our discussions of the emergence of the gentry as a social category in Tudor England or the rise of the burghers in the northern Netherlands. One of the ways they supported their claim to be a universal class was by the development of national sentiment, which gave a cultural veneer to their claim.

The deep dilemma of a bourgeoisie trapped by insurrection on the left, so to speak, and fearing an alliance between its two sets of opponents taking the form of regionalist claims, has been illustrated in our discussions of France in the "second" sixteenth century. The bourgeoisie there opted for temporary retreat. They perhaps had no viable alternative. But this retreat was to have its long term consequences in the later social radicalism of the French revolution (however momentary), and in the long-run lag in economic development of France behind England.

Our examples here are of bourgeoisies that became conscious, but conscious within the bounds of a nation-state. This was clearly not the only choice. They could have become conscious of themselves as a world class. And many groups pushed for such a definition. On the one hand, there were the various communities of international merchant–bankers. On the other hand, there were the many sets of capitalist farmers in the peripheral areas.

In the heyday of Charles V, there were many in the Low Countries, in southern Germany, in northern Italy and elsewhere who tied their hopes to the imperial aspirations of the Hapsburgs (some prudentially keeping a foot in the door of the Valois as well). If these groups remained a social stratum and did not yet form a conscious class, they were moving in that direction, and it seemed only a matter of time. But with the failure of empire, the bourgeoisies of Europe realized that their economic and social future was tied to the core-states. And those who, by virtue of their ethnic–religious affiliations, could turn to the national state as their arena of political operation did so.

As for the capitalist farmers of the periphery, they would gladly have thought of themselves as part of an international gentry class. They willingly sacrificed local cultural roots for participation in "world" cultures. But to constitute an international class, they needed the cooperation of the capitalist strata of the core-states, and this was not to be forthcoming. So increasingly these peripheral capitalist farmers became the antiquated and snobbish Spanish-American *hacenderos* or east European nobility of later centuries, retreating from potential international class-consciousness into local status solidarities—which served well the interests of Western European bourgeoisies.

Geographic concentration of particular economic activities serves as a continuing pressure to status-group formation. When the local dominant strata are threatened by any incipient class-consciousness of lower strata, emphasis on local culture serves well to deflect local internal conflict, creating instead local solidarity against the outside. If, in addition, these local dominant strata feel themselves oppressed by higher strata of the world-system, they are doubly motivated to pursue the creation of a local identity.

Obviously, one does not construct an identity out of thin air. One builds on what one finds—in terms of language, religion, and distinctive life-styles. Nonetheless it is quite clear that both linguistic and religious homogeneity and passion (*a fortiori* devotion to separate life-styles) are social creations which cannot be accounted for as simple continuities of tradition eternal. They are social creations molded with difficulty in times of travail.

The sixteenth century was such a time of travail in much of Europe. It was of course the era of the Reformation and the Counter–Reformation. It was the era of great religious civil wars. It was the era of international religious "parties." But in the end, as the dust settled, all the religious upheaval resulted in a pattern of relative religious homogeneity of the various political entities within the framework of international laissez-faire—*cuius regio eius religio.*

We have tried to indicate in our discussion of various specific developments why various forms of Protestantism ended up as the religion of the core-states (except France, and again why) and Catholicism as the religion of the periphery and semiperiphery. We have been skeptical that the tenets of the various theologies had too much to do with it, although they may have facilitated the task. Rather the tenets of the theologies, as they evolved in practice as opposed to their original conception, reflected and served to sustain the roles of the various areas in the world-system.

It is often said that Charles V missed a great opportunity of creating a united German Protestant state by attempting to remain an arbiter of the religious split instead of a protagonist. But such a critique neglects the fact that Charles V sought to create a world-empire, not a core-state within a world-economy. Empires thrive on multiple religions reflecting multiple roles, few of which are concentrated within specific political boundaries. National homogeneity within international heterogeneity is the formula of a world-economy.

At least this is the formula at the simple beginnings. Core-states because of their complex internal division of labor begin to reflect the pattern of the system as a whole. In the sixteenth century, England was already moving in the direction of becoming Britain, which would have regional homogeneity within a relative heterogeneity for the nation as a whole.

Religion does not have to be the defining cultural trait of the major status-groups; one can use language. Language indeed began to play such a role in the sixteenth century, and its importance was to increase as the centuries passed. Religious reinforcement of role specialization in a world-economy has, however, advantages over linguistic reinforcement. It interferes less with the ongoing communications process within the world-economy. And it lends itself less (only less) to isolationist closures, because of the underlying universalist themes of world religions.

The European world-economy of the sixteenth century tended overall to be a one-class system. It was the dynamic forces profiting from economic expansion and the capitalist system, especially those in the core-areas, who tended to be class-conscious, that is to operate within the political arena as a group defined primarily by their common role in the economy. This common role was in fact defined somewhat broadly from a twentieth-century perspective. It included persons who were farmers, merchants, and industrialists. Individual entrepreneurs often moved back and forth between these activities in any case, or combined them. The crucial distinction was between these men, whatever their occupation, principally oriented to obtaining profit in the world market, and the others not so oriented.

The "others" fought back in terms of their status privileges—those of the traditional aristocracy, those which small farmers had derived from the feudal system, those resulting from guild monopolies that were outmoded. Under the cover of cultural similarities, one can often weld strange alliances. Those strange alliances can take a very activist form and force the political centers to take account of them. We pointed to such instances in our discussion of France. Or they can take a politically passive form that serves well the needs of the dominant forces in the world-system. The triumph of Polish Catholicism as a cultural force was a case in point.

The details of the canvas are filled in with the panoply of multiple forms of status-groups, their particular strengths and accents. But the grand sweep is in terms of the process of class formation. And in this regard, the sixteenth century was indecisive. The capitalist strata formed a class that survived and gained *droit de cité,* but did not yet triumph in the political arena.

The evolution of the state machineries reflected precisely this uncertainty. Strong states serve the interests of some groups and hurt those of others. From however the standpoint of the world-system as a whole, if there is to be a multitude of political entities (that is, if the system is not a world-empire), then it cannot be the case that all these entities be equally strong. For if they were, they would be in the position of blocking the effective operation of transnational economic entities whose locus were in another state. It would then follow that the world division of labor would be impeded, the world-economy decline, and eventually the world-system fall apart.

It also cannot be that *no* state machinery is strong. For in such a case, the capitalist strata would have no mechanisms to protect their interests, guaranteeing their property rights, assuring various monopolies, spreading losses among the larger population, etc.

It follows then that the world-economy develops a pattern where state structures are relatively strong in the core areas and relatively weak in the periphery. Which areas play which roles is in many ways accidental. What is necessary is that in some areas the state machinery be far stronger than in others.

What do we mean by a strong state-machinery? We mean strength vis-à-vis other states within the world-economy including other core-states, and strong vis-à-vis local political units within the boundaries of the state. In effect, we mean a sovereignty that is *de facto* as well as *de jure*. We also mean a state that is strong vis-à-vis any particular social group within the state. Obviously, such groups vary in the amount of pressure they can bring to bear upon the state. And obviously certain combinations of these groups control the state. It is not that the state is a neutral arbiter. But the state is more than a simple vector of given forces, if only because many of these forces are situated in more than one state or are defined in terms that have little correlation with state boundaries.

A strong state then is a partially autonomous entity in the sense that it has a margin of action available to it wherein it reflects the compromises of multiple interests, even if the bounds of these margins are set by the existence of some groups of primordial strength. To be a partially autonomous entity, there must be a group of people whose direct interests are served by such an entity: state managers and a state bureaucracy.

Such groups emerge within the framework of a capitalist world-economy because a strong state is the best choice between difficult alternatives for the two groups that are strongest in political, economic, and military terms: the emergent capitalist strata, and the old aristocratic hierarchies.

For the former, the strong state in the form of the "absolute monarchies" was a prime customer, a guardian against local and international brigandage, a mode of social legitimation, a preemptive protection against the creation of strong state barriers elsewhere. For the latter, the strong state represented a brake on these same capitalist strata, an upholder of status conventions, a maintainer of order, a promoter of luxury.

No doubt both nobles and bourgeois found the state machineries to be a burdensome drain of funds, and a meddlesome unproductive bureaucracy. But what options did they have? Nonetheless they were always restive and the immediate politics of the world-system was made up of the pushes and pulls resulting from the efforts of both groups to insulate themselves from what seemed to them the negative effects of the state machinery.

A state machinery involves a tipping mechanism. There is a point where strength creates more strength. The tax revenue enables the state to have a larger and more efficient civil bureaucracy and army which in turn leads to greater tax revenue—a process that continues in spiral form. The tipping mechanism works in other direction too—weakness leading to greater weakness. In between these two tipping points lies the politics of state-creation. It is in this arena that the skills of particular managerial groups make a difference. And it is because of the two tipping mechanisms that at certain points a small gap in the world-system can very rapidly become a large one.

In those states in which the state machinery is weak, the state managers do not play the role of coordinating a complex industrial–commercial–agricultural mechanism. Rather they simply become one set of landlords amidst others, with little claim to legitimate authority over the whole.

These tend to be called traditional rulers. The political struggle is often phrased in terms of tradition versus change. This is of course a grossly misleading and ideological terminology. It may in fact be taken as a general sociological principle that, at any given point of time, what is thought to be traditional is of more recent origin than people generally imagine it to be, and represents primarily the conservative instincts of some group threatened with declining social status. Indeed, there seems to be nothing which emerges and evolves as quickly as a "tradition" when the need presents itself.

In a one-class system, the "traditional" is that in the name of which the "others" fight the class-conscious group. If they can encrust their values by legitimating them widely, even better by enacting them into legislative barriers, they thereby change the system in a way favorable to them.

The traditionalists may win in some states, but if a world-economy is to survive, they must lose more or less in the others. Furthermore, the gain in one region is the counterpart of the loss in another.

This is not quite a zero-sum game, but it is also inconceivable that all elements in a capitalist world-economy shift their values in a given direction simultaneously. The social system is built on having a multiplicity of value systems within it, reflecting the specific functions groups and areas play in the world division of labor.

We have not exhausted here the theoretical problems relevant to the functioning of a world-economy. We have tried only to speak to those illustrated by the early period of the world-economy in creation, to wit, sixteenth-century Europe. Many other problems emerged at later stages and will be treated, both empirically and theoretically, in later volumes.

In the sixteenth century, Europe was like a bucking bronco. The attempt of some groups to establish a world-economy based on a particular division of labor, to create national states in the core areas as politico–economic guarantors of this system, and to get the workers to pay not only the profits but the costs of maintaining the system was not easy. It was to Europe's credit that it was done, since without the thrust of the sixteenth century the modern world would not have been born and, for all its cruelties, it is better that it was born than that it had not been.

It is also to Europe's credit that it was not easy, and particularly that it was not easy because the people who paid the short-run costs screamed lustily at the unfairness of it all. The peasants and workers in Poland and England and Brazil and Mexico were all rambunctious in their various ways. As R. H. Tawney says of the agrarian disturbances of sixteenth-century England: "Such movements are a proof of blood and sinew and of a high and gallant spirit. . . . Happy the nation whose people has not forgotten how to rebel."[1]

The mark of the modern world is the imagination of its profiteers and the counter-assertiveness of the oppressed. Exploitation and the refusal to accept exploitation as either inevitable or just constitute the continuing antinomy of the modern era, joined together in a dialectic which has far from reached its climax in the twentieth century.

---

[1] Tawney, *Agrarian Problems*, p. 340.

BIBLIOGRAPHY

Abel, Wilhelm, *Die Wüstungen des Ausgehenden Mittelalters*, 2d ed. Stuttgart: Fisher Verlag, 1955.

Abrate, Mario, "Creta, colonia veneziana nei secoli XIII–XV," *Economia e storia*, **IV**, 3, lugl.–sett., 1957, 251–277.

Actes du Colloque de la Renaissance. Paris: Lib. Philosophique J. Vrin, 1958.

Ardant, Gabriel, *Théorie sociologique de l'impôt*, 2 vol. Paris: S.E.V.P.E.N., 1965.

Arnold, Stanislaw, "Les idées politiques et sociaules de la Renaissance en Pologne," *La Pologne au Xe Congrès International des Sciences Historiques à Rome*. Warszawa: Académie Polonaise des Sciences, Institut d'Histoire, 1955, 147–165.

Ashton, Robert, "Revenue Farming under the Early Stuarts," *Economic History Review*, 2d ser., **VIII**, 3, 1956, 310–322.

Ashton, Robert, "Charles I and the City," in F. J. Fisher, ed., *Essays in the Economic and Social History of Tudor and Stuart England*. London and New York: Cambridge Univ. Press, 1961, 138–163.

Aspetti e cause della decadenza economica veneziana nel secolo XVII. Atti del Convegno (27 giugno–2 luglio 1957). Venezia-Roma: Istituto per la Collaborazione Culturale, 1961.

Aydelotte, Frank, *Elizabethan Rogues and Vagabonds*, Vol. I of Oxford Historical and Literary Studies. London and New York: Oxford Univ. Press (Clarendon), 1913.

Aylmer, G. E., *The King's Servants*. New York: Columbia Univ. Press, 1961.

Aznar, Luis, "Las etapas iniciales de la legislación sobre indios," *Cuadernos americanos*, **VII**, 5, sept.–oct., 1948, 164–187.

Baehrel, René, "Economie et histoire à propos des prix" in *Eventail de l'histoire vivante: hommage à Lucien Febvre*. Paris: Lib. Armand Colin, 1953, **I**, 287–310.

Baehrel, René, *Une croissance: la Basse-Provence rurale (fin XVIe siècle-1789)*. Paris: S.E.V.P.E.N., 1961.

Bagú, Sergio, "La economía de la sociedad colonial," *Pensamiento crítico*, No. 27, abril 1969, 30–65.

Balandier, Georges, *Daily Life in the Kingdom of the Kongo*. New York: Pantheon, 1968.

Bannon, John F., ed., *Indian Labor in the Spanish Indies: Was There Another Solution?* Boston, Massachusetts: D.C. Heath, 1966.

Barbour, Violet, "Dutch and English Merchant Shipping in the Seventeenth Century," in E. M. Carus-Wilson, ed., *Essays in Economic History*. New York: St. Martin's, 1965, **I**, 227–253. (Originally in *Economic History Review*, **II**, 1930.)

Barbour, Violet, *Capitalism in Amsterdam in the Seventeenth Century*. Ann Arbor, Michigan: Ann Arbor Paperbacks, 1963.

Barkan, Ömer Lutfi, "La 'Méditerranée' de Fernand Braudel vue d'Istamboul," *Annales E.S.C.*, **IX**, 2, avr.–juin 1954, 189–200.

Barley, M. W., "Rural Housing in England," in *The Agrarian History of England and Wales*, **IV**: Joan Thirsk, ed., *1500–1640*. London and New York: Cambridge Univ. Press, 1967, 696–766.

Baron, Salo W., *A Social and Religious History of the Jews*, 2nd ed., **III**: *Heirs of Rome and Persia*. Philadelphia: Jewish Publication Society of America, 1957.

Baron, Salo W., *A Social and Religious History of the Jews*, 2nd ed., **IV**: *Meeting of East and West*. Philadelphia: Jewish Publication Society of America, 1957.

Baron, Salo W., *A Social and Religious History of the Jews*, 2nd ed., **XI**: *Citizen or Alien Conjurer*. New York: Columbia Univ. Press, 1967.

Baron, Salo W., *A Social and Religious History of the Jews*, 2nd ed., **XII**: *Economic Catalyst*. New York: Columbia Univ. Press, 1967.

Barraclough, Geoffrey, *History in a Changing World*. Oxford: Blackwell, 1957.

Barraclough, Geoffrey, *The Origins of Modern Germany*. Oxford: Blackwell, 1962.

Barraclough, Geoffrey, "Universal History," in H. P. R. Finberg, ed., *Approaches to History: A Symposium.* Toronto: Univ. of Toronto Press, 1962, 83–109.

Batho, Gordon, "Landlords in England, A: The Crown," in *The Agrarian History of England and Wales,* **IV**: Joan Thirsk, ed., *1500–1640.* London and New York: Cambridge Univ. Press, 1967, 256–276.

Batho, Gordon, "Landlords in England, B: Noblemen, Gentlemen, and Yeomen," in *The Agrarian History of England and Wales,* **IV**: Joan Thirsk, ed. *1500–1640,* London and New York: Cambridge Univ. Press, 1967, 276–306.

Bauthier, Robert Henri, "The Fairs of Champagne," in Rondo E. Cameron, ed., *Essays in French Economic History.* Homewood, Illinois: Irwin, 1970, 42–63.

Becker, Marvin B., "Economic Change and the Emerging Florentine Territorial State," *Studies in the Renaissance,* **XIII**, 1966, 7–39.

Beloff, Max, *The Age of Absolutism, 1660–1815.* New York: Harper, 1962.

Bennett, M. K., *The World's Food.* New York: Harper, 1954.

Beresford, Maurice W., *The Lost Villages of England.* London: Lutterworth Press, 1954.

Berrill, K., "International Trade and the Rate of Economic Growth," *Economic History Review,* 2nd ser., **XII**, 3, 1960, 350–359.

Betts, Reginald R., "La société dans l'Europe centrale et dans l'Europe occidentale," *Revue d'histoire comparée,* n.s., **VII**, 1948, 167–183.

Bindoff, S. T., *Tudor England,* Vol. V of the Pelican History of England. London: Penguin Books, 1950.

Bindoff, S. T., "Economic Change: The Greatness of Antwerp," *New Cambridge Modern History,* **II**: G. R. Elton, ed., *The Reformation, 1520–1559.* London and New York: Cambridge Univ. Press, 1958, 50–69.

Bishko, Charles Julian, "The Castilian as Plainsman: The Medieval Ranching Frontier in La Mancha and Extremadura," in Archibald R. Lewis and Thomas F. McGann, eds., *The New World Looks at Its History.* Austin: Univ. of Texas Press, 1967, 47–69.

Bitton, Davis, *The French Nobility in Crisis.* Stanford, California: Stanford Univ. Press, 1969.

Blanchard, Ian, "Population Change, Enclosures, and the Early Tudor Economy," *Economic History Review,* 2nd ser., **XXIII**, 3, Dec. 1970, 427–445.

Bloch, Marc, "Medieval 'Inventions'" in *Land and Work in Medieval Europe.* Berkeley: Univ. of California Press, 1967, 169–185. (Translated from *Annales d'histoire économique et sociale,* No. 36, Nov. 1935.)

Bloch, Marc, "Economie-nature ou économie-argent: un pseudo-dilemme," *Annales d'histoire sociale,* **I**, 1939, 7–16.

Bloch, Marc, *Esquisse d'une histoire monétaire de l'Europe,* Cahiers des Annales, **9**, Paris: Lib. Armand Colin, 1954.

Bloch, Marc, *Seigneurie française et manoir anglais.* Paris. Lib. Armand Colin, 1960.

Bloch, Marc, *Feudal Society.* Chicago, Illinois: Univ. of Chicago Press, 1961.

Bloch, Marc, *Les caractères originaux de l'histoire rurale française,* 2 vol. Paris: Lib. Armand Colin, 1964.

Bloch, Marc, "The Rise of Dependent Cultivation and Seigniorial Institutions," *Cambridge Economic History of Europe,* **I**: M. M. Postan, ed., *The Agrarian Life of the Middle Ages,* 2nd ed. London and New York: Cambridge Univ. Press, 235–290.

Blum, Jerome, "Prices in Russia in the Sixteenth Century," *Journal of Economic History,* **XVI**, 2, June 1956, 182–199.

Blum, Jerome, "Rise of Serfdom in Eastern Europe," *American Historical Review,* **LXII**, 4, July 1957, 807–836.

Blum, Jerome, *Lord and Peasant in Russia from the Ninth to the Nineteenth Century.* Princeton, New Jersey: Princeton Univ. Press, 1961.

Borah, Woodrow, *Silk-raising in Colonial Mexico,* Ibero-Americana: **20**. Berkeley: Univ. of California Press, 1943.

Borah, Woodrow, *New Spain's Century of Depression,* Ibero-Americana: **35**. Berkeley: Univ. of California Press, 1951.

Borah, Woodrow, *Early Colonial Trade Between Mexico and Peru,* Ibero-Americana: **38**. Berkeley: Univ. of California Press, 1954.

Boserup, Ester, *The Conditions of Economic Growth.* Chicago, Illinois: Aldine, 1965.

Bouwsma, William J., "Politics in the Age of the Renaissance," in *Chapters in Western Civilization,* 3rd ed. New York: Columbia Univ. Press, 1961, **I**, 199–244.

Bouwsma, William J., *Venice and the Defenses of Republican Liberty.* Berkeley: Univ. of California Press, 1968.

Bowden, P. J., "Wool Supply and the Woollen Industry," *Economic History Review,* 2nd ser., **IX**, 1, 1956, 44–58.

Bowden, P. J., *The Wool Trade in Tudor and Stuart England.* New York: Macmillan, 1962.

Bowden, P. J., "Agricultural Prices, Farm Profits, and Rents," in *The Agrarian History of England and Wales,* **IV**: Joan Thirsk, ed., *1500–1640.* London and New York: Cambridge Univ. Press, 1967, 593–695.

Boxer, C. R., *The Christian Century in Japan.* Berkeley: Univ. of California Press, 1951.

Boxer, C. R., "The Portuguese in the East, 1500–1800," in H. V. Livermore, ed., *Portugal and Brazil, an Introduction.* London and New York: Oxford Univ. Press (Clarendon), 1953, 185–247.

Boxer, C. R., *Four Centuries of Portuguese Expansion, 1415–1825.* Johannesburg: Witswatersrand Univ. Press, 1961.

Boxer, C. R., *Race Relations in the Portuguese Colonial Empire, 1415–1825.* London and New York: Oxford Univ. Press (Clarendon), 1963.

Boxer, C. R., *The Portuguese Seaborne Empire, 1415–1825.* New York: Knopf, 1969.

Braudel, Fernand, "Monnaies et civilization: de l'or du Soudan à l'argent d'Amérique," *Annales E.S.C.,* **I**, 1, janv.–mars 1946, 9–22.

Braudel, Fernand, "La double faillite 'coloniale' de la France aux XVe et XVIe siècles," *Annales E.S.C.,* **IV**, 4, oct.–déc. 1949, 451–456.

Braudel, Fernand, "Qu'est-ce que le XVIe siècle?," *Annales E.S.C.,* **VIII**, 1, janv.–mars 1953, 69–73.

Braudel, Fernand, "L'économie de la Méditerranée au XVIIe siècle," *Les Cahiers de Tunisie,* **IV**, 14, 2e trimestre 1956, 175–196.

Braudel, Fernand, "Le pacte de ricorsa au service du roi d'Espagne et de ses prêteurs à la fin du XVIe siècle," in *Studi in onore di Armando Sapori.* Milano: Istituto Edit. Cisalpino, 1957, **II**, 1115–1125.

Braudel, Fernand, "Les emprunts de Charles-Quint sur la Place d'Anvers," *Charles Quint et son temps,* Colloques internationaux du C.N.R.S., Paris, 30 sept.–3 oct., 1958. Paris: Ed. du C.N.R.S., 1959, 191–201.

Braudel, Fernand, "European Expansion and Capitalism: 1450–1650" in *Chapters in Western Civilization,* 3rd ed. New York: Columbia Univ. Press, 1961, **I**, 245–288.

Braudel, Fernand, *La Méditerranée et le monde méditerranéen à l'époque de Philippe II,* 2e éd. revue et augmentée, 2 vol. Paris: Lib. Armand Colin, 1966.

Braudel, Fernand, *Civilisation matérielle et capitalisme (XVe–XVIIIe siècle).* Vol. I. Paris: Lib. Armand Colin, 1967.

Braudel, Fernand, and Romano, Ruggiero, *Navires et marchandises à l'entrée du Port de Livourne (1547–1611).* Paris: Lib. Armand Colin, 1951.

Braudel, Fernand, and Spooner, Frank C., "Les métaux monétaires et l'économie du XVIe siècle," in *Relazioni del X Congresso Internazionale di Scienze Storiche,* **IV**: *Storia moderna.* Firenze: G. B. Sansoni, 1955, 233–264.

Braudel, Fernand, and Spooner, Frank C., "Prices in Europe from 1450 to 1750," in *Cambridge Economic History of Europe,* **IV**: E. E. Rich and C. H. Wilson, eds., *The Economy of Expanding Europe in the 16th and 17th Centuries.* London and New York: Cambridge Univ.

Press, 1967, 374–486.

Brenner, Y. S., "The Inflation of Prices in Early Sixteenth-Century England," *Economic History Review*, 2nd ser., **XIV**, 2, 1961, 225–239.

Brinkmann, Carl, "The Hanseatic League: A Survey of Recent Literature," *Journal of Economic and Business History*, **II**, 4, Aug. 1930, 585–602.

Brulez, Wilfrid, "Les routes commerciales d'Angleterre en Italie au XVIe siècle," in *Studi in onore di Amintore Fanfani*, **IV**: *Evo moderno*. Milano: Dott. A. Giuffrè-Ed. 1962, 121–184.

Brunner, Otto, "Europäisches und Russisches Bürgertum," *Vierteljahrschrift für Sozial- und Wirtschaftsgeschichte*, **XL**, 1, 1953, 1–27.

Brutzkus, J., "Trade with Eastern Europe, 800–1200," *Economic History Review*, **XIII**, 1943, 31–41.

Bücher, Karl, *Industrial Evolution*. New York: Holt, 1901.

Buckatzsch, E. J., "The Geographical Distribution of Wealth in England, 1086–1843," *Economic History Review*, 2nd ser., **III**, 2, 1950, 180–202.

Bulferetti, Luigi, "L'oro, la terra e la società: una interpretazione del nostro Seicento," *Archivio storico lombardo*, 8th ser., **IV**, 1953, 5–66.

Burckhardt, Jacob, *The Civilization of the Renaissance in Italy*. New York: Modern Library, 1954.

Cahen, Claude, "A propos de la discussion sur la féodalité," *La Pensée*, No. 68, juil.–août 1956, 94–96.

Cahen, Claude, "Au seuil de la troisième année: Réflexions sur l'usage du mot 'féodalité,'" *Journal of the Economic and Social History of the Orient*, **III**, Pt. 1, Apr. 1960, 2–20.

Campbell, Mildred, *The English Yeomen Under Elizabeth and the Early Stuarts*. New Haven, Connecticut: Yale Univ. Press, 1942.

Capistrano de Abreu, J., *Capítulos de história colonial (1500–1800)*. Rio de Janeiro, Ed. da Soc. Capistrano de Abreu, Typ. Leuzinger, 1928.

Carande, Ramón, *El crédito de Castilla en el precio de la política imperial*, discurso leído ante la Real Academia de la Historia. Madrid, 1949.

Carande, Ramón, *Carlos V y sus banqueros: La vida económica en Castilla (1516–1556)*, 2a. ed corr. y aum., 2 vol. Madrid: Sociedad de Estudios y Publicaciones, 1965.

Carsten, F. L., *The Origins of Prussia*. London and New York: Oxford Univ. Press (Clarendon), 1954.

Carus-Wilson, E. M., "An Industrial Revolution of the Thirteenth Century," *Economic History Review*, **XI**, 1941, 39–60.

Chabod, F., "Y a-t-il un état de la Renaissance?" in *Actes du Colloque sur la Renaissance*. Paris: Lib. Philosophique J. Vrin, 1958, 57–74.

Chang, T'ien-Tsê, *Sino-Portuguese Trade from 1514 to 1644*. Leiden, Netherlands: Brill, 1934.

Chaudhuri, K. N., "The East India Company and the Export of Treasure in the Early 17th Century," *Economic History Review*, 2nd ser., **XVI**, 1, Aug. 1963, 23–38.

Chaunu, Pierre, "Le galion de Manille," *Annales E.S.C.*, **VI**, 4, oct.–déc. 1951, 447–462.

Chaunu, Huguette & Pierre, "Économie atlantique, économie-monde (1504–1650)," *Cahiers d'histoire mondiale*, **I**, 1, juil. 1953, 91–104.

Chaunu, Huguette & Pierre, *Séville et l'Atlantique (1504–1650)*, **I**: *Introduction méthodologique*. Paris: Lib. Armand Colin, 1955.

Chaunu, Pierre, "Pour une histoire économique de l'Amérique espagnole coloniale," *Revue historique*, **LXXX**, 216, oct.–déc. 1956, 209–218.

Chaunu, Pierre, *Séville et l'Atlantique (1504–1650)*, **VIII** (1): *Les structures géographiques*. Paris: S.E.V.P.E.N., 1959.

Chaunu, Pierre, *Séville et l'Atlantique (1504–1650)*, **VIII** (2): *La conjoncture (1504–1592)*. Paris: S.E.V.P.E.N., 1959.

Chaunu, Pierre, *Séville et l'Atlantique (1504–1650)*, **VIII** (2 bis): *La conjoncture (1593–1650)*. Paris: S.E.V.P.E.N., 1959.

Chaunu, Pierre, "Séville et la 'Belgique,' 1555–1648," *Revue du Nord,* **XLII,** 1960, 259–292.
Chaunu, Pierre, "Minorités et conjoncture: l'expulsion des Morèsques en 1609," *Revue historique,* **CCXXV,** 1, janv.–mars 1961, 81–98.
Chaunu, Pierre, "Le renversement de la tendance majeure des prix et des activités au XVIIe siècle," *Studi in onore di Amintore Fanfani,* **IV**: *Evo moderno.* Milano: Dott. A Giuffrè-Ed., 1962, 219–255.
Chaunu, Pierre, *L'Amérique et les Amériques.* Paris: Lib. Armand Colin, 1964.
Chaunu, Pierre, "Réflexions sur le tournant des années 1630–1650," *Cahiers d'histoire,* **XII,** 3, 1967, 249–268.
Chaunu, Pierre, *L'expansion européenne du XIIIe au XVe siècle,* Collection Nouvelle Clio 26. Paris: Presses Universitaires de France, 1969.
Chaunu, Pierre, *Conquète et exploitation des nouveaux mondes (XVIe siècle),* Collection Nouvelle Clio 26 bis. Paris: Presses Universitaires de France, 1969.
Chaussinand-Nogaret, Guy, "L'or, le poivre, le Portugal et l'économie mondiale," *Annales E.S.C.,* **XXV,** 6, nov.–déc. 1970, 1591–1596.
Cheung, Steven N. S., *The Theory of Share Tenancy.* Chicago, Illinois: Univ. of Chicago Press, 1969.
Chevalier, François, *Land and Society in Colonial Mexico.* Berkeley: Univ. of California Press, 1963.
Christensen, Aksel E., *Dutch Trade to the Baltic about 1600.* Copenhagen: Munksgaard, 1941.
Ciocca, Pierluigi, "L'ipotesi del 'ritardo' dei salari rispetto ai prezzi in periodi di inflazione: alcune considerazioni generali," *Bancaria,* **XXV,** 4, apr. 1969, 423–437; 5, maio 1969, 572–583.
Cipolla, Carlo M., *Mouvements monétaires dans l'Etat de Milan (1580–1700).* Paris: Lib. Armand Colin, 1952.
Cipolla, Carlo M., "Note sulla storia del saggio d'interesse—Corso, dividendi, e sconto dei dividendi del Banco de S. Giorgio nel secolo XVI," *Economia internazionale,* **V,** 2, magg. 1952, 255–274.
Cipolla, Carlo M., "La prétendue 'révolution des prix,' " *Annales E.S.C.,* **X,** 4, oct.–déc. 1955, 513–516.
Cipolla, Carlo M., "Four Centuries of Italian Demographic Development" in D. V. Glass & D. E. C. Eversley, eds., *Population in History.* London: Arnold, 1965, 570–587.
Cipolla, Carlo M., *Guns and Sails in the Early Phase of European Expansion, 1400–1700.* London: Collins, 1965. (1)
Cipolla, Carlo M., *Clocks and Culture, 1300–1700.* New York: Walker & Co., 1967.
Cipolla, Carlo M., *Money, Prices, and Civilization in the Mediterranean World: Fifth to Seventeenth Century.* New York: Gordian Press, Inc., 1967.
Cipolla, Carlo M., "The Economic Decline of Italy," in Brian Pullan ed., *Crisis and Change in the Venetian Economy in the Sixteenth and Seventeenth Centuries.* London: Methuen, 1968, 126–145. (Revised and expanded version of "The Decline of Italy: The Case of a Fully-Matured Economy," *Economic History Review,* V, 1952.)
Clark, G. N., *The Seventeenth Century.* London and New York: Oxford Univ. Press (Clarendon), 1929.
Clark, G. N., "The Birth of the Dutch Republic," *Proceedings of the British Academy,* 1946, 189–217.
Clark, G. N., *The Wealth of England from 1496 to 1760.* London: Oxford Univ. Press, 1946.
Coleman, D. C., "An Innovation and its Diffusion: the 'New Draperies,'" *Economic History Review,* 2nd ser., **XXII,** 3, Dec. 1969, 417–429.
Coles, Paul, "The Crisis of Renaissance Society: Genoa, 1448–1507," *Past & Present,* No. 11, April 1957, 17–47.
Colvin, H. M., "Castles and Government in Tudor England," *English Historical Review,* **LXXXIII,** No. 327, Apr. 1968, 225–234.
Cook, Sherburne F., and Simpson, Lesley Boyd, *The Population of Central Mexico in the*

Sixteenth Century, Ibero-Americana: **31**. Berkeley: Univ. of California Press, 1948.

Cooper, J. P., "The Counting of Manors," *Economic History Review*, 2nd ser., **VIII**, 3, 1956, 376–389.

Cooper, J. P., "Letter to the Editor," *Encounter*, **XI**, 3, Sept. 1958.

Cooper, J. P., "General Introduction," in *New Cambridge Modern History*, **IV**: J. P. Cooper, ed., *The Decline of Spain and the Thirty Years' War, 1609–48/59*. London and New York: Cambridge Univ. Press, 1970, 1–66.

Coornaert, Emile, "La genèse du système capitaliste: grande capitalisme et économie traditionelle au XVIe siècle," *Annales d'histoire économique et sociale*, **VIII**, 1936, 127–139.

Coornaert, Emile, "Les échanges de la France avec l'Allemagne et les pays du Nord au XVIe siècle," *Revue d'histoire économique et sociale*, **XXXV**, 3, 1959, 407–427.

Coulbourn, Rushton, ed., *Feudalism in History*. Princeton, New Jersey: Princeton Univ. Press, 1956.

Coulbourn, Rushton, "A Comparative Study of Feudalism," Part III of Rushton Coulbourn, ed., *Feudalism in History*. Princeton, New Jersey: Princeton Univ. Press, 1956, 183–395.

Craeybeckx, Jan, "Quelques grands marchés de vins français dans les anciens Pays-Bas et dans le Nord de la France à la fin du Moyen Age et au XVIe siècle: Contribution à l'étude de la notion d'étape," *Studi in onore di Armando Sapori*. Milano: Istituto Edit. Cisalpino, 1957, **II**, 849–882.

Craeybeckx, Jan, "Les français et Anvers au XVIe siècle," *Annales E.S.C.*, **XVII**, 3, mai–juin 1962, 542–554.

Craeybeckx, Jan, "Les industries d'exportation dans les villes flamandes au XVIIe siècle, particulièrement à Gand et à Bruges," *Studi in onore di Amintore Fanfani*, **IV**: *Evo moderno*. Milano: Dott. A. Giuffrè-Ed., 1962, 411–468.

Cromwell, Julian, "The Early Tudor Gentry," *Economic History Review*, 2nd ser., **XVII**, 3, 1965, 456–471.

Czalpinski, Wladyslaw, "Le problème baltique aux XVIe et XVIIe siècles," *International Congress of Historical Sciences*, Stockholm, 1960. *Rapports*, **IV**: *Histoire moderne*. Göteborg: Almqvist & Wiksell, 1960, 25–47.

Czarnowski, Stefan, "La réaction catholique en Pologne à la fin du XVIe siècle et au début du XVIIe siècle," *La Pologne au VIIe Congrès Internationale des Sciences Historiques*, Varsovie: Société Polonaise d'Histoire, 1933, **II**, 287–310.

Darby, H. C., "The Clearing of the Woodland in Europe," in William L. Thomas, Jr., ed., *Man's Role in Changing the Face of the Earth*. Chicago, Illinois: Univ. of Chicago Press, 1956, 183–216.

da Silva, José-Gentil, "Trafics du Nord, marchés du 'Mezziogiorno,' finances génoises: recherches et documents sur la conjoncture à la fin du XVIe siècle," *Revue du Nord*, **XLI**, 1959, 129–152.

da Silva, José-Gentil, "Villages castillans et types de production au XVIe siècle," *Annales E.S.C.*, **XVIII**, 4, juil.–août 1963, 729–744.

da Silva, José-Gentil, *En Espagne: développement économique, subsistence, déclin*. Paris: Mouton, 1965.

da Silva, José-Gentil, "L'autoconsommation au Portugal (XIVe–XXe siècles)," *Annales E.S.C.*, **XXIV**, 2, mars–avr. 1969, 250–288.

Davies, C. S. L., "Provisions for Armies, 1509–50: A Study in the Effectiveness of Early Tudor Government," *Economic History Review*, 2nd ser., **XVII**, 2, 1964, 234–248.

Davies, C. S. L., "Les révoltes populaires en Angleterre (1500–1700)," *Annales E.S.C.*, **XXIV**, 1, janv.–févr. 1969, 24–60.

Davis, Ralph, "England and the Mediterranean, 1570–1670," in F. J. Fisher, ed., *Essays in the Economic and Social History of Tudor and Stuart England*. London and New York: Cambridge Univ. Press, 1961, 117–137.

de Bary, William Theodore, "Introduction," to William Theodore de Bary, ed., *Self and Society in Ming Thought.* New York: Columbia Univ. Press, 1970, 1–27.

de Bary, William Theodore, "Individualism and Humanitarianism in Late Ming Thought," in William Theodore de Bary, ed., *Self and Society in Ming Thought.* New York: Columbia Univ. Press, 1970, 145–247.

de Falguerolles, G. E., "La décadence de l'économie agricole dans le Consulat de Lempaut aux XVIIe et XVIIIe siècles," *Annales du Midi,* **LIII**, 1941, 142–168.

de Lagarde, Georges, "Réflexions sur la cristallisation de la notion d'Etat au XVIe siècle," in Enrico Castelli, ed., *Umanesimo e scienza politica.* Milano: Dott. Carlo Marzorati, 1951, 247–256.

Delumeau, Jean, *Vie économique et sociale de Rome dans la seconde moitié du XVIe siècle,* 2 vol. Paris: Boccard, 1957.

de Maddalena, Aldo, "Il mondo rurale italiano nel cinque e nel seicento," *Rivista storica italiana,* **LXXVI**, 2, giug. 1964, 349–426.

de Oliveira Marques, António H., "Notas para a história da feitoria portuguésa na Flandres no século XV," *Studi in onore di Amintore Fanfani,* **II**: *Medioevo.* Milano: Dott. A. Giuffrè-Ed., 1962, 437–476.

de Roover, Raymond, "Anvers comme marché monétaire au XVIe siècle," *Revue belge de philologie et d'histoire,* **XXXI**, 4, 1953, 1003–1047.

de Vries, Jan, "The Role of the Rural Sector in the Development of the Dutch Economy: 1500–1700," *Journal of Economic History,* **XXXI**, 1, Mar. 1971, 266–268.

de Vries, Philip, "L'animosité anglo-hollandaise au XVIIe siècle," *Annales E.S.C.,* **V**, 1, janv.–mars 1950, 42–47.

Deyon, Pierre, "A propos des rapports entre la noblesse et la monarchie absolue pendant la première moitié du XVIIe siècle," *Revue historique,* **CCXXXI**, avr.–juin 1964, 341–356.

Dobb, Maurice, *Studies in the Development of Capitalism.* London: Routledge & Kegan Paul, 1946.

Dobb, Maurice, "Reply," *Science and Society,* **XIV**, 2, Spring 1950, 157–167.

Dobb, Maurice, *Papers on Capitalism, Development, and Planning.* New York: International Publ., 1967.

Dollinger, Philippe, *La Hanse (XIIe–XVIIe siècles).* Paris: Montaigne, 1964.

Domar, Evsey D., "The Causes of Slavery or Serfdom: A Hypothesis," *Journal of Economic History,* **XXX**, 1, Mar. 1970, 18–32.

Dowd, Douglas F., "The Economic Expansion of Lombardy, 1300–1500: A Study in Political Stimuli to Economic Change," *Journal of Economic History,* **XXI**, 2, June 1961, 143–160.

Duby, Georges, "Le grand domaine de la fin du moyen âge en France," *Première Conférence Internationale d'Histoire Economique,* Stockholm, August 1960: *Contributions.* Paris: Mouton, 1960, 333–342.

Duby, Georges, "The French Countryside at the End of the 13th Century" in Rondo E. Cameron, ed., *Essays in French Economic History.* Homewood, Illinois: Richard D. Irwin, Inc., 1970, 33–41. (Translated from *Bolletino dell'Istituto Storico Italiano per il Medio Evo,* No. 74, 1962.)

Duby, Georges, "Démographie et villages désertés," *Villages désertés et histoire économique, XIe–XVIIIe siècles.* Paris: S.E.V.P.E.N., 1965, 13–24.

Duby, Georges, *Rural Economy and Country Life in the Medieval West.* Columbia: Univ. of South Carolina Press, 1968.

Duby, Georges, and Mandrou, Robert, *Histoire de la civilisation française,* **I**: *Le Moyen Age et le XVIe siècle.* Paris: Lib. Armand Colin, 1958.

Duby, Georges, and Mandrou, Robert, *Histoire de la civilisation française,* **II**: *XVIIe–XXe siècle.* Paris: Lib. Armand Colin, 1958.

Eberhard, Wolfram, *Conquerors and Rulers: Social Forces in Medieval China,* 2nd ed. Leiden: Brill, 1965.

Edler, Florence, "The Effects of the Financial Measures of Charles V on the Commerce of Antwerp, 1539–42," *Revue belge de philologie et d'histoire,* **XVI**, 3–4, juil.–déc. 1937, 665–673.

Ehrenberg, Richard, *Capital and Finance in the Age of the Renaissance.* New York: Harcourt, 1928.

Eisenstadt, S. N., "Political Struggle in Bureaucratic Societies," *World Politics,* **IX**, 1, Oct. 1956, 15–36.

Eisenstadt, S. N., "The Causes of Disintegration and Fall of Empires: Sociological and Historical Analyses," *Diogenes,* No. 34, Summer 1961, 82–107.

Eisenstadt, S. N., "Empires," *International Encyclopedia of the Social Sciences.* New York: Macmillan and Free Press, 1968, **V**, 41–49.

Eitzen, Stanley D., "Two Minorities: The Jews of Poland and the Chinese of the Philippines," *Jewish Journal of Sociology,* **X**, 2, Dec. 1968, 221–240.

Elliott, J. H., "The Decline of Spain," *Past & Present,* No. 20, Nov. 1961, 52–75.

Elliott, J. H., *Imperial Spain, 1469–1716.* New York: Mentor, 1966.

Elliott, J. H., *Europe Divided, 1559–1598.* New York: Harper, 1968.

Elliott, J. H., *The Old World and the New, 1492–1650.* London and New York: Cambridge Univ. Press, 1970.

Elliott, J. H., "The Spanish Peninsula, 1598–1648," in *New Cambridge Modern History,* **IV**: J. P. Cooper, ed., *The Decline of Spain and the Thirty Years' War, 1609–48/59.* London and New York: Cambridge Univ. Press, 1970, 435–473.

Elman, P., "The Economic Causes of the Expulsion of the Jews in 1290," *Economic History Review,* **VII**, 1, Nov. 1936, 145–154.

Elton, G. R., *The Tudor Revolution in Government.* London and New York: Cambridge Univ. Press, 1953.

Elton, G. R., "The Tudor Revolution: A Reply," *Past & Present,* No. 29, Dec. 1964, 26–49.

Elton, G. R., "A Revolution in Tudor History?" *Past & Present,* No. 32, Dec. 1965, 103–109.

Emery, Frank, "The Farming Regions of Wales," in *The Agrarian History of England and Wales,* **IV**: Joan Thirsk, ed., *1500–1640.* London and New York: Cambridge Univ. Press, 1967, 113–160.

Engels, Frederick, *Socialism: Utopian and Scientific.* New York: International Publishers, 1935.

Engels, Frederick, *The Origins of the Family, Private Property and the State.* London: Lawrence & Wishart, 1940.

Engels, Frederick, *The Peasant War in Germany,* in *The German Revolutions.* Chicago, Illinois: Univ. of Chicago Press, 1967.

Espeiux, Henri, *Histoire de l'Occitanie.* Nîmes: Le Centre Culturel Occitan, Collection Cap-e-Cap, 1970.

Everitt, Alan, "Social Mobility in Early Modern England," *Past & Present,* No. 33, Apr. 1966, 56–73.

Everitt, Alan, "Farm Labourers," in *The Agrarian History of England and Wales,* **IV**: Joan Thirsk, ed., *1500–1640.* London and New York: Cambridge Univ. Press, 1967, 396–465.

Everitt, Alan, "The Marketing of Agricultural Produce," in *The Agrarian History of England and Wales,* **IV**: Joan Thirsk, ed., *1500–1640,* London and New York: Cambridge Univ. Press, 1967, 466–592.

Falls, Cyril, *Elizabeth's Irish Wars.* London, Methuen, 1950.

Fanfani, Amintore, *Storia del lavoro in Italia della fine del secolo XV agli inizi del XVIII.* Milano: Dott. A. Giuffrè-Ed., 1959.

Fanon, Frantz, *The Wretched of the Earth.* New York: Grove Press, 1966.

Favret, Jeanne, "Le traditionalisme par excès de modernité," *European Journal of Sociology,* **VIII**, 1, 1967, 71–93.

Febvre, Lucien, "Préface" to Huguette & Pierre Chaunu, *Séville et l'Atlantique (1504–1650),* Paris: Lib. Armand Colin, 1955, **I.** ix–xv.

Felix, David, "Profit Inflation and Industrial Growth: The Historic Record and Contemporary Analogies," *Quarterly Journal of Economics*, **LXX**, 3, Aug. 1956, 441–463.

Ferguson, Wallace, "Toward the Modern State," in Wallace Ferguson, ed., *Renaissance Studies*, No. 2. London, Ont.: University of Western Ontario, 1963, 137–153. (Originally in *The Renaissance: A Symposium*, 1953.)

Fernández Alvarez, Manuel, "La Paz de Cateau-Cambrésis," *Hispania, revista española de historia,* **XIX**, No. 77, oct.–dic. 1959, 530–544.

Fisher, F. J., "The Development of the London Food Market, 1540–1640," in E. M. Carus-Wilson, ed., *Essays in Economic History.* New York: St. Martin's, 1965, **I**, 135–151. (Originally in *Economic History Review*, V, 1935.)

Fisher, F. J., "The Development of London as a Centre of Conspicuous Consumption in the Sixteenth and Seventeenth Centuries," in E. M. Carus-Wilson, ed., *Essays in Economic History.* New York: St. Martin's, 1966, **II**, 197–207. (Originally in *Transactions of the Royal Historical Society*, 4th ser., XXX, 1948.)

Fisher, F. J., "London's Export Trade in the Early Seventeenth Century," *Economic History Review*, 2nd ser., **III**, 2, 1950, 151–161.

Fisher, F. J., "The Sixteenth and Seventeenth Centuries: The Dark Ages in English Economic History?," *Economica*, n.s., **XXIV**, 93, 1957, 2–18.

Fisher, F. J., "Tawney's Century," in F. J. Fisher, ed., *Essays in the Economic and Social History of Tudor and Stuart England.* New York and London: Cambridge Univ. Press. 1961, 1–14.

Fourastié, Jean, and Gradamy, René, "Remarques sur les prix salariaux des céréales et la productivité du travailleur agricole en Europe du XVe et XVIe siècles," *Third International Conference of Economic History*, Munich, 1965. Paris: Mouton, 1968, 647–656.

Foust, C. M., "Russian Expansion to the East Through the Eighteenth Century," *Journal of Economic History*, **XXI**, 4, Dec. 1961, 469–482.

Fox, P., "The Reformation in Poland," in *The Cambridge History of Poland*, **I**: W. F. Reddaway *et al.*, eds., *From the Origins to Sobieski (to 1696).* London and New York: Cambridge Univ. Press, 1950, 322–347.

François, Michel, "L'idée d'empire sous Charles-Quint," *Charles Quint et son temps*, Colloques internationaux du C.N.R.S., 30 sept.–3 oct. 1958. Paris: Ed. du C.N.R.S., 1959, 23–35.

Frank, André Gunder, *Capitalism and Underdevelopment in Latin America.* New York: Monthly Review Press, 1967.

Fried, Morton, "On the Concept of 'Tribe' and 'Tribal Society,' " in June Helm, ed., *Essays on the Problem of Tribe*, Proceedings of 1967 Annual Spring Meeting of the American Ethnological Society, 3–20.

Friedrich, Carl J., *The Age of the Baroque.* New York: Harper, 1952.

Friis, Astrid, *Alderman Cockayne's Project and the Cloth Trade.* Copenhagen: Levin and Munksgaard, 1927.

Friis, Astrid, "An Inquiry into the Relations between Economic and Financial Factors in the Sixteenth and Seventeenth Centuries, *Scandinavian Economic History Review*, **I**, 2, 1953, 193–241.

Furtado, Celso, *Economic Development of Latin America.* London and New York: Cambridge Univ. Press, 1970.

Gay, Edwin F., "The Midland Revolt and the Inquisitions of Depopulation of 1607," *Transactions of the Royal Historical Society*, n.s., **XVIII**, 1904, 195–244.

Génicot, Leopold, "Crisis: From the Middle Ages to Modern Times," in *Cambridge Economic History of Europe*, **I**: M. M. Postan, ed., *The Agrarian Life of the Middle Ages*, 2nd ed. London and New York: Cambridge Univ. Press, 1966, 660–741.

Gerschenkron, Alexander, "An Economic History of Russia," *Journal of Economic History*, **XII**, 2, Spr. 1952, 146–154.

Gerschenkron, Alexander, "Review article: Lord and Peasant in Russia from the Ninth to the Nineteenth Century," *Journal of Economic History*, **XXIV**, 1, Mar. 1964, 53–59.

Gerth, Hans, "Glossary" in Max Weber, *The Religion of China.* New York: Free Press, 1951, 298–308.

Gestrin, Ferdo, "Economie et société en Slovénie au XVIe siècle," *Annales E.S.C.,* **XVII**, 4, juil.–août, 1962, 663–690.

Geyl, Pieter, *The Revolt of the Netherlands (1559–1609).* London: Williams & Norgate, 1932.

Geyl, Pieter, *Debates with Historians.* New York: Meridian, 1958.

Gibson, Charles, *The Aztecs Under Spanish Rule.* Stanford, California: Stanford Univ. Press, 1964.

Glamann, Kristof, "European Trade, 1500–1700," *Fontana Economic History of Europe,* **II**, 6, 1971.

Godinho, Vitorino Magalhães, "Création et dynamisme économique du monde atlantique (1420–1670)," *Annales E.S.C.,* **V**, 1, janv.–mars 1950, 32–36.

Godinho, Vitorino Magalhães, "Le repli vénitien et égyptien et la route du Cap, 1496–1533," in *Eventail de l'histoire vivante: hommage à Lucien Febvre,* Paris: Lib. Armand Colin, 1953, **II.** 283–300.

Godinho, Vitorino Magalhães, *L'économie de l'empire portugais aux XVe et XVIe siècles.* Paris: S.E.V.P.E.N., 1969.

Goldmann, Lucien, *The Hidden God.* New York: Humanities Press, 1964.

Gordon-Walker, P. C., "Capitalism and the Reformation," *Economic History Review,* **VIII**, 1, Nov. 1937, 1–19.

Goubert, Pierre, "Recent Theories and Research in French Population between 1500 and 1700," in D. V. Glass and D. E. C. Eversley, eds., *Population in History.* London: Arnold, 1965, 457–473.

Gould, J. D., "The Trade Depression of the Early 1620's," *Economic History Review,* 2nd ser., **VII**, 1, 1954, 81–90.

Gould, J. D., "The Price Revolution Reconsidered," *Economic History Review,* 2nd ser., **XVII**, 2, 1964, 249–266.

Grabowski, Thadée, "La réforme réligieuse en Occident et en Pologne," *La Pologne au Ve Congrès International des Sciences Historiques,* Bruxelles, 1923. Warsaw: 1924, 67–72.

Gramsci, Antonio, *Il Risorgimento.* Roma: Giulio Einaudi, 1955.

Gras, N. S. B., *The Evolution of the English Corn Market.* Cambridge: Harvard Univ. Press, 1915.

Gray, H. L., "English Foreign Trade from 1446 to 1482," in Eileen E. Power and M. M. Postan, eds., *Studies in English Trade in the Fifteenth Century.* New York: Barnes & Noble, 1966, 1–38.

Griffiths, Gordon, "The Revolutionary Character of the Revolution of the Netherlands," *Comparative Studies in Society and History,* **II**, 4, July 1960, 452–472.

Guillén Martinez, Fernando, *Raíz y futuro de la revolución.* Bogotá: Ed. Tercer Mundo, 1963.

Habakkuk, H. John, "La disparition du paysan anglais," *Annales E.S.C.,* **XX**, 4, juil.–août 1965, 649–663.

Hall, A. Rupert, "Scientific Method and the Progress of Techniques," *Cambridge Economic History of Europe,* **IV**: E. E. Rich and C. H. Wilson, eds., *The Economy of Expanding Europe in the 16th and 17th Centuries.* London and New York: Cambridge Univ. Press, 1967, 96–154.

Hamilton, Earl J., "American Treasure and Andalusian Prices, 1503–1660," *Journal of Economic and Business History,* **I**, 1, Nov. 1928, 1–35.

Hamilton, Earl J., "American Treasure and the Rise of Capitalism," *Economica,* **IX,** 27, Nov. 1929, 338–357.

Hamilton, Earl J., "Origin and Growth of the National Debt in Western Europe," *American Economic Review,* **XXXVII**, 2, May 1947, 118–130.

Hamilton, Earl J., "Prices and Progress: Prices as a Factor in Business Growth," *Journal of Economic History,* **XII**, Fall 1952, 325–349.

Hamilton, Earl J., "The History of Prices Before 1750," in *International Congress of Historical Sciences*, Stockholm, 1960. *Rapports*, I: *Méthodologie, histoire des universités, histoire des prix avant 1750*. Göteborg: Almqvist & Wiksell, 1960, 144–164.

Hammarström, Ingrid, "The 'Price Revolution' of the Sixteenth Century: Some Swedish Evidence," *Scandinavian Economic History Review*, **V**, 1, 1957, 118–154.

Harrison, J. B., Colonial Development and International Rivalries Outside Europe, II: Asia and Africa," *New Cambridge Modern History*, **III**: R. B. Wernham, ed., *The Counter-Reformation and the Price Revolution, 1559–1610*. London and New York: Cambridge Univ. Press, 1968, 532–558.

Harriss, G. L., and Williams, Penry, "A Revolution in Tudor History?" *Past & Present*, No. 31, July 1965, 87–96.

Hartung, Fr., and Mousnier, R., "Quelques problèmes concernant la monarchie absolue," in *Relazioni del X Congreso Internazionale di Scienze Storiche*, **IV**: *Storia moderna*. Firenze: G. B. Sansoni, 1955, 1–55.

Hauser, Henri, "The European Financial Crisis of 1559," *Journal of European Business History*, **II**, 2, Feb. 1930, 241–255.

Hauser, Henri, "The Characteristic Features of French Economic History from the Middle of the Sixteenth Century to the Middle of the Eighteenth Century," *Economic History Review*, **IV**, 3, Oct. 1933, 257–272.

Heaton, Herbert, *Economic History of Europe,* rev. ed. New York: Harper, 1948.

Heckscher, Eli F., *An Economic History of Sweden*. Cambridge, Massachusetts: Harvard Univ. Press, 1954.

Heckscher, Eli F., *Mercantilism*, 2 vol., rev. ed. London: Allen & Unwin, 1955.

Heers, Jacques, "Les Génois en Angleterre: la crise de 1458–1466," *Studi in onore di Armando Sapori*. Milano: Istituto Edit. Cisalpino, 1957, **II**, 809–832.

Heers, Jacques, "Rivalité ou collaboration de la terre et de l'eau? Position générale des problèmes," in *Les grandes voies maritimes dans le monde, XVe–XIXe siècles*, VIIe Colloque, Commission Internationale d'Histoire Maritime. Paris: S.E.V.P.E.N., 1965, 13–63.

Helleiner, Karl, "The Population of Europe from the Black Death to the Eve of the Vital Revolution," in *Cambridge Economic History of Europe*, **IV**: E. E. Rich and C. H. Wilson, eds., *The Economy of Expanding Europe in the 16th and 17th Centuries*. London and New York: Cambridge Univ. Press, 1967, 1–95.

Hexter, J. H., "Letter to the Editor," *Encounter*, **XI**, 2, Aug., 1958.

Hexter, J. H., "The Myth of the Middle Class in Tudor England," *Reappraisals in History*. New York: Harper, 1963, 71–116.

Hexter, J. H., "A New Framework for Social History," *Reappraisals in History*. New York: Harper, 1963, 14–25.

Hexter, J. H., "Storm Over the Gentry," *Reappraisals in History.* New York: Harper, 1963, 117–162. (Originally appeared in *Encounter*, **X**, 5, May 1968.)

Hibbert, A. B., "The Origins of the Medieval Town Patriciate," *Past & Present*, No. 3, Feb. 1953, 15–27.

Hill, Christopher, "The Transition from Feudalism to Capitalism," *Science and Society*, **XVII**, 4, Fall 1953, 348–351.

Hill, Christopher, "Recent Interpretations of the Civil War," in *Puritanism and Revolution*. New York: Schocken Books, 1958, 3–31.

Hill, Christopher, "Some Social Consequences of the Henrician Revolution," in *Puritanism and Revolution*. New York: Schocken Books, 1958, 32–49.

Hill, Christopher, "Protestantism and the Rise of Capitalism," in F. J. Fisher, ed., *Essays in the Economic and Social History of Tudor and Stuart England*. London and New York: Cambridge Univ. Press, 1960, 15–39.

Hill, Christopher, *Reformation to the Industrial Revolution, 1530–1780*, Vol. II of The Pelican Economic History of Britain. London: Penguin Books, 1967.

Hilton, R. H., "Peasant Movements in England before 1381," in E. M. Carus-Wilson, ed.,

Essays in Economic History: New York: St. Martin's, 1966, **II,** 73–90. (Originally in *Economic History Review,* II, 1949.)

Hilton, R. H., "Y eut-il une crise générale de la féodalité?" *Annales E.S.C.,* **VI,** 1, janv.–mars 1951, 23–30.

Hilton, R. H., "The Transition from Feudalism to Capitalism," *Science and Society,* **XVII,** 4, Fall 1953, 340–348.

Hilton, R. H., "A Study in the Pre-History of English Enclosure in the Fifteenth Century," *Studi in onore di Armando Sapori.* Milano: Istituto Edit. Cisalpino, 1957, **I,** 673–685.

Hilton, R. H. and Smith, R. E. F., "Introduction" to R. E. F. Smith, *The Enserfment of the Russian Peasantry.* London and New York: Cambridge Univ. Press, 1968, 1–27.

Hinton, R. W. K., "Dutch Entrepôt Trade at Boston, Lincs., 1600–40," *Economic History Review,* 2nd ser., **IX,** 3, Apr., 1957, 467–471.

Hinton, R. W. K., "Letter to the Editor," *Encounter,* **XI,** 1, July 1958.

Hinton, R. W. K., *The Eastland Trade and the Common Weal in the Seventeenth Century.* London and New York: Cambridge Univ. Press, 1959.

Hobsbawm, E. J., "The Crisis of the Seventeenth Century," in Trevor Aston, ed., *Crisis in Europe, 1560–1660.* London: Routledge & Kegan Paul, 1965, 5–58.

Honjo, Eijiro, "Facts and Ideas of Japan's Over-sea Development Prior to the Meiji Restoration," *Kyoto University Economic Review,* **XVII,** 1, Jan. 1942, 1–13.

Hoskins, W. G., "The Rebuilding of Rural England, 1570–1640," *Past & Present,* No. 4, Nov. 1953, 44–57.

Hoszowski, Stanislaw, "The Polish Baltic Trade in the 15th–18th Centuries," *Poland at the XIth International Congress of Historical Sciences in Stockholm.* Warsaw: The Polish Academy of Sciences, The Institute of History, 1960, 117–154.

Hoszowski, Stanislaw, "L'Europe centrale dans la révolution des prix: XVIe et XVIIe siècles," *Annales E.S.C.,* **XVI,** 3, mai–juin 1961, 441–456.

Hudson, G. F., *Europe and China.* London: Arnold, 1931.

Hurstfield, J., "The Profits of Fiscal Feudalism, 1541–1602," *Economic History Review,* 2nd ser., **VIII,** 1, 1955, 53–61.

Hurstfield, J., "Social Structure, Office-Holding and Politics, Chiefly in Western Europe," *New Cambridge Modern History,* **III:** R. B. Wernham, ed., *The Counter-Reformation and the Price Revolution, 1559–1610.* London and New York: Cambridge Univ. Press, 1968, 126–148.

Innis, Harold A., "The Rise and Fall of the Spanish Fishery in Newfoundland," *Proceedings and Transactions of the Royal Society of Canada,* 3rd ser., **XXV,** Section II, 1931, 51–70.

Innis, Harold A., *The Cod Fisheries: The History of an International Economy.* New Haven, Connecticut: Yale Univ. Press, 1940.

Jara, Alvaro, "Una investigación sobre los problemas del trabajo en Chile durante el periodo colonial," *Hispanic American Historical Review,* **XXXIX,** 2, 1959, 239–244.

Jara, Alvaro, *Guerre et société au Chili: essai de sociologie coloniale.* Paris: Institut des Hautes Etudes de l'Amérique Latine, 1961.

Jara, Alvaro, "La producción de metales preciosos en el Perú en el siglo XVI," *Boletín de la Universidad de Chile,* No. 44, nov. 1963, 58–64.

Jara, Alvaro, "Estructuras de colonización y modalidades del tráfico en el Pacífico sur hispano-americano," *Les Grandes voies maritimes dans le monde XV–XIXe siècles,* VIIe Colloque, Commission Internationale d'Histoire Maritime. Paris: S.E.V.P.E.N., 1965, 247–275.

Jara, Alvaro, "Economía minera e historia económica hispanoamericana," in *Tres ensayos sobre economía minera hispanoamericana.* Santiago de Chile: Centro de Investigaciones de Historia Americana, 1966, 15–54.

Jara, Alvaro, "Salario en una economía caracterizada por las relaciones de dependencia personal," *Third International Conference of Economic History,* Munich 1965. Paris: Mouton, 1968, 601–615.

Jeannin, Pierre, "Anvers et la Baltique au XVIe siècle," *Revue du Nord,* **XXXVII,** avr.–juin 1955, 93–113.

Jeannin, Pierre, "Les relations économiques des villes de la Baltique avec Anvers au XVIe siècle," *Vierteljahrschrift für Sozial- und Wirtschaftsgeschichte,* **XLIII,** 3, Sept. 1956, 193–217; 4, Dez. 1956, 323–355.

Jeannin, Pierre, "Les comptes du Sund comme source pour la construction d'indices généraux de l'activité économique en Europe (XVI–XVIIIe siècles)," *Revue historique,* **CCXXXI,** janv.–mars 1964, 55–102; avr.–juin 1964, 307–340.

Johnsen, Oscar Albert, "Les relations commerciales entre la Norvège et l'Espagne dans les temps modernes," *Revue historique,* 55e Année, **CLXV,** 1, sept.–déc. 1930, 77–82.

Jones, E. L., and Woolf, S. J., "The Historic Role of Agrarian Change in Economic Development" in E. L. Jones and S. J. Woolf, eds., *Agrarian Change and Economic Development.* London: Methuen, 1969, 1–21.

Jones, P. J., "Per la storia agraria italiana nel medio evo: lineamenti e problemi," *Rivista storica italiana,* **LXXVI,** 2, giugno 1964, 287–348.

Kellenbenz, Herman, "Spanien, die nördlichen Niederlande und die Skandinavisch-baltische Raum in der Weltwirtschaft und Politik um 1600," *Vierteljahrschrift für Sozial- und Wirtschaftsgeschichte,* **XLI,** 4, 1954, 289–332.

Kellenbenz, Herman, "Autour de 1600: le commerce de poivre des Fuggers et le marché internationale de poivre," *Annales E.S.C.,* **XI,** 1, janv.–mars 1956, 1–28.

Kellenbenz, Herman, "Landverkehr, Fluss- und Seeschiffahrt im Europäischen Handel (Spätmitterlalter-Anfang des 19. Jahrhunderts)," in *Les grandes voies maritimes dans le monde, XVe–XIXe siècles,* VIIe Colloque, Commission Internationale d'Histoire Maritime. Paris: S.E.V.P.E.N., 1965, 65–174.

Kerridge, Eric, "The Movement in Rent, 1540–1640," in E. M. Carus-Wilson, ed., *Essays in Economic History.* New York: St. Martin's, 1966, **II,** 208–226. (Originally in *Economic History Review,* VI, 1953.)

Keynes, J. M., *A Treatise on Money,* 2 vol. New York: Macmillan, 1950.

Kiernan, V. G., "Foreign Mercenaries and Absolute Monarchy," *Past & Present,* No. 11, Apr. 1957, 66–83.

Kiernan, V. G., "State and Nation in Western Europe," *Past & Present,* No. 31, July 1965, 20–38.

Kingdon, Robert M., "The Political Resistance of the Calvinists in France and the Low Countries," *Church History,* **XXVII,** 3, Sept. 1958, 220–233.

Kingdon, Robert M., "Social Welfare in Calvin's Europe," *American Historical Review,* **LXXVI,** 1, Feb. 1971, 50–69.

Klein, Julius, *The Mesta: A Study in Spanish Economic History, 1273–1836.* Cambridge, Massachusetts: Harvard Univ. Press, 1919.

Klíma, A., and Macůrek, J., "La question de la transition du féodalisme au capitalisme en Europe centrale (16e–18e siècles)," *International Congress of Historical Sciences,* Stockholm, 1960. *Rapports,* **IV:** *Histoire moderne.* Göteborg: Almqvist & Wiksell, 1960, 84–105.

Kluchevsky, V. O., *A History of Russia,* 5 vol. London: J. M. Dent, 1911.

Kobata, A., "The Production and Uses of Gold and Silver in 16th and 17th Century Japan," *Economic History Review,* 2nd ser., **XVIII,** 2, Oct. 1965, 245–266.

Koenigsberger, H. G., *The Government of Sicily Under Philip II of Spain.* London: Staples Press, 1951.

Koenigsberger, H. G., "The Organization of Revolutionary Parties in France and the Netherlands During the Sixteenth Century," *The Journal of Modern History,* **XXVII,** 4, Dec. 1955, 335–351.

Koenigsberger, H. G., "Property and the Price Revolution (Hainault, 1474–1573)," *Economic History Review,* 2nd ser., **IX,** 1, 1956, 1–15.

Koenigsberger, H. G., "The Empire of Charles V in Europe," in *New Cambridge Modern*

History, **II**: G. R. Elton, ed., *The Reformation, 1520–1559.* London and New York: Cambridge Univ. Press, 1958, 301–333.

Koenigsberger, H. G., "Western Europe and the Power of Spain," *New Cambridge Modern History,* **III**: R. B. Wernham, ed., *The Counter-Reformation and the Price Revolution, 1559–1610.* London and New York: Cambridge Univ. Press, 1968, 234–318.

Koenigsberger, H. G., "The European Civil War," in *The Habsburgs and Europe, 1516–1660.* Ithaca, New York: Cornell Univ. Press, 1971, 219–285. (Originally in H. R. Trevor-Roper, ed., *The Age of Expansion.*)

Kosminsky, Eugen A. "The Evolution of Feudal Rent in England from the XIth to the XVth Centuries," *Past & Present,* No. 7, Apr. 1955, 12–36.

Kosminsky, Eugen A., "Peut-on considérer le XIVe et le XVe siècles comme l'époque de la décadence de l'économie européenne?" *Studi in onore di Armando Sapori.* Milano: Istituto Edit. Cisalpino, 1957, **I,** 551–569.

Kovacevic, Desanka, "Dans la Serbie et la Bosnie médiévales: les mines d'or et d'argent," *Annales E.S.C.,* **XV,** 2, mars–avr. 1960, 248–258.

Kula, Witold, *Théorie économique du système féodal: pour un modèle de l'économie polonaise, 16e–18e siècles.* Paris: Mouton, 1970.

Kuznets, Simon, "The State as the Unit of Study of Economic Growth," *Journal of Economic History,* **XI,** 1, Winter 1951, 25–41.

Lach, Donald F., *Asia in the Making of Europe,* Vol. I: *The Century of Discovery,* 2 books. Chicago, Illinois: Univ. of Chicago Press, 1965.

Laclau (h), Ernesto, "Feudalism and Capitalism in Latin America," *New Left Review,* No. 67, May–June 1971, 19–38.

Ladero Quesada, Miguel Angel, "Les finances royales de Castille à la veille des temps modernes," *Annales E.S.C.,* **XXV,** 3, mai–juin 1970, 775–788.

Lane, Frederic C., "The Rope Factory and Hemp Trade in the Fifteenth and Sixteenth Centuries," in *Venice and History.* Baltimore, Maryland: Johns Hopkins Press, 1966, 269–284. (Originally in *Journal of Economic and Business History,* IV, 1932.)

Lane, Frederic C., "Venetian Shipping during the Commercial Revolution," in *Venice and History.* Baltimore, Maryland: Johns Hopkins Press, 1966, 3–24. (Originally in *American Historical Review,* XXXVIII, 1937.)

Lane, Frederic C., "The Mediterranean Spice Trade: Its Revival in the Sixteenth Century," in *Venice and History.* Baltimore, Maryland: Johns Hopkins Press, 1966, 25–34. (Originally in *American Historical Review,* XLV, 1940.)

Lane, Frederic C., "National Wealth and Protection Costs," in *Venice and History.* Baltimore, Maryland: Johns Hopkins Press, 1966, 373–382. (Originally in Jesse Clarkson and Thomas C. Cochran, eds., *War as a Social Institution,* 1941.)

Lane, Frederic C., "The Economic Meaning of War and Protection," *Venice and History.* Baltimore, Maryland: Johns Hopkins Press, 1966, 383–398. (Originally in *Social Philosophy and Jurisprudence,* VII, 1942.)

Lane, Frederic C., "Force and Enterprise in the Creation of Oceanic Commerce," in *Venice and History.* Baltimore, Maryland: Johns Hopkins Press, 1966, 399–411. (Originally in *Journal of Economic History,* Supplement X, 1950.)

Lane, Frederic C., "Economic Consequences of Organized Violence," in *Venice and History.* Baltimore, Maryland: Johns Hopkins Press, 1966, 412–428. (Originally in *Journal of Economic History,* XVIII, 1958.)

Lapeyre, Henri, *Géographie de l'Espagne morisque.* Paris: S.E.V.P.E.N., 1959.

Lapeyre, Henri, *Les monarchies européennes du XVIe siècle,* Collection Nouvelle Clio 39. Paris: Presses Universitaires de France, 1967.

Larraz, José, *La época del mercantilismo en Castilla (1500–1700).* Madrid: Atlas, 1943.

Laskowski, Otton, "Infantry Tactics and Firing Power in the XVI Century," *Teki Historyczne,* **IV,** 2, 1950, 106–115.

Laslett, Peter, *The World We Have Lost*. New York: Scribner's, 1965.

Lattimore, Owen, *Inner Asian Frontiers of China*, 2nd edition. Irvington-on-Hudson: Capitol Publishing Co., and New York: American Geographical Society, 1940.

Lattimore, Owen "The Frontier in History," in *Relazioni del X Congresso di Scienze Storiche*, I: *Metodologia–Problemi generali–Scienze ausiliare della storia*. Firenze: G. C. Sansoni, 1955, 103–138.

Lattimore, Owen, "La civilisation, mère de Barbarie?," *Annales E.S.C.*, **XVII**, 1, janv.–févr. 1962, 95–108.

Lefebvre, Henri, "Une discussion historique: du féodalisme au capitalisme: observations," *La Pensée*, No. 65, janv.–févr. 1956, 22–25.

Lenin, V. I., *The Development of Capitalism in Russia*. Moscow: Foreign Languages Publishing House, 1956.

Le Roy Ladurie, Emmanuel, *Les paysans du Languedoc*, 2 vol. Paris: S.E.V.P.E.N., 1966.

Le Roy Ladurie, Emmanuel, *Histoire du climat depuis l'an mil*. Paris: Flammarion, 1967.

Levenson, Joseph R., ed., *European Expansion and the Counter-Expansion of Asia, 1300–1600*. Englewood Cliffs, New Jersey: Prentice-Hall, 1967.

Lewis, Archibald R., "The Closing of the European Frontier," *Speculum*, **XXXIII**, 4, Oct. 1958, 475–483.

Lewis, Bernard, "Some Reflections on the Decline of the Ottoman Empire," *Studia islamica*, **IX**, 1958, 111–127.

Livermore, H. V., "Portuguese History," in H. V. Livermore, ed., *Portugal and Brazil, an Introduction*. London and New York: Oxford Univ. Press (Clarendon), 1953, 48–81.

Lockhart, James, "Encomienda and Hacienda: The Evolution of the Great Estate in the Spanish Indies," *Hispanic American Historical Review*, **XLIX**, 3, Aug. 1969, 411–429.

Lockwood, David, "Social Integration and System Integration," in George K. Zollschan and Walter Hirsch, eds., *Explorations in Social Change*. Boston, Massachusetts: Houghton, 1964, 244–257.

Lonchay, H., "Etude sur les emprunts des souverains belges au XVIe et XVIIe siècles," *Académie Royale de Belgique, Bulletins de la Classe des Lettres et des Sciences Morales et Politiques et de la Classe des Beaux-Arts*, 1907, 923–1013.

Lopez, R. S., "The Trade of Medieval Europe: the South," in *Cambridge Economic History of Europe*, **II**: M. M. Postan and E. E. Rich, eds., *Trade and Industry in the Middle Ages*. London and New York: Cambridge Univ. Press, 1952, 257–354.

Lopez, R. S., and Miskimin, H. A., "The Economic Depression of the Renaissance," *Economic History Review*, 2nd ser., **XIV**, 3, 1962, 408–426.

Lopez, R. S., Miskimin, H. A., and Udovitch, Abraham, "England to Egypt, 1350–1500: Long-term Trends and Long-distance Trade," in M. A. Cook, ed., *Studies in the Economic History of the Middle East from the rise of Islam to the present day*. London: Oxford Univ. Press, 1970, 93–128.

Lowmianski, Henryk, "The Russian Peasantry," *Past & Present*, No. 26, Nov. 1963, 102–109.

Lubimenko, Inna, *Les relations commerciales et politiques de l'Angleterre avec la Russie avant Pierre le Grand*. Paris: Lib. Ancienne Honoré Champion, 1933.

Lublinskaya, A. D., "Préface à l'édition russe des *Caractères originaux de l'histoire rurale française*," *Annales E.S.C.*, **XIV**, 1, janv.–mars 1959, 91–105.

Lublinskaya, A. D., *French Absolutism: The Crucial Phase, 1620–1629*. London and New York: Cambridge Univ. Press, 1968.

Ludloff, R., "Industrial Development in 16th–17th Century Germany," *Past & Present*, No. 12, Nov. 1957, 58–75.

Lütge, Friedrich, "Economic Change: Agriculture," *New Cambridge Modern History*, **II**: G. R. Elton, ed., *The Reformation, 1520–1559*. London and New York: Cambridge Univ. Press, 1958, 23–50.

Luttrell, Anthony, "Slavery and Slaving in the Portuguese Atlantic (to about 1500)," in Centre of African Studies, University of Edinburgh, *The Transatlantic Slave Trade from West Africa* (mimeo, 1965), 61–79.

Luzzatto, Gino, *Storia economica dell'età moderna e contemporanea*, Part I, *L'età moderna.* Padova: CEDAM, 1955.

Lyashchenko, Peter I., *History of the National Economy of Russia to the 1917 Revolution.* New York: Macmillan, 1949.

Lybyer, A. H., "The Ottoman Turks and the Routes of Oriental Trade," *English Historical Review*, **XXX**, Oct. 1915, 577–588.

Lythe, S. G. E., *The Economy of Scotland in Its European Setting, 1550–1625.* Edinburgh: Oliver & Boyd, 1960.

Mączak, Antoni, "The Social Distribution of Landed Property in Poland from the Sixteenth to the Eighteenth Centuries," *Third International Conference of Economic History*, Paris: Mouton, 1968. **I**, 455–469.

Malowist, Marian, "Histoire sociale: époque contemporaine," *IXe Congrès Internationale des Sciences Historiques*, **I**: *Rapports.* Paris: Lib. Armand Colin, 1950, 305–322.

Malowist, Marian, "L'évolution industrielle en Pologne du XIVe au XVIIe siècle: traits généraux," *Studi in onore di Armando Sapori*, Milano: Istituto Edit. Cisalpino, 1957, **I**, 571–603.

Malowist, Marian, "Über die Frage des Handelspolitik des Adels in den Ostseeländern im 15. und 16. Jahrhundert," *Hansische Geschichtsblätter*, **75** Jh., 1957, 29–47.

Malowist, Marian, "Poland, Russia and Western Trade in the 15th and 16th Centuries," *Past & Present*, No. 13, Apr. 1958, 26–39.

Malowist, Marian, "The Economic and Social Development of the Baltic Countries from the 15th to the 17th Centuries," *Economic History Review*, 2nd ser., **XII**, 2, 1959, 177–189.

Malowist, Marian, "A Certain Trade Technique in the Baltic Countries in the Fifteenth to the Seventeenth Centuries," *Poland at the XIth International Congress of Historical Sciences.* Warsaw: Polish Academy of Sciences, The Institute of History, 1960, 103–116.

Malowist, Marian, "Un essai d'histoire comparée: les mouvements d'expansion en Europe au XVe et XVIe siècles," *Annales E.S.C.*, **XVII**, 5, sept.–oct. 1962, 923–929.

Malowist, Marian, "Les aspects sociaux de la première phase de l'expansion coloniale," *Africana Bulletin*, No. 1, 1964, 11–40.

Malowist, Marian, "Le commerce d'or et d'esclaves au Soudan Occidental," *Africana Bulletin*, No. 4, 1966, 49–72.

Malowist, Marian, "The Problem of the Inequality of Economic Development in Europe in the Latter Middle Ages," *Economic History Review*, 2nd ser., **XIX**, 1, Apr. 1966, 15–28.

Malowist, Marian, "The Social and Economic Stability of the Western Sudan in the Middle Ages," *Past & Present*, No. 33, Apr. 1966, 3–15.

Malowist, Marian, "Les débuts du système des plantations dans la période des grandes découvertes," *Africana Bulletin*, No. 10, 1969, 9–30.

Malowist, Marian, "Quelques observations sur le commerce de l'or dans le Soudan occidental au Moyen Age," *Annales E.S.C.*, **XXV**, 6, nov.–déc. 1970, 1630–1636.

Mandrou, Robert, "Les soulèvements populaires et la société française du XVIIe siècle," *Annales E.S.C.*, **XIV**, 4, oct.–déc. 1959, 756–765.

Mankov, A. G., *Le mouvement des prix dans l'état russe au XVIe siècle.* Paris: S.E.V.P.E.N., 1957.

Manning, Brian, "The Nobles, the People, and the Constitution," *Past & Present*, No. 9, Apr. 1956, 42–64.

Maravall, José A., "The Origins of the Modern State," *Cahiers d'histoire mondiale*, **VI**, 4, 1961, 789–808.

Margarido, Alfredo, "L'ancien royaume du Congo," *Annales E.S.C.*, **XXV**, 6, nov.–déc. 1970, 1718–1726.

Marrero, Manuela, "Los italianos en la fundación de Tenerife hispánico," *Studi in onore di*

Amintore Fanfani, **V:** *Evi moderno e contemporaneo,* Milano: Dott. A. Giuffrè-Ed., 1962, 329–337.

Marx, Karl, *The German Ideology.* New York: International Publ., 1947.

Marx, Karl, *Capital,* 3 vol. New York: International Publishers, 1967.

Masefield, G. B., "Crops and Livestock," in *Cambridge Economic History of Europe,* **IV**: E. E. Rich and C. H. Wilson, eds., *The Economy of Expanding Europe in the 16th and 17th Centuries.* London and New York: Cambridge Univ. Press, 1967, 276–301.

Mattingly, Garrett, *Renaissance Diplomacy.* London: Jonathon Cape, 1955.

Mauny, R. A., "The Question of Ghana," *Africa,* **XXIV,** 3, July 1954, 200–213.

Mauro, François, "Types de navires et constructions navales dans l'Atlantique portugais aux XVIe et XVIIe siècles," *Revue d'histoire moderne et contemporaine,* **VI,** juil.–août 1959, 185–193.

Mauro, François, "Toward an 'Intercontinental Model': European Overseas Expansion Between 1500–1800," *Economic History Review,* 2nd ser., **XIV,** 1, 1961, 1–17.

Mauro, François, *Le XVIe siècle européen: aspects économiques,* Collection Nouvelle Clio 32. Paris: Presses Universitaires de France, 1966.

McCracken, Eileen, "The Woodlands of Ireland circa 1600," *Irish Historical Studies,* **XI,** 44, Sept. 1959, 271–296.

Meilink-Roelofsz, M. A., *Asian Trade and European Influence in the Indonesian Archipelago between 1500 and about 1630.* The Hague: Nijhoff, 1962.

Meuvret, Jean, "Monetary Circulation and the Economic Utilization of Money in 16th- and 17th-Century France," in Rondo E. Cameron, ed., *Essays in French Economic History.* Homewood, Illinois: Irwin, Inc., 1970, 140–149. (Translated from *Etudes d'histoire moderne et contemporaine,* **I,** 1947.)

Meuvret, Jean, "Demographic Crisis in France from the Sixteenth to the Eighteenth Century," in D. V. Glass and D. E. C. Eversley, eds., *Population in History.* London: Arnold, 1965, 507–522.

Miller, A., "Considérations sur les institutions financières de l'état moscovite aux XVIe et XVIIe siècles," *Revue internationale de sociologie,* **XL,** 7–8, juil.–août 1932, 369–421.

Miller, Edward, "The Economic Policies of Governments: France and England," in *Cambridge Economic History of Europe,* **III**: M. M. Postan, E. E. Rich and Edward Miller, eds., *Economic Organization and Policies in the Middle Ages.* London and New York: Cambridge Univ. Press, 1963, 290–340.

Miller, Edward, "The Fortunes of the English Textile Industry During the Thirteenth Century," *Economic History Review,* 2nd ser., **XVIII,** 1, Aug. 1965, 39–60.

Miller, Edward, "Government Economic Policies and Public Finance, 900–1500," *Fontana Economic History of Europe,* **I,** 8, 1970.

Minchinton, W. E., "Introduction," *The Growth of English Overseas Trade in the Seventeenth and Eighteenth Centuries.* London: Methuen, 1969, 1–57.

Miranda, José, "La función económica del encomendero en los orígenes del régimen colonial, Nueva España (1525–1531)," *Anales del Instituto Nacional de Antropología e Historia,* **II,** 1941–1946, 421–462.

Miranda, José, *El tributo indígena en la Nueva España durante el siglo XVI.* México: El Colegio de México, 1957.

Miskimin, H. A., "Agenda for Early Modern Economic History," *Journal of Economic History,* **XXXI,** 1, Mar. 1971, 172–183.

Mollat, Michel, "Y a-t-il une économie de la Renaissance?" in *Actes du Colloque sur la Renaissance.* Paris: Lib. Philosophique J. Vrin, 1958, 37–54.

Mollat, Michel, Johansen, Paul M., Postan, M. M., Sapori, Armando, and Verlinden, Charles, "L'économie européenne aux derniers siècles du Moyen-Age," *Relazioni del X Congresso Internazionale di Scienze Storiche,* **III:** *Storia del medioevo.* Firenze: G. B. Sansoni, 1955, 655–811.

Molnar, Erik, "Les fondements économiques et sociaux de l'absolutisme," in *XIIe Congrès International des Sciences Historiques: Rapports,* **IV:** *Méthodologie et histoire contemporaine.* Wien: Verlag Ferdinand Berger & Söhne, 1965, 155–169.

Moore, Jr., Barrington, *Social Origins of Dictatorship and Democracy.* Boston: Beacon Press, 1966.

Morineau, Michel, "D'Amsterdam à Séville: de quelle réalité l'histoire des prix est-elle le miroir?," *Annales E.S.C.,* **XXIII,** 1, janv.–fevr. 1968, 178–205.

Morison, Samuel Eliot, *Admiral of the Ocean Sea.* Boston: Little Brown, 1942.

Mousnier, Roland, *La vénalité des offices sous Henri IV et Louis XIII.* Rouen: Ed. Maugard, n.d., ca. 1945.

Mousnier, Roland, *Les XVIe et XVIIe siècles,* Vol. IV of *Histoire Générale des Civilisations.* Paris: Presses Universitaires de France, 1954.

Mousnier, Roland, "Recherches sur les soulèvements populaires en France avant la Fronde," *Revue d'histoire moderne et contemporaine,* **V,** 1958, 81–113.

Mousnier, Roland, ed., *Lettres et mémoires addressées au Chancelier Séguier (1633–1649),* 2 vol. Paris: Presses Universitaires de France, 1964.

Mousnier, Roland, *Peasant Uprisings in Seventeenth-Century France, Russia, and China.* New York: Harper, 1970.

Mundy, John H., and Riesenberg, Peter, *The Medieval Town.* Princeton, New Jersey: Van Nostrand, 1958.

Murray, John J., "The Cultural Impact of the Flemish Low Countries on Sixteenth and Seventeenth Century England," *American Historical Review,* **LXII,** 4, July 1957, 837–854.

Myers, A. R., *England in the Late Middle Ages,* Vol. IV of The Pelican History of England, London: Penguin Books, 1952.

Nadal, Jorge, "La revolución de los precios españoles en el siglo XVI: estado actual de la cuestión," *Hispania, revista española de historia,* **XIX,** 77, oct.–dic. 1959, 503–529.

Nadal, Jorge, *La población española: siglos XVI a XX.* Collección de ciencia económica, **VII.** Barcelona: Ed. Ariel, 1966.

Needham, Joseph, *Science and Civilization in China,* **I.** London and New York: Cambridge Univ. Press, 1954.

Needham, Joseph, "Les contributions chinoises à l'art de gouverner les navires," *Colloque international d'histoire maritime,* 5e, Lisbonne, 1960 (Paris, 1966) with discussion, 113–134.

Needham, Joseph, "The Chinese Contributions to Vessel Control," *Scientia,* **XCVI,** 98, April 1961, 123–128; 99, May 1961, 163–168.

Needham, Joseph, "Commentary" on Lynn White, Jr., "What Accelerated Technological Change in the Western Middle Ages?" in A. C. Crombie, ed., *Scientific Change.* New York: Basic Books, 1963.

Needham, Joseph, "Poverties and Triumphs of Chinese Scientific Tradition," in A. C. Crombie, ed., *Scientific Change.* New York: Basic Books, 1963, 117–153.

Nef, John U., "Silver Production in Central Europe, 1450–1618," *Journal of Political Economy,* **XLIX,** 4, Aug. 1941, 575–591.

Nef, John U., *Industry and Government in France and England, 1540–1640.* Ithaca: Great Seal Books, 1957. (Originally in *Memoirs of the American Philosophical Society,* XV, 1940.)

Nef, John U., *War and Human Progress.* New York: Norton, 1963.

Nef, John U., "The Progress of Technology and Growth of Large-Scale Industry in Great Britain, 1540–1640," in *The Conquest of the Material World.* Chicago, Illinois: Univ. of Chicago Press, 1964, 121–143. (Originally in *Economic History Review,* V, 1934.)

Nef, John U., "A Comparison of Industrial Growth in France and England from 1540 to 1640," in *The Conquest of the Material World.* Chicago, Illinois: Univ. of Chicago Press, 1964, 144–212. (Originally in *Journal of Political Economy,* XLIV, 1936.)

Nef, John U., "Prices and Industrial Capitalism in France and England," in *The Conquest of the*

Material World. Chicago, Illinois: Univ. of Chicago Press, 1964, 240–267. (Originally in *Economic History Review,* VII, 1937.)

Nef, John U., "Industrial Europe at the Time of the Reformation, c. 1515–c. 1540," in *The Conquest of the Material World.* Chicago, Illinois: Univ. of Chicago Press, 1964, 67–117. (Originally in *Journal of Political Economy,* XLIX, 1941.)

Néré, Jean, "Le développement du capitalisme," *Revue historique,* **CCIII,** janv.–mars 1950, 64–69.

North, Douglas C., and Thomas, Robert Paul, "An Economic Theory of the Growth of the Western World," *Economic History Review,* 2nd ser., **XXIII,** 1, Apr. 1970, 1–17.

Ohlin, Goran, "Entrepreneurial Activities of the Swedish Aristocracy," *Explorations in Entrepreneurial History,* **VI,** 2, Dec. 1953, 147–162.

Oman, Sir Charles, *A History of the Art of War in the Sixteenth Century.* London: Methuen, 1937.

Ots Capdequí, J. M., *El estado español en las Indias.* México: Fondo de Cultura Económica, 1941.

Pach, Zs. P., "Die Abbiegung der Ungarischen Agrarentwicklung von den Westeuropäischen," *XIe Congrès International des Sciences Historiques,* Stockholm, 1960. *Résumés des communications.* Göteborg: Almqvist & Wiksell, 1960, 154–156.

Pach, Zs. P., "The Development of Feudal Rent in Hungary in the Fifteenth Century," *Economic History Review,* 2nd ser., **XIX,** 1, Apr. 1966, 1–14.

Pach, Zs. P., "En Hongrie au XVIe siècle: l'activité commerciale des seigneurs et leur production marchande," *Annales E.S.C.,* **XXI,** 6, nov.–déc. 1966, 1212–1231.

Pagès, G., "Essai sur l'évolution des institutions administratives en France du commencement du XVIe siècle à la fin du XVIIe," *Revue d'histoire moderne,* n.s., No. 1, janv.–févr. 1932, 8–57; No. 2, mars–avr. 1932, 113–151.

Pagès, G., "La vénalité des offices dans l'ancienne France," *Revue historique,* **CLXIX,** 3, 1932, 477–495.

Pannikar, K. M., *Asia and Western Dominance.* London: Allen & Unwin, 1953.

Parry, J. H., *The Age of Reconnaissance.* New York: Mentor Books, 1963.

Parry, J. H., "Transport and Trade Routes," in *Cambridge Economic History of Europe,* **IV:** E. E. Rich and C. H. Wilson, eds., *The Economy of Expanding Europe in the 16th and 17th Centuries.* London and New York: Cambridge Univ. Press, 1967, 155–219.

Parry, J. H., "Colonial Developments and International Rivalry Outside Europe, I. America," *New Cambridge Modern History,* **III:** R. B. Wernham, ed., *The Counter-Reformation and the Price Revolution, 1559–1610.* London and New York: Cambridge Univ. Press, 1968, 507–532.

Parsons, Talcott, *Structure and Process in Modern Societies.* New York: Free Press, 1960.

Pascu, S., Mavrodin, V. V., Porchnev, Boris, and Anteleva, I. G., "Mouvements paysans dans le centre et le Sudest de l'Europe du XVe au XXe siècles," *XIIe Congrès International des Sciences Historiques, Rapports,* **IV:** *Méthodologie et histoire contemporaine.* Wien: Verlag Ferdinand Berger & Söhne, 1965, 21–35.

Penrose, Boies, *Travel and Discovery in the Renaissance, 1420–1620.* Cambridge, Massachusetts: Harvard Univ. Press, 1952.

Perroy, Edouard, "A l'origine d'une économie contractée: les crises du XIVe siècle," *Annales E.S.C.,* **IV,** 2, avr.–juin 1949, 167–182.

Perroy, Edouard, *et al., Le Moyen Age,* Vol. III of *Histoire Générale des Civilisations.* Paris: Presses Universitaires de France, 1955.

Pesez, Jean-Marie, and Le Roy Ladurie, Emmanuel, "Le cas français: vue d'ensemble," *Villages désertés et histoire économique, XIe–XVIIIe siècles.* Paris: S.E.V.P.E.N., 1965, 127–252.

Petráň, Josef, "A propos de la formation des régions de la productivité spécialisée en Europe Centrale," in *Deuxième Conférence Internationale d'Histoire Economique,* Aix-en-Provence,

1962, **II:** *Middle Ages and Modern Times.* Paris: Mouton, 1965, 217–222.

Phelps-Brown, E. H., and Hopkins, Sheila V., "Wage-Rates and Prices: Evidence for Population Pressure in the Sixteenth Century," *Economica,* **XXIV,** No. 96, Nov. 1957, 289–306.

Phelps-Brown, E. H., and Hopkins, Sheila V., "Builders' Wage-Rates, Prices, and Population: Some Further Evidence," *Economica,* **XXVI,** No. 101, Feb. 1959, 18–38.

Phelps-Brown, E. H., and Hopkins, Sheila V., "Seven Centuries of Building Wages," in E. M. Carus-Wilson, ed., *Essays in Economic History,* New York: St. Martin's, 1966, **II,** 168–178. (Originally in *Economica,* XXII, 1955.)

Phelps-Brown, E. H., and Hopkins, Sheila V., "Seven Centuries of the Price of Consumables, Compared with Builders' Wage-Rates," in E. M. Carus-Wilson, ed., *Essays in Economic History,* New York: St. Martin's, 1966, **II,** 179–196. (Originally in *Economica,* XXIII, 1956.)

Pierce, T. Jones, "Landlords in Wales, A.: The Nobility and Gentry," in *The Agrarian History of England and Wales,* **IV:** Joan Thirsk, ed. *1500–1640.* London and New York: Cambridge Univ. Press, 1967, 357–381.

Pike, Ruth, "The Genoese in Seville and the Opening of the New World," *Journal of Economic History,* **XXII,** 3, Sept. 1962, 348–378.

Pirenne, Henri, "The Stages in the Social History of Capitalism," *American Historical Review,* **XIX,** 3, Apr. 1914, 494–515.

Pirenne, Henri, *Economic and Social History of Medieval Europe.* London: Routledge & Kegan Paul, 1936.

Pirenne, Henri, *Early Democracies in the Low Countries.* New York: Norton, 1971.

Pocock, J. G. A., "Letter to the Editor," *Encounter,* **XI,** 4, Oct. 1958.

Polanyi, Karl, *The Great Transformation.* Boston: Beacon Press, 1944.

Porchnev, Boris, "Les rapports politiques de l'Europe Occidentale et de l'Europe Orientale à l'époque de la Guerre des Trente Ans," *International Congress of Historical Sciences,* Stockholm, 1960. *Rapports,* **IV:** *Histoire moderne.* Göteborg: Almqvist & Wiksell, 1960, 136–163.

Porchnev, Boris, *Les soulèvements populaires en France de 1623 à 1648.* Paris: S.E.V.P.E.N., 1963.

Portal, Roger, *Les Slaves.* Paris: Lib. Armand Colin, 1965.

Postan, M. M., "The Chronology of Labour Services," *Transactions of the Royal Historical Society,* 4th ser., **XX,** 1937, 169–193.

Postan, M. M., "The Fifteenth Century," *Economic History Review,* **IX,** 2, May 1939, 160–167.

Postan, M. M., "Some Social Consequences of the Hundred Years' War," *Economic History Review,* **XII,** 1 & 2, 1942, 1–12.

Postan, M. M., "The Rise of a Money Economy," in E. M. Carus-Wilson, ed., *Essays in Economic History.* New York: St. Martin's, 1965, **I,** 1–12. (Originally in *Economic History Review,* XIV, 1944.)

Postan, M. M., "Some Economic Evidence of Declining Population in the Later Middle Ages," *Economic History Review,* 2nd ser., **II,** 3, 1950, 221–246.

Postan, M. M., "Italy and the Economic Development of England in the Middle Ages," *Journal of Economic History,* **XI,** 4, Fall 1951, 339–346.

Postan, M. M., "The Trade of Medieval Europe: The North," in *Cambridge Economic History of Europe,* **II:** M. M. Postan and E. E. Rich, eds., *Trade and Industry in the Middle Ages.* London and New York: Cambridge Univ. Press, 1952, 119–256.

Postan, M. M., "Note" (on article by W. C. Robinson), *Economic History Review,* 2nd ser., **XII,** 1, 1959, 77–82.

Postan, M. M., "The Economic and Political Relations of England and the Hanse (1400 to 1475)," in Eileen E. Power and M. M. Postan, eds., *Studies in English Trade in the Fifteenth Century.* New York: Barnes & Noble, 1966, 91–153.

Pounds, Norman J. G., "Overpopulation in France and the Low Countries in the Later Middle Ages," *Journal of Social History,* **III,** 3, Spring 1970, 225–247.

Power, Eileen E., "The Wool Trade in the Fifteenth Century," in Eileen E. Power and M. M. Postan, eds., *Studies in English Trade in the Fifteenth Century.* New York: Barnes & Noble, 1966, 39–90.

Prawer, Joshua, and Eisenstadt, S. N., "Feudalism," in *International Ecyclopedia of the Social Sciences,* New York: Macmillan and Free Press, 1968, **V**, 393–403.

Prestwick, Minna, review of Boris Porchnev in *English Historical Review,* **CCCXX**, July 1966, 565–572.

Pullan, Brian, "Wage-earners and the Venetian Economy, 1500–1630," *Economic History Review,* 2nd ser., **XVI**, 3, 1964, 407–26.

Quinn, D. B. "Ireland and Sixteenth-Century European Expansion," in T. Desmond Williams, ed., *Historical Studies.* London: Bowes & Bowes, 1958, 20–32.

Ramsey, Peter, *Tudor Economic Problems.* London: Gollancz, 1968.

Rau, Virginia, "A Family of Italian Merchants in Portugal in the Fifteenth Century: the Lomellini," *Studi in onore di Armando Sapori.* Milano: Istituto Edit. Cisalpino, 1957, **I**, 715–726.

Redlich, Fritz, "European Aristocracy and Economic Development," *Explorations in Entrepreneurial History,* **VI**, 2, Dec. 1953, 78–91.

Redlich, Fritz, "De Praeda Militari: Looting and Booty, 1500–1815," *Vierteljahrschrift für Sozial- und Wirtschaftsgeschichte,* Supplement No. 39, 1956.

Redlich, Fritz, "Military Entrepreneurship and the Credit System in the 16th and 17th Centuries," *Kyklos,* **X**, 1957, 186–193.

Redlich, Fritz, "The German Military Enterpriser and His Work Force," Vol. I, *Vierteljahrschrift für Sozial- und Wirtschaftsgeschichte,* Suppl. No. 47, 1964.

Reglá, Juan "La cuestión morisca y la conyuntura internacional en tiempos de Felipe II," *Estudios de historia moderna,* **III**, 1953, 219–234.

Reglá, Juan, "La expulsión de los moriscos y sus consecuencias," *Hispania, revista española de historia,* **XIII**, No. 51, 1953, 215–267; No. 52, 1953, 402–479.

Reglá, Juan, "La expulsión de los moriscos y sus consecuencias en la economia valenciana," *Studi in onore di Amintore Fanfani,* **V**: *Evi moderni e contemporaneo.* Milano: Dott. A. Giuffrè-Ed., 1962, 525–545.

Renouard, Yves, "1212–1216: Comment les traits durables de l'Europe occidentale moderne se sont définis au début du XIIIe siècle," *Annales de l'Université de Paris,* **XXVIII**, 1, janv.–mars 1958, 5–21.

Revah, I. S., "L'hérésie marrane dans l'Europe Catholique du 15e au 18e siècle," in Jacques LeGoff, *Hérésies et sociétés dans l'Europe pré-industrielle, 11e–18e siècles.* Paris: Mouton, 1968, 327–337.

Reynolds, Robert L., *Europe Emerges.* Madison: Univ. of Wisconsin Press, 1967.

Rich, E. E., "Expansion as a Concern of All Europe," *New Cambridge Modern History,* **I**: G. R. Potter, ed., *The Renaissance, 1493–1520.* London and New York: Cambridge Univ. Press, 1957, 445–469.

Rich, E. E., "Colonial Settlement and its Labour Problems," in *Cambridge Economic History of Europe,* **IV**: E. E. Rich and C. H. Wilson, eds., *The Economy of Expanding Europe in the 16th and 17th Centuries.* London and New York: Cambridge Univ. Press, 1967, 302–373.

Rich, E. E., "Preface," in *Cambridge Economic History of Europe,* **IV**: E. E. Rich and C. H. Wilson, eds., *The Economy of Expanding Europe in the 16th and 17th Centuries.* London and New York: Cambridge Univ. Press, 1967, xi–xxxii.

Robertson, H. M., "European Economic Developments in the Sixteenth Century," *South African Journal of Economics,* **XVIII**, 1, Mar. 1950, 36–53.

Robinson, W. C., "Money, Population and Economic Change in Late Medieval Europe," *Economic History Review,* 2nd ser., **XII**, 1, 1959, 63–76.

Romano, Ruggiero, "La pace di Cateau-Cambrésis e l'equilibrio europeo a metà del secolo XVI," *Rivista storica italiana,* **LXI**, 3, sett. 1949, 526–550.

Romano, Ruggiero, "A Florence au XVIIe siècle: industries textiles et conjoncture," *Annales E.S.C.,* **VII**, 7, oct.–déc. 1952, 508–512.

Romano, Ruggiero, "A propos du commerce de blé dans la Méditerranée des XIVe et XVe siècles," in *Eventail de l'histoire vivante: Hommage à Lucien Febvre,* Paris: Lib. Armand Colin, 1953, **II,** 149–161.

Romano, Ruggiero, "La marine marchande vénitienne au XVIe siècle," in M. Mollat *et al.,* eds., *Les sources de l'histoire maritime en Europe, du Moyen Age au XVIIIe siècle,* Actes du IVe Colloque International d'Histoire Maritime. Paris: S.E.V.P.E.N., 1962, 33–55.

Romano, Ruggiero, "Tra XVI e XVII secolo. Una crisi economica: 1619–1622," *Rivista storica italiana,* **LXXIV,** 3, sett. 1962, 480–531.

Romano, Ruggiero, "Encore la crise de 1619–22," *Annales E.S.C.,* **XIX,** 1, janv.–févr. 1964, 31–37.

Roorda, D. J., "The Ruling Classes in Holland in the Seventeenth Century," in J. S. Bromley and E. H. Kossman, eds., *Britain and the Netherlands.* Groningen: Wolters, 1964, **II,** 109–132.

Rosenberg, Hans, "The Rise of the Junkers in Brandenburg–Prussia, 1410–1653," *American Historical Review,* Part I, **XLIX,** 1, Oct. 1943, 1–22; Part II, **XLIX,** 2, Jan. 1944, 228–242.

Rosenberg, Hans, *Bureaucracy, Aristocracy and Autocracy: The Prussian Experience, 1660–1815.* Cambridge, Massachusetts: Harvard Univ. Press, 1966.

Roth, Cecil, *The History of the Jews of Italy.* Philadelphia: Jewish Publication Society of America, 1946.

Rowse, A. L., "Tudor Expansion: The Transition from Medieval to Modern History," *William & Mary Quarterly,* 3rd ser., **XIV,** 4, July 1957, 309–316.

Rowse, A. L., *The Elizabethans and America.* New York: Macmillan, 1959.

Ruddock, Alwyn A., *Italian Merchants and Shipping in Southampton, 1270–1600.* Southampton: University College, 1951.

Ruîz Almansa, Javier, "Las ideas y las estadísticas de población en España en el siglo XVI," *Revista internacional de sociología,* **I,** 1947, 89–107.

Rusche, Georg, and Kirchheimer, Otto, *Punishment and Social Structure.* New York: Russell & Russell, 1939.

Salmon, J. H. M., "Venality of Office and Popular Sedition in Seventeenth Century France," *Past & Present,* No. 37, July 1967, 21–43.

Samsonowicz, Henryk, "Salaires et services dans les finances citadines de la Prusse au XVe siècle et dans la première moitié du XVIe siècle," *Third International Conference of Economic History,* Munich 1965. Paris: Mouton, 1968, 533–551.

Sansom, George B., *The Western World and Japan.* New York: Knopf, 1950.

Sansom, George B. A., *A History of Japan: II: 1334–1615.* Stanford, California: Stanford University Press, 1961.

Savine, Alexander, "Bondmen under the Tudors," *Transactions of the Royal Historical Society,* n.s., **XVII,** 1903, 235–289.

Sayous, André-E., "Le rôle d'Amsterdam dans l'histoire du capitalisme commercial et financier," *Revue historique,* **CLXXXIII,** 2, oct.–déc. 1938, 242–280.

Schöffer, I., "The Dutch Revolution Anatomized: Some Comments," *Comparative Studies in Society and History,* **III,** 4, July 1961, 470–477.

Schumpeter, Joseph A., *Business Cycles,* 2 vol. New York: McGraw-Hill, 1939.

Schumpeter, Joseph A., *Capitalism, Socialism and Democracy.* London: Allen & Unwin, 1943.

Schumpeter, Joseph A., *The Sociology of Imperialism,* in *Social Classes, Imperialism.* New York: Meridian Books, 1955.

Schurz, Walter L., "Mexico, Peru, and the Manila Galleon," *Hispanic American Historical Review,* **I,** 4, Nov. 1918, 389–402.

Sée, Henri, *Modern Capitalism.* New York: Adelphi Co., 1928.

Sella, Domenico, "Les mouvements longs de l'industrie lainière à Venise aux XVIe et XVIIe siècles," *Annales E.S.C.,* **XII,** 1, janv.–mars 1957, 29–45.

Sella, Domenico, "Crisis and Transformation in Venetian Trade," in Brian Pullan, ed., *Crisis and Change in the Venetian Economy in the Sixteenth and Seventeenth Centuries*. London: Methuen, 1968, 88–105.

Sella, Domenico, "European Industries, 1500–1700," *Fontana Economic History of Europe*, **II**, 5, 1970.

Serraîma Cirici, Enrique, "Hugonotes y bandidos en el Pirineo catalán," *Estudios de historia moderna*, **IV**, 1954, 207–223.

Serrão, Joël, "Le blé des îles atlantiques: Madère et Açores aux XVe et XVIe siècles," *Annales E.S.C.*, **IX**, 3, juil.–sept. 1954, 337–341.

Servoise, R., "Les relations entre la Chine et l'Afrique au XVe siècle," *Le mois en Afrique*, No. 6, juin 1966, 30–45.

Shneidman, J. Lee, *The Rise of the Aragonese-Catalan Empire, 1200–1350*, 2 vol. New York: N.Y. Univ. Press, 1970.

Siemenski, J., "Constitutional Conditions in the Fifteenth and Sixteenth Centuries," *Cambridge History of Poland*, **I**: W. F. Reddaway *et al.*, eds., *From the Origins to Sobieski (to 1696)*. London and New York: Cambridge Univ. Press, 1950, 416–440.

Skeel, Caroline, "The Cattle Trade between Wales and England From the Fifteenth to the Nineteenth Centuries," *Transactions of the Royal Historical Society*, 4th ser., **IX**, 1926, 135–158.

Slicher van Bath, B. H., "The Rise of Intensive Husbandry in the Low Countries," in J. S. Bromley and E. H. Kossman, eds., *Britain and the Netherlands*. London: Chatto, 1960, **I**, 130–153.

Slicher van Bath, B. H., *The Agrarian History of Western Europe, A.D. 500–1850*. New York: St. Martin's, 1963.

Slicher van Bath, B. H., "Les problèmes fondamentaux de la société pré-industrielle en Europe occidentale," *Afdeling Agrarische Geschiedenis Bijdragen*, No. 12, 1965, 3–46.

Sluiter, Engel, "Dutch-Spanish Rivalry in the Caribbean Area, 1594–1609," *Hispanic American Historical Review*, **XXVIII**, 2, May 1948, 165–196.

Smit, J. W., "The Present Position of Studies Regarding the Revolt of the Netherlands," in J. S. Bromley and E. H. Kossman, eds., *Britain and the Netherlands*. Groningen: Wolters, 1964, **I**, 11–28.

Smit, J. W., "The Netherlands Revolution," in Robert Forster and Jack P. Greene, eds., *Preconditions of Revolution in Early Modern Europe*. Baltimore, Maryland: The Johns Hopkins Press, 1970, 19–54.

Smith, R. E. F., *The Enserfment of the Russian Peasantry*. London and New York: Cambridge Univ. Press, 1968.

Smith, Robert S., "Indigo Production and Trade in Colonial Guatemala," *Hispanic American Historical Review*, **XXXIX**, 2, May 1959, 181–211.

Smolar, Jr., Frank J., "Resiliency of Enterprise: Economic Causes and Recovery in the Spanish Netherlands in the Early Seventeenth Century," in Charles H. Carter, ed.: *From the Renaissance to the Counter-Reformation*. New York: Random House, 1965, 247–268.

Soldevila, Ferran, "Barcelona demana à l'emperador Carles V l'autorització per a comerciar directament amb America (1522)," *Studi in onore di Amintore Fanfani*, **V**: *Evi moderno e contemporaneo*. Milano: Dott. A Giuffrè-Ed., 1962, 633–641.

Solt, Leo F., "Revolutionary Calvinist Parties in England Under Elizabeth I and Charles I," *Church History*, **XXVII**, 3, Sept. 1958, 234–239.

Spooner, Frank C., "A la côte de Guinée sous pavillon français (1559–1561)," *Studi in onore di Armando Sapori*. Milano: Istituto Edit. Cisalpino, 1957, **II**, 1001–1008.

Spooner, Frank C., "The Habsburg-Valois Struggle," *New Cambridge Modern History*, **II**: G. R. Elton, ed., *The Reformation, 1520–1559*. London and New York: Cambridge Univ. Press, 1958, 334–358.

Spooner, Frank C., "Venice and the Levant: An Aspect of Monetary History (1600–1614)," in *Studi in onore di Amintore Fanfani*, **V**: *Evi moderno e contemporaneo*. Milano: Dott. A.

Giuffrè-Ed., 1962, 643–667.

Spooner, Frank C., "The Economy of Europe, 1559–1609," in *New Cambridge Modern History*, **III**: R. B. Wernham, ed., *The Counter-Reformation and the Price Revolution, 1559–1610*. London and New York: Cambridge Univ. Press, 1968, 14–93.

Spooner, Frank C., "The European Economy, 1609–50," *New Cambridge Modern History*, **IV**: J. P. Cooper, ed., *The Decline of Spain and the Thirty Years' War, 1609–48/59*. London and New York: Cambridge Univ. Press, 1970, 67–103.

Stahl, Henri H., *Les anciennes communautés villageoises roumaines—asservissement et pénétration capitaliste*. Bucarest: Ed. de l'Académie de la République Socialiste de Roumanie, 1969.

Stein, Stanley J. and Barbara H., *The Colonial Heritage of Latin America*. London and New York: Oxford Univ. Press, 1970.

Stephens, W. B., "The Cloth Exports of the Provincial Ports, 1600–1640," *Economic History Review*, 2nd ser., **XXII**, 2, Aug. 1969, 228–243.

Stoianovich, Traian, "Material Foundations of Preindustrial Civilization in the Balkans," *Journal of Social History*, **IV**, 3, Spring 1971, 205–262.

Stone, Lawrence, "State Control in Sixteenth-Century England," *Economic History Review*, **XVII**, 1, 1947, 103–120.

Stone, Lawrence, "The Anatomy of the Elizabethan Aristocracy," *Economic History Review*, **XVIII**, 1 & 2, 1948, 1–53.

Stone, Lawrence, "Elizabethan Overseas Trade," *Economic History Review*, 2nd ser., **II**, 1, 1949, 30–58.

Stone, Lawrence, "The Elizabethan Aristocracy—A Restatement," *Economic History Review*, 2nd ser., **IV**, 1, 2, & 3, 1951–52, 302–321.

Stone, Lawrence, "The Nobility in Business, 1540–1640," *Explorations in Entrepreneurial History*, **X**, 2, Dec. 1957, 54–61.

Stone, Lawrence, "Letter to the Editor," *Encounter*, **XI**, 1, July 1958.

Stone, Lawrence, "Social Mobility in England, 1500–1700," *Past & Present*, No. 33, Apr. 1966, 16–55.

Stone, Lawrence, *The Crisis of the Aristocracy, 1558–1641*, abr. ed. London: Oxford Univ. Press, 1967.

Strauss, Gerald, *Nuremberg in the Sixteenth Century*. New York: Wiley, 1966.

Strayer, Joseph, *On the Medieval Origins of the Modern State*. Princeton, New Jersey: Princeton Univ. Press, 1970.

Streider, Jacob, "Origin and Evolution of Early European Capitalism," *Journal of Economic and Business History*, **II**, 1, Nov. 1929, 1–19.

Supple, Barry, *Commercial Crisis and Change in England, 1600–1642*. London and New York: Cambridge Univ. Press, 1959.

Swart, K. W., *The Sale of Offices in the Seventeenth Century*. The Hague: Nijhoff, 1949.

Sweezy, Paul, "The Transition from Feudalism to Capitalism," *Science and Society*, **XIV**, 2, Spring 1950, 134–157.

Szeftel, Marc, "Aspects of Feudalism in Russian History," in Rushton Colbourn, ed., *Feudalism in History*. Princeton, New Jersey: Princeton Univ. Press, 1956, 167–182.

Takahashi, H. K., "The Transition from Feudalism to Capitalism: A Contribution to the Sweezy–Dobb Controversy," *Science and Society*, **XVI**, 4, Fall 1952, 313–345.

Takahashi, H. K., "On the 'Transition' from Feudalism to the Bourgeois Revolution," *Indian Journal of Economics*, **XXXV**, 140, 1955, 143–151.

Tapié, Victor-L., *La France de Louis XIII et de Richelieu*. Paris: Flammarion, 1952.

Taube, Edward, "German Craftsmen in England During the Tudor Period," *Journal of Economic History*, **IV**, 14, Feb. 1939, 167–178.

Tawney, R. H., *The Agrarian Problem in the Sixteenth Century*. New York: Longmans, 1912.

Tawney, R. H., "Introduction" to Thomas Wilson, *A Discourse Upon Usury*. London: Bell & Sons, 1925, 1–172.

Tawney, R. H., "Harrington's Interpretation of His Age," *Proceedings of the British Academy,* 1941, 199–223.

Tawney, R. H., "The Rise of the Gentry, 1558–1640," in E. M. Carus-Wilson, ed., *Essays in Economic History.* New York: St. Martin's, 1965, **I,** 173–206. (Originally in *Economic History Review,* XI, 1941.)

Tawney, R. H., "Postscript," in E. M. Carus-Wilson, ed., *Essays in Economic History.* New York: St. Martin's, 1965, **I,** 206–214. (Originally in *Economic History Review,* VII, 1954.)

Taylor, A. J. P., *The Course of German History.* London: Hamilton, 1945.

Taylor, K. W., "Some Aspects of Population History," *Canadian Journal of Economics and Political Sciences,* **XVI,** Aug. 1950, 301–313.

Tazbir, Janusz, "The Commonwealth of the Gentry," in Aleksander Gieysztor *et al., History of Poland.* Warszawa: PWN—Polish Scientific Puslishers, 1968, 169–271.

Teall, Elizabeth S., "The Seigneur of Renaissance France," *Journal of Modern History,* **XXXVII,** 2, June 1965, 131–150.

Thiriet, Freddy, *La Romanie vénitienne au Moyen Age,* Bibliothèque des Ecoles Française d'Athènes et de Rome, fasc. 183. Paris: Boccard, 1959.

Thirsk, Joan, "Industries in the Countryside," in F. J. Fisher, ed., *Essays in the Economic and Social History of Tudor and Stuart England.* London and New York: Cambridge Univ. Press, 1961, 70–88.

Thirsk, Joan, "Enclosing and Engrossing," in *The Agrarian History of England and Wales,* **IV:** Joan Thirsk, ed., *1500*–1640. London and New York: Cambridge Univ. Press, 1967, 200–255.

Thirsk, Joan, "The Farming Regions of England," in *The Agrarian History of England and Wales,* **IV:** Joan Thirsk, ed., *1500–1640.* London and New York: Cambridge Univ. Press, 1967, 1–112.

Thirsk Joan "Farming Techniques," in *The Agrarian History of England and Wales,* **IV:** Joan Thirsk, ed., *1500–1640.* London and New York: Cambridge Univ. Press, 1967, 161–199.

Thompson, F. M. L., "The Social Distribution of Landed Property in England Since the Sixteenth Century," *Economic History Review,* 2nd ser., **XIX,** 3, Dec. 1966, 505–517.

Thorner, Daniel, "L'économie paysanne: concept pour l'histoire économique," *Annales E.S.C.,* **XIX,** 3, mai–juin 1964, 417–432.

Thrupp, Sylvia, "Medieval Industry, 1000–1500," *Fontana Economic History of Europe,* **I,** 6, 1971.

Tilly, Charles, "Food Supply and Public Order in Modern Europe," mimeo, forthcoming in Charles Tilly, ed., *The Building of States in Western Europe.* Princeton, New Jersey: Princeton Univ. Press.

Tilly, Charles, "Reflections on the History of European Statemaking," mimeo., forthcoming in Charles Tilly, ed., *The Building of States in Western Europe.* Princeton, New Jersey: Princeton Univ. Press.

Topolski, Jerzy, "La régression économique en Pologne," *Acta poloniae historica,* **VII,** 1962, 28–49.

Trevor-Roper, H. R., "The Elizabethan Aristocracy: An Anatomy Anatomized," *Economic History Review,* 2nd ser., **III,** 3, 1951, 279–298.

Trevor-Roper, H. R., "The Gentry, 1540–1640," *Economic History Review,* Supplement 1, 1953.

Trevor-Roper, H. R., "Letter to the Editor," *Encounter,* **XI,** 1, July 1958.

Trevor-Roper, H. R., "England's Moderniser: Thomas Cromwell," in *Historical Essays.* New York: Harper, 1966, 74–78.

Trevor-Roper, H. R., "The Jesuits in Japan," in *Historical Essays.* New York: Harper, 1966, 119–124.

Trevor-Roper, H. R., "The General Crisis of the Seventeenth Century," in *The European Witch-Craze of the 16th and 17th Centuries and Other Essays.* New York: Harper, 1969,

46–89.

Trevor-Roper, H. R., "Religion, the Reformation, and Social Change," in *The European Witch-Craze of the Sixteenth and Seventeenth Centuries and other Essays.* New York: Harper, 1969, 1–45. (Previously published as part of *The Crisis of the Seventeenth Century: Religion, the Reformation, and Social Change.*)

Tyminiecki, Kazimierz, "Le servage en Pologne et dans les pays limitrophes au moyen âge," *La Pologne au Xe Congrès International des Sciences Historiques à Rome.* Warszawa: Académie Polonaise des Sciences, Institut d'Histoire, 1955, 5–28.

Ullman, Joan Connelly, "Translator's footnotes," in Jaime Vicens Vives, *Approaches to the History of Spain,* 2nd ed. Berkeley: Univ. of California Press, 1970.

Umiński, J., "The Counter-Reformation in Poland," in *The Cambridge History of Poland,* I: W. F. Reddaway *et al.,* eds., *From the Origins to Sobieski (to 1696).* London and New York: Cambridge Univ. Press, 1950, 394–415.

Utterström, Gustaf, "Climatic Fluctuations and Population Problems in Early Modern History," *Scandinavian Economic History Review,* III, 1, 1955, 3–47.

Vaccari, Pietro, "I lavatori della terra nell'occidente e nell'oriente dell'Europa nella età moderna," *Studi in onore di Armando Sapori.* Milano: Istituto Edit. Cisalpino, 1957, II, 969–978.

Válka, Josef, "La structure économique de la seigneurie tchèque au XVIe siècle," *Deuxième Conférence Internationale d'Histoire Economique,* II: *Middle Ages and Modern Times.* Paris: Mouton, 1965, 211–215.

van der Sprenkel, Otto B., "Population Statistics of Ming China," *Bulletin of the SOAS,* XV, Part 2, 1953, 289–326.

van der Wee, Herman, *The Growth of the Antwerp Market and the European Economy,* 3 vol. The Hague: Nijhoff, 1963.

van Dillen, J. G., "Amsterdam's Role in Seventeenth-Century Dutch Politics and its Economic Background," in J. S. Bromley and E. H. Kossman, eds.: *Britain and the Netherlands.* Groningen: Wolters, 1964, II, 133–147.

van Houtte, J. A., "Bruges et Anvers: marchés 'nationaux' ou 'internationaux' du XIVe au XVIe siècles," *Revue du Nord,* XXXIV, 1952, 89–108.

van Houtte, J. A., "Anvers aux XVe et XVIe siècles: expansion et apogée," *Annales E.S.C.,* XVI, 2, mars–avr. 1961, 248–278.

van Houtte, J. A., "Déclin et survivance d'Anvers (1550–1700)," *Studi in onore di Amintore Fanfani,* V: *Evi moderno e contemporaneo.* Milano: Dott. A. Giuffrè-Ed., 1962, 703–726.

van Houtte, J. A., "L'approvisionnement des villes dans les Pays-Bas (Moyen Age et Temps Modernes)," *Third International Conference of Economic History,* Munich 1965. Paris: Mouton, 1968, 73–77.

van Leur, J. C., *Indonesian Trade and Society.* The Hague: van Hoeve, Ltd., 1955.

Veblen, Thorstein, *Imperial Germany and the Industrial Revolution.* Ann Arbor, Michigan: Ann Arbor Paperbacks, 1966.

Verlinden, Charles, "The Rise of Spanish Trade in the Middle Ages," *Economic History Review,* X, 1, 1940, 44–59.

Verlinden, Charles, "Deux aspects de l'expansion commerciale du Portugal au moyen âge," *Revista portuguêsa de história,* IV, 1949, 169–209.

Verlinden, Charles, "Italian Influence in Iberian Colonization," *Hispanic American Historical Review,* XXXIII, 2, May 1953, 199–211.

Verlinden, Charles, *L'esclavage dans l'Europe médiévale,* 2 vol. Brugge: De Tempel, 1955.

Verlinden, Charles, "La colonie italienne de Lisbonne et le développement de l'économie métropolitaine et coloniale portugaise," *Studi in onore di Armando Sapori.* Milano: Istituto Edit. Cisalpino, 1957, I, 615–628.

Verlinden, Charles, "Crises économiques et sociales en Belgique à l'époque de Charles Quint," in *Charles Quint et son temps,* Colloques internationaux du C.N.R.S., Paris, 30 sept.–3 oct. 1958. Paris: Ed. du C.N.R.S., 1959, 177–190.

Williams, Eric, *Capitalism and Slavery*. London: Deutsch, 1964.

Williams, Penry, and Harriss, G. L., "A Revolution in Tudor History?" *Past & Present*, No. 25, July 1963, 3–58.

Wilson, C. H., "Cloth Production and International Competition in the 17th Century," *Economic History Review*, 2nd ser., **XIII**, 2, 1960, 209–221.

Wilson, C. H., "Trade, Society and the State," in *Cambridge Economic History of Europe*, **IV:** E. E. Rich and C. H. Wilson, eds., *The Economy of Expanding Europe in the 16th and 17th Centuries*. London and New York: Cambridge Univ. Press, 1967, 487–575.

Wittman, T., "Quelques problèmes relatifs à la dictature révolutionnaire des grandes villes de Flandres, 1577–1579," *Studia historica*, Academicae Scientarum Hungaricae, No. 40, 1960.

Wolf, Eric, *Sons of the Shaking Earth*. Chicago, Illinois: Univ. of Chicago Press, 1959.

Wolf, Eric, *Peasants*. Englewood Cliffs, New Jersey: Prentice-Hall, 1966.

Wolfe, Martin, "Fiscal and Economic Policy in Renaissance France," *Third International Conference of Economic History*, Munich 1965. Paris: Mouton, 1968, 687–689.

Woolf, S. J., "Venice and the Terraferma: Problems of the Change from Commercial to Landed Activities," in Brian Pullan, ed., *Crisis and Change in the Venetian Economy in the Sixteenth and Seventeenth Centuries*. London: Methuen, 1968, 175–203.

Wright, L. P., "The Military Orders in Sixteenth and Seventeenth-Century Spanish Society," *Past & Present*, No. 43, May 1969, 34–70.

Youings, Joyce, "Landlords in England, C: The Church," in *The Agrarian History of England and Wales*, **IV:** Joan Thirsk, ed., *1500–1640*. London and New York: Cambridge Univ. Press, 1967, 306–356.

Zagorin, Perez, "The Social Interpretation of the English Revolution," *Journal of Economic History*, **XIX**, 3, Sept. 1959, 376–401.

Zavala, Silvio, *La encomienda indiana*. Madrid: Centro de Estudios Históricos, 1935.

Zavala, Silvio, *New Viewpoints on the Spanish Colonization of America*. Philadelphia: Univ. of Pennsylvania Press, 1943.

Zeller, Gaston, "Industry in France Before Colbert," in Rondo E. Cameron, ed., *Essays in French Economic History*. Homewood, Illinois: Irwin, Inc., 1970, 128–139. (Translated from *Revue d'histoire économique et sociale*, XXVIII, 1950.)

Verlinden, Charles, "L'état et l'administration des communautés indigènes dar espagnol d'Amérique." *International Congress of Historical Sciences,* Stockho *Résumés des communications.* Göteborg: Almqvist & Wiksell, 1960, 133–134.

Verlinden, Charles, "La Crète, débouché et plaque tournante de la traite des es XIVe et XVe siècles," *Studi in onore di Amintore Fanfani,* **III:** *Medioevo.* Milanc Giuffrè-Ed., 1962, 593–669.

Verlinden, Charles, *et al.,* "Mouvements des prix et des salaires en Belgique au X\ *Annales E.S.C.,* **X,** 2, avr.–juin 1955, 173–198.

Vernadsky, George, "Feudalism in Russia," *Speculum,* **XIV,** 3, July 1939, 300–323.

Vernadsky, George, *The Tsardom of Muscovy, 1547–1682,* Vol. **V** of *A History of* parts. New Haven, Connecticut: Yale Univ. Press, 1969.

Vicens Vives, Jaime, "Discussion" of Charles Verlinden, "Crises économiques et s Belgique à l'époque de Charles-Quint," in *Charles Quint et son temps,* Colloq¹ nationaux du C.N.R.S., 30 sept.–3 oct. 1958. Paris: Ed. du C.N.R.S., 1959.

Vicens Vives, Jaime, *An Economic History of Spain.* Princeton, New Jersey: Prince Press, 1969.

Vicens Vives, Jaime, *Approaches to the History of Spain,* 2nd ed. Berkeley: Univ. of (Press, 1970.

Vilar, Pierre, "Le temps de Quichotte," *Europe,* **34,** Nos. 121–122, janv.–févr. 195(

Vilar, Pierre, "Problems on the Formation of Capitalism," *Past & Present,* No. 1956, 15–38.

Vilar, Pierre, *La Catalogne dans l'Espagne moderne,* 3 vol. Paris: S.E.V.P.E.N., 1962.

Villari, Rosario, *La rivolta anstispagnola a Napoli: le origini (1585–1647).* Bari: Later

Vitale, Luis, "Latin America: Feudal or Capitalist?," in James Petras and Mauric eds., *Latin America: Reform or Revolution?* Greenwich, Conn.: Fawcett, 1968, 32–4!

Vitale, Luis, "España antes y después de la conquista de América," *Pensamien* No. 27, abril 1969, 3–28.

Vivante, Corrado, "Le rivolte popolari in Francia prima della Fronde e la crisi d XVII," *Rivista storica italiana,* **LXXVI,** 4, dic. 1964, 957–981.

Warriner, Doreen, "Some Controversial Issues in the History of Agrarian Europe," and *East European Review,* **XXXI,** No. 78, Dec. 1953, 168–186.

Watson, Andrew M., "Back to Gold—and Silver," *Economic History Review,* 2nd ser 1967, 1–34.

Webb, Walter Prescott, *The Great Frontier.* Boston, Massachusetts: Houghton Miffli

Weber, Max, *General Economic History.* New York: Free Press, 1950.

Weber, Max, *The Religion of China.* New York: Free Press, 1951.

Weber, Max, *The Religion of India.* New York: Free Press, 1958.

Weber, Max, *Economy and Society.* Totowa, New Jersey: Bedminster Press, 1968.

Wernham, R. B., "English Policy and the Revolt of the Netherlands," in S. Bromley ar Kossman, eds., *Britain and the Netherlands,* Groningen: Wolters, 1964, **I,** 29–40.

Wernham, R. B., "The British Question, 1559–69," *New Cambridge Modern Hist* R. B. Wernham, ed., *The Counter-Reformation and the Price Revolution, 155!* London and New York: Cambridge Univ. Press, 1968, 209–233.

Wernham, R. B., "Introduction," *New Cambridge Modern History,* **III:** R. B. Wernha *The Counter-Reformation and the Price Revolution, 1559–1610.* London and New Cambridge Univ. Press, 1968, 1–13.

White, Jr., Lynn, "What Accelerated Technological Progress in the Western Middle Ag A. C. Crombie, ed., *Scientific Change.* New York: Basic Books, 1963, 272–291.

Willan, T. S., "Trade Between England and Russia in the Second Half of the Si: Century," *English Historical Review,* **LXIII,** No. 247, July 1948, 307–321.

Willetts, William, "The Maritime Adventures of the Great Eunuch Ho," in Colin Jack-I ed., *Papers on Early South-East Asian History.* Singapore: Journal of Southeast History, 1964, 25–42.

INDEX

The use of this index is complicated by the fact that the same terms were often used to denote somewhat different phenomena in the feudal and capitalist systems. This failure of terminology to follow institutional change is discussed in the book, and therefore reading the book is a desirable preliminary to using the index. As a general rule, we have tried to separate the different institutions under distinct headings: for example, Manors versus Estates (capitalist).

There are three other general principles used in constructing this index. Time periods, such as the Middle Ages or the sixteenth century, are not indexed, except when referring to a specific regime (for example, the Tudor Monarchy).

All names of peoples are included under the corresponding name of the country, except when there is no such corresponding name (for example, Slavs) or at least none in the time periods covered (for example, Turks).

Each manufactured product may be listed in four ways: as a raw material, as a product, as an industry, as a trade. A good example is: Wool; Textiles, woollen; Industries, textile; Clothier.

J

Jack-Hinton, Colin, 54
Jacobean era, 243, *see also* James I
Jacobins, 206
Jacqueries, 24, 268, *see also* Peasants, rebellions
James I, King of England, 238, 243, 259, 281
Jansenism, 288, 295, *see also* Catholic Church
Japan, 55–56, 60, 301, 329, 337, 342–343
Jara, Alvaro, 89, 93–94, 99–100, 168, 170, 189, 337
Java, 54, 342
Jeannin, Pierre, 76, 101, 111, 175, 201, 211, 264, 272
Jesuits, *see* Catholic Church, Jesuits
Jewels, 41, 45
Jews, 92, 118, 147–151, 167, 193, 195, 211, 341
   expulsion of, 47, 117, 147, 149, 166, 193–194
   Portuguese, 192, *see also* Jews, Sephardic; Marranos
   Sephardic, 211, *see also* Marranos
John II, King of Aragon, 166
John II, King of Portugal, 326
Johnsen, Oscar Albert, 211
Joint-stock companies, *see* Companies, joint-stock
Jones, E. L., 85, 118
Jones, P. J., 217
Journeymen, 267
Junkers, 91, 95, 160, 310–311, *see also* Aristocracy; Farmers, capitalist; Seigniors
Junks, *see* Transport, maritime

K

Kazan, 303
Kellenbenz, Herman, 273, 301, 341, 342
Kent, 111
Kerridge, Eric, 78
Keynes, J. M., 83, 280–281
Kholop labor, *see* Coerced labor, cash-crop
Kiernan, V. G., 33, 139–140, 146, 157, 196
Kiev, 323
King, Gregory, 251
King, the, *see* State
Kingdon, Robert M., 208, 254
Kinglets, 321, *see also* Aristocracy
King's household, *see* State, bureaucracy
Kirchheimer, Otto, 143
Klein, Julius, 109, 116, 167, 191, 193–194
Klíma, A., 324
Kluchevsky, V. O., 302–303,

313–315, 319, 322
Kniazhata, 320, *see also* Aristocracy
Knights, 240, 243, 267, 289
Kobata, A., 329
Königsberg, 154, 322
Koenigsberger, H. G., 179–180, 195, 203, 206–209, 215, 221, 267–268, 292, 294
Kongo, 339
Koppelwirtschaft, see Agriculture, rotation systems
Korea, 55
Kormlenie system, 316, *see also* Taxes, tax-farming
Kosminsky, E., 23–24, 27–28, 69, 112
Kossman, E. H., 42, 200, 202
Kovacevic, Desanka, 40
Kula, Witold, 101
Kulaki, 249, *see also* Peasants
Kuznets, Simon, 162

L

Labor,
   division of, *see also* Capitalism, World-economy
   European or international, 63, 67–129, 139, 157, 162, 200, 276, 290, 302, 307, 332, 349, 335–357
   national, 281, 354
   shortage of, 26, 135, 295
Labor control, modes of, 38, 84, 87, 90, 92, 99–100, 102–103, 116, 127, 162, *see also* Coerced labor; Farmers, tenant, Laborers; Sharecropping; Slavery
Labor force, *see* Workers
Laborers, (common), 251, 268, 275, 307
   migratory, 117
   rural, 86, 91, 93, 99, 113, 117, 120, 142, 157, 192, 194, 246, 251–253, *see also* Coerced labor, Cottagers, Farmers, Husbandmen, Peasants
   seasonal wage-workers, 256
   urban, *see* Workers
Labrador, 96
Lace, 324
Lach, Donald F., 328, 330–331
Laclau (h), Ernesto, 126
Ladero Quesada, Miguel Angel, 169
Lake district (England), 229
Lancaster, House of, 243
Land/labor ratio, 69, 104, 107, 112
Landlords, 18, 58–59, 62, 78, 83, 93, 95, 99, 101, 107, 115, 122, 124, 157, 234–235, 238–242, 244, 246–248, 255, 258, 302, 305, 313, 321, 356, *see also* Farmers,

capitalist; Gentry; Seigniors
Landowners, *see* Seigniors; Landlords
Lane, Frederic C., 16, 45, 51, 120, 135, 140, 215, 220, 332, 334, 339–340
Language, 353–354
Languedoc, 101–102, 106, 267, 295, *see also* France, southern
Lapeyre, Henri, 194, 206
Larraz, José, 166, 213
Laskowski, Otton, 139
Laslett, Peter, 251
Latifundia, see Estates, *latifundia*
Latimer, Hugh, Bishop of Worcester, 251
Latin America, *see* America, Latin
Latins, 43, *see also* Italy, (northern)
Lattimore, Owen, 21, 61, 98, 246
Lawyers, 248, 258, *see also* Professions, members of
Lease, *see* Tenure
Leaseholder, *see* Farmer, tenant
Leather, 108–109, 227, 281, 337, *see also* Industries, tanning; Leather goods
Leather goods, 305
Lefebvre, Henri, 26, 90
Leghorn, 217
Legitimacy, *see* State, legitimacy
Lenin, V. I., 120
Le Roy Ladurie, Emmanuel, 25, 35, 101–102, 221, 268, 287, 312
Levant, 19, 39–40, 43, 85, 89, 171, 173, 215, 218, 274, 317, 325–326, 336, 339, *see also* Empire, (Ottoman); Mediterranean, eastern; Orient; Trade, Levantine
Levellers, 209
Levenson, Joseph R., 59
Lewis, Archibald R., 38, 48, 135
Lewis, Bernard, 325
Liberalism, 135, 144, 243
Liège, 83, 206, 226
Lima, 189–190
Liquidity crisis, *see* Money, liquidity crisis
Lisbon, 47, 49–50, 76, 165, 174, 183, 200, 327, 329, 331, 336–337, 340–341
Lithuania, 94, 122, 148, 317, 319
Livermore, H. V., 46, 327, 329
Livestock, 44–45, 106–109, 159, 188–189, *see also* Agriculture, pasturage; Cattle; Dairy products; Horses; Meat; Mules; Sheep
Livonia, 307, 321
Livonian War, 316–319
Locher, T.J.G., 8
Lockhart, James, 190

STUDIES IN SOCIAL DISCONTINUITY

Under the Consulting Editorship of:

CHARLES TILLY
University of Michigan

EDWARD SHORTER
University of Toronto

The list of titles in this series continues on the last page of this volume